D0743114

COLLINS GEM

WELSH DICTIONARY

WELSH•ENGLISH
SAESNEG•CYMRAEG

HarperCollins*Publishers*

First published in this edition 1992

© HarperCollins Publishers 1992

Latest reprint 1997

ISBN 0 00 470199-2

*in collaboration with/
mewn cydweithrediad â'r*

Dr. David A. Thorne and the Department of
Welsh Language and Literature,
St. David's University College, Lampeter

Dr. David A. Thorne ac Adran Iaith a
Llenyddiaeth Cymru, Coleg Prifysgol Dewi Sant,
Llanbedr Pont Steffan

editor/golygydd
Anne Convery

editorial staff/staff golygyddol
Lesley Johnston

*A catalogue record for this book is
available from the British Library*

*Printed and bound in Great Britain by
Caledonian International Book Manufacturing Ltd,
Glasgow, G64*

INTRODUCTION

The first Spurrell Welsh-English dictionary appeared in 1848 published by William Spurrell (1813–89) the Carmarthen printer and publisher. One of his sons, Walter Spurrell (1858–1934), joined his father in the business and the family firm published a series of distinguished Welsh-English, English-Welsh dictionaries and influential Welsh grammars during the latter part of last century and the first half of the present century. William Spurrell was advised by and well-acquainted with Daniel Silvan Evans (1818–1903), one of the father figures of Welsh lexicography, sometime lecturer in Welsh at St David's University College, Lampeter and the first professor of Welsh to be appointed by the University of Wales.

The Collins-Spurrell Welsh Dictionary was first published in 1960 and quickly became an essential tool of general reference for Welsh learners as well as those anxious to interpret literature. It was edited by Henry Lewis, Professor of Welsh Language and Literature at University College, Swansea. The staff of the Department of Welsh Language and Literature at St David's University College, Lampeter are happy to cooperate with the editorial staff at Collins to produce this latest edition of a famous dictionary.

D A THORNE

CONTENTS

THE WELSH LANGUAGE

MOST of the languages of Europe, and some of the languages of Asia, can be traced back to a common ancestor to which the name Indo-European is commonly given. From this ancestor were derived a dozen or so branches, one of which is called Celtic. This branch probably had its beginning in the upper Danube valley, and from there spread in many directions over Europe, and even to Galatia in Asia Minor. As the Celtic-speaking people became scattered, changes naturally occurred in the language, resulting in the growth of dialects. Of these the best known on the continent is that which was spoken in Gaul, to which the name Gaulish is given. Gaulish became extinct in the early Christian period, and was displaced by Latin.

In the meantime people speaking different forms of Celtic had crossed over from the Continent to the British Isles. One group established itself in Ireland. This is known as the Goidelic or Gaelic group, and from it descended the Irish language, which spread from Ireland to the Isle of Man, developing later to Manx, and also to Scotland, eventually becoming Scottish Gaelic. The other group prevailed in Britain and the language is called British or Brythonic or Brittonic. Prior to the Roman Conquest this language was spoken throughout what later became England, Wales and southern Scotland. It was from this descendant of the original Common Celtic language that ultimately sprang the Welsh, Cornish and Breton languages.

The language of the Goidelic group is referred to also as Q Celtic, and that of the British group as P Celtic. The reason for this is that the Indo-European consonant written 'qu' has given 'c' in the former and 'p' in the latter. An example is found in the forms corresponding to the English interrogative pronoun 'who', which in Irish is 'cia' or 'cé', in Welsh 'pwy', and in Latin 'quis'. It may be mentioned that Gaulish shows the same development as the British languages. Thus whereas the word for 'head, end' is in Irish 'ceann' (earlier 'cenn'), it is in Welsh 'pen', while the corresponding form is found in Gaulish 'penne' in a compound name.

One of the oldest poems in Welsh literature is a eulogy to Cynan Garwyn, son of Brochwel Ysgithrog. Cynan's son Selyf is known to have been killed as he led the Welsh in the battle of Chester about the year 615. The eulogy is attributed to Taliesin, whom persistent tradition acclaims as author of eulogies and elegies to princes in southern Scotland and northern England who struggled against the Saxon invader in the late sixth century. Another name that has been handed down from these early times is Aneirin, whose long poem *Y Gododdin* refers to a great tragic exploit at Catraeth, somewhere in the neighbourhood of Catterick. These early traditions have tenaciously persisted throughout the long story of Welsh poetic literature.

Recorded Welsh prose goes back to the early ninth century. The earliest remains are scanty, but it can hardly be contested that prose writing must have long preceded what little has had the good fortune to escape oblivion. It is free from the crudeness that would be expected from initial efforts, and the way in which difficult and somewhat abstruse material is expressed with clarity, economy and directness goes a long way to prove that the writers were inheritors rather than initiators. The splendour and exactness of medieval Welsh prose, quite apart from its literary content, is striking evidence of the mastery of the writers of the prose medium. These qualities appear not least in the unlikely realm of legal writing.

During its long history the Welsh language has naturally undergone changes, but far from the extent to which English, for example, has changed since the days of Chaucer. He was a contemporary of Dafydd ap Gwilym, but whereas Chaucer has to be practically translated into Modern English, Dafydd is using to all intents the same language as any present-day poet expressing himself in the same type of poem. Similarly, if most of the earlier prose literature were printed in accordance with modern orthographical usage, the reader would not experience excessive difficulty in comprehending it. There have been changes in syntax, and still more in vocabulary. Idiomatic expressions have become obsolete from age to age, and new ones have grown. But substantially the literary language has been strikingly uniform.

The vocabulary has naturally been greatly affected from time to time by contact with peoples speaking a different language. Like many other languages Welsh has rarely been afraid of borrowing words from foreign languages. In the period of Roman occupation, and later under the influence of the Church, hundreds of Latin words were borrowed and submitted to the same treatment as native words. The same is to a less extent true of the period of contact with Anglo-Saxons. Then came the influence of the Normans, followed ultimately by the great pressure of English. All these accretions have been from non-Celtic sources, but the Welsh vocabulary is not without borrowings taken from time to time from Irish.

The written, and especially the printed, literary language always tends to be more static and conservative than the spoken. This results in the retention in the literary language of forms which have long since vanished completely from everyday colloquial speech, thus giving the printed literary language a somewhat artificial appearance. But the spoken language also differs from area to area. Indeed a brook seems a sufficient barrier to create divergence in expression between the inhabitants on either side. It is well known that speakers of dialect in one locality can hardly understand compatriots speaking another dialect of the same language. To secure, therefore, that all speakers, of whatever dialects, should have access to all that is of value in enlightened minds, the standard literary language must retain a high level of permanence, but should also avoid pedantic rigidity and scholastic snobbery.

NOTES ON THE PRONUNCIATION OF WELSH

VOWELS

They are sounded, long or short, as the vowels in the English words given.

A	*palm, pat.*
E	*gate* (without diphthongization), *get.*
I	*feet, fit.*
O	*more, not.*
U (1)	North Wales: like French *u* or German *ü* without rounding lips.
(2)	South Wales: as I.
W	*cool, full.*
Y (1)	In monosyllables generally, and in final syllables, as U (the 'clear' sound).
(2)	In all but final syllables, and in **y, yr** (the), **fy** (my), **dy** (thy), **yn, yng, ym** (in), the adverbial **yn**, the preverbal and relative particle **y, yr** (**y'm, y'th** etc), **syr** (sir), **nyrs** (nurse), as English *fun*, (the 'obscure' sound).

DIPHTHONGS

(1) Falling diphthongs, in which the second sound is consonantal: the two vowels have the sound noted above: **ae, oe, ai, oi**, the diphthong **ei** as English *by*, **aw, ew, iw, ow, uw, ŵy, yw**.

(2) Rising diphthongs, in which the first sound is consonantal: **ia, ie, io, iw, iy**, ('obscure' y); **wa, we, wi, wo, wy**, ('clear' y), **wy**, ('obscure' y).

viii

CONSONANTS

Only such as differ from English need be noted.

CH	(following C in the alphabet), as Scottish lo*ch*.
DD	(following D in the alphabet), as *th* in English *th*is, brea*the*.
F	as English *v*.
FF	As English *f*.
G	always as in English *go*.
NG	(following G in the alphabet), as in English si*ng*. In some words (e.g. **dangos**), however, it is sounded *ng-g*, as in English lo*ng*er. Alphabetically this follows after N.
LL	produced by placing the tongue to pronounced *l*, then emitting breath without voice.
PH	(following P in the alphabet), as English *f*.
TH	always as th in English *th*in.

ACCENT

Welsh words are generally accented on the last syllable but one. There are certain exceptions:

(1) The reduplicated personal pronouns **myfi, tydi, efe, efô, hyhi, nyni, chwychwi, hwynt-hwy,** accented on the final syllable.

(2) Verbs in -(h)au, -(h)oi, -eu, accented on the final syllable.

(3) A few dissyllabic words beginning **y** + consonant, accented on the final syllable.

(4) Certain polysyllabic words with a diphthong resulting in contraction in the final syllable, such as **Cymraeg**.

(5) Some late borrowings accented as in the language of origin, generally English.

INITIAL MUTATIONS

Certain initial consonants are mutated under certain conditions, as shown in the following table. Only the radical form is given in the dictionary.

SOUNDS	EXAMPLES			
	Radical	*Soft*	*Nasal*	*Spirant*
p	pren	bren	mhren	phren
t	tad	dad	nhad	thad
c	cam	gam	ngham	cham
b	baich	faich	maich	
d	dyn	ddyn	nyn	
g	gŵr	-ŵr	ngŵr	
ll	llais	lais		
rh	rhes	res		
m	mam	fam		

ABBREVIATIONS

BYRFODDAU

abbreviation	**abbr**	byrfodd
adjective	**adj**	ansoddair
adverb	**adv**	adferf
collective noun	**coll n**	enw torfol
colloquial	**col**	tafodieithol
conjunction	**conj**	cysylltiad
contraction	**contr**	cywasgiad
demonstrative	**dem**	dangosol
dual noun	**dn**	enw deuol
emphatic	**emphat**	pwyslais
exclamation	**excl**	ebychiad
feminine	**f**	benywaidd
grammatical	**gram**	gramadegol
imperative	**imper**	gorchmynnol
masculine	**m**	gwrywaidd
mutation	**mut**	treiglad
noun dual	**nd**	enw deuol
plural	**pl**	lluosog
pronoun	**pron**	rhagenw
preposition	**prep**	arddodiad
relative	**rel**	perthynol
singular	**sg**	unigol
verb	**vb**	berf
intransitive verb	**vi**	berf gyflawn
transitive verb	**vt**	berf anghyflawn

GEIRIADUR CYMRAEG A SAESNEG

A

a *interrogative particle* ♦ *preverbal particle* ♦ *rel pron* who, that, which

a, ac *conj* and

â, ag *conj* as

â, ag *prep* with

a *excl* ah, oh

ab, ap *nm* son (*before name, in place of surname, like 'Mac', and 'Fitz'*)

abad (-au) *nm* abbot

abadaeth (-au) *nf* abbacy, abbotship

abades (-au) *nf* abbess

abatir (-oedd) *nm* abbey-land

abaty (abatai) *nm* abbey

aber (-oedd, ebyr) *nm* confluence; mouth of river, estuary; brook, stream

aberfa (-oedd) *nf* mouth of river, estuary

abergofiant *nm* forgetfulness, oblivion

aberth (-au, ebyrth) *nm* sacrifice

aberthged *nf* oblation; offering of fruits

aberthol *adj* sacrificial

aberthu *vb* sacrifice

aberthwr (-wyr) *nm* sacrificer

aberu *vb* flow into, disembogue

abid *nmf* apparel; dress of religious order

abiéc *nm/f* alphabet

abl *adj* able; well-off

abladol *adj* ablative

abledd *nm* ability; plenty

abrwysg *adj* clumsy, drunken

absen *nm* absence; slander

absennol *adj* absent

absennu *vb* backbite, slander

absennwr (absenwyr) *nm* backbiter

absenoldeb *nm* absence

absenoli *vb* absent

absenoliaeth (-au) *nm* absenteeism

abwyd, -yn (-od) *nm* worm; fishing-bait

ac, a *conj* and

academaidd *adj* academic

academi (-iau) *nm* academy

acen (-ion) *nf* accent

aceniad *nm* accentuation

acennod *nf* accent mark

acennu *vb* accent, stress

acenyddiaeth *nf* accentuation

acer (-i) *nf* acre

acrilig *adj* acrylic

act (-au) *nf* act

actio *vb* act

actor (-ion) *nm* actor

actores (-au) *nf* actress

acw *adv* there, yonder

ach *excl* ugh

ach (-au, -oedd) *nf* degree of kinship; (*pl*) pedigree, ancestry

aches *nm* tide, flood; eloquence

achlân *adv* wholly, entirely

achles (-oedd) *nf* succour, protection; manure

achlesol *adj* succouring

achlesu *vb* succour, cherish; manure

achlod *nm* shame, disgrace

achlust *nm* rumour ♦ *adj* attentive

achlysur (-on) *nm* occasion

achlysuro *vb* occasion

achlysurol *adj* occasional

achos (-ion) *nm* cause, case

achos *conj* because, for

achosi vb cause

achres (-i, -au) nf genealogical table

achub vb seize, snatch; save, rescue. **a. y blaen** forestall. **a. y cyfle** seize the opportunity

achubiaeth nf salvation

achubol adj saving

achubwr (-wyr), -ydd (-ion) nm saviour, rescuer

achul adj thin, emaciated

achwre, ach(f)re n under-thatch, protection; covering, garment

achwyn vb complain ♦ (-ion) nm complaint, plaint

achwyngar adj querulous

achwyniad (-au) nm complaint, accusation

achwynwr (-wyr) nm complainer; complainant, plaintiff

achwynyddes (-au) nf complainant

achydd (-ion) nm genealogist

achyddiaeth nf genealogy

achyddol adj genealogical

ad- prefix very; second; bad, re-

adail nf building, edifice, structure

adain, aden (adenydd) nf wing; fin; spoke

adamant nm adamant, diamond

adamantaidd adj adamantine

adar npl (aderyn nm) birds, fowls. **a. drudwy, a. yr eira**, starlings. **a y to** sparrows

adara vb catch birds, fowl

adardy (-dai) nm aviary

adareg nf ornithology

adargi (-gwn) nm retriever, setter, spaniel

adargraffiad (-au) nm reprint

adarwr (-wyr) nm fowler

adarwriaeth nf fowling

adarydd (-ion) nm ornithologist

adaryddiaeth nf ornithology

ad-dalu vb repay, requite

ad-drefnu vb rearrange

adeg (-au) nf time, occasion,

opportunity

adeilad (-au) nm/f building, edifice

adeiladaeth nf building; edification, construction

adeiladol adj edifying, constructive

adeiladu vb build, edify

adeiladwr (-wyr), -ydd (-ion) nm builder

adeiledd nm structure

adeiniog adj winged

aden (-ydd, edyn) nf wing (adain)

adenedigaeth nf regeneration

adeni vb regenerate

adennill vb regain, recover

aderyn (adar) nm bird

adfach (-au) nm barb; liver-fluke

adfail (-feilion) nm ruin

adfeddiannu vb repossess

adfeiliad nm decay, ruin

adfeiliedig adj decayed, in ruins

adfeilio vb decay, moulder

Adfent nm Advent

adfer, -u, -yd vb restore

adferf (-au) nf adverb

adferfol adj adverbial

adferiad nm restoration

adferol adj restorative; remedial

adferwr (-wyr) nm restorer

adflas nm after-taste, bad taste

adfyd nm adversity

adfydus adj adverse, miserable

adfynach nm renegade monk

adfyw adj half alive, half dead

adfywhau vb revive, reanimate

adfywiad (-au) nm revival

adfywio vb revive, resuscitate

adfywiol adj refreshing

adg- see **atg-**

adiad nm drake

adio nm addition ♦ vb add

adiolyn (adiolion) nm additive

adladd, adlodd nm aftermath

adlais (-leisiau) nm echo

adlam (-au) nm home; rebound. **cic a.** drop-kick

adlamu vb rebound

adleisio vb resound

adlewyrch, -iad (-au) *nm* reflection

adlewyrchu *vb* reflect

adlewyrchydd (-ion) *nm* reflector

adlog (-au) *nm* compound interest

adloniadol *adj* of or for entertainment

adloniant *nm* recreation, entertainment

adlonni *vb* entertain, refresh

adlunio *vb* remodel, reconstruct

adnabod *vb* know, recognize

adnabyddiaeth *nf* knowledge, acquaintance

adnabyddus *adj* known, familiar

adnabyddwr *nm* knower

adnau (adneuon) (-au) *nm* deposit, pledge. **ar a.** on deposit

adneuo *vb* deposit

adneuol *adj* depositing

adneuwr (-wyr) *nm* depositor

adnewyddiad (-au) *nm* renewal, renovation

adnewyddu *vb* renew, renovate

adnewyddwr (-wyr) *nm* renewer, renovator

adnod (-au) *nf* verse

adnoddau *npl* resources

adolygiad (-au) *nm* review

adolygu *vb* review

adolygydd (-ion) *nm* reviewer

adran (-nau) *nf* division, section, department

adref *adv* homewards, home

adrodd *vb* relate, recite

adroddgan *nf* recitative

adroddiad (-au) *nm* report; recitation

adroddwr (-wyr) *nm* narrator, reciter

ads- see **ats-**

aduniad *nm* reunion

aduno *vb* reunite

adwaith (-weithiau) *nm* reaction

adweithiol *adj* reactionary

adweithydd (-ion) *nm* reactor

adwr *nm* coward, churl

adwy (-au, -on) *nf* gap, breach; pass

adwyth (-au) *nm* evil, misfortune, illness

adwythig *adj* cruel; evil, baneful; sore, sick; harmful

adyn (-od) *nm* wretch

adysgrif (-au) *nf* copy, transcript

adysgrifio *vb* copy, transcribe

addas *adj* suitable, proper

addasiad (-au) *nm* adjustment, adaptation

addasrwydd *nm* suitableness, fitness

addasu *vb* suit, adapt, fit

addawol *adj* promising

addef *vb* acknowledge, own, admit

addefiad *nm* admission, confession

addewid (-ion) *nf* promise

addfain *adj* slender, shapely

addfed see **aeddfed**

addfwyn *adj* gentle, meek, mild

addfwynder *nm* gentleness, meekness

addien *adj* fair, beautiful

addo *vb* promise

addod *nm*: **wy a.** nest-egg

addoed *nm* death, hurt

addoedi *vb* delay, postpone, prorogue

addoediad *nm* prorogation

addoer *adj* sad, cruel; chilling

addoldy (-dai) *nm* place of worship

addolgar *adj* devout, reverent

addolgarwch *nm* devoutness, reverence

addoli *vb* worship, adore

addoliad *nm* worship

addolwr (-wyr) *nm* worshipper

adduned *nf* vow

addunedu *vb* vow

addurn (-au, -iadau) *nm* ornament, adornment

addurnedig *adj* decorated

addurniad *nm* ornamentation

addurno *vb* adorn, ornament

addurnol adj ornamental, decorative

addurnwr (-wyr) nm decorator

addysg nf education, instruction

addysgiadol adj instructive, educational

addysgiaeth nf instruction, training

addysgol adj educational

addysgu vb educate, instruct

addysgwr (-wyr), -ydd (-ion) nm educator, instructor, tutor

aeddfed adj ripe, mature

aeddfedrwydd nm ripeness, maturity

aeddfedu vb ripen; mature

ael (-iau) nf brow

aele adj sad, wretched

aelgerth, -geth see **elgeth**

aelod (-au) nm member, limb. **A. Seneddol** Member of Parliament

aelodaeth nf membership

aelodi vb become a member; enrol

aelwyd (-ydd) nf hearth, fireside

aer (-ion) nm heir

aer nm air

aeres (-au) nf heiress

aerfa nf slaughter, battle

aerglo nm air-lock

aeron npl fruit, fruits, berries

aerwy (-au, -on) nm collar, torque; neck-chain

aes nf shield

aestheteg nf aesthetics

aesthetig adj aesthetic

aeth nm pain, grief, fear, shock

aethnen nf aspen, poplar

aethus adj poignant, grievous, severe

afal (-au) nm apple

afaleua vb gather apples

afallen (-nau) nf apple-tree

afan npl (afanen nf) raspberries

afanc (-od) nm beaver

afiach adj unwell, unhealthy, morbid

afiachus adj sickly; unwholesome

afiaith nm zest, mirth, glee

afiechyd (-on) nm disease, malady

afieithus adj mirthful, gleeful

aflafar adj harsh, unmelodious

aflan adj unclean, polluted, foul

aflawen adj fierce; sad, cheerless, dismal; awful

aflednais adj immodest, indelicate

afledneisrwydd nm immodesty, indelicacy

aflem adj obtuse

aflendid nm uncleanness; pollution

aflêr adj untidy, slovenly

aflerwch nm untidiness, slovenliness

afles nm disadvantage, hurt

aflesol adj disadvantageous, unprofitable

afliwiog adj pale, colourless

aflonydd adj unquiet, restless

aflonyddu vb disquiet, disturb, molest

aflonyddwch nm disturbance, unrest

aflonyddwr (-wyr) nm disturber

afloyw adj turbid; opaque

afluniaidd adj mis-shapen, deformed

aflunio vb disfigure, deform

aflwydd nm misfortune, calamity

aflwyddiannus adj unsuccessful

aflwyddiant nm failure

aflwyddo vb fail

aflywodraeth nf misrule, anarchy

aflywodraethus adj ungovernable, uncontrollable

afon (-ydd) nf river

afonig nf rivulet, streamlet, brook

afradlon adj wasteful, prodigal

afradlonedd nm prodigality

afradloni, afradu vb waste, lavish, squander

afraid adj unnecessary, needless

afrasol adj graceless, impious

afreidiau nm superfluity

afreidiol adj needless, superfluous

afreol nf misrule, disorder

afreolaidd adj irregular; disorderly

afreoleidd-dra nm irregularity

afreolus adj unruly, disorderly

afreswm nm absurdity

afresymol adj unreasonable

afresymoldeb nm unreasonableness

afrifed adj innumerable

afrllad, -en (-au, -ennau) nf wafer

afrosgo adj clumsy, unwieldy

afrwydd adj difficult, stiff, awkward

afrwyddineb nm difficulty

afrwyddo vb obstruct, hinder

afrywiog adj perverse, crossgrained, improper

afrywiogrwydd nm churlishness, roughness

afu liver ♦ nmlf a. (g)las gizzard

afwyn (-au) nf rein

affeithiad nm affection (in grammar)

afflau nm grip, hug, embrace

affliw nm shred, particle

Affrica nf Africa

affwysol adj abysmal

ag conj as ♦ prep with. see â

agen (-nau) nf cleft, chink, fissure

agendor nmlf gulf, abyss

agennu vb split, crack

ager, agerdd nm steam, vapour

agerfad (-au) nm steamboat

agerlong (-au) nf steamship, steamer

ageru vb steam, evaporate

agerw adj bitter, fierce

agor, -yd vb open, expand

agorawd (-au) nf overture

agored adj open; liable

agorfa (-oedd) nf opening, orifice

agoriad (-au) nm opening; key

agoriadol adj opening, inaugural

agorwr (-wyr), -ydd (-ion) nm opener

agos adj near, nigh

agosaol adj approaching

agosatrwydd nm intimacy

agosáu vb draw near, approach

agosrwydd nm nearness, proximity

agwedd (-au) nf form; aspect; attitude

agweddi nm dowry, marriage gift

agwrdd adj strong, mighty

angall adj unwise, foolish

angau nmlf death

angel (angylion, engyl) nm angel

angen (anghenion) nm need, want

angenrheidiol adj necessary, needful

angenrheidrwydd nm necessity

angerdd nm heat; passion; force

angerddol adj ardent, intense, passionate

angerddoldeb nm vehemence, intensity

anghaffael nm mishap; defect, flaw

anghallineb nm unwisdom, imprudence

angharedig adj unkind

angharedigrwydd nm unkindness

anghelfydd adj unskilful, clumsy

anghenfil (angenfilod) nm monster

anghenraid (angenrheidiau) nf necessity

anghenus adj needy, necessitous, indigent

angheuol adj deadly, mortal, fatal

anghlod nm dispraise, dishonour

anghoelio vb disbelieve

anghofiedig adj forgotten

anghofio vb forget

anghofrwydd nm forgetfulness

anghofus adj forgetful, oblivious

anghred nf unbelief, infidelity

anghredadun (anghredinwyr) nm unbeliever

anghrediniaeth nf unbelief, infidelity

anghrediniol adj unbelieving

anghredu vb disbelieve

anghrefyddol adj irreligious

anghrist (**-iau**) *nm* antichrist
anghryno *adj* incompact, prolix
anghwrtais *adj* discourteous
anghwrteisi *nm* discourtesy
anghydbwysedd *nm* imbalance
anghydfod *nm* disagreement, discord
Anghydffurfiaeth *nf* Nonconformity
Anghydffurfiwr (**-wyr**) *nm* Nonconformist
anghydnaws *adj* uncongenial
anghydsynio *vb* dissent, disagree
anghydweddol *adj* incompatible
anghyfaddas *adj* unsuitable, unfit
anghyfaddasu *vb* unfit, disqualify
anghyfamodol *adj* uncovenanted
anghyfanhedd-dra *nm* desolation
anghyfanheddle (**-aneddleoedd**) *nm* desolate place
anghyfanheddol *adj* desolating; desert
anghyfannedd *adj* uninhabited, desert
anghyfansoddiadol *adj* unconstitutional
anghyfartal *adj* unequal, uneven
anghyfartaledd *nm* disparity
anghyfarwydd *adj* unfamiliar, unskilled
anghyfeillgar *adj* unfriendly
anghyfiaith *adj* foreign, alien
anghyfiawn *adj* unjust, unrighteous
anghyfiawnder *nm* injustice
anghyflawn *adj* incomplete
anghyfleus *adj* inconvenient
anghyfleustra (**-terau**) *nm* inconvenience
anghyflogaeth *nm* unemployment
anghyfnewidiol *adj* immutable
anghyfraith *nf* transgression, crime
anghyfranogol *adj* incommunicable
anghyfreithlon *adj* unlawful, illegal, illegitimate

anghyfrifol *adj* irresponsible
anghyffredin *adj* uncommon, rare
anghyffwrdd *adj* intangible
anghyffyrddus *adj* uncomfortable
anghymedrol *adj* immoderate
anghymen *adj* rash, coarse, untidy
anghymeradwy *adj* unacceptable
anghymeradwyo *vb* disapprove
anghymesur *adj* inordinate
anghymharol *adj* incomparable
anghymharus *adj* ill-matched
anghymhendod *nm* foolishness, indelicacy, untidiness
anghymhwyso *vb* unfit, disqualify
anghymhwyster *nm* incapacity, disqualification
anghymodlon *adj* implacable
anghymwys *adj* unfit, unsuitable
anghynefin *adj* unfamiliar
anghynefindra *nm* unfamiliarity
anghynhyrchiol *adj* unproductive
anghynnes *adj* odious, loathsome
anghysbell *adj* out-of-the-way; remote
anghyson *adj* inconsistent
anghysondeb, -der (**-au**) *nm* inconsistency
anghysur (**-on**) *nm* discomfort
anghysuro *vb* discomfort
anghysurus *adj* uncomfortable
anghytbwys *adj* unbalanced, lopsided
anghytgord (**-iau**) *nm* discord, dissension
anghytûn *adj* not agreeing, discordant
anghytundeb *nm* disagreement
anghytuno *vb* disagree
anghywair *adj* ill-equipped; discordant ♦ *nm* disrepair
anghyweithas *adj* froward, uncivil
anghywir *adj* incorrect, inaccurate, false
anghywirdeb (**-au**) *nm* inaccuracy, falseness
anghywrain *adj* unskilful; slovenly
angladd (**-au**) *nm/f* burial, funeral

angladdol adj funeral

angof nm forgetfulness, oblivion

angor (-au, -ion) nf anchor

angorfa (-oedd, -feydd) nf anchorage

angori vb anchor

angylaidd adj angelic

angyles (-au) nf female angel

ai adv is it? what? **a. e?** is it so?

ai conj or; either; if

aidd nm zeal, ardour, zest

Aifft: yr A. nf Egypt

aig, eigiau nf host, shoal

aig nf (late corrupt form) sea, ocean

ail adj second ♦ adv a second time, again

ailadrodd vb repeat

ailadroddiad (-au) nm repetition

ailenedigaeth nf rebirth

aileni vb bear again, regenerate

Ailfedyddiwr (-wyr) nm Anabaptist

ail-law adj second-hand

aillt nm vassal, villain, slave

ais npl (eisen nf) laths; ribs

alaeth nm wailing, lamentation, grief

alaethu vb lament

alaethus adj mournful, lamentable

alarch (-od, elyrch) nm swan

alaru vb surfeit; loathe

alaw (-on) nf lily; air, melody, tune

Alban: yr A. nf Scotland

Albanwr (-wyr) nm Scot

alcali (-iau) nf alkali

alcam nm tin

alcohol nm alcohol

alch (-au, eilch) nf grate, grill

ale (-au, -on) nf aisle; gangway; alley

algebra nm algebra

Algeria nf Algeria

Almaen: yr A. nf Germany

Almaeneg nf German

Almaenwr (-wyr) nm German

almon nm almond

aloi (**aloeon**) nm alloy

Alpau: yr A. npl the Alps

allan adv out

allanol adj outward, external

allblyg adj extrovert

allforio vb export

allfro nm foreigner; foreign land

allfudwr (-wyr) nm emigrant

allgarwch nm altruism

allor (-au) nf altar

allt (elltydd) nf hill; cliff; wood

alltud (-ion) nm alien; exile

alltudiaeth nf banishment, exile

alltudio vb banish, exile

allwedd (-au, -i) nf key, clef (music)

am prep round, about; for; at; on ♦ conj for, because; so long as

am see **ym**

amaeth nm husbandman; agriculture

amaethdy (-dai) nm farm-house

amaethu vb farm, till

amaethwr (-wyr) nm farmer

amaethwraig nf farm-wife

amaethyddiaeth nf agriculture

amaethyddol adj agricultural

amarch nm disrespect, dishonour

amau vb doubt, suspect ♦ (-heuon) nm doubt

ambell adj occasional. **a. waith** sometimes

amcan (-ion) nm purpose, aim; guess. **ar a.** at random, approximately, at a guess

amcangyfrif vb estimate ♦ (-on) nm estimate

amcanu vb purpose; aim; guess

amdo (-oeau) nm shroud, winding-sheet

amdoi vb shroud, enshroud

amdorch (-dyrch) nf chaplet, wreath

amddifad adj destitute, orphan

amddifadrwydd nm destitution, privation

amddifadu vb bereave, deprive
amddifaty (-tai) nm orphanage
amddifedi nm destitution, privation
amddiffyn vb defend, protect, shield ♦ (-ion) nm defence
amddiffynfa (-feydd) nf fortress
amddiffyniad nm protection, defence
amddiffynnwr (-ynwyr), **-ynnydd** (-ynyddion) nm defender, protector
amddyfrwys adj mighty, rugged; marshy
America Ladin nf Latin America
Amerig: yr A. nf America
amfesur (-au) nm perimeter
amgáu vb enclose, shut in
amgen adj, adv other, else, otherwise; different. **nid a.** that is to say, namely
amgenach adj, adv otherwise; better
amgueddfa (-feydd) nf museum
amgyffred vb comprehend, comprise ♦ (-ion) nm comprehension
amgyffrediad nm comprehension
amgylch (-oedd) nm circuit; environs, surroundings. **o (oddi amgylch** round about, about
amgylchedd nm circumference; environment
amgylchfyd nm environment
amgylchiad (-au) nm circumstance; occasion
amgylchiadol adj circumstantial
amgylchu vb surround
amgylchynol adj surrounding
amgylchynu vb surround
amharchu vb dishonour, disrespect
amharchus adj disrespectful, disreputable
amhariad nm impairment, damage
amharod adj unprepared, unready
amharodrwydd nm unreadiness
amharu vb impair, harm, injure, damage

amhendant adj indefinite, vague
amhenderfynol adj irresolute
amhenodol adj indefinite
amherchi vb dishonour, insult
amherffaith adj imperfect
amherffeithrwydd nm imperfection
amhersonol adj impersonal
amherth(y)nasol adj irrelevant
amheuaeth nf doubt, scepticism
amheugar adj suspicious; sceptical
amheuol adj doubting, doubtful
amheus adj doubting, doubtful, dubious
amheuthun adj dainty, savoury ♦ (-ion) nm dainty, delicacy, treat
amheuwr (-wyr) nm doubter, sceptic
amhlantadwy adj childless, barren
amhleidiol, amhleitgar adj impartial
amhoblog adj sparsely populated
amhoblogaidd adj unpopular
amhosibl adj impossible
amhriodol adj improper
amhrisiadwy adj priceless
amhrofiadol adj inexperienced
amhrydlon adj unpunctual
amhûr adj impure, foul
amhwrpasol adj irrelevant
amhwyllo vb lose one's senses, go mad
aml adj frequent, abundant ♦ adv often
amider, amldra nm abundance
amldduwiad (-iaid) nm polytheist
amldduwiaeth nf polytheism
amleiriog adj wordy, verbose, prolix
amlen (-ni) nf envelope, wrapper
amlhad nm increasing, increase
amlhau vb increase, multiply
amlinelliad (-au) nm outline
aml-lawr adj multi-storey

amlochrog adj many-sided
amlosgfa nf crematorium
amlosgi vb cremate
amlwg adj plain, clear, manifest, evident, prominent
amlwreigiaeth nf polygamy
amlwreigiwr (-wyr) nm polygamist
amlygiad (-au) nm manifestation
amlygrwydd nm prominence, limelight
amlygu vb manifest, reveal, evince
amnaid (-neidiau) nf beck, nod
amneidio vb beckon, nod
amnest (-au) nm amnesty
amod (-au) nmf condition
amodi vb covenant, stipulate
amodol adj conditional
amrant (-au, -rannau) nm eyelid
amrantiad nm wink, twinkling, second
amreiniol adj unprivileged
amrwd adj uncooked, raw, crude
amryddawn adj versatile
amryfal adj sundry, manifold
amryfus adj erroneous, inadvertent
amryfusedd (-au) nm error, oversight
amryliw adj variegated; multicoloured
amryw adj several, sundry, various
amrywiad (-au) nm variant
amrywiaeth nf variety, diversity
amrywio vb vary, differ
amrywiol adj sundry
amser (-oedd, -au) nmf time
amseriad (-au) nm timing, dating, date
amserlen (-ni) nf time-table
amserol adj timely; temporal
amseru vb time, date
amserydd (-ion) nm chronologist
amseryddiaeth nf chronology
amseryddol adj chronological
amwisg (-oedd) nf covering,

shroud
amwisgo vb enwrap, shroud
amwys adj ambiguous
amwysedd nm ambiguity
amyn conj, prep unless, except, but
amynedd nm patience
amyneddgar adj patient
an- prefix un-, in-, de-, dis-
anabl adj disabled
anabledd nm disability
anad adj: **yn a.** above all, more than
anadferadwy adj irreparable
anadl (-au, -on) nf/m breath
anadliad nm breath, breathing
anadlu vb breathe
anadnabyddus adj unknown
anaddas adj unfit, unsuitable
anaddasu vb unfit, disqualify
anaeddfed, anaddfed adj unripe, immature
anaeddfedrwydd nm unripeness, immaturity
anaele adj awful, direful; incurable
anaesthetig adj anaesthetic
anaf (-au) nm blemish, defect; wound
anafu vb blemish, maim, hurt
anafus adj maimed, disabled
anair (-eiriau) nm ill report, slander
anallu nm inability
analluog adj unable
analluogi vb disenable; disable
anaml adj infrequent, rare ♦ adv rarely, seldom
anamlwg adj obscure, inconspicuous
anamserol adj untimely, mistimed
anap (-hapon) nm/f mischance, mishap
anarchiaeth nm anarchy
anarchydd (-ion) nm anarchist
anarferol adj unusual, extraordinary
anarfog adj unarmed

anchwiliadwy *adj* unsearchable

ancr *nm/f* anchorite, anchoress

ancwyn (-ion) *nm* dinner, supper; delicacy

andras *nm* curse; devil, deuce

andwyo *vb* spoil, ruin, undo

andwyol *adj* harmful, ruinous

anedifeiriol *adj* impenitent

aneddfa see **anheddfa**

aneffeithiol *adj* ineffectual

aneglur *adj* indistinct; illegible

aneirif *adj* innumerable

anelu *vb* bend, aim

anenwog *adj* unrenowned, ignoble, mean

anerchiad (-au) *nm* salutation, address

anesboniadwy *adj* inexplicable

anesgusodol *adj* inexcusable

anesmwyth *adj* uneasy, restless

anesmwythder, -dra *nm* uneasiness, unrest

anesmwytho *vb* be or make uneasy

anesmwythyd *nm* uneasiness, disquiet

anewyllysgar *adj* unwilling

anfad *adj* wicked, nefarious

anfadwaith *nm* wickedness, villainy

anfadwaith *nm* villainy; crime

anfadwr (-wyr) *nm* villain, scoundrel

anfaddeugar *adj* unforgiving

anfaddeuol *adj* unpardonable

anfantais (-teision) *nf* disadvantage

anfanteisiol *adj* disadvantageous

anfarwol *adj* undying, immortal

anfarwoldeb *nm* immortality

anfedrus *adj* unskilful

anfedrusrwydd *nm* unskilfulness

anfeidrol *adj* infinite

anfeidroldeb *nm* infinity

anferth *adj* huge, monstrous

anferthedd *nm* hugeness, monstrosity

anfodlon *adj* unwilling

anfodloni *vb* discontent, dissatisfy

anfodlonrwydd *nm* discontent

anfodd *nm* unwillingness, displeasure

anfoddio *vb* displease, disoblige

anfoddlon *etc* see **anfodlon**

anfoddog *adj* discontented, dissatisfied

anfoddogrwydd *nm* discontentment

anfoesgar *adj* unmannerly, rude

anfoesgarwch *nm* rudeness, incivility

anfoesol *adj* immoral

anfoesoldeb *nm* immorality

anfon *vb* send, transmit, dispatch

anfoneddigaidd *adj* ungentlemanly

anfonheddig *adj* impolite, discourteous

anfoniad *nm* sending, transmission

anfri *nm* disrespect, dishonour

anfucheddol *adj* immoral

anfuddiol *adj* unprofitable

anfwriadol *adj* unintentional

anfwyn *adj* unkind, ungentle, uncivil

anfynych *adj* infrequent, seldom, rare

anffaeledig *adj* infallible

anffaeledigrwydd *nm* infallibility

anffafriol *adj* unfavourable

anffawd (-ffodion) *nf* misfortune

anffodus, anffortunus *adj* unfortunate

anffrwythlon *adj* unfruitful, barren

anffurfio *vb* disfigure, deform

anffurfiol *adj* informal

anffyddiaeth *nf* atheism

anffyddiwr (-wyr) *nm* infidel, atheist

anffyddlon *adj* unfaithful

anhaeddiannol *adj* unmerited, undeserved

anhaeddiant *nm* demerit, unworthiness

anhapus *adj* unhappy, unlucky

anhardd *adj* unhandsome, unseemly, ugly

anhawdd *adj* hard, difficult

anhawddgar *adj* unamiable, unlovely

anhawster (anawsterau) *nm* difficulty

anheddfa (aneddfaoedd) *nf*, **-le (aneddleoedd)** *nm/f* dwelling-place

anhepgor (-ion) *nm* essential

anhepgorol *adj* indispensable

anhoffter *nm* hatred, dislike

anhraethadwy *adj* unutterable

anhraethol *adj* unspeakable, ineffable

anhrefn *nm* disorder, confusion

anhrefnu *vb* disorder, disarrange

anhrefnus *adj* disorderly, untidy

anhreiddiol *adj* impervious, impenetrable

anhreuliedig *adj* undigested; unspent

anhrugarog *adj* unmerciful, merciless

anhuddo *vb* cover (a fire)

anhunedd *nm* wakefulness, disquiet

anhwyldeb *nm* disorder, complaint, illness

anhwylustod *nm* inconvenience

anhyblyg *adj* inflexible, stiff, rigid

anhydawdd *adj* insoluble

anhyder *nm* distrust, diffidence

anhyderus *adj* diffident

anhydrin *adj* unmanageable

anhydyn *adj* intractable, obstinate

anhyddysg *adj* unversed, ignorant

anhyfryd *adj* unpleasant

anhyfrydwch *nm* unpleasantness

anhygar *adj* unpleasant, unamiable

anhygoel *adj* incredible

anhygyrch *adj* inaccessible

anhylaw *adj* unhandy, unwieldy

anhynod *adj* indistinctive; uncertain

anhysbys *adj* unknown; unversed

anhywaith *adj* intractable, refractory

anial *adj* desert, wild ♦ *nm* wilderness

anialwch *nm* wilderness

anian (-au) *nf* nature, instinct, genius

anianawd *nm* temperament, disposition

anianol *adj* natural

anianyddol *adj* physical

anifail (-feiliaid) *nm* animal, beast

anifeilaidd *adj* beastly, brutish

anifeileiddio *vb* animalize, brutalize

anlwc *nm* bad luck, misfortune

anlwcus *adj* unlucky

anllad *adj* wanton, lascivious, lewd

anlladrwydd *nm* wantonness, lewdness

anlladu *vb* wanton

anllygredig *adj* incorrupt, incorruptible

anllygredigaeth *nf* incorruption

anllythrennog *adj* illiterate

anllywodraeth *nf* misrule, anarchy

annaearol *adj* unearthly, weird

annatodol *adj* indissoluble, that cannot be undone

annaturiol *adj* unnatural

annealladwy *adj* unintelligible

anneallus *adj* unintelligent

annedwydd *adj* unhappy, miserable

annedwyddwch *nm* unhappiness

annedd (anheddau) *nf* dwelling

anneddfol *adj* lawless

annefnyddiol *adj* useless; immaterial

annel (anelau) *nm/f* trap; purpose, aim

annelwig *adj* shapeless, unformed; vague

anner (aneirod, -i, -au) *nf* heifer

annerbyniol *adj* unacceptable

annerch *vb* salute, greet, address ♦ **(anerchion)** *nm* salutation, greeting

annewisol adj ineligible, undesirable, unwelcome

annhebyg adj unlike, dissimilar

annhebygol adj unlikely, improbable

annhebygolrwydd nm improbability

annhebygrwydd nm unlikeness, unlikelihood

annheg adj unfair

annhegwch nm unfairness

annheilwng adj unworthy

annheilyngdod nm unworthiness

annherfynol adj endless; infinitive, infinite

annhirion adj ungentle, cruel

annhosturiol adj pitiless, ruthless

annhuedd nf disinclination

annhueddol adj disinclined, indisposed

anniben adj untidy, slovenly

annibendod nm untidiness

annibyniaeth nf independence

annibynnol adj independent

Annibynnwr (-ynwyr) nm Independent

annichellgar adj guileless, simple

annichon, -adwy adj impossible

anniddan adj comfortless, miserable

anniddig adj peevish, irritable, fretful

anniddigrwydd nm peevishness

anniddos adj leaky, comfortless

annifeiriol adj innumerable, countless

annifanedig adj unfading, imperishable

annifyr adj miserable, wretched

annifyrrwch nm misery

anniffoddadwy adj unquenchable

annigonedd nm insufficiency

annigonol adj insufficient, inadequate

annigonolrwydd nm inadequacy

annileadwy adj indelible,

ineffaceable

annilys adj unauthentic, spurious, insincere

annillyn adj inelegant, clumsy

annioddefol adj unbearable, intolerable

anniogel adj unsafe, insecure

anniolchgar adj unthankful, ungrateful

anniolchgarwch nm ingratitude

annirnadwy adj incomprehensible

annisgrifiadwy adj indescribable

annisgwyliadwy adj unexpected

anniwair adj unchaste, incontinent, lewd

anniwall adj insatiable

anniweirdeb nm unchastity, incontinence

anniwylliedig adj uncultured

annoeth adj unwise, imprudent

annoethineb nm unwisdom, folly

annog vb incite, urge; exhort

annormal adj abnormal

annos vb incite, set (a dog) on

annosbarthus adj unruly, disorderly

annuw, -iad (-iaid) nm atheist

annuwiaeth nf atheism

annuwiol adj ungodly, godless

annuwioldeb nm ungodliness

annwn, annwfn nm the underworld; hell

annwyd (anwydau, -on) nm cold

annwyl adj dear, beloved

annyledus adj undue, wrongful

annymunol adj unpleasant, disagreeable

annynol adj inhuman, cruel

annysgedig adj unlearned

anobaith nm despair

anobeithio vb despair

anobeithiol adj hopeless

anochel, -adwy adj unavoidable, inevitable

anodd adj hard, difficult

anoddefgar adj impatient, intolerant

anogaeth (-au) nf exhortation
anolrheinadwy adj untraceable
anolygus adj unsightly
anonest adj dishonest
anonestrwydd nm dishonesty
anorchfygol adj irresistible; unconquerable
anorfod adj insuperable; unavoidable
anorffen adj endless, unending
anorffenedig adj incomplete, unfinished
anorthrech adj invincible
anrasol adj graceless
anrhaith (-rheithiau) nf prey, spoil, booty
anrheg (-ion) nf present, gift
anrhegu vb present, give
anrheithio vb prey, spoil, plunder
anrheithiwr (-wyr) nm spoiler, pillager
anrhydedd (-au) nm honour
anrhydeddu vb honour
anrhydeddus adj honourable
anrhydeddwr (-wyr) nm honourer
ansad adj unsteady, unstable
ansadrwydd nm instability
ansafadwy adj unstable; fickle
ansathredig adj untrodden, unfrequented
ansawdd (-soddau) nm/f quality, state
ansefydlog adj unsettled, unstable; fickle
ansefydlogi vb unsettle
ansicr adj uncertain, doubtful
ansicrwydd nm uncertainty, doubt
ansoddair (-eiriau) nm adjective
ansoddeiriol adj adjectival
ansyber adj untidy, slovenly
Antartica nf the Antarctic
anterliwt (-iau) nm/f interlude
anterth nm meridian, zenith, prime
antur (-iau) nm attempt, venture; adventure; enterprise. **ar a.** at random

anturiaeth (-au) nf adventure, enterprise
anturiaethus adj adventurous, enterprising
anturiaethwr (-wyr) nm adventurer
anturio vb venture, adventure
anturus adj adventurous
anthem (-au) nf anthem
anudon (-au) nm false oath, perjury
anudoniaeth nf perjury
anudonwr (-wyr) nm perjurer
anufudd adj disobedient
anufudd-dod nm disobedience
anufuddhau vb disobey
anundeb nm disunion
anunion adj crooked; unjust
anuniondeb nm injustice, iniquity
anurddo vb spoil, mar, disfigure
anwadal adj unstable, fickle, changeable
anwadalu vb waver, vacillate
anwadalwch nm fickleness
anwar adj wild, barbarous, savage
anwaraidd adj uncivilized, barbarous
anwarddyn (-wariaid) nm barbarian, savage
anwaraidd-dra nm barbarity
anwastad adj uneven, unstable, fickle
anwe (-oedd) nf woof
anwedd nm vapour, steam
anweddaidd adj unseemly, indecent
anweddus adj improper, indecent
anweledig adj unseen, invisible
anwes nm indulgence; caress
anwesog adj pampered, affectionate
anwesu vb fondle, caress, pamper, indulge
anwir adj untrue, lying, false; wicked
anwiredd (-au) nm untruth; iniquity

anwireddu *vb* falsify

anwireddus *adj* untruthful, false, lying

anwr (-wyr) *nm* wretch, coward

anwybod *nm* ignorance

anwybodaeth *nf* ignorance

anwybodus *adj* ignorant

anwybyddu *vb* ignore

anwydog *adj* cold, chilly; having a cold

anwydwst *nf* influenza

anwyldeb *nm* belovedness, dearness

anwyliaid *npl* beloved ones, favourites

anwylo *vb* cherish, fondle, caress

anwylyd (-liaid) *nm* beloved

anwylyn *nm* favourite

anwythiad *nm* induction

anwytho *vb* induce

anwythol *adj* inductive

anymarferol *adj* impractical, impracticable

anymddiried *vb, nm* mistrust, distrust

anymwybodol *adj* unconscious

anymwybyddiaeth *nf* unconsciousness

anynad *adj* peevish, petulant; brawling

anysgrifenedig *adj* unwritten

anysgrythurol *adj* unscriptural

anystwyth *adj* stiff, rigid

anystwytho *vb* stiffen

anystyriaeth *nf* heedlessness, rashness

anystyriol *adj* heedless, reckless, rash

anystywallt, -ell *adj* unmanageable

apêl (apelion) *nm/f*, **apeliad (-au)** *nm* appeal

apelio *vb* appeal

apostol (-ion) *nm* apostle

apostolaidd, -ig *adj* apostolic

apostoliaeth *nf* apostleship

apwyntiad (-au) *nm* appointment

apwyntio *vb* appoint

âr *nm* ploughed land, tilth; ground

ar *prep* on, upon, over

arab *adj* facetious, merry, pleasant

arabedd *nm* facetiousness, wit

arabus *adj* witty

aradr (erydr) *nm* plough

araf *adj* slow, soft, gentle, still

arafu *vb* slow; quiet; moderate

arafwch *nm* slowness; moderation

arail *vb* guard, care for, foster ♦ *adj* attending, careful

araith (areithiau) *nf* speech

arall (eraill) *adj, pron* another, other; else

aralleg (-au) *nf/m* allegory

aralleiriad (-au) *nm* paraphrase

aralleirio *vb* paraphrase

araul *adj* sunny, sunlit; serene

arawd *nf* speech, oration

arbed *vb* spare, save

arbediad (-au) *nm* save, salvage

arbedol *adj* sparing, saving

arbenigaeth *nf* expertise; specialisation

arbenigo *vb* specialise

arbenigrwydd *nm* speciality; prominence

arbenigwr (-wyr) *nm* specialist

arbennig *adj* special

arbrawf (arbrofion) *nm* experiment

arbrofi *vb* experiment

arbrofol *adj* experimental

arch (eirchion) *nf* request, petition; bidding

arch (eirch) *nf* ark, coffin; trunk, waist

archaeoleg *nf* archaeology

archangel (-ylion) *nm* archangel

archddiacon (-iaid) *nm* archdeacon

archeb (-ion) *nf* order

archebu *vb* order

archen *nf*, **-ad** *nm* shoe; clothing

archesgob (-ion) *nm* archbishop

archesgobaeth (-au) *nf* archbishopric

archfarchnad (-oedd) *nf*

supermarket

archiad nm bidding

archif (-au) nm archive

archifdy (-dai) nm record office

archifydd (-ion) nm archivist

archoffeiriad (-iaid) nm high priest

archoll (-ion) nf wound

archolli vb wound

archwaeth nm taste, appetite

archwaethu vb taste, savour

archwilio vb examine, audit; explore

archwiliwr (-wyr) nm examiner, auditor; explorer

ardal (-oedd) nf region, district

ardalydd (-ion) nm marquis

ardreth (-i) nf rent

ardrethu vb rent

ardystiad (-au) nm pledge, attestation

ardystio vb pledge, attest

arddangos vb show, exhibit, indicate

arddangosfa (-feydd) nf show, exhibition

arddegol adj teenage

arddel vb avow, own

arddeliad nm claim, avowal; unction

ardderchog adj excellent, noble, splendid

ardderchowgrwydd nm excellency

arddodi vb prefix; impose

arddodiad (-iaid) nm preposition

arddu vb plough (properly **aredig**)

arddull (-iau) nf style

arddulleg nf stylistics

ardduniant nm sublimity

arddunol adj sublime

arddwr (-wyr) nm ploughman

arddwrn (-ddyrnau) nm wrist

arddywediad (-au) nm dictation

aredig vb plough

areitheg nf rhetoric

areithio vb speak, make a speech

areithiwr (-wyr) nm speaker, orator

areithyddiaeth nf oratory; elocution

arel nm laurel

aren (-nau) nf kidney; (pl.) reins

arestio vb arrest

arf (-au) nm/f weapon, (pl.) arms; tool

arfaeth (-au) nf purpose; decree

arfaethu vb purpose, intend

arfbais (-beisiau) nf coat of arms

arfdy (-dai) nm armoury

arfer vb use, accustom ♦ (-ion) nf/m use, custom, habit

arferiad nm/f use, custom, habit

arferol adj usual, customary

arfod nf stroke of a weapon, fight; armour; opportunity

arfog adj armed

arfogaeth nf armour

arfogi vb arm

arfoll (-au) nm pledge, oath

arfordir (-oedd) nm coast

arforol adj maritime

arffed (-au) nf lap

argae (-au) nm dam, embankment; enclosed place

argeisio vb seek

argel nm/f concealment, refuge ♦ adj hidden, occult

arglwydd (-i) nm lord

arglwyddaidd adj lordly

arglwyddes (-au) nf lady

arglwyddiaeth (-au) nf lordship, dominion

arglwyddiaethu vb have dominion

argoed (-ydd) vb enclosure of trees

argoel (-ion) nf sign, token, omen

argoeli vb betoken, portend, augur

argoelus adj ominous

argraff (-ion, -au) nf print, impression

argraffdy (-dai) nm printing-house

argraffiad (-au) nm impression; edition

argraffu vb print, impress

argraffwaith *nm* print, typography

argraffwasg *nf* printing-press

argraffwr (-wyr), **-ydd** (-ion) *nm* printer

argrwm, -wn *adj* convex

argyfwng (-yngau, -yngoedd) *nm* crisis

argyhoeddi *vb* reprove; convince, convict

argyhoeddiad (-au) *nm* conviction

argyhoeddiadol *adj* convincing

argymell *vb* urge, recommend

argymhelliad *nm* recommendation

arholi *vb* examine

arholiad (-au) *nm* examination

arholwr (-wyr) *nm* examiner

arhosfa *nf* abode; stopping-place (*bus*)

arhosiad *nm* staying, stay

arhosol *adj* abiding, permanent

arial *nm/f* vigour, mettle

arian *nm* silver ♦ *coll n* money, cash. **a. breiniol** currency. **a. byw** mercury. **a. gleision** silver. **a. parod** cash. **a. pen** exact money. **a. treigl** current money

ariandy (-dai) *nm* bank

ariangar *adj* fond of money, avaricious

ariangarwch *nm* love of money, avarice

ariannaid *adj* silver, silvern

ariannaidd *adj* silvery

arianneg *nm/f* finance

Ariannin *nf* Argentina

ariannog *adj* moneyed, wealthy, rich

ariannol *adj* financial, monetary

ariannu *vb* silver; finance/fund

ariannydd (arianyddion) *nm* banker, investor, financier

arlais (-leisiau) *nf* temple

arloesi *vb* clear, prepare the way, pioneer

arloesydd *nm* pioneer

arluniaeth *nf* portraiture, painting

arlunio *vb* draw, paint, portray

arlunydd (-wyr) *nm* artist

arlwy (-au, -on) *nm/f* provision, feast, menu

arlwyaeth *nf* catering

arlwyo *vb* prepare, provide; cook

arlwydd (-ion) *nm* president

arlwyddiaeth *nf* presidency

arlwyddol *adj* presidential

arlliw (-iau) *nm* varnish, tint, shade, trace

arlliwio *vb* colour, tint, paint

arllwys *vb* pour out, empty

arllwysfa *nf* outfall, outlet, vent

armel *nm* second milk

armes *nf* prophecy; calamity

arobryn *adj* worthy, prize-winning

arofun *vb* intend, purpose

arogl (-au), **aroglau** (-euon) *nm* scent, smell

arogl-darth *nm* incense

arogldarthu *vb* burn incense

arogli, arogleuo *vb* scent; smell

arogliad *nm* smelling, sense of smell

arolwg *nm* survey

arolygiaeth *nf* superintendency

arolygu *vb* superintend

arolygwr (-wyr), **-ydd** (-ion) *nm* superintendent, inspector

aros *vb* wait, await, stay, stop, tarry, abide, remain

arswyd *nm* dread, terror, horror

arswydo *vb* dread; shudder

arswydus *adj* fearful, terrible, dreadful

arsyllfa (-feydd) *nf* observatory

arsylwi *vb* observe

artaith (-teithiau) *nf* torture, torment, pang

arteithio *vb* torture, rack

arteithiol *adj* racking, excruciating

arth (eirth) *nm/f* bear

arthes (-au) *nf* she-bear

arthio, -u *vb* bark, growl

Artig: yr A. *nf* the Arctic

artistig *adj* artistic

aruchel *adj* lofty, sublime

arucheledd *nm* loftiness, sublimity

aruthr *adj* marvellous, strange

aruthredd *nm* amazement, horror

aruthrol *adj* huge, prodigious

arwahanrwydd *nm* uniqueness, individuality

arwain *vb* conduct, lead, guide, carry

arwedd (-au, -ion) *nf* bearing, aspect

arweddu *vb* bear

arweddwr (-wyr) *nm* bearer

arweiniad *nm* guidance; introduction

arweiniol *adj* leading, introductory

arweinydd (-ion) *nm* guide, leader; conductor

arweinyddiaeth *nf* leadership

arwerthiant (-iannau) *nm* auction

arwerthu *vb* sell by auction

arwerthwr (-wyr) *nm* auctioneer

arwisgiad *nm* investiture

arwisgo *vb* enrobe, array, invest

arwr (-wyr) *nm* hero

arwraidd *adj* heroic, epic

arwres (-au) *nf* heroine

arwrgerdd (-i) *nf* epic poem

arwriaeth *nf* heroism

arwrol *adj* heroic, gallant

arwybod *nm* awareness

arwydd (-ion) *nm/f* sign, signal; ensign

arwyddair (-eiriau) *nm* motto

arwyddlun (-iau) *nm* emblem, symbol

arwyddluniol *adj* emblematic, symbolic

arwyddnod (-au) *nm* mark, token

arwyddo *vb* sign; signify

arwyddocâd *nm* signification, significance

arwyddocaol *adj* significant

arwyddocáu *vb* signify, denote

arwyl (-ion) *nf* funeral, funeral rites

arwylo *vb* mourn over the dead

arwynebedd *nm* surface, superficies

arwynebol *adj* superficial

arwyrain *nm/f* praise, panegyric ♦ *vb* rise, extol

arwystlo *vb* pledge, mortgage

arysgrif (-au), -en (-nau) *nf* inscription, epigraph

asb (-iaid) *nf* asp

asbri *nm* animation, vivacity, spirits

asen (-nau) *nf* rib

asen (-nod) *nf* she-ass

asesu *vb* assess

aseth *nf* stake, spar, lath

asgell (esgyll) *nf* wing, fin. **a. fraith** chaffinch

asgellog *adj* winged

asgellwr (-wyr) *nm* wing, outside-forward

asglod, asglodion *npl* **(asglodyn** *nm)* chips

asgre *nf* bosom, heart

asgwrn (esgyrn) *nm* bone

asiad (-au) *nm* joint, weld

asiant (-au) *nm* agent

asio *vb* join, weld; solder; cement

astell (estyll, ystyllod) *nf* plank, shelf

astroleg *nf* astrology

astrus *adj* abstruse, difficult

astud *adj* attentive

astudiaeth (-au) *nf* study

astudio *vb* study

astudrwydd *nm* attentiveness

aswy *adj* left

asyn (-nod) *nm* he-ass

asynnaidd *adj* asinine

at *prep* to, towards; for; at; by

atafaeliad *nm* confiscation, distraint

atafaelu *vb* distrain, confiscate

atal *vb* stop, hinder, withhold ♦ **(-ion)** *nm* hindrance, impediment. **a. dweud** stammering

ataleb (-au) *nf* injunction

atalfa (-feydd) *nf* check; stoppage

ataliad (-au) *nm* stoppage

ataliol adj preventive
atalnod (-au) nf stop, point
atalnodi vb point, punctuate
atblygol adj reflexive
ateb vb answer, reply ♦ (-ion) nf answer
atebol adj answerable, responsible
ateg (-ion) nf prop, stay, support
ategiad (-au) nm affirmation
ategol adj confirming; auxiliary
ategu vb support
atgas adj odious, hateful
atgasedd nm hatred
atgasrwydd nm odiousness, hatefulness
atgenhedliad nm regeneration
atgenhedlu vb regenerate
atgno (-oeau, -oeon) nm remorse
atgof (-ion) nm remembrance, reminiscence
atgofio vb recollect, remember, remind
atgofus adj reminiscent
atgoffa vb recall, remind
atgyfnerthion npl reinforcements
atgyfnerthu vb reinforce
atgyfodi vb rise, raise again
atgyfodiad nm resurrection
atgynhyrchu vb reproduce
atgyweiriad (-au) nm repair
atgyweirio vb repair, mend
atgyweiriwr (-wyr) nm repairer, mender
Athen nf Athens
atig (-au) nm/f attic
atodi vb add, append, affix
atodiad (-au) nm addition, appendix
atodlen (-ni) nf supplement; schedule
atodol adj supplementary
atolwg, atolygu vb pray, beseech
atom (-au) nm/f atom
atomfa (-feydd) nf nuclear power station
atomig adj atomic
atsain (-seiniau) nf echo

atseinio vb resound, echo
atwf (atyfion) nm second growth
atyniad nm attraction
atyniadol adj attractive
atynnu vb attract
athletau npl athletics
athrawes (-au) nf teacher, governess
athrawiaeth (-au) nf doctrine
athrawiaethol adj doctrinal
athrist adj very sad, pensive, sorrowful
athro (-athrawon) nm teacher, master
athrod (-ion) nm slander, libel
athrodwr (-wyr) nm slanderer, libeller
athrofa (-feydd) nf college, academy, institute
athrofaol adj academic
athroniaeth nf philosophy
athronydd (-ion, -wyr) nm philosopher
athronyddol adj philosophical
athronyddu vb philosophize
athrylith (-oedd) nf genius
athrylithgar adj of genius, talented
athrywyn nm mediation, intervention ♦ vb mediate, arbitrate
aur nm gold
awch nm edge; ardour, zest; relish, appetite
awchlym adj sharp, keen, acute
awchlymu vb sharpen, whet
awchus adj sharp, keen; eager; greedy
awdl (-au, odlau) nf ode
awdur (-on, -iaid) nm author
awdurdod (-au) nm/f authority
awdurdodedig adj authorised
awdurdodi vb authorize
awdurdodol adj authoritative
awdures (-au) nf authoress
awduriaeth nf authorship
awel (-on) nf breeze, wind
awelog adj breezy, windy

awen (-au) *nf* muse
awen (-au) *nf* rein
awenydd (-ion) *nm* poet
awenyddiaeth *nf* poetry, poesy
awenyddol *adj* poetical
awenyddu *vb* poetize
awgrym (-au, -iadau) *nm* hint, suggestion
awgrymiadol *adj* suggestive
awgrymog *adj* suggestive
awgrymu *vb* hint, suggest
awr (oriau) *nf* hour
Awst *nm* August
Awstralia *nf* Australia
Awstria *nf* Austria
awtistig *adj* autistic
awydd (-au) *nm* desire, eagerness
awyddfryd *nm* vehement desire, zeal
awyddu *vb* desire
awyddus *adj* desirous, eager, zealous
awyr *nf* air, sky
awyrdrom (-au) *nf* aerodrome
awyren (-nau, -ni) *nf* balloon, aeroplane
awyrendy (-dai) *nm* hangar
awyrgylch (-au, -oedd) *nm/f* atmosphere
awyriad *nm* ventilation
awyrlong (-au) *nf* airship
awyro, -u *vb* air, ventilate

B

baban (-od) *adj* baby
babanaidd *adj* babyish
babandod *nm* babyhood, infancy
babi *nm/f* baby
bacas (bacs(i)au) *nf* footless stocking; hair on horse's fetlocks
baco *nm* tobacco
bacwn *nm* bacon
bach (-au) *nm* hook. **bachau petryal** square brackets
bach *adj* little, small

bachell (-au, -ion) *nf* nook, corner; snare
bachgen (bechgyn) *nm* boy
bachgendod *nm* boyhood
bachgennaidd *adj* boyish
bachgennyn (bechgynnos) *nm* little boy
bachigyn (bachigion) *nm* little bit, diminutive
bachog *adj* hooked
bachu *vb* hook, grapple
bachwr (-wyr) *nm* hooker (*rugby*)
bad (-au) *nm* boat. **b. achub** lifeboat
badwr (-wyr) *nm* boatman
badd (-au), **baddon** (-au) *nm* bath
bae (-au) *nm* bay
baedd (-od) *nm* boar
baeddu *vb* beat, buffet; soil
baetio *vb* bait, maltreat
bag (-iau) *nm* bag
bagad (-au) *nm* cluster; troop, multitude
bagl (-au) *nf* crook; crutch; leg
baglor (-ion) *nf* bachelor
bagloriaeth *nf* bachelorship
baglu *vb* entangle, ensnare, trip
bai (beiau) *nm* fault, vice; defect; blame
baich (beichiau) *nm* burden, load
bais *nm* bottom, ford; walking
bala *nm* efflux of river from lake
balch *adj* proud; glad
balchder *nm* pride
balchdra *nm* joy, gladness
balchïo *vb* pride
baldordd *nm* babble, balderdash
baldorddi *vb* babble
bale *nm* ballet
baled (-i) *nf* ballad
baledwr (-wyr) *nm* ballad-monger
balm *nm* balm
balmaidd *adj* balmy
balog (-au, -ion) *nf* fly, cod-piece; flap
balleg *nf* hamper, net, purse
ballegrwyd (-au) *nf* drag-net

ban (-nau) *nm/f* peak; horn; corner; stanza
banadl *npl* (-badlen *nf*) broom
banc (-iau) *nm* bank
banc (bencydd) *nm* bank, mound, hill
bancaw (-iau) *nm* band, tuft
baner (-au, -i) *nf* banner, flag
banerog *adj* with banners, bannered
banerwr (-wyr) *nm* standard-bearer; ensign
banffagl (-au) *nf* bonfire, blaze
bangaw *adj* eloquent, melodious, skilful
bangor (-au, bangyr) *nf/m* upper row of rods in wattle fence; monastery
baniar (-ieri) *nf/m* shout; banner
banllawr (-lloriau) *nm* platform
banllef (-au) *nf* loud shout
bannod (banodau) *nf* article
bannog *adj* elevated, conspicuous; horned
bar (-rau) *nm* bar
bâr *nm* fury, greed
bara *nm* bread
barbaraidd *adj* barbarous
barbareidd-dra *nm* barbarity
barbareiddio *vb* barbarize
barbariad (-iaid) *nm* barbarian
barbariaeth *nm* barbarism
barbwr (-wyr) *nm* barber
barcer (-iaid) *nm* tanner
barclod (-iau) *nm* apron
barcud (-iaid), **barcutan** (-od) *nm* kite
bardd (beirdd) *nm* bard, poet
barddas *nm/f* bardism
barddol *adj* bardic
barddoni *vb* compose poetry, poetize
barddoniaeth *nf* poetry, verse
barddonol *adj* poetic, poetical
barf (-au) *nf* beard, whiskers
barfog *adj* bearded
bargeinio, bargenna *vb* bargain

bargen (-einion) *nf* bargain
bargod (-ion) *nm* eaves
bargyfreithiwr (-wyr) *nm* barrister
bariaeth *nf/m* evil, grief, wrath; greed
baril (-au) *nf* barrel
barilaid (-eidiau) *nf* barrelful
bario *vb* bar, bolt
barlad *nm* drake
barlys *nm* barley
barn (-au) *nf* judgment; opinion; sentence
barnais *nf* varnish
barnedigaeth (-au) *nf* judgment
barneisio *vb* varnish
barnol *adj* judicial, condemnatory, annoying
barnu *vb* judge
barnwr (-wyr) *nm* judge
baromedr *nm* barometer
barrug *nm* hoar-frost
barugo *vb* cast hoar-frost
barugog *adj* white with hoar-frost
barus *adj* voracious, greedy
barwn (-iaid) *nm* baron
barwnes (-au) *nf* baroness
barwniaeth (-au) *nf* barony
barwnig (-iaid) *nm* baronet
bas *adj* shallow ♦ (bais, beis) *npl* shallows
bas *adj, nm* bass
basged (-i, -au) *nf* basket
basgedaid (-eidiau) *nf* basketful
basgedwr (-wyr) *nm* basket-maker
basn (-au, -ys) *nm* basin
bastard (-iaid) *nm* bastard
bastardiaeth *nf* bastardy
batri *nm* battery
bath (-au) *nm* kind, sort; stamp; coin
bathdy (-dai) *nm* mint
bathodyn (-odau) *nm* medal, badge
bathol *adj* coin, coined
bathu *vb* coin
baw *nm* dirt, mire, dung, filth
bawaidd *adj* dirty, vile; sordid,

mean

bawd (**bodiau**) *nf* thumb, toe

bechan *adj* f. of **bychan**

bechgynnos *npl* little boys, youngsters

bedw *npl* (**-en** *nf*) birch

bedydd *nm* baptism

bedyddfa (**-fâu, -feydd**) *nf* baptistry

bedyddfaen (**-feini**) *nm* font

bedyddio *vb* baptize

bedyddiol *adj* baptismal; baptized

Bedyddiwr (**-wyr**) *nm* Baptist

bedd (**-au**) *nm* grave, tomb, sepulchre

beddargraff (**-iadau**) *nm* epitaph

beddfaen (**-feini**) *nm* tombstone

beddgell (**-oedd**) *nf* vault, catacomb

beddrod (**-au**) *nm* tomb, sepulchre

Beibl (**-au**) *nm* Bible

Beiblaidd *adj* Biblical

beichio *vb* burden; low; sob

beichiog *adj* pregnant

beichiogi *vb* conceive

beichus *adj* burdensome, oppressive

beicio *vb* cycle

beiddgar *adj* daring, audacious

beiddgarwch *nm* daring, audacity

beiddio *vb* dare, presume

beili (**beiliaid**) *nm* bailiff

beio *vb* blame, censure

beirniad (**-iaid**) *nm* adjudicator; critic

beirniadaeth (**-au**) *nf* adjudication; criticism

beirniadol *adj* critical

beirniadu *vb* adjudicate; criticize

beisgawn (**-au**) *nf* stack, heap of corn sheaves

beiston *nf* sea-shore, beach; surf

beius *adj* faulty; blameworthy

bellach *adv* now, at length

bendigaid, bendigedig *adj* blessed

bendigedigrwydd *nm* blessedness

bendith (**-ion**) *nf* blessing, benediction

bendithio *vb* bless

bendithiol *adj* conferring blessings

benthyca, -io *vb* borrow, lend

benthyciwr (**-wyr**) *nm* borrower, lender

benthyg *nm* loan

benyw *adj* female ♦ (**-od**) *nf* female, woman

benywaidd *adj* feminine; effeminate

benywol *adj* feminine, female

ber *adj* f. of **byr**

bêr (**berau, -i**) *nm* spear; roasting-spit

bera *nf/m* rick; pyramid

berdys *npl* (**-yn** *nm*, **-en** *nf*) shrimps

berf (**-au**) *nf* verb. **b. anghyflawn** transitive verb. **b. gyflawn** intransitive verb

berfa (**-fâu, -feydd**) *nf* barrow

Berlin *nf* Berlin

berth *adj* beautiful, valuable

berthog *adj* wealthy, fair

berw *nm, adj* boiling, seething, ebullition

berwedig *adj* boiling

berwedydd (**-ion**) *nm* boiler

berwedd-dy (**-dai**) *nm* brewery

berweddu *vb* brew

berwi *vb* boil, seethe, effervesce

berwr *coll n* cress

betgwn *nm/f* bedgown

betws *nm* oratory, chapel; birch grove

beudy (**-dai**) *nm* cow-house, byre

beunoeth, beunos *adv* nightly, every night

beunydd *adv* daily, every day, always

beunyddiol *adj* daily, quotidian

bidog (**-au**) *nf* dagger; bayonet

bil (**-iau**) *nm* bill

bilidowcar *nm* cormorant

bilwg (**-ygau**) *nm* billhook

bing (-oedd) nm alley, bin

biocemeg nm/f biochemistry

bir (-oedd) nm beer

biswail nm filth

blaen adj fore, foremost, first; front ♦ (-au, -ion) nm point, end, top, tip; front, van, priority, precedence; edge

blaenasgellwr (-wyr) nm wing-forward

blaenbrawf (-brofion) nm foretaste

blaendal nm prepayment, deposit

blaendarddu vb sprout

blaenddalen (-nau) nf title page

blaenddodi vb prefix

blaenddodiad (-iaid) nm prefix

blaenffrwyth nm first-fruits

blaengar adj prominent, progressive

blaengroen (-grwyn) nm foreskin

blaenllaw adj forward, prominent

blaenllym adj sharp, keen

blaenllymu adj sharpen, whet

blaenor (-iaid) nm leader; elder

blaenoriaeth nf preference; precedence

blaenorol adj previous, antecedent

blaenu vb point; outrun; precede

blaenwr (-wyr) nm leader; forward

blagur coll n sprouts, buds, shoots

blaguro vb sprout, bud; flourish

blaguryn nm sprout, bud, shoot

blaidd (bleiddiaid, bleiddiau) nm wolf

blas nm taste, savour, relish

blasio, -u vb taste

blasus adj tasty, savoury, delicious

blawd (blodion, -iau) nm flour, meal

blêr adj untidy, slovenly

blerwm nm blabberer; blab-blab

blew npl (-yn nm) hairs; hair; fur

blewog adj hairy, shaggy

bliant nm lawn, fine linen

blif (-iau) nm catapult

blingo vb skin, flay

blin adj tired, weary; peevish, irritable

blinder (-au) nm weariness; trouble

blinderog, -derus adj wearisome

blinfyd nm tribulation

blino vb tire, weary; trouble, vex

blith (-ion) nm milk ♦ adj milch

blith draphlith adv helter-skelter

blodeugerdd (-i) nf anthology

blodeuglwm nm bunch, nosegay

blodeuo vb flower, bloom, flourish

blodeuog adj flowery; flourishing

blodeuyn, blodyn (blodau) nm flower

blodiog adj floury, mealy

bloddest nf rejoicing, acclamation

bloedd (-iau, -iadau) nf shout

bloeddio, -ian vb shout, cry

bloeddiwr (-wyr) nm shouter

bloesg adj lisping, faltering, indistinct

bloesgi vb lisp, falter, speak indistinctly

bloneg nm, -en nf lard, grease

blwch (blychau) nm box

blwng adj angry, sullen, cheerless ♦ nm anger

blwydd (-au, -i) nf, adj year of age; year-old

blwydd-dal nm annuity, pension

blwyddiad (-iaid) nm yearling, annual

blwyddiadur (-on) nm yearbook, annual

blwyddyn (blynyddoedd) nf year

blychaid (-eidiau) nm boxful

blynedd npl/f years (after numerals)

blynyddol adj annual, yearly

blys (-iau) nm craving, lust

blysig adj greedy, lustful

blysigrwydd nm greediness

blysio vb crave, lust

bocs (-ys) nm box

bocsach nm vaunt, boast, brag

boch (-au) nf check

bochgoch adj rosy-cheeked
bod vb be, exist ♦ (-au) nm being, existence. **Y Bod Mawr** nm God
boda nmf buzzard
bodio vb thumb, finger
bodlon adj content, willing
bodloni vb satisfy, content; be content
bodlonrwydd nm contentment
bodolaeth nf existence
bodoli vb exist
bodd nm pleasure, will, consent
boddfa nf flood, drenching
boddhad nm pleasure, satisfaction
boddhaol adj pleasing, satisfactory
boddhau vb please, satisfy
boddhaus adj pleased
boddi vb drown; flood
boddio vb please, satisfy
boddlon etc see **bodlon**
bogail (-eiliau) nmf navel; boss, hub
boglwm (-lymau), **-lyn** (-lynnau) nm boss, knob, stud, bud, bubble
bol, bola (boliau) nm belly
bolaid (-eidiau) nm bellyful
bolera vb gorge, guzzle; sponge (fig)
bolerwr (-wyr) nm sponge, parasite
bolgi (-gwn) nm gourmand, glutton
bolgno nm, **-fa** nf gripes, colic
bolheulo vb bask in the sun
bolio vb belly, gorge
boliog adj big-bellied, corpulent
boloch nm pain, anxiety, destruction
bolrwth adj gluttonous, greedy
bolrwym adj costive, constipated
bollt (-au, -ydd, byllt) nf bolt
bolwst nf/m gripes, colic
bol(y)sothach nm hotchpotch; jargon
bom (-iau) nm/f bomb
bomio vb bomb
bôn (bonau, bonion) nm bottom; stump
boncath (-od) nm buzzard
bonclust (-iau) nm box on the ear
boncyff (-ion) nm stump, trunk, stock
bondigrybwyll adv forsooth ♦ adj hardly mentionable
bondo nm eaves
bonedd nm gentility, nobility
boneddigaidd adj noble; gentlemanly
boneddigeiddrwydd nm gentlemanliness
boneddiges (-au) nf lady
bonesig nf lady; Miss
bonet (-i) nf bonnet
bongam adj bandy-legged
bonheddig adj noble, gentle, gentlemanly ♦ (boneddigion) nmpl gentlemen
bonheddwr (-wyr) nm gentleman
bonllef (-au) nf shout
bonllwm adj bare-bottomed, breechless; bare-backed
Bonn nf Bonn
bonyn (bonion) nm stump
bord (-ydd, -au) nf table, board
bore (-au) nm morning ♦ adj early
boreddydd nm day-break, morning
borefwyd nm breakfast
boreol adj morning
bors nf hernia
bos nf palm of the hand, fist
bost (-ydd, -au) nf boast, brag
bostio vb boast, brag
botas, en (-asau) nf boot
botwm (-ymau) nm button
botymog adj buttoned
botymu vb button
both (-au) nf nave of wheel; boss
brac adj free, frank, talkative
bracso vb wade, paddle
bracty (-tai) nm malt-house, brewery
brad (-au) nm treason; plot
bradfwriadu vb plot, conspire
bradlofrudd (-ion) nm assassin

bradlofruddiaeth (-au) *nf* assassination

bradlofruddio *vb* assassinate

bradwr (-wyr) *nm* traitor

bradwriaeth (-au) *nf* treason, treachery

bradwrus *adj* traitorous, treacherous

bradychu *vb* betray

braen *adj* rotten, corrupt

braenar (-au) *nm* fallow

braenaru *vb* fallow, pioneer

braenu *vb* rot, putrify

braf *adj* fine

brag *nm* malt

bragad *nf* army, battle; offspring

bragaldian *vb* jabber, gabble, prate

bragio *vb* brag, boast

bragiwr (-wyr) *nm* bragger, boaster

bragod (-au, -ydd) *nm* bragget

bragu *vb* malt, brew

bragwair *nm* moorland hay, coarse grass

bragwr (-wyr) *nm* maltster, brewer

braich (breichiau) *nf* arm; branch, handle; headland

braidd *adv* rather, somewhat

braint (breintiau) *nf* privilege

braisg *adj* gross, thick, large; pregnant

braith *adj* f. of **brith**

brân (brain) *nf* crow, rook, raven

bras (breision) *adj* fat; coarse; rich; luxuriant

brasáu *vb* grow fat or gross

brasbwytho *vb* baste, tack

brasgamu *vb* stride

Brasil *nf* Brazil

braslun (-iau) *nm* sketch, outline

braslunio *vb* sketch, outline

brasnaddu *vb* rough-hew

braster *nm* fat

brasterog *adj* fat, greasy

brat (-iau) *nm* rag, clout; pinafore

bratiaith *nf* debased language

bratiog *adj* ragged, tattered

brath (-au) *nm* stab, wound; sting; bite

brathog *adj* that bites; biting

brathu *vb* stab, wound; sting; bite

brau *adj* brittle, frail, fragile; kindly; prompt

braw (-iau) *nm* terror, dread, fright

brawd (brodyr) *nm* brother; friar

brawd (brodiau) *nf* judgment

brawdgarwch *nm* brotherly love

brawdle (-oedd) *nf/m* judgement-seat

brawdlys (-oedd) *nf/m* assize-court

brawdmaeth *nm* foster-brother

brawdol *adj* brotherly, fraternal

brawdoliaeth (-au) *nf* brotherhood, fraternity

brawddeg (-au) *nf* sentence

brawddegu *vb* construct sentences

brawl *nm* boast, brag; gabble, tattle

brawychu *vb* frighten, terrify

brawychus *adj* frightful, terrible

bre (-on, -oedd) *nf* hill, highland

brebwl (-yliaid) *nm* blockhead; prattler

breci *nm* wort; spree

brecwast (-au) *nm/f* breakfast

brecwasta *vb* breakfast

brech *nf* eruption, pox

brech *adj* f. of **brych**

brechdan (-au) *nf* slice of bread and butter

brechiad (-au) *nm* inoculation, vaccination

brechu *vb* vaccinate, inoculate

bredych (-au, -ion) *nm* betrayal; fear; rascal

bref (-iadau) *nf* lowing; bleat; bray

breferad (-au) *nm* bellowing

brefiad (-au) *nm* lowing; bleating

brefu *vb* low; bleat; bray

breg *nm* guile, blemish; breach ♦ *adj* fragile, faulty

bregliach vb jabber

bregus adj frail, brittle, rickety

breichled (-au) nf bracelet

breichrwy(f) (-au) nm/f bracelet

breinio vb privilege, enfranchise

breiniol adj privileged, free

breinlen (-ni) nf charter

breintal nm bonus; royalty

breintiedig adj patented, patent

breintio vb privilege, favour

brenhinaidd adj kingly, regal

brenhindod nm royalty

brenhindref (-i) nf royal city

brenhindy (-dai) nm royal palace

brenhines (breninesau) nf queen

brenhinfainc nf throne

brenhiniaeth (breniniaethau) nf
kingdom

brenhinol adj royal, regal

brenin (-hinoedd) nm king

brest (-iau) nf breast, chest

bresych npl (-en nf) cabbages

brethyn (-nau) nm cloth

brethynnwr (-ynwyr) nm clothier;
cloth-worker

breuan (-au) nf quern; print of
butter

breuder nm brittleness, frailty

breuddwyd (-ion) nm/f dream. b.
gwrach wishful thinking

breuddwydio vb dream

breuddwydiol adj dreaming,
dreamy

breuddwydiwr (-wyr) nm dreamer

brëyr, brehyr (brehyrion, -iaid) nm
nobleman, chief, baron

bri nm honour, renown, distinction

briallu npl (briallen nf) primroses

bribys npl fragments, scraps

brifo vb hurt

brig (-au) nm top; (pl) twigs

brigâd (-au) nf brigade. b. dân
fire-brigade

briger (-au) nm hair of head; top

brigo vb top; branch

brigog adj branching; flourishing

brigwyn adj white-topped, white-

crested

brigyn (brigau) nm twig

brith adj mottled, speckled; f
braith

britho vb mottle, speckle; dazzle

Brithwr (-wyr) nm Pict

brithyll (-od, -iaid) nm trout

briw adj broken, bruised, sore ♦
(-iau) nm wound, sore

briwfwyd nm crumbs, mince

briwlaw nm drizzling rain

briwlio vb broil

briwo vb wound, hurt

briwsion npl (-yn nm) crumbs,
fragments.

briwsioni vb crumble

briwsyn (briwsion) nm crumb,
morsel

bro (-ydd) nf land; region; vale

broch nm badger

broch nm froth, anger, tumult

brochi vb chafe, fume; bluster

brochus adj fuming; blustering

brodio vb embroider; darn

brodor (-ion) nm native; fellow
countryman

brodorol adj native, indigenous

broga (-od) nm frog

brol nf boast, brag

brolio vb boast, brag, vaunt

broliwr (-wyr) nm boaster,
braggart

bron (-nau, -nydd) nf breast;
hillside

bron adv almost, nearly. o'r b.
completely, in succession

bronfraith (-freithod) nf thrush

brongoch (-iaid) nf/m robin
redbreast

bronwen nf weasel

bru nm womb

brud (-iau) nm chronicle;
divination

brudio vb prognosticate, divine

brudiwr (-wyr) nm wizard,
soothsayer

brwd adj hot, fervent ♦ nm boil,

heat

brwdfrydedd *nm* ardour, enthusiasm

brwdfrydig *adj* ardent, enthusiastic

brwmstan *nm* brimstone, sulphur

brwmstanaidd *adj* brimstony, sulphury

brwnt *adj* foul, nasty, dirty; harsh; *f* bront

brwyd *nm* embroidering frame; skewer

brwyd *adj* variegated; bloodstained; shattered

brwydo *vb* embroider; tear, consume

brwydr (-au) *nf* battle, combat

brwydro *vb* battle, combat

brwydrwr (-wyr) *nm* fighter, combatant

brwydwaith *nm* embroidery

brwylio *vb* broil

brwyn *nm* grief, sadness

brwynen (brwyn) *nf* rush

brwynog *adj* rushy

brwysg *adj* drunk; vigorous

brycan, brecan (-au) *nf/m* blanket, rug

brych *adj* mottled, brindled, freckled; *f* brech ◆ *nm* the after-birth of a cow

brychau *npl* spots, freckles

brycheulyd *adj* spotted, brindled

brychni *nm* spots, freckles

brychu *vb* spot, freckle

bryd *nm* mind, heart, will

brydio *vb* burn, inflame, boil, throb

brygawthan *vb* jabber, prate, rant

bryn (-iau) *nm* hill

bryncyn (-nau) *nm* hillock

bryniog *adj* hilly

brynti, bryntni *nm* filthiness, filth

brys *nm* haste, hurry

brysio *vb* hasten, hurry

brysiog *adj* hurried, hasty

bryslythyr (-au) *nm* dispatch

brysneges (-au) *nf* telegram

brytheirio *vb* belch; utter oaths, threats *etc*

Brython (-iaid) *nm* Briton, Welshman

Brythoneg *nf* British language, Welsh

brythwch *nm* storm, tumult; groan

bryweddu *vb* brew

brywes *nm* brewis

bual (buail) *nm* buffalo, drinking horn

buan *adj* fast, quick, swift, fleet; soon

buander, -dra *nf* swiftness, speed

buandroed *adj* swift-footed

buarth (-au) *nm* yard

buchdraeth (-au) *nf* biography, memoir

buchedd (-au) *nf* life, conduct

bucheddol *adj* right-living, virtuous

bucheddu *vb* live, flourish

buches (-au) *nf* herd of cows

buchfrechu *vb* vaccinate

budr *adj* dirty, filthy, foul, vile

budreddi *nm* filthiness, filth

budro *vb* dirty, soil, foul

budd (-ion) *nm* benefit, profit, gain

buddai (-eiau) *nf* churn

buddel (-wydd) *nm/f* cow-house post, pillar

buddiant (-iannau) *nm* interest

buddio *vb* profit, avail

buddiol *adj* profitable, beneficial, useful

buddioldeb *nm* profitableness, expediency

buddsodd (-ion), **-iad** (-au) *nm* investment

buddsoddi *vb* invest

buddugol *adj* winning, victorious

buddugoliaeth (-au) *nf* victory

buddugoliaethus *adj* victorious, triumphant

buddugwr (-wyr) *nm* winner,

victor
bugail (-eiliaid) *nm* shepherd;
pastor
bugeiles (-au) *nf* shepherdess
bugeiliaeth (-au) *nf* pastorate
bugeilio, -a *vb* watch, shepherd
bugeiliol *adj* pastoral
bugunad *nm* bellowing, roar
bun *nf* maid, maiden
burgyn (-nod, iaid) *nm* carcass,
carrion
burman, burum *nm* barm, yeast
busnes (-ion) *nm/f* business
busnesa *vb* interfere, meddle
busnesgar, busneslyd *adj*
meddlesome
bustach (-tych) *nm* bullock, steer
bustachu *vb* buffet about, bungle
bustl *nm* gall, bile
bustlaidd *adj* like gall; bitter as
gall
buwch (buchod) *nf* cow. **b. goch
gota** ladybird
bwa (bwâu) *nm* bow; arch
bwaog *adj* arched, vaulted
bwbach (-od) *nm* bugbear, bogey,
scarecrow
bwced (-i) *nm/f* bucket
bwci (-iod) *nm* bugbear, bogey,
ghost
bwcl (byclau) *nm* buckle
bwcled (-au) *nf* buckler
bwch (bychod) *nm* buck. **b.
dihangol** scapegoat. **b. gafr** he-
goat
bwgan (-od) *nm* bogey, ghost,
scarecrow
bwgwl (bygylau) *nm* threat,
menace
bwgwth see **bygwth, bygythio**
bwhwman *vb* beat about;
vacillate
bŵl (bylau) *nm* globe, ball, knob
bwlch (bylchau) *nm* gap; pass;
notch
bwled (-i) *nf* bullet
bwn (bynnoedd, byniaid) *nm*

bittern
bwndel (-i) *nm* bundle
bwngler (-iaid) *nm* bungler
bwnglera *vb* bungle
bwngleraidd *adj* bungling, clumsy
bwnglerwaith *nm* bungle, botch
bwnglerwch *nm* clumsiness
bwr (byr) *adj* fat, big, strong
bwrdais (-deisiaid) *nm* burgess
bwrdeistref (-i) *nm* borough
bwrdd (byrddau) *nm* table; deck;
board. **b. du** black-board
bwriad (-au) *nm* purpose, intention
bwriadol *adj* intentional
bwriadu *vb* purpose, intend
bwrlwm (byrlymau) *nm* bubble;
gurgling
bwrn (byrnau) *nm* burden,
incubus; bale
bwrw *vb* cast, shed; strike;
imagine, suppose; spend ♦ *nm*
cast, throw; woof
bwtler (-iaid) *nm* butler
bwtri *nm* buttery, pantry, dairy
bwth (bythod) *nm* hut, booth, cot
bwthyn (bythynnod) *nm* cottage,
cabin, hut
bwyall, -ell (-eill, -yll) *nf* axe
bwyd (-ydd) *nm* food
bwyda, bwydo *vb* feed
bwyd-offrwm (-ymau) *nm* meat-
offering
bwydwr (-wyr) *nm* feeder
bwygilydd *adv* (from one) to the
other
bwylltid (-au) *nm* swivel
bwyllwr(w) (-yriau) *nm* provisions
for journey
bwysel (-au, -i) *nm* bushel
bwystfil (-od) *nm* (wild) beast
bwystfilaidd *adj* beastly, brutish
bwystfiles (-au) *nf* beast
bwyta *vb* eat; corrode
bwytadwy *adj* eatable, edible
bwytawr (-wyr) *nm* eater
bwyteig *adj* greedy, voracious
bwyty (-tai, -tyau) *nm* restaurant

bychan adj little, small; f **bechan**

bychander, -dra nm littleness, smallness

bychanu vb belittle, minimize

bychanus adj derogatory

byd (-oedd) nm world; state; life

bydaf (-au) nmf beehive

bydio vb live, fare

bydol adj worldly, secular

bydolddyn (-ion) nm worldling

bydolrwydd nm worldliness

bydwraig (-wragedd) nf midwife

bydwreigiaeth nf midwifery

bydysawd nm universe

byddag (-au) nf running knot, noose

byddar adj deaf ♦ (-iaid, byddair) nm deaf person

byddardod nm deafness

byddarol adj deafening

byddaru vb deafen, stun

byddin (-oedd) nf army, host

byddino vb set army in array, embattle

byddinog adj with armies

bygwth vb threaten, menace ♦ (-ython, -ythiau) nm threat, menace

bygythiad (-au) nm threat

bygythio vb threaten, menace

bygythiol adj threatening, menacing

byl (-au) nmf edge, brim (of vessel). hyd y f. to the brim

bylb (-au) nm bulb

bylchog adj gapped, gappy; notched

bylchu vb make a gap, breach; notch

byngalo (-s, -au) nm bungalow

bynnag pron -ever, -soever

byr adj short, brief; f **ber**

byrbryd (-iau) nm luncheon, snack

byrbwyll adj impulsive, rash

byrbwylltra nm impulsiveness

byrder, -dra nm shortness, brevity

byrdwn nm burden, refrain, chorus

byrddaid (-eidiau) nm tableful

byrddio vb board

byrddiwr (-wyr) nm boarder

byrfyfyr adj impromptu

byrgorn adj shorthorn

byrhau vb shorten, abridge

byrhoedlog adj short-lived

byrlymu vb bubble, gurgle

byrllysg (-au) nmf mace

byrnio (-u) vb bale, bundle

byrnwr (-wyr) nm baler

bys (-edd) nm finger; toe; hand of dial, latch

bysaid (-eidiau) nm pinch

byseddu vb finger

bysled(r) (-au) nm finger-stall

byth adv ever, for ever ♦ nm eternity

bytheiad (-aid) nm hound

bytheirio vb belch, threaten

bythfywiol adj everliving

bythgofiadwy adj memorable

bythol adj everlasting, eternal, perpetual

bytholi vb perpetuate

bytholwyrdd (-ion) adj, nm evergreen

bythynnwr (-ynwyr) nm cottager

byw vb live ♦ adj alive, living, quick ♦ nm life

bywgraffiad (-au) nm biography

bywgraffiadol adj biographical

bywgraffiadur (-on) nm biographical dictionary

bywgraffydd (-ion) nm biographer

bywgraffyddol adj biographical

bywhau, bywiocâu vb animate, vivify, quicken

bywin nm soft part of bread

bywiog adj lively, animated, vivacious

bywiogi vb enliven, animate

bywiol adj living, animate

bywoliaeth (-iolaethau) nf living

bywyd (-au) nm life

bywydeg nf biology

bywydegwr (-wyr) *nm* biologist

bywydfad (-au) *nm* lifeboat

bywydol *adj* of life, vital

bywyn (-nau) *nm* pith, core

C

cabaets *npl* (**cabaetsen** *nf*) cabbage

caban (-au) *nm* cabin

cabidwl *nm* consistory, chapter

cabl (-au) *nm* blasphemy, reviling

cabledd (-au) *nm* blasphemy

cableddus *adj* blasphemous

cablu *vb* blaspheme, revile

cablwr (-wyr), **-ydd** (-ion) *nm* blasphemer

caboli *vb* polish

cacamwci *nm* burdock

cacen (-nau, -ni) *nf* cake

cacwn *npl* (**cacynen** *nf*) wasps; wild bees

cachfa (-feydd) *nf* excretion; closet

cachgi (-gwn) *nm* coward; sneak

cachiad *nm* excretion, jiffy; coward

cachlyd *adj* befouled, dirty

cachu *vb* defecate

cachwr (-wyr) *nm* coward; sneak; one who excretes

cad (-au, -oedd) *nf* battle; army, host

cadach (-au) *nm* cloth, kerchief, clout

cadair (-eiriau) *nf* chair, seat; cradle; udder

cadarn (cedyrn) *adj* strong, mighty; firm

cadarnhad *nm* affirmation, confirmation

cadarnhaol *adj* affirmative

cadarnhau *vb* strengthen, confirm

cadeirfardd (-feirdd) *nm* chaired bard

cadeirio *vb* chair

cadeiriog *adj* chaired

cadeiriol *adj* pertaining to a chair, cathedral

cadeirydd (-ion) *nm* chairman

cadernid *nm* strength; stability

cadfarch (-feirch) *nm* war-horse

cadfridog (-ion) *nm* general

cadfwyall (-eill, -yll) *nf* battleaxe

cadlas (-lesydd) *nf* close, enclosure

cadlong (-au) *nf* warship, battleship

cadlys (-oedd) *nf* camp, headquarters

cadno (cadnoid, cadnawon) *nm* fox

cadnöes, cadnawes (-au) *nf* vixen

cadoediad (-au) *nm* armistice, truce

cadofydd (-ion) *nm* tactician, strategist

cadofyddiaeth *nf* tactics, strategy

cadofyddol *adj* tactical, strategic

cadw *vb* keep, preserve, save; hold

cadwedig *adj* saved

cadwedigaeth *nf* salvation

cadw-mi-gei *nf* money-box

cadwraeth *nf* keeping; observance; conservation

cadwyn (-au, -i) *nf* chain

cadwyno *vb* chain

cadwynog *adj* chained, in chains

caddug *nm* darkness; mist, fog

caddugo *vb* darken, obscure

cae (-au) *nm* field; fence, hedge; brooch

caead (-au) *nm* cover, lid ♦ *adj* shut, closed

caeadle (-oedd) *nm* enclosure

caeëdig *adj* closed, fenced

cael *vb* have; get; find

caen (-au) *nf* surface; peel; coating

caenen (-nau) *nf* layer, film, flake

caentach (-au) *nf* wrangle, grumbling ♦ *vb* wrangle, grumble

caenu *vb* coat, finish

caer (-au, ceyrydd) *nf* wall; castle; city

Caerdydd *nf* Cardiff

Caeredin *nf* Edinburgh
caeriwrch *nm* roebuck
caerog *adj* walled, fortified; brocaded
Caersalem *nf* Jerusalem
caeth *adj* bound, captive, confined
♦ **(-ion)** *nm* bondman, slave
caethder *nm* strictness; restraint; asthma
caethfab (-feibion) *nm* slave
caethfasnach *nf* slave-trade
caethferch (-ed) *nf* slave
caethforwyn (-forynion) *nf* slave
caethglud *nf* captivity
caethgludiad (-au) *nm* captivity
caethgludo *vb* lead captive
caethiwed *nm* slavery, bondage, captivity, detention
caethiwo *vb* bind, confine, enslave
caethiwus *adj* confining; confined, tied
caethlong (-au) *nf* slave-ship
caethwas (-weision) *nm* slave
caethwasanaeth, -wasiaeth *nm* slavery
cafell (-au) *nf* cell; sanctuary, oracle
cafn (-au) *nm* trough, gutter
cafnedd *nm* concavity
cafnio, -u *vb* hollow out, scoop, gouge
cafod see **cawod**
caffael *vb* get, obtain
caffaeledd *nm* availability; acquisitiveness
caffaeliad (-au) *nm* acquisition, asset; prey, spoil
caffe, -i (-s) *nm* café, restaurant
caffio *vb* snatch, grapple
cafflo *vb* cheat; entangle
cagl *nm* clotted dirt
caglu *vb* befoul, bedraggle
cangell (-hellau) *nf* chancel
cangelloriaeth *nf* chancellorship
cangen (-hennau) *nf* branch, bough
canghellor (cangellorion) *nm* chancellor

canghennog *adj* branching
canghennu *vb* branch, ramify
caib (ceibiau) *nf* pickaxe, mattock
cail (ceiliau) *nf* sheepfold, flock of sheep
caill (ceilliau) *nf* testicle
cain *adj* fair, fine, elegant
cainc (cangau, ceinciau) *nf* branch; strand; strain
cais (ceisiadau) *nm* application; attempt; try
cal(a) (-iau) *nf* penis
calan (-nau) *nm* first day of month. Dydd C. New Year's Day
calch *nm* lime
calchaidd *adj* calcareous
calchbibonwy *nm* stalactite
calchbost (-byst) *nm* stalagmite
calchen *nf* limestone; lump of lime
calchfaen (-feini) *nm* limestone
calcho, calchu *vb* lime
calclwys (calcwli) *nm* calculus
caled *adj* hard; severe; harsh; dry
caledfwrdd *nm* hardboard
caledi *nm* hardness; hardship
caledu *vb* harden, dry
caledwch *nm* hardness
calen (-nau, -ni) *nf* whetstone; bar
calendr *nm* calendar
calennig *nm/f* New Year's gift
calon (-nau) *nf* heart
calondid *nm* encouragement
calon-dyner *adj* tender-hearted
calon-galed *adj* hard-hearted
calon-galedwch *nm* hard-heartedness
calonnog *adj* hearty; high-spirited
calonogi *vb* hearten, encourage
calori (-iau) *nm* calorie
call *adj* wise, sensible, rational
callestr (cellystr) *nf* flint
callineb *nm* wisdom, sense
calsiwm *nm* calcium
cam (-au) *nm* step
cam *adj* crooked, wry; wrong ♦ **(-au)** *nm* injury, wrong
cam- *prefix* wrong, mis-

camarfer vb misuse, abuse ♦
(-**ion**) nm/f misuse, malpractice
camargraff nf/m wrong impression
camarwain vb mislead
camarweiniol adj misleading
Cambodia nf Cambodia
cambren (-**ni**) nm swingletree
camchwarae nm foul play
camdafliad (-**au**) nm foul throw
camdaflu vb foul throw
camder, -dra nm crookedness
cam-drefn nf disorder
camdreuliad nm indigestion
camdreulio vb mis-spend
cam-drin vb ill-treat, abuse
camdriniaeth (-**au**) nf ill-treatment
camdystiolaeth nf false
witness
camdystiolaethu vb bear false
witness
camddeall vb misunderstand
camddealltwriaeth nm
misunderstanding
camddefnydd nm misuse
camddefnyddio vb misuse
camedd nm bend, curvature. **c. y
droed** instep. **c. y gar** knee-joint
cameg (-**au, cemyg**) nf felloe
camel (-**od**) nm camel
camenw (-**au**) nm misnomer
camenwi vb misname
camfa (-**feydd**) nf stile
camfarnu vb misjudge
camgred (-**oau, -au**) nf misbelief,
heresy
camgredu vb misbelieve
camgredwr (-**wyr**) nm heretic
camgwl nm penalty, fine; blame
camgyfrif vb miscalculate
camgyhuddiad (-**au**) nm false
accusation
camgyhuddo vb accuse falsely
camgymeriad (-**au**) nm mistake
camgymryd vb mistake, err
camlas (-**lesi, -lesydd**) nf/m canal
camliwio vb misrepresent
camochri vb be offside

camog (-**au**) nf felloe
camp (-**au**) nf feat, exploit; game;
prize
campfa (-**feydd**) nf gymnasium
campus adj excellent, splendid,
grand
campwaith (-**weithiau**) nm
masterpiece, feat
campwr (-**wyr**) nm champion
camre nm walk, footstep(s)
camsyniad (-**au**) nm mistake
camsynied vb mistake
camsyniol adj mistaken
camu vb bow, bend, stoop
camu vb step, stride
camwedd (-**au**) nm iniquity,
transgression
camweddu vb transgress
camwri nm injury, wrong
camymddwyn vb misbehave
camymddygiad (-**au**) nm
misconduct
cân (**caniadau, caneuon**) nf song
can adj white ♦ nm flour
Canada nf Canada
cancr nm canker; cancer
cancro vb canker, corrode
candryll adj shattered, wrecked
canfasio vb canvass
canfed adj hundredth
canfod vb see, perceive, behold
canfyddadwy adj perceptible
canfyddiad nm perception
canhwyllbren (**canwyllbrenni, -au**)
nm/f candlestick
canhwyllwr (**canhwyllwyr**) nm
chandler
caniad nm singing; ringing;
crowing
caniad (-**au**) nf song, poem
caniadaeth nf singing, psalmody
caniatâd nm leave, permission,
consent
caniataol adj permissive; granted
caniatáu vb permit, allow
caniedydd (-**ion**) nm singer,
songster; song-book

canlyn vb follow, pursue
canlyniad (-au) nm consequence, result
canlynol adj following, consequent
canlynwr (-wyr) nm follower
canllaw (-iau) nf/m hand-rail, parapet, aid
canmlwyddiant nm centenary
canmol vb praise, commend
canmoladwy adj praiseworthy
canmoliaeth (-au) nf praise, commendation
canmoliaethus adj eulogistic, complimentary
cannaid adj white, bright, luminous
cannu vb whiten, bleach
cannwr (canwyr) nm bleacher
cannwyll (canhwyllau) nf candle
canol adj ♦ (-au) nm middle, centre, midst
canolbarth (-au) nm middle part, midland
canolbwynt (-iau) nm centre, focus
canolbwyntio (-iau) vb centre, concentrate
canoldir (-oedd) nm inland region
canolddydd nm mid-day, noon
canolfan (-nau) nm/f centre
canoli vb centre; arbitrate; centralize
canoloesol adj mediaeval
canolog adj central
canolradd (-ol) adj intermediate
canolwr (-wyr) nm mediator, referee; centrehalf, centre. **c. blaen** centreforward
canon (-au) nm/m, (-iaid) nm canon
canonaidd adj canonical
canoneiddio vb canonize
canoniaeth (-au) nf canonry
canonwr (-wyr) nm canon, canonist
canradd (-au) adj, nf centigrade, percentile

canran (-nau) nm percentage
canrif (-oedd) nf century
cansen (-ni) nf cane
canser nm cancer
canslo vb cancel
cant (-au) nm circle, ring, rim; tyre
cant (cannoedd) nm hundred
cantel (-au) nm rim, brim
cantîn (cantinoedd) nf canteen
cantor (-ion) nm singer
cantores (-au) nf songstress, singer
cantref (-i, -ydd) nm hundred
cantwr (-orion) nm singer, songster
cantwraig nf songstress, singer
canu vb sing, chant; play; crow; ring. **c. gwlad** country music
canŵ (-od) nm canoe
canŵo vb canoe
canwr (-wyr) nm singer
canwriad (-iaid) nm centurion
canwyr (-au, -ion) nm plane (in carpentry)
canys conj because, for
cap (-iau) nm cap
capan (-au) nm cap; lintel
capel (-i, -ydd, -au) nm chapel
capelwr (-wyr) nm chapel-goer
caplan (-iaid) nm chaplain
caplaniaeth (-au) nf chaplaincy
capteiniaeth nf captaincy
capten (-einiaid) nm captain
car (ceir) nm car. **c. campau** sports car
câr (ceraint) nm friend; relation
carafán (-au) nf caravan
carbohydrad (-au) nm carbohydrate
carbon (-au) adj, nm carbon
carbwl adj clumsy, awkward
carco vb take care
carcus adj solicitous, anxious, careful
carchar (-au) nm prison; restraint
carchardy (-dai) nm prison-house

carchariad nm imprisonment
carcharor (-ion) nm prisoner
carcharu vb imprison
carden (cardiau) nf card
cardigan (-au) nf cardigan
cardod (-au) nf charity, alms, dole
cardota vb beg
cardotyn (-ion) nm beggar
cardydwyn, -odwyn nm., **-wen** nf weakest of brood or litter
caredig adj kind
caredigrwydd nm kindness
caregog adj stony
caregu vb stone; petrify; gather stones
carennydd nm friendship; kinship
caretsen (carets) nf carrot
carfaglog adj clumsy
carfan (-au) nf beam; swath; party, faction
cariad (-au) nm love
cariad (-au, -on) nm/f lover, sweetheart
cariadfab nm lover, sweetheart
cariadferch nf sweetheart, mistress
cariadlawn adj full of love, loving
cariadus adj loving, beloved, dear
caridým (-s) nm ragamuffin
cario vb carry, bear
carismatig adj charismatic
carlam (-au) nm prance, gallop
carlamu vb prance, gallop
carlwm (-lymod) nm ermine, stoat
carn (-au) nm hoof; hilt, haft, handle
carn (-au), **carnedd** (-au) nf cairn
cárnifal nm carnival
carniforus adj carnivorous
carnog, -ol adj hoofed
carol (-au) nm/f carol
carp (-iau) nm clout, rag
carped (-au, -i) nm carpet
carpiog adj ragged, tattered
carrai (careiau) nf lace, thong
carreg (cerrig) nf stone
cart (ceirt) nm/f cart

cartaid, certaid (-eidiau) nm cartful
cartilag (-au) nm cartilage
cartref (-i, -ydd) nm home, abode
cartrefle (-oedd) nm abode
cartreflu nm militia
cartrefol adj homely, domestic, home; civil
cartrefu vb make one's home, settle
cartwn (cartwnau) nm cartoon
cartwnydd (-ion) nm cartoonist
carth (-ion) nm tow, oakum; off-scouring
carthen (-ni, -nau) nf Welsh blanket, coverlet
carthffos (-ydd) nf sewer
carthffosaeth nf sewage
carthu vb cleanse, purge, scavenge
caru vb love; like; court
caruaidd adj loving, kind
carw (ceirw) nm stag, deer
carwden (-ni) nf back-chain; tall awkward fellow
carwr (-wyr) nm lover, wooer
carwriaeth (-au) nf courtship
cas adj hateful, odious; nasty, disagreeable ♦ nm hatred, aversion
cas (caseion) nm hater, foe, enemy
casáu vb hate, detest, abhor
casbeth (-au) nm aversion, nuisance
caseg (cesig) nf mare
casét (-iau) nm cassette
casgen (-ni, casgiau) nf cask
casgl nf/m collection
casgliad (-au) nm collection; gathering
casglu vb collect, gather; infer
casglwr (-wyr), **-ydd** (-ion) nm collector
casineb nm hatred
cast (-iau) nm vice, knack
castan (-au) nf chestnut
castanwydd npl (-en nf) chestnut-trees

castell (cestyll) nm castle

castellog adj castled, castellated

castellu vb castle, encamp

castio vb trick, cheat; cast, calculate

castiog adj full of tricks, tricky

casul (-(i)au) nm/f chasuble, cassock

caswir nm unpalatable truth

casyn (casiau) nm case, casing

cat (-iau) nm bit, piece, fragment; pipe

catalog (-au) nm catalogue

catalogio vb catalogue

catalydd (-ion) nm catalyst

categori (-iau) nm category

catel coll n chattels; cattle

catgor (-(i)au) nm ember day(s)

catrawd (-rodau) nf regiment

cath (-od, -au) nf cat

cathl (-au) nf melody, hymn, lay

cathlu vb sing, hymn

cathod (-au) nf cathode

catholig adj catholic

Catholigiaeth nf Catholicism

catholigrwydd nm catholicity

cau adj hollow, concave

cau vb shut, close, enclose

caul (ceulion) nm maw; rennet; curd

caw (-(i)au) nm band, swaddling-clothes

cawdel nm hotchpotch, mess

cawell (cewyll) nm hamper, basket, cradle

cawellaid (-eidiau) nm hamperful

cawellwr (-wyr) nm basket-maker

cawg (-iau) nm basin, bowl, pitcher

cawl nm broth, soup; hotchpotch

cawn npl (-en) reeds

cawod (-ydd) nf shower

cawodi vb shower

cawodog adj showery

cawr (cewri) nm giant

cawraidd adj gigantic

cawres (-au) nf giantess

caws nm cheese; curd

cawsai, cawsi nf/m causeway

cawsaidd adj cheesy, caseous

cawsellt (-ydd, -i, -au) nm cheese-vat

cawsio vb curd, curdle

cawsiog adj curdled

cecian vb stammer

cecren (-nod) nf shrew, scold, cantankerous woman

cecru vb wrangle, bicker

cecrus adj cantankerous, quarrelsome

cecryn (-nod) nm wrangler, brawler

cedor nm/f pubic hair

cedrwydd npl (-en nf) cedars

cefn (-au) nm back; support

cefndedyn nm mesentery; diaphragm, pancreas

cefnder (-dyr) nm first cousin

cefndir (-oedd) nm background

cefnen (-nau) nf ridge

cefnfor (-oedd) nm main sea, ocean

cefngrwm adj hump-backed

cefnog adj well-off, well-to-do

cefnogaeth nf encouragement, support

cefnogi vb encourage, support

cefnogol adj encouraging

cefnu vb back, turn the back, forsake

cefnwlad (-wledydd) nf hinterland

cefnwr (-wyr) nm back, full-back

ceffyl (-au) nm horse

ceg (-au) nf mouth

cega vb mouth, prate

cegaid (-eidiau) nf mouthful

cegen (-nau) nf gullet, windpipe

cegid, -en (-au) nf green woodpecker, jay

cegin (-au) nf kitchen

cegrwth adj gaping

cegyr npl hemlock

cengl (-au) nf band; girth; hank

cenglu vb hank; girth; wind

cei (-au) *nm* quay
ceibio *vb* pick with pickaxe
ceidwad (-aid) *nm* keeper, saviour
ceidwadaeth *nf* conservatism; conservancy
ceidwadol *adj* conservative
Ceidwadwr (-wyr) *nm* Conservative
ceiliagwydd (-au) *nm* gander
ceiliog (-od) *nm* cock. **c. rhedyn** grasshopper
ceinach (-od) *nf* hare
ceincio *vb* branch out, ramify
ceinciog *adj* branched, branching
ceinder *nm* elegance, beauty
ceiniog (-au) *nf* penny
ceiniogwerth (-au, -i) *nf* pennyworth
ceinion *npl* beauties, gems
ceintach *vb* grumble, croak
ceintachlyd *adj* querulous
ceintachwr (-wyr) *nm* grumbler, croaker
ceirch (-en) *coll n* oats
ceirios *npl* (-en *nf*) cherries
ceisbwl (-byliaid) *nm* catchpole, bailiff
ceisio *vb* seek; ask; try, attempt, endeavour; fetch, get
cêl *adj* hidden, concealed ♦ *nm* concealment ♦ *npl* kale
celain (celanedd) *nf* dead body
celanedd *coll nf* carnage, slaughter
celc *nm/f* concealment; hoard
celf (-au) *nf* art, craft
celfi *npl* (-cyn *nm*) tools, gear; furniture
celfydd *adj* skilled, skilful
celfyddgar *adj* ingenious; artistic
celfyddwr (-wyr) *nm* artificer, artist
celfyddyd (-au) *nf* art, craft; skill.
celfyddau graffig graphic arts
celfyddydol *adj* relating to art/the Arts
celu *vb* hide, conceal
celwrn (-yrnau) *nm* tub, bucket, pail

celwydd (-au) *nm* lie, falsehood, untruth
celwyddog *adj* lying, mendacious; false
celwyddwr (-wyr) *nm* liar
celyn *npl* (-nen *nf*) holly
cell (-oedd, -au) *nf* cell, chamber.
celloedd cenhedlu germ cells.
enyniad y celloedd cellulitis
celli (celliau, -ïoedd) *nf* grove
cellog *adj* cellular
cellwair *vb* jest, trifle ♦ *nm* fun
cellweiriwr (-wyr) *nm* jester, trifler
cellweirus *adj* playful, jocular
cemeg *nm* chemistry
cemegol *adj* chemical
cemegwr, -ydd (-wyr) *nm* chemist
cemegyn (cemegau) *nm* chemical
cen *coll n* skin, peel, scales, scurf, film, lichen
cenadwri *nf* message
cenau (cenawon) *nm* cub, whelp; rascal
cenedl (-hedloedd) *nf* nation; gender
cenedlaethol *adj* national
cenedlaetholdeb *nm* nationalism
cenedlaetholi *vb* nationalize
cenedlaetholi *adj* nationalist
cenedlaetholwr (-wyr) *nm* nationalist
cenedl-ddyn (-ion) *nm* gentile
cenfaint (-feiniau) *nf* herd
cenfigen (-nau) *nf* envy, jealousy
cenfigennu *vb* envy
cenfigennus, -enllyd *adj* envious, jealous
cenhadaeth (cenadaethau) *nf* mission
cenhadol *adj* missionary
cenhadu *vb* permit; propagate, conduct a mission
cenhadwr (-hadon) *nm* missionary
cenhedlaeth (cenedlaethau) *nf* generation
cenhedlig *adj* gentile, pagan

cenhedlu vb beget, generate
cenllif nm flood, torrent, deluge
cenllysg coll nm hailstones, hail
cennad (-hadau, -hadon) nf leave; messenger
cennin npl (-hinen nf) leeks
cennog adj scaly, scurfy
cennu vb scale, scurf
cêr nm gear, tools, trappings
cerameg nm/f ceramics
ceramig adj ceramic
cerbyd (-au) nm chariot, coach, car
cerbydwr (-wyr) nm coachman
cerdyn (cardiau) nm card
cerdd (-i) nf song, poem; music, poetry
cerddbrenni npl woodwinds
cerddbres npl brass section (orchestra)
cerdded vb walk; go; travel
cerddediad nm walking, going; pace
cerddgar adj harmonious, musical
cerddin, cerdin npl (-en nf) rowan
cerddor (-ion) nm singer, musician
cerddorfa (-feydd) nf orchestra
cerddorfaol adj orchestral
cerddoriaeth nf music
cerddorol adj musical
cerddwr (-wyr) nm walker
cerfddelw (-au) nf graven image, statue
cerfio vb carve
cerflun (-iau) nf statue; engraving
cerfluniaeth nf sculpture
cerflunydd (-lunwyr) nm sculptor
cerfwaith nm carving, sculpture
cern (-au) nf cheek, jaw
cernod (-iau) nf buffet
cernodio vb buffet, clout
cerpyn (carpiau) nm clout, rag
cerrynt nm/f course, road; current
cert (-i) nf cart
certiwr (-wyr) nm carter
certh adj right; awful
cerub, ceriwb (-iaid) nm cherub

cerwyn (-i) nf tub; vat; winepress
cerydd (-on) nm correction, chastisement; rebuke, reproof, censure
ceryddol adj chastising, chastening
ceryddu vb correct, chastise; rebuke
ceryddwr (-wyr) nm chastiser; rebuker
cesail (-eiliau) nf arm-pit; bosom
cesair npl, coll n hailstones, hail
cest (-au) nf belly, paunch
cestog adj corpulent
cetyn (catiau) nm piece, bit; pipe
cethin adj dark, fierce, ugly
ceubren (-nau) nm hollow tree
ceubwll (-byllau) nm pit
ceudod nm cavity; abdomen; thought, heart
ceufford (-ffyrdd) nf tunnel
ceuffos (-ydd) nf drain, ditch
ceugrwm adj concave
ceulan (-nau, -lennydd) nf bank, brink
ceulo vb curdle, coagulate
ceunant (-nentydd) nm ravine, gorge
cewyn (-nau, cawiau) nm napkin
ci (cŵn) nm dog, hound
ciaidd adj dog-like, houndish; brutal
cib (-au) nm pod, husk
cibddall adj purblind
cibo vb frown, scowl
cibog adj scowling
cibws, cibwst nf kibes, chilblains
cibwts nm kibbutz
cibyn (-nau) nm shell; husk; half a bushel
cic (-iau) nm/f kick
cicio vb kick
ciciwr (-wyr) nm kicker
cidwm (-ymiaid, -ymod) nm wolf; rascal
cieidd-dra nm houndishness, brutality
cig (-oedd) nm flesh, meat

cigfran (-frain) *nf* raven
cignoeth *adj* touching to the quick, caustic
cigog *adj* fleshy
cigwain (-weiniau) *nf* flesh-hook
cigydd (-ion) *nm* butcher
cigyddiaeth *nf* butchery
cigysol *adj* carnivorous
cigysydd (-ion) *nm* carnivore
cil (-iau, -ion) *nm* back; retreat; corner
cilagor *vb* open partly
cilagored *adj* ajar
cilbost (cilbyst) *nm* gate-post
cilchwyrn *npl* (-en *nf*), (-au, -od *nm*) glands
cildrem (-iau) *nf* leer
cildremio *vb* leer
cildroi *vb* reverse
cildwrn *nm* tip, bribe
cildyn *adj* obstinate, stubborn
cildynnu *vb* be obstinate
cildynnus *adj* obstinate, stubborn
cildynrwydd *nm* obstinacy
cilddant (-ddannedd) *nm* molar
cilfach (-au) *nf* nook; creek, bay
cilfilyn (-filod) *nm* ruminant
cilgnoi *vb* chew the cud, ruminate
cilgwthio *vb* push, shove, jostle
cilgynnyrch (-gynhyrchion) *nm* by-product
cilio *vb* retreat, recede, swerve
cilocalori (-iau) *nm* kilocalorie
cilogram (-au) *nm* kilogram
cilomedr (-au) *nm* kilometre
cilwen (-au) *nf* half smile
cilwenu *vb* simper, smile, leer
cilwg (-ygon) *nm* frown, scowl
cilyddol *adj* reciprocal
cimwch (-ychiaid) *nm* lobster
cingroen *nf* stink-horn
ciniawa *vb* dine
cinio (ciniawau) *n* dinner
cip (-ion) *nm* pluck, snatch; glimpse
cipdrem (-iau) *nf/m* glance, glimpse
cipedrych *vb* glance, glimpse
cipio *vb* snatch
cipiwr (-wyr) *nm* snatcher
cipolwg *nm/f* glance, glimpse
ciprys (-ion) *nm* scramble
cis (-iau) *nm/f* buffet; slap, touch
cist (-iau) *nf* chest, coffer, box; bin
ciw (-iau) *nm* cue, queue
ciwb *nm* cube
ciwed *coll nf* rabble, mob, crew
ciwrad (-iaid) *nm* curate
ciwt *adj* cute, clever, ingenious
claddedigaeth (-au) *nf/m* burial
claddfa (-feydd) *nf* burial-ground, cemetery
claddu *vb* bury
claear *adj* lukewarm, tepid; mild; cool
claearineb *nm* lukewarmness
claearu *vb* make mild or tepid; soothe
claer *adj* clear, bright, shining
claerder *nm* clearness, brightness
claf (cleifion) *adj* sick, ill ♦ *nm* sick person, patient
clafdy (-dai) *nm* hospital, infirmary
clafr *nm* itch, mange
clafrllyd *adj* mangy
clafychu *vb* sicken, fall ill
clai (cleiau) *nm* clay
clais (cleisiau) *nm* stripe; bruise
clamp (-iau) *nm* mass, lump; monster
clap (-iau) *nm* lump
clapgi (-gwn) *nm* telltale
clapio *vb* lump; strike; gossip
clapiog *adj* lumpy
clas *nm* monastic community, cloister, college
clasur (-on) *nm* classic
clasurol *adj* classical
clau *adj* quick, swift, soon; true; audible
clawdd (cloddiau) *nm* hedge; dyke, embankment
clawr (cloriau) *nm* face, surface;

cover, lid; board

clebar, **cleber** nf/m idle talk, gossip, tattle

clebran vb chatter, gossip, tattle

clebryn nm, **clebren** nf tattler

clec (**-iau, -s**) nf click; clack; crack; gossip

cleci (**-cwn**) nf telltale

clecian vb click; clack; crack, snap

clecyn nm, **clecen** nf gossip, telltale

cledr (**-au**) nf pole; rail; palm (of hand)

cledren (**-nau, -ni**) nf pale, pole, rail

cleddyf, cleddau, cledd (**cleddyfau**) nm sword; brace

cleddyfwr (**-wyr**) nm swordsman

clefyd (**-au**) nm disease; fever. **c. melys** diabetes

clegar vb clack, cluck, cackle

clegyr, clegr nm rock; cairn, stony place

cleigio adj clayey

cleiriach nm decrepit one

cleisio vb bruise

cleisiog adj bruised

clem (**-iau**) nf notion, idea; look, gaze; pl grimaces

clep (**-iau**) nf clack, clap; gossip

clepgi (**-gwn**) nm babbler; telltale

clepian vb clap; slam; blab

clêr coll nf itinerant minstrels; bards

clêr npl (**cleren** nf) flies

clera vb stroll as minstrels

clerc (**-od**) nm clerk

clercio vb serve as clerk

clerigol adj clerical

clerigwr (**-wyr**) nm clergyman

clerwr (**-wyr**) nm itinerant minstrel

clerwriaeth nf minstrelsy

clewt (**-iau**) nm clout

clewtian vb clout

clic (**cliciau**) nm clique

clicied (**-au**) nf clicket; trigger

cliciedu vb latch, fasten

clindarddach vb crackle ♦ nm crackling

clinig (**-au**) nm clinic

clir adj clear

clirio vb clear

clo (**cloeau, cloeon**) nm lock, conclusion

clobyn nm, **cloben** nf monster

cloc (**-iau**) nm clock

clocian vb cluck

clocsiau npl (**clocsen** nf) clog

cloch (**clych, clychau**) nf bell. **o'r/ar gloch** o'clock

clochaidd adj sonorous, noisy

clochdar vb cluck, cackle

clochdy (**-dai**) nm belfry, steeple

clochydd (**-ion**) nm bell-man; sexton

clod (**-ydd**) nm/f praise, fame, renown

clodfori vb praise, extol

clodwiw adj commendable, praiseworthy

cloddfa (**-feydd**) nf quarry, mine

cloddio vb dig, delve; quarry, mine

cloddiwr (**-wyr**) nm digger, navvy

cloëdig adj locked, closed

cloer (**-(i)au**) nm/f locker; niche, embrasure; pigeon-hole

cloff adj lame

cloffi vb lame, halt ♦ nm lameness

cloffni nm lameness

cloffrwym (**-au**) nm fetter, hobble. **c. y cythraul, c. y mwci** great bindweed

clog (**-au**) nf rock, precipice

clog (**-au**) nm/f cloak

clogfaen (**-feini**) nm boulder

clogwyn (**-i**) nm cliff, crag, precipice

clogwynog adj craggy, precipitous

clogyn (**-nau**) nm cloak, cape

clogyrnaidd adj rough, rugged, clumsy

cloi vb lock

clonc nf clank; gossip ♦ adj addled

clopa (-âu) nf/m noddle; knob; club

cloren (-nau) nf rump, tail

clorian (-nau) nm/f pair of scales

cloriannu vb weigh, balance

clorin nm chlorine

clorinio, -adu vb chlorinate

clos (-ydd) nm yard

clos (closau) nm pair of breeches

clòs adj close

closio vb close, near

cludadwy adj portable

cludair (-eiriau) nf heap, load, wood-pile

cludiad nm carriage

cludiant (-nnau) nm transport, haulage

cludo vb carry, convey

cludwr (-wyr), **-ydd** (-ion) nm porter

clul (-iau) nm knell

clun (-iau) nf hip, haunch, thigh, leg; moor

cluro vb rub, smear

clust (-iau) nf/m ear; handle

clustfeinio vb prick up the ears; eavesdrop

clustfys nm little finger

clustffon (-ffonau) nm earphone

clustlws (-lysau) nm earring

clustnod (-au) nm earmark

clustog (-au) nf/m cushion, pillow

clwb (clybiau) nm club

clwc adj addled

clwcian vb cluck

clwm (clymau) nm knot, tie

clwpa (-od) nm knob, boss; club; dolt

clws adj pretty, nice; f **clos**

clwstwr (clystyrau) nm cluster

clwt (clytiau) nm patch, clout, rag

clwyd (-au, -i, -ydd) nf hurdle; gate; roost

clwydo vb roost

clwyf (-au) nm wound; disease

clwyfo vb wound

clwyfus adj wounded; sore; sick

clybodeg nf acoustics

clybodig adj acoustic

clyd adj warm, sheltered, snug, cosy

clydwch, clydwr nm warmth, shelter

clyfar adj clever; pleasant, agreeable

clymblaid (-bleidiau) nf clique, cabal

clymog adj knotty, entangled

clymu vb knot, tie

clytio vb patch, piece

clytiog adj patched; ragged

clytwaith (-weithiau) nm patchwork

clyw nm sense of hearing

clywadwy adj audible

clywed vb hear; feel; taste; smell

clywedigaeth nf hearing

clywedol adj aural

clywedydd (-ion) nm hearer, auditor

clyweled adj audio-visual

cnaf (-on, -iaid) nm knave, rascal

cnafaidd adj knavish, rascally

cnaif (cneifion) nm shearing, fleece

cnap (-iau) nm lump, knob, boss

cnapan (-au) nm ball, bowl, kind of ball game

cnapiog adj lumpy

cnau npl (cneuen nf) nuts

cnawd nm flesh

cnawdol adj carnal, fleshly, fleshy

cneifio vb shear, fleece

cneifiwr (-wyr) nm shearer

cneua vb nut

cneuen (cnau) nf nut

cnewyllyn (cnewyll) nm kernel, nucleus

cnith (-iau, -ion) nm slight touch; blow; pluck

cno nm bite, chewing, gnawing

cnoc (-iau) nm/f knock

cnocio vb knock

cnofa (-**feydd**) *nf* gnawing, pang
cnofil (-**od**) *nf* rodent
cnoi *vb* gnaw, chew, bite; ache
cnot (-**iau**) *nm* knot, bunch
cnu (-**au**), **cnuf** (-**iau**) *nm* fleece
cnud (-**oedd**) *nf* pack (*of wolves, etc.*)
cnùl, cnul (-**iau**) *nm* knell
cnwd (**cnydau**) *nm* crop; covering
cnydfawr *adj* fruitful, productive
cnydio *vb* crop, yield increase
cnydiog *adj* fruitful, productive
cob (**cobau**) *nf* coat, cloak, robe
còb (-**iau**) *nm* embankment; miser; wag; cob
coban (-**au**) *nf*: **c. nos** nightshirt
coblyn (-**nod**) *nm* sprite, goblin, imp
cocos *npl* cogs. **olwyn g.** cog-wheel
cocos, cocs *npl* (**cocsen** *nf*) cockles
coch *adj, nm* red
coch-gam *nf* robin
cochi *vb* redden, blush
cochi, cochder *nm* redness
cochl (-**au**) *nmf* mantle, cloak
cod (-**au**) *nf* bag, pouch
codaid (-**eidiau**) *nf* bagful
codi *vb* rise, raise, lift, erect
codiad (-**au**) *nm* rise, rising; erection
codog *adj* baggy ♦ (-**ion**) *nmf* rich man; miser
codwm (**codymau**) *nm* fall, tumble
codwr (-**wyr**) *nm* riser; raiser, lifter. **c. canu** precentor
codymu *vb* wrestle
codymwr (-**wyr**) *nm* wrestler
codded *nm* anger; grief
coddi *vb* anger, offend
coed (-**ydd**) *coll vb* wood, timber, trees
coeden (**coed**) *nf* tree
coedio *vb* timber
coediog *adj* wooded, woody
coedwig (-**oedd**) *nf* wood, forest
coedwigaeth *nf* forestry

coedwigwr (-**wyr**) *nm* woodman, forester
coedd *adj* public
coeg *adj* empty, vain; one-eyed, blind
coegddyn (-**ion**) *nm* fop, coxcomb, fool
coegedd *nm* emptiness, silliness
coegen (-**nod**) *nf* minx, coquette
coegennaidd *adj* coquettish
coegfalch *adj* vain, foppish
coegi *vb* jeer at, mock
coeglyd *adj* vain, sarcastic
coegni *nm* vanity; spite; sarcasm
coegwr (-**wyr**) *nm* fool
coegwych *adj* gaudy, garish, tawdry
coegyn (-**nod**) *nm* coxcomb
coel (-**ion**) *nf* belief, trust, credit
coelbren (-**nau, -ni**) *nm* lot
coelcerth (-**i**) *nf* bonfire, blaze
coelgrefydd (-**au**) *nf* superstition
coelgrefyddol *adj* superstitious
coelio *vb* believe, credit, trust
coes (-**au**) *nf* leg, shank ♦ *nm/f* handle; stem, stalk
coetgae *nm* hedge; enclosure
coetmon (-**myn**) *nm* lumberjack
coetref (-**i**) *nf* woodland, homestead
coeth *adj* fine, refined; elegant
coethder *nm* refinement, elegance
coethi *vb* refine; chastise; babble
coethwr (-**wyr**) *nm* refiner
cof (-**ion**) *nm* memory; remembrance
cofadail (-**eiladau**) *nf* monument
cofeb (-**ion**) *nf* memorandum; memorial
cofgolofn (-**au**) *nf* monument
cofiadur (-**on, -iaid**) *nm* recorder
cofiadwy *adj* memorable
cofiannydd (-**anyddion**) *nm* biographer
cofiant (-**iannau**) *nm* memoir, biography
cofio *vb* remember, recollect
cofl (-**au**) *nf* embrace; bosom

coflaid (-eidiau) *nf* armful; bundle

coflech (-au) *nf* memorial tablet

cofleidio *vb* embrace, hug

coflyfr (-au) *nm* record, chronicle

cofnod (-ion) *nm* memorandum, minute

cofnodi *vb* record, register

cofrestr (-au) *nf* register, roll

cofrestrfa *nf* registry

cofrestru *vb* register

cofrestrydd (-ion) *nm* registrar

cofus *adj* mindful

cofweini *vb* prompt

cofweinydd (-ion) *nm* prompter

coffa *vb* remember ♦ *nm* remembrance

coffâd *nm* remembrance

coffadwriaeth *nf* remembrance, memory

coffadwriaethol *adj* memorial

coffáu *vb* remember; remind; commemorate

coffi *nm* coffee

coffr (-au) *nm* coffer, trunk, chest

cog (-au) *nf* cuckoo

cog (-au) *nm* cook

coginiaeth *nf* cookery

coginio *vb* cook

cogio *vb* cog; sham, feign, pretend

cogiwr (-wyr) *nm* pretender, swindler

cogor *vb* chatter, caw, croak ♦ *nm* chattering

cogwrn (-yrnau, cegyrn) *nm* knob, cone; cock (of corn); shell

cogydd (-ion) *nm*, **cogyddes** (-au) *nf* cook

cogyddiaeth *nf* cookery

congl (-au) *nf* corner

côl *nf* bosom, embrace

col (-ion) *nm* awn, beard

coladu *vb* collate

coledd, -u *vb* cherish, foster

coleddwr (-wyr) *nm* cherisher, fosterer, patron, supporter

coleg (-au) *nm* college

colegol *adj* collegiate

colegwr (-wyr) *nm* collegian

coler (-i) *nf/m* collar

colfen (-nau, -ni) *nf* bough, branch; tree

colofn (-au) *nf* column, pillar

colomen (-nod) *nf* dove, pigeon

colomendy (-dai) *nm* dove-cot

colomennaidd *adj* dove-like

coluddion *npl* (-yn *nm*) bowels

colur (-au) *nm* make-up, colour

coluro *vb* make-up, paint; conceal

colwyn (-od) *nm* puppy

colyn (-nau) *nm* pivot; sting; tail

colynnog *adj* stinging; hinged

colynnu *vb* sting

coll (-iadau) *nm* loss; failing, defect

colladwy *adj* perishable

colldail *adj* deciduous

colled (-ion) *nm/f* loss

colledig *adj* lost, damned

colledigaeth *nf* perdition

colledu *vb* occasion loss

colledus *adj* fraught with loss

colledwr (-wyr) *nm* loser

collen (cyll) *nf* hazel

collfarn (-au) *nf* doom, condemnation

collfarnu *vb* condemn

colli *vb* lose; be lost, perish; spill, shed

collnod (-au) *nm* apostrophe

collwr (-wyr) *nm* loser

côma (comâu) *nm* coma

coma (-s) *nm* comma

comed (-au) *nf* comet

comedi (-iau) *nm/f* comedy

comig *adj* comic, comical ♦ *nm* comic (paper)

comisiwn (-iynau) *nm* commission

comisiynu *vb* commission

comiwnydd (-ion) *nf* communist

comiwnyddiaeth *nf* communism

comiwnyddol *adj* communist

conach *vb* grumble

conclaf *nm* conclave

concro *vb* conquer

concwerwr (-wyr) nm conqueror

concwest (-au) nf conquest, victory

condemniad nm condemnation

condemnio vb condemn

confensiwn (-iynau) nm convention

conffederasiwn (-asiynau) nm confederation

conffirmasiwn nm confirmation

conffirmio vb confirm

conifferaidd adj coniferous

cono nm rascal; wag; old fogey

consesiwn (-iynau) nm concession

consuriaeth nf conjuring

consurio vb conjure

consuriwr (-wyr) nm conjurer

conwydd npl (-en nf) coniferous trees

cop, copyn (-nod, -nau) nm spider

copa (-âu) nf top, crest; head

copi (-ïau) nm copy; copy-book

copïo vb copy, transcribe

copïwr (-wyr) nm copyist, transcriber

copr nm copper

côr (corau) nm choir; stall, pew. **c. feistr** choirmaster

cor (-rod) nm dwarf; spider

corachaidd adj dwarfish, stunted

corawl adj choral

corbwll (-byllau) nm whirlpool; puddle

corcyn (cyrc) nm cork

cord (-iau) nm cord; chord

cordeddu vb twist, twine

corddi vb churn; turn; agitate

corddiad (-au) nm churning

corddwr (-wyr) nm churner

cored (-au) nf weir, dam

coreograffiaeth nf choreography

corfan (-nau) nm metrical foot

corff (cyrff) nm body

corfflu (-oedd) nm corps

corfol adj corpulent; physical

corfolaeth nf bodily form; stature

corfforaeth (-au) nf corporation

corffori vb embody, incorporate

corfforiad (-au) nm embodiment

corfforol adj bodily, corporeal, corporal

corgan, côr-gân (-au) nf chant

corganu vb chant

corgi (-gwn) nm cur, corgi

corgimwch (-ychiaid) nm prawn

corhwyad (-aid) nf teal; moorhen

corlan (-nau) nf fold

corlannu vb fold

corn (cyrn) nm horn; pipe; tube; roll; corn; stethoscope. **c. gwddw(f), c. gwynt** windpipe. **c. siarad** loudspeaker

cornant (-nentydd) nm brook, rill

cornboer nm phlegm

cornchwiglen (-chwiglod) nf lapwing

cornel (-i, -au) nf/m corner

cornelu vb corner

cornicyll (-od) nm lapwing, plover, peewit

cornio vb horn, butt; examine with a stethoscope

corniog adj horned

cornwyd (-ydd) nm boil, abscess, sore

coron (-au) nf crown

coroni vb crown ♦ nm coronation

coroniad nm coronation

coronog adj crowned

corpws nm body (facetious)

corrach (corachod) nm dwarf, pygmy

corryn (corynnod) nm spider

cors (-ydd) nf bog, swamp

corsen (-nau, cyrs) nf reed; stem, stalk; cane

cortyn (-nau) nm cord, rope

corun (-au) nm crown of the head; tonsure

corwg(l) (-yg(l)au) nm coracle

corws nm chorus

corwynt (-oedd) nm whirlwind

cosb (-au) nf punishment, penalty. **c. ddihenydd** capital punishment

cosbadwy adj punishable
cosbedigaeth nf punishment
cosbi vb punish
cosbol adj punitive, penal
cosbwr (-wyr) nm punisher
cosfa (-feydd) nf itch, itching; thrashing
cosi vb scratch, itch ♦ nm itching
cosmetigau npl cosmetics
cosmig adj cosmic
cost (-au) nf cost, expense
costiad (-au) nm costing
costio vb cost
costiwm (-tiymau) nm/f costume
costog (-ion) nm mastiff; cur ♦ adj surly
costowci (-cwn) nm mastiff, mongrel
costrel (-au, -i) nf bottle
costrelaid (-eidiau) nf bottleful
costrelu vb bottle
costus adj costly, expensive
cosyn (-nau, -nod) nm a cheese
côt, cot (cotiau) nf coat
cotwm nm cotton
cowlas (-au) nm/f bay of building; hay-mow
cownter (-au, -i) nm counter
cowntio vb count, account, esteem
crac (-iau) nm crack
cracio vb crack
craciog adj cracked
crach npl (-en nf) scabs ♦ adj scabby; petty ♦ -**ach** npl snobs
crachboer nm phlegm
crachfardd (-feirdd) nm poetaster
crachfeddyg (-on) nm quack doctor
crachfonheddwr (-wyr) nm snob
crafangio, -u vb claw, grab
crafanc (-angau) nf claw; talon; clutch
crafiad (-au) nm scratch
crafog adj cutting, sarcastic
crafu vb scrape; scratch ♦ nm itch
crafwr (-wyr) nm scraper
craff adj close; keen; sagacious ♦

nm hold, grip
craffter nm keenness, sagacity
craffu vb look closely, observe intently
craffus adj keen, sagacious
cragen (cregyn) nf shell
crai adj new, fresh, raw
craidd (creiddiau) nm middle, centre
craig (creigiau) nf rock
crair (creiriau) nm relic
craith (creithiau) nf scar
cramen (-nau) nf crust, scab
cranc (-od) nm crab
crand adj grand
crandrwydd nm grandeur, finery
crap (-iau) nm hold; smattering
crapio vb grapple; pick up
cras (creision) adj parched, dry; harsh
crasiad nm baking
craslyd adj harsh, grating
craster nm dryness; harshness
crasu vb parch, scorch; bake
crau (creuau) nm hole, eye, socket
crau nm blood, gore
crau (creuau) nm sty; stockade
crawcian, crawcio vb croak, caw
crawen (-nau) nf crust
crawn nm matter, pus
crawni vb gather, suppurate
crawnllyd adj purulent
cread nm creation
creadigaeth (-au) nf creation
creadigol adj creative
creadur (-iaid) nm creature; animal
creadures nf female creature
creawdwr (-wyr) nm creator
crebach adj shrunk, withered
crebachlyd adj crabbed, wrinkled
crebachu vb shrink, shrivel, wrinkle, pucker
crebwyll (-ion) nm invention, understanding, fancy
crecian vb cluck; crackle
crechwen nf loud laughter, guffaw

crechwenu vb laugh loud, guffaw

cred (-au) nf belief; trust; pledge, troth

credadun (credinwyr) nm believer

credadwy adj credible

crediniaeth nf belief

crediniol adj believing

credo nm/f creed, belief

credu vb believe

credwr (-wyr) nm believer

credyd (-on) nm credit

credydu vb credit

cref f. of **cryf**

crefu vb crave, beg, implore

crefydd (-au) nf religion

crefydda vb profess or practise religion

crefyddol adj religious, pious

crefyddolder nm religiousness, piety

crefyddwr (-wyr) nm religioner, religionist

crefft (-au) nf handicraft, trade

crefftus adj skilled, workmanlike

crefftwaith nm craftwork

crefftwr (-wyr) nm craftsman

cregyn npl (cragen nf) shells

creider nm freshness

creifion npl scrapings

creigiog adj rocky

creigiwr (-wyr) nm quarryman

creigle (-oedd) nm rocky place

creinio vb wallow, lie or fall down; cringe

creision npl flakes, crisps

crempog (-au) nf pancake

crensio vb grind (the teeth)

crepach adj numb ♦ nf numbness

crest nm crust, scurf

Creta nf Crete

creu vb create

creulon adj cruel

creulondeb (-derau) nm cruelty

crëwr (crewyr) nm creator

crëyr (crehyrod) nm heron

cri (-au) nm cry, clamour

cri adj new, fresh, raw; unleavened

criafol, -en nf mountain ash

crib (-au) nf/m comb, crest; ridge

cribddeilio vb grab, extort

cribddeiliwr (-wyr) nm extortioner; speculator

cribin (-iau) nf/m rake; skinflint

cribinio vb rake

cribo vb comb; card

criced nm cricket

cricedwr (-wyr) nm cricketer

crimog (-au) nf, **crimp (-(i)au)** nm shin

crin adj withered, sear, dry

crino vb wither, dry up

crintach, -lyd adj niggardly, stingy

crintachrwydd nm niggardliness

crintachu vb scrimp, skimp, stint

crio vb cry, weep

cripio vb scratch; climb, creep

cris-groes nf criss-cross

crisial (-au, -on) adj crystal

crisialu vb crystallise

Cristion (-ogion, Cristnogion) nm Christian

Cristionogaeth nf Christianity

Cristionogol adj Christian

criw (-iau) nm crew

criwr (-wyr) nm crier

crocbont (-ydd) nf suspension bridge

crocbren (-ni) nm/f gallows, gibbet

crocbris (-iau) nm exorbitant price

croch adj loud, vehement

crochan (-au) nm pot, cauldron

crochanaid (-eidiau) nm potful

crochenydd (-ion) nm potter

crochenwaith (-weithiau) nm pottery

croen (crwyn) nm skin; hide; peel, rind

croendenau adj thin-skinned

croeni, -io vb form skin, skin over

croes (-au) nf cross ♦ nm transept

croes (-ion) adj cross, contrary

croesair (-eiriau) nm crossword

croesawgar adj hospitable

croesawiad nm welcome,

reception

croesawu vb welcome

croesawus adj hospitable

croesbren (-nau) nmf cross

croesddweud vb contradict

croesfan (-nau) nf crossing

croesffordd (-ffyrdd) nf crossroad

croesgad (-au) nf crusade

croesgadwr (-wyr) nm crusader

croeshoeliad nm crucifixion

croeshoelio vb crucify

croesholi vb cross-examine

croesholiad (-au) nm cross-examination

croesi vb cross

croeso nm welcome

croesymgroes adj criss-cross; vice-versa

crofen (-nau, -ni) nf rind, crust

crog (-au) nf cross, rood ♦ adj hanging

crogi vb hang, suspend

croglath (-au) nf springe, snare, gibbet

Croglith nmf: **Dydd Gwener y G.** Good Friday

croglofft (-ydd, -au) nf garret; rood-loft

crogwr (-wyr) nm hangman

cronglwyd (-ydd) nf: **tan fy ngh.** under my roof

crombil (-iau) nf crop; gizzard; bowels

cromen (-ni, -nau) nf dome

cromfach (-au) nf bracket, parenthesis

cromlech (-au, -i) nf cromlech

cromosom (-au) nm chromosome

cron adj f. of **crwn**

cronfa (-feydd) nf reservoir; fund

cronicl (-au) nm chronicle

croniclo vb chronicle

cronnell (cronellau) nf sphere, globe

cronni vb collect, hoard; dam

cronolegol adj chronological

cropian vb creep, crawl, grope

crosiet (-au, -i) nm crotchet

croth (-au) nf womb; calf (of leg)

croyw adj clear, plain, distinct; fresh

croywder nm clearness; freshness

croywi vb clear; freshen

crud (-au) nm cradle

crug (-iau) nm hillock; tumulus; heap; multitude; abscess, blister

cruglwyth (-i) nm heap, pile

cruglwytho vb heap, pile up; overload

crugo vb fester, vex, plague

crwban (-od) nm tortoise, turtle

crwca adj crooked, bowed, bent

crwm adj convex, curved, bowed; f **crom**

crwn adj round; complete; f **cron**

crwner (-iaid) nm coroner

crwsâd (-adau) nmf crusade

crwst (crystiau) nm crust

crwt (cryts) nm boy, lad

crwth (crythau) nm crowd, fiddle; purring; hump

crwybr nm honeycomb; mist; hoarfrost

crwydr nm wandering, **ar g.** astray

crwydro vb wander, stray, roam

crwydrol, crwydrus adj wandering

crwydrwr (-wyr) nm wanderer, rover

crwydryn (-riaid) nm vagrant, tramp

crwys nf, npl cross, crucifix. **dan ei g.** laid out for burial

crybwyll vb mention ♦ **(-ion)** nm mention

crybwylliad nm mention, notice

crych adj rippling; curly; quavering ♦ **(-au)** nm crease, ripple, wrinkle

crychlais (-leisiau) nm trill, tremolo

crychlyd adj wrinkled, puckered

crychnaid (-neidiau) nf leap, gambol

crychneidio vb skip, frisk

crychni nm curliness; wrinkle

crychu vb wrinkle, pucker; ruffle, ripple

cryd (-iau) nm shivering; fever; ague

crydd (-ion) nm cobbler, shoemaker

crydda vb cobble

cryf adj strong; f **cref**

cryfder, -dwr nm strength

cryfhaol adj strengthening

cryfhau vb strengthen; grow strong

cryg adj hoarse; f **creg**

cryglyd adj hoarse, raucous

crygni nm hoarseness

crygu vb hoarsen

cryman (-au) nm reaping-hook, sickle

crymanwr (-wyr) nm reaper

crymu vb bow, bend, stoop

cryn adj considerable, much

crŷn, cryn nm, adj shivering

crynder nm roundness

cryndod nm trembling, shivering

crynedig adj trembling, tremulous

crynfa (-feydd) nf tremble, tremor

crynhoad (-noadau) nm collection, digest

crynhoi vb gather together, collect

cryno adj compact; neat, tidy

crynodeb (-au) nm summary

crynswth nm mass, bulk, whole

crynu vb shiver, tremble, quake

Crynwr (-wyr) nm Quaker

crys (-au) nm shirt

crysbais (-beisiau) nf jacket, jerkin

crystyn (crystiau) nm crust

crythor (-ion) nm fiddler, violinist

cryw (-iau) nm creel; weir

cu adj dear, fond, kind

cuchio vb scowl, frown

cuchiog adj scowling, frowning

cudyll (-od) nm hawk

cudyn (-nau) nm lock (of hair), tuft

cudd adj hidden, concealed

cuddfa (-feydd) nf hiding-place; hoard

cuddiad nm hiding

cuddiedig adj hidden, concealed

cuddio vb hide, conceal

cufydd (-au) nm cubit

cul (-ion) adj narrow, lean

culfor (-oedd) nm strait

culhau vb narrow; grow lean

culni nm narrowness

cun adj dear, beloved; lovely

cunnog (cunogau) nf pail

cur nm throb, ache, pain; care, trouble

curad (-iaid) nm curate

curadiaeth (-au) nf curacy

curfa (-feydd) nf beating, flogging

curiad (-au) nm beat, throb, pulse

curio vb pine, waste

curlaw nm pelting rain

curn (-au), **curnen** (-nau) nf mound, core, rick

curnennu vb heap, stack

curo vb beat, strike, knock; throb; clap

curwr (-wyr) nm beater

curyll (-od) nm hawk

cusan (-au) nf/m kiss

cusanu vb kiss

cut (-iau) nm hovel, shed, sty

cuwch (cuchiau) nm scowl, frown

cwafrio vb quaver, trill

cwar (-rau) nm quarry

cwb (cybiau) nm kennel, coop, sty

cwbl adj, nm all, whole, total

cwblhad nm fulfilment

cwblhau vb fulfil, complete, finish

cwcer (-au) nm cooker

cwcw nf cuckoo

cwcwallt (-iaid) nm cuckold

cwcwalltu vb cuckold

cwcwll (cycyllau) nm hood, cowl

cwch (cychod) nm boat; hive. **c. gwyllt** speed boat

cwd (cydau) nm pouch, bag

cweir (-iau) *nm* thrashing, hiding
cweryl (-on) *nm* quarrel
cweryla *vb* quarrel
cwerylgar *adj* quarrelsome
cwest (-au) *nm* inquest
cwestiwn (-iynau) *nm* question
cwestiynu *vb* question
cwffio *vb* fight, box
cwgn (cygnau) *nm* knot; knuckle; joint
cwilt (-iau) *nm* quilt
cwlbren (-ni) *nm* bludgeon
cwliff, -yn (cyffiau) *nm* chunk
cwlwm see clwm
cwlltwr (cylltyrau) *nm* coulter
cwm (cymau, cymoedd) *nm* valley
cwman *nm* rump; stoop; stoop
cwmanu *vb* stoop
cwmni (-iau, -ïoedd) *nm* company
cwmnïaeth *nf* companionship
cwmpas (-oedd) *nm* round. o.g. about
cwmpasog *adj* round about, circuitous
cwmpasu *vb* round, wind, surround
cwmpawd (-odau) *nm* compass
cwmpeini, cwmpni *nm* company
cwmwd (cymydau) *nm* commot
cwmwl (cymylau) *nm* cloud
cwn see ci
cwndid (-au) *nm* song, carol
cwningen (-ingod) *nf* rabbit
cwnsel (-au, -oedd, -i) *nm* council; counsel, advice, secret
cwnsela *vb* counsel
cwnsler (-iaid) *nm* counsellor
cwnstabl (-iaid) *nm* constable
cworwm *nm* quorum
cwota (-au) *nm* quota
cwpan (-au) *nm/f* cup, goblet; chalice
cwpanaid (-eidiau) *nm/f* cupful
cwpl (cyplau) *nm* couple; tie beam
cwplhad, cwpláu see cwblhad, cwbláu
cwpled (-i, -au) *nm* couplet

cwplws (cyplysau) *nm* coupling; brace
cwpwrdd (cypyrddau) *nm* cupboard
cwr (cyrau) *nm* edge, border, skirt
cwrcwd *nm* stooping; squatting
cwrdd (cyrddau) *nm* meeting
cwrdd, cwrddyd *vb* meet, touch
cwrel *nm* coral
cwricwlwm (cwricwla) *nm* curriculum
cwrlid (-au) *nm* coverlet
cwrs (cyrsiau) *nm* course; fit
cwrt (cyrtiau) *nm* court
cwrtais *adj* courteous
cwrteisi, cwrteisrwydd *nm* courtesy
cwrw (cyrfau) *nm* ale, beer
cwrwg(l) see corwg(l)
cwsg *nm* sleep
cwsmer (-iaid) *nm* customer
cwsmeriaeth *nf* custom
cwstard (-iau) *nm* custard
cwstwm (cystymau) *nm* custom, patronage
cwt (cytiau) *nf/m* tail, skirt, queue
cwt (cytiau) *nm* hut, sty
cwta *adj* short, curt
cwter (-i, -ydd) *nf* gutter, channel
cwtogi *vb* shorten, curtail
cwthr (cythrau) *nm* anus, rectum
cwthwm (cythymau) *nm* puff of wind, storm
cwympo (-au) *nm* fall, tumble
cwympo *vb* fall; fell
cwyn (-ion) *nm/f* complaint, plaint
cwynfan *vb* complain, lament
cwynfanllyd *adj* querulous
cwynfanus *adj* plaintive, mournful
cwyno *vb* complain, lament
cwyr *nm* wax
cwyro *vb* wax
cwys (-au, -i) *nf* furrow-slice, furrow
cybôl *nm* nonsense, rubbish
cybolfa *nf* hotchpotch, medley
cyboli *vb* muddle; talk nonsense;

mess, bother

cybydd (**-ion**) *nm* miser, niggard

cybydda *vb* stint, hoard

cybydd-dod, -dra *nm* miserliness

cybyddlyd *adj* miserly

cycyllog *adj* hooded, cowled

cychaid (**-eidiau**) *nm* boatful; hiveful

cychwr (**-wyr**) *nm* boatman

cychwyn *vb* rise, stir, start

cychwynfa *nf* start, starting-point

cychwyniad (**-au**) *nm* start, beginning

cyd *adj* joint, united, common; fellow ♦ *prefix* together

cydadrodd *vb* to recite together

cydaid (**-eidiau**) *nm* bagful

cydbwysedd *nm* balance

cyd-destun (**-au**) *nm* context

cydfod *nm* agreement, concord

cydfodolaeth *nf* coexistence

cydfyned *vb* go with, concur, agree

cydfyw *vb* cohabit

cydffurfio *vb* conform

cydgordio *vb* agree, harmonize

cydgwmni (**-iau**) *nm* consortium

cydiedig *adj* adjoined

cydio *vb* join; bite; take hold

cydnabod *vb* acknowledge ♦ *nm* acquaintance

cydnabyddiaeth *nf* acquaintance; recognition

cydnabyddus *adj* acquainted, familiar

cydnaws *adj* congenial

cydnerth *adj* well set

cydol *nf/m, adj* whole

cydradd *adj* equal

cydraddoldeb *nm* equality

cyd-rhwng *prep* between

cydsyniad *nm* consent

cydsynio *vb* consent

cydwastad *adj* level (with), even

cydweddog *adj* conjugal

cydweddu *vb* accord, agree

cydweithfa (**-feydd**) *nf* co-

operative

cydweithrediad *nm* co-operation

cydweithredol *adj* co-operative

cydweithredu *vb* co-operate

cydweled *vb* agree

cydwladol *adj* international

cyd-wladwr (**-wyr**) *nm* compatriot

cydwybod (**-au**) *nf* conscience

cydwybodol *adj* conscientious

cydwybodolrwydd *nm* conscientiousness

cydymaith (**cymdeithion**) *nm* companion

cydymdeimlad *nm* sympathy

cydymdeimlo *vb* sympathize

cydymffurfiad *nm* conformity

cydymffurfio *vb* conform

cydymgais *nm* competition, rivalry, joint effort

cydymgeisydd (**-wyr**) *nm* rival

cyddwysiad (**-au**) *nm* condensation

cyfadran (**-nau**) *nf* faculty (*in college*); period (*in music*)

cyfaddas *adj* fit, suitable, convenient

cyfaddasiad (**-au**) *nm* adaptation

cyfaddaster *nm* fitness, suitability

cyfaddasu *vb* fit, adapt

cyfaddawd (**-odau**) *nm* compromise

cyfaddawdu *vb* compromise

cyfaddef *vb* confess, own, admit

cyfaddefiad (**-au**) *nm* confession, admission

cyfaenad *nm, adj* harmonious song

cyfagos *adj* near, adjacent, neighbouring

cyfaill (**-eillion**) *nm* friend

cyfair (**-eiriau**) *nm* acre

cyfair, -er *nm* direction. **ar g.** for; opposite

cyfalaf *nm* capital

cyfalafiaeth *nf* capitalism

cyfalafol *adj* capitalistic

cyfalafwr (**-wyr**) *nm* capitalist

cyfamod (**-au**) *nm* covenant

cyfamodi *vb* covenant

cyfamodol *adj* federal; covenanted
cyfamodwr (**-wyr**) *nm* covenanter
cyfamser *nm* meantime
cyfamserol *adj* timely;
synchronous
cyfan *adj, nm* whole
cyfandir (**-oedd**) *nm* continent
cyfandirol *adj* continental
cyfanfor (**-oedd**) *nm* main sea,
ocean
cyfanfyd *nm* whole world, universe
cyfangorff *nm* whole, bulk, mass
cyfan gwbl *adj*: **yn g**. altogether,
complete
cyfanheddol *adj* habitable,
inhabited
cyfanheddu *vb* dwell, inhabit
cyfannedd *adj* inhabited ♦
(**-anheddau**) *nf* inhabited place,
habitation
cyfannol *adj* integrated, integral
cyfannu *vb* make whole, complete
cyfanrwydd *nm* wholeness,
entirety
cyfansawdd *adj* composite,
compound
cyfansoddi *vb* compose, constitute
cyfansoddiad (**-au**) *nm*
composition; constitution
cyfansoddiadol *adj* constitutional
cyfansoddwr (**-wyr**) *nm* composer
cyfansoddyn (**-ion**) *nm*
constituent, compound
cyfanswm (**-symiau**) *nm* total
cyfantoledd (**-au**) *nm* equilibrium
cyfanwaith (**-weithiau**) *nm*
complete composition, whole
cyfarch *vb* greet, salute, address
cyfarchiad (**-au**) *nm* greeting,
salutation
cyfaredd (**-ion**) *nf* charm, spell
cyfareddol *adj* enchanting
cyfareddu *vb* charm, enchant
cyfarfod *vb* meet ♦ (**-ydd**) *nm*
meeting
cyfarfyddiad (**-au**) *nm* meeting
cyfarpar *nm* provision, equipment;

diet. **c. rhyfel** munitions of war
cyfarparu *vb* equip
cyfartal *adj* equal, even
cyfartaledd *nm* proportion,
average
cyfartalu *vb* proportion, equalize
cyfarth *vb, nm* bark
cyfarwydd *adj* skilled; familiar ♦
(**-iaid**) *nm* storyteller
cyfarwyddo *vb* direct; become
familiar
cyfarwyddwr (**-wyr**) *nm* director
cyfarwyddyd (**-iadau**) *nm*
direction, instruction
cyfatal *adj* unsettled, hindering
cyfateb *vb* correspond, agree, tally
cyfatebiaeth (**-au**) *nf*
correspondence, analogy
cyfatebol *adj* corresponding,
proportionate
cyfathrach (**-au**) *nf* affinity;
intercourse
cyfathrachu *vb* have intercourse
cyfathrachwr (**-wyr**) *nm* kinsman
cyfathreb (**-au**) *nm* communication
cyfathrebu *vb* communicate
cyfddydd *nm* day-break, dawn
cyfeb, cyfebr *adj* pregnant (*of
mare, ewe*)
cyfebol *adj* in foal
cyfeddach (**-au**) *nf* carousal
cyfeddachwr (**-wyr**) *nm* carouser
cyfeiliant *nm* musical
accompaniment
cyfeilio *vb* accompany
cyfeiliorn *nm* error; wandering,
lost (*person etc*). **ar g**. astray
cyfeiliornad (**-au**) *nm* error,
heresy
cyfeiliorni *vb* err, stray
cyfeiliornus *adj* erroneous,
mistaken
cyfeilydd (**-ion**) *nm* accompanist
cyfeillach (**-au**) *nf* fellowship;
fellowship-meeting
cyfeillachu *vb* associate
cyfeilles (**-au**) *nf* female friend

cyfeillgar adj friendly
cyfeillgarwch nm friendship
cyfeiriad (-au) nm direction; reference; (postal) address
cyfeiriannu nm orienteering
cyfeirio vb point; direct; refer; address (letter)
cyfeirnod (-au) nm mark of reference; aim; direct (in music)
cyfeirydd (-ion) nm indicator, guide
cyfenw (-au) nm surname; namesake
cyfenwi vb surname
cyfer nm: **ar g.** for; opposite
cyferbyn adj opposite
cyferbyniad (-au) nm contrast
cyferbyniol adj opposing, opposite, contrasting
cyferbynnu vb contrast, compare
cyfethol vb co-opt
cyfiaith adj of the same language
cyfiawn adj just, righteous
cyfiawnder (-au) nm justice, righteousness
cyfiawnhad nm justification
cyfiawnhau vb justify
cyfieithiad (-au) nm translation, version
cyfieithu vb translate, interpret
cyfieithydd (-wyr) nm translator, interpreter
cyfisol adj of the present month, instant
cyflafan (-au) nf outrage; massacre
cyflafareddiad nm arbitration
cyflafareddu vb arbitrate
cyflafareddwr (-wyr) nm arbitrator
cyflaith nm toffee
cyflawn adj full, complete
cyflawnder nm fullness; abundance
cyflawni vb fulfil, perform, commit
cyflawniad (-au) nm fulfilment, performance

cyfle (-oedd) nm place; chance, opportunity
cyfled adj as broad as
cyflegr (-au) nm gun, cannon, battery
cyflegru vb bombard
cyflenwad (-au) nm supply
cyflenwi vb supply
cyfleu vb place, set; convey
cyfleus adj convenient
cyfleustra (-terau) nm opportunity, convenience
cyflin adj parallel
cyfliw adj of the same colour
cyflo adj in calf
cyflog (-au) nm/f hire, wage, wages
cyflogaeth nf employment
cyflogedig (-ion) nm employee
cyflogi vb hire; engage in service
cyflogwr (-wyr) nm hirer, employer
cyflwr (-lyrau) nm condition; case
cyflwyniad nm presentation; dedication
cyflwyno vb present; dedicate
cyflwynydd (-ion) nm compère, presenter
cyflychwr, -wyr nm evening twilight, dusk
cyflym adj quick, fast, swift
cyflymder, -dra nm swiftness, speed
cyflymu vb speed, accelerate
cyflynu vb stick together
cyflyru vb condition
cyflythreniad (-au) nm alliteration
cyfnerthu vb confirm; aid, help
cyfnerthydd (-ion, -wyr) nm strengthener, booster
cyfnesaf (-iaid, -eifiaid) nm/f next of kin, kinsman ♦ adj next, nearest
cyfnewid vb change, exchange
cyfnewidfa (-oedd, -feydd) nf exchange
cyfnewidiad (-au) nm change,

alteration

cyfnewidiol *adj* changeable

cyfnewidiwr (-wyr) *nm* changer, trader

cyfnither (-oedd) *nf* female cousin

cyfnod (-au) *nm* period

cyfnodol *adj* periodic(al) ♦ **-yn** (-ion) *nm* periodical publication

cyfnos *nm* evening twilight, dusk

cyfochredd *nm* parallelism

cyfochrog *adj* parallel

cyfodi *vb* rise, arise; raise

cyfodiad *nm* rise, rising

cyfoed *adj* contemporary, of the same age ♦ (-ion) *nm* contemporaries

cyfoes *adj* contemporary

cyfoesi *vb* be contemporary

cyfoeswr (-wyr) *nm* contemporary

cyfoeth *nm* power; riches, wealth

cyfoethog *adj* powerful; rich, wealthy

cyfoethogi *vb* make or grow rich

cyfog *nm* sickness

cyfogi *vb* vomit

cyfor *nm* flood, abundance; rim, brim, edge ♦ *adj* entire, brim-full

cyforiog *adj* brim-full, overflowing

cyfosodiad *nm* apposition

cyfradd (-au) *nf* rate. **c. llog** rate of interest ♦ *adj* of equal rank

cyfraid (-reidiau) *nm* necessity

cyfraith (-reithiau) *nf* law

cyfran (-nau) *nf* part, portion, share

cyfranc (-rangau) *nfm* meeting; combat; incident; story, tale

cyfranddaliad (-au) *nm* share

cyfranddaliwr (-wyr) *nm* shareholder

cyfraniad (-au) *nm* contribution

cyfrannog *adj* participating, partaking

cyfrannol *adj* contributing

cyfrannu *vb* contribute; impart

cyfrannwr (-anwyr) *nm* contributor

cyfranogi *vb* participate, partake

cyfranogwr (-wyr) *nm* partaker

cyfredol *adj* current, concurrent

cyfreithio *vb* go to law, litigate

cyfreithiol *adj* legal

cyfreithiwr (-wyr) *nm* lawyer

cyfreithlon *adj* lawful, legitimate

cyfreithlondeb *nm* lawfulness

cyfreithloni *vb* legalize; justify

cyfreithus *adj* legitimate

cyfres (-i) *nf* series

cyfresol *adj* serial

cyfresu *vb* serialise

cyfresymiad (-au) *nm* syllogism

cyfresymu *vb* syllogise

cyfrgolli *vb* lose utterly; damn

cyfrif *vb* count, reckon; account; impute ♦ (-on) *nm* account, reckoning

cyfrifeg *nmf* accountancy

cyfrifiad (-au) *nm* counting; census

cyfrifiadur (-on) *nm* computer

cyfrifiadureg *nf* computer science

cyfrifiannell *nf* calculator

cyfrifol *adj* of repute; responsible

cyfrifoldeb (-au) *nm* responsibility

cyfrifydd (-ion) *nm* statistician, accountant

cyfrin *adj* secret, subtle

cyfrinach (-au) *nf* secret

cyfrinachol *adj* secret, private, confidential

cyfrinfa *nf* lodge of friendly society or trade union

cyfrin-gyngor (-nghorau) *nm* privy council

cyfriniaeth *nf* mystery; mysticism

cyfriniol *adj* mysterious, mystic

cyfriniwr (-wyr) *nm* mystic

cyfrodedd *adj* twisted, twined

cyfrodeddu *vb* twist, twine

cyfrol (-au) *nf* volume

cyfrwng (-ryngau) *nm* medium, means

cyfrwy (-au) *nm* saddle

cyfrwyo *vb* saddle

cyfrwys *adj* cunning

cyfrwystra *nm* cunning

cyfrwywr (-wyr) nm saddler
cyfryngdod nm mediation,
intercession; mediatorship
cyfryngiad nm mediation;
intervention
cyfryngol adj mediatorial
cyfryngu vb mediate; intervene
cyfryngwr (-wyr) nm mediator
cyfryngwriaeth nf mediatorship
cyfryw adj like, such
cyfuchlinedd (-au) nm contour
cyfuchliniau npl contours
cyfundeb (-au) nm union;
connexion
cyfundebol adj connexional;
denominational
cyfundrefn (-au) nf system
cyfundrefnol adj systematic
cyfundrefnu vb systematize
cyfuniad (-au) nm combination
cyfuno vb unite, combine
cyfunol adj united
cyfunrywiol adj homosexual
cyfuwch adj as high
cyfweld vb interview
cyfweliad (-au) nm interview
cyfwerth adj equivalent
cyfwng (-yngau) nm space;
interval
cyfwrdd vb meet
cyfyng adj narrow, confined
cyfyngder (-au) nm trouble,
distress
cyfyngdra nm narrowness;
distress
cyfyngedig adj confined,
restricted, limited
cyfyng-gyngor nm perplexity
cyfyngu vb narrow, confine, limit
cyfyl nm neighbourhood. **ar ei g.**
near him
cyfyrder (-dyr) nm second cousin
cyfystlys adj side by side
cyfystyr adj synonymous
cyfystyron npl synonyms
cyff (-ion) nm stock
cyffaith (-ffeithiau) nm confection

cyffelyb adj like, similar
cyffelybiaeth (-au) nf likeness,
similitude
cyffelybiaethol adj figurative
cyffelybrwydd nm likeness,
similarity
cyffelybu vb liken, compare
cyffes (-ion) nf confession
cyffesgell (-oedd) nf confessional
cyffesu vb confess
cyffeswr (-wyr), **-ydd** (-ion) nm
confessor
cyffin (-iau, -ydd) nf/m border,
confine
cyffindir (-oedd) nm frontier,
march
cyffio vb stiffen; fetter, shackle;
beat
cyffion npl stocks
cyffordd (-ffyrdd) nf junction
cyffredin adj common; general
cyffredinedd nm mediocrity,
banality
cyffredinol adj general, universal
cyffredinoli vb universalize,
generalize
cyffredinolrwydd nm universality
cyffredinwch nm commonness
cyffro (-adau) nm motion, stir;
excitement
cyffroi vb move, excite; provoke
cyffrous adj exciting; excited
cyffur (-iau) nm/f ingredient, drug
cyffuriwr (-wyr) nm apothecary,
druggist
cyffwrdd vb meet, touch
cyffylog (-od) nm woodcock
cyffyrddiad (-au) nm touch,
contact
cyffyrddus adj comfortable
cygnog adj knotted, gnarled
cyngaf, cyngaw nm burdock; burs
cyngan adj suitable, harmonious
cynganeddol adj in cynghanedd
cynganeddu vb form cynghanedd;
harmonize
cynganeddwr (-wyr) nm writer of

cynghanedd

cyngaws (cynghawsau, -ion) *nm*
lawsuit, action; trial; battle

cyngerdd (-ngherddau) *nm/f*
concert

cynghanedd (cynganeddion) *nf*
music, harmony; Welsh metrical
alliteration

cynghori *vb* counsel, advise;
exhort

cynghorwr (-wyr) *nm* councillor;
counsellor; exhorter

cynghrair (-eiriau) *nm/f* alliance,
league

cynghreiriad (-iaid) *nm*
confederate, ally

cynghreirio *vb* league, confederate

cynghreiriwr (-wyr) *nm*
confederate, ally

cyngor (-nghorion) *nm* counsel,
advice ♦ (-nghorau) *nm* council.
C. Bro Community Council. C.
Tref Town Council. C. Sir County
Council

cyngres (-au, -i) *nf* congress

cyngresydd (-wyr) *nm*
congressman

cyngwystl (-i)(on) *nm/f* wager,
pledge

cyhoedd *adj, nm* public

cyhoeddi *vb* publish, announce

cyhoeddiad (-au) *nm* publication;
announcement; (preaching)
engagement

cyhoeddus *adj* public

cyhoeddusrwydd *nm* publicity

cyhoeddwr (-wyr) *nm* publisher

cyhuddiad (-au) *nm* accusation,
charge

cyhuddo *vb* accuse, charge

cyhuddwr (-wyr) *nm* accuser

cyhwfan *vb* wave, heave

cyhyd *adj* as long, so long

cyhydedd *nm* equator

cyhydeddol *adj* equatorial,
equinoctial

cyhyr (-au) *nm* flesh, muscle

cyhyrog *adj* muscular

cylch (-au, oedd) *nm* round, circle,
sphere, hoop

cylchdaith (-deithiau) *nf* circuit

cylchdro (-eon, -adau) *nm* orbit

cylchdroi *vb* rotate, revolve

cylched (-au) *nm* coverlet, blanket

cylchedd (-au) *nm/f* compass,
circle, circuit

cylchgrawn (-gronau) *nm*
magazine

cylchlythyr (-au) *nm* circular

cylchredeg *vb* circulate

cylchrediad *nm* circulation

cylchres (-i) *nf* round, rota

cylchwyl (-iau) *nf* anniversary,
festival

cylchynol *adj* surrounding

cylchynu *vb* surround, encompass

cylion *npl* (-yn *nm*, -en *nf*) flies,
gnats

cylymu *vb* knot, tie

cyll *npl* (collen *nf*) hazel-trees

cylla (-on) *nm* stomach

cyllell (-yll) *nf* knife

cyllid (-au) *nm* revenue, income

cyllideb (-au) *nf* budget

cyllidol *adj* financial, fiscal

cyllidwr (-wyr), **cyllidydd** (-ion)
nm taxgatherer, revenue or
excise officer, financier

cymaint *adj* as big, as much, as
many; so big, *etc*

cymal (-au) *nm* joint; clause
(*gram.*)

cymalwst *nf* rheumatism

cymanfa (-oedd) *nf* assembly;
festival

cymantoledd (-au) *nm* equilibrium

cymanwlad *nf* commonwealth

cymar (-heiriaid) *nm* fellow,
partner

cymathiad *nm* assimilation

cymathu *vb* assimilate

cymdeithas (-au) *nf* society,
association. C. yr Iaith Gymraeg
The Welsh Language Society

cymdeithaseg *nf/m* sociology
cymdeithasegol *adj* sociological
cymdeithasgar *adj* sociable
cymdeithasol *adj* social
cymdeithasu *vb* associate
cymdogaeth (-au) *nf*
neighbourhood
cymdogol *adj* neighbourly
cymedr (-au) *nm* mean (*maths*),
average
cymedrol *adj* moderate, temperate
cymedroldeb *nm* moderation,
temperance
cymedroli *vb* moderate
cymedrolwr (-wyr) *nm* moderator;
moderate drinker
cymell *vb* urge, press, persuade,
induce
cymen *adj* wise, skilful, neat,
becoming
cymer (-au) *nm* confluence
cymeradwy *adj* acceptable,
approved, commendable
cymeradwyaeth *nf* approval;
applause
cymeradwyo *vb* approve;
recommend
cymeradwyol *adj* commendary
cymeriad (-au) *nm* character,
reputation
cymesur *adj* proportionate,
symmetrical
cymesuredd *nm* proportion,
symmetry
cymesurol *adj* commensurate,
proportionate
cymhareb (cymarebau) *nf* ratio
cymhariaeth (cymariaethau) *nf*
comparison
cymharol *adj* comparative
cymharu *vb* pair; compare
cymhathu *vb* assimilate
cymhelliad (-hellion) *nm* motive,
inducement
cymhelliant (-nnau) *nm* motivation
cymhendod *nm* knowledge;
proficiency; tidiness; eloquence;
affection
cymhennu *vb* put in order; trim;
scold, reprove
cymhercyn *adj* limping, infirm ♦
nm valetudinarian
cymhleth (-au) *adj* complex,
complicated
cymhlethdod (-au) *nm* complexity
cymhlethu *vb* complicate
cymhorthdal (cymorthdaloedd) *nm*
subsidy, grant
cymhwysiad *nm* application,
adjustment
cymhwyso *vb* apply, adjust
cymhwyster (cymwysterau) *nm*
fitness, suitability; (*pl*)
qualifications
cymod *nm* reconciliation
cymodi *vb* reconcile; be reconciled
cymodol *adj* reconciliatory,
propitiatory
cymodwr (-wyr) *nm* reconciler
cymon *adj* orderly, tidy; seemly
cymorth *vb* assist, aid, help ♦ *nm*
assistance, aid, help
Cymraeg *nf/m, adj* Welsh
Cymraes *nf* Welshwoman
cymrawd (-odyr) *nm* comrade,
fellow
Cymreictod *nm* Welshness
Cymreig *adj* Welsh
Cymreigaidd *adj* Welshy
Cymreiges (-au) *nf* Welshwoman
Cymreigio *vb* translate into Welsh
Cymreigiwr (-wyr) *nm* one versed
or skilled in Welsh; Welsh-
speaking Welshman
Cymro (Cymry) *nm* Welshman
cymrodedd *nm* arbitration;
compromise
cymrodeddu *vb* compromise,
reconcile
cymrodor (-ion) *nm* consociate,
fellow
cymrodoriaeth *nf* fellowship
Cymru *nf* Wales
cymrwd *nm* mortar, plaster

Cymry see **Cymro**
cymryd vb take, accept. **c. ar** pretend
cymun, -deb nm communion, fellowship
cymuned nf community
cymunedol adj community
cymuno vb commune
cymunwr (-wyr) nm communicant
cymwy (-au) nm affliction
cymwynas (-au) nf kindness, favour
cymwynasgar adj obliging, kind
cymwynasgarwch nm obligingness, kindness
cymwynaswr (-wyr) nm benefactor
cymwys adj fit, proper, suitable; exact
cymwysedig adj applied
cymwysiadol adj applicable
cymydog (cymdogion) nm neighbour; f **cymdoges**
cymylog adj cloudy, clouded
cymylu vb cloud, dim, obscure
cymyndod nm committal
cymynnu vb bequeath
cymynrodd (-ion) nf legacy, bequest
cymynroddi vb bequeath
cymynu vb hew, fell
cymynwr (-wyr) nm hewer, feller
cymysg adj mixed
cymysgedd nm/f mixture
cymysgfa nf mixture, medley, hotchpotch
cymysgliw adj motley
cymysglyd adj muddled, confused
cymysgryw adj mongrel; heterogeneous
cymysgu vb mix, blend; confuse
cymysgwch nm mixture, jumble
cymysgwr (-wyr) nm mixer, blender
cyn prefix before, previous, first, former, pre-, ex-
cyn adv: **cyn wynned â** as white as

cŷn (cynion) nm wedge, chisel
cynadledda vb meet in conference
cynaeafu vb harvest
cynamserol adj premature, untimely
cynaniad nm pronunciation
cynanu vb pronounce
cyndad (-au) nm forefather, ancestor
cynderfynol adj semi-final
cyndyn adj stubborn, obstinate
cyndynnu vb be obstinate
cyndynrwydd nm stubborness, obstinacy
cynddaredd nf madness; rabies
cynddeiriog adj mad, rabid
cynddeiriogi vb madden, enrage
cynddeiriogrwydd nm rage, fury
cynddrwg adj as bad
cynddydd nm day-break, dawn
cynefin adj acquainted, accustomed, familiar ♦ nm haunt, habitat
cynefindra nm use, familarity
cynefino vb get used, become accustomed
cynefinol adj usual, accustomed
cynfas (-au) nm/fm (bed) sheet; canvas
cynfyd nm primitive world, antiquity
cynffon (-nau) nf tail; tang
cynffonna vb fawn, toady, cringe
cynffonnwr (-onwyr) nm toady, sycophant; sneak
cyn-geni adj antenatal
cynhadledd (cynadleddau) nf conference
cynhaeaf (cynaeafau) nm harvest
cyn(h)aeafa vb dry in the sun
cyn(h)aeafu vb harvest
cyn(h)aeafwr (-wyr) nm harvester
cynhaliaeth nf maintenance, support
cynhaliol adj sustaining
cynhaliwr (-wyr) nm supporter, sustainer

cynhanesiol adj prehistoric
cynhebrwng (-yngau) nm funeral
cynhenid adj innate
cynhennu vb contend, quarrel
cynhennus adj contentious, quarrelsome
cynhennwr (-henwyr) nm wrangler
cynhesol adj agreeable, amiable
cynhesrwydd nm warmth
cynhesu vb warm, get warm
cynhorthwy (cynorthwyon) nm help, aid
cynhwynol adj natural, congenital, innate
cynhwysedd (cynwyseddau) nm capacity, capacitance
cynhwysfawr adj comprehensive
cynhwysiad nm contents
cynhyrchiad (-au) nm production
cynhyrchiol adj productive
cynhyrchu vb produce
cynhyrchydd (-ion, cynhyrchwyr) nm producer, generator
cynhyrfiad (cynyrfiadau) nm stirring, agitation
cynhyrfiol adj stirring, thrilling
cynhyrfu vb stir, agitate
cynhyrfus adj agitated; exciting
cynhyrfwr (-wyr) nm agitator, disturber
cynhysgaeth nf dower, portion, fortune
cyni nm anguish, distress, adversity
cynifer adj, nm as many, so many
cynigiad (-au) nm proposal, motion
cynigiwr (-wyr), -ydd (-ion) nm proposer, mover
cynildeb nm frugality, economy
cynilion npl savings
cynilo vb save, economise
cynio vb chisel, gouge
cyniwair vb go to and fro, frequent
cyniweirfa (-feydd) nf resort, haunt

cyniweirydd nm wayfarer
cynllun (-iau) nm pattern; plan
cynllunio vb plan, design
cynlluniydd (-ion, -wyr) nm designer
cynllwyn vb plot, conspire ♦ (-ion) nm plot
cynllwynio vb conspire, plot
cynllwynwr (-wyr) nm conspirator
cynnal vb hold, uphold, support, sustain
cynnar adj early
cynnau vb kindle, light
cynneddf (cyneddfau) nf quality, faculty
cynnen (cynhennau) nf contention, strife. **asgwrn y g.** bone of contention
cynnes adj warm
cynnig vb offer; attempt; propose, move; bid; apply ♦ (cynigion) nm offer; attempt; motion
cynnil adj economical; delicate
cynnor (cynhorau) nf door-post
cynnud nm firewood, fuel
cynnull vb collect, gather, assemble
cynnwrf nm stir, commotion, agitation
cynnwys vb contain, include, comprise, comprehend ♦ nm content(s)
cynnydd nm increase, growth, progress
cynnyrch (cynhyrchion nm produce, product; (pl) productions
cynoesol adj primeval
cynorthwyo vb help, assist
cynorthwyol adj auxiliary; assistant
cynorthwywr (-wyr) nm helper, assistant
cynradd adj primary
cynrhon npl (-yn nm) maggots
cynrhoni vb breed maggots
cynrhonllyd adj maggoty

cynrychioladol *adj* representative
cynrychiolaeth *nf* representation
cynrychioli *vb* represent
cynrychiolwr (-wyr), -ydd (-ion) *nm* representative, delegate
cynt *adj* earlier, sooner, quicker ♦ *adv* see **gynt**
cyntaf *adj, adv* first
cyntedd (-au) *nm* court; porch, foyer
cyntefig *adj* prime, primitive
cyntun *nm* nap
cynulleidfa (-oedd) *nf* congregation
cynulleidfaol *adj* congregational
cynulliad (-au) *nm* gathering
cynulla *vb* gather fuel
cynyddol *adj* increasing, growing
cynyddu *vb* increase
cynysgaeddu *vb* endow, endue
cyplad *nm* copula
cypladu *vb* copulate
cyplu, cyplysu *vb* couple
cyraeddadwy *adj* attainable
cyraeddiadau *npl* attainments
cyrbibion *npl* atoms, smithereens
cyrcydu *vb* squat, cower
cyrch (-au) *nm* attack
cyrchfa (-feydd) *nf* resort
cyrchu *vb* go, resort, repair
cyrhaeddgar *adj* telling, incisive
cyrhaeddiad (cyraeddiadau) *nm* reach, attainment
cyrliog *adj* curly
cyrraedd *vb* reach, attain; arrive
cyrren (cyrensen *nf*) currants
cyrydiad *nm* corrosion
cyrydu *vb* corrode
cysawd (-odau) *nm* system; constellation
cysefin *adj* original, primordial
cysegr (-au, -oedd) *nm* sanctuary
cysegredig *adj* consecrated, sacred
cysegredigrwydd *nm* sacredness
cysegriad (-au) *nm* consecration
cysegr-ladrad *nm* sacrilege

cysegr-lân *adj* holy
cysegru *vb* consecrate, dedicate, devote
cyseinedd *nm* alliteration
cysetlyd *adj* fastidious
cysgadrwydd *nm* sleepiness, drowsiness
cysgadur (-iaid) *nm* sleeper
cysglyd *adj* sleepy
cysgod (-au, -ion) *nm* shade, shadow; shelter; type
cysgodi *vb* shadow, shade; shelter
cysgodol *adj* shady, sheltered
cysgu *vb* sleep
cysgwr (-wyr) *nm* sleeper
cysidro *vb* consider
cysodi *vb* set type, compose
cysodydd (-ion, -wyr) *nm* compositor
cyson *adj* consistent, constant
cysondeb *nm* consistency; regularity
cysoni *vb* harmonize; reconcile
cysonwr (-wyr), -ydd (-ion) *nm* harmonist
cystadleuaeth (-au) *nf* competition
cystadleuol *adj* competitive
cystadleuwr, -ydd (-wyr) *nm* competitor
cystadlu *vb* compete; compare
cystal *adj* as good, so good ♦ *adv* as well, so well
cystrawen (-nau) *nf* construction, syntax
cystudd (-iau) *nm* affliction; illness
cystuddiedig *adj* afflicted, contrite
cystuddio *vb* afflict, trouble
cystuddiol *adj* afflicted
cystuddiwr (-wyr) *nm* afflicter, oppressor
cystwyo *vb* chastise, castigate, trounce
cysur (-on) *nm* comfort, consolation
cysuro *vb* comfort, console
cysurus *adj* comfortable

cysurwr (-wyr) *nm* comforter

cyswllt (-ylltiadau) *nm* joint, junction

cysylltiad (-au) *nm* conjunction; joining, connexion

cysylltiol *adj* connecting; connected

cysylltnod (-au) *nm* ligature, hyphen

cysylltu *vb* join, connect

cysylltydd (-ion) *nm* connector, contact

cysyniad (-au) *nm* concept

cytbell *adj* equidistant

cytbwys *adj* of equal weight

cytbwysedd *nm* balance

cytew *nm* batter

cytgan (-au) *nm/f* chorus

cytgord *nm* concord

cytir (-oedd) *nm* common

cytras *adj* allied, related; cognate

cytsain (-seiniaid) *nf* consonant

cytûn *adj* agreed, of one accord, unanimous

cytundeb (-au) *nm* agreement, consent

cytuno *vb* agree, consent

cythlwng *nm* fasting, fast, hunger

cythraul (-euliaid) *nm* devil, demon

cythreuldeb *nm* devilment

cythreulig *adj* devilish, fiendish

cythru *vb* snatch, rush

cythruddo *vb* annoy, provoke, irritate

cythrwfl *nm* uproar, tumult

cythryblu *vb* trouble, agitate

cythryblus *adj* troubled, agitated

cyw (-ion) *nm* young bird, chick, chicken; baby

cywain *vb* convey, carry; garner

cywair (-eiriau) *nm* order; key; tune

cywaith (-weithiau) *nm* collective work, project

cywarch *nm* hemp

cywasg, -edig *adj* compressor, diminished

cywasgiad (-au) *nm* contraction, compression

cywasgu *vb* contract, compress

cywasgydd (-ion) *nm* compressor

cyweiriad (-au) *nm* repair

cyweiriadur (-on) *nm* modulator

cyweirio *vb* set in order; prepare, dress

cyweirnod (-au) *nm* key-note

cywen (-nod) *nf* pullet, young hen

cywerth *nm* equivalent

cywilydd *nm* shame; shyness

cywilydd-dra *nm* shamefulness

cywilyddgar *adj* bashful, shy

cywilyddio *vb* shame; be ashamed

cywilyddus *adj* shameful, disgraceful

cywir *adj* correct, accurate, true, faithful

cywirdeb *nm* correctness; integrity

cywiriad (-au) *nm* correction

cywiro *vb* correct; make good; perform

cywirwr (-wyr) *nm* corrector

cywladu *vb* naturalize

cywrain *adj* skilful; curious

cywreinbeth (-au, -einion) *nm* curiosity

cywreindeb *nm* skill, ingenuity

cywreinrwydd *nm* skill; curiosity

cywydd *nm* alliterative Welsh poem

cywyddwr (-wyr) *nm* composer of *cywyddau*

CH

Chile *nf* Chile

China *nf* China

chwa (-on) *nf* puff, gust, breeze

chwaer (chwiorydd) *nf* sister

chwaeroliaeth *nf* sisterhood

chwaeth (-au, -oedd) *nf* taste

chwaethu *vb* taste

chwaethus *adj* tasteful; decent

chwaith adv nor either, neither

chwâl adj scattered, loose

chwalfa (-feydd) nf upset, rout

chwalu vb scatter, spread

chwalwr (-wyr) nm scatterer, demolisher

chwaneg adj, nm more

chwanegiad (-au) nm addition

chwanegol adj additional

chwanegu vb add, augment, increase

chwannen (chwain) nf flea

chwannog adj desirous; addicted; prone

chwant (-au) nm desire, craving, lust

chwantu vb desire, lust

chwap nm sudden blow, moment ♦ adv instantly

chwarae, chware vb play ♦ (-on) nm play

chwaraedy (-dai) nm playhouse, theatre

chwaraefa (-feydd) nf pitch, playground

chwaraegar adj playful, sportive

chwaraewr (-wyr) nm player, actor, performer

chwaraeydd (-ion) nm actor

chwarddiad (-au) nm laugh

chwarel (-au, -i, -ydd) nf quarry

chwarelwr (-wyr) nm quarryman

chwareus adj playful

chwarren (-arennau) nf gland; kernel

chwart (-iau) nm quart

chwarter (-i, -au) nm quarter

chwarterol adj quarterly

chwarterolyn (-olion) nm quarterly (magazine)

chwarteru vb quarter

chwe adj six (before a noun)

chweban (-nau) nm sestet, sextain

chwech adj six ♦ (-au) nm six; sixpence

chwechawd (-au) nm sextet

chwedl (-au) nf story, tale

chwedleua vb talk, gossip

chwedleuwr (-wyr) nm story-teller

chwedloniaeth nf mythology

chwedlonol adj mythical, mythological

chwedlonydd (-wyr) nm mythologist

chwedyn adv: **na chynt na ch.** neither before nor after

Chwefror, Chwefrol nm February

chwennych, chwenychu vb covet, desire

chwenychiad (-au) nm desire

chweongl (-au) nm hexagon

chwephlyg adj sixfold

chwerthin vb laugh ♦ nm laughter

chwerthiniad (-au) nm laugh

chwerthinllyd adj laughable, ridiculous

chwerthinog adj laughing, merry

chwerw adj bitter

chwerwder, -dod nm bitterness

chwerwedd nm bitterness

chwerwi vb grow bitter, embitter

chwi pron you

chwib (-iau) nm whistle

chwiban vb, nm whistle

chwibaniad nm whistling, whistle

chwibanogl (-au) nf whistle, flute

chwibanu vb whistle

chwibon (-iaid) nm curlew, stork

chwifio vb wave, flourish, brandish

chwiff (-iau) nf whiff, puff

chwifflad nm whiff, jiffy

chwil (-od) nm/f beetle, chafer

chwil adj whirling, reeling

chwilboeth adj scorching, piping hot

chwildroi vb whirl, spin

chwilen (chwilod) nf beetle

chwilenna vb rummage; pry; pilfer

chwiler (-od) nm chrysalis, pupa

chwilfriw adj smashed to atoms

chwilfriwio vb smash, shatter

chwilfrydedd nm curiosity

chwilfrydig adj curious, inquisitive

chwilgar *adj* curious, inquisitive

chwilgarwch *nm* inquisitiveness

chwiliad (-au) *nm* search, scrutiny

chwilibawa(n) *vb* dawdle, trifle

chwilio *vb* search; examine

chwiliwr (-wyr) *nm* searcher

chwil-lys *nm* inquisition

chwilmantan *vb* pry, rummage

chwilolau (-oleuadau) *nm* searchlight

chwilota *vb* rummage, pry

chwilotwr (-wyr) *nm* searcher, rummager

chwim *adj* nimble, quick, agile

chwimder, -dra *nm* nimbleness

chwimio *vb* move, stir, accelerate

chwimwth *adj* nimble, brisk

chwinc *nm* wink

chwinciad *nm* twinkling, trice

chwiorydd see **chwaer**

chwip (-iau) *nf* whip; whipping

chwipiad (-au) *nm* whipping

chwipio *vb* whip

chwipyn *adv* instantly

chwirligwgan *nf* whirligig

chwisgi *nm* whisky

chwisl (-au) *nm* whistle

chwistrell (-au, -i) *nf* squirt, syringe

chwistrelliad (-au) *nm* injection

chwistrellu *vb* squirt, syringe, inject

chwit-chwat *adj* fickle, inconstant

chwith *adj* left; wrong; sad; strange

chwithau *pron conj* you (on your part), you also

chwithdod, -dra *nm* strangeness

chwithig *adj* strange, wrong, awkward

chwithigrwydd *nm* awkwardness

chwiw (-iau) *nf* fit, attack, malady

chwiwgar *adj* fickle

chwychwi *pron* you yourselves

chwyd, chwydiad *nm* vomit

chwydu *vb* vomit, spew

chwydd, chwyddi *nm* swelling

chwyddiant (-nnau) *nm* inflation; inflammation

chwyddo *vb* swell, increase, magnify

chwyddwydr (-au) *nm* microscope

chwŷl (chwylion) *nm/f* turn, rotation

chwyldro (-ion) *nm* rotation; orbit

chwyldroad (-au) *nm* revolution

chwyldroadol *adj* revolutionary

chwyldroadwr (-wyr) *nm* revolutionary

chwyldroi *vb* whirl, revolve, rotate

chwyldrowr see **chwyldroadwr**

chwylolwyn (-ion) *nf* flywheel

chwyn (chwynnyn *nm*) *coll n, npl* weeds

chwynladdwr *nm* weed-killer

chwynnu *vb* weed

chwyrligwgan (-od) *nm* spinning top, whirligig

chwyrlïo *vb* whirl, spin, speed

chwyrlwynt (-oedd) *nm* whirlwind

chwyrn *adj* rapid, swift

chwyrnellu *vb* whirl, whiz

chwyrnu *vb* hum; snore; snarl

chwyrnwr (-wyr) *nm* snorer; snarler

chwys *nm* sweat, perspiration

chwysfa (-feydd) *nf* sweating

chwysiant *nm* exudation

chwysigen (-igod) *nf* blister, vesicle

chwyslyd *adj* sweaty

chwystyllau *npl* pores

chwysu *vb* sweat, perspire; exude

chwyswr (-wyr) *nm* sweater

chwyth, chwythad *nm* breath

chwythbib (-au) *nf* blowpipe

chwythbrenni *npl* woodwinds

chwythell (-i) *nf* jet

chwythiad (-au) *nm* blow, blast

chwythu *vb* blow, blast; breathe; hiss

chwythwr (-wyr) *nm* blower

D

da adj good, well ♦ (**-oedd**) nm good; goods; stock, cattle

da-da nm sweets

dacw adv there is, are; behold there

dad-, dat- prefix un-, dis- re-, back

dadansoddi vb analyse

dadansoddiad (**-au**) nm analysis

dadansoddol adj analytic(al)

dadansoddwr (**-wyr**) nm analyst

dadansoddydd (**-wyr**) nm analyser

dadchwyddiant (**-nnau**) nm deflation

dad-ddyfrio vb dehydrate

dadebriad nm resuscitation

dadebru vb resuscitate, revive

dadelfeniad (**-au**) nm decomposition

dadelfennu vb decompose; refine

dadeni vb regenerate, reanimate ♦ nm rebirth, renascence, renaissance

dadfachu vb unhook

dadfathiad nm dissimulation

dadfeiliad nm decay

dadfeilio vb fall to ruin, decay

dadflino vb rest (after exertion)

dadl (**-euon**) nf debate; doubt; plea

dadlaith vb thaw; dissolve

dadlau vb argue, debate; plead

dadleniad (**-au**) nm disclosure, exposure

dadlennol adj revealing, disclosing, exposing

dadlennu vb disclose, expose

dadleoli vb dislocate

dadleoliad (**-au**) nm dislocation

dadleuaeth nf polemics, controversy

dadleugar adj argumentative

dadleuol adj controversial, polemical

dadleuwr (**-wyr**), **-ydd** (**-ion**) nm debater, controversialist; advocate

dadluddedu vb rest (after exertion)

dadlwytho vb unload, unburden

dadlygru vb decontaminate

dadmer vb thaw; dissolve

dadnitreiddiad nm denitrification

dadolwch nm propitiation ♦ vb worship, seek forgiveness

dadorchuddio vb unveil, uncover

dadreolaeth nf decontrol

dadrewlifiant nm deglaciation

dadrithiad (**-au**) nm disillusionment

dadrithio vb disillusion

dadsefydlu vb disestablish

dadwaddoli vb disendow

dadwaddoliad nm disendowment

dadwneuthur, dadwneud vb undo, unmake

dadwrdd nm noise, uproar, hubbub

dadymchwel, -yd vb overturn, overthrow

daear (**-oedd**) nf earth, ground, soil

daeardy (**-dai**) nm dungeon

daeareg nf geology

daearegol adj geological

daearegwr (**-wyr**), **-ydd** (**-ion**) nm geologist

daearen nf the earth; land, country

daearfochyn (**-foch**) nm badger

daeargell (**-oedd**) nf dungeon, vault

daeargi (**-gwn**) nm terrier

daeargryd (**-iau**) nm earth tremor

daeargryn (**-fâu**) nm/f earthquake

daearol adj terrestrial, earthly, earthy

daearu vb earth; inter

daearyddiaeth nf geography

daearyddol adj geographical

daearyddwr (-wyr) nm geographer

dafad (defaid) nf sheep; wart

dafaden (-ennau) nf wart

dafn (-au) nm drop

dafnu vb trickle

dagr (-au) nm dagger, bayonet, dirk

dagrau npl (**deigryn** nm) tears

dagreuol adj tearful, sad

dangos see **dan-**

dail npl (**dalen, deilen** nf) leaves

daioni nm goodness, good

daionus adj good; beneficial; beneficent

dal, -a vb hold; catch; arrest; last

dalen (-nau, dail) nf leaf

dalfa (-feydd) nf hold; arrest, custody; prison

dalgylch (-oedd) nm catchment area

daliad (-au) nm holding; tenet; spell

daliwr (-wyr) nm jig, catcher

dall (deillion) adj blind

dallbleidiaeth nf bigotry

dallbleidiol adj bigoted

dallbleidiwr (-wyr) nm bigot

dallineb nm blindness

dallu vb blind; dazzle

damcaniaeth (-au) nf theory

damcaniaethol adj theoretical

damcaniaethwr (-wyr) nm theorist

damcanu vb theorize, speculate

dameg (-hegion) nf parable

damhegol adj parabolic(al), allegorical

damhegwr (-wyr) nm allegorist

damnedig adj damned, damnable

damnedigaeth nf damnation, condemnation

damnio vb damn

damniol adj damning, damnatory

damsang vb tread, trample

damwain (-weiniau) nf accident, chance, fate

damweinio vb befall, happen

damweiniol adj accidental, casual

dan see **tan**

danadl npl (**danhadlen** nf) nettles

danas coll n deer. **bwch d.** buck

danfon vb send, convey; escort

dangos vb show

dangoseg (-ion) nf index; indication

dangosol adj indicative, demonstrative

danheddog adj jagged, serrated, toothed

dannod vb reproach, upbraid, taunt, twit

dannoedd nf toothache

dansoddol adj abstract

dant (dannedd) nm tooth

danteithfwyd (-teithion) nm dainty

danteithiol adj dainty, delicious

danteithion npl delicacies

darbodus adj provident, thrifty

darbwyllo vb persuade, convince

darfod vb finish, end; perish; happen

darfodadwy adj transitory, perishable

darfodedig adj perishable, transient

darfodedigaeth nm consumption

darfudiad (-au) nm convection

darfudol adj convectional

darganfod vb discover

darganfyddiad (-au) nm discovery

darganfyddwr (-wyr) nm discoverer

dargludedd nm conductivity

dargludo vb conduct

dargludydd (-ion) nm conductor

dargyfeiredd nm divergence

dargyfeirio vb diverge, divert

darlith (-iau, -oedd) nf lecture

darlithfa (-feydd) nf lecture room

darlithio vb lecture

darlithiwr (-wyr), -ydd (-ion) nm lecturer

darlun (-iau) nm picture

darluniad (-au) nm portrayal, description

darluniadol adj pictorial, illustrated

darluniaeth nf imagery

darlunio vb portray, depict, describe

darluniol adj pictorial

darllediad (-au) nm broadcast

darlledu vb broadcast

darlledwr (-wyr) nm broadcaster

darllen vb read

darllenadwy adj readable, legible

darllenfa (-feydd) nf reading room; reading-desk; lectern

darllengar adj fond of reading, studious

darlleniad (-au) nm reading

darllenwr (-wyr), -ydd (-ion) nm reader

darn (-au) nm piece, fragment, part

darnguddio vb conceal or withhold a part

darniad (-au) nm fragmentation

darnio vb cut up, hack

darn-ladd vb beat mercilessly

darogan vb predict, foretell, forebode ♦ (-au) nf prediction, foreboding

daroganu vb predict, foretell

daroganwr (-wyr) nm predictor, prophet, soothsayer, forecaster

darostwng vb lower; subdue; subject, humiliate

darostyngiad nm humiliation; subjection

darpar (-ion, -iadau) nm preparation, provision ♦ adj intended, elect

darpariaeth (-au) nf preparation, provision

darparu vb prepare, provide

darparwr (-wyr) nm provider

darwden nf ringworm

das (-au, deisi) nf rick, stack

dat- prefix see **dad-**

data nm data

datblygiad (-au) nm development,
evolution

datblygol adj nascent, developing

datblygu vb develop, evolve

datblygus adj developmental

datblygydd (-ion) nm developer

datchwyddiant nm deflation

datgan vb declare; recount; render

datganiad (-au) nm declaration; rendering

datganoli vb devolve, decentralize

datganoli(ad) nm devolution

datganu vb declare; sing, render

datgeliad (-au) nm detection; revelation

datgelu vb detect; reveal

datgloi vb unlock

datglymu vb unhitch, undo

datgorffori vb dissolve (parliament)

datgorfforiad nm dissolution

datguddiad (-au) nm revelation, disclosure

datguddio vb reveal, disclose

datgyffesiad nm recantation

datgyffesu vb recant

datgymalu vb dislocate, dismember

datgysylltiad nm disestablishment

datgysylltu vb disconnect; disestablish

datod vb undo, untie, dissolve

datrannu vb dissect

datro vb change; undo

datru vb de-code

datrys vb solve

datrysiad (-au) nm solution, resolution

datseinio vb resound, reverberate

datsgwar (-au) nm square root

datysen (datys) nf date

dathliad (-au) nm celebration

dathlu vb celebrate

dau adj, nm two; f dwy

dau-, deu- prefix two, bi-

dauddyblyg adj twofold, double

daufiniog adj double-edged

dauwynebog adj two-faced

dawn (doniau) nmf gift, talent

dawns (-iau) nf dance

dawnsio vb dance

dawnsiwr (-wyr) nm dancer

dawnus adj gifted, talented

de see **deau**

De Affrica nf South Africa

deall vb understand ♦ nm understanding, intellect, intelligence

dealladwy adj intelligible

deallgar adj intelligent

deallol adj intellectual

dealltwriaeth (-au) nf understanding, intelligence

deallus adj understanding, intelligent

deallusion npl intelligentsia

deallusrwydd nm intelligence

deau adj, nm right; south

debentur (-on) nm debenture

debyd (-au) nm debit

debydu vb debit

dec (-iau, -s) nm deck

decilitr (-au) nm decilitre

decimetr (-au) nm decimetre

decstros nm dextrose

dectant nm ten-stringed instrument, psaltery

dechrau vb begin ♦ nm beginning

dechreuad (-au) nm beginning

dechreunos nf nightfall, dusk

dechreuol adj initial

dechreuwr (-wyr) nm beginner

dedfryd (-au) nf verdict; sentence

dedfrydu vb sentence

dedwydd adj happy, blessed

dedwyddwch, **-yd** nm happiness, bliss

deddf (-au) nf law, statute, act

deddfeg nf jurisprudence

deddfegwr (-wyr) nm jurist

deddfol adj legal, lawful

deddfu vb legislate, enact

deddfwr (-wyr) nm legislator

deddfwriaeth nf legislation,

legislature

deddfwriaethol adj legislative

deddlyfr (-au) nm statute book

defni vb drip, trickle

defnydd (-iau) nm material, stuff; use

defnyddio vb use, utilize, employ

defnyddiol adj useful

defnyddioldeb nm usefulness, utility

defnyddiwr (-wyr) nm user, consumer

defnyn (-nau) nm drop

defnynnu vb drop, drip, dribble, distil

defod (-au) nf custom; rite, ceremony

defodaeth nf ritualism

defodol adj ritualistic

defosiwn (-ynau) nm devotion

defosiynol adj devotional, devout

deffiniad, **-io** see **diff-**

deffro, **deffroi** vb rouse; wake

deffroad (-au) nm awakening

deg adj ten ♦ (-au) nm ten

degawd (-au) nm decade

degaidd adj denary

degiad (-au) nm decimal

degol (-ion) nm, adj decimal

degoli vb decimalise

degoliad nm decimalisation

degolyn (degolion) nm decimal

degwm (-ymau) nm tenth, tithe

degymu vb tithe

deng adj ten (before certain words)

dehau, **deheu** see **deau**

deheubarth, **-dir** nm southern region, south

deheuig adj dexterous, skilful

deheulaw nf right hand

deheuol adj southern

deheurwydd nm dexterity, skill

deheuwr (-wyr) nm southerner, southman

deheuwynt nm south wind

dehongli vb interpret

dehongliad (-au) nm interpretation

dehonglwr (-wyr), -ydd (-ion) *nm* interpreter

dehydrad (-au) *nm* dehydration

dehydru *vb* dehydrate

deial (-au) *nm* dial

deialog (-au) *nm/f* dialogue

deialu *vb* dial

deifio *vb* singe, scorch; blast; dive

deifiol *adj* scorching, scathing

deifiwr (-wyr) *nm* diver

deigryn (dagrau) *nm* tear

deilbridd *nm* humus

deildy (-dai) *nf/m* bower, arbour

deilen (dail) *nf* leaf

deilgoll *adj* deciduous

deiliad (-on, deiliaid) *nm* tenant; subject

deiliant (-nnau) *nm* foliage

deilio *vb* leaf

deiliog *adj* leafy

deillio *vb* proceed, emanate, issue

deinameg *nf/m* dynamics

deinamig *adj* dynamic

deinamo (-s, -au) *nm* dynamo

deincod *nm* teeth on edge

deincryd *nm* chattering or gnashing of teeth

deintio *vb* nibble

deintrod (-au) *nf* cog

deintydd (-ion) *nm* dentist

deintyddiaeth *nf* dentistry

deintyddol *adj* dental

deiseb (-au) *nf* petition

deisebu *vb* petition

deisebwr, -ydd (-wyr) *nm* petitioner

deisyf, **deisyfu** *vb* desire, wish; beseech, entreat

deisyfiad (-au) *nm* request, petition

del *adj* pretty, neat

delfryd (-au) *nm* ideal

delfrydiaeth *nf* idealism

delfrydol *adj* ideal

delfrydwr (-wyr) *nm* idealist

delff *nm* churl, oaf, dolt, rascal

delio *vb* deal

delw (-au) *nf* image; form, mode, manner

delwedd (-au) *nf* image

delweddaeth *nf* imagery

delweddu *vb* portray

delwi *vb* be wool-gathering; pale, be paralysed with fright.

dellni *nm* blindness

dellt *npl* (-en *nf*) laths, lattice, splinters

democratiaeth (-au) *nf* democracy

democratig *adj* democratic

demograffeg *nf* demography

demograffig *adj* demographic

dengar *adj* attractive

dengarwch *nm* attractiveness

deniadau *npl* attractions, allurements

deniadol *adj* attractive

Denmarc *nf* Denmark

denu *vb* attract, allure, entice

deon (-iaid) *nm* dean

deondy (-dai) *nm* deanery

deoniaeth (-au) *nf* deanery

deor *vb* brood, hatch, incubate

deorfa (-fâu, -feydd) *nf* hatchery

deorydd (-ion) *nf* incubator

derbyn *vb* receive; accept; admit

derbyniad (-au) *nm* receipt; reception

derbyniadwy *adj* admissible

derbyniol *adj* acceptable

derbyniwr (-wyr), -nnydd (-ynyddion) *nm* receiver, acceptor

derbynneb (-ynebau, -ynebion) *nf* receipt, voucher

derbynnydd (-ynyddion) *nm* receiver

deri *npl* (dâr *nf*) oak-trees, oak

dernyn (-nau) *nm* piece, scrap

derwen (derw, deri) *nf* oak-tree, oak

derwydd (-on) *nm* druid

derwyddiaeth *nf* druidism

derwyddol *adj* druidic(al)

desg (-iau) *nf* desk

desgant (-au) *nm* descant

desibel (-au) *nm* decibel

destlus *adj* neat

destlusrwydd *nm* neatness

detector (-au) *nm* detector

dethol *vb* select, pick, choose ♦ *adj* select

detholedd *nm* selectivity

detholiad (-iau, detholion) *nm* selection, anthology

deu- see **dau-**

deuawd (-au) *nm/f* duet

deublyg *adj* double, twofold

deuddeg *adj*, *nm* twelve

deufin *adj* two-edged

deuffocal *adj* bifocal

deugain *adj*, *nm* forty

deugraff *nm* digraph

deunaw *adj*, *nm* eighteen

deunydd (-iau) *nm* stuff, material

deuocsid *nm* dioxide

deuod (-au) *nm* diode, binary

deuol *adj* dual

deuoliaeth *nf* dualism, duality

deuparth *nd* two-thirds

deuris *adj* two-tier

deurudd *nd* the cheeks

deuryw *adj* bisexual

deusain *nd* diphthong

deutu *nd*: **o dd.** about

dewin (-iaid) *nm* diviner, magician, wizard

dewines (-au) *nf* witch, sorceress

dewiniaeth *nf* divination, witchcraft

dewinio *vb* divine

dewin(i)ol *adj* prophetic, divinatory

dewis *vb* choose, select ♦ *nm* choice

dewisiad *nm* choice, option

dewisol *adj* choice, desirable

dewr *adj* brave ♦ (-ion) *nm* brave man, hero

dewrder *nm* bravery, valour

di- *neg prefix* without, not, un-, non-, -less

diabetig *adj*, *nm/f* diabetic

diacon (-iaid) *nm* deacon

diacones (-au) *nf* deaconess

diaconiaeth *nf* diaconate

diadell (-au, -oedd) *nf* flock

diaddurn *adj* unadorned, plain, rude

dialedi *vb* dismember; expel a member

diafael *adj* slippery, careless

diafol (diefyl, dieifl) *nm* devil

diaffram (-au) *nm* diaphragm

diagnosis *nm* diagnosis

diangen *adj* unnecessary, free from want

dianghenraid *adj* unnecessary, needless

di-ail *adj* unequalled, unrivalled

dial *vb* avenge, revenge ♦ *nm* vengeance, revenge

dialedd (-au) *nm* vengeance, nemesis

dialgar *adj* revengeful, vindictive

dialgarwch *nm* vindictiveness

di-alw-amdano *adj* redundant, uncalled for

dialwr (-wyr), **-ydd** (-ion) *nm* avenger

diamau *adj* doubtless

diamcan *adj* aimless, purposeless

diamedr (-au) *nm* diameter

diamedral *adj* diametral

diamheuol *adj* undoubted, indisputable

diamod *adj* unconditional, absolute

diamodol *adj* unconditional, unqualified

diamwys *adj* unambiguous

diamynedd *adj* impatient

dianc *vb* escape

dianwadal *adj* unwavering, immutable

dianwadalwch *nm* immutability

diarddel *vb* expel, excommunicate

diarddeliad *nm* expulsion, excommunication

diarfogi *vb* disarm

diarfogiad *nm* disarmament

diarffordd *adj* out of the way, inaccessible

diargyhoedd *adj* blameless

diarhebol *adj* proverbial

diaroglydd (**-ion**) *nm* deodorant

diarwybod *adj* unawares

diasbad *nf* cry, scream

diasbedain *vb* resound, ring

diatreg *adj* immediate

diau *adj* true, certain; doubtless

diawl (**-iaid**) *nm* devil

diawledig *adj* devilish

di-baid, dibaid *adj* unceasing, ceaseless

di-ball, diball *adj* unfailing, infallible, sure

diben (**-ion**) *nm* end, purpose, aim

di-ben-draw *adj* endless

dibeniad (**-au**) *nm* ending, conclusion, predicate

di-benllanw *adj* off-peak

dibennu *vb* end, conclude, finish

diberfeddu *vb* disembowel, eviscerate

dibetrus *adj* unhesitating

dibl (**-au**) *nm* border, edge

diboblogaeth *nf* depopulation

diboblogi *vb* depopulate

dibrin *adj* abundant, plentiful

dibriod *adj* unmarried, single

dibris *adj* reckless, contemptuous

dibrisio *vb* depreciate, despise

dibristod *nm* depreciation, contempt

dibwys *adj* trivial, unimportant

dibwysiant (**-nnau**) *nm* depression

dibyn (**-nau**) *nm* steep, precipice

dibynadwy *adj* reliable

dibynadwyedd *nm* reliability

dibyniad *nm* dependence

dibyniant *nm* dependence

dibynnedd *nm* reliability

dibynnol *adj* depending; subjunctive

dibynnu *vb* depend, rely

dibynnydd (**dibynyddion**) *nm* dependant

dicllon *adj* wrathful, angry

dicllonrwydd *nm* wrath, indignation

dicotomi (**-iau**) *nm* dichotomy

dicra *adj* squeamish, fastidious, slow

dicter *nm* anger, wrath, displeasure

dichell (**-ion**) *nf* wile, craft, guile

dichellgar *adj* wily, crafty, cunning

dichlyn *vb* choose, pick ♦ *adj* careful, circumspect, exact

dichon *vb* be able; it may be

di-dact *adj* tactless

didactig *adj* didactic

didaro *adj* unaffected, unconcerned, cool

di-daw *adj* ceaseless, clamant

diden (**-nau**) *nf* nipple, teat

diderfyn *adj* unlimited

didoli *vb* separate, segregate

didoliad *nm* separation, segregation

didolnod (**-au**) *nm/f* diæresis

di-dor, didor *adj* unbroken, uninterrupted

didoreth *adj* shiftless, silly, fickle

didoriad *adj* unbroken, untamed, rough

di-drais, didrais *adj* non-violent, meek

diduedd *adj* impartial, unbiassed

didwyll *adj* guileless, sincere

didwylledd *nm* guilelessness, sincerity

di-ddadl *adj* unquestionable, indisputable

diddan *adj* amusing, diverting, pleasant

diddanion *npl* pleasantries, jokes

diddanu *vb* amuse, divert; comfort

diddanwch *nm* comfort, consolation

diddanwr (**-wyr**), **-ydd** (**-ion**) *nm* comforter

diddarbod *adj* shiftless

di-dderbyn-wyneb *adj* outspoken
diddig *adj* contented, pleased
diddigrwydd *nm* contentment, placidity
diddim *adj* nm void
diddordeb *nm* interest
diddori *vb* interest
diddorol *adj* interesting
diddos *adj* watertight, sheltered; snug
diddosi *vb* shelter
diddosrwydd *nm* shelter, safety
di-dduw, didduw *adj* ungodly ♦ *nm* atheist
di-ddweud *adj* taciturn, stubborn
diddwythiad *nm* deduction
diddwytho *vb* deduce
diddyfnu *vb* wean
diddymdra *nm* nothingness, void
diddymiad, -iant *nm* annihilation
diddymu *vb* annihilate, abolish
dieflig *adj* devilish, diabolical, fiendish
diegwyddor *adj* unprincipled
dieisiau *adj* unnecessary, needless
dieithr *adj* strange, alien, foreign ♦ (**-iaid**) *nm* stranger
dieithrio *vb* estrange, alienate
dieithrwch *nm* strangeness
dienaid *adj* soulless, senseless
dienyddiad (-au) *nm* execution
dienyddio *vb* put to death, execute
dienyddiwr (-wyr) *nm* executioner
dieuog *adj* guiltless, innocent
difa *vb* consume, destroy, devour
di-fai, difai *adj* blameless, faultless
difalch *adj* humble
difancoll *nf* total loss, perdition
difaol *adj* consuming, devouring
difater *adj* indifferent, unconcerned
difaterwch *nm* indifference, apathy
difeddiannu *vb* dispossess, deprive
di-feind *adj* heedless
difenwad *nm* (-au) *nm* defamation
difenwi *vb* revile, abuse, belittle
diferlif *nm* stream, issue

diferol *adj* dripping, dropping
diferu *vb* drip, drop, dribble, distil
diferyn (-nau, diferion) *nm* drop
difesur *adj* huge, immeasurable, unstinted
di-feth, difeth *adj* infallible, certain
difetha *vb* destroy, spoil, waste
difethwr (-wyr) *nm* destroyer
Difiau *nm* Thursday
difidend (-au) *nm* dividend
diflanbwynt *nm* vanishing point
diflanedig *adj* evanescent, fleeting
diflannu *vb* vanish, disappear
di-flas *adj* tasteless
diflas *adj* insipid, dull, wearisome
diflastod *nm* disgust
diflasu *vb* disgust; weary, surfeit
diflin, -o *adj* untiring, indefatigable
difodi *vb* annihilate, exterminate
difodiad, -iant *nm* annihilation
di-foes, difoes *adj* rude, unmannerly
difreiniad *nm* disfranchisement
difreinio *vb* disfranchise, deprive
difriaeth *nf* abuse, calumny
difrif *nm* seriousness, earnestness
difrifddwys *adj* solemn
difrifol *adj* serious, earnest, solemn, grave
difrifoldeb see **difrifwch**
difrifoli *vb* sober, solemnize
difrifwch *nm* seriousness, earnestness, solemnity
difrio *vb* scold, abuse, malign
difrod *nm* waste, havoc, damage
difrodi *vb* waste, spoil, ravage
difrodol *adj* destructive
difrodwr (-wyr) *nm* spoiler, devastator
difrycheulyd *adj* spotless, immaculate
di-fudd, difudd *adj* unprofitable, useless, futile
di-fwlch, difwlch *adj* without a break, continuous
difwyniad (-au) *nm* adulteration,

pollution
difwyniant nm defilement
difwyno vb mar, soil, sully, defile
difyfyr adj impromptu
difynio vb dissect, vivisect
difyr adj pleasant, diverting,
amusing
difyrion npl diversions,
amusements
difyrru vb divert, amuse, beguile
difyrrus adj diverting, amusing
difyrrwch nm diversion,
amusement, fun
difyrrwr (-yrwyr) nm entertainer
difyrwaith (-weithiau) nm hobby
difwyd adj inert
diffaith adj waste, desert; base,
mean ♦ (-ffeithydd) nm
wilderness, desert
diffeithdra nm dereliction
diffeithio vb lay waste
diffeithwch (-ychau) nm desert,
wilderness
diffiniad (-au) nm definition
diffinio vb define
diffodd, -i vb quench, extinguish
diffoddiad nm quenching,
extinction
diffoddwr (-wyr), -ydd (-ion) nm
quencher
diffrwyth adj barren; numb,
paralysed
diffrwythder, -dra nm barrenness;
numbness
diffrwytho vb make barren;
paralyse
diffuant adj unfeigned, sincere,
genuine
diffuantrwydd nm genuineness
di-ffurf adj amorphous
diffwys adj wild, waste; high,
steep; huge, awful
difyg (-ion) nm defect, want,
lack; eclipse
diffygiant nm deficiency
diffygio vb fail; faint, weary
diffygiol adj defective; faint,

weary
diffyndoll (-au) nf tariff
diffyndollaeth nf protectionism
diffynnydd (-ynyddion) nm
defendant
dig adj angry, wrathful ♦ nm
anger, wrath
digalon adj disheartened,
depressed, dejected, sad
digalondid nm depression,
dejection
digaloni vb dishearten,
discourage
digamsyniol adj unmistakable
digasedd nm hatred, enmity
digid (-au) nm digit
digidiad (-au) nm digitation
digidol adj digital
digio vb anger, offend; take
offence
di-glem adj inept
digllon see **dicllon**
digofaint nm anger, wrath,
indignation
digofus adj angry, indignant
digolledu vb indemnify,
compensate
digon nm, adj, adv enough; done
(of cooking)
digonedd nm abundance, plenty
digoni vb suffice; satisfy; cook
digonol adj satisfying; sufficient,
adequate; satisfied
digonolrwydd nm sufficiency,
abundance
digornio vb dehorn
di-gred adj infidel
di-grefft, digrefft adj unskilled
digrif, -ol adj mirthful, funny
digriflun (-iau) nm caricature,
cartoon
digrifwas (-weision) nm clown,
buffoon
digrifwch nm mirth, fun
digroeso adj inhospitable
digwydd vb befall, happen, occur
digwyddiad (-au) nm happening,

occurrence, event

digyfnewid adj unchangeable
digyffelyb adj incomparable
digymysg adj unmixed
digyswllt adj incoherent
digywilydd adj impudent
digywilydd-dra nm impudence
dihafal adj unequalled, peerless
dihangfa (diangfâu) nf escape
dihangol adj escaped, safe
dihareb (diarhebion) nf proverb
dihatru vb strip, undress
dihefelydd adj unequalled
diheintio vb disinfect
diheintydd (-ion) nm disinfectant, sterilizer
di-hid(io) adj heedless, indifferent, reckless
dihidlo vb drop, distil; shed
dihidrwydd nm indifference, recklessness
dihiryn (-hirod) nm rascal, scoundrel
dihoeni vb languish, pine
dihuno vb wake, rouse
di-hwyl adj out of sorts
dihyder adj lacking confidence
dihydradu vb dehydrate
dihysbydd adj inexhaustible
dihysbyddu vb empty, exhaust
dil (-iau) nm: d. mêl honeycomb
dilead nm abolition, deletion
dilechdid nm dialectic
diledryw adj pure, genuine
dileu vb blot out, delete; abolish
dilewyrch adj dismal; unprosperous
dilorni vb abuse, revile
di-lun adj slovenly
diluw see **dilyw**
dilyffethair adj unencumbered, unfettered
dilyn vb follow, pursue; imitate
dilyniad nm following; imitation
dilyniant (-nnau) nm sequence, progression
dilynol adj following; consequent

dilynwr (-wyr) nm follower; imitator
dilys adj sure, certain; genuine
dilysiant (-nnau) nm validation
dilysnod (-au) nm hallmark
dilysrwydd nm genuineness
dilysu vb certify, warrant, guarantee
dilyw nm flood, deluge
dillad (dilledyn nm) npl clothes, clothing
dilladu vb clothe
dilledydd nm clothier
dilledyn nm garment
dim adj any; (with negative understood) no ♦ nm anything; none, nothing
dimensiwn (-iynau) nm dimension
dimensiynol adj dimensional
di-nam, dinam adj faultless
dinas (-oedd) nf city
dinasol adj municipal
dinasyddiaeth nf citizenship
dincod see **deincod**
dinesig adj civil, civic
dinesydd (dinasyddion) nm citizen
dinistr nm destruction
dinistrio vb destroy
dinistriol adj destroying, destructive
dinistriwr (-wyr) nm destroyer
dinistrydd (-ion) nm destroyer
diniwed adj harmless, innocent
diniweidrwydd nm innocence
di-nod, dinod, adj insignificant, obscure
dinodedd nm insignificance, obscurity
dinoethi vb bare, denude, expose
diod (-ydd) nf drink, beverage
diodi vb give drink
dioddef vb suffer, bear; wait ♦ (-iadau) nm suffering
dioddefaint nm suffering, passion
dioddefgar, -efus adj patient
dioddefgarwch nm patience
dioddefwr, -ydd (-wyr) nm

sufferer, patient

di-oed, dioed adj without delay, immediate

diofal adj careless

diofalwch nm carelessness

diog adj slothful, indolent, lazy

diogel adj safe, secure; sure, certain

diogelu vb make safe, secure

diogelwch nm safety, security

diogi vb be lazy, idle ♦ nm laziness

dioglyd adj lazy, sluggish, indolent

diogyn nm lazy one, idler, sluggard

diolch vb thank, give thanks ♦ (-iadau) nm thanks, thanksgiving

diolchgar adj thankful, grateful

diolchgarwch nm thankfulness, gratitude, thanksgiving

diolwg adj ugly

diorseddu vb dethrone, depose

di-os adj without doubt

diosg vb undress, put off, strip, divest

diota vb tipple

diotwr (-wyr) nm boozer, drunkard

dioty (-tai) nm ale-house, public-house

diploma (-âu) nm/f diploma

diplomateg nf diplomacy

diplomydd (-ion) nm diplomat

diplomyddol adj diplomatic

dipton (-au) nf diphthong

dir adj certain, necessary

diraddiad (-au) nm degradation

diraddio vb degrade

diraddiol adj degrading

di-raen adj shabby, dull

dirboeni vb torture, excruciate

dirdyniad (-au) nm convulsion

dirdynnol adj excruciating

dirdynnu vb rack, torture

direidi nm mischievousness, mischief

direidus adj mischievous

direol adj unruly, disorderly

direwydd nm defroster

direwyn nm antifreeze

dirfawr adj vast, huge, immense, enormous

dirgel adj secret ♦ (-ion) nm secret

dirgeledig adj hidden, secret; mystical

dirgeledigaeth (-au) nm/f mystery

dirgelu vb secrete, conceal, hide

dirgelwch nm secrecy, mystery, secret

dirgryniad (-au) nm tremor, vibration

dirgrynol adj vibrating

dirgrynu vb tremble, vibrate

diriaethol adj concrete

dirlawn adj saturated

dirmyg nm contempt, scorn

dirmygu vb despise, scorn

dirmygus adj contemptuous; contemptible

dirnad vb discern, comprehend

dirnadaeth nf discernment, comprehension

dirnadwy adj discernible

dirprwy (-on) nm deputy; delegate

dirprwyaeth (-au) nf commission; deputation

dirprwyo vb deputise, delegate

dirprwyol adj vicarious

dirprwywr (-wyr) nm commissioner

dirwasgiad (-au) nm depression

dirwest nm/f abstinence, temperance

dirwestol adj temperate

dirwestwr (-wyr) nm abstainer

dirwy (-on) nf fine

dirwyn vb wind, twist, twine

dirwynwr (-wyr) nm winder

dirwyo vb fine

di-rym adj powerless, void

dirymu vb nullify, annul, cancel

diryw adj neuter

dirywiad nm degeneration, deterioration

dirywiaeth nf degeneracy

dirywiedig *adj* degenerate
dirywio *vb* degenerate, deteriorate
dirywiol *adj* decadent, retrograde
dis (-iau) *nm* die, dice
di-sail *adj* groundless, baseless
disbaddu *vb* castrate, geld, spay
disbaddwr (-wyr) *nm* castrator
disberod *nm*: **ar dd.** wandering, astray
disbyddedig *adj* exhausted
disbyddu *vb* empty, exhaust
disbyddwr *nm* exhaust
disco (-au) *nm* disco
diserch *adj* sullen, sulky, loveless
disg (-iau) *nm* disk, record
disgen (disgiau) *nf* discus
disglair *adj* bright, brilliant
disgleirdeb, -der *nm* brightness, brilliance
disgleirio *vb* shine, glitter
disgloff *adj* free from lameness
disgownt (-iau, -s) *nm* discount
disgrifiad (-au) *nm* description
disgrifiadol *adj* descriptive
disgrifio *vb* describe
disgwyl *vb* look, expect, wait
disgwylfa (-feydd) *nf* watch-tower
disgwylgar *adj* watchful, expectant
disgwyliad (-au) *nm* expectation
disgybl (-ion) *nm* disciple, pupil
disgyblaeth *nf* discipline
disgyblu *vb* discipline
disgyblwr (-wyr) *nm* disciplinarian
disgyn *vb* descend; fall, drop; let down
disgynfa (-feydd) *nf* descent, declivity; landing place
disgyniad (-au) *nm* descent
disgynnol *adj* descending
disgynnydd (-ynyddion) *nm* descendant
disgyrchedd *nm* gravitation
disgyrchiad, -iant *nm* gravity.
craidd **d.** centre of gravity
disgyrchu *vb* gravitate
di-sigl *adj* unshaken, steadfast, firm
disiog *adj* diced
disodli *vb* trip up, supplant
dist (-iau) *nm* joist, beam
distadl *adj* insignificant, low, base, mean
distadledd *nm* insignificance, obscurity
distain (-einiaid) *nm* steward
distaw *adj* silent, quiet
distawrwydd *nm* silence, quiet
distewi *vb* silence; calm, quiet
distryw *nm* destruction
distrywgar *adj* destructive, wasteful
distrywio *vb* destroy
distrywiwr (-wyr) *nm* destroyer
distyll *nm* ebb; **-iad** distillation
distyllio *vb* distil
di-sut *adj* unwell; small
diswta *adj* sudden, abrupt
diswyddiad (-au) *nm* dismissal
diswyddo *vb* dismiss from office, discharge
disychedu *vb* quench thirst
di-syfl *adj* immovable, impregnable
disyfyd *adj* sudden, instantaneous
disyml *adj* simple, artless, ingenuous
disymwth *adj* sudden, instantaneous
disynnwyr *adj* senseless
ditectif (-s) *nm* detective
diwahân *adj* inseparable, indiscriminate
diwair *adj* chaste
di-waith, diwaith *adj* unemployed, idle
diwall *adj* satisfied, full, perfect
diwallu *vb* satisfy, supply
diwarafun *adj* unforbidden, ungrudging
diwasgedd (-au) *nm* depression (weather)
diwedydd (-iau) *nm* evening, eventide
diwedd *nm* end, conclusion

diweddar adj late, modern
diweddaru vb modernize
diweddarwch nm lateness
diweddeb nf cadence
diweddglo nm conclusion
diweddu vb end, finish, conclude
diweirdeb nm chastity
diweithdra nm unemployment
diwelfa (-feydd) nf watershed
diwethaf adj last
diwinydd (-ion) nm divine, theologian
diwinyddiaeth nf divinity, theology
diwinyddol adj theological
diwreiddio vb uproot, eradicate
diwrnod (-iau) nm day
diwrthdro adj inexorable
diwyd adj diligent, industrious
diwydianfa nf industrial estate
diwydiannaeth nf industrialization, industrialism
diwydiannol adj industrial
diwydiannwr (-ianwyr) nm industrialist
diwydiant (-iannau) nm industry
diwydrwydd nm diligence, industry
diwyg nm form, dress, garb
diwygiad (-au) nm reform, reformation; revival
diwygiadol adj reformatory; revivalistic
diwygiedig adj reformed; revised
diwygio vb amend, reform, revise
diwygiol adj reformatory
diwygiwr (-wyr) nm reformer; revivalist
diwylliadol adj cultural
diwylliannol adj cultural
diwylliant (-nnau) nm culture
diwylliedig adj cultured
diwyllio vb cultivate
diymadferth adj helpless
diymadferthedd nm helplessness
diymdroi adj without delay
diymhongar adj unassuming

diymod adj steadfast, immovable
diymwad adj undeniable, indisputable
diysgog adj steadfast, firm, stable
diystyr adj contemptuous; contemptible; meaningless
diystyrllyd adj contemptuous, disdainful
diystyru vb disregard, despise
diystyrwch nm contempt, disdain, scorn
do adv yes (to questions in preterite tense)
doc (-iau) nm dock
docfa (-feydd) nf berth
docio vb shorten; dock, berth
doctor (-iaid) nm doctor
doctora vb doctor
dod see **dyfod**
dodi vb put, place; give
dodrefn npl (-yn nm) furniture
dodrefnu vb furnish
dodrefnwr (-wyr) nm furnisher
dodwy vb lay eggs
doe adv yesterday
doeth (-ion) adj wise
doethineb nmf wisdom
doethinebu vb discourse wisely, pontificate
doethor (-iaid) nm doctor (of university)
doethur (-iaid) nm doctor (of university)
doethuriaeth (-au) nf doctorate
dof adj tame, domesticated; garden
dofednod npl fowls, poultry
dofi vb tame, domesticate; assuage
dofn adj f of **dwfn**
Dofydd nm God
dogfen (-ni, -nau) nf document
dogfennaeth nf documentation
dogfennen (-ennau) nf documentary
dogfennol adj documentary
dogn (-au) nm share, portion; dose

dogni vb ration
doili nm doyley
dol (-iau) nf doll
dôl nm dole
dôl (dolydd, dolau) nf meadow
dolbridd (-oedd) nm alluvium, meadow soil
doldir (-oedd) nm meadow-land
dolef (-au) nf cry
dolefain vb cry out
dolefus adj wailing, plaintive
dolen (-nau) nf loop, link, ring, bow
dolennog adj ringed, looped; winding
dolennu vb loop; wind, meander
doler (-i) nf dollar
dolffin nm dolphin
dolur (-iau) nm sore; ailment; grief
dolurio vb hurt, wound; grieve
dolurus adj sore
dominyddu vb dominate
donio vb endow, gift
doniol adj gifted; witty, humorous
donioldeb, -wch nm wit, humour
dôr (dorau) nf door
dos (-ys, -au) nf dose
dosbarth (au, -iadau) nm reason; class; district
dosbarthiad nm distribution
dosbarthu vb class, classify; distribute
dosbarthwr (-wyr) nm distributor
dosio vb dose
dosran (-nau) nf division, section
dosrannu vb separate, analyse
dot (-iau) nm/f dot
dot nf giddiness, vertigo
dotio vb dote
drachefn adv again
dracht (-iau) nm draught (of liquor)
drachtio vb drink deep
draen (-iau) nf drain
draen (drain) nf prickle, thorn
draen, -en (drain) nf thorn

draeniad (-au) nm drainage
draenio vb drain
draenog (-od) nm hedgehog
drafft (-iau) nm draft, draught
draffts npl draughts
dragio vb drag, tear, mangle
draig (dreigiau) nf dragon
drain see draen, draenen
drama (dramâu) nf drama
dramateiddio vb dramatize
dramatig adj dramatic
dramodiad (-au) nm dramatization
dramodwr (-wyr) nm dramatist
draw adv yonder, away
dreflan vb dribble
dreng adj morose, surly, sullen, harsh
dresel, -er (-i, -ydd) nm dresser
drewdod nm stink, stench
drewi vb, nm stink
drewllyd adj stinking
driblo vb dribble
drifft (-iau) nm drift
dril (-iau) nm drill
drilio vb drill
dringad vb, nm climb
dringfa (-feydd) nf climb, ascent
dringo vb climb
dringwr (-wyr) nm climber
dripsych adj dripdry
drôr (drors) nm drawer
dros see tros
drud adj dear, precious, costly; reckless
drudfawr adj costly, expensive
drudwen nf, **drudwy** nm starling
drwg adj evil, bad, naughty, wicked ♦ (drygau) nm evil, harm, hurt
drwgdybiaeth (-au) nf suspicion
drwgdybio vb suspect
drwgdybus adj suspicious
drwglosgiad nm arson
drwgweithredwr (-wyr) nm evildoer
drwm (drymiau) nm drum
drws (drysau) nm door

drwy see trwy

drycin (-oedd) nf foul weather

drycinog adj stormy

drych (-au) nm spectacle; mirror; object, pattern

drychfeddwl (-yliau) nm idea

drychiolaeth (-au) nf apparition, phantom

drygair nm ill report; scandal

dryganadl nm halitosis

drygfyd nm adversity

drygioni nm badness, wickedness

drygionus adj bad, wicked

drygu vb hurt, harm, injure

dryll (-iau) nm piece; part ♦ nm/f gun, rifle

drylliad (-au) nm breaking; wreck

drylliedig adj broken

dryllio vb break in pieces, shatter

drylliog adj broken, contrite

drysi npl (-ien nf) thorns, briers

dryslwyn (-i) nm thicket

dryslyd adj perplexing; confused

drysu vb tangle; perplex; be confused

dryswch nm tangle; perplexity; confusion

dryw (-od) nm/f wren

du adj, nm black

duc, dug (-iaid) nm duke

dugiaeth nf duchy

dull (-iau) nm form, manner, mode

dullwedd (-au) nm mannerism

Dulyn nf Dublin

duo vb black, blacken

dur nm steel

duw (-iau) nm god. Duw God

dũwch nm blackness

duwdod nm godhead, divinity, deity

duwies (-au) nf goddess

duwiol (-ion) adj godly, pious

duwioldeb nm godliness, piety

duwiolfrydedd nm godliness, piety

duwiolfrydig adj god-fearing, pious

dwbl adj double

dweud, dwyd see dywedyd

dwfn adj deep, profound; f dofn

dwfr, dŵr (dyfroedd) nm water

dwl adj dull, stupid, foolish

dwlu vb dote

dwmbwr-dambar adv helter-skelter

dwndwr nm din, babble, hubbub

dwnsiwn (-iynau) nm dungeon

dŵr see dwfr

dwrdio vb scold

dwrn (dyrnau) nm fist; knob, handle, hilt

dwsin (-au) nm dozen

dwst nm dust, powder

dwster (-i) nm duster

dwthwn nm day

dwy see dau

dwyfol adj divine

dwyfoldeb nm divinity, deity

dwyfoli vb deify

dwyfron (-nau) nf breast, chest

dwyfronneg nf breastplate

dwyieithedd nm bilingualism

dwyieitheg nf study of bilingualism

dwyieithog adj bilingual, duoglot

dwyieithrwydd nm bilingualism

dwylaw, -lo nd, pl two hands, hands

dwyn vb bear; bring; steal

dwyochredd nm bilateralism

dwyochrol adj bilateral

dwyradd adj quadratic, two-tier

dwyrain nm, adj east. D. yr Almaen East Germany

dwyraniad nm dichotomy

dwyrannu vb bisect

dwyreiniol adj easterly, eastern, oriental

dwyreiniwr (-wyr) nm easterner, oriental

dwys adj dense, grave, deep, intense

dwysáu vb deepen, intensify

dwysbigo vb prick, sting

dwysedd (-au) *nm* density
dwyster *nm* gravity, solemnity
dwythell (-au) *nf* duct
dwywaith *adv* twice
dy *pron* thy, thine
dyblu *vb* double; repeat
dyblyg *adj* twofold, double
dyblygiad (-au) *nm* duplication, duplicate
dyblygu *vb* double, fold
dyblygydd (-ion) *nm* duplicator
dybryd *adj* sore, dire; flagrant
dychan (-au) *nf* lampoon, satire
dychangerdd (-i) *nf* satirical poem, satire
dychanol *adj* satirical
dychanu *vb* lampoon, satirize, revile
dychanwr (-wyr) *nm* satirist
dychmygadwy *adj* imaginable
dychmygol *adj* imaginary
dychmygu *vb* imagine
dychmygus *adj* imaginative, inventive
dychryn (-iadau) *nm* fright, terror
♦ *vb* frighten
dychrynllyd *adj* frightful, terrible
dychrynu *vb* frighten, be frightened
dychweledig *adj* returned
dychweliad (-au) *nm* return; conversion
dychwelyd *vb* return
dychymyg (dychmygion) *nm* imagination, fancy; riddle, device
dydd (-iau) *nm* day. **dyddiau cŵn** silly season
dyddfu *vb* flag, pine, faint
dyddiad (-au) *nm* date
dyddiadur (-on) *nm* diary, journal
dyddiedig *adj* dated
dyddio *vb* become day, dawn; date
dyddiol *adj* daily
dyddlyfr (-au) *nm* diary, journal
dyddodyn (-odion) *nm* deposit
dyfais (-feisiau) *nf* device,

invention
dyfal *adj* diligent
dyfalbarhad *nm* perseverance
dyfalbarhau *vb* persevere
dyfaliad (-au) *nm* guess, conjecture
dyfalu *vb* guess, conjecture
dyfalwch *nm* diligence, assiduity
dyfarniad (-au) *nm* decision, verdict
dyfarnu *vb* adjudge
dyfarnwr (-wyr) *nm* judge, umpire
dyfeisio *vb* devise, invent, imagine; guess
dyfeisiwr (-wyr) *nm* inventor
dyfnant (-nentydd) *nf* ravine
dyfnder (-au, -oedd) *nm* deep, depth
dyfnhau *vb* deepen
dyfod, dod *vb* come, become
dyfodfa *nf* access, entrance
dyfodiad *nm* coming, arrival, advent
dyfodiad (-iaid) *nm* incomer, stranger
dyfodol *adj* coming, future ♦ *nm* future
dyfradwy *adj* watered; watering
dyfredig *adj* irrigated
dyfrffos (-ydd) *nf* canal, watercourse
dyfrgi (-gwn) *nm* otter
dyfrhad *nm* irrigation
dyfrhau, dyfrio *vb* water
dyfrllyd *adj* watery
dyfyniad (-au) *nm* citation, quotation
dyfynnod (-ynodau) *nm* quotation mark
dyfynnol *adj* citatory, summoned
dyfynnu *vb* cite, quote; summon
dyffryn (-noedd) *nm* valley
dyffryndir (-oedd) *nm* low country; vale
dygn *adj* hard, severe, grievous, dire
dygnu *vb* strive, persevere

dygnwch *nm* perseverance, assiduity

dygwyl *nm* holiday, feast day

dygymod *vb* agree (with), put up (with)

dyhead (-au) *nm* aspiration

dyheu *vb* pant; long, yearn, aspire

dyhiryn see **dihiryn**

dyladwy *adj* due

dylanwad (-au) *nm* influence

dylanwadol *adj* influential

dylanwadu *vb* influence

dyled (-ion) *nf* debt, obligation

dyledog *adj* in debt, indebted

dyledus *adj* due

dyledwr (-wyr) *nm* debtor

dyletswydd (-au) *nf* duty, obligation

dylif *nm* flood, deluge ♦ *nf* warp

dylifo *vb* flow, stream, pour

dylni *nm* stupidity, dullness

dyluniad (-au) *nm* design, drawing

dylunio *vb* design

dylunydd (-ion) *nm* designer

dylyfu gên *vb* yawn, gape

dylluan see **tylluan**

dyma here is, here are; this is, these are

dymchweliad *nm* overthrow

dymchwelyd *vb* overthrow, upset, subvert

dymuniad (-au) *nm* wish, desire

dymuno *vb* wish, desire

dymunol *adj* desirable, agreeable, pleasant

dyn (-ion) *nm* man, person

dyna *adv* there is, there are; that is, those are

dynad *npl* nettles

dyndod *nm* manhood, humanity

dyneiddiaeth *nf* humanism

dyneiddiol *adj* humanistic

dyneiddiwr (-wyr) *nm* humanist

dynes *nf* woman

dynesiad *nm* approach

dynesu *vb* draw near, approach

dyngar *adj* humane

dyngarol *adj* philanthropic

dyngarwch *nm* philanthropy

dyngarwr (-wyr) *nm* philanthropist

dyniawed (-iewaid) *nm* yearling, steer

dyn-laddiad *nm* manslaughter

dynodi *vb* denote, signify

dynodiad (-au) *nm* denotation

dynol *adj* human; man-like; manly

dynoliaeth *nf* humanity

dynoliaethau *npl* humanities

dynolryw *coll n* mankind

dynwared *vb* imitate, mimic

dynwarededd *nm* mimicry

dynwarediad (-au) *nm* imitation, mimicry

dynwaredol *adj* imitative

dynwaredwr (-wyr) *nm* imitator, mimic

dyraddiant *nm* degradation

dyraniad (-au) *nm* allocation

dyrchafael *vb* rise, ascend ♦ *nm* ascension

dyrchafedig *adj* exalted

dyrchafiad *nm* elevation, promotion

dyrchafol *adj* elevating

dyrchafu *vb* raise, elevate; rise, ascend

dyri (-iau), **dyrif** (-au) *nf* ballad, lyric

dyrnaid (-eidiau) *nm* handful

dyrnio *vb* punch

dyrnod (-iau) *nm/f* blow, stroke

dyrnu *vb* thump; thresh

dyrnwr (-wyr) *nm* thresher

dyrnwr medi *nm* combine harvester

dyrys *adj* tangled; difficult; perplexing

dyryslyd, dyrysu, dyryswch see **dryslyd, drysu, dryswch**

dysg *nm/f* learning

dysgedig (-ion) *adj* learned

dysgeidiaeth *nf* teaching, doctrine

dysgl (-au) *nf* dish

dysglaid (-eidiau) *nf* dishful, dish

dysgu *vb* learn, teach
dysgwr (-wyr) *nm* learner, teacher
dywalgi (-gwn) *nm* tiger
dywediad (-au) *nm* saying
dywedwst *adj* taciturn ♦ *nm* taciturnity
dywedyd *vb* say, speak, tell
dyweddi (-iau) *nf* betrothal, fiancé(e) ♦ *n coll* betrothed
dyweddïad *nm* betrothal
dyweddïo *vb* betroth

E

eang *adj* wide, broad, immense
eangder, eangu see ehangder, ehangu
eangfrydedd *nm* magnanimity
eangfrydig *adj* broad-minded, magnanimous
eb, ebe, ebr *vb* said, quoth
ebargofiant *nm* oblivion
ebill (-ion) *nm* auger, borer; peg
ebillio *vb* bore
ebol (-ion) *nm* colt, foal
eboles (-au) *nf* foal, filly
eboni *nm* ebony
ebran (-nau) *nm* provender, fodder
Ebrill *nm* April
ebrwydd *adj* quick, swift, soon
ebwch (-ychau) *nm* gasp
ebychiad (-au) *nm* interjection, ejaculation
ebychu *vb* gasp, interject, ejaculate
eciwmenaidd *adj* ecumenical
ecliptig *adj* *nm* ecliptic
ecoleg (-au) *nf/m* ecology
ecolegol *adj* ecological
ecolegwr (-wyr) *nm* ecologist
economaidd *adj* economic
economeg *nf* economics
economegol *adj* economic
economegwr (-wyr) *nm* economist
economegydd (-ion) *nm* economist

economi (-ïau) *nm* economy
economydd *nm* economist
ecsbloetio *vb* exploit
ecsbloetiwr (-wyr) *nm* exploiter
ecseis *nm* excise
ecseismon (-myn) *nm* exciseman
ecsema *nm* eczema
ecsentredd (-au) *nm* eccentricity
ecsentrig *adj* eccentric (*maths*)
ecstasi *nm* ecstasy
ecstatig *adj* ecstatic
echblyg *adj* explicit, outward
echblygol *adj* extrovert
echdoe *adv* day before yesterday
echdoriad (-au) *nm* eruption
echel (-au) *nf* axle, axletree; axis
echelin (-au) *nm* axis
echnos *nm* night before last
echrydus *adj* fearful, frightful, shocking
echwyn (-ion) *nm* loan
echwynna *vb* borrow, lend
echwynnwr (-wynwyr) *nm* lender, creditor
edau (edafedd) *nf* thread; (*pl*) yarn, wool
edfryd *vb* restore
edifar *adj* penitent, sorry
edifarhau, -faru *vb* repent, be sorry
edifarus, -feiriol *adj* repentant, penitent
edifeirwch *nm* repentance, penitence
edliw *vb* upbraid, reproach, taunt
edmygedd *nm* admiration
edmygol *adj* admiring
edmygu *vb* admire
edmygwr, -ydd (-wyr) *nm* admirer
edrych *vb* look, examine
edrychiad *nm* look
edrychwr (-wyr) *nm* beholder, spectator
edwi (edwino) *vb* fade, wither, decay
eddi *npl* thrums; fringe, nap

ef, efe pron he, him; it
efallai adv perhaps, peradventure
efengyl (-au) nf gospel
efengylaidd adj evangelical
efengyleiddio vb evangelize
efengyles (-au) nf female evangelist
efengylu vb evangelize
efengylwr, -ydd (-wyr) nm evangelist
efelychiad (-au) nm imitation
efelychiadol adj imitative
efelychu vb imitate
efelychwr (-wyr) nm imitator
efelychydd (-ion) nm simulator
eferw adj effervescent
eferwad (-au) nm effervescence
eferwi vb effervesce
efo prep with
efô pron he, him; it
efrau npl tares
Efrog Newydd nf New York
efrydiaeth (-au) nf study
efrydu vb study
efrydydd (-ion, -wyr) nm student
efydd nm bronze, copper, brass
effaith (-eithiau) nf effect
effeithio vb effect, affect
effeithiol adj effectual, effective, efficient
effeithiolrwydd nm render effectual
effeithiolrwydd nm efficacy
effeithlon adj efficient
effeithlonedd nm efficiency (of machines etc)
effeithlonrwydd nm efficiency
effro adj awake, vigilant
eger (-au) nm bore, eagre
egin npl (-yn nm) germs, sprouts
eginhad, eginiad (-au) nm germination, sprouting
egino vb germinate, shoot, sprout
eginol adj germinal, shooting
eginyn (egin) nm sprout
eglur adj clear, plain, evident
eglurdeb, -der nm clearness
eglureb (-au) nf illustration

eglurhad nm explanation, demonstration
eglurhaol adj explanatory
egluro vb make clear, explain
eglwys (-i, -ydd) nf church
eglwysig adj church, ecclesiastical
eglwyswr (-wyr) nm churchman
eglwyswraig (-wragedd) nf churchwoman
egni (-ion) nm effort, might, energy
egnio vb endeavour, make an effort
egniol adj energetic
egnioli vb energise
ego nm ego
egoistiaeth nm egoism
egosentrig adj egocentric
egoÿdd nm egoist
egr adj sharp; sour; severe; savage; cheeky
egroes npl (-en nf) hips
egwan adj weak, feeble
egwyd (-ydd) nf fetlock; fetter
egwyddor (-ion, -au) nf rudiment; principle; alphabet
egwyddorol adj high-principled
egwyl nf lull, respite; opportunity
enghraifft (-eifftiau) nf example, instance
enghreifftiol adj exemplary, illustrative
englyn (-ion) nm Welsh alliterative stanza
englyna, -u vb compose englynion
englynwr (-wyr) nm composer of englynion
engyl see angel
ehangder (eangderau) nm breadth, immensity
ehangu vb enlarge, extend
ehedeg vb fly; run to seed
ehedfa (-feydd) nf flight
ehedfan vb hover, fly
ehediad (-au) nm flight
ehediad (-iaid) nm fowl, bird
ehedog adj flying

ehedydd (-ion) *nm* lark

ehofndra *nm* fearlessness, boldness

ei *pron* his, hers; its

eich *pron* your

Eidal: yr E. Italy

eidion (-nau) *nm* ox

eiddew *coll n* ivy

eiddgar *adj* zealous, ardent

eiddgarwch *nm* zeal, ardour

eiddigedd *nm* jealousy; zeal

eiddigeddu *vb* be jealous, envy; have zeal

eiddigeddus *adj* jealous, envious

eiddigus *adj* jealous; zealous

eiddil *adj* slender, feeble

eiddilwch *nm* slenderness, feebleness

eiddiorwg *coll n* ivy

eiddo *nm* property, possessions ♦ *pron* his, *etc*

eidduno *vb* desire, wish, pray

Eifftaidd *adj* Egyptian

Eifftiwr (-wyr), **Eifftiad** (-iaid) *nm* Egyptian

eigion *nm* depth, ocean

eigioneg *nf/m* oceanography

eigionol *adj* pelagic

eingion (-au) *nf* anvil

Eingl *npl* Angles, Englishmen

Eingl-Gymro (-Gymry) *nm* Anglo-Welshman

Eingl-Sais (-Saeson) *nm* Anglo-Saxon

Eingl-Seisnig *adj* Anglo-Saxon

eil- *prefix* second (ail)

eilchwyl *adv* again

eiliad (-au) *nm/f* second, moment

eiliadur (-on) *nm* alternator

eilio *vb* weave, plait; sing; second

eiliwr (-wyr) *nm* seconder

eilradd (-ol) *adj* secondary, inferior

eilrif (-au) *nm* even number

eilun (-od) *nm* image, idol

eilunaddolgar *adj* idolatrous

eilunaddoli *vb* worship idols

eilunaddolwr (-wyr) *nm* idolator

eilwaith *adv* again

eilydd (-ion) *nm* seconder, reserve

eillio *vb* shave

eilliwr (-wyr) *nm* shaver, barber

ein *pron adj* our

einioes *nf* life, lifetime

einion (-au) *nf* anvil

eira *nm* snow

eirchion see **arch**

eirias *adj* burning, glowing, fiery

eirin *npl* (-en *nf*) plums. **e. gwlanog** peaches. **e. duon** damsons. **e. duon bach** sloes. **e. Mair** gooseberries

eiriol *vb* plead, pray, intercede

eirioaeth *nf* intercession

eiriolwr (-wyr) *nm* intercessor, mediator

eirlaw *nm* sleet

eirlin (-iau) *nm* snowline

eirlithrad (-au) *nm* avalanche

eirlys (-iau) *nm* snowdrop

eironi *nm* irony

eisen (ais) *nf* rib; lath

eisglwyf *nm* pleurisy

eisiau *nm* want, need, lack

eisin *coll n* bran, husk

eising *nm* icing

eisio *vb* ice

eisoes *adv* already

eistedd *vb* sit, seat

eisteddfa (-oedd, -fâu) *nf* seat

eisteddfod (-au) *nf* session; eisteddfod

eisteddfodol *adj* eisteddfodic

eisteddfodwr (-wyr) *nm* frequenter of *eisteddfodau*

eisteddfota *vb* frequent *eisteddfodau*

eisteddiad (-au) *nm* sitting, session

eisteddle (-oedd) *nm* seat, sitting, pew

eitem (-au) *nf* item

eithaf (-ion) *adj, nm* extreme; superlative ♦ *adv* very, quite

eithafbwynt (-iau) *nm* extremity; apogee

eithafiaeth *nf* extremism

eithafion *npl* extremes, extremities

eithafol *adj* extreme

eithafwr (-wyr) *nm* extremist

eithin *npl* (-en *nf*) furze, gorse

eithinog *adj* furzy

eithr *prep* except; besides ♦ *conj* but

eithriad (-au) *nm* exception

eithriadol *adj* exceptional

eithrio *vb* except, exclude

elastig *adj*, *nm* elastic

elastigedd *nm* elasticity

electromagneteg *nf/m* electromagnetism

electromedr (-au) *nm* electrometer

electron (-au) *nm* electron

electroneg *nf/m* electronics

electronig *adj* electronic

elegeiog *adj* elegiac, mournful

eleni *adv* this year

elfen (-nau) *nf* element

elfennig *adj* elemental

elfennol *adj* elementary

eli (elïoedd) *nm* ointment, salve

elifiant (-nnau) *nm* effluence

elifyn (elifion) *nm* effluent

eliffant (-od, -iaid) *nm* elephant

eliffantaidd *adj* elephantine

elin (-au, -oedd) *nf* elbow; angle, bend

elips (-au) *nm* ellipse

eliptig *adj* elliptical

elor (-au) *nf* bier

elusen (-nau) *nf* alms

elusendy (-dai) *nm* almshouse

elusengar *adj* charitable, benevolent

elusengarwch *nm* charity, benevolence

elusennol *adj* eleemosynary

elusennwr (-enwyr) *nm* almoner

elw *nm* possession, gain, profit

elwa *vb* gain, profit

elwlen (-wlod) *nf* kidney

ellyll (-on) *nm* fiend; goblin

ellyllaidd *adj* fiendish; elfish

ellylles (-au) *nf* fury, she-goblin

ellyn (-au, -od) *nm* razor

embryo *nm* embryo

embryoleg *nf* embryology

emosiwn (-iynau) *nm* emotion

emosiynol *adj* emotional

empeiraeth *nf* empiricism

empeiraidd *adj* empirical

empirig *adj* empirical

emrallt *nm* emerald

emyn (-au) *nm* hymn

emyn-dôn (-au) *nf* hymn-tune

emyniadur (-on) *nm* hymnal

emynwr (-wyr) *nm* hymnist

emynydd (-ion, -wyr) *nm* hymnist

emynyddiaeth *nf* hymnody, hymnology

enaid (eneidiau) *nm* life, soul

enamel (-au) *nm* enamel

enamlio *vb* enamel

enbyd, -us *adj* dangerous, perilous

enbydrwydd *nm* peril, danger, jeopardy

encil (-ion) *nm* retreat, flight

encilfa (-feydd) *nf* retreat

enciliad (-au) *nm* retreat; desertion

encilio *vb* retreat; desert

enciliwr (-wyr) *nm* retreater; deserter

enclitig *adj* enclitic

encôr *nm* encore

encyd *nm* space; while

enchwythu *vb* inflate

endemig *adj* endemic

endid *nm* entity, existence

endothermig *adj* endothermic

eneidiog *adj* animate

eneidiol *adj* animate, living

eneiniad (-au) *nm* anointing, unction

eneinio *vb* anoint

Eneiniog *nm* The Messiah, Christ

eneiniog *adj*, *nm* anointed

enfawr *adj* enormous, huge, immense

enfys (-au) *nf* rainbow

engiriol *adj* nefarious, cruel, terrible

engrafiad (-au) *nm* engraving

engrafu *vb* engrave

enhuddo see **anhuddo**

enigma *nm* enigma

enigmatig *adj* enigmatic

enillfawr *adj* lucrative, remunerative

enillgar *adj* gainful; winsome

enillion *npl* profits, earnings

enillwr, -ydd (-wyr) *nm* gainer, winner

enllib (-ion, -iau) *nm* slander, libel

enllibaidd *adj* slanderous, libellous

enllibio *vb* slander, libel

enllibiwr (-wyr) *nm* slanderer, libeller

enllibus *adj* slanderous, libellous

enllyn *nm* relish eaten with bread

ennaint (eneiniau) *nm* ointment

ennill *vb* gain, win, earn ♦ (enillion) *nm* gain, profit; (*pl*) earnings

ennyd *nm/f* while, moment

ennyn *vb* kindle, burn, inflame; excite

ensyniad (-au) *nm* insinuation

ensynio *vb* insinuate

entrych (-ion) *nm* firmament, height, zenith

enw (-au) *nm* name; noun

enwad (-au) *nm* denomination, sect

enwadaeth *nf* sectarianism

enwadol *adj* sectarian; nominative

enwadwr (-wyr) *nm* sectarian, sectary

enwaediad *nm* circumcision

enwaedu *vb* circumcise

enwebai (-eion) *nm* nominee

enwebiad (-au) *nm* nomination

enwebu *vb* nominate

enwedig *adj*: yn e. particularly, especially

enwi *vb* name

enwog (-ion) *adj* famous, renowned, noted

enwogi *vb* make famous

enwogrwydd *nm* fame, renown

enwol *adj* nominal, nominative

enwyn *nm*: llaeth e. buttermilk

enynfa *nf* inflammation; itching

enyniad (-au) *nm* inflammation

enynnol *adj* inflammatory; inflamed

eofn *adj* fearless, bold

eog (-iaid) *nm* salmon

eos (-au) *nf* nightingale

eosaidd *adj* like a nightingale

epa (-od) *nm* ape, monkey

epidemig *adj*, *nm* epidemic

epig *nf* epic

epiglotis (-au) *nm* epiglottis

epigram (-au) *nm* epigram

epil *nm* offspring, brood

epilepsi *nm* epilepsy

epilgar *adj* prolific, teeming

epiliad (-au) *nm* reproduction

epilio *vb* bring forth, teem, breed

epilog *nm* epilogue

episeicloid (-au) *nm* epicycloid

epistol (-au) *nm* epistle

eples *nm* leaven, ferment

eplesiad *nm* fermentation

eplesu *vb* leaven, ferment

er *prep* for, in order to; since ♦ *conj* though

eraill see **arall**

erbyn *vb* receive, meet ♦ *prep* against, by

erch *adj* speckled; frightful

erchi *vb* ask, pray, command, demand

erchwyn (-ion) *nm* side, bed-side

erchyll *adj* hideous, horrible

erchyllter (-au) *nm* atrocity

erchylltod, -tra *nm* hideousness, horror

eres *adj* wonderful, strange

erestyn *nm* minstrel, buffoon

erfin npl (**-en** nf) turnips
erfyn vb beg, pray, implore, expect
erfyniad (**-au**) nm prayer, petition
ergyd (**-ion**) nm/f blow, stroke; shot; cast
ergydio vb strike; throw, cast
ergydiwr (**-wyr**) nm striker
erial (**-au**) nm aerial
erioed adv ever
erledigaeth (**-au**) nf persecution
erlid vb persecute ♦ (**-iau**) nm persecution
erlidiwr (**-wyr**) nm persecutor
erlyn vb pursue, prosecute
erlyniad nm prosecution
erlynydd (**-ion**) nm prosecutor
ern, ernes (**-au**) nf earnest, pledge, deposit
ers prep since (**er ys**)
erthwch nm grunt, pant
erthygl (**-au**) nf article
erthyl (**-od**) nm abortion
erthylaidd adj abortive
erthyliad (**-au**) nm abortion, miscarriage
erthylu vb abort, miscarry
erw (**-au**) nf acre
erwain nf meadow-sweet
erwydd npl stave (in music)
erydiad (**-au**) nm erosion
erydol adj erosive
erydu vb erode
erydydd (**-ion**) nm erosive agent
eryr (**-od**) nm eagle; shingles
eryraidd adj eagle-like, aquiline
esblygiad (**-au**) nm evolution
esblygiadaeth nf evolutionism
esboniad (**-au**) nm explanation; commentary
esboniadaeth nf exposition, exegesis
esboniadol adj expository, explanatory
esbonio vb explain, expound
esboniwr (**-wyr**) nm expositor, commentator

esbonydd (**-ion**) nm exponent
esbonyddol adj exponential
escaladur (**-on**) nm escalator
esgair (**-eiriau**) nf shank, leg; ridge
esgeirlwm adj exposed, wind-swept
esgeulus adj neglectful, negligent
esgeuluso vb neglect
esgeulustod, -tra nm negligence
esgid (**-iau**) nf boot, shoe
esgob (**-ion**) nm bishop
esgobaeth (**-au**) nf bishopric, see, diocese
esgobyddiaeth nf episcopalianism
esgoli vb escalate
esgor vb bring forth, bear
esgud adj quick, swift, active
esgus (**-ion, -odion**) nm excuse, pretext
esgusodi vb excuse
esgusodol adj excusable, excused
esgymun adj execrable, excommunicate
esgymuno vb excommunicate
esgyn vb ascend, rise
esgynbren (**-nau**) nm perch
esgynfa (**-feydd**) nf ascent, rise
esgynfaen nm horse-block
esgyniad nm ascension
esgynneb (**esgynebau**) nf climax
esgynnol adj ascending
esgyrn see **asgwrn**
esgyrnog adj bony
esiampl (**-au**) nf example
esmwyth adj soft, smooth; easy
esmwythâd nm ease, relief
esmwytháu vb soothe, ease
esmwythder, -dra nm ease
esmwytho, -áu vb ease, soothe, soften
esmwythyd nm ease, luxury
estron (**-iaid**) nm foreigner, alien
estron adj foreign, strange, alien
estrones (**-au**) nf alien woman
estronol adj strange, foreign, alien
estrys (**-od**) nm/f ostrich
estyll npl (**-en** nf) planks, boards

estyn *vb* extend, reach; stretch, prolong
estynadwy *adj* extensible
estyniad *nm* extension, prolongation
estheteg *nm/f* aesthetics
esthetig *adj* aesthetic
etifedd (-ion) *nm* heir, inheritor
etifeddeg *nm/f* heredity
etifeddes (-au) *nf* heiress
etifeddiaeth (-au) *nf* inheritance
etifeddol *adj* hereditary
etifeddu *vb* inherit
eto *conj* yet, still ♦ *adv* again; yet, still
ether *nm* ether
ethnig *nm* ethnic
ethnoleg *nf* ethnology
ethol *vb* elect
etholaeth (-au) *nf* constituency
etholedig (-ion) *adj* elect
etholedigaeth *nf* election (*theol.*)
etholiad (-au) *nm* election
etholiadol *adj* electoral, elective
etholwr (-wyr) *nm* elector, voter
ethos *nm* ethos
eu *pron* their
euog *adj* guilty
euogrwydd *nm* guiltiness, guilt
euraid, -aidd *adj* golden, (of) gold
euro *vb* apply or bestow gold; gild
eurych (-od) *nm* goldsmith
ewig (-od) *nf* hind
ewin (-edd) *nm/f* nail, talon, claw; hoof
ewino *vb* claw
ewinog *adj* having nails or claws
ewinrhew *nf* frost-bite
Ewrop *nf* Europe
Ewropead (-aid) *nm* European
Ewropeaidd *adj* European
ewyllys (-iau) *nf* will
ewyllysio *vb* will, wish
ewyn *nm* foam, froth, surf
ewynnog *adj* foaming, foamy, frothy
ewynnu *vb* foam, froth

ewythr (-edd) *nm* uncle

F

fagddu *nf:* **y f.** gross darkness
falf (-iau) *nf* valve
fan (-iau) *nf* van
fandal (-iau) *nm* vandal
fandaleiddio *vb* vandalise
fandaliaeth *nf* vandalism
farnais (-eisiau) *nm* varnish
farneisio *vb* varnish
fe *pron* he, him ♦ *preverbal particle*
feallai *adv* perhaps, peradventure
fel *adv, conj, prep* so, as, that, thus, like; how
felly *adv* so, thus
festri (-ioedd) *nf* vestry
ficer (-iaid) *nm* vicar
ficerdy (-dai) *nm* vicarage
finegr *nm* vinegar
fiola (-s) *nf* viola
firws (-au, fira) *nm* virus
fitamin (-au) *nm* vitamin
folt (-iau) *nm* volt
foltamedr (-au) *nm* voltameter
foltedd (-au) *nm* voltage
foltmedr (-au) *nm* voltmeter
fortais (-eisiau) *nm* vortex
fory *adv* tomorrow (**yfory**)
fry *adv* above, aloft
fwltur (-iaid) *nm* vulture
fy *pron* my
fyny *adv* up, upwards

FF

ffa *npl* (**ffäen, ffeuen** *nf*) beans. **ffa'r gors** buckbeans. **ffa pob** baked beans
ffabrigo *vb* fabricate
ffacbys *npl* fitches, vetches
ffactor (-au) *nm/f* factor. **ff. cyffredin mwyaf** highest common factor. **ff. cysefin** prime factor

ffactori, -o vb factorize
ffactri (-ioedd) nf factory, mill
ffaeledig adj fallible, ailing
ffaeledigrwydd nm fallibility
ffaeledd (-au) nm failing, defect, fault.
ffaelu vb fail
ffafr (-au) nf favour
ffafraeth nf favouritism
ffafrio vb favour
ffafriol adj favourable
ffagl (-au) nf blaze, flame; torch
ffagotsen (ffagots) nf faggot
ffair (ffeiriau) nf fair, exchange.
ffair sborion jumble sale
ffaith (ffeithiau) nf fact
ffald (-au) nf fold; pound
ffals (ffeilsion) adj false, deceitful
ffalsedd nm falsehood, deceit
ffalster nm deceitfulness, cunning
ffalwm nm whitlow
ffan (-nau) nf fan
ffanatig nm fanatic
ffansi nf fancy
ffansïo vb fancy
ffansïol adj fanciful, pleasing to the fancy
ffanatigiaeth nf fanaticism
ffantasi(a) (-iau) nf/m fantasy
ffarm (ffermydd) nf farm
ffarmio vb farm
ffarmwr (ffermwyr) nm farmer
ffarmwraig (-wragedd) nf farmwoman
ffârs (-iau) nf farce
ffarwél nf farewell
ffarwelio vb bid farewell
ffaryncs (-au) nm pharynx
ffas (-ys, -au) nf face, coal-face
ffasâd (ffasadau) nm facade
ffasiwn (-iynau) nm fashion
ffasiynol adj fashionable
ffasner (-i) nm fastener
ffasnin (-au) nm fastening
ffasno vb fasten
ffasnydd (-ion) nm fastener
ffatri (-ioedd) nf factory, mill

ffatrïaeth nf manufacturing
ffau (ffeuau) nf den
ffawd (ffodion) nf fortune, fate
ffawdheglu vb hitch-hike
ffawdheglwr (-wyr) nm hitch-hiker
ffawna nf fauna
ffawydd npl (-en nf) beech trees
ffederal adj federal
ffederaliaeth nf federalism
ffederasiwn (-iynau) nm federation
ffed(e)reiddio vb federate
ffefryn (-nau) nm favourite
ffeil (-iau) nf file
ffein, ffeind adj fine
ffeirio vb barter, exchange
ffelt nm felt
ffelwm nm whitlow
ffemwr (ffemora) nm femur
ffendir nm fenland
ffenestr (-i) nf window
ffenigl nm fennel
ffenomen (-au) nf phenomenon
ffens (-ys) nf fence
ffensio vb fence
ffêr (fferau) nf ankle
fferdod nm numbness
fferi (-iau) nf ferry
fferins npl sweets
fferm (-ydd) nf farm
ffermdy (-dai) nm farm-house
ffermio vb farm
ffermwr (-wyr) nm farmer
fferru vb congeal, freeze; perish with cold
fferyllfa (-feydd) nf dispensary
fferylliaeth nf pharmacy
fferyllol adj chemical, pharmaceutical
fferyllydd (-wyr) nm chemist, pharmacist
ffesant (-s, -au) nm pheasant
ffest adj fast
ffest nf feast
ffetan (-au) nf sack, bag
ffi (-oedd) nf fee
ffiaidd adj loathsome, abominable
ffibr (-au) nm fibre

ffibrog, -us adj fibrous
Ffichtiad (-iaid) nm Pict
ffidil (ffidlau) nf fiddle
ffidlan vb fiddle, dawdle
ffidler (-iaid) nm fiddler
ffidlo vb fiddle
ffieiddbeth (-au) nm abomination
ffieidd-dra nm abomination
ffieiddio vb loathe, abominate, abhor
ffigur (-au) nf figure, type
ffigurol adj figurative
ffigys npl (**-en** nf) figs
ffigysbren (-nau) nm fig-tree
ffiled (-au, -i) nf fillet
ffilharmonig adj philharmonic
ffilm (-iau) nf film
ffilmio vb film
ffiloreg nf rigmarole, nonsense
ffilter (-au, -i) nm filter
ffin (-iau) nf boundary, limit
Ffindir: y F. nf Finland
ffindir (-oedd) nm borderland
ffinedig adj bounded
ffinio vb border (upon), abut
ffiniol adj bordering
ffiol (-au) nf vial; cup
ffiseg nm physics
ffisegol adj physical
ffisegwr (-wyr) nm physicist
ffisig nm physic, medicine
ffisigwr (-wyr) nm physician
ffisigwriaeth nm physic, medicine
ffisioleg nf/m physiology
ffit adj fit ♦ (**-iau**) nm fit, paroxysm
ffit-ffatio vb flip-flop
ffitrwydd nm fitness
ffiwdal adj feudal
ffiwg (-iau) nf fugue
ffiws (-iau) nm fuse
ffiwsio vb fuse
fflach (-iau) nf, **fflachiad (-au)** nm flash
fflachio vb flash
fflachiog adj flashing
fflag (-iau) nf flag
fflagen (-ni) nf flagon, flag-stone

fflangell (-au) nf scourge
fflangelliad (-au) nm flagellation
fflangellu vb scourge, whip, flog
fflam (-au) nf flame
fflamadwy adj (in)flammable
fflamio vb flame, blaze
fflamllyd adj flaming, blazing
fflan (-iau) nm flan
fflap (-iau) nm flap
fflasg (-iau) nf flask, basket
fflat adj flat ♦ (**-iau**) nm flat-iron ♦ (**-au, -iau**) nf a flat
fflatio vb flat, flatten
fflatwadn adj flatfooted
fflecs (-ys) nm flex
fflêm, fflem nf phlegm
fflint nm flint
ffliwt (-iau) nf flute
ffloch (-au) nm floe. **ffloch iâ** ice floe
fflodiad, -iart nf floodgate
ffo nm flight
ffoadur (-iaid) nm fugitive, refugee
ffodus adj fortunate, lucky
ffoedigaeth nf flight
ffoi vb flee
ffôl adj foolish, silly ♦ (**ffôls**) nf fall (in a slate quarry)
ffoledd nm foolishness, folly, fatuity
ffolen (-nau) nf buttock
ffoli vb infatuate, dote; fool
ffolineb nm foolishness; folly
ffon (ffyn) nf stick, staff
ffonnod (ffonodiau) nf stroke, blow, stripe
ffonodio vb cudgel, beat
fforc (ffyrc) nf (table) fork
fforch (-au, ffyrch) nf fork
fforchi vb fork
fforchog adj forked, cleft, cloven
ffordd (ffyrdd) nf way, road; distance
fforddio vb afford
fforddol (-ion) nm wayfarer, passer-by
fforest (-ydd, -au) nf forest

fforffedu vb forfeit

ffortiwn (-iynau), **-un** (-au) nf fortune

fforwm (-ymau) nm forum

ffos (-ydd) nf ditch, trench

ffosffad (-au) nm phosphate

ffosil (-au) nm fossil

ffracsiwn (-iynau) nf fraction

ffrae (-au) nf quarrel

ffraeo vb quarrel

ffraeth adj fluent; witty, facetious

ffraetheb (-ion) nf joke, witticism

ffraethineb nm wit, facetiousness

Ffrangeg nf French (language)

Ffrainc nf France

ffrâm (framiau) nf frame

fframio vb frame

fframwaith nm framework

Ffrances (-au) nf Frenchwoman

Ffrancwr (-wyr, Ffrancod) nm Frenchman

Ffrengig adj French. llygod ff. rats

ffrenoleg nmf phrenology

ffres adj fresh

ffresgo (-au) nm fresco

ffresni nm freshness

ffretwaith nm fretwork

ffreutur nf refectory

ffrewyll (-au) nf whip, scourge

ffridd (-oedd) nf mountain pasture, sheep-walk

ffrimpan (-au) nf frying pan

ffrind (-iau) nm friend

ffrio vb fry; hiss

ffris (-iau) nf frieze

ffrit (-iau) nm frit, flop ♦ adj worthless, unsubstantial

ffrith (-oedd) nf mountain pasture, sheep-walk

ffrithiant (-nnau) nm friction

ffroch, ffrochwyllt adj furious

ffroen (-au) nf nostril; muzzle (of gun)

ffroenell (-au) nf nozzle

ffroeni vb snort, snuff, sniff

ffroenuchel adj haughty, disdainful

ffroes npl (-en nf) pancakes

ffrog (-iau) nf frock

ffrom adj angry, irascible, testy, touchy

ffromi vb fume, chafe, rage

ffrostgar adj boastful

ffrwd (ffrydiau) nf stream, torrent

ffrwgwd (ffrygydau) nm squabble

ffrwst nm hurry, haste, bustle

ffrwtian vb splutter

ffrwydriad (-au) nm explosion

ffrwydro vb explode

ffrwydrol adj explosive

ffrwydryn (-nau, ffrwydron) nm mine, explosive

ffrwyn (-au) nf bridle

ffrwyno vb bridle, curb

ffrwyth (-au, -ydd) nm fruit; vigour, use

ffrwythlon adj fruitful, fertile

ffrwythlondeb, -der nm fruitfulness, fertility

ffrwythlonedd nm fecundity

ffrwythloni vb become fruitful; fertilize

ffrwytho vb bear fruit

ffrydio vb stream, gush

ffrydlif nmf stream, flood, torrent

ffug adj fictitious, false, sham ♦ (-ion) nm fiction, sham

ffug-bas (-ys) nf dummy (pass)

ffugbasio vb dummy

ffugenw (-au) nm pseudonym

ffugiad (-au) nm forgery

ffugio vb feign; forge

ffugiwr (-wyr) nm impostor; forger

ffuglen nf fiction

ffugliw (-iau) nm camouflage

ffugliwio vb camouflage

ffunud nm form, manner. yr un ffunud â exactly like

ffured (-au) nf ferret

ffureta vb ferret

ffurf (-iau) nf form, shape

ffurfafen nf firmament, sky

ffurfdro (-eon) nm inflection

ffurfeb (-au) nf formula

ffurfiad (-au) *nm* formation

ffurfiant (-nnau) *nm* accidence; formation

ffurfio *vb* form

ffurfiol *adj* formal

ffurfioliaeth *nf* formalism

ffurfioldeb *nm* formality, formalism

ffurflen (-ni) *nf* form (*to fill*)

ffurflin (-iau) *nm* formline

ffurfwasanaeth (-au) *nm* liturgy

ffurfwedd (-au) *nf* configuration

ffust (-iau) *nf* flail

ffustio, -o *vb* beat

ffwdan *nf* fuss, bustle, flurry

ffwdanllyd *adj* fussy, bustling

ffwdanu *vb* fuss, bustle

ffwdanus *adj* fussy, fidgety, flurried

ffwng (ffyngoedd, ffyngau) *nm* fungus

ffwngleiddiad (-au) *nm* fungicide

ffŵl (ffyliaid) *nm* fool

ffwlbart (-iaid) *nm* polecat

ffwlbri *nm* fudge, nonsense, tomfoolery

ffwlcyn *nm* fool, ninny, nincompoop

ffwndro *vb* founder, become confused

ffwndrus *adj* confused, bewildered

ffwndwr *nm* confusion, hurly-burly

ffwr *nm* fur

ffwrdd *nm* way. **I ff.** away

ffwrn (ffyrnau) *nf* furnace, oven

ffwrnais (-eisiau) *nf* furnace

ffwrwm (ffyrymau) *nf* form, bench

ffydd *nf* faith

ffyddiog *adj* strong in faith, trustful

ffyddlon *adj* faithful

ffyddlondeb *nm* faithfulness, fidelity

ffyddloniaid *npl* faithful ones

ffynhonnell (ffynonellau) *nf* fount, source

ffyniannus *adj* prosperous

ffyniant *nm* prosperity

ffynidwydd *npl* (-en *nf*) fir-trees, pine-trees

ffynnon (ffynhonnau) *nf* fountain, well, spring

ffynnu *vb* prosper, thrive

ffyrf *adj* thick, stout; *f* **fferf**

ffyrfder *nm* thickness, stoutness

ffyrling (-au, -od) *nf* farthing

ffyrnig *adj* fierce, savage, ferocious

ffyrnigo *vb* grow fierce; enrage

ffyrnigrwydd *nm* fierceness, ferocity

G

gadael, gadu *vb* leave, forsake; let, allow

gaeaf (-au, -oedd) *nm* winter

gaeafaidd, -ol *adj* wintry

gaeafu *vb* winter, hibernate

gafael, -yd *vb* hold, grasp ♦ (-ion) *nf* hold, grasp

gafaelgar *adj* gripping, tenacious

gafl (-au, geifl) *nf* fork, groin

gafr (geifr) *nf* goat

gafrewig (-od) *nf* gazelle, antelope

gagendor see **agendor**

gaing (geingau) *nf* chisel. **g. gau** gouge

gair (geiriau) *nm* word

galanas (-au) *nf* murder, massacre

galanastra *nm* slaughter; mess

galar *nm* mourning, grief, sorrow

galarnad (-au) *nf* lamentation

galarnadu *vb* bewail, lament

galaru *vb* mourn, grieve, lament

galarus *adj* mournful, lamentable, sad

galarwr (-wyr) *nm* mourner

galw *vb* call ♦ *nm* call, demand

galwad (-au) *nm/f* call, demand

galwedigaeth (-au) *nf* occupation, vocation, calling

galwyn (-i) *nm* gallon

gallt (gelltydd) *nf* wooded slope;

hill, rise
gallu vb be able ♦ (-oedd) nm
power, ability
galluog adj able, powerful, mighty
galluogi vb enable, empower
gan prep with, by; of, from
gar (-rau) nf/m thigh, shank
garan (-od) nf heron, crane
Garawys nm Lent
gardas, -ys (-ysau) nm/f garter
gardd (gerddi) nf garden; garth,
yard
garddio vb garden ♦ nm gardening
garddwr (-wyr) nm gardener
garddwriaeth nf horticulture
gargam adj knock-kneed
garlant (-au) nm garland
garlleg npl (-en nf) garlic
gartref adv at home (mut. of
cartref)
garth nm hill; enclosure
garw (geirwon) adj coarse, rough,
harsh
garwedd nm roughness
garwhau (-wyr) vb roughen; ruffle
gast (geist) nf bitch
gau adj false; hollow
gefail (-eiliau) nf smithy
gefel (-eiliau) nf tongs, pincers
gefell (-eilliaid) n coll twin
gefelldref (-i) nf twinned town
gefyn (-nau) nm fetter, shackle
gefynnu vb fetter, shackle
geingio vb chisel, gouge
geilwad (-waid) nm caller
geirfa (-oedd) nf vocabulary,
glossary
geiriad nm wording, phraseology
geiriadur (-on) nm dictionary,
lexicon
geiriadurol adj lexicographical
geiriadurwr (-wyr) nm
lexicographer
geirio vb word, phrase
geirlyfr (-au) nm word-book,
dictionary
geirwir adj truthful, truth-speaking

geirwiredd nm truthfulness
gelau, gelen (gelod) nf leech
gelyn (-ion) nm foe, enemy
gelyniaeth nf enmity, hostility
gelyniaethus adj hostile, inimical
gelynol adj hostile, adverse
gellyg npl (-en nf) pears
gem (-au) nf gem, jewel
gêm (gêmau) nf game
gemog adj gemmed, jewelled
gemydd (-ion) nm jeweller
gên nf jaw, chin
genau (-euau) nm mouth, orifice
genau-goeg, geneuoeg (-ion) nf
lizard; newt
genedigaeth (-au) nf birth
genedigol adj native
Genefa nf Geneva
geneth (-od) nf girl
genethaidd adj girlish
genethig nf little girl, maiden
geni vb be born
genni vb be contained
genwair (-eiriau) nf fishing-rod
genweirio vb angle, fish
genweiriwr (-wyr) nm angler
ger prep by, near
gêr coll n gear, tackle
gerbron prep before (place); in the
presence of
gerfydd prep by
geri nm bile, gall. **g. marwol**
cholera morbus
geriach coll n gear, odds and ends
gerllaw prep near ♦ adv at hand
gerwin adj rough, severe, harsh
gerwindeb, -der nm roughness,
severity
gerwino vb roughen
gewyn (-nau, gïau) nm sinew,
tendon
gewynnog adj sinewy
Ghana nf Ghana
giach (-od) nm snipe
Gibralter n Gibraltar
gieuwst nf neuralgia
gildio vb yield; gild

gilydd *nm:* **ei g.** each other. **gyda'i**
g. together
gimbill *nf* gimlet
glafoerio *vb* drivel, slobber
glafoerion *npl* drivel, slobber
glaif, gleifiau *nm* lance, sword,
glaive
glain (gleiniau) *nm* gem, jewel;
bead
glan (-nau, glennydd) *nf* bank,
shore
glân *adj* clean; holy; fair,
beautiful
glanhad *nm* cleansing, purification
glanhaol *adj* cleansing, purging
glanhau *vb* cleanse, purify
glaniad *nm* landing,
disembarkation
glanio *vb* land, disembark
glanwaith *adj* clean, tidy
glanweithdra *nm* cleanliness
glas (gleision) *adj* blue, green,
grey, silver ♦ *nm* blue
glasgoch *adj, nm* purple
glaslanc (-iau) *nm* youth, stripling
glasog (-au) *nf* crop, gizzard
glastwr *nm* milk and water
glastwraidd *adj* watered down,
feeble; muddled
glasu *vb* become blue, green or
grey; turn pale
glaswellt *coll n* grass
glaswelltyn *nm* blade of grass;
tigridia
glaw (-ogydd) *nm* rain
glawiad (-au) *nm* rainfall
glawio *vb* rain
glawlen (-ni) *nf* umbrella
glawog *adj* rainy
gleisiad (-iaid) *nm* sewin
gleision *npl* whey
glendid *nm* cleanness; fairness,
beauty
glesni *nm* blueness, verdure
glew (-ion) *adj* brave, daring;
astute
glewdra, -der *nm* courage,
resource
glin (-iau) *nm* knee
glo *nm* coal
gloddest (-au) *nm* carousal,
revelling
gloddesta *vb* carouse, revel
gloddestwr (-wyr) *nm* reveller
gloes (-au, -ion) *nf* pang; qualm
glofa (-feydd) *nf* colliery
glôwr (-wyr) *nm* collier
glowty (-tai) *nm* cow-house,
shippon
glôyn *nm* coal. **g. byw** butterfly
gloyw (-on) *adj* bright, clear;
shiny, glossy
gloywder *nm* brightness, clearness
gloywi *vb* brighten, polish
glud (-ion) *nm* glue; bird-lime
gludio *vb* glue
gludiog *adj* sticky
glwth (glythau) *nm* couch
glwth (glythion) *adj* gluttonous ♦
nm glutton
glwys *adj* fair; holy
glyn (-noedd) *nm* glen, valley
glynu *vb* stick, adhere, cleave
glythineb, glythni *nm* gluttony
glythinebu, glythu *vb* glut,
gormandize
go *adv* rather, somewhat
goachul *adj* lean; puny; sickly,
poorly
gobaith (-eithion) *nm* hope
gobeithio *vb* hope
gobeithiol *adj* hopeful
gobeithlu (-oedd) *nm* Band of
Hope
gobennydd (-enyddiau) *nm*
bolster, pillow
goblygu *vb* fold, wrap
gochel see **gochelyd**
gocheladwy *adj* avoidable
gochelgar *adj* wary, cautious
gocheliad *nm* avoidance. **ar ei o.**
on his guard
gochelyd *vb* avoid, shun
godidog *adj* excellent, splendid

godidowgrwydd nm excellence
godineb nm adultery
godinebu vb commit adultery
godinebus adj adulterous
godinebwr (**-wyr**) nm adulterer
godre (**-on**) nm skirt, border, edge
godriad (**-au**) nm milking
godro vb milk
goddaith (**-eithiau**) nf fire, bonfire
goddef vb bear, suffer, allow, permit
goddefgar adj forbearing, tolerant
goddefgarwch nm forbearance, tolerance
goddefiad (**-au**) nm licence; toleration
goddefol adj tolerable; passive
goddiweddyd, goddiwes vb over-take
goddrych nm subject (in grammar)
goddrychol adj subjective
gof (**-aint**) nm smith
gofal (**-on**) nm care, charge
gofalu vb care, mind, take care
gofalus adj careful
gofaniaeth nf smith's craft
gofer (**-oedd, -ydd**) nm overflow of well; rill
gofid (**-iau**) nm grief, sorrow, trouble
gofidio vb afflict, grieve, vex
gofidus adj grievous, sad
gofod nm space. **llong o.** nf spaceship
gofodwr (**-wyr**) nm astronaut
gofyn vb ask, demand, require ♦ (**-ion**) nm demand, requirement
gofyniad (**-au**) nm question, query
gofynnod (**-ynodau**) nm note of interrogation, question-mark
gofynnol adj necessary, requisite; interrogative (pronoun etc)
gogan nf defamation, satire
goganu vb defame, satirize, lampoon
goganwr (**-wyr**) nm satirist
goglais vb, nm tickle

gogledd nm, adj north
Gogledd Iwerddon nf Northern Ireland
gogleddol adj northern
gogleddwynt nm north wind
gogleddwr (**-wyr**) nm northman; North Walian
gogleisio vb tickle
gogleisiol adj tickling, titillating, amusing
gogoneddu vb glorify
gogoneddus adj glorious
gogoniant nm glory
gogor (**-ion**) nm fodder, provender
gogr (**-au**) nm sieve, riddle
gogri, gogrwn, gogryn vb sift, riddle
gogwydd nm slant, inclination, bent
gogwyddiad (**-au**) nm inclination
gogwyddo vb incline, slope, lean
gogyfer adj opposite; for, by
gogyfuwch adj, prep of equal height
gogyhyd adj of equal length
gogymaint adj equal in size
gohebiaeth (**-au**) nf correspondence
gohebol adj corresponding
gohebu vb correspond (by letter etc); reply
gohebydd (**-wyr**) nm correspondent, reporter
gohiriad (**-au**) nm postponement
gohirio vb delay, postpone, defer
golau adj, nm, vb light
golau-leuad nm moonlight
golch (**-ion**) nm wash; coating; lye
golchdy (**-dai**) nm wash-house, laundry
golchfa nf wash; lathering
golchi vb wash; coat
golchiad (**-au**) nm washing; plating, coating
golchion npl slops; suds
golchwr (**-wyr**), **-ydd** (**-ion**) nm washer

golchwraig (-wragedd) *nf* washerwoman

golchyddes (-au) *nf* laundry

goledd(f) *nm* slant, slope

goledd(f)u *vb* slant, slope

goleuad (-au) *nm* light, luminary

goleudy (-dai) *nm* lighthouse

goleuni *nm* light

goleuo *vb* light, enlighten, illuminate

golosg *nm* coke, charcoal

golud (-oedd) *nm* wealth, riches

goludog *adj* wealthy, rich

golwg (-ygon) *nm/f* sight, look; (*pl*) eyes

golwr (-wyr) *nm* goalkeeper

golwyth (-ion) *nm* chop, slice, cut

golygfa (-feydd) *nf* scene, view; (*pl*) scenery

golygiad (-au) *nm* view

golygu *vb* view; mean; edit

golygus *adj* slightly, comely, handsome

golygwedd (-au) *nf* feature, aspect

golygydd (-ion, -wyr) *nm* editor

golygyddiaeth *nf* editorship

golygyddol *adj* editorial

gollwng *vb* drop, release, let go; discharge; dismiss; leak

gollyngdod *nm* release; absolution

gomedd *vb* refuse

gomeddiad *nm* refusal, omission

gonest, onest *adj* honest

gonestrwydd *nm* honesty

gôr *nm* pus

gor- *prefix* over-, super-

gorau (-euon) *adj* best. **o'r g.** very well

gorawen *nf* joy, ecstasy

gorblu *npl* immature feathers

gorboblogi *vb* overpopulate

gorbwyso *vb* outweigh, overweigh

gorchest (-ion) *nf* feat, exploit

gorchestol *adj* excellent, masterly

gorchfygu *vb* overcome, conquer

gorchfygwr (-wyr) *nm* victor;

conqueror

gorchudd (-ion) *nm* cover, covering, veil

gorchuddio *vb* cover

gorchwyl (-ion) *nm* task, undertaking

gorchymyn *vb* command ♦ (-gorchmynion) *nm* command, commandment

gordoi *vb* overspread, cover

gordyfu *vb* overgrow

gordd (gyrdd) *nf* sledge-hammer, mallet

gordderch (-adon) *nf* concubine; lover; bastard

goresgyn *vb* overrun, invade; conquer

goresgyniad *nm* invasion; conquest

goresgynnydd *nm* invader; conqueror

goreuro *vb* gild

gorfod *vb* be obliged ♦ *nm* obligation, necessity

gorfodaeth *nf* obligation, compulsion

gorfodi *vb* oblige, compel

gorfodol *adj* obligatory, compulsory

gorfoledd *nm* joy, rejoicing, triumph

gorfoleddu *vb* rejoice, triumph

gorfoleddus *adj* jubilant, triumphant

gorffen *vb* finish, complete, conclude

gorffeniad *nm* finishing, finish

Gorffennaf *nm* July

gorffennol *adj, nm* past

gorffwyll *adj* mad, frenzied

gorffwyllo *vb* rave

gorffwyllog *adj* mad, insane

gorffwylltra *nm* madness, insanity

gorffwys *vb, nm* rest, repose

gorffwysfa (-oedd) *nf* resting-place, rest

gorffwysiad (-au) *nm* rest, pause

gorffwyso, gorffwystra see gorffwys

gorhendaid nm great-great-grandfather

gorhennain nf great-great-grandmother

gori vb hatch

gorifyny nm ascent, hill, steep climb

goris prep below, beneath, under

goriwaered nm descent, declivity

gorlawn adj superabundant

gorlenwi vb overfill

gorliwio vb colour too highly, exaggerate

gorllewin nm west. G. yr Almaen West Germany

gorllewinol adj westerly, western

gorllewinwr (-wyr) nm westerner

gormes nm oppression, tyranny

gormesol adj oppressive, tyrannical

gormesu vb oppress, tyrannize

gormeswr (-wyr), -ydd (-ion) nm oppressor, tyrant

gormod (-ion) nm too much, excess

gormodedd nm excess, superfluity

gormodiaith nf hyperbole, exaggeration

gormodol adj excessive

gormwyth nm catarrh

gornest, ornest (-au) contest, match

goroesi vb outlive, survive

goroesiad (-au) nm survival

goroeswr (-wyr) nm survivor

goror (-au) nm border, coast, frontier

gorsaf (-oedd) nf station

gorsedd (-au) nf, **gorseddfa** (-oedd) nf, **gorseddfainc** (-feinciau) nf throne

gorseddu vb throne, enthrone, install

gorsin, gorsing (-au) nf door-post

gorthrech nm oppression; coercion

gorthrechu vb oppress; coerce

gorthrwm nm oppression

gorthrymder nm oppression, tribulation

gorthrymedig adj oppressed

gorthrymu vb oppress

gorthrymus adj oppressive

gorthrymwr, -ydd (-wyr) nm oppressor

goruchaf adj most high, supreme

goruchafiaeth nf supremacy; triumph

goruchel adj high, exalted

goruchwyliaeth (-au) nf oversight, supervision; dispensation

goruchwylio vb oversee, supervise

goruchwyliwr (-wyr) nm supervisor, steward

goruwch prep above, over

goruwchnaturiol adj supernatural

goruwchreoli vb overrule

gorwedd vb lie

gorweddfa (-oedd), -fan (-nau) nf bed, couch

gorweddian vb lounge, loll

gorweiddiog adj bedridden

gorwel (-ion) nm horizon

gorwych adj gorgeous

gorwyr (-ion) nm great-grandson

gorwyres (-au) nf great-granddaughter

gorymdaith (-deithiau) nf procession

gorymdeithio vb walk in procession

gorynys (-oedd) nf peninsula

gosber (-au) nm vespers

gosgedd (-au) nm form, figure

gosgeiddig adj comely, graceful

gosgordd (-ion) nf retinue, train, escort

gosgorddlu (-oedd) nm bodyguard

goslef (-au) nf tone, intonation (oslef)

gosod vb put, place, set; let ♦ adj false, artificial

gosodiad (-au) *nm* proposition, statement

gosteg (-ion) *nf* silence; (*pl*) banns

gostegu *vb* silence, still, quell

gostwng *vb* lower, reduce; bow; put down, humble

gostyngedig *adj* humble

gostyngeiddrwydd *nm* humility

gostyngiad *nm* reduction; humiliation

gowt *nm* gout

gradell (-gredyll) *nf* griddle

gradd (-au) *nmf* grade, degree, stage

graddedigion *npl* graduates

graddfa (-feydd) *nf* scale

graddio *vb* graduate

graddol *adj* gradual

graddoli *vb* grade, graduate

graean *coll n* (greyenyn *nm*) gravel

graeanu *vb* granulate

graeanwst *nf* gravel (*complaint*)

graen *nm* grain, gloss, lustre

graenus *adj* of good grain, glossy, sleek

graff (-iau) *nm* graph

gramadeg (-au) *nm* grammar

gramadegol *adj* grammatical

gramadegwr, -ydd (-wyr) *nm* grammarian

gran (-nau) *nm* cheek

gras (-au, -usau) *nm* grace

graslawn, -lon *adj* full of grace, gracious

graslonrwydd *nm* graciousness, grace

grasol, grasusol *adj* gracious

grât (gratiau) *nm* grate

grawn *npl* (gronyn *nm*) grain; grapes; roe

grawnfwyd (-ydd) *coll n* cereal

grawnwin *npl* grapes

Grawys *nm* Lent

gre (-oedd) *nf* stud, flock

greddf (-au) *nf* instinct, intuition

greddfol *adj* instinctive, intuitive,

rooted

greddfu *vb* become ingrained

grefi *nm* gravy

gresyn *nm* pity

gresyni, -dod *nm* misery, wretchedness

gresynu *vb* commiserate, pity

gresynus *adj* miserable, wretched

gridyll (-au) *nmf* griddle

griddfan *vb* groan, moan ♦ (-nau) *nm* groan

grillian, -io *vb* squeak, creak; chirp; crunch

gris (-iau) *nm* step, stair

grisial *nm* crystal

grisialaidd *adj* crystal, crystalline

gro *coll n* (grôyn *nm*) gravel, pebbles

Groeg *nf* Greek language; Greece ♦ *adj* Greek

Groegaidd *adj* Grecian, Greek

Groeges (-au) *nf* Greek woman

Groegwr (-wyr, -iaid) *nm* Greek

gronell (-au) *nf* roe

Grønland *nm* Greenland

gronyn (-nau) *nm* grain, particle; while

grot (-iau) *nm* groat, fourpence

grual *nm* gruel

grud *nm* grit

grudd (-iau) *nf* cheek

gruddfan see **griddfan**

grug *nm* heather

grugiar (-ieir) *nf* moor-hen, grouse

grugog *adj* heathery

grwgnach *vb* grumble, murmur

grwgnachlyd *adj* given to grumbling

grwgnachwr (-wyr) *nm* grumbler

grwn (grynnau) *nm* ridge (*in ploughing*)

grŵn, grwndi *nm* purr

grwnan *vb* croon, purr

grwndwal (-au) *nm* foundation

grydian *vb* murmur; grunt

grym (-oedd) *nm* force, power, might

grymial *vb* mutter, murmur, grumble

grymus *adj* strong, powerful, mighty

grymuso *vb* strengthen

grymuster, -tra *nm* power, might

gwacáu *vb* empty

gwacsaw *adj* trivial, frivolous

gwacsawrwydd *nm* levity, vanity

gwacter *nm* emptiness, vacuity

gwachul see **goachul**

gwad, gwadiad *nm* denial, disavowal

gwadn (-au) *nm* sole

gwadnu *vb* sole; foot it

gwadu *vb* deny, disown; renounce, forsake

gwadwr (-wyr) *nm* denier

gwadd (-od) *nf* mole

gwadd see **gwahodd**

gwaddod (-ion) *nm* sediment, lees, dregs

gwaddodi *vb* deposit sediment

gwaddol (-ion, -iadau) *nm* endowment; dowry

gwaddoli *vb* endow

gwae (-au) *nm/f* woe

gwaed *nm* blood

gwaedlif, gwaedlyn *nm* hæmorrhage, dysentery

gwaedlyd *adj* bloody, sanguinary

gwaedoliaeth *nf* blood, consanguinity

gwaedu *vb* bleed

gwaedd (-au) *nf* cry, shout

gwaeddi see **gweiddi**

gwaeg (gwaegau) *nf* buckle, clasp

gwael *adj* poor, vile; poorly, ill

gwaelder, -dra *nm* poorness, vileness

gwaeledd *nm* illness

gwaelod (-ion) *nm* bottom; *(pl)* sediment

gwaelodi *vb* settle, deposit sediment

gwaelu *vb* sicken

gwaell (gwêyll, gweill) *nf* knitting-needle

gwaered *nm* descent. **I w.** down

gwaeth *adj* worse

gwaethwaeth *adj* worse and worse

gwaethygu *vb* worsen

gwaew see **gwayw**

gwag (gweigion) *adj* empty, vacant, vain

gwagedd *nm* vanity

gwagelog *adj* wary, circumspect

gwagen (-i) *nf* waggon

gwagenwr (-wyr) *nm* waggoner

gwagfa (-feydd) *nf* vacuum

gwagle (-oedd) *nm* space, void

gwagu *vb* empty

gwahadden (gwahaddod) *nf* mole

gwahan, gwahân *nm*: **ar w.** apart, separately

gwahangleifion *npl* lepers

gwahanglwyf *nm* leprosy

gwahanglwyfus *adj* leprous ♦ *nm* leper

gwahaniaeth (-au) *nm* difference

gwahaniaethol *adj* distinguishing

gwahaniaethu *vb* differ; distinguish

gwahanol *adj* different

gwahanu *vb* divide, part, separate

gwahardd *vb* forbid, prohibit

gwaharddiad (-au) *nm* prohibition, veto

gwahodd *vb* invite

gwahoddedigion *npl* guests

gwahoddiad (-au) *nm* invitation

gwahoddwr (-wyr) *nm* inviter, host

gwain (gweiniau) *nf* sheath, scabbard

gwair (gweiriau) *nm* hay

gwaith (gweithiau) *nm* work

gwaith (gweithiau) *nf* time, turn

gwal (-iau, gwelydd) *nf* wall

gwâl (gwalau) *nf* couch, bed; lair

gwala *nf* enough, plenty

gwalch (gweilch) *nm* hawk; rogue, rascal

gwaled (-au) nf wallet

gwalio vb wall, fence

gwall (-au) nm defect, want; mistake, error

gwallgof adj mad, insane

gwallgofdy (-dai) nm madhouse, lunatic asylum

gwallgofddyn (-gofiaid) nm madman

gwallgofi vb go mad, rave

gwallgofrwydd nm madness, insanity

gwallt (-iau) nm, coll n hair of the head

gwalltog adj hairy

gwallus adj faulty, incorrect, inaccurate

gwamal adj fickle, frivolous

gwamalio, -u vb waver; behave frivolously

gwamalrwydd nm frivolity, levity

gwan (gweiniaid, gweinion) adj weak, feeble

gwanaf (-au) nf layer; row, swath

gwanc nm greed, voracity

gwancus adj greedy, voracious

gwaneg (-au, gwenyg) nf wave, billow

gwangalon adj faint-hearted

gwangalonni vb lose heart

gwanhau vb weaken, enfeeble

gwanllyd, gwannaidd adj weakly, delicate

gwant nm caesura; division

gwantan adj unsteady, fickle; feeble, poor

gwanu vb pierce, stab

gwanwyn (-au) nm spring

gwanwynol adj vernal, spring-like

gwanychu vb weaken, enfeeble

gwar (-rau) nm/f (nape of) neck

gwâr adj civilised, tame, gentle

gwaradwydd (-iadau) nm shame, disgrace

gwaradwyddo vb shame, disgrace

gwaradwyddus adj shameful, disgraceful

gwarafun vb forbid, refuse, grudge

gwaraidd adj gentle, civilized

gwarant (-au) nf warrant

gwarantu vb warrant, guarantee

gwarchae vb besiege ♦ nm siege

gwarcheidiol adj guardian, tutelary

gwarcheidwad (-waid) nm guardian

gwarchod vb watch, ward, mind

gwarchodaeth nf ward, custody

gwarchodlu (-oedd) nm garrison, guards

gward (-iau) nm/f ward

gwarden (-deiniaid) nm warden

gwared vb rid; deliver, redeem

gwaredigaeth (-au) nf deliverance

gwaredigion npl redeemed, ransomed

gwaredu vb save, deliver, redeem; rid

gwaredwr (-wyr), -ydd (-ion) nm saviour

gwaredd nm mildness, gentleness

gwareiddiad nm civilization

gwareiddiedig adj civilized

gwareiddio vb civilize

gwargaled adj stiffnecked, stubborn

gwargaledwch nm stubbornness

gwargam adj stooping

gwargamu vb stoop

gwarged nm remains

gwargrwm adj round-shouldered

gwargrymu vb stoop

gwario vb spend

gwarogaeth see **gwrogaeth**

gwarth nm shame, disgrace

gwarthaf nm top, summit. **ar w.** on top of, upon

gwarthafl (-au) nf stirrup

gwartheg npl cows, cattle

gwarthnod (-au) nm stigma

gwarthnodi vb stigmatize

gwarthol (-ion) nf stirrup

gwarthrudd nm shame, disgrace

gwarthruddo vb shame, disgrace
gwarthus adj shameful, disgraceful
gwas (gweision) nm lad; servant
gwasaidd adj servile, slavish
gwasanaeth (-au) nm service
gwasanaethferch (-ed) nf handmaid
gwasanaethgar adj serviceable; obliging
gwasanaethu vb serve, minister
gwasanaethwr (-wyr) nm manservant, servant
gwasanaethwraig (-wragedd) nf maidservant
gwasanaethydd (-ion) nm servant
gwasanaethyddes (-au) nf handmaid
gwaseidd-dra nm servility
gwasg (-au, -oedd, gweisg) nf press ♦ nm waist; bodice
gwasgar nm dispersion. **ar w.** scattered, dispersed
gwasgaredig (-ion) adj scattered
gwasgarog adj scattered; divided
gwasgaru vb scatter, disperse; spread
gwasgarwr (-wyr) nm scatterer; spreader
gwasgfa (-feydd, -feuon) nf squeeze; fit
gwasgod (-au) nf waistcoat
gwasgu vb press, squeeze, crush, wring
gwasod adj in heat (of a cow)
gwastad adj level, flat; even; constant, continual
gwastadedd (-au) nm plain
gwastadol adj continual, perpetual
gwastadrwydd nm evenness
gwastatáu vb make even, level; settle
gwastatir (-oedd) nm level ground, plain
gwastraff nm waste, extravagance
gwastraffu vb waste, squander
gwastraffus adj wasteful, extravagant

gwastrawd (-odion) nm groom, ostler
gwastrodaeth, -odi vb grooming; discipline
gwatwar vb mock; mimic ♦ nm mockery
gwatwareg nf sarcasm, satire, irony
gwatwarus adj mocking, scoffing
gwatwarwr (-wyr) nm mocker, scoffer
gwau vb knit, weave
gwaun (gweunydd) nf moor, meadow
gwawch (-iau) nf, -io vb scream, yell
gwawd nm scoff, scorn, ridicule
gwawdiaeth nf ridicule
gwawdio vb mock, scoff, jeer, ridicule
gwawdiwr (-wyr) nm mocker, scoffer
gwawdlyd adj mocking, jeering, sneering
gwawl nm light
gwawn nm gossamer
gwawr nf dawn, day-break; hue, nuance
gwawrio vb dawn
gwayw (gwewyr) nm pang, pain, stitch
gwaywffon (-ffyn) nf spear
gwden (-ni, gwdyn) nf withe
gwdihŵ nm owl
gwddf (gyddfau) nm neck, throat
gwe (-oedd) nf web; texture
gwead nm weaving, knitting; texture
gwedd (-au) nf aspect, form; appearance
gwedd (-oedd) nf yoke; team
gweddaidd adj seemly, decent
gweddeidd-dra nm seemliness, decency
gwedder (gweddrod) nm wether. **cig g.** mutton

gweddgar *adj* plump, sleek
gweddi (**-iau**) *nf* prayer
gweddigar *adj* prayerful
gweddill (**-ion**) *nm* remnant, remainder, rest; (*pl*) remains
gweddillio *vb* leave spare, leave a remnant
gweddïo *vb* pray
gweddïwr (**-ïwyr**) *nm* one who prays
gweddol *adj* fair, fairly
gweddu *vb* suit, become, befit
gweddus *adj* seemly, decent, proper
gweddustra *nm* decency, propriety
gweddw *adj* single; widow, widowed. **gŵr g.** widower ♦ (**-on**) *nf* widow
gweddwdod *nm* widowhood
gweddwi *vb* widow
gwefl (**-au**) *nf* lip (*usu.* of animal)
gwefr *nm* thrill, excitement; charge
gwefreiddio *vb* electrify, thrill
gwefreiddiol *adj* thrilling
gwefus (**-au**) *nf* (human) lip
gwefusol *adj* of the lip, labial
gwegi *nm* vanity, levity
gwegian *vb* sway, totter
gwegil *nm* back of head
gwehelyth *nmf* lineage, pedigree
gwehilion *npl* refuse, trash, riffraff
gwehydd (**-ion**) *nm* weaver
gwehynnu *vb* draw, pour, empty
gweiddi *vb* cry, shout
gweilgi *nf* sea, torrent
gweili *adj* empty, idle
gweini *vb* serve, minister; be in service
gweinidog (**-ion**) *nm* minister, servant
gweinidogaeth (**-au**) *nf* ministry, service
gweinidogaethol *adj* ministerial
gweinidogaethu *vb* minister

gweinio *vb* sheathe
gweinyddes (**-au**) *nf* attendant, nurse; waitress
gweinyddiaeth (**-au**) *nf* administration
gweinyddol *adj* administrative
gweinyddu *vb* administer, officiate
gweirglodd (**-iau**) *nf* meadow
gweitied, -io *vb* wait
gweithdy (**-dai**) *nm* workshop
gweithfa (**-oedd, -feydd**) *nf* works
gweithfaol *adj* industrial
gweithgar *adj* hard-working, industrious
gweithgaredd (**-au**), **-garwch** *nm* activity
gweithio *vb* work; ferment; purge
gweithiwr (**-wyr**) *nm* workman, worker
gweithred (**-oedd**) *nf* act, deed, work
gweithrediad (**-au**) *nm* action, operation
gweithredol *adj* active, actual, virtual
gweithredu *vb* act, work, operate
gweithredwr (**-wyr**) *nm* doer
gweithredydd (**-ion**) *nm* doer, factor, agent
gweladwy *adj* perceptible, visible
gweled, gweld *vb* see, perceive
gwelediad *nm* sight, appearance
gweledig *adj* seen, visible
gweledigaeth (**-au**) *nf* vision
gweledydd (**-ion**) *nm* seer
gwelw *adj* pale
gwelwi *vb* pale
gwely (**-au, gwelâu**) *nm* bed; river basin; sea bed; stratum; flat surface
gwell *adj* better, superior
gwella *vb* better, mend, improve, recover
gwellau, gwellaif (**-eifiau**) *nf* shears
gwellen (**gweill**) *nf* knitting-needle
gwellhad *nm* recovery,

improvement
gwellhau vb better, improve
gwelliant (**-iannau**) nm
amendment, improvement
gwellt coll n grass; sward; straw
gwelltglas nm grass, greensward
gwelltog adj grassy, green
gwelltyn nm blade of grass; a
straw
gwellwell adv better and better
gwen adj f. of **gwyn**
gwên (**gwenau**) nf smile
gwenci (**-iod**) nf stoat, weasel
gwendid (**-au**) nm weakness,
frailty
Gwener nf Venus. **Dydd G.** Friday
gwenerol adj venereal
gwenfflam adj blazing, ablaze
gweniaith nf flattery
gwenieithio vb flatter
gwenieithiwr (**-wyr**) nm flatterer
gwenieithus adj flattering
gwenith npl (**-en** nf) wheat
gwenithfaen nm granite
gwennol (**gwenoliaid**) nf swallow,
martin; shuttle
gwenu vb smile
gwenwisg (**-oedd**) nf surplice
gwenwyn nm poison, venom;
jealousy
gwenwynig, -wynol adj
poisonous, venomous
gwenwynllyd adj peevish; jealous
gwenwyno vb poison; fret; be
jealous
gwenyn npl (**-en** nf) bees
gwep nf visage, grimace
gwêr nm tallow, suet etc
gwer nm shade
gwerchyr nm cover, lid, valve
gwerdd adj f. of **gwyrdd**
gwerin coll nf men, people;
democracy; crew
gweriniaeth (**-au**) nf democracy;
republic
Gweriniaeth Iwerddon nf Eire
gwerinlywodraeth (**-au**) nf

republic
gwerinol adj plebian, vulgar
gwerinos coll nf the rabble, the
mob
gwerinwr (**-wyr**) nm democrat
gwern (**-i, -ydd**) nf swamp,
meadow; alder-grove
gwern npl (**-en** nf) alder-trees
gwerog adj tallowy, suety
gwers (**-i**) nf verse; lesson
gwersyll (**-oedd**) nm camp,
encampment
gwersyllu, -a vb encamp
gwerth nm worth, value. **ar w.** for
sale
gwerthfawr adj valuable, precious
gwerthfawredd nm preciousness
gwerthfawrogi vb appreciate
gwerthfawrogiad nm appreciation
gwerthu vb sell
gwerthwr (**-wyr**) nm seller
gwerthyd (**-au**) nf spindle, axle
gweryd (**-au**) nm earth, soil;
sward ♦ nf groin
gweryriad nm neighing
gweryru vb neigh
gwestai (**-eion**) nm guest
gwesty (**-au, -tai**) nm inn, hotel
gweu vb weave, knit
gwewyr nm anguish
gwg nm frown, scowl; disapproval
gwgu vb frown, scowl, lower
gwialen (**gwiail**) nf rod, switch
gwialennod (**-enodiau**) nf stroke,
stripe
gwialenodio vb beat with a rod
gwib nf wandering, jaunt ♦ adj
wandering
gwibdaith (**-deithiau**) nf excursion
gwiber (**-od**) nf viper
gwibio vb flash, flit, dart, wander
gwibiog adj flitting, darting,
wandering
gwiblong (**-au**) nf cruiser
gwich nf squeak; creak; wheeze,
wheezing
gwichiad (**-iaid**) nm periwinkle

gwichian vb squeak, squeal; creak; wheeze

gwichlyd adj creaking; wheezy

gwiddon (-od) nf witch

gwiddon npl mites

gwif (-iau) nm lever, crowbar

gwig (-oedd) nf wood

gwingo vb wriggle, fidget; writhe; kick, struggle

gwin (-oedd) nm wine

gwinau adj bay, brown, auburn

gwinc (-od) nf chaffinch

gwinegr nm vinegar

gwinllan (-noedd, -nau) nf vineyard

gwinllannwr, -nydd nm vinedresser

gwinwryf (-oedd) nm wine-press

gwinwydd npl (-en nf) vines

gwir adj true ♦ nm truth

gwireb (-au, -ion) nf truism, axiom

gwireddu vb verify, substantiate

gwirfodd nm goodwill; own accord

gwirfoddol adj voluntary, spontaneous

gwirfoddolwr (-wyr) nm volunteer

gwirio vb verify

gwirion (-iaid) adj innocent; silly

gwiriondeb nm innocence; silliness

gwirionedd (-au) nm truth, verity, reality

gwirioneddol adj true, real, genuine

gwirioni vb infatuate, dote

gwirionyn nm simpleton

gwirod (-ydd) nm liquor, spirits

gwisg (-oedd) nf dress, garment, robe

gwisgi adj brisk, lively, nimble; ripe

gwisgo vb dress; wear

gwisgwr (-wyr) nm wearer

gwiw adj fit, meet; worthy

gwiwer (-od) nf squirrel

gwlad (gwledydd) nf country, land

gwladaidd adj countrified, rustic

Gwlad Belg nf Belgium

Gwlad yr Iâ nf Iceland

Gwlad Thai nf Thailand

gwladfa (-oedd) nf colony, settlement

gwladgar see gwlatgar

gwladgarol adj patriotic

gwladgarwch nm patriotism

gwladgarwr (-wyr) nm patriot

gwladol adj of a country, civil, state

gwladoli vb nationalize

gwladweiniaeth nf statesmanship

gwladweinydd (-ion, -wyr) nm statesman

gwladwr (-wyr) nm countryman, peasant

gwladwriaeth (-au) nf state

gwladwriaethol adj state, political

gwladychfa (-oedd) nf settlement, colony

gwladychu vb inhabit, settle, colonize; rule

gwladychwr (-wyr) nm settler, colonist

gwlân (gwlanoedd) nm wool

gwlana vb gather wool

gwlanen (-ni) nf flannel

gwlanog adj woolly

gwlatgar adj patriotic

gwlaw see glaw

gwledig adj countrified, country, rural

gwledd (-oedd) nf feast, banquet

gwledda vb feast

gwleddwr (-wyr) nm feaster

gwleidydd (-ion) nm politician, statesman

gwleidyddiaeth nf politics

gwleidyddol adj political

gwleidyddwr (-wyr) nm politician

gwlith (-oedd) nm dew

gwlitho vb dew, bedew

gwlithog adj dewy; inspiring

gwlithyn nm dewdrop

gwlyb (-ion) adj wet, fluid, liquid ♦ nm fluid, liquid

gwlybaniaeth *nm* wet, moisture

gwlybwr *nm* wet, moisture, liquid, fluid

gwlybyrog *adj* wet, damp, rainy

gwlych *nm* wet. **rhoi yng ng.** steep

gwlychu *vb* wet, moisten; get wet; dip

gwlydd *npl, coll n* (**-yn** *nm*) haulm

gwn (**gynnau**) *nm* gun

gŵn (**gynau**) *nm* gown

gwndwn see **gwyndwn**

gwneud, gwneuthur *vb* do, make

gwneuthuriad *nm* make, making

gwneuthurwr (**-wyr**) *nm* maker, doer, manufacturer

gwniad *nm* sewing, stitching, seam

gwniadur (**-iau, on**) *nm/f* thimble

gwniadwraig *nf* stitcher, seamstress

gwniadyddes (**-au**) *nf* seamstress

gwnio *vb* sew, stitch

gwniyddes (**-au**) *nf* seamstress

gwobr (**-au**) *nf/m*, **gwobrwy** (**-au, -on**) *nm* reward, prize

gwobrwyo *vb* reward

gwobrwywr (**-wyr**) *nm* rewarder

gŵr (**gwŷr**) *nm* man; husband

gwra *vb* seek or marry a husband

gwrach (**-iod, -od**) *nf* hag, witch.
    breuddwyd g. wishful thinking

gwrachïaidd *adj* old-womanish

gwraidd (**gwreiddiau**) *coll n* roots

gwraig (**gwragedd**) *nf* woman; wife

gwrandaw see **gwrando**

gwrandawiad *nm* listening, hearing

gwrandawr (**-wyr**) *nm* listener, hearer

gwrando *vb* listen, hearken

gwrcath (**-od**) *nm* tom-cat

gwregys (**-au**) *nm* girdle, belt, truss; zone

gwregysu *vb* girdle, gird

gwrêng *nm, coll n* (one of the) common people

gwreica *vb* seek or marry a wife

gwreichion *npl* (**-en** *nf*) sparks

gwreichioni *vb* emit sparks, sparkle

gwreiddio *vb* root

gwreiddiol *adj* radical, rooted; original

gwreiddioldeb *nm* originality

gwreiddyn (**gwreiddiau**) *nm* root

gwres *nm* heat, warmth

gwresfesurydd (**-ion**) *nm* thermometer

gwresog *adj* warm, hot; fervent

gwresogi *vb* warm, heat

gwrhyd (**-oedd**), **gwryd** *nm* fathom

gwrhydri *nm* exploit; valour

gwrid *nm* blush, flush

gwrido *vb* blush, flush

gwridog, gwritgoch *adj* rosy-cheeked, ruddy

gwrogaeth *nf* homage

gwrogi *vb* do homage

gwrol *adj* brave, courageous

gwroldeb *nm* bravery, courage

gwroli *vb* hearten

gwron (**-iaid**) *nm* hero

gwroniaeth *nf* heroism

gwrtaith (**-teithiau**) *nm* manure, fertiliser

gwrteithiad *nm* cultivation, culture

gwrteithio *vb* manure; cultivate, culture

gwrth- *prefix* counter-, contra-, anti-

gwrthban (**-au**) *nm* blanket

gwrthblaid *nf* (party in) opposition

gwrthbrofi *vb* disprove, refute

gwrthbwynt *nm* counterpoint

gwrthdaro *vb* clash, collide

gwrthdrawiad *nm* collision

gwrthdystiad (**-au**) *nm* protest

gwrthdystio *vb* protest

gwrthddadl (**-euon**) *nf* objection

gwrthddadlau *vb* object,

controvert

gwrthddywediad (-au) *nm* contradiction

gwrthddywedyd *vb* contradict

gwrthgiliad (-au) *nm* backsliding

gwrthgilio *vb* backslide, secede

gwrthgiliwr (-wr) *nm* backslider, seceder

gwrthglawdd (-gloddiau) *nm* rampart

gwrthgyferbyniad (-au) *nm* contrast, antithesis

gwrthgyferbynnu *vb* contrast

gwrthnaws *nm* antipathy ♦ *adj* repugnant

gwrthnysig *adj* obstinate, stubborn

gwrthod *vb* refuse, reject

gwrthodedig *adj* rejected, reprobate

gwrthodiad *nm* refusal, rejection

gwrthodwr (-wyr) *nm* refuser, rejecter

gwrthol *nm, adv* back. ôl a g. to and fro

gwrthrych (-au) *nm* object; subject (*of biography*)

gwrthrychol *adj* objective

gwrthryfel (-oedd) *nm* rebellion, mutiny

gwrthryfela *vb* rebel

gwrthryfelgar *adj* rebellious, mutinous

gwrthryfelwr (-wyr) *nm* rebel, mutineer

gwrthsafiad *nm* resistance

gwrthsefyll *vb* withstand, resist

gwrthun *adj* repugnant, odious, absurd

gwrthuni *nm* odiousness, absurdity

gwrthuno *vb* mar, deform, disfigure

gwrthweithio *vb* counteract

gwrthwyneb *nm* opposite, contrary

gwrthwynebiad (-au) *nm* objection

gwrthwynebol *adj* opposed

gwrthwynebu *vb* resist, oppose

gwrthwynebus *adj* repugnant; antagonistic

gwrthwynebwr, -ydd (-wyr) *nm* opponent, adversary

gwrych (-oedd) *nm* hedge

gwrych *npl, coll n* (-yn *nm*) bristles

gwryd see **gwrhyd**

gwryf (-oedd) *nm* press

gwrym (-iau) *nm* seam; wale

gwrysg *npl* (-en *nf*) stalks, haulm

gwryw *adj* male ♦ (-od) *nm* male

gwrywaidd, -ol *adj* masculine

gwrywgydiaeth *nm* homosexuality

gwrywgydiol *adj* homosexual

gwrywgydiwr (-wyr) *nm* homosexual

gwth *nm* push, thrust, shove; gust

gwthio *vb* push, thrust, shove

gwthiwr (-wyr) *nm* pusher

gwyar *nm* gore, blood

gwybed *npl* (-yn *nm*) flies

gwybod *vb* know ♦ (-au) *nm* knowledge. **gwybodau** studies

gwybodaeth (-au) *nf* knowledge

gwybodeg *nm* epistemology

gwybodus *adj* knowing, well-informed

gwybyddus *adj* known, aware of

gwych *adj* fine, splendid, brilliant

gwychder *nm* splendour, pomp

gwŷd (**gwydiau**) *nm* vice

gwydn *adj* tough

gwydnwch *nm* toughness

gwydr (-au) *nm* glass

gwydraid (-eidiau) *nm* glassful, glass

gwydro *vb* glaze

gwydrwr (-wyr) *nm* glazier

gwydryn (**gwydrau**) *nm* drinking-glass

gwŷdd *nm* presence

gwŷdd (**gwyddau**) *nm* goose

gwŷdd (**gwehyddion, gwyddion**) *nm* loom; plough

gwŷdd *npl* (**gwydden** *nf*) trees

gwyddbwyll *nf* chess

Gwyddel (-od, Gwyddyl) *nm* Irishman

Gwyddeleg *nf* Irish language

Gwyddeles (-au) *nf* Irishwoman

Gwyddelig *adj* Irish

gwyddfa *nf* tumulus, grave

gwyddfid *nm* honeysuckle

gwyddfod *nm* presence

gwyddoniadur (-on) *nm* encyclopaedia

gwyddoniaeth *nf* science

gwyddonol *adj* scientific

gwyddonydd (-wyr) *nm* scientist

gwyddor (-ion) *nf* rudiment; science. **yr w.** the alphabet

gwyddori *vb* instruct, ground

gwyfyn (-od) *nm* moth

gwyg *coll n* vetch

gwŷl *adj* bashful, modest

gŵyl (-iau) *nf* holiday, feast, festival

gwylaidd *adj* bashful, modest

gwylan (-od) *nf* sea-gull

gwylder *nm* bashfulness, modesty

gwyleidd-dra *nm* bashfulness, modesty

gwylfa (-fâu, -feydd) *nf* watch; lookout

gwyliadwriaeth *nm* watchfulness, caution ♦ (-au) *nf* watch; guard

gwyliadwrus *adj* watchful, cautious

gwyliedydd (-ion) *nm* watchman, sentinel

gwylio *vb* watch, mind, beware

gwyliwr (-wyr) *nm* watchman, sentinel

gwylmabsant (-au) *nf* wake

gwylnos (-au) *nf* watch-night, wake, vigil

gwyll *nm* darkness, gloom

gwylliad (-iaid) *nm* robber, bandit

gwyllt *adj* wild, savage, mad; rapid ♦ (-oedd) *nm* wild

gwylltineb *nm* wildness, rage, fury

gwylltio, -u *vb* frighten; fly into a passion

gwymon *nm* seaweed

gwyn *adj* white; blessed; *f* gwen

gwŷn (gwyniau) *nm/f* ache, smart; lust

gwynder, -dra *nm* whiteness

gwyndwn *nm* unploughed land

gwyneb see **wyneb**

gwynegon *nm* rheumatism

gwynegu *vb* throb, ache

gwynfa *nf* paradise

gwynfyd (-au) *nm* blessedness, bliss; (pl) beatitudes

gwynfydedig *adj* blessed, happy, beatific

gwyngalch *nm* whitewash

gwyngalchog *adj* whitewashed

gwyngalchu *vb* whitewash

gwyniad (-iaid) *nm* whiting

gwynias *adj* white-hot

gwyniedyn *nm* sewin

gwynio *vb* throb, ache

gwynnu *vb* whiten, bleach

gwynnwy *nm* white of egg

gwynt (-oedd) *nm* wind; breath; smell

gwyntell (-i) *nf* round basket without handle

gwyntio *vb* smell

gwyntog *adj* windy

gwyntyll (-au) *nf* fan

gwyntylliad *nm* ventilation

gwyntyllio, -u *vb* ventilate, winnow

gŵyr *adj* crooked, oblique, sloping

gwŷr see **gŵr**

gwyrdraws *adj* perverse

gwyrdro (-ion) *nm* perversion

gwyrdroi *vb* pervert, distort

gwyrdd (-ion) *adj*, *nm* green

gwyrddlas *adj* green, verdant

gwyrddlesni *nm* verdure

gwrddni *nm* greenness, verdure

gwyrgam *adj* crooked

gwyrni *nm* crookedness, perverseness

gwyro *vb* swerve; slope; stoop;

tilt; deviate

gwyrth (-iau) *nf* miracle

gwyrthiol *adj* miraculous

gwyry, gwyryf (**gwyryfon**) *nf* virgin

gwyryfdod *nm* virginity

gwyryfol *adj* virgin

gwŷs (**gwysion**) *nf* summons

gwysio *vb* summon

gwystl (-on) *nm* pledge; hostage

gwystlo *vb* pledge, pawn

gwystno *vb* dry, wither, flag

gwythien (**gwyth, gwythiennau**) *nf* vein, blood vessel, artery. **cwlwm gwythi** cramp

gwyw *adj* withered, faded, sere

gwywo *vb* wither, fade

gyda, -g *prefix* with

gyddfol *adj* guttural

gyferbyn *prefix* over against, opposite

gylfin (-od) *nm* bill, beak

gylfinir *nm* curlew

gynfad (-au) *nm* gunboat

gynnau *adv* a little while ago, just now

gynt *adv* formerly, of yore

gyr (-roedd) *nm* drove

gyrfa (-oedd, -feydd) *nf* race; course; career

gyriedydd (-ion) *nm* driver

gyrru *vb* drive; send; work, forge

gyrrwr (**gyrwyr**) *nm* driver; sender

gyrwynt (-oedd) *nm* hurricane, tornado

gysb *nm* staggers

H

ha *excl* ha

hac (-iau) *nf* cut, notch, hack

hacio *vb* hack

had (-au) *nm, coll n* (**hedyn** *nm*) seed

hadlif *nm* seminal fluid

hadog *nm* haddock

hadu *vb* seed

hadyd *coll n* seed-corn

haearn (**heyrn**) *nm* iron. **h. bwrw** cast iron. **h. gyr** wrought iron

haearnaidd *adj* like iron

haeddiannol *adj* meritorious; merited

haeddiant (-iannau) *nm* merit, desert

haeddu *vb* deserve, merit

hael *adj* generous, liberal

haelfrydedd *nm* liberality

haelfrydig *adj* generous, free

haelioni *nm* generosity

haelionus *adj* generous, liberal

haen (-au) *nf* layer, stratum; seam

haenen (-nau) *nf* layer, film

haenu *vb* stratify

haeriad (-au) *nm* assertion

haerllug *adj* importunate; impudent

haerllugrwydd *nm* importunity; impudence

haeru *vb* affirm, assert

haf (-au) *nm* summer

hafaidd *adj* summer-like, summery

hafal *adj* like, equal

hafaliad *nm* equation

hafn *nf* haven

hafn (-au) *nf* hollow, gorge, ravine

hafod (-ydd) *nf* summer dwelling, upland farm

hafog *nm* havoc

hafoty (-tai) *nm* summer residence

hagr *adj* ugly

hagru *vb* mar, disfigure

hagrwch *nm* ugliness

haid (**heidiau**) *nf* swarm, drove, horde

haidd (**heiddiau**) *nm, coll n* (**heidden** *nf*) barley

haig (**heigiau**) *nf* shoal

haint (**heintiau**) *nm/f* pestilence; faint

hala *vb* send, spend

halen *nm* salt, brine

halog, -edig adj defiled, polluted
halogi vb defile, profane, pollute
halogrwydd nm defilement, pollution
halogwr (-wyr) nm defiler, profaner
hallt adj salt, salty; severe
halltedd, -rwydd nm saltness, saltiness
halltu vb salt
halltwr (-wyr) nm salter
hambwrdd (-byrddau) nm tray
hamdden nf leisure, respite
hamddenol adj leisurely
hanerob (-au) nf flitch of bacon
haneru vb halve
hanes (-ion) nm history, story, account
hanesydd (-wyr) nm historian
hanesyddol adj historical
hanesyn (-nau) nm anecdote
hanfod vb descend from, issue ♦ nm essence
hanfodol adj essential
haniad nm derivation, descent
haniaeth nf abstraction
haniaethol adj abstract
hanner (hanerau, haneri) nm, adj, adv half
hanu vb proceed, be derived, be descended
hapus adj happy
hapusrwydd nm happiness
hardd adj beautiful, handsome
harddu vb beautify, embellish, adorn
harddwch nm beauty
harnais (-eisiau) nm harness
harneisio vb harness
hatling (-au, -od) nf tithe, half a farthing
hau vb sow, disseminate
haul (heuliau) nm sun
hawdd adj easy
hawddamor nm, excl good luck, welcome
hawddfyd nm ease, prosperity

hawddgar adj amiable; comely
hawddgarwch nm amiability
hawl (-iau) nf claim; right. **h. ac ateb** question and answer
hawlio vb claim, demand
hawlydd (-ion) nm claimant, plaintiff
haws adj easier
heb prep without
heblaw prep beside(s)
hebog (-au) nm hawk, falcon
Hebraeg nf, adj Hebrew (language)
Hebreaidd, Hebreig adj Hebrew, Hebraic
Hebrees (-au) nf Hebrew woman
Hebreigydd (-ion) nm Hebraist
Hebrëwr (-wyr) nm a Hebrew
hebrwng vb accompany, conduct, convey, escort
hebryngydd (-ion) nm conductor, guide
hedeg vb fly; run to seed
hedegog adj flying; high-flown
hedfa (-feydd) nf flight
hedfan vb fly, hover
hedydd (-ion) nm lark
hedyn (hadau) nm seed, germ
hedd nm peace, tranquillity
heddgeidwad (-waid) nm policeman
heddiw adv today
heddlu nm police force
heddwas (-weision) nm policeman
heddwch nm peace, quiet, tranquillity
heddychiaeth nf pacifism
heddychlon adj peaceful, peaceable
heddychol adj peaceable, pacific
heddychu vb pacify, appease
heddychwr (-wyr) nm pacifist, peace-maker
heddyw see **heddiw**
hefelydd adj similar
hefyd adv also, besides
heffer (heffrod) nf heifer
hegl (-au) nf leg, shank

heglog adj leggy, long-legged

heglu vb foot it, 'hook it'

heibio adv past

heidio vb swarm, throng, flock

heidden nf grain of barley

heigio vb shoal, teem

heini adj active, lively, nimble, brisk

heintio vb infect

heintus adj infectious, contagious

heislan (-od) nf hackle, hatchel

heislanu vb hackle flax

hel vb gather, collect; drive, chase

hela vb hunt, spend (money, time). **cŵn h.** hounds

helaeth adj ample, abundant, extensive

helaethrwydd nm abundance

helaethu vb enlarge, extend, amplify

helaethwych adj sumptuous

helbul (-on) nm trouble

helbulus adj troubled, troublous

helcyd vb hunt ♦ nm worry, trouble

helfa (-fâu, -feydd) nf hunt, catch

helfarch (-feirch) nf hunter (horse)

helgi (-gwn) nm hound

heli nm salt water, brine

heliwr (-wyr) nm hunter, huntsman

helm (-au) nf helm, helmet, stack

help nm help, aid, assistance

helpio, -u vb help, aid, assist

helwriaeth nf game, hunting; chase

helyg npl (-en nf), willows

helynt (-ion) nf trouble, fuss, bother

helltni nm saltiness, saltness

hem nm rivet

hem (-iau) nf hem, border

hen adj old, aged, ancient, of old

henadur (-iaid) nm alderman

henaduriad (-iaid) nm Presbyterian, elder

henaduriaeth (-au) nf presbytery

henafgwr, henafol see hy-

henaint nm old age

hendaid (-deidiau) nm great-grandfather

hender nm oldness

hendref (-i, -ydd) nf winter dwelling, lowland farm

heneb (-ion) nf ancient monument

heneiddio vb grow old, age

henfam nf grandmother

henffasiwn adj old-fashioned

hennain (heneiniau) nf great-grandmother

heno adv tonight

henoed coll n elderly people, the aged

henuriad (-iaid) nm elder, presbyter

heol (-ydd) nf road

hepgor vb spare, dispense with ♦ (-ion) nm what may be dispensed with

hepian vb slumber, doze

her (-iau) nf challenge

herc (-iau) nf hop; limp

hercian vb hop, hobble, limp

heresi (-iau) nf heresy

heretic (-iaid) nm heretic

hereticaidd adj heretical

herfeiddio vb dare, brave, defy

herfeiddiol adj daring, defiant

hergwd nm push, thrust, shove

herio vb challenge, dare, brave, defy

herw nm raid; outlawry

herwa vb scout, prowl, raid

herwgipio vb kidnap

herwgipiwr (-wyr) nm kidnapper

herwhela vb poach (game)

herwr (-wyr) nm scout, raider; outlaw

herwydd see oherwydd

hesb adj f. of **hysb**

hesben (-nau) nf hasp

hesbin (-od) nf yearling ewe

hesbio vb dry up

hesbwrn (**-yrniaid**) *nm* young ram
hesg *npl* (**-en** *nf*), sedge, rushes
het (**-iau**) *nf* hat
heulo *vb* shine (*as the sun*); sun
heulog *adj* sunny
heulwen *nf* sunshine
heuwr (**-wyr**) *nm* sower
hi *pron* she, her; it
hidio *vb* heed
hidl *adj:* **wylo yn h.** weep
    abundantly
hidl (**-au**) *nf* strainer, sieve
hidlen (**-ni**) *nf* strainer, sieve
hidlo *vb* distil, run; strain, filter
hil *nf* race, lineage, posterity
hilio *vb* bring forth, teem, breed
hiliogaeth *nf* offspring, issue,
    posterity
hilydd (**-ion**) *nm* racist
hilyddiaeth *nf* racism
hin *nf* weather
hinfynegydd (**-ion**) *nm* barometer
hiniog (**-au**) *nf* threshold, door-
    frame
hinon *nf* fair weather
hinsawdd (**-soddau**) *nf* climate
hinsoddol *adj* climatic
hir (**hirion**) *adj, prefix* long
hiraeth *nm* longing, nostalgia,
    grief; homesickness
hiraethu *vb* long, yearn, sorrow
hiraethus *adj* longing; homesick
hirbell *adj:* **o h.** from afar
hirben *adj* long-headed, shrewd
hirhoedledd *nm* longevity
hirhoedlog *adj* long-lived
hirymarhous *adj* longsuffering
hirymaros *nm* longsuffering
hithau *pron conj* she (on her part),
    she also
hobaid (**-eidiau**) *nf* peck
hobi (**hobïau**) *nm* hobby
hoced (**-ion**) *nf* deceit, fraud
hocedu *vb* cheat, deceive, defraud
hocedwr (**-wyr**) *nm* cheat, fraud
hoci *nm* hockey
hocys *npl* mallows

hodi *vb* shoot, ear, run to seed
hoe *nf* spell, rest
hoeden (**-nau**) *nf* hoyden
hoedl (**-au**) *nf* lifetime, life
hoel, -en (**-ion**) *nf* nail
hoelio *vb* nail
hoeliwr (**-wyr**) *nm* nailer
hoen *nf* joy, gladness; vigour
hoenus *adj* joyous, blithesome,
    gay
hoenusrwydd *nm* liveliness,
    sprightliness
hoenyn (**-nau**) *nm* snare
hoew see **hoyw**
hofran *vb* hover
hogi *vb* sharpen, whet
hoff *adj* dear, fond; favourite
hoffi *vb* like, love
hoffter *nm* fondness; delight
hoffus *adj* lovable, amiable,
    affectionate
hogen (**-nod**) *nf* girl; **-naidd** *adj*
    girlish
hogfaen (**-feini**) *nm* whetstone,
    hone
hogi *vb* sharpen, whet
hogyn (**hogiau**) *nm* boy, lad
hongiad (**-au**) *nm* suspension
hongian *vb* hang, dangle
holgar *adj* inquisitive, curious
holi *vb* ask, question, inquire
holiad (**-au**) *nm* interrogation,
    question
holiadur (**-on**) *nm* questionnaire
holwr (**-wyr**) *nm* questioner,
    interrogator; catechist, question-
    master
holwyddoreg (**-au**) *nf* catechism
holwyddori *vb* catechize
holl *adj* all, whole
hollalluog *adj* almighty,
    omnipotent
hollalluowgrwydd *nm*
    omnipotence
hollbresennol *adj* omnipresent
hollbresenoldeb *nm* omnipresence
hollfyd *nm* universe
hollgyfoethog *adj* almighty

holliach adj whole, sound

hollol adj quite

hollt (-au) nf split, slit, cleft

hollti vb split, cleave, slit

hollwybodaeth nf omniscience

hollwybodol adj omniscient

homili (-iau) nf homily

hon pron f. of **hwn**

honcian vb waggle; jolt; limp

honedig adj alleged

honiad (-au) nm claim, assertion, allegation

honni vb assert, allege, profess, pretend

honno pron f. of **hwnnw**

hopran (-au) nf mill-hopper; mouth

hosan (-au) nf stocking

hoyw adj alert, sprightly, lively, gay

hoywdeb, -der nm sprightliness

hoywi vb brighten, smarten

hual (-au) nm fetter, shackle

hualu vb fetter, shackle

huan nf the sun

huawdl adj eloquent

hud nm magic, illusion, charm, enchantment

hudlath (-au) nf magic wand

hudo vb charm, allure, beguile

hudol adj enchanting ♦ (-ion) nm enchanter

hudoles (-au) nf enchantress, sorceress

hudoliaeth (-au) nf enchantment, allurement

hudolus adj enchanting, alluring

hudwr (-wyr) nm enticer, allurer

huddygl nm soot

hufen nm cream

hugan (-au) nf cloak, covering; rug

hulio vb cover, spread

hun (-au) nf sleep, slumber

hun pron self. **yn ei dŷ ei h.** his own house

hunan (-ain) pron self ♦ prefix self-

hunan-dyb nm self-conceit

hunangar adj self-loving, selfish

hunaniaeth nf identity

hunanladdiad nm self-murder, suicide

hunanol adj selfish, conceited

hunanoldeb nm selfishness; conceit

hunanymwadiad nm self-denial

hunanymwadu vb deny oneself

hunell (-au) nf wink (of sleep)

hunllef (-au) nf nightmare

huno vb sleep

huodledd nm eloquence

hur (-iau) nm hire, wage

hurio vb hire

huriwr (-wyr) nm hirer; hireling

hurt adj stunned, stupid

hurtio vb stun, stupefy

hurtrwydd nm stupidity

hurtyn (-nod) nm stupid, blockhead

hwb (hybiau) nm push; effort; lift

hwde (hwdiwch) vb imper take, accept

Hwngari nf Hungary

hwn adj, pron this (one); f **hon**

hwnnw adj, pron that one (absent); f **honno**

hwnt adv beyond, away, aside. **tu h.** beyond

hwp nm push; **-io, -o** vb push

hwrdd (hyrddod) nm ram

hwrdd (hyrddiau) nm impulse, stroke

hwre vb see **hwde**

hwsmon (-myn) nm farm-bailiff

hwtio vb hoot, hiss

hwy pron they, them

hwyad, -en (hwyaid) nf duck

hwyhau vb lengthen, elongate

hwyl (-iau) nf sail; humour; religious fervour

hwylbren (-nau, -ni) nm mast

hwylio vb sail; prepare, order

hwyliog adj fervent, eloquent

hwylus adj easy, convenient,

comfortable

hwyluso vb facilitate

hwylustod nm ease, facility, convenience

hwynt pron them, they

hwynt-hwy pron they, they themselves

hwyr adj late ♦ nm evening

hwyrach adv perhaps ♦ adj later

hwyrdrwm adj sluggish, drowsy, dull

hwyrfrydig adj slow, tardy, reluctant

hwyrfrydigrwydd nm tardiness, reluctance

hwyrhau vb get late

hwyrol adj evening

hwythau pron conj they (on their part), they also

hy adj bold

hybarch adj venerable

hyblyg adj flexible, pliant, pliable

hyblygrwydd nm flexibility, pliancy

hybu vb improve in health; promote

hyd (-au, -oedd) nm length ♦ prep to, till, as far as

hyder nm confidence, trust

hyderu vb confide, rely, trust

hyderus adj confident

hydred (-ion) nm longitude

hydredol adj longitudinal

hydref (-au) nm autumn. H. October

hydrefol adj autumnal

hydrin adj tractable, docile

hydwyll adj gullible

hydwylledd nm gullibility

hydwyth adj supple, elastic

hydwythedd nm elasticity

hydyn adj tractable, docile

hydd (-od) nm stag

hyddysg adj well versed, learned

hyf see hy

hyfder, -dra nm boldness

hyfedr adj expert, skilful, clever

hyfryd adj pleasant, delightful, agreeable

hyfrydu vb delight

hyfrydwch nm delight, pleasure

hyfwyn adj kindly, genial

hyfforddi vb direct, instruct, train

hyfforddiadol adj training

hyfforddiant nm instruction, training

hyfforddwr (-wyr) nm guide, instructor

hygar adj amiable

hygarwch nm amiability

hyglod adj celebrated, renowned, famous

hyglyw adj audible

hygoel adj credible

hygoeledd nm credibility; credulity

hygoelus adj credulous, gullible

hygyrch adj accessible

hyhi pron f emphat. of hi

hylaw adj handy, convenient; dexterous

hylif (-au) nm, adj fluid, liquid

hylithr adj slippery, fluent

hylosg adj combustible, inflammable

hylwydd adj prosperous

hyll adj ugly, hideous

hylltra nm ugliness

hyllu vb mar, disfigure

hyn adj, pron this; these; that

hynafgwr (-gwyr) nm old man, elder

hynafiad (-iaid) nm ancestor

hynafiaeth (-au) nf antiquity

hynafiaethol adj antiquarian

hynafiaethwr, -ydd (-wyr) nm antiquary

hynafol adj ancient

hynaws adj kind, genial

hynawsedd nm kindness, geniality

hynny adj, pron that; those

hynod adj noted, notable, remarkable

hynodi vb distinguish, characterize

hynodion *npl* peculiarities

hynodrwydd *nm* peculiarity

hynt (-iau, -oedd) *nf* way, course

hyrddio, -u *vb* hurl, impel

hyrddwynt (-oedd) *nm* hurricane

hyrwyddo *vb* facilitate, promote

hyrwyddwr (-wyr) *nm* sponsor, promoter

hysb *adj* dry, barren; *f* hesb

hysbio *vb* dry

hysbyddu *vb* exhaust, drain

hysbys *adj* known, evident. **dyn h.** *nm* wise man, sorcerer

hysbyseb (-ion) *nf* advertisement

hysbysebu *vb* advertise

hysbysebwr (-wyr) *nm* advertiser

hysbysiad (-au) *nm* announcement, advertisement

hysbysrwydd *nm* information

hysbysu *vb* inform, announce

hysbyswr (-wyr) *nm* informant, informer

hysian, -io *vb* hiss; set on, incite

hytrach *adv* rather

hywaith *adj* industrious, dexterous

hywedd *adj* trained, tractable

I

i *prep* to, into

i *pron* I, me

iâ *nm* ice

iach *adj* healthy, well

iachâd *nm* healing

iacháu *vb* heal; save

iachawdwr (-wyr) *nm* saviour

iachawdwriaeth *nf* salvation

iachawr (-wyr) *nm* healer

iachus, -ol *adj* healthy, healthful, wholesome

iad (-au) *nf* pate, cranium

iaith (ieithoedd) *nf* language. **yr i. fain** English

iâr (ieir) *nf* hen

iard (ierdydd) *nf* yard

iarll (ieirll) *nm* earl

iarllaeth (-au) *nf* earldom

iarlles (-au) *nf* countess

ias (-au) *nf* shiver; thrill

Iau *nm* Jupiter. **Dydd I.** Thursday

iau (ieuau) *nf* liver

iau (ieuau, ieuoedd) *nf* yoke

iawn *adj* right ♦ *nm* right; atonement ♦ *nf* very

iawndal *nm* compensation

iawnder (-au) *nm* right, equity

iawnol *adj* atoning, expiatory

idealaeth *nf* idealism

ideoleg (-au) *nf* ideology

idiom (-au) *nm* idiom

Iddew (-on) *nm* Jew

Iddewiaeth *nf* Judaism

Iddewes (-au) *nf* Jewess

Iddewig *adj* Jewish

iddwf *nm*: **tân i.** erysipelas

ie *adv* yes, yea

iechyd *nm* health

iechydaeth *nf* hygiene, sanitation

iechydol *adj* hygienic, sanitary

iechydwriaeth *nf* salvation

ieitheg *nf* philology

ieithegydd (-ion, -wyr) *nm* philologist

ieithwedd (-au, -ion) *nf* diction, (literary) style

ieithydd (-ion) *nm* linguist

ieithyddiaeth *nf* linguistics, philology

ieithyddol *adj* linguistic, philological

iet (-au, -iau) *nf* gate

ieuanc (-ainc) *adj* young

ieuenctid *nm* youth

ieuo *vb* yoke

ifanc (-ainc) *adj* young

ifori *nm* ivory

ig (-ion) *nm* hiccup

igam-ogam *adj* zigzag

igian *vb* hiccup

ing (-oedd) *nm* agony, anguish

ingol *adj* agonizing, agonized

ill *pron* they. **i. dau** they both

impio *vb* sprout, shoot; bud, graft

impyn nm graft; scion

inc nm ink

incil (-iau) nm tape

incwm nm income

India nf India

India'r Gorllewin npl West Indies

iod nm iota, jot

lôn nm the Lord

lonawr nm January

lôr nm the Lord

lorddonen nf Jordan

iorwg nm ivy

ir adj fresh, green, raw

irai nm ox-goad

iraid (ireidiau) nm grease

iraidd adj fresh, succulent, luxuriant

Iran nf Iran

Iraq nf Iraq

irder nm freshness, greenness

ireidd-dra nm freshness, vigour

ireiddio vb freshen

iriad (-au) nm lubrication, greasing

iro vb grease, smear, rub, anoint

irwr (-wyr) nm greaser

is adj inferior, lower ♦ prep below, under ♦ prefix under-, sub-, vice-

isadran (-nau) nf subsection

Isalmaen nf Holland

isel adj low; base; humble; depressed

iselder (-au) nm lowness, depth; depression

iseldir (-oedd) nm lowland

Iseldiroedd: Yr I. npl Netherlands

iselfryd adj humble-minded

iselfrydedd nm humility, condescension

iselhau vb lower, abase, degrade

isetholiad (-au) nm by-election

is-gadeirydd nm vice-chairman

is-ganghellor nm vice-chancellor

is-gapten (-iaid, -einiaid) nm lieutenant

isgell nm broth, stock

isiarll (-ieirll) nm viscount

islaw prep below, beneath

isod adv below, beneath

isop nm hyssop

isosod vb sublet

isradd (-iaid) nm inferior, subordinate

israddol adj inferior

israddoldeb nm inferiority

Israel nf Israel

iswasanaethgar adj subservient

isymwybod nm subconscious

isymwybyddiaeth nf subconsciousness

ithfaen nm granite

Iwerddon nf Ireland

Iwerddon Rydd nf Eire

Iwerydd nm the Atlantic

Iwgoslavia nf Yugoslavia

iwrch (iyrchod) nm roebuck

J

jac codi baw nm JCB

jac-y-do nm jackdaw

jam nm jam ♦ -io vb preserve

Jamaica nf Jamaica

jar (-iau) nf jar, hot water bottle

jersi (-s) nf jersey

jest adv just, almost

jeti (-iau) nm jetty

jetlif nm jet stream

ji-binc (-od) nf chaffinch

jîns npl jeans

job (-sys) nf job

jobyn nm job

jôc nf joke

jocan vb joke

joci (-s) nm jockey

jwg (jygiau) nf jug

jyngl (-oedd) nm jungle

L

label (-i) nf label

labelu vb label

labordy (-dai) nm laboratory

labro vb labour
labrwr (-wyr) nm labourer
lafant nm lavender
lamp (-au) nf lamp
lamplen (-ni) nf lampshade
lapio vb lap, wrap
larwm nm alarm
lawnt (-iau) nf lawn
lefain nm leaven
lefeinio vb leaven
lefeinllyd adj leavened
lefel (-au) nf level
leicio vb like
lein (-iau) nf clothes line, line-out
   (rugby)
lesbiad (-iaid) nf lesbian
letys npl (-en nf) lettuce
Libanus nf Lebanon
libart nm back-yard
Libya nf Libya
lifft (-iau) nm lift
lifrai nm/f livery
lili nf lily
lindys npl (-yn nm) caterpillars
locust (-iaid) nm locust
lodes see **herlodes**
loetran vb loiter
lol nf nonsense
lolfa (-feydd) nf lounge
lolian vb talk nonsense
lôn (lonydd) nf lane
loncian vb jog
lonciwr (-wyr) nm jogger
lori (-iau) nf lorry
losin npl (-en nf) sweets
lot (-iau) nf lot
Luxembourg nf Luxembourg
lwans, lwfans nm allowance
lwc nf luck
lwcus adj lucky
lwmp (lympiau) nm lump

LL

llabed (-au) nf lappet, lapel, flap
llabwst (-ystiau) nm lubber, lout

llabyddio vb stone
llac adj slack, loose, lax
llacio vb slacken, loosen, relax
llacrwydd nm slackness, laxity
llacs nm mud, dirt
llacsog adj muddy, dirty
llach (-iau) nf lash, slash
llachar adj bright, brilliant,
   flashing
llachio vb lash, slash
Lladin nf Latin
lladmerydd (-ion) nm interpreter
lladrad (-au) nm theft, robbery
lladradaidd adj stealthy, furtive
lladrata vb thieve, steal
lladron see **lleidr**
lladrones (-au) nf female thief
lladronllyd adj thievish, pilfering
lladd vb cut; kill, slay, slaughter
lladd-dy (-dai) nm slaughter-house
lladdedig (-ion) adj killed, slain
lladdedigaeth (-au), **lladdfa**,
   (-fau, -feydd) nf slaughter, a
   tiring job
lladdwr (-wyr) nm killer, slayer
llaes adj long, loose. **Y treiglad ll.**
   spirant mutation
llaesod(r) nf litter (for animals)
llaesu vb slacken, loosen, relax,
   droop, flag
llaeth nm milk
llaetha vb yield milk
llaethdy (-dai) nm milk-house,
   dairy
llaethog adj rich in milk; milky
llafar nm utterance, speech ♦ adj
   vocal; loud
llafariad (-iaid) nf vowel
llafn (-au) nm blade
llafrwyn npl (-en nf) bulrushes
llafur (-iau) nm labour; corn
llafurfawr adj elaborate; laborious
llafurio vb labour, toil; till
llafurlu (-oedd) nm manpower,
   labour force, workforce
llafurus adj laborious, toilsome,
   painstaking

llafurwr (-wyr) nm labourer, husbandman

llai adj smaller

llaid nm mud, mire

llain (lleiniau) nf patch, piece, narrow strip

llais (lleisiau) nm voice, vote

llaith adj damp, moist

llall (lleill) pron other, another

llam (-au) nm stride, leap, jump, bound

llamhidydd (llamidyddion) nm porpoise

llamsachus adj prancing, frisky

llamu vb stride, leap, bound

llan (-nau) nf church; village

llanast(r) nm confusion, mess

llanc (-iau) nm young man, youth, lad

llances (-au, -i) nf young woman, lass

llannerch (llennyrch), **llanerchau** (-i, -ydd) nf spot, patch, glade

llanw nm flow (of tide) ♦ vb flow, fill

llaprwth nm lout

llariaidd adj mild, meek, gentle

llarieidd-dra nm meekness, gentleness

llarieiddio vb soothe, mollify

llarp (-iau) nm shred, clout

llarpio vb rend, tear, mangle, maul

llarpiog adj tattered, ragged

llaswyr (-au) nm psalter

llatai (-eion) n coll love-messenger

llath (-au) nf yard, wand

llathen (-ni) nf yard

llathr adj bright, glossy, smooth

llathraidd adj smooth; of fine growth

llathru vb polish

llau npl (lleuen npl) lice

llaw (dwylaw, dwylo) nf hand

llawcio vb gulp, gorge, gobble

llawchwith adj left-handed

llawdde adj dexterous

llawddryll (-iau) nm pistol, revolver

llawen adj merry, joyful, glad, cheerful

llawenhau vb rejoice, gladden

llawenychu vb rejoice

llawenydd nm joy, gladness, mirth

llawer (-oedd) nm, adj, adv many, much

llawes (llewys) nf sleeve

llawfaeth adj reared by hand

llawfeddyg (-on) nm surgeon

llawfeddygaeth nf surgery

llawfeddygol adj surgical

llaw-fer nf shorthand

llawfom (-iau) nf grenade

llawforwyn (-forynion) nf handmaid

llawn adj full ♦ adv quite

llawnder, -dra nm fullness, abundance

llawr (lloriau) nm floor, ground, earth

llawryf (-oedd) nm laurel, bay

llawryfog, -ol adj laureate

llawysgrif (-au) nf manuscript

llawysgrifen nf handwriting

lle (-oedd, llefydd) nm place

llecyn (-nau) nm place, spot

llech (-au) nf slab, flag, slate

llechgi (-gwn) nm sneak

llechres (-i) nf table, catalogue, list

llechu vb hide, shelter; lurk, skulk

llechwedd (-au, -i) nf slope, hillside

llechwraidd adj stealthy, underhand, insidious

lled (-au) nm breadth, width

lled adv partly, rather

lledaenu vb spread, disseminate, circulate

lleden (lledod) nf flat-fish

llediaith nf/m foreign accent

llednais adj modest, delicate; meek

llednant (-nentydd) nf tributary

lledneisrwydd nm modesty,

delicacy

lled-orwedd *vb* recline, lounge, loll

lledr (-au) *nm* leather. ll. y gwefusau gums

lledred (-ion) *nm* latitude

lledrith *nm* magic, illusion, phantasm

lledrithio *vb* appear, haunt

lledrithiol *adj* illusory, illusive

lledrwr (-wyr) *nm* leather-merchant

lledryw *adj* degenerate

lledu *vb* widen, broaden, expand, spread

lleddf *adj* slanting; flat, minor; plaintive

lleddfolyn (-olion) *nm* sedative

lleddfu (-iaid) *vb* flatten; soften, soothe, allay

llef (-au) *nf* voice, cry

llefain *vb* cry

llefareg *nf* speech training

llefaru *vb* speak, utter

llefarwr (-wyr), -ydd (-ion) *nm* speaker

lleferydd *nm/f* utterance, voice, speech

llefn *adj* f. of llyfn

llefrith *nm* sweet milk, new milk, milk

llegach *adj* weak, feeble, infirm, decrepit

lleng (-oedd) *nf* legion

lleiaf *adj* least, smallest

lleiafrif (-au) *nm* minority

lleian (-od) *nf* nun

lleiandy (-dai) *nm* nunnery, convent

lleibio *vb* lap, lick

lleidiog *adj* miry

lleidr (lladron) *nm* thief, robber

lleiddiad (-iaid) *nm* assassin

lleihad *nm* diminution, decrease

lleihau *vb* lessen, diminish, decrease

lleill see llall

lleisio *vb* sound, utter, voice

lleisiol *adj* vocal

lleisiwr (-wyr) *nm* vocalist

lleithder, -dra *nm* damp, moisture

lleithig *nf* couch; footstool

lleitho *vb* damp, moisten

llem *adj* f. of llym

llen (-ni) *nf* sheet; veil, curtain

llên *nf* literature, lore, learning

llencyn *nm* stripling, lad

llencynod *nm* adolescence

llengar *adj* literary, learned

llengig *nf* diaphragm, midriff. tor ll. rupture

llên-ladrad (-au) *nm* plagiarism

llenor (-ion) *nm* literary man

llenwi *vb* fill; flow in

llenydda *vb* practise literature

llenyddiaeth (-au) *nf* literature

llenyddol *adj* literary

lleol *adj* local

lleoli *vb* locate; localize

lleoliad *nm* location; localization

llercian *vb* lurk, loiter

lles *nm* benefit, profit, good, advantage. y wladwriaeth les the welfare state

llesâd *nm* advantage, profit, benefit

llesáu *vb* benefit, advantage

llesg *adj* feeble, faint; languid, sluggish

llesgáu *vb* weaken, languish, faint

llesgedd *nm* weakness, languor, debility

llesmair (-meiriau) *nm* faint, swoon

llesmeirio *vb* faint, swoon

llesol *adj* advantageous, profitable, beneficial

llestair, llesteirio *vb* hinder, impede, baulk

llestr (-i) *nm* vessel

llesyddiaeth *nf* utilitarianism

lletbai *adj* askew, awry; oblique

lletchwith *adj* awkward, clumsy

lletem (-au) *nf* wedge, stud, rivet

lletraws *adj* diagonal

lletwad (-au) *nf* ladle

llety (-au) *nm* lodging(s)

lletya *vb* lodge

lletygar *adj* hospitable

lletygarwch *nm* hospitality

lletywr (-wyr) *nm* lodger; host

lletywraig (-wragedd) *nf* landlady

llethol *adj* oppressive, overpowering

llethr (-au) *nf* slope, declivity

llethrog *adj* sloping, steep, declining

llethu *vb* overlie; smother; oppress, overpower, overwhelm

lleuad (-au) *nf* moon

lleuog *adj* lousy

llew (-od) *nm* lion. **dant y ll.** dandelion

llewaidd *adj* lionlike, leonine

llewes (-au) *nf* lioness

llewpart (-pardiaid) *nm* leopard

llewych *nm* light, brightness

llewyg (-on) *nm* faint, swoon

llewygu *vb* faint, swoon

llewyrch *nm* brightness, radiance, gleam

llewyrchu *vb* shine

llewyrchus *adj* flourishing, prosperous

lleyg (-ion) *adj* lay

lleygwr (-wyr) *nm* layman

lliain (-einiau) *nm* linen; cloth; towel

lliaws *nm* host, multitude

llibin *adj* limp, feeble; awkward, clumsy

llid *nm* wrath; irritation, inflammation

llidiart (-ardau) *nm* gate

llidio *vb* be angry, chafe, inflame

llidiog *adj* angry, wrathful; inflamed

llidiowgrwydd *nm* wrath, indignation

llidus *adj* inflamed

llieiniwr (-wyr) *nm* linen-draper

llif (-iau) *nf* saw

llif (-ogydd) *nm* stream, flood, current

llifbridd *nm* alluvium

llifddor (-au) *nf* floodgate

llifddwfr (-ddyfroedd) *nm* flood, torrent

llifeiriant (-iaint) *nm* flood

llifeirio *vb* flow, stream

llifeiriol *adj* streaming, overflowing

llifio *vb* saw

llifiwr (-wyr) *nm* sawyer

llifo *vb* flow, stream

llifo *vb* grind (*tool*)

llifo *vb* dye

llifolau (-euadau) *nm* floodlight

llifwr (-wyr) *nm* dyer

llifyn (-nau, -ion) *nm* dye

llininio *vb* streamline

llin *nm* flax. **had ll.** linseed

llinach (-au) *nf* lineage, pedigree

llindagu *vb* strangle, throttle, choke

llinell (-au) *nf* line. **ll. gais** try line. **ll. gwsg** touch-in-goal

llinelliad (-au) *nm* lineation, drawing

llinellog *adj* lined, ruled

llinellol *adj* lineal

llinglwm *nm*: **cwlwm ll.** tight knot

lliniaru *vb* ease, soothe, allay

llinorog *adj* eruptive; purulent; suppurating

llinos (-od) *nf* linnet

llinyn (-nau) *nm* line, string, twine

llinynnu *vb* string

llipa *adj* limp, weak

llipryn (-nod) *nm* hobbledehoy, weakling

lliprynnaidd *adj* limp, flabby

llith (-iau, -oedd) *nf* lesson, lecture; bait, mash

llithio *vb* entice, allure, seduce; feed

llithriad (-au) *nm* slip, glide

llithren (-nau) *nf* chute

llithrig *adj* slippery, glib, fluent

llithrigrwydd *nm* slipperiness, glibness

llithro vb slip, glide, slide
lliw (-iau) nm colour, hue, dye
lliwio vb colour, dye
lliwiog adj coloured
llo (lloi) nm calf
lloc (-iau) nm fold, pen
lloches (-au) nf refuge, shelter, den
llochesu vb harbour, shelter
llochi vb stroke, caress, fondle
llodig adj in heat (of a sow)
llodrau npl trousers, breeches
Lloegr nf England
lloer (-au) nf moon
lloeren (-ni, -nau) nf satellite
lloerig adj, nm lunatic
llofnod, -iad (-au) nm signature
llofnodi vb sign
llofrudd (-ion) nm murderer
llofruddiaeth (-au) nf murder
llofruddio vb murder
llofruddiog adj guilty of murder
lloffa vb glean
lloffion npl gleanings
llofft (-ydd) nf loft, bedroom, gallery
lloffwr (-wyr) nm gleaner
lloffyn nm bundle of gleanings
llog (-au) nm interest
llogi vb hire
llogwr (-wyr) nm hirer
llong (-au) nf ship
llongddrylliad (-au) nm shipwreck
llongwr (-wyr) nm sailor
llongwriaeth nf seamanship
llom adj f. of **llwm**
llon adj glad, merry
llonaid, llond nm full
llonder nm gladness, joy
llongyfarch vb congratulate
llongyfarchiad (-au, -archion) nm congratulation
lloniant nm joy, cheer
llonni vb cheer, gladden
llonydd adj quiet, still ♦ nm quiet, calm
llonyddu vb quiet, still, calm

llonyddwch nm quietness, quiet
llorgynllun (-iau) nm ground plan
llorio vb floor, ground (rugby)
llorwedd adj horizontal
llosg nm, adj burning
llosgach nm incest
llosgadwy adj combustible
llosgfa (-fâu, -feydd) nf burning, inflammation
llosgfynydd (-oedd) nm volcano
llosgi vb burn, scorch; smart
llosgwrn (-yrnau) nm tail
llosgydd (-ion) nm incinerator
llu (-oedd) nm host
lluched npl (-en nf) lightning
lluchfa (-feydd) nf snowdrift
lluchio vb throw, fling, pelt
lluchiwr (-wyr) nm thrower
lludlyd adj ashy
lludu, lludw nm ashes, ash
lludded nm weariness, fatigue
lluddedig adj wearied, tired, fatigued
lluddedu vb tire, weary
lluddias, -io vb hinder; forbid
lluest (-au) nm tent, booth
lluestfa (-feydd) nf encampment
lluestu vb encamp
lluesty (-tai) nm tent, booth
llugoer adj lukewarm
lluman (-au) nm banner, standard, ensign
llumanwr (-wyr) nm linesman
llumon nm chimney stack, peak
llun (-iau) nm form, image, picture
Llun, Dydd Llun nm Monday
Llundain nf London
lluniad (-au) nm drawing
lluniadaeth (-au) nf draughtsmanship
lluniaeth nm food, nourishment
lluniaethu vb order, ordain, decree
lluniedydd nm draughtsman
lluniaidd adj shapely
llunio vb form, shape, fashion
lluniwr (-wyr) nm former, maker
llun-recordydd (-ion) nm video-

tape recorder

lluosflwydd adj perennial

lluosi vb multiply

lluosiad nm multiplication

lluosill, -afog adj polysyllabic

lluosog adj numerous; plural

lluosogi vb multiply

lluosogiad nm multiplication

lluoswm nm product (maths)

lluosydd nm multiplier

llurgunio vb mangle, mutilate

llurguniwr (-wyr) nm mangler, mutilator

llurig (-au) nf coat of mail, cuirass

llurigog adj mail-clad

llus npl (-en nf) bilberries, whinberries

llusern (-au) nf lantern, lamp

llusg (-ion) nm draught; drag

llusgfad (-au) nm tugboat

llusgo vb drag; trail; crawl; drawl

llusgwr (-wyr) nm dragger, slowcoach

llutrod nm mire, ashes, debris

lluwch nm dust; spray; snowdrift

lluydd nm host, army

lluyddu vb mobilise

llw (-on) nm oath

llwch nm dust, powder

llwdn (llydnod) nm young of animals

llwfr adj timid, cowardly

llwfrdra nm cowardice

llwfrddyn, -gi nm coward

llwfrhau vb faint

llwglyd adj hungry, famished

llwgr nm corruption ♦ adj corrupt

llwgrwobrwy (-on) nm bribe

llwgrwobrwyo vb bribe

llwgu vb starve, famish

llwm adj bare; destitute; poor; f **llom**

llwnc nm gulp, swallow; gullet

llwncdestun nm toast (health)

llwr, llwrw nm track. **ll. ei ben** headlong. **ll. ei gefn** backwards

llwy (-au) nf spoon; ladle

llwyaid (-eidiau) nf spoonful

llwybr (-au) nm path, track

llwybreiddio vb direct, forward

llwybro vb walk

llwyd adj brown; grey; pale; hoary

llwydaidd adj greyish, palish

llwydi, llwydni nm greyness; mould, mildew

llwydnos nf dusk, twilight

llwydo vb turn grey; become mouldy

llwydrew nm hoar-frost

llwydrewi vb cast hoar-frost

llwydd, -iant nm success, prosperity

llwyddiannus adj successful, prosperous

llwyddo vb succeed, prosper

llwyfan (-nau) nm/f platform, stage

llwyfandir (-oedd) nm plateau

llwyfannu vb stage

llwyfen (llwyf) nf elm

llwyn (-i) nm grove; bush

llwyn (-au) nf loin

llwynog (-od) nm fox

llwynoges (-au) nf vixen

llwynwst nf lumbago

llwyo vb use a spoon; ladle

llwyr adj entire, complete, total ♦ adv entirely, altogether ♦ prefix total

llwyredd nm entireness, completeness

llwyrymatal, -ymwrthod vb abstain totally

llwyrymwrthodwr (-wyr) nm teetotaller

llwyth (-au) nm tribe, clan

llwyth (-i) nm load, burden

llwytho vb load, burden

llwythog adj laden, burdened

llychlyd adj dusty

Llychlyn nf Scandinavia

llychwino vb spot, tarnish, soil, sully

llychyn nm particle of dust, mote

llydan adj broad, wide

Llydaw nf Brittany

llydnu vb bring forth, foal

llyfn adj smooth, sleek; f **llefn**

llyfnder, -dra nm smoothness, sleekness

llyfndew adj plump, sleek

llyfnhau vb smooth, level

llyfnu vb smooth, level; harrow

llyfr (-au) nm book

llyfrbryf (-ed) nm bookworm

llyfrgell (-oedd) nf library

llyfrgellydd (-ion) nm librarian

llyfrifeg nm/f book-keeping

llyfrnod (-au) nm bookmark

llyfrwerthwr (-wyr) nm bookseller

llyfrydd (-ion) nm bibliographer, transcriber of books

llyfryddiaeth nf bibliography

llyfrfa nf (-feydd) library; bookroom; official publishing house of religious denomination, government etc

llyfryn (-nau) nm booklet, pamphlet

llyfu vb lick

llyffant (-od, llyffaint) nm frog, toad

llyffethair (-eiriau) nf fetter, shackle

llyffetheirio vb fetter, shackle

llyg (-od) nm/f shrew (-mouse)

llygad (llygaid) nm eye. **ll. y dydd** daisy

llygad-dynnu vb bewitch

llygadog adj eyed, sharp-eyed

llygadrwth adj wide-eyed, staring

llygadrythu vb stare

llygadu vb eye

llygatgraff adj keen-eyed, sharp-sighted

llygedyn nm ray of light

llygeidiog adj eyed

llygoden (llygod) nf mouse. **ll. fawr, ll. ffrengig** rat

llygota vb catch mice

llygotwr (-wyr) nm mouser,

ratter; f **llygotwraig**

llygradwy adj corruptible

llygredig adj corrupt, depraved, degraded

llygredigaeth (-au) nf corruption

llygredd nm corruptness, depravity

llygriad (-au) nm corruption, adulteration

llygru vb corrupt, adulterate

llygrwr (-wyr) nm corrupter, adulterator

llynges (-au) nf fleet, navy

llyngeswr (-wyr) nm navy-man

llyngesydd (-ion) nm admiral

llyngyr npl (-en nf) (intestinal) worms

llym adj sharp, keen, severe; f **llem**

llymaid (-eidiau) nm sip, drink

llymarch (llymeirch) nm oyster

llymder nm sharpness, keenness, severity

llymder, -dra nm bareness, poverty

llymeitian, -io vb sip, tipple

llymeitiwr (-wyr) nm tippler, sot

llymhau vb make bare (from **llwm**)

llymhau vb sharpen (from **llym**)

llymriaid npl (-ien nf) sand-eels

llymru nm flummery

llymsur adj acrid

llymu vb sharpen, whet

llyn (-noedd) nm lake, pond, pool

llynciad (-au) nm draught, gulp

llyncu vb swallow, gulp, absorb

llyncwr (-wyr) nm swallower, guzzler

llynedd nf last year

llyo vb lick

llys (-oedd) nm court, hall, palace

llysaidd adj courtly, polite

llysblant npl step-children

llyschwaer nf step-sister

llysenw (-au) nm nickname

llysenwi vb nickname

llysfab nm step-son

llysfam nf step-mother

llysferch *nf* step-daughter

llysfrawd *nm* step-brother

llysgenhadaeth *nf* embassy, legation

llysgenhadol *adj* ambassadorial

llysgenhadwr, llysgennad (-genhadon) *nm* ambassador

llysiau *npl* (-ieuyn *nm*) herbs, vegetables

llysieuol *adj* herbal, vegetable

llysieuydd (-ion, -wyr) *nm* botanist; vegetarian

llysnafedd *nm* snivel, slime

llystad *nm* step-father

llyswenwyn *nm* herbicide

llysysol *adj* herbivorous

llysywen (llysywod) *nf* eel

llysywenna *vb* catch eels

llythrennol *adj* literal

llythyr (-au) *nm* letter, epistle

llythyrdy (-dai) *nm* post-office

llythyren (llythrennau) *nf* letter, type

llythyrwr (-wyr) *nm* letter-writer

llyw (-iau) *nm* ruler; rudder, helm

llywaeth *adj* hand-fed, tame, pet

llywiawdwr (-wyr) *nm* ruler, governor

llywio *vb* rule, govern, direct, steer

llywiwr (-wyr) *nm* steersman, helmsman

llywodraeth (-au) *nf* government

llywodraethol *adj* governing, dominant

llywodraethu *vb* govern, rule

llywodraethwr (-wyr) *nm* governor, ruler

llywydd (-ion) *nm* president

llywyddiaeth (-au) *nf* presidency

llywyddol *adj* presidential

llywyddu *vb* preside

M

mab (meibion) *nm* boy, son; man, male

mabaidd *adj* filial

maban (-od) *nm* babe, baby

mabandod *nm* childhood, infancy

mabinogi *nm* tale, story

mablygad *nm* eyeball

mabmaeth (-au, -od) *nm* foster-son

maboed *nm* childhood, infancy, youth

mabolaeth *nf* sonship; boyhood, youth

mabolaidd *adj* youthful, boyish

mabolgamp (-au) *nf* game, sport, feat

mabsant *nm* patron saint

mabwysiad *nm* adoption

mabwysiadol *adj* adoptive; adopted

mabwysiadu *vb* adopt

macrell (mecryll) *nf/m* mackerel

macsu *vb* to brew

macwy (-aid) *nm* youth, page

machlud, -o *vb* set, go down. m. haul sunset

machludiad *nm* setting, going down

machnïydd *nm* mediator

madarch *npl* (-en *nf*) mushrooms

madfall (-od) *nm* lizard

madrondod *nm* giddiness, stupefaction

madroni *vb* make or become giddy

madru *vb* putrefy, fester, rot

madruddyn *nm* cartilage. m. y cefn spinal cord

maddau *vb* pardon, forgive, remit

maddeuant *nm* pardon, forgiveness

maddeugar *adj* of a forgiving disposition

maddeuol *adj* pardoning, forgiving

maddeuwr (-wyr) *nm* pardoner

mae vb is, are; there is, there are

maeden nf slut, jade

maeddu see **baeddu**

maen (**meini**) nm stone

maenol, maenor (-**au**) nf manor

maentumio vb maintain

maer (-**od, meiri**) nm mayor

maeres (-**au**) nf mayoress

maerol adj mayoral

maeryddiaeth nf mayoralty

maes (**meysydd**) nm field. **i. m.** out.
m. glanio airport

maesglaf (-**gleifion**) nm outpatient

maeslywydd (-**ion**) nm field-
marshal

maestir (-**oedd**) nm open country,
plain

maestref (-**i, -ydd**) nf suburb

maeth nm nourishment, nutriment

maethlon adj nourishing,
nutritious

maethu vb nourish, nurture

maethydd (-**ion**) nm nourisher

maethyn (-**nau**) nm nutrient;
suckling

mafon npl (-**en** nf) raspberries

magl (-**au**) nf snare; mesh

maglu vb snare, mesh, trip

magnel (-**au**) nf gun, cannon

magnelaeth nf artillery

magnelwr (-**wyr**) nm gunner

magnesiwm nm magnesium

magnetedd nm/f magnetism

magneteiddio vb magnetise

magu vb breed, rear, nurse; gain,
acquire

magwraeth nf nourishment,
nurture

magwyr (-**ydd**) nf wall

maharen (**meheryn**) nm ram;
wether

Mai nm May

mai conj that it is

maidd nm whey

main (**meinion**) adj fine, slender,
thin. **m. y cefn** small of the back

mainc (**meinciau**) nf bench, form,
seat

maint nm size, quantity, number

maintioli nm size, stature

maip npl (**meipen** nf) turnips

maith (**meithion**) adj long, tedious

mâl adj ground

malais nm malice

maldod nm dalliance, affection

maldodi vb pet, pamper, indulge

maleisus adj malicious

maleithiau npl chilblains

malio vb care, mind, heed

Malta nf Malta

malu vb grind, mince, chop, smash

malurio vb pound; crumble,
moulder

malurion npl fragments, debris

malwod npl (-**en, malwen** nf)
snails

malwr (-**wyr**) nm grinder

mall nf blight. **y f.** Belial, perdition

malltod nm rot, blight, blast

mallu vb rot, blast

mam (-**au**) nf mother. **mam-gu**
grandmother

mamaeth (-**od**) nf nurse

mamal (-**iaid**) nm mammal

mamiaith (-**ieithoedd**) nf mother-
tongue

mamog (-**iaid**) nf dam, sheep with
young

mamolaeth (-**au**) nf maternity

mamwlad (-**wledydd**) nf
motherland

man (-**nau**) nm/f place, spot;
blemish

mân adj small, fine, petty

mandyllog adj porous

maneg (**menig**) nf glove, gauntlet

mangre nf place, spot

manion npl scraps, trifles, minutiæ

mantais (-**eision**) nf advantage

manteisio vb take advantage,
profit

manteisiol adj advantageous

mantell (-**oedd, mentyll**) nf mantle

mantellog adj mantled

mantol (**-ion**) *nf* balance
mantolen (**-ni**) *nf* balance-sheet
mantoli *vb* turn scale, balance, weigh
manwaidd *adj* delicate, fine
mân-werthu *vb* retail
manwl *adj* exact, precise, strict, particular
manwl-gywir *adj* precise
manylion *npl* particulars, details
manylrwydd *nm* exactness, precision
manylu *vb* go into detail, particularize
manylwch *nm* exactness, precision
map (**-iau**) *nm* map
mapio *vb* map
mapiwr (**-wyr**) *nm* cartographer
marblen (**marblys**) *nf* marble
marc (**-iau**) *nm* mark
marcio *vb* mark
march (**meirch**) *nm* horse, stallion
marchlu (**-oedd**) *nm* cavalry
marchnad (**-oedd**) *nf* market
marchnadfa (**-oedd**) *nf* marketplace
marchnata *vb* market, trade
marchnatwr (**-wyr**) *nm* merchant
marchnerth (**-oedd**) *nm* horsepower
marchocáu *vb* ride a horse
marchog (**-ion**) *nm* horseman, rider; knight
marchogaeth *vb* ride
marchogwr (**-wyr**) *nm* rider, horseman
marchredyn *npl* (**-en** *nf*) polypody fern
marchwellt *nm* tall, coarse grass
marian *nm* holm, strand, moraine
marlad *nm* drake
marmalêd (**-au**) *nm* marmalade
marmor *nm* marble
marsialydd (**-ion**) *nm* marshal
marsiandïaeth *nf* merchandise
marsiandïwr (**-wyr**) *nm* merchant
marsipan *nm* marzipan

marw *vb* die
marw (**meirw, meirwon**) *n, adj* dead
marwaidd *adj* lifeless, sluggish, moribund
marwdon *nf* dandruff
marweidd-dra *nm* deadness, sluggishness
marweiddio *vb* deaden, mortify
marwhad *nm* mortification
marwhau *vb* deaden, mortify
marwnad (**-au**) *nf* lament, elegy
marwol *adj* deadly, mortal, fatal
marwolaeth (**-au**) *nf* death
marwoldeb *nm* mortality
marwolion *npl* mortals
marwor *npl* (**-yn** *nm*) embers; charcoal
marwydos *npl* embers
masarnen (**masarn**) *nf* sycamore
masgl (**-au**) *nf* shell, pod
masglo, -u *vb* shell; interlace
masnach (**-au**) *nf* trade, traffic, commerce
masnachol *adj* commercial, business
masnachu *vb* do business, trade, traffic
masnachwr (**-wyr**) *nm* dealer, merchant
masw *adj* wanton
maswedd *nm* wantoness, ribaldry
masweddol *adj* wanton, ribald
maswr (**-wyr**) *nm* outside half
mat (**-iau**) *nm* mat
mater (**-ion**) *nm* matter
materol *adj* material; materialistic
materoliaeth *nf* materialism
matog (**-au**) *nf* mattock
matras (**-resi**) *nm* mattress
matrics (**-au**) *nm* matrix
matsien (**matsys**) *nf* match
math (**-au**) *nm* sort, kind
mathemateg *nm* mathematics
mathru *vb* trample, tread
mathrwr (**-wyr**) *nm* trampler
mawl *nm* praise

mawn coll n (-en nf) peat

mawnog adj peaty ♦ nf peat-bog

mawr (-ion) adj big, great, large

mawredd nm greatness, grandeur, majesty

mawreddog adj grand, majestic; grandiose

mawrfrydig adj magnanimous

mawrfrydigrwydd nm magnanimity

mawrhau vb magnify, enlarge

mawrhydi nm majesty

Mawrth nm Mars; March. **Dydd M.** Tuesday

mawrygu vb magnify, extol

mebyd nm childhood, infancy, youth

mecaneg nf mechanics

mecanwaith (-weithiau) nm mechanism

mecanyddol adj mechanical

mechniaeth nf surety, bail

mechnio vb go bail, become surety

mechniol adj vicarious

mechnïydd (-ion) nm surety, bail

medel (-au) nf reaping; reaping party

medelwr (-wyr) nm reaper

medi vb reap

Medi nm September

medr nm skill, ability

medru vb know, be able

medrus adj clever, skilful

medrusrwydd nm cleverness, skilfulness, skill

medrydd (-ion) nm gauge

medd nm mead

medd vb says

meddal adj soft, tender

meddalhau, meddalu vb soften

meddalwch nm softness

meddalwedd nm softwear

meddiannol adj possessing, possessive

meddiannu vb possess, occupy

meddiant (-iannau) nm possession

meddu vb possess, own

meddw (-on) adj drunk, intoxicated

meddwdod nm drunkenness, intoxication

meddwi vb get drunk, intoxicate, inebriate

meddwl vb think; mean ♦ (-yliau) nm thought; meaning; opinion

meddwol adj intoxicating

meddwyn (-won) nm drunkard, inebriate

meddyg (-on) nm physician, doctor

meddygaeth nf medicine

meddygfa (-feydd) nf surgery

meddyginiaeth (-au) nf medicine, remedy

meddyginiaethol adj medicinal, remedial

meddyginiaethu vb cure, remedy, heal

meddygol adj medicinal; medical

meddylfryd nm mind, affection, bent

meddylgar adj thoughtful

meddylgarwch nm thoughtfulness

meddyliol adj mental, intellectual

meddyliwr (-wyr) nm thinker

mefus npl (-en nf) strawberries

megin (-au) nf bellows

megino vb work bellows, blow

megis conj, prep as, so as, like a

Mehefin nm June

meicrobioleg nmlf microbiology

meicro-brosesydd nm microprocessor

meicroffon (-au) nm microphone

meicro-sglodyn (-ion) nm microchip

meicrosgop (-au) nm microscope

meichiad (-iaid) nm swineherd

meichiau (-iafon) nm surety, bail

meidrol adj finite

meidroldeb nm finiteness

meiddio vb dare, venture

meiddion npl curds and whey

meiddlyd *adj* wheyey, curdled

meilart *nm* drake

meillion *npl* (-en *nf*) clover

meim (-iau) *nm/f* mime

meimio *vb* mime

meinder *nm* fineness, slenderness

meindio *vb* mind, care

meinedd *nm* slender part, small

meingefn *nm* small of the back

meinhau *vb* grow slender, taper

meini see **maen**

meinllais *nm* shrill voice, treble

meintoli *vb* quantify

meintoliad *nm* quantification

meinwe (-bledd) *nf* tissue

meipen (maip) *nf* turnip

meirch see **march**

meirioli *vb* thaw

meirw see **marw**

meistr (-iaid, -i, -adoedd) *nm* master

meistres (-i) *nf* mistress

meistrolaeth *nf* mastery

meistrolgar *adj* masterful, masterly

meistroli *vb* master

meitin *nm:* **ers m.** some time since

meitr (-au) *nm* mitre

meithder *nm* length

meithrin *vb* nurture, rear, foster

meithrinfa (-oedd) *nf* nursery

mêl *nm* honey

mela *vb* gather honey

melan *nf* melancholy

melen *adj* f. of **melyn**

melfared *nm* corduroy

melfed *nm* velvet

melin (-au) *nf* mill

melinydd (-ion) *nm* miller

melodaidd *adj* melodious

melodi *nm* melody

melyn *adj* yellow; *f* **melen** ♦ *nm* yellow. **m. wy** yolk of egg. **Y clefyd m.** jaundice

melynaidd *adj* yellowish, tawny

melynder, -dra *nm* yellowness

melynddu *adj* tawny, swarthy

melyngoch *adj* yellowish red, orange

melyni *nm* yellowness; jaundice

melynu *vb* yellow

melynwyn *adj* yellowish white, cream

melys *adj* sweet ♦ (-ion) *npl* sweets

melyster, -tra *nm* sweetness

melysu *vb* sweeten

mellt *npl* (-en *nf*) lightning

melltennu *vb* flash lightning

melltigaid, -edig *adj* accursed, cursed

melltith (-ion) *nf* curse

melltithio *vb* curse

memorandwm (-anda) *nm* memorandum

memrwn (-rynau) *nm* parchment, vellum

men (-ni) *nf* wain, waggon, cart

mên *adj* mean

mendio *vb* mend, heal, recover

menestr *nm* cup-bearer

menig see **maneg**

mentr *nf* venture, hazard

mentro *vb* venture, hazard

mentrus *adj* adventurous

mentrwr (-wyr) *nm* entrepreneur

menyw (-od) *nf* woman

mêr (merion) *nm* marrow

mercwri *nm* mercury

merch (-ed) *nf* daughter, woman

Mercher *nm* Mercury. **Dydd M.** Wednesday

mercheta *vb* womanise

merchetaidd *adj* effeminate

merddwr (-ddyfroedd) *nm* stagnant water

merf, -aidd *adj* insipid, tasteless, flat

merfdra, merfeidd-dra *nm* insipidity

merlota *vb* pony-trek

merlyn (-nod, merlod) *nm* pony; *f* **merlen**

merllyd *adj* insipid

merthyr (-on, -i) *nm* martyr

merthyrdod *nm* martyrdom

merthyru *vb* martyr

merwindod *nm* numbness, tingling

merwino *vb* benumb, tingle, smart

meryw *npl* (**-en** *nf*) juniper trees

mes *npl* (**-en** *nf*) acorns

mesa *vb* gather acorns

mesur (**-au**) *nm* measure; metre; tune; bill

mesur, mesuro *vb* measure, mete

mesureg *nf* mensuration

mesuriad (**-au**) *nm* measurement

mesurwr (**-wyr**) *nm* measurer; surveyor

mesurydd (**-ion**) *nm* measurer, meter

metamorffedd *nm* metamorphism

metel (**-oedd**) *nm* metal; mettle

metelaidd *adj* metallic

metelydd (**-ion**) *nm* metallurgist

metelyddiaeth *nf* metallurgy

metr (**-au**) *nm* metre

metrig *adj* metric

metrigeiddio *vb* metricate

meth (**-ion**) *nm* miss, failure

methdaliad (**-au**) *nm* bankruptcy

methdalwr (**-wyr**) *nm* bankrupt

methedig (**-ion**) *adj* decrepit, infirm, disabled

methiannus *adj* failing, decayed

methiant *nm* failure

methodoleg *nf* methodology

methu *vb* fail, miss

meudwy (**-aid, -od**) *nm* hermit, recluse

meudwyaidd *adj* hermit-like, retiring

meudwyol *adj* eremitic

mewian *vb* mew

mewn *prep* in, within

mewnadlu *vb* inhale

mewnforio *vb* import ♦ (**-ion**) *npl* imports

mewnfudwr (**-wyr**) *nm* immigrant

mewnol *adj* inward, internal; subjective

mewnwr (**-wyr**) *nm* scrum-half

mewnyn (**mewnion**) *nm* filling

México *nf* Mexico

mi *pron* I, me

mieri *npl* (**miaren** *nf*) brambles

mig *nf*: **chwarae m.** play bo-peep

mign, -en *nf* bog, quagmire

migwrn (**-yrnau**) *nm* knuckle; ankle

mil (**-od**) *nm* animal

mil (**-oedd**) *nf* thousand

milain *adj* angry, fierce, savage, cruel

mileindra *nm* savageness, ferocity

mileinig *adj* savage, ferocious, malignant

milfed *adj* thousandth

milfeddyg (**-on**) *nm* veterinary surgeon

miffil *nf* million, an indefinite number

milflwyddiant *nm* millennium

milgi (**-gwn**) *nm* greyhound

miliast (**-ieist**) *nf* greyhound bitch

militariaeth *nf* militarism

militarydd *nm* militarist

miliwn (**-iynau**) *nf* million

miliynydd (**-ion**) *nm* millionaire

milodfa (**-oedd, -feydd**) *nf* menagerie

milwr (**-wyr**) *nm* soldier

milwraidd *adj* soldierly

milwriad (**-iaid**) *nm* colonel

milwriaeth *nf* warfare

milwriaethus *adj* militant

milwrio *vb* militate

milwrol *adj* military

milltir (**-oedd**) *nf* mile

min (**-ion**) *nm* edge; brink; lip

mindlws *adj* simpering, affected, precious

mingamu *vb* grimace

minio *vb* edge, sharpen; make impression

miniog *adj* sharp, keen, cutting

minlliw (**-iau**) *nm* lipstick

minnau *pron conj* I (on my part), I also

mintai (-eioedd) nf band, troop

mintys nm mint

mirain adj fair, beautiful, comely

mireinder nm beauty, comeliness

miri nm merriment, fun, festivity

mis (-oedd) nm month

misio vb miss, fail

misol (-ion) adj monthly

misolyn (-olion) nm monthly (magazine)

mitsio vb mitch, play truant

miwsig nm music

mo contr. of dim o: **nid oes mo'i debyg** there is none like him

moch npl (-yn nm) swine, pigs, hogs

mocha vb pig, litter

mochaidd adj swinish, hoggish

mochynnaidd adj piggish, swinish

modfedd (-i) nf inch

modrwy (-au) nf ring

modrwyo vb ring

modrwyog adj ringed

modryb (-edd) nf aunt

modur (-on) nm motor

modurdy (-dai) nm garage

modurwr (-wyr) nm motorist

modylu vb modulate

modylydd (-ion) nm modulator

modd (-ion, -au) nm mode, manner; means; mood

moddion npl means; medicine

moddol adj modal

moel (-ion) adj bare, bald; hornless, polled

moel (-ydd) nf hill

moeli vb make or become bald; hang (ears)

moelni nm bareness, baldness

moelyn nm bald-head

moes vb imper give, bring hither

moes (-au) nf morality; (pl) manners, morals

moeseg nf ethics

Moesenaidd adj Mosaic

moesgar adj mannerly, polite

moesgarwch nm politeness

moesol adj moral, ethical

moesoldeb nm morality

moesoli vb moralize

moesolwr (-wyr) nm moralist

moeswers (-i) nf moral

moesymgrymu vb bow

moeth (-au) nm luxury, indulgence

moethi vb pamper, indulge

moethlyd adj pampered, spoilt

moethus adj luxurious, pampered

moethusrwydd nm luxuriousness, luxury

molawd nm/f eulogy, panegyric

molecwl (-cylau) nm molecule

moleewlar adj molecular

moled (-au) nf kerchief; muffler

moli, moliannu vb praise, laud

moliannus adj praised, praiseworthy

moliant (-iannau) nm praise

mollt (myllt) nm wether

molltig nm mutton

moment (-au) nf moment

momentwm (momenta) nm momentum

monarchiaeth nf monarchy

monarchydd (-ion) nm monarchist

monni vb sulk, pout

monocsid (-au) nm monoxide

monópoli (-ïau) nm monopoly

môr (moroedd) nm sea, ocean

Môr: Y M. Canoldir nm Mediterranean Sea. **Y M. Coch** nm Red Sea. **Y M. Tawel** nm Pacific Ocean. **M. Udd** nm English Channel. **M. y Gogledd** nm North Sea

mor adv how, so, as

moratoriwm (-atoria) nm moratorium

mordaith (-deithiau) nf voyage

mordeithiwr (-wyr) nm voyager

mordwyaeth nf navigation

mordwyo vb go by sea, voyage, sail

mordwywr (-wyr) nm mariner, sailor

morddwyd (-ydd) nf/m thigh

morfa (-feydd) nm moor, fen, marsh

morfil (-od) nm whale

môr-forwyn (-forynion) nf mermaid

morfran (-frain) nf cormorant

morffoleg nmf morphology

morffolegol adj morphological

morgainc (-geinciau) nf gulf

morgais (-geisiau) nm mortgage

morgeisi nm mortgagee

morgeisio vb mortgage

môr-gerwyn nf whirlpool, vortex, abyss

morglawdd (-gloddiau) nm embankment, mole

morgrug npl (-yn nm) ants

morio vb voyage, sail

môr-ladrad (-au) nm piracy

môr-leidr (-ladron) nm pirate

morlen (-ni) nm chart

morlo (-loi) nm sea-calf, seal

morllyn (-noedd) nf/m lagoon

Moroco nf Morocco

morol adj maritime

moron npl (-en nf) carrots

mortais (-eisiau) nf mortise

morteisio vb mortise

morter (-au) nm mortar

morthwyl (-ion) nm hammer

morthwylio vb hammer

morthwyliwr (-wyr) nm hammerer

morwr (-wyr) nm seaman, sailor, mariner

morwriaeth nf seamanship, navigation

morwydd npl (-en nf) mulberry-trees

morwyn (-ynion) nf maid, virgin

morwyndod nm virginity

morwynol adj virgin, maiden

moryd (-iau) nf estuary

moryn (-nau) nm billow, breaker

mosaig (-au) nm, adj mosaic

Moscow nf Moscow

motif (-au) nm motive

motiff (-au) nm motif

muchudd nm jet

mud adj dumb, mute; dull

mudan (-od) nm mute

mudandod nm muteness

mudanes (-au) nf dumb woman

mudferwi vb simmer

mudiad (-au) nm removal; movement

mudo vb move, remove

mudol adj mobile, moving, migratory

mudwr (-wyr) nm remover

mul (-od) nm mule; donkey

mulaidd adj mulish, asinine

mules (-au) nf she-mule, she-ass

mulfran (-frain) nf cormorant

mun see **bun**

munud (-au) nm/f minute, moment

munud (-iau) nm sign, gesture; nod

munudio vb make gestures, gesticulate

mur (-iau) nm wall

murddun (-od) nm ruin, ruins

murio vb wall

murlun (-iau) nm mural

murmur vb murmur ♦ (-on) nm murmur

mursen (-nod) nf coquette; prude

mursendod nm prudery, affectation

mursennaidd adj prudish, affected

mursennu vb coquette, mince

musgrell adj feeble, decrepit

musgrellni nm feebleness, debility

mwd nm mud

mwdwl (mydylau) nm cock (of hay)

mwg nm smoke

mwgwd (mygydau) nm blind mask

mwng (myngau) nm mane

mwngial vb mumble

mwlsyn nm nincompoop; mule

mwlwg nm refuse, sweepings,

chaff

mwll *adj* close, warm, sultry
mwmian *vb* hum, mumble
mŵn see **mwyn**
mwnci (-iod) *nm* monkey
mwnciaidd *adj* monkeyish, apish
mwnglawdd see **mwyn-**
mwnwgl (mynyglau) *nm* neck
mwnws *coll n* small particles,
dust, debris
mwrdro *vb* murder
mwrllwch *nm* fog, mist, vapour
mwrn *adj* sultry, close, warm
mwrndra *nm* sultriness
mwrthwl (myrthylau) *nm* hammer
mws *adj* stale, rank, stinking
mwsg *nm* musk
mwsged (-i) *nm/f* musket
mwsogl, -wgl *nm* moss
mwstard, -tart *nm* mustard
mwstro *vb* fidget, hurry
mwstwr *nm* muster; bustle,
commotion
mwy *adj* more, bigger ♦ *adv* more,
again
mwyach *adv* any more, henceforth
mwyafrif (-au) *nm* majority
mwyalch, -en (-od) *nf* blackbird
mwyar *npl* (**-en** ♦ **-od**) blackberries
mwyara *vb* gather blackberries
mwydion *npl* crumb; pith, pulp
mwydo *vb* moisten, soak, steep
mwydro *vb* moider, bewilder
mwydyn (mwydod) *nm* worm
mwyfwy *adv* more and more
mwyhau *vb* increase, enlarge,
magnify
mwyn *nm* sake
mwyn, mŵn (-au) *nm* ore,
mineral
mwyn *adj* kind, gentle, mild; dear
mwynder (-au) *nm* gentleness;
(*pl*) delights
mwyndoddi *vb* refine
mwyneidd-dra *nm* kindness,
gentleness
mwynglawdd (-gloddiau) *nm* mine

mwyngloddio *vb* mine
mwynhad *nm* enjoyment, pleasure
mwynhau *vb* enjoy
mwyniant (-iannau) *nm* pleasure
mwynofydd (-ion) *nm*
mineralogist
mwynoleg *nf* mineralogy
mwynwr (-wyr) *nm* miner
mwys *adj* ambiguous, equivocal
mwythau *npl* indulgence, caresses
mwytho *vb* pet, fondle, pamper
mwythus *adj* pampered
myctod *nm* asphyxia
mydr (-au) *nm* metre, verse
mydryddiaeth *nf* versification
mydryddol *adj* metrical
mydryddu, mydru *vb* versify
mydylu *vb* cock
myfi *pron* I, me, myself
myfiaeth *nf* egotism
myfiol *adj* egotistic
myfyrdod (-au) *nm* meditation
myfyrgar *adj* studious,
contemplative
myfyrgell (-oedd) *nf* study
myfyrio *vb* meditate, study
myfyriol *adj* meditative
myfyriwr (-wyr) *nm* student
mygedol *adj* honorary
mygfa (-feydd) *nf* suffocation
myglyd *adj* smoky; close;
asthmatic
myglys *nm* tobacco
mygu *vb* smoke; suffocate, stifle,
smother
mygydu *vb* blindfold
mygyn *nm* a smoke
myngial *vb* mumble, mutter
myngog *adj* maned
myngus *adj* indistinct, mumbling
myllni *nm* sultriness
mympwy (-on) *nm* whim, caprice,
fad
mympwyol *adj* arbitrary,
capricious
mymryn (-nau) *nm* particle, bit,
mite

myn prep by (in swearing)
myn (-nod) nm kid
mynach (-aich, -od) nm monk
mynachaeth nf monasticism
mynachdy (-dai) nm monastery, convent
mynachlog (-ydd) nf monastery, abbey
mynawyd (-au) nm awl
mynci (-iau) nm hame(s)
myned, mynd vb go, proceed
mynedfa (-oedd, -feydd) nf entrance, passage
mynediad nm going; access, admission
mynegai (-eion) nm index, exponent
mynegair (-eiriau) nm concordance
mynegfys (-edd) nm forefinger, index
mynegi vb tell, express, relate, declare
mynegiad (-au) nm statement, declaration·
mynegiant nm expression
mynnu vb will, wish; insist; get, obtain
mynor (-ion) nm marble
mynwent (-au, -ydd) nf churchyard, graveyard
mynwes (-au) nf breast, bosom
mynwesol adj bosom
mynwesu vb cherish
mynych adj frequent, often
mynychiad nm frequenting; repetition
mynychu vb frequent, attend; repeat
mynydd (-oedd) nm mountain
mynydda vb mountaineer
mynydd-dir nm hill-country
mynyddig adj mountainous, hilly
mynyddwr (-wyr) nm mountaineer
myrdd, -iwn (-iynau) nm myriad
myrllyd adj myrrhy
myrndra nm sultriness
myrr nm myrrh

myrtwydd npl (-en nf) myrtles
mysg nm middle, midst. **ymysg** among
mysgu vb loose, undo
myswynog (-ydd) nf barren cow
mysglog adj mossy
mytholeg nf mythology
mytholegol adj mythological

N

na conj nor, neither; than ♦ adv no, not
nac adv no, not ♦ conj nor, neither
nacâd nm refusal, denial
nacaol adj negative
nacáu vb refuse, deny
nad adv not
nâd (nadau) nf cry, howl; clamour
Nadolig nm Christmas
Nadoligaidd adj Christmassy
nadu vb cry (out), howl
nadu vb stop, hinder
nadd adj hewn, wrought
naddion npl chips; shreds; lint
naddo adv no (to questions in preterite tense)
naddu vb hew, chip, whittle
Naf nm Lord
nag conj than
nage adv not so, no
nai (neiaint) nm nephew
naid (neidiau) nf jump, leap, bound
naïf adj naïve
naïfder nm naïveté
naill dem pron the one ♦ conj either
nain (neiniau) nf grandmother
nam (-au) nm mark, blemish, flaw
namyn pron except, but, save
nant (nentydd) nf brook; gorge, ravine
napcyn (-au) nm napkin
narcotig nm, adj narcotic
natur nf nature; temper
naturiaeth (-au) nf nature
naturiaethwr (-wyr) nm naturalist

naturiol *adj* natural
naturioldeb *nm* naturalness
naturus *adj* angry, quick-tempered
naw *adj, nm* nine
nawdd *nm* protection; patronage
nawddogaeth *nf* patronage,
protection
nawfed *adj* ninth
nawn *nm* noon
naws *nf* nature, disposition;
essence, tincture
nawseiddio *vb* temper, soften
neb *nm* any one; *(with negative
understood)* no one
nedd *npl* (**-en** *nf*) nits
neddau, neddyf (**neddyfau**) *nf*
adze
nef (**-oedd**) *nf* heaven
nefol, -aidd *adj* heavenly, celestial
nefoli *vb* make or become
heavenly
nefrosis *nm* neurosis
neges (**-au, -euau**) *nf* errand,
message
negesa, -eua *vb* run errands;
trade
negeseuwr (**-wyr**) *nm* messenger
negodi *vb* negotiate
negyddiaeth *nf* negativism
negyddol *adj* negative
neidio *vb* leap, jump; throb
neidiwr (**-wyr**) *nm* leaper, jumper
neidr (**nadroedd, nadredd**) *nf* snake
neiedd *nm* nepotism
neillog (**-ion**) *nm* alternative
neilltu *nm* one side. **o'r n.** aside,
apart
neilltuad *nm* separation
neilltuaeth *nf* separation, privacy,
seclusion
neilltuedig *adj* separated, secluded
neilltuo *vb* set apart, separate
neilltuol *adj* particular, peculiar,
special
neilltuolion *npl* peculiarities
neilltuolrwydd *nm* peculiarity,
distinction

neis *adj* nice
neisied (**-i**) *nf* kerchief
neithdar *nm* nectar
neithior (**-au**) *nf* marriage feast
neithiwr *adv* last night
nemor *adj* few. **nid n.** hardly any
nen (**-nau, -noedd**) *nf* ceiling;
heaven. **n. tŷ** house-top
nenbren *nm* roof-tree
nenfwd (**-fydau**) *nm* ceiling
nepell *adv* far. **nid n.** not far
nerf (**-au**) *nf* nerve
nerfwst *nm* neurasthenia
nerth (**-oedd**) *nm* might, power,
strength
nerthol *adj* strong, powerful,
mighty
nerthu *vb* strengthen
nes *adj* nearer. **yn n. ymlaen**
further on
nes *adv* till, until
nesaf *adj* nearest, next
nesáu *vb* draw near, approach
nesnes *adv* nearer and nearer
nesu *vb* draw near. **n draw** move
away
neu *conj* or
neuadd (**-au**) *nf* hall
newid *vb* change, alter ♦ *nm*
change
newidiant *nm* variability
newidiol *adj* changeable, variable
newidydd (**-ion**) *nm* transformer
newidyn (**-nau**) *nm* variable
newydd *adj* new, novel; fresh ♦
(**-ion**) *nm* news
newyddbeth (**-au**) *nm* novelty
newydd-deb, -der *nm* newness,
novelty
newyddiadur (**-on**) *nm* newspaper
newyddiaduriaeth *nf* journalism
newyddiadurwr (**-wyr**) *nm*
journalist
newyddian (**-od**) *n coll* novice,
neophyte
newyn *nm* hunger, famine
newynog *adj* hungry, starving

newynu vb starve, famish
ni pron we, us
ni, nid adv not
nifer (-oedd, -i) nm/f number
nifwl nm mist, fog; nebula
Nigeria nf Nigeria
Nihon nf Japan
ninnau pron conj we (on our part), we also
nionyn (nionod) nm onion
nis adv not ... it. **n. cafodd** he did not find it
nitrad (-au) nm nitrate
nith (-oedd) nf niece
nithio vb sift, winnow
nithiwr (-wyr) nm sifter, winnower
nithlen (-ni) nf winnowing-sheet
niwed (-eidiau) nm harm, injury
niweidio vb harm, hurt, injure, damage
niweidiol adj harmful, injurious
niwl (-oedd) nm, **-en** nf mist, fog, haze
niwliog, niwlog adj misty, foggy, hazy
niwmatig adj pneumatic
niwmonia nm pneumonia
niwtral adj neutral
niwtraleiddio vb neutralise
niwtraliaeth nf neutrality
nobyn (nobiau) nm knob
nod (-au) nm/f note; mark, token
nodachfa (-feydd) nf bazaar
nodedig adj appointed, set; remarkable
nodi vb mark, note, appoint, state
nodiad (-au) nm note
nodiadur (-on) nm notebook
nodiant nm notation
nodwedd (-ion) nf character, characteristic, feature
nodweddiadol adj characteristic
nodweddu vb characterize
nodwydd nf needle
nodyn (-nau, nodau, nodion) nm note

nodd (-ion) nm moisture; juice, sap
nodded nm refuge, protection
noddfa (-fâu, -feydd) nf refuge
noddi vb protect
noddlyd adj juicy, sappy
noddwr (-wyr) nm protector; patron
noe (-au) nf dish; kneading-trough
noeth adj naked, bare, exposed, raw
noethder nm bareness, nakedness
noethi vb bare, denude
noethlymun adj nude
noethlymunwr (-wyr) nm streaker
noethlymunwraig nf stripper
noethni nm nakedness, nudity
noethwr (-wyr) nm nudist
nofel (-au) nf novel
nofelwr, -ydd (-wyr) nm novelist
nofiadwy adj swimmable
nofiedydd (-ion) nm swimmer
nofio vb swim; float
nofiwr (-wyr) nm swimmer
nogio vb jib
noglyd adj jibbing
nôl vb fetch, bring
Norwy nf Norway
nos (-au, nosweithiau) nf night
nosi vb become night
noson, nosweth (nosweithiau) nf a night, an evening
noswyl (-iau) nf eve of festival, vigil
noswylio vb cease work at eve
nudden nf fog, mist, haze
nwy (-on) nm gas
nwyd (-au) nm passion; emotion
nwydd (-au) nm substance, article; (pl) goods
nwyf nm vivacity, energy, vigour
nwyfiant nm vivacity, vigour
nwyfus adj sprightly, spirited, lively
nwyol adj gaseous
nychdod nm feebleness, infirmity
nychlyd adj sickly, feeble

nychu *vb* sicken, pine, languish
nydd-dro (-droeau, -droeon) *nm* twist
nydd-droi *vb* twist, screw
nyddu *vb* spin, twist
nyddwr (-wyr) *nm* spinner
nyf *coll n* snow
nyni *pron* we, us
nyrs (-ys) *nm/f* nurse
nyrsio *adj* nurse
nytmeg *nm* nutmeg
nyth (-od) *nm/f* nest
nythu *vb* nest, nestle

O

o *prep* from; of, out of; by
o *excl* oh!, O!
oblegid *conj, prep* because, for
obry *adv* beneath, below
obstetreg *nm* obstetrics
obstetregydd (-wyr) *nm* obstetrician
ocsid (-iau) *nm* oxide
ocsidiad *nm* oxidisation
ocsidio *vb* oxidise
ocsidydd (-ion) *nm* oxidising agent
ocsigen *nm* oxygen
och *excl* oh, alas, woe
ochenaid (-eidiau) *nf* sigh
ocheneidio, ochneidio *vb* sigh
ochr (-au) *nf* side
ochrgamu *vb* sidestep
ochri *vb* side
ôd *nm* snow
od *adj* odd, remarkable
odiaeth *adj* excellent, exquisite ♦ *adv* very, most, extremely
odid *adv* perchance, peradventure
odl (-au) *nf* rhyme; ode, song
odli *vb* rhyme
odrif (-au) *nm* odd number
odrwydd *nm* oddity
odyn (-au) *nf* kiln
oddeutu *prep* about
oddi *prep* out of, from

oddieithr, oddigerth *prep* except, unless
oed (-au) *nm* age; time
oed-dâl (-iadau) *nm* superannuation
oedfa (-on, -feuon) *nf* meeting, service
oedi *vb* delay; postpone, defer
oediad (-au) *nm* delay
oedran *nm* age, full age
oedrannus *adj* aged
oedd *vb* was, were
oen (wyn) *nm* lamb
oena *vb* lamb, yean
oenig *nf* ewe-lamb
oer *adj* cold, chill, frigid; sad
oeraidd *adj* coldish, cool, chilly
oerddrws (-ddrysau) *nm* wind gap
oerfel *nm* cold
oergell (-oedd) *nf* refrigerator
oeri *vb* cool, chill
oerllyd *adj* chilly, frigid; cool
oernad (-au) *nf* howl, wail, lamentation
oernadu *vb* howl, wail, lament
oerni *nm* cold, coldness, chillness
oes (-oedd, -au) *nf* age, lifetime.
 yn o. oesoedd for ever and ever
oes *vb* there is, there are; is there?
oesoffagws *nm* oesophagus
oesol *adj* age-long, perpetual
ofer *adj* vain, idle; prodigal, dissipated; waste
ofera *vb* waste, squander, idle
oferedd *nm* vanity, dissipation
ofergoel (-ion) *nf* superstition
ofergoeledd, -iaeth *nf* superstition
ofergoelus *adj* superstitious
oferwr (-wyr) *nm* idler, waster
ofn (-au) *nm* fear, dread
ofnadwy *adj* awful, terrible, dreadful
ofnadwyaeth *nf* awe, terror, dread
ofni *vb* fear, dread

ofnog *adj* fearful, timorous

ofnus *adj* timid, nervous

ofnusrwydd *nm* timidity, nervousness

ofwl (-au) *nm* ovule

ofydd (-ion) *nm* ovate

offeiriad (-iaid) *nm* priest, clergyman

offeiriadaeth *nf* priesthood

offeiriades (-au) *nf* priestess

offeiriadol *adj* priestly, sacerdotal

offeiriadu *vb* officiate, minister

offer *npl* implements, tools, gear

offeren (-nau) *nf* mass

offeryn (-nau, offer) *nm* instrument, tool

offerynnol *adj* instrumental

offerynoliaeth *nf* instrumentality

offrwm (-ymau) *nm* offering, oblation

offrymu *vb* offer, sacrifice

offrymwr (-wyr) *nm* offerer, sacrificer

offthalmia *nm* ophthalmia

offthalmosgop (-au) *nm* ophthalmoscope

og (-au), **oged** (-au, -i) *nf* harrow

ogof (-au, -fâu, -feydd) *nf* cave, cavern; den

ogylch *prep* about

ongl (-au) *nf* angle, corner

onglog *adj* angled, angular

oherwydd *conj, prep* because, for

ôl *adj* back, hind, hindmost ♦ (olion) *nm* mark, print, trace, track. **Yn ôl** according to; ago

ôl-dâl (-oedd) *nm* back-pay

ôl-ddodiad (-iaid) *nm* suffix

ôl-dyddio *vb* post-date

ôl-ddyled (-ion) *nf* arrears

olew (-au) *nm* oil

olewydd *npl* (-en *nf*) olive-trees

olifaid *npl* olive-berries

oirhain *vb* trace

olwr (-wyr) *nm* back (*rugby*)

olwyn (-ion) *nf* wheel

olwyno *vb* wheel, cycle

olwynog *adj* wheeled

olyniaeth *nf* succession, sequence

olynol *adj* successive, consecutive

olynu *vb* succeed (to)

olynwr (-wyr), **-ydd** (-ion) *nm* successor

ôlysgrif (-au) *nf* postscript

oll *adv* all, wholly; ever, at all

ombwdsman (-myn) *nm* ombudsman

omlet (-i) *nm* omelette

ond *conj* but, only ♦ *prep* except, save, but

onest *adj* honest

onestrwydd *nm* honesty

oni, onid *adv* not?, is it not? ♦ *conj* if not, unless ♦ *prep* except, save, but

onid e *adv* otherwise, else; is it not?

onis *conj* if it is not. **o. caiff** if he does not get it

onnen (onn, ynn) *nf* ash

opiniwn (-ynau) *nm* opinion

opiniynllyd, -iynus *adj* opinionated

optimistaeth *nf* optimism

optimistaidd *adj* optimistic

optimwm (-tima) *nm* optimum

oracl (-au) *nm* oracle

oracladd *adj* oracular

oraens *nm* orange

ordeiniad (-au) *nm* ordination, ordinance

ordeinio *vb* ordain

ordinhad (-au) *nf* ordinance, sacrament

oren (-nau) *nm/f* orange

organ (-au) *nf/m* organ

organaidd *adj* organic

organeb (-au) *nf* organism

organig *adj* organic

organydd (-ion) *nm* organist

orgraff (-au) *nf* orthography

orgraffyddol (-au) *adj* orthographical

oriawr (-oriorau) *nf* watch

oriel (-au) *nf* gallery

orig *nf* little while

oriog adj fickle, changeable, inconstant

os conj if

osgo nm slant, slope, inclination

osgoi vb swerve, avoid, evade, shirk

oslef nf tone, voice

ow excl oh!, alas!

P

pa adj what, which

pab (-au) nm pope

pabaeth nf papacy

pabaidd adj papal, popish

pabell (pebyll) nf tent, tabernacle

pabellu vb tent, tabernacle, encamp

pabi nm poppy

pabwyr npl (-en nf, -yn nm) rushes

pabwyr nm wick, candle-wick

pabydd (-ion) nm Roman Catholic

pabyddiaeth nf Roman Catholicism

pabyddol adj Roman Catholic

pac (-iau) nm pack, bundle

pacio vb pack

padell (-au, -i, pedyll) nf pan, bowl

padellaid (-eidiau) nf panful

pader (-au) nm paternoster, Lord's Prayer

padera vb repeat prayers, patter

pae nm pay, wage

paediatreg nm paediatrics

paediatregydd nm paediatrician

paent nm paint

paentiad (-au) nm painting

pafiliwn nm pavilion

paffio vb box, fight

paffiwr (-wyr) nm boxer

pagan (-iaid) nm pagan, heathen

paganaidd adj pagan, heathen

paganiaeth nf paganism, heathenism

pang (-au) nm, **pangfa (-feydd)** nf pang, fit

paham adv why, wherefore

paill nm flour; pollen

pair (peiriau) nm cauldron, furnace

pais (peisiau) nf coat, petticoat

paith (peithiau) nm prairie

Pacistan nf Pakistan

pâl (palau) nf spade

paladr (pelydr) nm ray, beam; staff; stem

palaeolithig adj palaeolithic

palas (-au) nm palace

Palestina nf Palestine

palf (-au) nf palm, hand; paw

palfais (-eisiau) nf shoulder

palfalu vb feel, grope

palfod (-au) nf smack, slap, buffet

palff nm fine, well-built man

pali nm silk brocade

palis (-au) nm pale, partition, wainscot

palmant (-mentydd) nm pavement

palmantu vb pave

palmwydd npl (-en nf) palm-trees

palu vb dig, delve

palwr (-wyr) nm digger

pall (-au) nm mantle; tent

pall nm fail, failing; lack; lapse

pallu vb fail, cease; neglect; refuse

pam adv why, wherefore (**paham**)

pamffled (-i, -au), -yn nm pamphlet

pan conj when

pandy (-dai) nm fulling-mill

pannas npl (**panasen** nf) parsnips

pannu vb full cloth

pannwl (panylau) nm dimple, hollow

pannwr (panwyr) nm fuller

pant (-iau) nm hollow, valley

pantio vb depress, dent, sink

pantiog adj hollow, sunken; dimpled

papur (-au) nm paper

papuro vb paper

papurwr (-wyr) nm paperer, paperhanger

papuryn *nm* scrap of paper

pâr (**parau**) *nm* pair; suit

pâr (**peri**) *nm* spear, lance

para *vb* last, endure, continue

parabl (**-au**) *nm* speech, discourse

parablu *vb* speak

paradeim (**-au**) *nm* paradigm

paradwys *nf* paradise

paradwysaidd *adj* paradisean

paragraff (**-au**) *nm* paragraph

paratoad (**-au**) *nm* preparation

paratoawl *adj* preparatory

paratoi *vb* prepare, get ready

parc (**-iau**) *nm* park, field

parch *nm* respect, reverence

parchedig (**-ion**) *adj* reverend; reverent

parchedigaeth *nf* reverence

parchu *vb* respect, revere, reverence

parchus *adj* respectful; respectable

parchusrwydd *nm* respectability

pardwn (**-ynau**) *nm* pardon

pardynu *vb* pardon

parddu *nm* fire-black, smut; soot

pardduo *vb* blacken, vilify, defame

pared (**parwydydd**) *nm* partition wall, wall

paredd *nm* parity

parhad *nm* continuance, continuation

parhaol *adj* lasting, perpetual

parhau *vb* last, continue; persevere

parhaus *adj* lasting; continual, perpetual

Paris *nf* Paris

parlwr (**-yrau**) *nm* parlour

parlys *nm* paralysis, palsy

parlysu *vb* paralyse

parod *adj* ready, prepared; prompt

parodrwydd *nm* readiness, willingness

parôl (**-ion**) *nm* parole

parsel (**-i, -ydd**) *nm* parcel

parti (**-ïon**) *nm* party

partïaeth *nf* partisanship

partïol *adj* partial, biassed, partisan

parth (**-au**) *nm* part, region; floor

parthed *prefx* about, concerning

parthu *vb* part, divide

parwyden (**-nau**) *nf* wall, side; breast

pas *nm* whooping-cough

Pasg *nm* Passover, Easter

pasgedig (**-ion**) *adj* fatted, fattened, fat

pasiant (**-iannau**) *nm* pageant

pasio *vb* pass

past *nm* paste

pastai (**-eiod**) *nf* pasty, pie

pastio *vb* paste

pasturedig *adj* pasteurised

pasturo *vb* pasteurise

pastwn (**-ynau**) *nm* baton, club, cudgel

pastynu *vb* club, cudgel, bludgeon

patriarch (**-iaid, patrieirch**) *nm* patriarch

patriarchaeth (**-au**) *nf* patriarchate

patriarchaidd *adj* patriarchal

patrwm (**-ymau**) *nm* pattern

patrymlun (**-iau**) *nm* template

pathew (**-od**) *nm* dormouse

patholeg *nf* pathology

patholegol *adj* pathological

patholegydd (**-egwyr**) *nm* pathologist

pau *nf* country

paun (**peunod**) *nm* peacock

pawb *pron* everybody, all

pawen (**-nau**) *nf* paw

pawl (**polion**) *nm* pole, stake

pe *conj* if

pebyll see **pabell**

pecyn (**-nau**) *nm* packet, package

pech-aberth (**-au**) *nm* sin-offering

pechadur (**-iaid**) *nm* sinner, offender

pechadures (**-au**) *nf* woman sinner

pechadurus *adj* sinful, wicked

pechadurusrwydd *nm* sinfulness

pechod (-au) *nm* sin, offence
pechu *vb* sin, offend
ped *conj* if
pedair *adj* f. of **pedwar**
pedeirongl *adj* foursquare
pedi *vb* worry, grieve
pedol (-au) *nf* horseshoe
pedoli *vb* shoe
pedrain *nf* haunches, crupper
pedrongl *adj* square ♦ (-au) *nf* square
pedronglog *adj* quadrangular
pedryfan *adj* four-cornered ♦ **-noedd** *nm* four quarters
pedryfwrdd (-fyrddau) *nm* quarter-deck
pedwar *adj* four; f **pedair**
pedwarawd *nm* quartette
pedwarcarnol (-ion) *adj* four-footed, quadruped
pedwaredd *adj* f. of **pedwerydd**
pedwarplyg *adj* fourfold, quarto
pedwerydd *adj* fourth; f **pedwaredd**
peddestr *nm* pedestrian
peddestrig *nm* walking; pedestrian
pefr *adj* radiant, bright, beautiful
pefrio *vb* radiate, sparkle
peg (-iau) *nm* peg
pegio *vb* peg
pegor (-au) *nm* manikin; dwarf; imp
pegwn (-ynau) *nm* pivot, pole, axis
Pegwn y Gogledd *nm* North Pole
pegynol *adj* axial, polar
peidio *vb* cease, stop, desist
peilon (-au) *nm* pylon
peilot (-iaid) *nm* pilot
peillio *vb* bolt, sift
peint (-iau) *nm* pint
peintiad (-au) *nm* painting
peintio *vb* paint
peintiwr (-wyr) *nm* painter
peipen (peipiau) *nf* pipe
peirianneg *nm* engineering
peiriannol *adj* mechanical
peiriannydd (-ianyddion) *nm*
engineer
peiriant (-iannau) *nm* machine, engine. **p. golchi** washing machine
peirianwaith *nm* mechanism
peiswyn *nm* chaff
peithyn (-au) *nm* ridge-tile
Pecing *nf* Peking
pêl (pelau, peli) *nf* ball
pelawd *nf* over (cricket)
pêl-droed *nf* football
pêl-fasged *nf* basket-ball
pelferyn (-nau) *nm* ball-bearing
pêl-foli *nf* volley-ball
pêl-rwyd *nf* netball
pelten (pelts) *nf* blow
pelydr (-au) *nm* ray, beam
pelydru *vb* beam, gleam, radiate
pelydryn *nm* ray, beam
pell *adj* far, distant, remote, long
pellen (-nau, -ni) *nf* ball (of yarn)
pellennig *adj* far, distant, remote
pellhau *vb* put or remove far off
pellter (-au, -oedd) *nm* distance
pen (-nau) *nm* head; chief; end; top
pen *adj* head, chief, supreme
penadur (-iaid) *nm* sovereign
penaduriaeth *nf* sovereignty
penagored *adj* open, indefinite, undecided
penarglwyddiaeth *nf* sovereignty
penbaladr *adj* general, universal
penben *adv* at loggerheads
penbleth *nf* perplexity, quandary
pen-blwydd (-i) *nm* birthday
penboeth *adj* hot-headed, fanatical
penboethni *nm* fanaticism
penboethyn (-boethiaid) *nm* fanatic
penbwl (-byliaid) *nm* blockhead; tadpole
pencadlys *nm* head-quarters
pencampwr (-wyr) *nm* champion
pencampwriaeth (-au) *nf* championship
pencerdd (-ceirddiaid) *nm* chief musician

penchwiban adj giddy, flighty
pendant adj positive, emphatic
pendantrwydd nm positiveness
pendefig (-ion) nm prince, peer, noble
pendefigaeth nf aristocracy, peerage
pendefigaidd adj noble, aristocratic
pendefiges (-au) nf peeress
penderfyniad (-au) nm determination, resolution
penderfynol adj determined, resolute
penderfynu vb determine, resolve
pendew adj thick-headed, stupid
pendifaddau adj: **yn b.** especially
pendil (-iau) nm pendulum
pendramwnwgl adj topsyturvy; headlong
pendraphen adj helter-skelter, confused
pendro nf giddiness, vertigo; staggers
pendroni vb perplex oneself, worry over
pendrwm adj top-heavy; drowsy
pendrymu vb drowse, droop
pendwmpian vb nod, doze, slumber
penddaredd nm giddiness
penddaru vb make or become giddy
pendduyn (-nod) nm botch, boil
penelin (-oedd) nm/f elbow
penelino vb elbow
penffest (-au) nm headgear
penffol adj silly, idiotic
penffrwyn (-au) nm/f head-stall, halter
pengaled adj headstrong ♦ nf knapweed
pengaledwch nm stubbornness
pengam adj wrong-headed, perverse
pen-glin (-iau) nf knee
penglog (-au) nf skull

pengryf adj headstrong, stubborn
pengryniad (-iaid) nm roundhead
peniad (-au) nm header
penigamp adj excellent, splendid
penisel adj downcast, crestfallen
penlinio vb kneel
penllwyd adj grey-headed
penllwydni nm grey hair, white hair
penllywydd (-ion) nm sovereign
penllywyddiaeth nf sovereignty
pennaeth (penaethiaid) nm chief
pennaf adj chief, principal
pennawd (penawdau) nm heading; headline
pennill (penillion) nm verse, stanza
pennod (penodau) nf chapter
pennoeth adj bare-headed
pennog (penwaig) nm herring
pennu vb specify, appoint, determine
penodi vb appoint
penodiad (-au) nm appointment
penodol adj particular, specific
penrhydd adj unbridled, loose
penrhyddid nm licence, licentiousness
penrhyn (-noedd, -nau) nm cape, foreland
pensaer (-seiri) nm architect
pensaerniaeth nf architecture
pensil (-iau) nm pencil
pensiwn (-iynau) nm pension
pen-swyddog (-ion) nm chief officer
pensyfrdan adj stunned, dazed
pensyfrdandod nm giddiness, dizziness
pensyfrdanu vb stun, daze
pensyth adj perpendicular
pentan (-au) nm hob
penteulu (pennau teuluoedd) nm head of family
pentewyn (-ion) nm firebrand
pentir (-oedd) nm headland
pentis nm pentice, penthouse
pentref (-i, -ydd) nm village;

homestead

pentrefan (-nau) *nm* hamlet
pentrefol *adj* village
pentrefwr (-wyr) *nm* villager
pentwr (-tyrrau) *nm* heap, pile
penty (-tai) *nm* cottage, shed
pentyrru *vb* heap, pile, accumulate
penuchel *adj* proud, haughty
penwan *adj* weak-minded
penwyn *adj* white-headed
penwynni *nm* white hair, grey hair
penyd (-iau) *nm* penance, punishment
penyd-wasanaeth *nm* penal servitude
penysgafn *adj* light-headed, giddy, dizzy
penysgafnder *nm* giddiness, dizziness
pêr *adj* sweet, delicious, luscious
peraidd *adj* sweet, mellow
perarogl (-au) *nm* perfume, fragrance
perarogli *vb* perfume; embalm
peraroglus *adj* fragrant, scented
percoladur (-on) *nm* percolator
perchen, -nog (perchenogion) *nm* owner
perchenogaeth *nf* ownership
perchenogi *vb* possess, own
perchentywr (-wyr) *nm* householder
pereidd-dra *nm* sweetness
pereiddio *vb* sweeten
pererin (-ion) *nm* pilgrim
pererindod (-au) *nm/f* pilgrimage
pererinol *adj* pilgrim
perfedd (-ion) *nm* guts, bowels
perfeddwlad (-wledydd) *nf* interior, heartland
perffaith *adj* perfect
perffeithio *vb* perfect
perffeithrwydd *nm* perfection
perffeithydd (-ion) *nm* perfecter
perfformiad (-au) *nm* performance
perfformio *vb* perform

perfformiwr (-wyr) *nm* performer
peri *vb* cause, bid
perl (-au) *nm* pearl
perlewyg (-on) *nm* ecstasy, trance
perlysiau *npl* aromatic herbs; spices
perllan (-nau) *nf* orchard
perocsid (-au) *nm* peroxide
peroriaeth *nf* melody, music
persain *adj* euphonious, melodious
  ◆ (-seiniau) *nf* euphony
persawr (-au) *nm* fragrance
perseiniol *adj* melodious
persli *nm* parsley
person (-au) *nm* person
person (-iaid) *nm* parson, clergyman
personadu *vb* impersonate
personadwr (-wyr) *nm* impersonator
persondy (-dai) *nm* parsonage
personol *adj* personal
personoli *vb* personify
personoliad (-au) *nm* personification
personoliaeth (-au) *nf* personality
perswâd *nm* persuasion
perswadio *vb* persuade
pert *adj* quaint, pretty; pert
perth (-i) *nf* bush, hedge
perthnasedd (-au) *nm* relativity, relevance
perthnasiad (-au) *nf* affiliation
perthnasol *adj* relevant
perthyn *vb* belong, pertain, be related
perthynas (-au) *nf* relation; relationship
perthynol *adj* relative
perwyl *nm* purpose, effect
perygl (-on) *nm* danger, peril, risk
peryglu *vb* endanger, imperil
peryglus *adj* dangerous, perilous
pes *conj* if ... it. **p. adwaenasent** had they known him
pesgi *vb* feed, fatten
pesimist (-iaid) *nm* pessimist

pesimistaidd *adj* pessimistic
pesimistiaeth *nf* pessimism
pestl (-au) *nm* pestle
peswch *nm* cough
pesychiad (-au) *nm* cough
pesychu *vb* cough
petris *npl* (-en *nf*) partridges
petrocemogolau (petrocemogolyn *nm*) *npl* petrochemicals
petrol (-au) *nm* petrol
petroleg *nm/f* petrology
petrus *adj* hesitating; doubtful
petruso *vb* hesitate, doubt
petruster *nm* hesitation, doubt
petryal *nm, adj* square
peth (-au) *nm* thing; part, some
petheuach *npl* odds and ends, trifles
peunes (-od) *nf* peahen
pianydd (-ion) *nm* pianist
piau *vb* own, possess
pib (-au) *nf* pipe, tube; diarrhœa
pibell (-au, -i) *nf* pipe, tube
pibgorn (-gyrn) *nm* recorder (music)
pibo *vb* pipe; squirt
pibonwy (-en *nf*) *npl* icicles
pibydd (-ion) *nm* piper
picell (-au) *nf* dart, javelin, spear
picellu *vb* spear, stab
picfforch (-ffyrch) *nf* pitchfork
picil *nm* pickle, trouble
picio *vb* dart, hie
piclo *vb* pickle
pictiwr (-tiyrau) *nm* picture
picwns (-nen *nf*) *npl* wasps
piff (-iau) *nm* puff, sudden blast
piffian *vb* snigger, giggle
pig (-au) *nf* point, spike; beak; spout
pigan *vb* drizzle
pigdwr (-dyrau) *nm* spire, steeple
pigiad (-au) *nm* prick, sting; injection
pigion *npl* pickings, selections
pigo *vb* pick; peck; prick; sting
pigog *adj* prickly

pigyn *nm* thorn, prickle
pilcod *npl* (-yn *nm*) minnows
pilen (-nau) *nf* membrane, film; cataract
piler (-au, -i) *nm* pillar
pilio *vb* peel, pare
pili-pala *nm* butterfly
Pilipinas *npl* the Philippines
pilsen (pils) *nf* pill
pilyn *nm* garment, rag, clout
pin (-nau) *nm/f* pin ♦ *nm* pen
pinacl (-au) *nm* pinnacle
pinaclog *adj* pinnacled
pinafal (-au) *nm* pineapple
pinbwyntio *vb* pinpoint
pinc (-od) *nm* finch, chaffinch
pincio *vb* pink. **parlwr p.** beauty parlour
pincws (-cysau) *nm* pincushion
pindwll (-dyllau) *nm* pinhole
pinsiad (-au) *nm* pinch
pinsio *vb* pinch
pioden (piod) *nf* magpie
piser (-au) *nm* pitcher, jug, can
pistyll (-oedd) *nm* spout; cataract
pistyllio *vb* spout, gush
pisyn (-nau, pisiau) *nm* piece
piti *nm* pity
pitw *adj* petty, puny, paltry
piw (-od) *nm* dug, udder
Piwritan (-iaid) *nm* Puritan
piwritanaidd *adj* puritan, puritanical
piwritaniaeth *nf* puritanism
pla (plâu) *nm/f* plague, pestilence; nuisance
pladur (-au) *nf* scythe
pladurwr (-wyr) *nm* mower
plaen *adj* plain, clear
plaen (-au) *nm* plane
plaenio *vb* plane
plagio *vb* plague, tease, torment
plagus *adj* annoying, troublesome
plaid (pleidiau) *nf* side, party. **P. Cymru** The Welsh National Party
planced (-i) *nf* blanket

planed (-au) *nf* planet
planhigfa (-feydd) *nf* plantation
planhigyn (-higion) *nm* plant
plannu *vb* plant; dive
plannwr (planwyr) *nm* planter
plant *npl* (plentyn *nm*) children
planta *vb* beget or bear children
plantos *npl* (little) children
plas (-au) *nm* hall, mansion,
 palace
plasaidd *adj* palatial
plastr (-au) *nm* plaster
plastro *vb* plaster
plastrwr (-wyr) *nm* plasterer
plât, plat (-iau) *nm* plate
platwn (-tynau) *nm* platoon
platwydr *nm* plate-glass
ple *nm* plea
pledio *vb* plead, argue
pledren (-nau, -ni) *nf* bladder
pleidgarwch *nm* partisanship
pleidio *vb* side with, support
pleidiol *adj* favourable, partial
pleidiwr (-wyr) *nm* partisan,
 supporter
pleidlais (-leisiau) *nf* vote, suffrage
pleidleisio *vb* vote
pleidleisiwr (-wyr) *nm* voter
plencyn (planciau) *nm* plank
plentyn (plant) *nm* child, infant
plentyndod *nm* childhood, infancy
plentyneiddiwch *nm* childishness
plentynnaidd *adj* childish, puerile
plentynrwydd *nm* childishness
pleser (-au) *nm* pleasure
pleserdaith (-deithiau) *nf* trip,
 excursion
pleserus *adj* pleasurable, pleasant
plesio *vb* please
plet, pleten (pletiau) *nf* pleat
pletio *vb* pleat
pletiog *adj* pleated
pleth (-au) *nf* plait
plethdorch (-au) *nf* wreath
plethu *vb* plait, weave, fold
plewra (-e) *nm* pleura
plicio *vb* pluck, peel, strip

plisg *coll n* (-yn *nm*) shells, husks,
 pods
plisgo *vb* shell, husk
plisman, -mon (-myn) *nm*
 policeman
plismones (-au) *nf* policewoman
plith *nm* midst
pliwrisi *nm* pleurisy
plocyn (plociau) *nm* block
plod *adj, nm* plaid, tartan
ploryn (-nod) *nm* pimple
plu *npl* (-en *nf*), **pluf** *npl* (-yn *nm*)
 feathers. **p. eira** snow-flakes
pluo, plufio *vb* pluck, deplume;
 plume
pluog *adj* feathered, fledged
plwc (plyciau) *nm* pluck; space,
 while
plwg (plygiau) *nm* plug
plwm *nm* lead
plws *nm* plus
plwtoniwm *nm* plutonium
plwyf (-i, -ydd) *nm* parish
plwyfol *adj* parochial
plwyfolion *npl* parishioners
plycio *vb* pluck
plyg (-ion) *nm* fold, double; hollow
plygain *nm* cock-crow, dawn;
 matins
plygeiniol *adj* dawning; very early
plygell (-au) *nm* folder
plygiad (-au) *nm* folding, fold
plygu *vb* fold; bend, stoop; bow
plymen *nf* plummet
plymio *vb* plumb, sound
plymwr (-wyr) *nm* plumber
po *particle used before superlative.*
 gorau po gyntaf the sooner the
 better
pob *adj* each, every; all
pobi *vb* bake; roast; toast
pobiad (-au) *nm* baking, batch
pobl (-oedd) *nf* people
poblog *adj* populous
poblogaeth (-au) *nf* population
poblogaidd *adj* popular
poblogeiddio *vb* popularize

poblogi *vb* people, populate
poblogrwydd *nm* popularity
pobwr (-wyr), **-ydd** (-ion) *nm* baker
poced (-i) *nf* pocket
pocedu *vb* pocket
pocer (-i, -au) *nm* poker
poen (-au) *nmf* pain, torment
poenedigaeth *nf* torment
poeni *vb* pain, torment; worry, grieve
poenus *adj* painful
poenwr (-wyr) *nm* tormentor, torturer
poenydio *vb* torment, torture; fret, vex
poenydiwr (-wyr) *nm* tormentor
poer (-ion) *nm* spittle, saliva
poeri *vb* spit, expectorate
poeryn *nm* spittle
poeth *adj* hot; burning. **dŵr p.** heart-burn
poethder, **-ni** *nm* hotness, heat
poethdon (-nau) *nf* heatwave
poethi *vb* heat
pôl (polau) *nm* poll
polaredd *nm* polarity
polareiddiad *nm* polarisation
polareiddio *vb* polarise
polymorff *nm* polymorph
polymorffedd *nm* polymorphism
polyn (polion) *nm* pole
pomgranad (-au) *nm* pomegranate
pompiwn (-iynau) *nm* pumpkin, gourd
pompren *nf* plank bridge, footbridge
ponc (-iau), **-en** *nf*, **-yn** *nm* hillock, tump; bank
pont (-ydd) *nf* bridge, arch
pontffordd (-ffyrdd) *nf* fly-over, viaduct
pontio *vb* bridge
popeth *nm* everything
polys *npl* (**-en** *nf*) poplar-trees
popty (-tai) *nm* bakehouse; oven
porc *nm* pork

porchell (**perchyll**) *nm* little pig
porfa (-feydd) *nf* pasture, grass
porffor *adj, nm* purple
pori *vb* graze, browse; eat
pornograffiaeth *nf* pornography
Portiwgal *nf* Portugal
portread (-au) *nm* portrayal, pattern
portreadu *vb* portray
porth *nm* aid, help, succour
porth (pyrth) *nm* gate, gateway; porch door. **p. awyr** airport
porthfa (-feydd) *nf* port, harbour; ferry
porthi *vb* feed
porthiannus *adj* well-fed, high-spirited
porthiant *nm* food, sustenance, support
porthladd (-oedd) *nm* port, harbour, haven
porthmon (-myn) *nm* cattle-dealer
porthor (-ion) *nm* porter, door-keeper, commissionaire
pôs (-au) *nm* riddle, conundrum, puzzle
posibilrwydd *nm* possibility
posib(l) *adj* possible
positif *adj* positive
positifiaeth *nf* positivism
post (pyst) *nm* post; pillar
poster (-i) *nm* poster
postfarc (-iau) *nm* postmark
postio *vb* post
postman, **-mon** (-myn) *nm* postman
postyn (pyst) *nm* post
pot (-iau) *nm* pot
potel (-i) *nf* bottle
potelaid (-eidiau) *nf* bottleful
potelu *vb* bottle
poten (-ni) *nf* paunch; pudding
potensial (-au, *adj*) potential
potes *nm* pottage, broth, soup
potio *vb* pot; tipple
potsiar (-s) *nm* poacher
potsio *vb* poach

pothell (-au, -i) nf blister
powdr (-au) nm powder
powl, -en (powliau) nf bowl, basin
powlio vb roll; wheel, trundle
powltis (-au) nm poultice
practis nm practice
praff adj thick, stout
praffter nm thickness, stoutness, girth
pragmatiaeth nf pragmatism
praidd (preiddiau) nf flock
pranc (-iau) nm frolic, prank
prancio vb caper, prance
pratio vb pat, stroke, caress
praw, prawf (profion) nm test, trial, proof
preblan vb chatter, babble
pregeth (-au) nf sermon, discourse
pregethu vb preach
pregethwr (-wyr) nm preacher
pregethwrol adj preacher-like
pregowtha vb jabber, rant
preifat adj private
preifatrwydd nm privacy
preimin nm ploughing match
prelad (-iaid) nm prelate
preladiaeth nf prelacy
preliwd (-au) nm prelude
premiwm (-iymau) nm premium
pren (-nau) nm tree, timber; wood
prentis (-iaid) nm apprentice
prentisiaeth nf apprenticeship
prentisio vb apprentice
prepian vb babble, blab
pres nm brass; bronze; copper; money
preseb (-au) nm crib, stall
presennol adj nm present
presenoldeb nm presence; attendance
presenoli vb be present (reflexive)
presgripsiwn (-iynau) nm prescription
preswyl nm, -fa (-feydd) nf, -fod nm abode, dwelling
preswylio vb dwell, reside, inhabit
preswylydd (-ion, -wyr) nm

dweller, inhabitant
pric (-iau) nm stick, chip
prid adj dear, costly ♦ nm price, value
pridwerth nm ransom
pridd nm mould, earth, soil, ground
priddell (-au, -i) nf clod
priddglai nm loam
priddlech (-au, -i) nf tile
priddlestr (-i) nm earthenware vessel
priddlyd adj earthy
pridd(i)o vb earth
priddyn nm earth, soil, mould
prif adj prime, principal, chief
prifardd (-feirdd) nm chief bard
prifathro (-athrawon) nm headmaster, principal
prifddinas (-oedd) nf metropolis, capital
prifiant nm growth
prifio vb grow
prifodl (-au) nf chief rhyme
prifysgol (-ion) nf university
priffordd (-ffyrdd) nf highway
prin adj scarce, rare ♦ adv scarcely
prinder, -dra nm scarceness, scarcity
prinhau vb make or grow scarce, diminish
print (-iau) nm print
printiedig adj printed
printio vb print
printiwr (-wyr) nm printer
priod adj own; proper; married ♦ n coll husband or wife
priodas (-au) nf marriage, wedding
priodasfab (-feibion) nm bridegroom
priodasferch (-ed) nf bride
priodasol adj matrimonial
priod-ddull (-iau) nm idiom
priodfab (-feibion) nm bridegroom
priodferch (-ed) nf bride

priodi vb marry

priodol adj proper, appropriate

priodoldeb (-au) nm propriety

priodoledd (-au) nf attribute

priodoli vb attribute

prior (-iaid) nm prior

priordy (-dai) nm priory

pris (-iau) nm price, value

prisiad, -iant nm valuation

prisio vb price, value; prize

prisiwr (-wyr) nm valuer

problem (-au) nm/f problem

proc (-iau) nm poke

procer (-au, -i) nm poker

procio vb poke; throb

procsi nm proxy

prodin (-au) nm protein

profedig adj approved, tried

profedigaeth (-au) nf trouble, tribulation

profedigaethus adj beset with trials

profi vb prove; taste; try; experience

profiad (-au) nm experience

profiadol adj experienced

profiannaeth (-au) nf probation

proflen (-ni) nf proof-sheet

profocio vb provoke, tease

profoclyd adj provoking, provocative

profwr (-wyr) nm taster, tester

proffes (-au) nf profession

proffesiwn (-iynau) nm profession

proffesu vb profess

proffid nf profit

proffidio vb profit, benefit

proffidiol adj profitable

proffwyd (-i) nf prophet

proffwydes (-au) nf prophetess

proffwydo vb prophesy

proffwydol adj prophetic

proffwydoliaeth (-au) nf prophecy

project nm project

proses (-au) nm/f process

prosesu vb process

prosesydd nm processor. **p. geiriau**

word processor

protest (-au) nf protest

Protestannaidd adj Protestant

Protestant (-aniaid) nm Protestant

protestio vb protest

protestiwr (-wyr) nm protestor

prudd adj grave, serious, sad; wise

pruddaidd adj sad, gloomy, mournful

prudd-der nm sadness, gloom

pruddglwyf nm depression, melancholy

pruddglwyfus adj depressed, melancholy

pruddhau vb sadden, depress

Prwsia nf Prussia

pryd (-iau) nm time; season ♦ (-au) nm meal

pryd adv while, when, since

pryd nm form, aspect; complexion

Prydain nf Britain

Prydeindod nm Britishness

Prydeinig adj British

Prydeiniwr (-wyr) nm Britisher

pryder (-on) nm anxiety, solicitude

pryderu vb be anxious

pryderus adj anxious, solicitous

prydferth adj beautiful, handsome

prydferthu vb beautify

prydferthwch nm beauty

prydles (-au, -i) nf lease

prydlon adj timely, punctual

prydlondeb nm punctuality

prydydd (-ion) nm poet

prydyddu vb compose poetry, poetize

pryddest (-au) nf poem in free metre

pryf (-ed) nm insect; worm; vermin

pryfedog adj verminous

pryfleiddiad (-au) nm insecticide

pryfyn nm worm

prȳn adj bought, purchased

prynedigaeth nf/m redemption

prynhawn (-au) nm afternoon

prynhawnol *adj* afternoon, evening

pryniad *nm* purchase

prynu *vb* buy, purchase; redeem

prynwr (-wyr) *nm* buyer; redeemer

prysg *nm* bush, wood

prysgwydd *npl* brushwood

prysur *adj* busy, hasty; diligent; serious

prysurdeb *nm* haste, hurry; busyness

prysuro *vb* hurry, hasten

publican (-od) *nm* publican (New Test.)

pulpud (-au) *nm* pulpit

pulsau *npl* pulses

pum, pump *adj* five

pumawd (-au) *nm* quintet

pumed *adj* fifth

pumongl (-au) *nm* pentagon

punt (punnoedd, punnau) *nf* pound (money)

pupur *nm* pepper

pur *adj* pure, sincere ♦ *adv* very, fairly

purdan *nm* purgatory

purdeb *nm* purity, sincerity

puredigaeth *nf* purification

puredd *nm* purity, innocence

purfa (-feydd) *nf* refinery

purion *adj* very well; right enough

puro *vb* purify, cleanse

puror *nm* harpist

purwr (-wyr) *nm* purifier, refiner

purydd (-ion) *nm* purist

putain (-einiaid) *nf* prostitute

puteindra *nm* prostitution

puteinio *vb* commit fornication

puteiniwr (-wyr) *nm* fornicator

pw *excl* pooh

pwbig *adj* pubic

pwdin *nm* pudding, dessert

pwdlyd *adj* sulking

pwdr *adj* rotten, corrupt, putrid

pwdu *vb* pout, sulk

pŵer (-au) *nm* power

pwerus *adj* powerful

pwff (pyffiau) *nm* puff, blast

pwffian *vb* puff

pŵl (pyliau) *nm* fit, attack, paroxysm

pŵl *adj* blunt, obtuse; dull, dim

pwl (pyliau) *nm* fit, attack, paroxysm

pwll (pyllau) *nm* pit, pool, pond. **p. glo** coal pit. **p. tro** whirlpool

pwmp (pympiau) *nm* pump

pwn (pynnau) *nm* pack, burden

pwnc (pynciau) *nm* point, subject, question

pwniad (-au) *nm* nudge, dig

pwnio *vb* nudge; beat, thump, wallop

pwrcas (-au) *nm* purchase

pwrcasu *vb* purchase

pwrffil *nm* purfle, train

pwrpas (-au) *nm* purpose

pwrpasol *adj* suitable

pwrpasu *vb* purpose, intend

pwrs (pyrsau) *nm* purse, bag; udder; scrotum

pwt (pytiau) *nm* anything short; stump

pwt, -ian *vb* prod, poke

pwti *nm* putty

pwy *pron* who

Pŵyl *nf* Poland

pwyll *nm* sense, discretion

pwyllgor (-au) *nm* committee

pwyllgorwr (-wyr) *nm* committee-man

pwyllo *vb* pause, consider, reflect

pwyllog *adj* discreet, prudent, deliberate

pwynt (-iau) *nm* point

pwyntil *nm* tab, tag; pencil

pwyntio *vb* point; batten

pwyo *vb* beat, batter, pound

pwys (-au, -i) *nm* weight, burden, pressure; pound (lb.); importance

pwysau *nm* weight

pwysedd *nm* pressure

pwysi (-au) *nm* posy

pwysig *adj* important

pwysigrwydd *nm* importance

pwyslais (-leisiau) *nm* emphasis

pwysleisio *vb* emphasize

pwyso *vb* weigh, press; lean, rest; rely

pwyswr (-wyr) *nm* weigher

pwyth (-au) *nm* stitch. **talu'r p.** requite

pwytho *vb* stitch

pwythwr (-wyr) *nm* stitcher

pybyr *adj* strong, stout, staunch, valiant

pybyrwch *nm* stoutness, vigour, valour

pydew (-au) *nm* well, pit

pydredig *adj* rotten, putrid

pydredd *nm* rottenness, putridity, rot

pydru *vb* rot, putrefy

pyg *nm* pitch, bitumen

pygddu *adj* pitch-black

pygu *vb* pitch

pyngad, pyngu *vb* cluster

pylni *nm* bluntness, dullness

pylor *nm* dust, powder

pylu *vb* blunt, dull

pyllog *adj* full of pits

pyllu *vb* pit

pymtheg *adj, nm* fifteen

pymthegfed *adj* fifteenth

pyncio *vb* sing, play, make melody

pynfarch (-feirch) *nm* pack-horse; mill-race

pynio *vb* burden, load

pys *npl* (-en *nf*) peas

pysgod *npl* (-yn *nm*) fishes, fish. **p. a sglodion** fish and chips

pysgodfa (-feydd) *nf* fishery

pysgota *vb* fish

pysgotwr (-wyr) *nm* fisherman

pystylad *vb* stamp with the feet

pytaten (-tws) *nf* potato

pythefnos (-au) *nm/f* fortnight

PH

Pharisead (-aid) *nm* Pharisee

Phariseaeth *nf* Pharisaism

Phariseaidd *adj* Pharisaic(al)

Philistiad (-iaid) *nm* Philistine

Philistiaeth *nf* Philistinism

R

rabi (-niaid) *nm* rabbi

rabinaidd *adj* rabbinical

radio *nm* radio

radioleg *nf* radiology

radiws *nm* radius

ras (-ys) *nf* race

rasal, raser (-elydd, -erydd) *nf* razor

record (-iau) *nf/m* record

recordiad (-au) *nm* recording

reiat *nf* row, riot

reis *nm* rice

reit *adv* right, very, quite

ridens *nf* fringe, nap

riwl *nf* ruler

robin goch *nm* robin

robin y gyrrwr *nm* gadfly

roced (-i) *nf* rocket

România *nf* Romania

ruban (-au) *nm* ribbon

rŵan *adv* now

rwbel *nm* rubble, rubbish

rwber *nm* rubber

rwdins *npl* (rwden *nf*) swedes

Rwsia *nf* Russia

Rwsiad (Rwsiaid) *nm* Russian (citizen)

Rwsieg *nm* Russian (language)

RH

rhaca (-nau) *nf*, **-nu** *vb* rake

rhacs (rhecsyn *nm*) *npl* rags

rhad *adj* free; cheap

rhad (-au) *nm* grace, favour, blessing

rhadlon *adj* gracious, kind; genial

rhadlondeb, -rwydd *nm* graciousness, cheapness

rhadus *adj* economical

rhaeadr (-au) *nf* cataract, waterfall

rhaeadru *vb* pour, gush

rhaff (-au) *nf* rope, cord

rhaffo, -u *vb* rope

rhag *prep* before, against; from; lest ♦ *prefix* pre-, fore-, ante-

rhagafon (-ydd) *nf* tributary

rhagair (-au) *nm* preface

rhagarfaethiad *nm* predestination

rhagarfaethu *vb* predestine

rhagarweiniad *nm* introduction

rhagarweiniol *adj* introductory, preliminary

rhagarwyddo *vb* foretoken, portend

rhagbaratoawl *adj* preparatory

rhagbrawf (-brofion) *nm* foretaste; preliminary test

rhagdraeth (-au) *nm* preface, introduction

rhag-dyb (-ion) *nm* presupposition

rhagdybied, -io *vb* presuppose

rhagddodiad (-iaid) *nm* prefix

rhagddywedyd, rhagddweud *vb* foretell

rhagenw (-au) *nm* pronoun

rhagenwol *adj* pronominal

rhagfarn (-au) *nf* prejudice

rhagfarnllyd *adj* prejudiced

rhagferf (-au) *nf* adverb

rhagflaenor (-iaid) *nm* forerunner

rhagflaenu *vb* precede, anticipate, forestall

rhagflaenydd (-ion, -wyr) *nm* predecessor, precursor

rhagflas *nm* foretaste

rhagfur (-iau) *nm* bulwark

rhagfyfyrio *vb* premeditate

rhagfynegi *vb* foretell

Rhagfyr *nm* December

rhaglaw (-iaid, -lofiaid) *nm* prefect, viceroy, governor

rhaglawiaeth *nf* prefecture, governorship

rhaglen (-ni) *nf* programme

rhagluniaeth (-au) *nf* providence

rhagluniaethol *adj* providential

rhaglunio *vb* predestine, predestinate

rhagod *vb* ambush, hinder, waylay

rhagofnau *npl* forebodings

rhagolwg (-ygon) *nm* prospect, outlook

rhagor (-au, -ion) *nm* difference; more

rhagorfraint (-freintiau) *nf* privilege

rhagori *vb* exceed, excel, surpass

rhagoriaeth (-au) *nf* superiority; excellence

rhagorol *adj* excellent, splendid

rhagoroldeb *nm* excellence

rhagorsaf (-oedd) *nf* out-station; outpost

rhagredegydd (-ion) *nm* forerunner

rhagrith (-ion) *nm* hypocrisy

rhagrithio *vb* practise hypocrisy

rhagrithiol *adj* hypocritical

rhagrithiwr (-wyr) *nm* hypocrite

rhagrybuddio *vb* forewarn

rhagweld *vb* foresee

rhagwelediad *nm* foresight, prescience

rhagwybod *vb* foreknow

rhagwybodaeth *nf* foreknowledge

rhagymadrodd (-ion) *nm* introduction

rhai *pron* ones ♦ *adj* some

rhaib *nf* rapacity, greed; spell

rhaid (rheidiau) *nm* need, necessity

rhaidd (rheiddiau) *nf* antler

rhain *pron* these

rhamant (-au) *nf* romance

rhamantus *adj* romantic

rhan (-nau) *nf* part, portion; fate

rhanbarth (-au) *nm* division,

district

rhandir (-oedd) nm/f division, district

rhangymeriad (-iaid) nm participle

rhaniad (-au) nm division

rhannu vb divide, share, distribute

rhannwr (rhanwyr) nm divider, sharer

rhanrif nm fraction

rhathell (-au) nf rasp

rhathiad nm friction, chafing

rhathu vb rub, rasp, file

rhaw (-iau, rhofiau) nf spade, shovel

rhawd nf course, career

rhawg adv for a long time (to come)

rhawio, rhofio vb shovel

rhawn coll n coarse long hair, horse-hair

rhech nf fart

rhechain vb fart

rhedeg vb run; flow

rhedegfa (-feydd) nf racecourse, race

rhedegog adj running, flowing

rhedegydd (-ion, -wyr) nm runner

rhedfa (-u) running, course, race

rhediad nm running, trend; slope

rhedweli (-iau) nf artery

rhedyn npl (-en nf) fern

rheffyn (-nau) nm cord; string, rigmarole

rheg (-au, -feydd) nf curse

rhegen yr ŷd, rhegen ryg nf corncrake

rhegi vb curse

rheglyd adj given to cursing, profane

rheng (-au, -oedd) nf row, rank

rheibio vb raven, ravage, ravish

rheibus adj rapacious, of prey

rheidiol adj necessary, needful

rheidrwydd nm necessity, need

rheidus adj necessitous, needy

rheilffordd (-ffyrdd) nf railway

rheini pron those

rheitheg nf rhetoric

rheithfarn (-au) nf verdict

rheithgor (rheithwyr) nm jury

rheithiwr (-wyr) nm juryman, juror

rheithor (-ion, -iad) nm rector

rhelyw nm residue, rest, remainder

rhemp nf excess; defect

rhent (-i) nm rent

rhentu vb rent

rheol (-au) nf rule, regulation

rheolaeth nf rule, management, control

rheolaidd adj regular

rheoleiddio vb regulate; regularize

rheoli vb rule, govern, control

rheolwr (-wyr) nm ruler, controller

rhes (-i) nf line, stripe; row, rank

rhesen (rhesi) nf line, parting, streak, stripe

rhesin (-au, -ingau) nm raisin

rhesog adj striped; ribbed

rhestl (-au) nm rack

rhestr (-au, -i) nf list; row

rhestru vb list

rheswm (-ymau) nm reason

rhesymeg nf logic

rhesymegol adj logical

rhesymol adj reasonable, rational

rhesymoldeb nm reasonableness

rhesymolwr (-wyr) nm rationalist

rhesymu vb reason

rhetoreg, rhethreg nf rhetoric

rhew (-oedd, -ogydd) nm frost, ice

rhewfryn (-iau) nm iceberg

rhewgell (-oedd) nf freezer

rhewi vb freeze

rhewllyd adj icy, frosty, frigid

rhewyn (-au) nm ditch, stream

rhewynt (-oedd) nm freezing wind

rhi nm king, lord

rhiain (rhianedd) nf maiden

rhialtwch nm pomp; festivity, jollity

rhibidirês *nf* rigmarole
rhibin *nm* streak
rhic (-iau) *nm* notch, nick; groove
rhiciog *adj* notched; grooved; ribbed
rhidyll (-iau) *nm* riddle, sieve
rhidyllio, -u *vb* riddle, sift
rhieingerdd (-i) *nf* love-poem
rhieni *npl* parents
rhif (-au) *nm*, **rhifedi** *nm* number
rhifo *vb* number, count, reckon
rhifol (-ion) *nm* numeral
rhifyddeg, -yddiaeth *nf* arithmetic
rhifyddwr (-wyr) *nm* arithmetician
rhifyn (-nau) *nm* number
rhigol (-au, -ydd) *nf* rut, groove
rhigwm (-ymau) *nm* rigmarole; rhyme
rhigymu *vb* rhyme, versify
rhigymwr (-wyr) *nm* rhymester
rhingyll (-iaid) *nm* sergeant, bailiff
rhimyn (-nau) *nm* strip, string
rhin (-iau) *nf* virtue, essence
rhincian *vb* creak; gnash
rhiniog (-au) *nm* threshold
rhinwedd (-au) *nm/f* virtue
rhinweddol *adj* virtuous
rhip *nm* strickle
rhisgl *nm* bark
rhith (-iau) *nm* form, guise, appearance, image; foetus
rhithio *vb* appear
rhithyn *nm* atom, particle, scintilla
rhiw (-iau) *nf* hill, acclivity
rhoch *nf* grunt, groan; deathrattle
rhochain, -ian *vb* grunt
rhod (-au) *nf* wheel, orb; ecliptic
rhodfa (-feydd) *nf* walk, promenade, avenue
rhodiad *nm* walk
rhodianna *vb* stroll
rhodio *vb* walk, stroll
rhodres *nm* ostentation, affectation
rhodresa *vb* behave ostentatiously
rhodresgar *adj* ostentatious, affected
rhodreswr (-wyr) *nm* swaggerer

rhodd (-ion) *nf* gift, present
rhoddi *vb* give, bestow, yield; put
rhoddwr (-wyr) *nm* giver, donor
rhoi *vb* give, bestow, yield; put
rhôl (-iau) *nf*, **rholyn** *nm* roll
rholbren (-ni) *nm* rolling-pin
rholio *vb* roll
rhombws (**rhombi**) *nm* rhombus
rhonc *adj* rank, stark, out-and-out
rhos (-ydd) *nf* moor, heath; plain
rhos *npl* (-yn *nm*) roses
rhost *adj* roast, roasted
rhostio *vb* roast
rhosyn (-nau) *nm* rose
rhuad (-au) *nm* roaring, roar
rhuadwy *adj* roaring
rhuchen (**rhuchion**) *nf* husk; film, pellicle
rhudd *adj* red, crimson
rhuddell *nf* rubric
rhuddem (-au) *nf* ruby
rhuddin *nm* heart of timber
rhuddion *npl* bran
rhuddygl *nm* radish
Rhufain *nf* Rome
Rhufeinaidd *adj* Roman
Rhufeiniad (-iaid), **-iwr** (-wyr) *nm* Roman
Rhufeinig *adj* Roman
rhugl *adj* free, fluent, glib
rhuglen (-ni) *nf* rattle
rhuglo *vb* rattle
rhuo *vb* roar, bellow, bluster
rhusio *vb* start, scare, take fright
rhuthr (-au) *nm* rush; attack; sally
rhuthro *vb* rush; attack, assault
rhwbio *vb* rub, chafe
rhwd *nm* rust
rhwng *prep* between, among
rhwnc *nm* snort, snore; deathrattle
rhwth *adj* gaping, distended
rhwyd (-au, -i) *nf* net, snare
rhwydo *vb* net, ensnare
rhwydog *adj* reticulated, netted
rhwydwaith (-weithiau) *nm*

network

rhwydd adj easy, expeditious, prosperous

rhwyddhau vb facilitate

rhwyddineb nm ease, facility

rhwyf (-au) nf oar

rhwyflong (-au) nf galley

rhwyfo vb row; sway; toss about

rhwyfus adj restless

rhwyfwr (-wyr) nm rower, oarsman

rhwyg (-iadau) nf rent, rupture; schism

rhwygo vb rend, tear

rhwyll (-au) nf, -yn nm buttonhole, aperture; lattice

rhwyllwaith nm fretwork, lattice-work

rhwym adj bound ♦ (-au) nm bond, tie; obligation

rhwymedig adj bound, obliged

rhwymedigaeth (-au) nf bond, obligation

rhwymedd nm constipation

rhwymiad (-au) nm binding

rhwymo vb bind, tie; constipate

rhwymwr (-wyr) nm binder

rhwymyn (-nau) nm band, bond, bandage

rhwysg (-au) nm sway; pomp

rhwysgfawr adj pompous, ostentatious

rhwystr (-au) nm hindrance, obstacle

rhwystro vb hinder, prevent, obstruct

rhwystrus adj embarrassed, confused

rhy adv too

rhybedio vb rivet

rhybudd (-ion) nm notice, warning

rhybuddio vb warn, admonish, caution

rhybuddiwr (-wyr) nm warner

rhych (-au) nm/f furrow, rut, groove

rhychog adj furrowed, seamed

rhychwant (-au) nm span

rhychwantu vb span

rhyd (-au, -iau) nf ford

rhydio vb ford

rhydlyd adj rusty

rhydu vb rust

rhydd adj free; loose; liberal

Rhyddfrydiaeth nf Liberalism

rhyddfrydig adj liberal, generous

Rhyddfrydol adj liberal (in politics)

Rhyddfrydwr (-wyr) nm Liberal, Radical

rhyddhad nm liberation, emancipation

rhyddhau vb free, release, liberate

rhyddhawr (-wyr) nm liberator

rhyddiaith nf prose

rhyddid nm freedom, liberty

rhyddieithol adj prose, prosaic

rhyddni nm looseness, diarrhœa

rhyfedd adj strange, queer, wonderful

rhyfeddnod (-au) nm note of exclamation

rhyfeddod (-au) nm/f wonder, marvel

rhyfeddol adj wonderful, marvellous

rhyfeddu vb wonder, marvel

rhyfel (-oedd) nm/f war, warfare

rhyfela vb wage war, war

rhyfelgar adj warlike, bellicose

rhyfelgri nm war-cry, battle-cry

rhyfelgyrch (-oedd) nm campaign

rhyfelwr (-wyr) nm warrior

rhyferthwy nm torrent, inundation

rhyfon npl currants

rhyfyg nm presumption, foolhardiness

rhyfygu vb presume, dare

rhyfygus adj presumptuous; foolhardy

rhyg nm rye

rhyglyddu vb deserve, merit

rhygnu vb rub, grate, jar; harp

rhygyngu vb amble; caper, mince

rhyngu *vb*: **rh. bodd** please
rhyngwladol *adj* international
rhyndod *nm* shivering, chill
rhynion *npl* grits, groats
rhynllyd *adj* shivering, chilly
rhynnu *vb* starve with cold
rhysedd *nm* abundance, excess
rhython *npl* cockles
rhythu *vb* gape; stare
rhyw *adj* some, certain ♦ (**-iau**)
     nf/m sort; sex
rhywbeth *nm* something
rhywfaint *nm* some amount
rhywfodd, rhywsut *adv* somehow
rhywiog *adj* kindly, genial; fine;
     tender
rhywiol *adj* sexual
rhywle *adv* somewhere, anywhere
rhywogaeth (**-au**) *nf* species, sort,
     kind
rhywun (**rhywrai**) *nm* someone,
     anyone

S

Sabath, -oth (**-au**) *nm* Sabbath
Sabothol *adj* Sabbath, sabbatic(al)
sacrament (**-au**) *nm/f* sacrament
sacramentaidd *adj* sacramental
sach (**-au**) *nf/m* sack
sachaid (**-eidiau**) *nf* sackful
sachlen *nf*, **sachliain** *nm* sack-
     cloth
sachu *vb* sack, bag
sad *adj* firm, steady, solid; sober
sadio *vb* firm, steady
sadistiaeth *nf* sadism
sadrwydd *nm* firmness, steadiness
Sadwrn (**-yrnau**) *nm* Saturn;
     Saturday
saer (**seiri**) *nm* wright, mason,
     carpenter
saerniaeth *nf* workmanship,
     construction
saernïo *vb* fashion, construct

Saesneg *nf, adj* English
Saesnes (**-au**) *nf* Englishwoman
saets *nm* sage
saeth (**-au**) *nf* arrow, dart
saethiad (**-au**) *nm* shooting
saethu *vb* shoot, dart; blast
saethwr (**-wyr**) *nm* shooter, shot
saethydd (**-ion**) *nm* shooter,
     archer
saethyddiaeth *nf* archery
saethyn (**-nau**) *nm* projectile
safadwy *adj* stable
safanna *nm* savannah
safbwynt (**-iau**) *nm* standpoint
safiad *nm* standing; stature; stand
safio *vb* save
safle (**-oedd**) *nm* position, station,
     situation
safn (**-au**) *nf* mouth, jaws
safnrhwth *adj* open-mouthed,
     gaping
safnrhythu *vb* gape, stare
safon (**-au**) *nf* standard, criterion
safoni *vb* standardise
safonol *adj* standard
saffir *nm* sapphire
saffrwm, saffron *nm* crocus
sagrafen (**-nau**) *nf* sacrament
sang (**-au**) *nf* pressure, tread
sangu, sengi *vb* tread, trample
saib (**seibiau**) *nm* leisure; pause,
     rest
saig (**seigiau**) *nf* meal, dish
sail (**seiliau**) *nf* base, foundation
saim (**seimiau**) *nm* grease
sain (**seiniau**) *nf* sound, tone
Sais (**Saeson**) *nm* Saxon,
     Englishman
saith *adj, nm* seven
sâl *adj* poor; poorly, ill
saldra *nm* poorness; illness
salm (**-au**) *nf* psalm
salmydd (**-ion**) *nm* psalmist
salw *adj* poor, mean, vile; ugly
salwch *nm* illness
Sallwyr *nm* Psalter
sampl (**-au**) *nf* sample

samplu vb sample
Sanct nm the Holy One
sanctaidd adj holy
sancteiddio vb sanctify, hallow
sancteiddrwydd nm holiness, sanctity
sandal (-au) nm sandal
sant (saint, seintiau) nm saint
santes (-au) nf female saint
sarff (seirff) nf serpent
sarhad (-au) nm insult, disgrace, injury
sarhau vb insult, affront, injure
sarhaus adj insulting, offensive, insolent
sarn (-au) nf causeway ♦ nm litter, ruin, destruction
sarnu vb trample; litter; spoil, ruin
sarrug adj gruff, surly, morose
sarugrwydd nm gruffness, surliness
sasiwn (-iynau) nf C.M. Association
satan (-iaid) nm satan
sathredig adj common, vulgar
sathru vb tread, trample
Saudi Arabia nf Saudi Arabia
sawdl (sodlau) nm/f heel
sawl pron whoso, he that. **Pa s.** how many
sawr, sawyr nm savour
sawrio, -u vb savour
sawrus adj savoury
saws nm sauce
sba (-on) nm spa
Sbaen nf Spain
sbageti nm spaghetti
sbaner (-i) nm spanner
sbâr (sbarion) nm spare; (pl) leavings
sbario vb spare, save
sbectol nf spectacle(s)
sbeit nf spite
sbeitio vb spite
sbeitlyd adj spiteful
sbel (-iau) nf spell

sbon adv: **newydd s.** brand-new
sbonc (-iau) nm leap, jerk
sboncen nf squash
sbort nf sport, fun, game
sbri nm spree, fun
sbring nm spring
sbwylio vb spoil
sebon (-au) nm soap
seboni vb soap, lather; soft-soap, flatter
sebonwr (-wyr) nm flatterer
sect (-au) nf sect
sectyddiaeth nf sectarianism
sectyddol adj sectarian
sech adj f. of **sych**
sedd (-au) nf seat, pew
sef conj that is to say, namely, to wit
sefnig nm pharynx
sefydledig adj established
sefydliad (-au) nm establishment, institution
sefydlog adj fixed, settled, stationary, stable
sefydlo(w)grwydd nm stability
sefydlu vb establish, found, settle
sefyll vb stand; stop; stay
sefyllfa (-oedd) nf situation, position
sefyllian vb stand about, loiter
sefyllwyr npl bystanders
segur adj idle
segura vb idle
segurdod nm idleness
segurwr (-wyr) nm idler
seguryd nm idleness
seguryn, segurwr (-wyr) nm idler
sengi vb tread, trample
sengl adj single
seiat (-adau) nf fellowship meeting, 'society'
seibiant nm leisure, respite
seibio vb pause
seiciatreg nf psychiatry
seiciatrydd nm psychiatrist
seicoleg nf psychology
seidin nm sidings

seilio *vb* ground, found
seimio *vb* grease
seimllyd *adj* greasy
seinber *adj* melodious, euphonious
seindorf (-dyrf) *nf* band
seineg *nf* phonetics
seinfawr *adj* loud
seinfforch (-ffyrch) *nf* tuning-fork
seinio *vb* sound, resound;
pronounce
seintio *vb* saint, canonize
seintwar *nf* sanctuary
seinyddol *adj* phonetic
Seisnig *adj* English
Seisnigaidd *adj* English,
Anglicized
Seisnigeiddio, -igo *vb* Anglicize
seithblyg *adj* sevenfold
seithfed *adj* seventh
seithongl (-au) *nf* septangle,
heptagon
seithug *adj* futile, fruitless,
bootless
sêl *nf* zeal
sêl (seliau) *nf* seal
Seland Newydd *nf* New Zealand
seld (-au) *nf* dresser, sideboard,
bookcase
seler (-au, -i, -ydd) *nf* cellar
selio *vb* seal
selni *nm* illness
selog *adj* zealous, ardent
selsig (-od) *nf* black-pudding,
sausage
semanteg *nf* semantics
seml *adj* f. of **syml**
sen (-nau) *nf* reproof, rebuke,
censure, snub
senedd (-au) *nf* senate;
parliament
seneddol *adj* senatorial,
parliamentary
seneddwr (-wyr) *nm* senator
sennu *vb* rebuke, censure
sentimentaleiddiwch *nm*
sentimentality
sêr see **seren**

seraff (-iaid) *nm* seraph
serch *conj, prep* although,
notwithstanding
serch (-iadau) *nm* affection, love
serchog *adj* affectionate, loving
serchowgrwydd *nm*
affectionateness, love
serchu *vb* love
serchus *adj* loving, affectionate,
pleasant
sêr-ddewin (-iaid) *nm* astrologer
sêr-ddewiniaeth *nf* astrology
seremoni (-ïau) *nf* ceremony
seremonïol *adj* ceremonial
seren (sêr) *nf* star; asterisk
serennog *adj* starry
serennu *vb* sparkle, scintillate
serfyll *adj* unsteady
seri *nm* causeway, pavement
serio *vb* sear
sero (-au) *nm* zero
serth *adj* steep, precipitous;
obscene
serthedd *nm* ribaldry, obscenity
serwm *nm* serum
seryddiaeth *nf* astronomy
seryddol *adj* astronomical
seryddwr (-wyr) *nm* astronomer
sesbin *nm* shoehorn
set (-iau) *nf* set
sêt (seti) *nf* seat, pew. **s. fawr**
deacons' pew
setl (-au) *nf* settle
setlo *vb* settle
sethrydd (-ion) *nm* treader,
trampler
sew (-ion) *nm* juice; pottage;
delicacy
sffêr *nf* sphere
sg- see also **ysg-**
sgâm (sgamiau) *nf* scheme, dodge
sgamio *vb* scheme, dodge
sgarff (-iau) *nf* scarf
sgaprwth *adj* uncouth, rough
sgil *nm* pillion. **s. effaith** side effect
sgiw *nf* settle. **ar y s.** askew
sglefren *nf* slide

sglefrio vb skate, slide
sgolor (-ion) nm scholar
sgôr nm score
sgrafell (-i) nf scraper
sgrechian vb shriek
sgrin (-au) nf screen
sgriw (-iau) nf screw
sgwâr (-iau) nm square
sgwd (sgydiau) nf cataract, waterfall
sgwrs (sgyrsiau) nf talk, chat, conversation
sgwrsio vb talk, chat
si nm whiz, buzz; rumour, murmur
siaced (-i) nf jacket, coat
siâd (sidau) nf pate
sialc nm chalk
sialens nf challenge
sialensio vb challenge
siambr nf chamber
sianel (-i, -ydd) nf channel
siant (-au) nf chant
siâr nf share
siarad vb talk, speak ♦ nm talk
siaradus adj talkative, garrulous
siaradwr (-wyr) nm talker, speaker
siario vb share
siars nf charge, command
siarsio vb charge, enjoin, warn
siart (-iau) nm chart
siartr (-au) nf charter
siasbi nm shoehorn
siawns nf chance
siawnsio vb chance
sibrwd vb whisper, murmur ♦ (-ydion) nm whisper, murmur
sicr adj sure, certain; secure
sicrhau vb assure, affirm, confirm; secure
sicrwydd nm certainty, assurance
sidan (-au) nm silk
sidanaidd adj silky
sidanbryf (-ed) nm silkworm
siêd nm escheat, forfeit
sied (-au) nf shed

siesbin nm shoehorn
siew nf show
siffrwd vb rustle, shuffle
sigâr nf cigar
sigaret (sigaretau) nf cigarette
sigledig adj shaky, rickety, unstable
siglen (-nydd) nf swing; bog, swamp
siglo vb shake, quake, rock, swing, wag
sil (-od) nm spawn; fry
silff (-oedd) nf shelf
silwair nm silage
sill (-iau), -af (-au) nf syllable
sillafiaeth nf spelling
sillafu vb spell
sillgoll (-au) nf apostrophe
simnai (-neiau) nf chimney
simsan adj unsteady, tottering, rickety
simsanu vb totter
sinach (-od) nf balk, waste ground; skinflint
sinc nm zinc
sinema (sinemâu) nf cinema
sinig nm cynic
sinigaidd adj cynical
sinsir nm ginger
sio vb hiss, whiz; murmur, purl
sioe (-au) nf show
siól (-au) nf skull, pate
siôl (siolau) nf shawl
siom (-au) nm disappointment
siomedig adj disappointed, disappointing
siomedigaeth (-au) nf disappointment
siomi vb disappoint; balk, thwart; deceive
siomiant nm disappointment
sionc adj brisk, nimble, agile, active
sioncio vb brisk
sioncrwydd nm briskness, agility
sioncyn y gwair nm grasshopper
siop (-au) nf shop

siopwr (-wyr) *nm* shopman, shopkeeper

sipian *vb* sip, sup, suck

siprys *nm* mixed corn (oats and barley)

sipsiwn *npl* gipsies

sir (-oedd) *nf* shire, county

siriol *adj* cheerful, bright, pleasant

sirioldeb *nm* cheerfulness

sirioli *vb* cheer, brighten

sirydd, -yf (-ion) *nm* sheriff

siryddiaeth *nf* shrievalty

sisial *vb* whisper

siswrn (-yrnau) *nm* scissors

siwgr *nm* sugar

siwmper (-i) *nf* jumper

siwr, siwr *adj* sure, certain

siwrnai (-eiau) *nf* journey ♦ *adv* once

siwt (-iau) *nf* suit

slaf (slafiaid) *nm* slave, drudge

slei *adj* sly

sleifio *vb* slink

sleisen *nf* slice

slic *adj* slick

slotian *vb* paddle, dabble; tipple

slumyn see **ystlum**

slwt *nf* slut

smala *adj* droll

smalio *vb* joke

sment *nm* cement

smocio *vb* smoke (tobacco)

smociwr (-wyr) *nm* smoker

smotyn (smotiau) *nm* spot

smygu see **smocio**

snisin *nm* snuff

snwffian *vb* snuff, sniff; snuffle; whimper

sobr *adj* sober, serious

sobreiddio, sobri *vb* sober

sobrwydd *nm* sobriety, soberness

socas (-au) *nf* gaiter, legging

sodomiaeth *nf* sodomy

sodr *nm* solder

soddi *vb* submerge

soeg *nm* brewers' grains, draff

sofl *npl* (**-yn** *nm*) stubble

sofliar (-ieir) *nf* quail

sofraniaeth *nf* sovereignty

sofren (sofrod) *nf* sovereign (coin)

solas *nm* solace, joy

sol-ffa *nm*, **solffaeo** *vb* sol-fa

sôn *vb, nm* talk, mention, rumour

soned (-au) *nf* sonnet

sonedwr (-wyr) *nf* composer of sonnets

soniarus *adj* melodious, tuneful; loud

soriant *nm* indignation, displeasure

sorod *npl* dross, dregs, refuse

sorri *vb* chafe, sulk, be displeased

sosban (-nau, -benni) *nf* saucepan

sosej (-ys) *nf* sausage

soser (-i) *nf* saucer

sosialaeth *nf* socialism

sothach *coll n* refuse, rubbish, trash

st- see also **yst-**

stac (-iau) *nf* stack

staen *nm, nm*, **-io** *vb* stain

stâl (-au) *nf* stall

stamp (-iau) *nm/f* stamp

stampio *vb* stamp

starts *nm* starch

stên (stenau) *nf* pitcher

stesion (-au) *nf* station

sticil, -ill *nf* stile

stilio *vb* question

stiward (-iaid) *nm* steward

stiwdio *nf* studio

stoc (-iau) *nf* stock

stomp *nf* bungle, mess, muddle

stompio *vb* beat, pound; bungle, mess

stompiwr (-wyr) *nm* bungler

stori (-iau, -ïau, straeon) *nf* story, tale

stormus *adj* stormy

stor(o)m (stormydd) *nf* storm

straegar *nf* gossiping, gossipy

strancio *vb* play tricks

strategaeth *nf* strategy

strategol *adj* strategic

strategydd (-ion) *nm* strategist**

streic (-iau) *nf* strike
strwythur *nm* structure
stryd (-oedd) *nf* street
stwc (styciau) *nm* pail, bucket
stwff (styffiau) *nm* stuff
stwffio *vb* stuff, thrust
stwffwl (styfflau) *nm* post; staple
styfflylydd (-ion) *nm* stapler
su *nm* buzz, murmur, hum
suad *nm* buzzing, lulling; hum
sucan *nm* gruel
sudd (-ion) *nm* juice, sap
suddgloch (-glychau) *nf* diving-bell
suddlong (-au) *nf* submarine
suddo *vb* sink, dive; invest (money)
sug (-ion) *nm* juice, sap
sugn *nm* suck; suction; sap
sugno *vb* suck, imbibe, absorb
Sul (-iau) *nm* Sunday
Sulgwyn *nm* Whitsunday
suo *vb* buzz, hum; lull, hush
sur (-ion) *adj* sour, acid
surdoes *nm* leaven
surni *nm* sourness, staleness, tartness
suro *vb* sour
suryn *nm* acid
sut *nm* manner; plight. **pa sut?**
  sut? how? what sort of?
swalpio *vb* flounder, jump, bounce
swci *adj* tame, pet
swcro *vb* succour
swcwr *nm* succour
swch (sychau) *nf* ploughshare; tip, grimble; lips
Sweden *nf* Sweden
swil *adj* shy, bashful
swilder *nm* shyness, bashfulness
swllt (syltau) *nm* shilling
Swistir: y S. *nf* Switzerland
swm (symiau) *nm* sum, bulk
swmbwl (symbylau) *nm* goad
swmer (-au) *nm* beam; pack
swmp *nm* bulk
swmpus *adj* bulky
swn *nm* noise, sound

swnian *vb* murmur, grumble, nag
swnio *vb* sound, pronounce
swnllyd *adj* peevish, querulous
swnt *nm* sound, strait
swoleg *nf* zoology
swp (sypiau) *nm* mass, heap; cluster
swper (-au) *nmf* supper
swpera, -u *vb* give or take supper
swrn (syrnau) *nf* fetlock, ankle ♦
  nm good number
swrth *adj* heavy, sluggish; sullen
sws (-ys) *nf* kiss
swta *adj* abrupt, curt
swydd (-au, -i) *nf* office; county
swyddfa (-feydd) *nf* office
swyddog (-ion) *nm* officer, official
swyddogaeth *nf* office, function
swyddogol *adj* official
swyn (-ion) *nm* charm, fascination, spell, magic
swyngyfaredd (-ion) *nf* sorcery, witchcraft
swyngyfareddwr (-wyr) *nm* sorcerer
swyno *vb* charm, enchant, bewitch
swynol *adj* charming, fascinating
swynwr (-wyr) *nm* magician, wizard
swynwraig (-wragedd) *nf* sorceress
sy see **sydd**
syber *adj* sober, decent; clean, tidy
sych *adj* dry; *f* **sech**
sychder *nm* dryness, drought
sychdir (-oedd) *nm* dry land
syched *nm* thirst
sychedig *adj* thirsty, parched, dry
sychedu *vb* thirst
sychin *nf* drought
sychlyd *adj* dry
sychu *vb* dry, dry up; wipe dry, wipe
sychydd *nm* dryer
sydyn *adj* sudden, abrupt
sydynrwydd *nm* suddenness

sydd vb is, are

syfi npl (**syfien** nf) strawberries

syflyd vb stir, move, budge

syfrdan adj giddy, dazed, stunned

syfrdandod nm giddiness, stupor

syfrdanol adj stunning

syfrdanu vb daze, bewilder, stupefy, stun

sylfaen (**-feini**) nf foundation

sylfaenol adj basic

sylfaenu vb found

sylfaenwr (**-wyr**), **-ydd** (**-ion**) nm founder

sylw (**-adau**) nm notice, attention, remark

sylwadaeth nf observation

sylwebaeth nf commentary

sylwedydd (**-ion**) nm observer

sylwedd (**-au**) nm substance, reality

sylweddol adj substantial, real

sylweddoli vb realize

sylweddoliad nm realization

sylwi vb observe, regard, notice

syllu vb gaze

symbal (**-au**) nm cymbal

symbol nm symbol

symboliaeth nf symbolism

symbyliad nm stimulus, encouragement

symbylu vb goad, spur, stimulate

symbylydd (**-ion**) nm stimulant

symio vb sum

syml adj simple; f **semi**

symledd nm simplicity

symleiddiad nm simplification

symleiddio vb simplify

symlrwydd nm simplicity

symol adj middling, fair

symud vb move, remove

symudiad (**-au**) nm movement, removal

symudol adj moving, movable, mobile

syn adj amazed; astonishing, surprising

synagog (**-au**) nm synagogue

synamon nm cinnamon

syndod nm marvel, amazement, surprise

synfyfyrrdod nm reverie

synfyfyrio vb muse

synhwyro vb sense

synhwyrol adj sensible

syniad (**-au**) nm notion, idea, view

syniadaeth nf conception

synied, -io vb think, believe, feel

synnu vb marvel, be amazed, surprise, be surprised

synnwyr (**synhwyrau**) nm sense

synwyroldeb nm sensibleness

synwyrusrwydd nm sensuousness

sypio vb pack, heap, bundle

sypyn (**-nau**) nm package, packet

syr nm sir

syrcas nf circus

syrffed nm surfeit

syrffedu vb surfeit

Syria nf Syria

syrthiedig adj fallen

syrthio vb fall, tumble

syrthni nm listlessness, sloth; inertia

system nmf system

systematig adj systematic

syth adj stiff; straight

sythu vb stiffen, straighten; starve with cold

sythwelediad nm intuition

T

tabernacl (**-au**) nm tabernacle

tabl (**-au**) nm table

tablen nf ale, beer

tabŵ nm taboo

tabwrdd (**-yrddau**) nm drum

tabyrddu vb drum, thrum

taclau npl (**teclyn** nm) tackle, gear

taclo vb tackle

taclu vb put in order, trim

taclus adj neat, trim, tidy

tacluso vb trim, tidy

taclusrwydd *nm* tidiness

Tachwedd *nm* November

tacteg (-au) *nf* tactic

tad (-au) *nm* father. **tad-cu** grandfather

tadmaeth (-au, -od) *nm* fosterfather

tadogaeth *nf* paternity; derivation

tadogi *vb* father

tadol *adj* fatherly, paternal

taenelliad *nm* sprinkling, affusion

taenellu *vb* sprinkle

taenellwr (-wyr) *nm* sprinkler

taenu *vb* spread, expand, stretch

taenwr (-wyr) *nm* spreader, disseminator

taeog *adj* churlish, blunt ♦ **(-au, -ion)** *nm* churl

taeogaidd *adj* churlish, rude

taer *adj* earnest, importunate, urgent

taerineb, taerni *nm* earnestness, importunity

taeru *vb* insist, maintain; contend, wrangle

tafarn (-au) *nf/m* tavern, inn, public-house

tafarndy (-dai) *nm* public-house

tafarnwr (-wyr) *nm* inn-keeper, publican

tafell (-au, -i, tefyll) *nf* slice

tafl (-au) *nf* cast; scale. **ffon d.** sling

tafledigion *npl* projectiles

taflegryn (taflegrau) *nm* missile

tafleisiaeth *nf* ventriloquism

tafleisydd (-ion, -wyr) *nm* ventriloquist

taflen (-nau, -ni) *nf* table, list, leaflet

taflennu *vb* tabulate

tafliad (-au) *nm* throw; set-back

taflod (-ydd) *nf* loft. **t. y genau** palate

taflodol *adj* palatal

taflu *vb* throw, fling, cast, hurl

tafluniad *nm* projection

taflunio *vb* project

taflunydd *nm* projector

tafod (-au) *nm* tongue

tafodi *vb* berate, scold

tafodiaith (-ieithoedd) *nf* speech, language, dialect

tafod-leferydd *nm* speech, utterance, **ar d.** by rote

tafol *nf* scales, balance

tafol *coll n* dock

tafoli *vb* weigh up, assess

tafotrwg *adj* foul-mouthed, abusive

tafotrydd *adj* garrulous, flippant

tagell (-au, tegyll) *nf* gill; wattle; dewlap; double chin

tagellog *adj* wattled; doublechinned

tagfa (-feydd) *nf* choking, strangling

tagu *vb* choke, stifle; strangle

tangnefedd *nm/f* peace

tangnefeddu *vb* make peace; appease

tangnefeddus *adj* peaceable, peaceful

tangnefeddwr (-wyr) *nm* peacemaker

tai see **tŷ**

taid (teidiau) *nm* grandfather

tail *nm* dung, manure

tair *adj* f. of **tri**

taith (teithiau) *nf* journey, voyage, progress

tal *adj* tall, high, lofty

tâl (talau, taloedd) *nm* end, forehead

tâl (taliadau) *nm* pay, payment. **taloedd** rates

talaith (-eithiau) *nf* diadem; province, state

talar *(-au)* *nf* headland in field

talcen (-nau, -ni) *nm* forehead; gable

taldra *nm* tallness, loftiness, stature

taleb (-au, -ion) *nf* receipt, voucher

taledigaeth *nf* payment,

recompense

taleithiol adj provincial

talent (-au) nf talent

talentog adj talented

talfyriad (-au) nm abbreviation, abridgement

talfyrru vb abbreviate, abridge

talgryf adj sturdy, robust; impudent

taliad (-au) nm payment

talm nm space, while; quantity, number. **er ys t.** long ago

talog adj jaunty

talp (-au, -iau) nm mass, lump

talpiog adj lumpy

talu vb pay, render; answer, suit; be worth

talwr (-wyr) nm payer

talwrn nm threshing floor; poetic contest

tamaid (-eidiau) nm morsel, bit, bite

tan prep to, till, until, as far; under

tân (tanau) nm fire

tanbaid adj fiery, hot, fervent; brilliant

tanbeidrwydd nm fierce heat, ardour

tanchwa (-oedd) nf fire-damp; explosion

tanddaearol adj underground, subterranean

tanforol adj submarine

taniad nm ignition, firing

tanio vb fire, stoke

taniwr (-wyr) nm firer, fireman, stoker

tanlinellu vb underline

tanlwybr nm subway

tanlli adj: **newydd sbon danlli** brand new

tanllwyth (-i) nm blazing fire

tanllyd adj fiery

tannu vb adjust, spread, make (bed)

tanodd adv below, beneath

tant (tannau) nm chord, string

tanwent nm fuel

tanwydd coll n firewood, fuel

tanysgrifiad (-au) nm subscription

tanysgrifio vb subscribe

tanysgrifiwr (-wyr) nm subscriber

taradr (terydr) nm auger. **t. y coed** woodpecker

taran (-au) nf (peal of) thunder

taranfollt (-au) nf thunderbolt

taranu vb thunder

tarddell nf source, spring

tarddiad (-au) nm source, derivation

tarddle (-oedd) nm source

tarddu vb sprout, spring; derive, be derived

tarfu vb scare, scatter

targed (-au) nm target

tarian (-au) nf shield

tario vb tarry

taro vb strike, smite, hit, knock; tap; stick; hot; suit

tarren (tarenni, -ydd) nf knoll, rock

tarth (-oedd) nm mist, vapour

tarw (teirw) nm bull

tarwden nf ringworm

tas (teisi) nf rick, stack

tasel nm tassel

tasg (-au) nf task

tasgu vb task; start, jump; splash, spirt

tato, tatws npl (**taten, tatysen** nf) potatoes

taw nm silence. **rhoi t.** ar silence

taw conj that

tawch nm vapour, haze, t. mist, fog

tawdd adj melted, molten, dissolved

tawedog adj silent, taciturn

tawedogrwydd nm taciturnity

tawel adj calm, quiet, still, tranquil

tawelu vb calm; grow calm

tawelwch nm calm, quiet, tranquillity

tawelydd nm silencer

tawlbwrdd nm draughtboard, backgammon

tawtologiaeth nf tautology

te nm tea

tebot (-au) nm teapot

tebyg adj similar, like, likely

tebygol adj likely, probable

tebygolrwydd nm likelihood, probability

tebygrwydd nm likeness, resemblance

tebygu vb liken, resemble; suppose

tecáu vb beautify, adorn, embellish

teclyn (**taclau**) nm tool, instrument

techneg nf technique ♦ -ol adj technical

teg adj fair, beautiful, fine

tegan (-au) nm plaything, toy, bauble

tegell (-au, -i) nm kettle, teakettle

tegwch nm fairness, beauty

tei nm/f tie

teiar nm tyre

teigr (-od) nm tiger

teilchion npl fragments, atoms, shivers

teiliwr (-eilwriaid) nm tailor

teilo vb dung, manure

teilwng adj worthy; deserved

teilwra vb tailor

teilwres (-au) nf tailoress

teilwriaeth nf tailoring

teilyngdod nm worthiness, merit

teilyngu vb deserve, merit; deign

teim nm thyme

teimlad (-au) nm feel, feeling, sensation, emotion ♦ -ol adj emotional

teimladrwydd nm feelingness, sensibility

teimladwy adj feeling; sensitive

teimlo vb feel, touch, handle, manipulate

teimlydd (-ion) nm feeler, antenna, tentacle

teios npl cottages

teip (-iau) nm type

teipiadur (-ion) nm typewriter

teipio vb type

teipydd (-ion) nm typist

teisen (-nau) nf cake

teitl (-au) nm title

teithi coll n traits, characteristics, qualities

teithio vb travel, journey

teithiol adj travelling, itinerant

teithiwr (-wyr) nm traveller, passenger

telathrebiaeth nf telecommunication

teledu nm television ♦ vb televise

teleffon (-au) nm telephone

teler (-au) nm term, condition

teligraff nm telegraph

telm (-au) nf snare

telori vb warble; quaver

telyn (-au) nf harp

telyneg (-ion) nf lyric

telynegol adj lyrical

telynegwr nm lyric poet

telynor (-ion) nm harpist

telynores (-i) nf female harpist

teml (-au) nf temple

tempro vb temper

temtasiwn (-iynau) nm/f temptation

temtio vb tempt

temtiwr (-wyr) nm tempter

tenant (-iaid) nm tenant

tenantiaeth nf tenancy

tenau adj thin, lean; slender; rarified; sensitive

tendio vb tend, mind

teneuad nm dilution

teneuo vb thin, become thin, dilute

teneuwch nm thinness, leanness; tenuity

tenewyn (-nau) nm flank

tenis nm tennis

tenlli(f) nm lining

tennyn (**tenynnau**) nm cord, rope, halter

têr adj clear, refined, pure, fine

teras (-au) *nm* terrace

terfyn (-au) *nm* end, extremity, bound

terfyniad (-au) *nm* ending, termination

terfynol *adj* final; conclusive

terfynu *vb* end, terminate, determine

terfysg (-oedd) *nm* tumult, riot

terfysgaeth *nf* terrorism

terfysgaidd, -lyd *adj* riotous, turbulent

terfysgu *vb* riot, rage, surge

terfysgwr (-wyr) *nm* rioter, insurgent

term (-au) *nm* term

terminoleg *nf* terminology

tes *nm* sunshine, warmth, heat; haze

tesog *adj* sunny, hot, close, sultry

testament (-au) *nm* testament

testamentwr (-wyr) *nm* testator

testun (-au) *nm* text, theme, subject

testunio *vb* taunt, deride

tetanws *nm* tetanus

teth (-au) *nf* teat

teulu (-oedd) *nm* family

teuluaidd *adj* family, domestic

tew *adj* thick, fat, plump

tewdra, -dwr *nm* thickness, fatness

tewhau *vb* thicken, fatten

tewi *vb* keep silence, be silent

tewychu *vb* thicken, fatten; condense

tewychydd *nm* condenser

tewyn (-ion) *nm* ember, brand

teyrn (-edd, -oedd) *nm* monarch, sovereign

teyrnas (-oedd) *nf* kingdom, realm. **y Deyrnas Gyfunol** the United Kingdom

teyrnasiad (-au) *nm* reign

teyrnasu *vb* reign

teyrnfradwr (-wyr) *nm* traitor

teyrnfradwriaeth *nf* (high)

treason

teyrngar *adj* loyal

teyrngarwch *nm* loyalty

teyrnged (-au) *nf* tribute

teyrnwialen (-wiail) *nf* sceptre

ti *pron* you (*fam*)

ticed (-i) *nm/f* ticket

tician *vb* tick

tid (-au) *nf* chain

tila *adj* feeble, puny, insignificant

tim (timau) *nm* team

tin (-au) *nf* bottom; rump; tail

tinc (-iadau) *nm* clang, tinkle

tincian *vb* tinkle, chink, clink, clank

tip (-iadau) *nm* tick (of clock)

tipian *vb* tick

tipyn (-nau, tipiau) *nm* bit

tir (-oedd) *nm* land, ground, territory

tirio *vb* land, ground

tiriog *adj* landed

tiriogaeth (-au) *nf* territory

tiriogaethol *adj* territorial

tirion *adj* kind, tender, gentle, gracious

tiriondeb *nm* kindness, tenderness

tirlun (-iau) *nm* landscape

tirol *adj* relating to land

tirwedd *nf* relief (*GEOG*)

tisian *vb* sneeze

titw *nf* puss, pussy

tithau *pron conj* thou (on thy part), thou also

tiwmor *nm* tumour

tiwn (-iau) *nf* tune

tiwnio *vb* tune

tlawd (tlodion) *adj* poor

tlodaidd *adj* poorish, mean, dowdy

tlodi *vb* impoverish ♦ *nm* poverty

tlos *adj* f. of **tlws**

tloty (-ai) *nm* poorhouse, workhouse

tlotyn (tlodion) *nm* pauper

tlws *adj* pretty; *f* **tlos**

tlws (tlysau) *nm* jewel, gem; medal

tlysni nm prettiness

to (toeau) nm roof; generation

toc adv shortly, presently, soon

tocio vb clip, dock, prune

tocyn (tociau) nm pack, heap, hillock; slice of bread

tocyn (-nau) nm ticket

tocynnwr (-ynwyr) nm bus conductor

toddedig adj molten; melting

toddi vb melt, dissolve, thaw

toddiant (-nnau) nm solution

toddion npl dripping

toddwr (-wyr), -ydd (-ion) nm melter

toes nm dough

toi vb cover; roof; thatch

toili nm spectral funeral

tolach vb fondle

tolc (-iau) nm dent, dinge

tolchen (-au) nf clot

tolchennu vb clot

tolcio vb dent, dinge

tolciog adj dented, dinged

toll (-au) nf toll, custom

tolli vb take toll

tom nf dirt, mire, dung

tomen (-nydd) nf heap; dunghill

tomlyd adj dirty, miry

ton (-nau) nf wave, billow, breaker

ton (-nau) nm lay-land

tôn (tonau) nf tone; tune

tonc (-iau) nf tinkle, ring, clash

toncio, -ian vb tinkle, ring

tonfedd (-i) nf wavelength

tonig (-iau) adj tonic (MED) tonic (MUSIC)

tonnen (tonenydd, -au) nf skin; sward; bog

tonni vb wave, undulate

tonnog adj wavy, billowy

tonyddiaeth nf tone, intonation

topio vb plug, stop up

topyn nm plug, stopper

tor (-ion) nm break, interruption

tor (-rau) nf belly; palm (of hand)

torcalonnus adj heartbreaking

torch (-au) nf wreath; coil

torchi vb wreathe; coil; roll, tuck

torchog adj wreathed; coiled

tordyn adj tight-bellied; hectoring

toreithiog adj abundant, teeming

toreth nf abundance

torf (-eydd) nf crowd, multitude

torfynyglu vb break neck of; behead

torgoch (-ion) nm roach

torgwmwl nm cloudburst

torheulo vb bask, sunbathe

tori (-iaid) nm tory

toriad (-au) nm cut, break; fraction

toriaeth nf toryism

toriaidd adj tory, conservative

torlan (-nau, -lennydd) nf river bank

torllengig nm rupture

torllwyth (-i), torraid nf litter

torogen (-ogod) nf tick (in cattle)

torri vb break, cut; dig; write, trace

torrwr (torwyr) nm breaker, cutter

tors nm/f torch

torsyth adj swaggering

torsythu vb strut, swagger

torth (-au) nf loaf

tost adj severe, sharp, sore; ill

tost nm toast

tosturi (-aethau) nm compassion, pity

tosturio vb be compassionate, pity

tosturiol adj compassionate

tosyn (tosau) nm pimple

tôwr (towyr) nm tiler

tra adv over; very ♦ conj while, whilst

tra-arglwyddiaeth (-au) nf tyranny

tra-arglwyddiaethu vb tyrannize

tra-awdurdodi vb lord it over, domineer

trabludd nm trouble, tumult, turmoil

trac (-iau) nm track

trachefn adv again

trachwant (-au) nm lust, covetousness

trachwanta, -tu vb lust, covet

trachwantus adj covetous

tradwy adv three days hence

traddodi vb deliver; commit

traddodiad (-au) nm tradition; delivery

traddodiadol adj traditional

traddodwr (-wyr) nm deliverer

traean nm one third, the third part

traed see **troed**

traeth (-au) nm strand, shore, beach

traethawd (-odau) nm treatise; essay; tract

traethell (-au) nf strand, sandbank

traethiad (-au) nm predicate

traethodydd (-ion) nm essayist

traethu vb utter, declare; treat

trafael (-ion) nf travail, trouble

trafaelio vb travel

trafaeliwr (-wyr) nm traveller

trafaelu vb travel; travail

traflyncu vb guzzle, gulp, devour

trafnidiaeth nf traffic

trafod vb handle; discuss; transact

trafodaeth (-au) nf discussion, transaction

trafodion npl transactions

trafferth (-ion) nf/m trouble

trafferthu vb trouble

trafferthus adj troublesome; troubled

tragwyddol adj everlasting, eternal

tragwyddoldeb nm eternity

tragywydd adj everlasting, eternal

traha nm arrogance, presumption

trahaus adj arrogant, haughty

trahauster nm arrogance, presumption

trai nm ebb

trais nm oppression, force, violence

trallod (-ion, -au) nm trouble, tribulation

tralloddi vb afflict, vex, trouble

trallodus adj troubled; troublous

trallodwr (-wyr) nm troubler, afflicter

tramgwydd (-iadau) nm stumbling; offence

tramgwyddo vb stumble; offend; take offence

tramgwyddus adj scandalous; offensive

tramor adj foreign

tramorwr (-wyr) nm foreigner

tramwy, -o vb pass, traverse

tramwyfa (-feydd) nf passage, thoroughfare

tranc nm end, dissolution, death

trancedig adj deceased

trancedigaeth nf death, decease

trannoeth adv next day ♦ nm the morrow

trapio vb trap

traphlith adv: blith d. higgledy-piggledy

tras nf kindred, affinity

traserch nm great love, infatuation

trasiedi (trasiediau) nf tragedy

traul (treuliau) nf wear; cost, expense; digestion

trawiad (-au) nm stroke, beat, flash

trawiadol adj striking

traws adj cross; froward, perverse

trawsblannu vb transplant

trawsdoriad nm cross-section

trawsenwad nm metonymy

trawsfeddiannu vb usurp

trawsfudo vb transmigrate

trawsffurfio vb transform

trawsgludo vb transport, conduct

trawsgyweiriad nm transposition, modulation

trawsgyweirio vb transpose, change key

trawslif nm cross-saw

trawslythrennu vb transliterate

traws-sylweddiad nm transubstantiation

trawst (-iau) *nm* beam
trebl *nm, adj* treble
treblu *vb* treble
trech *adj* superior, stronger, mightier
trechu *vb* overpower, overcome, conquer
tref (-i, -ydd) *nf* home; town
trefedigaeth (-au) *nf* settlement, colony
trefgordd (-au) *nf* township
treflan (-nau) *nf* small town, townlet
trefn (-au) *nf* order, method, system
trefniad (-au) *nm* arrangement, ordering
trefniant *nm* arrangement, organization
trefnlen (-ni) *nf* schedule
trefnu *vb* order, arrange, dispose
trefnus *adj* orderly, methodical
trefnusrwydd *nm* orderliness
trefnydd (-ion) *nm* arranger; Methodist
trefol *adj* town, urban
treftadaeth *nf* patrimony, inheritance
trengi *vb* die, perish, expire
treial (-on) *nm* trial
treiddgar *adj* penetrating, keen
treiddgarwch *nm* penetration, acumen
treiddio *vb* pass, penetrate
treiddiol *adj* penetrating
treigl (-au) *nm* turn, revolution, course
treigl(i)ad (-au) *nm* mutation; inflection
treiglo *vb* roll; mutate; inflect; decline
treio *vb* ebb
treio *vb* try
treisiad (-iedi) *nf* heifer
treisio *vb* force, ravish, violate, oppress, rape
treisiwr (-wyr) *nm* violator, oppressor; rapist
trem (-iau) *nf* sight, look, aspect
tremio *vb* look, gaze
trên (trenau) *nm* train
trennydd *adv* day after tomorrow
tres (-i) *nf* trace, chain; tress
tresbasu, tresmasu *vb* trespass
tresglen *nf* thrush
treth (-i) *nf* rate, tax, tribute. **t. y pen** community charge, poll tax
trethadwy *adj* rateable, taxable
trethdalwr (-wyr) *nm* ratepayer
trethu *vb* tax, rate, assess
trethwr (-wyr) *nm* taxer
treuliad *nm* digestion
treulio *vb* wear, consume; spend; digest
tri *adj, nm* three; *f* **tair**
triagl *nm* treacle, balsam, balm
triawd (-au) *nm* trio
triban (-au) *nm* triplet (*metre*); Plaid Cymru badge
tribiwnlys (-oedd) *nm* tribunal
tric (-iau) *nm* trick
tridiau *npl* three days
trigain *adj, nm* sixty
trigfa (-feydd), **-fan** (-nau) *nf* dwelling-place, abode
trigiannol *adj* residentiary
trigiannu *vb* reside, dwell
trigiannydd (-ianwyr) *nm* resident
trigo *vb* stay, abide; dwell; die (*animals*)
trigolion *npl* inhabitants, dwellers
trimio *vb* trim
trin (-oedd) *nf* battle
trin *vb* handle; treat; dress; till; transact
trindod (-au) *nf* trinity
tringar *adj* skilful, tender
triniaeth (-au) *nf* treatment
trioedd *npl* triads
triongl (-au) *nm/f* triangle
trionglog *adj* triangular
trist *adj* sad, sorrowful
tristáu *vb* sadden, grieve
tristwch *nm* sadness, sorrow

triw *adj* loyal, faithful
tro (**troeau, troeon**) *nm* turn, twist; conversion
troad (**-au**) *nm* bend, turning; figure of speech
trobwll (**-byllau**) *nm* whirlpool
trobwynt (**-iau**) *nf* turning-point
trochfa (**-feydd**) *nf* plunge, immersion
trochi *vb* dip, plunge, immerse; soil
trochion *npl* lather, suds, foam
trochioni *vb* lather, foam
trochwr (**-wyr**) *nm* immerser, immersionist
troed (**traed**) *nm/f* foot, base; leg; handle
troedfainc (**-feinciau**) *nf* footstool
troedfedd (**-i**) *nf* foot (=12 inches)
troedig *adj* turned, converted, perverse
troedigaeth (**-au**) *nf* turning, conversion
troedio *vb* foot, tread, trudge
troednodyn *nm* footnote
troednoeth *adj* barefoot, barefooted
troedwst *nf* gout
troell (**-au**) *nf* wheel, spinning-wheel
troelli *vb* spin; twist, wind
troellog *adj* winding, tortuous
troellwr (**-wyr**) *nm* disc-jockey
troetffordd (**-ffyrdd**) *nf* footway, footpath
trofa (**-feydd**) *nf* turn; bend, turning
trofan (**-nau**) *nf* tropic
trofannol *adj* tropical
trofaus *adj* perverse
trofwrdd (**-fyrddau**) *nm* turntable
trogen see **torogen**
trogylch (**-au**) *nm* orbit
troi *vb* turn, revolve; convert; plough
trol (**-iau**) *nf* cart
trolian, -io *vb* roll

troliwr (**-wyr**) *nm* carter
trom *adj* f. of **trwm**
tros *prep* over, for, instead of, on behalf of
trosedd (**-au**) *nm* transgression, offence, crime
troseddol *adj* criminal
troseddu *vb* transgress, trespass, offend
troseddwr (**-wyr**) *nm* transgressor, trespasser, offender; criminal
trosgais (**trosgeisiau**) *nm* converted try
trosglwyddiad *nm* transference, transfer
trosglwyddo *vb* hand over, transfer
trosgynnol *adj* transcendental
trosi *vb* turn; translate; convert (a try)
trosiad (**-au**) *nm* translation; metaphor; conversion (*rugby*)
trosodd *adv* over, beyond
trosol (**-ion**) *nm* lever, crow-bar, bar; staff
trostan *nf* pole
trotian *vb* trot
trothwy (**-au**) *nm* threshold
trowr (**-wyr**) *nm* ploughman
trowsus (**-au**) *nm* trousers
trowynt (**-oedd**) *nm* whirlwind, tornado
truan (**truin**) *adj* poor, wretched, miserable ♦ (**trueiniaid**) *nm* wretch; *f* **truanes**
trueni *vb* wretchedness; misery; pity
truenus *adj* wretched, miserable
trugaredd (**-au**) *nf/m* mercy, compassion
trugarhau *vb* have mercy, take pity
trugarog *adj* merciful, compassionate
trugarogrwydd *nm* mercifulness
trulliad (**-iaid**) *nm* butler, cupbearer

trum (**-au, -iau**) nm ridge
truth nm flattery; rigmarole
trwbl nm, **-o** vb trouble
trwch nm thickness. **t. y blewyn** hair's breadth
trwch adj broken; unfortunate; wicked
trwchus adj thick
trwm (**trymion**) adj heavy; f **trom**
trwnc (**trynciau**) nm trunk
trwodd adv through
trwsgl adj awkward, clumsy, bungling
trwsiad nm dress, attire
trwsiadus adj well-dressed, smart
trwsio vb dress, trim; mend, repair
trwsiwr (**-wyr**) nm mender, repairer
trwst nm noise, din, tumult
trwstan adj awkward, clumsy, untoward
trwstaneiddiwch nm awkwardness
trwy prep through, by, by means of
trwyadl adj thorough
trwydded (**-au**) nf leave, licence
trwyddedu vb license
trwyn (**-au**) nm nose, snout; point, cape
trwyno vb nose, nuzzle, sniff
trwynol adj nasal
trwynsur adj sour, morose
trwyth (**-i**) nf decoction, infusion, urine
trwytho vb steep, saturate, imbue
trybedd, trybed nf tripod, trivet
trybelid adj bright, brilliant
trybestod nm commotion, bustle, fuss
trybini nm trouble, misfortune, misery
tryblith nm muddle, chaos
trychfil (**-od**) nm insect, animalcule

trychiad (**-au**) nm cutting, fracture, section
trychineb (**-au**) nm/f disaster, calamity
trychinebus adj disastrous, calamitous
trychu vb cut, hew, pierce, lop
trydan nm electric fluid, electricity
trydaneg nm/f electrical engineering
trydaniaeth nf electricity; thrill
trydanol adj electric, electrical
trydanu vb electrify
trydar nm, vb chirp, chatter
trydydd adj third; f **trydedd**
tryfer (**-i**) nf harpoon, trident
tryferu vb spear, harpoon
tryfesur nm diameter
tryfrith adj speckled; swarming, teeming
trylediad (**-au**) nm diffusion
tryledu vb diffuse
tryloyw adj pellucid, transparent
tryloywder nm transparency
trylwyr adj thorough
trylwyredd nm thoroughness
trymaidd adj heavy, close, oppressive
trymder nm heaviness, drowsiness
trymfryd nm sadness, sorrow
trymhau vb make or grow heavy
trymllyd adj heavy, close, oppressive
tryryw adj thoroughbred
trysor (**-au**) nm treasure
trysordy (**-dai**) nm treasurehouse
trysorfa (**-feydd**) nf treasury, fund
trysori vb treasure
trysorlys nm treasury, exchequer
trysorydd (**-ion**) nm treasurer
trystio vb make a noise; trust
trystiog adj noisy, rowdy
trythyll adj wanton, lascivious
trythyllwch nm lasciviousness
trywanu vb transfix, stab, pierce
trywel nm trowel
trywydd nm scent, trail

Tseina nf China

Tsiecoslofacia nf Czechoslovakia

tu nm side, part, direction

tua, tuag prep towards; about

tuchan vb grumble, groan, murmur

tudalen (-nau) nm/f page

tudded (-i) nf covering; pillowcase

tuedd (-iadau) nf tendency, inclination

tuedd (-au) nm district, region

tueddfryd nm inclination, bent

tueddol adj inclined, apt

tueddu vb incline, tend, trend

tufewnol adj inward, internal

tulath (-au) nf beam, rafter

Tunisia nf Tunisia

tunnell (tunelli) nf ton; tun

turio vb root up, burrow, delve

turn nm lathe

turniwr (-wyr) nm turner

turtur (-od) nf turtle-dove

tusw (-au) nm wisp, bunch

tuth (-iau) nm trot

tuthio vb trot

twb (tybiau) nm tub

twca nm tuck-knife

twffyn (twffiau) nm tuft

twlc (tylciau) nm sty

twlcio vb horn, butt, gore

twlciog adj given to horning

twll (tyllau) nm hole

twmpath (-au) nm tump, hillock; bush; folk-dance

twndis (-au) nm funnel

twndra (-âu) nm tundra

twnffed (-i) nm funnel

twnnel (twnelau) nm tunnel

twp adj stupid, dull, obtuse

twpdra nm stupidity

twpsyn nm stupid person

tŵr (tyrau) nm tower

twr (tyrrau) nm heap; group, crowd

Twrc (Tyrciaid) nm Turk

Twrci nf Turkey

twrci (-ïod) nm turkey

twrch (tyrchod) nm hog. **t. daear** mole

twrf (tyrfau) nm noise; (pl.) thunder

twrnai (-eiod) nm attorney, lawyer

twrw nm noise (**twrf**)

twt excl tut!

twt adj tidy, neat, smart

twtio vb tidy

twyll nm deceit, deception, fraud

twyllo vb deceive, cheat, swindle

twyllodrus adj deceitful, false

twyllresymeg nf sophism

twyllresymiad (-au) nm sophistry

twyllwr (-wyr) nm deceiver

twym adj warm, hot, sultry

twymder, twymdra nm warmness, warmth

twymgalon adj warm-hearted

twymo, twymno vb warm, heat

twymyn (-au) nf fever. **y dwymyn goch** scarlet fever. **y dwymyn doben** mumps

twyn (-i) nm hill, hillock, knoll; bush

twysged nf lot, quantity

tŷ (**tai, teiau**) nm house

tyaid (-eidiau) nm houseful

tyb (-iau) nm/f opinion, notion, surmise

tybaco nm tobacco

tybed adv I wonder; is that so?

tybiaeth (-au) nf supposition

tybied, tybio vb suppose, think, imagine

tybiedig adj supposed, putative

tycio vb prosper, succeed, avail

tydi pron thou, thyself

tyddyn (-nod) nm (small) farm, holding

tyddynnwr (-ynwyr) nm smallholder

tyfadwy adj growing

tyfiant nm growth

tyfu vb grow

tyfwr (-wyr) nm grower

tynged nf destiny, fate

tyngedfennol adj fateful, fatal

tynghedu vb destine; fate; adjure

tyngu vb swear, vow

tyngwr (-wyr) nm swearer

tylath see **tulath**

tyle nm slope, hill

tylino vb knead. **t. y corff** massage

tylinwr (-wyr) nm kneader, masseur

tylwyth (-au) nm household, family. **t. teg** fairies

tyllog adj holey

tyllu vb hole, bore, perforate, pierce

tylluan (-od) nf owl

tyllwr (-wyr) nm borer

tymer (-herau) nf temper

tymestl (-hestloedd) nf tempest, storm

tymheredd nm temperature

tymherus adj temperate

tymhestlog adj tempestuous, stormy

tymhoraidd adj seasonable

tymhorol adj temporal

tymor (-horau) nm season

tymp (-au) (appointed) time, season

tympan (-au) nm drum; timbrel

tyn adj tight

tynder, -dra nm tightness, tension

tyndro (tyndroeon) nm wrench

tyner adj tender, gentle

tyneru vb make tender, soften

tynerwch nm tenderness, gentleness

tynfa (-feydd) nf draw, attraction

tynfaen (-feini) nm loadstone, magnet

tynhau vb tighten, strain

tynnu vb draw, pull; take off, remove

tyno nm hollow; tenon

tyrchu vb root up, burrow

tyrchwr (-wyr) nm mole-catcher

tyrfa (-oedd) nf multitude, host, crowd

tyrfau npl thunder

tyrfedd (-au) nm turbulence, thunder

tyrfo, tyrfu vb make a noise or commotion

tyrpant nm turpentine

tyrpeg nm turnpike

tyrru vb heap, amass; crowd together

tyst (-ion) nm witness

tysteb (-au) nf testimonial

tystio vb testify, witness

tystiolaeth (-au) nf testimony, evidence

tystiolaethu vb bear witness, testify

tystlythyr (-au) nm testimonial

tystysgrif (-au) nf certificate

tywallt vb pour, shed, spill

tywalltiad (-au) nm outpouring

tywarchen (tywyrch) nf sod, turf

tywel (-ion) nm towel

tywod nm sand

tywodfaen nm sandstone

tywodlyd, -odog adj sandy

tywodyn nm grain of sand

tywydd nm weather

tywyll adj dark, obscure; blind

tywyllu vb darken, obscure

tywyllwch nm darkness

tywyn (-au) nm sea-shore, strand

tywynnu vb shine

tywys vb lead, guide

tywysen (-nau, tywys) nf ear of corn

tywysog (-ion) nm prince

tywysogaeth (-au) nf principality

tywysogaidd adj princely

tywysoges (-au) nf princess

tywysydd (-ion) nm leader, guide

TH

theatr (-au) nf theatre

thema (themâu) nf theme

theorem (-au) nf theorem

theori (-iau) nf theory

thermomedr *nm* thermometer
thesis (-au) *nm* thesis
thus *nm* frankincense

U

ubain *vb* howl, wail, moan; sob
uchaf *adj* uppermost, highest
uchafbwynt (-iau) *nm* climax; zenith
uchafiaeth *nf* supremacy; ascendancy
uchafion *npl* heights
uchafrif (-au) *nm* maximum
uchder *nm* height; top
uchel *adj* high, lofty; uppish; loud
uchelder (-au) *nm* highness, height
ucheldir (-oedd) *nm* highland
uchelfryd *adj* high-minded
uchelgais *nm/f* ambition
uchelgeisiol *adj* ambitious
uchelion *npl* heights
uchelradd *adj* of high degree, superior
uchelseinydd (-ion) *nm* loudspeaker
uchelwr (-wyr) *nm* gentleman, nobleman
uchelwydd *coll n* mistletoe
uchgapten (-teiniaid) *nm* major
uchod *adv* above
udo *vb* howl
udd *nm* lord
ufudd *adj* obedient, humble
ufudd-dod *nm* obedience, humility
ufuddhau *vb* obey
uffern *nf* hell
uffernol *adj* infernal, hellish
ugain (ugeiniau) *adj*, *nm* twenty, score
Ulster *nf* Ulster
ulw *coll n* ashes, powder ♦ *adv* utterly
un *adj* one, only; same ♦ (-au) *coll n* one, unit
unawd (-au) *nm/f* solo

unawdydd (-wyr) *nm* soloist
unben (-iaid, unbyn) *nm* sovereign lord, despot
unbenaethol *adj* despotic
unbennaeth *nf* sovereignty, despotism
undeb (-au) *nm* unity, union. **yr U. Sofietaidd** the Soviet Union
undebaeth *nf* unionism
undebol *adj* united, union
undebwr (-wyr) *nm* unionist
undod (-au) *nm* unity; unit
Undodaidd *adj* Unitarian
Undodiaeth *nf* Unitarianism
Undodwr (-wyr, -iaid) *nm* Unitarian
undonedd *nm* monotony
undonog *adj* monotonous
uned (-au) *nf* unit
unfan *nm* same place
unfarn *adj* unanimous
unfryd, -ol *adj* unanimous
unfrydedd *nm* unanimity
unffurf *adj* uniform
unffurfiaeth *nf* uniformity
ungell *adj* monocellular
uniaith *adj* monoglot
uniawn *adj* straight; right, upright; just
unig *adj* sole, only; alone, lonely
unigedd *nm* loneliness, solitude
unigol *adj* singular; individual ♦ (-ion) *nm* individual
unigoliaeth *nf*, **-rwydd** *nm* individuality
unigrwydd *nm* loneliness, solitude
union *adj* straight, direct; just, exact
uniondeb *nm* straightness; rectitude
uniongred *adj* orthodox
uniongrededd *nm/f* orthodoxy
uniongyrch, -ol *adj* immediate, direct
unioni *vb* straighten; rectify; make for
unionsgwar *adj* perpendicular

unionsyth adj straight, direct; erect

unllygeidiog adj one-eyed

unman adv anywhere

unnos adj of one night

uno vb join, unit, amalgamate

unochrog adj unilateral, biased

unodl adj of the same rhyme

unol adj united. **yr U. Daleithiau** npl the United States

unoli vb unify

unoliaeth nf unity, oneness, identity

unplyg adj of one fold; folio; simple, ingenuous

unplygrwydd nm sincerity

unrhyw adj same; any

unrhywiol adj unisexual

unsain adj unison. **yn u.** in unison

unsill adj monosyllabic

unswydd adj of one purpose

unwaith adv once

unwedd adj like ♦ adv likewise

urdd (-au) nf order; rank

urddas (-au) nm dignity, honour

urddasol adj dignified, noble

urddo vb ordain, confer degree or rank

us coll n chaff

ust excl, nm hush

ustus (-iaid) nm justice, magistrate

usuriaeth nf usury

utgan vb sound a trumpet

utganwr (-wyr) nm trumpeter

utgorn (-gyrn) nm trumpet

uwch adj higher ♦ prep above, over

uwchbridd (-oedd) nm topsoil

uwchgapten (-iaid) nm major

uwchradd nm, adj superior

uwchsonig adj ultrasonic, supersonic

uwd nm porridge

W

wadi (-iau) nm wadi

wagen (-ni) nf truck, waggon

waldio vb wallop, beat

warws (warysau) nm warehouse

wats (-iau) nm watch

wedi prep after ♦ adv afterwards

wedyn adv afterwards, then

weiren nf wire

weir(i)o vb wire

weithian, -ion adv now, now at length

weithiau adv sometimes

wel excl well

wele excl behold, lo

wermod nf wormwood

wfft excl fie, for shame

wfftio vb cry fie, flout, scout

whado vb beat, thrash

wiced (-i) nf wicket

wicedwr (-wyr) nm wicket-keeper

widw nf widow

Wien nf Vienna

wlser (-au) nm ulcer

wmbredd nm abundance

wraniwm nm uranium

wrth prep by; with; to; because, since

wy (-au) nm egg

wybr (-au), **wybren** (-nau, -nydd) nf sky; cloud

wybrol adj ethereal

wyf vb I am

wygell (-oedd) nf ovary

wylo vb weep, cry

wylofain vb wail, weep ♦ nm wailing

wylofus adj wailing, doleful, tearful

ẁyn see oen

ẁyna vb lamb

wyneb (-au) nm face, surface; front

wyneb-ddalen nf title-page

wynebgaled adj barefaced, impudent

wyneblun (-iau) nm frontispiece

wynebu vb face, front

wynepryd nm countenance

wynwyn npl onions

ŵyr (wyrion) n coll grandchild, grandson

wysg nm track. **yn w. ei gefn** backwards

wystrys npl, coll n oysters

wyth (-au) adj, nm eight

wythawd (-au, -odau) nf octave

wythblyg adj octavo

wythfed adj eighth

wythnos (-au) nf week

wythnosol (-ion) adj weekly

wythnosolyn (-olion) nm weekly paper

wythongl (-au) nf octagon

wythwr (-wyr) nm number eight (rugby)

Y

y, yr, 'r adj the

y, yr preverbal and relative particle

ych (-en) nm ox

ychwaith adv (nor) either, neither

ychwaneg nm more

ychwanegiad (-au) nm addition

ychwanegol adj additional

ychwanegu vb add, augment, increase

ychydig adj, adv, nm little, few

ŷd (ydau) nm corn

ydlan (-nau) nf stack-yard, rickyard

ydwyf vb I am

ydys vb: **yr ydys yn disgwyl** it is expected

ydyw vb is, are

yfed vb drink; absorb

yfory adv tomorrow

yfwr (-wyr) nm drinker

yfflon npl (**yfflyn** nm) shivers,

pieces, bits ♦ adj highly annoyed

yng prep in (mutation of **yn**)

yngan, -u vb utter, speak

ynghyd adv together

ynghylch prep about, concerning

ynglŷn â prep in connection with

ym prep in (mutation of **yn**)

ym- prefix (usu. reflexive or reciprocal)

yma adv here, in this place; this

ymadael, ymadaw vb depart

ymadawedig adj departed, deceased

ymadawiad nm departure; decease

ymadawol adj farewell, valedictory

ymado vb depart

ymadrodd (-ion) nm speech, saying, expression

ymadroddus adj eloquent

ymaddasu vb adjust, adapt

ymaelodi vb become a member, join

ymaelyd, ymafael, ymaflyd vb take hold

ymageru vb evaporate

ymagor vb open, unfold, expand

ymagweddiad (-au) nm demeanour, attitude

ymaith adv away, hence

ymarfer vb practise, exercise ♦ (-ion) nf practice, exercise

ymarferiad (-au) nm exercise

ymarhous adj dilatory; long-suffering, patient

ymaros vb bear with, endure ♦ nm long-suffering, patience

ymarweddiad nm conduct, behaviour

ymatal vb forbear, refrain, abstain

ymateb vb answer, respond, correspond

ymbalfalu vb grope

ymbaratoi vb get oneself ready

ymbarél nm umbrella

ymbelydredd nm radiation

ymbelydrol adj radioactive
ymbellhau vb go further away
ymbil (-iau) nm supplication, entreaty
ymbil, -io vb implore, beseech, entreat
ymboeni vb take pains
ymborth nm food, sustenance
ymbortheg n/m dietetics
ymborthi vb feed
ymbriodi vb marry; intermarry
ymbwyllo vb pause, reflect
ymchwelyd vb turn, return; overturn
ymchwil nf search, research, quest
ymchwiliad (-au) nm investigation
ymchwydd (-iadau) nm swelling, surge
ymchwyddo vb swell; surge
ymdaith (-deithiau) nf journey, march ♦ (-deithiau) nf journey, march
ymdebygu vb grow like; resemble
ymdeimlad nm feeling, sense
ymdeimlo vb feel; be conscious of
ymdeithio vb travel, journey; sojourn
ymdoddi vb melt, become dissolved
ymdopi vb manage
ymdrech (-ion) nm/f effort, endeavour, struggle
ymdrechgar adj striving, energetic
ymdrechu vb wrestle; strive, endeavour
ymdrin vb treat, deal with
ymdriniaeth nf treatment; discussion
ymdrochi vb bathe
ymdrochwr (-wyr) nm bather
ymdroi vb linger, loiter, dawdle
ymdrybaeddu vb wallow
ymdynghedu vb vow
ymddangos vb appear, seem
ymddangosiad (-au) nm appearance
ymddangosiadol adj seeming,

apparent
ymddarostwng vb submit
ymddarostyngiad nm humiliation, submission
ymddatod vb dissolve
ymddeol vb resign, retire
ymddeoliad (-au) nm retirement
ymddiddan vb talk, converse ♦ (-ion) nm talk, conversation
ymddihatru vb divest, undress
ymddiheuriad nm apology
ymddiheuro vb apologize
ymddiosg vb strip, undress
ymddiried vb trust ♦ nm trust, confidence
ymddiriedaeth nf trust, confidence
ymddiriedolwr (-wyr) nm trustee
ymddiswyddo vb resign
ymddwyn vb behave, act
ymddygiad (-au) nm behaviour, conduct; (pl) actions
ymddyrchafu vb exalt oneself; rise, ascend
ymegnio vb exert oneself
ymehangu vb become enlarged, expand
ymennydd (ymenyddiau) nm brain
ymenyn nm butter
ymerawdwr (-wyr) nm emperor
ymerodraeth (-au) nf empire
ymerodres (-au) nf empress
ymerodrol adj imperial
ymesgusodi vb excuse oneself, apologise
ymestyn vb stretch, extend, reach
ymestyniad (-au) nm extension
ymfalchïo vb pride oneself
ymfodloni vb acquiesce
ymfudo vb emigrate
ymfudwr (-wyr) nm emigrant
ymffrost nm boast
ymffrostio vb boast, vaunt
ymffrostiwr (-wyr) nm boaster
ymgadw vb keep oneself (from), forbear
ymgais nm/f effort, attempt
ymgasglu vb gather together

ymgecru vb quarrel, wrangle
ymgeisio vb try, apply; aim at
ymgeisydd (-wyr) nm applicant, candidate
ymgeledd nm succour, care
ymgeleddu vb cherish, succour
ymgeleddwr (-wyr) nm succourer; tutor, guardian
ymgilio vb retreat, recede
ymgiprys vb, nm scramble
ymglymu vb involve, bind together
ymglywed vb feel (oneself), be inclined
ymgnawdoliad nm incarnation
ymgodymu vb wrestle, fight
ymgofleidio vb mutually embrace
ymgom (-ion) nf chat, conversation
ymgomio vb chat, converse
ymgorfforiad nm embodiment
ymgreinio vb prostrate oneself; grovel
ymgroesi vb cross oneself; beware
ymgryfhau vb strengthen oneself, be strong
ymgrymu vb bow down, stoop
ymguddfa nf shelter, hiding-place
ymguddio vb hide
ymgydio vb copulate
ymgydnabod vb acquaint oneself
ymgyfathrachu vb have dealings with
ymgyfeillachu vb associate
ymgyfoethogi vb get rich
ymgynghori vb consult, confer
ymgynghoriad nm consultation
ymgymeriad (-au) nm undertaking
ymgymryd vb undertake
ymgynefino vb become familiar, get used to
ymgynnal vb bear up; support oneself; control oneself
ymgynnull vb assemble, congregate
ymgyrch (-oedd) nm/f campaign, expedition
ymgyrraedd vb stretch, strive after

ymgysegriad nm devotion, consecration
ymgysegru vb devote oneself
ymhél vb meddle
ymhelaethu vb abound; enlarge
ymhell adv far, afar
ymhellach adv further, furthermore
ymherodr etc see ymerawdwr
ymhlith prep among
ymhlyg adj implicit
ymhoelyd vb overturn, topple
ymhoffi vb take delight; boast
ymholi vb inquire
ymholiad (-au) nm inquiry
ymhonni vb lay claim to, pretend
ymhonnwr (-honwyr) nm pretender
ymhŵedd vb beseech, implore, crave
ymhyfrydu vb delight (oneself)
ymiacháu vb become healed, get well
ymlacio vb relax
ymladd vb fight ♦ (-au) nm fighting
ymlâdd vb kill oneself (with exertion), tire oneself out. wedi y. dead beat
ymladdfa (-feydd) nf fight
ymladdgar adj pugnacious, warlike
ymladdwr (-wyr) nm fighter, combatant
ymlaen adv on, onward
ymlafnio vb toil, strive, struggle
ymlawenhau vb rejoice
ymledu vb spread, expand
ymlenwi vb fill oneself
ymlid vb pursue, chase
ymlidiwr (-wyr) nm pursuer
ymlonyddu vb grow calm or still
ymlosgiad nm combustion
ymlusgiad (-iaid) nm reptile
ymlusgo vb creep, crawl
ymlwybro vb make one's way
ymlyniad nm attachment
ymlynu vb attach, adhere, cleave

(to)

ymlynwr (-wyr) nm adherent

Ymneilltuaeth nf Nonconformity

ymneilltuo vb retire

Ymneilltuol adj Nonconformist

Ymneilltuwr (-wyr) nm Nonconformist

ymnesáu vb approach, draw near

ymochel, -yd vb shelter; beware

ymod, -i vb move, stir

ymofyn vb ask, inquire, seek ♦ (-ion) nm inquiry

ymofynnydd (-ofynwyr) nm inquirer

ymolchfa (-feydd) nf wash; lavatory

ymolchi vb wash oneself, bathe

ymollwng vb sink, drop, give way, collapse

ymorchestu vb strive, labour

ymorffwys vb rest, repose

ymorol vb seek; take care, attend to, see to it

ymosod vb attack, assail, assault

ymosodiad (-au) nm attack, assault

ymosodol adj aggressive, offensive, forward

ymosodwr (-wyr) nm attacker, assailant

ymostwng vb stoop; humble oneself; submit

ymostyngar adj submissive

ymostyngiad nm submission

ympryd (-ion) nm fast

ymprydio vb fast

ymprydiwr (-wyr) nm faster

ymrafael (-ion) nm quarrel, contention

ymrafaelgar adj quarrelsome, contentious

ymraniad (-au) nm division, schism

ymrannu vb part, divide, separate

ymrannwr (-ranwyr) nm separatist

ymreolaeth nf self-government, Home Rule

ymrestru vb enlist

ymresymiad (-au) nm reasoning, argument

ymresymu vb reason, argue

ymresymwr (-wyr) nm reasoner

ymrithio vb appear

ymroad nm application, devotion

ymroddedig adj devoted

ymroddgar adj of great application

ymroddi, ymroi vb apply or devote oneself; yield or resign oneself, surrender, do one's best

ymroddiad nm application, devotion

ymron adv nearly, almost

ymrous adj assiduous

ymrwyfo vb struggle, toss about

ymrwygo vb tear, burst

ymrwymiad (-au) nm engagement

ymrwymo vb bind or engage oneself

ymryson vb contend, strive ♦ (-au) nm contention, strife, rivalry

ymrysongar adj contentious

ymsefydlu vb establish oneself, settle

ymsefydlwr (-wyr) nm settler

ymserchu vb cherish, dote

ymson vb soliloquize ♦ (-au) nm soliloquy

ymsuddiant nm subsidence

ymswyno vb cross oneself; beware

ymsymud vb move

ymuno vb join, unite

ymwacâd nm kenosis

ymwacáu vb empty oneself

ymwadiad nm denial, abnegation

ymwadu vb deny (oneself); renounce

ymwahanu vb part, divide, separate

ymwahanwr (-wyr) nm separatist

ymwared nm deliverance

ymwasgu vb embrace, hug

ymweithydd (-ion) nm reactor

ymweld vb visit

ymweliad (-au) nm visit, visitation

ymwelwr, -ydd (-wyr) nm visitor, visitant

ymwrando vb hearken

ymwroli vb take heart, be of good courage

ymwrthod vb abstain; renounce

ymwrthodiad nm abstinence

ymwthgar adj pushing, obtrusive

ymwthio vb push oneself, obtrude

ymwthiol adj obtrusive, intrusive

ymwybodol adj conscious

ymwybyddiaeth nf consciousness

ymwylltio vb fly into a passion

ymyl (-au, -on) nm/f edge, border, margin

ymylu vb border

ymylwe nf selvedge

ymyrgar adj meddlesome, officious

ymyrraeth, ymyrru, -yd nf meddle, interfere ♦ nf interference

ymyrrwr (-yrwyr) nm meddler

ymysg prep among, amid

ymysgaroedd npl bowels

ymysgwyd vb bestir oneself

yn prep in, at, into; for ♦ also introduces verb-nouns

yn adj particle

yna adv there; then; thereupon; that

ynad (-on) nm judge, justice, magistrate

yn awr adv now, at present

yndeintiad (-au) nm indentation

ynfyd (-ion) adj foolish, rash

ynfydrwydd nm foolishness, folly

ynfydu vb rave, be mad

ynfytyn (-fydion) nm fool, madman

ynni nm energy, vigour

yno adv there

yntau pron conj he (on his part), he also

ynteu, ynte conj or, or else, otherwise; then

Ynyd nm Shrovetide

ynys (-oedd) nf island, river meadow

ynysfor (-oedd) nm archipelago

Ynysoedd Dedwydd: yr Y. npl the Canary Islands

ynysol adj island, insular

ynyswr (-wyr) nm islander

ynysydd (-ion) nm insulator

yr see y

yrhawg adv for a long time (to come)

yrwân adv now (N.W.)

ys vb it is ♦ conj as

ysbaddu vb castrate

ysbaid (-beidiau) nm/f space (of time)

ysbail (-beiliau) nf spoil, plunder

ysbardun nm/f spur

ysbarduno vb spur

ysbeidiol adj occasional, intermittent

ysbeilio vb spoil, plunder

ysbeiliwr (-wyr) nm spoiler, robber

ysbienddrych (-au) nm spying-glass

ysbïo vb spy, look

ysbïwr (-wyr) nm spy

ysblander nm splendour

ysblennydd adj splendid

ysbonc (-iau) nf jump, bound; spurt

ysboncio vb jump, bounce; spurt, splash

ysborion npl cast-offs

ysbrigyn nm sprig, twig

ysbryd (-ion, -oedd) nm spirit, ghost

ysbrydegaeth nf spiritualism

ysbrydegol adj spiritualistic

ysbrydegydd (-ion) nm spiritualist

ysbrydiaeth nf encouragement, inspiration

ysbrydol adj spiritual; high-spirited

ysbrydoli vb spiritualize; inspire; inspirit

ysbrydoliaeth *nf* inspiration

ysbwng *nm* sponge

ysbwrial, -iel *nm* rubbish, refuse

ysbwylio *vb* spoil

ysbyty (-tai) *nm* hospital; hospice

ysfa (-feydd) *nf* itching; hankering

ysg- see **sg-**

ysgadan *npl* (**-enyn** *nm*) herrings

ysgafala *adj* secure, careless, free

ysgafn *adj* light ♦ *nm* stack

ysgafnder *nm* lightness, levity

ysgafnhau, ysgafnu *vb* lighten

ysgafnu *vb* heap, pile

ysgall *npl* (**-en** *nf*) thistles

ysgariad *nm*, **-iaeth** *nf* separation, divorce

ysgarlad *nm* scarlet

ysgarmes (-oedd, -au) *nf* skirmish

ysgaru *vb* part, separate, divorce

ysgatfydd *adv* perhaps, peradventure

ysgathru *vb* spread, scatter

ysgaw *coll n* (**-en** *nf*) elder

ysgeler *adj* wicked, villainous, infamous

ysgerbwd (-bydau) *nm* skeleton, carcase

ysgithr (-edd) *nm* tusk, fang

ysgithrog *adj* fanged, tusked; craggy, rugged

ysgiw *nf* settle

ysglefrio *vb* slide (on ice); skate

ysglyfaeth (-au) *nf* prey, spoil; carrion, filth

ysglyfaethus *adj* of prey; rapacious

ysgogi *vb* move, stir

ysgogiad (-au) *nm* movement, motion

ysgol (-ion) *nf* school; schooling

ysgol (-ion) *nf* ladder

ysgoldy (-dai) *nm* schoolhouse, schoolroom

ysgolfeistr (-i, -iaid) *nm* schoolmaster

ysgolfeistres (-i) *nf* schoolmistress

ysgolhaig (-heigion) *nm* scholar

ysgolheictod *nm* scholarship

ysgolheigaidd *adj* scholarly

ysgolor (-ion) *nm* scholar

ysgoloriaeth (-au) *nf* scholarship

ysgorpion (-au) *nm* scorpion

Ysgotyn (-gotiaid) *nm* Scot, Scotsman

ysgrafell (-od, -i) *nf* scraper; curry-comb

ysgrafellu *vb* scrape, curry

ysgraff (-au) *nf* boat, barge, ferry-boat

ysgraffinio *vb* scarify, graze, abrade

ysgrech (-feydd) *nf* scream, shriek

ysgrechian, -in *vb* scream, shriek

ysgrepan (-au) *nf* wallet, scrip

ysgrif (-au) *nf* writing, article, essay

ysgrifbin (-nau) *nm*, **-grifell (-au)** *nf* pen

ysgrifen, -eniad (-iadau) *nf* writing

ysgrifennu *vb* write

ysgrifennwyr (-enwyr) *nm* writer

ysgrifennydd (-enyddion) *nm* scribe, secretary

ysgrifenyddiaeth *nf* secretaryship

ysgriw (-iau) *nf* screw

ysgriwio *vb* screw

ysgrwbio *vb* scrub

ysgryd *nm* shiver

ysgrythur (-au) *nf* scripture

ysgrythurol *adj* scriptural

ysgrythurwr (-wyr) *nm* scripturist

ysgub (-au) *nf* sheaf; broom

ysgubo *vb* sweep

ysgubol *adj* sweeping

ysgubor (-iau) *nf* barn, granary

ysgubwr (-wyr) *nm* sweeper, sweep

ysgutor (-ion) *nm* executor

ysguthan (-od) *nf* wood-pigeon; jade

ysgwâr *adj*, *nf* square

ysgwario *vb* square

ysgŵd *nm* jerk, toss, fling, shove

ysgwïer (-iaid) nm squire

ysgwrfa nf scouring, lathering

ysgwrio vb scour, scrub; lather

ysgwyd vb shake; flutter; wag

ysgwydd (-au) nf shoulder

ysgwyddo vb shoulder, jostle

ysgydwad nm shaking, shake

ysgyfaint npl lungs, lights

ysgyfarnog (-od) nf hare

ysgymun adj excommunicate, accursed

ysgymundod nm excommunication, ban

ysgymuno vb excommunicate

ysgyrion npl staves, splinters, shivers

ysgyrnygu vb grind the teeth, snarl

ysgytiad (-au) nm shock

ysgytio vb shake violently, shock

ysgythru vb cut, carve; prune

ysictod nm contusion; sprain

ysig adj bruised, sore, sprained

ysigo vb bruise, crush; sprain

yslotian vb dabble, tipple

ysmala adj droll, funny, amusing

ysmaldod nm fun, drollery

ysmalio vb joke, jest

ysmaliwr (-wyr) nm joker, wit

ysmotyn (ysmotiau) nm spot

ysmwddio vb iron

ysmygu vb smoke (tobacco)

ysmygwr (-wyr) nm smoker

ysol adj consuming, devouring; corrosive

yst- see also **st-**

ystabl (-au) nf stable

ystad (-au) nf estate; estate; furlong

ystadegau npl statistics

ystadegol adj statistical

ystadegydd (-ion) nm statistician

ystafell (-oedd) nf chamber, room

ystalwyn (-i) nm stallion

ystanc (-iau) nm stake, bracket

ystarn (-au) nf stern

ystelcian vb skulk, loaf, loiter

ystelciwr (-wyr) nm loafer, loiterer

ystên (-enau) nf pitcher, ewer, milk-can

ystinos nm asbestos

ystiwart (-wardiaid) nm steward

ystlum (-od) nm bat

ystlys (-au) nf side, flank

ystlyswr (-wyr) nm linesman

ystod (-ion) nf course; swath. **Yn y.** during

ystof nm/f warp

ystofi vb warp; weave, plan

ystôl (-olion) nf stool, chair

ystôr (-orau) nm store, abundance

ystordy (-dai) nm storehouse, warehouse

ystorfa (-feydd) nf store, storehouse

ystorio vb store

ystorïwr (-iwyr) nm storyteller

ystorm (-ydd) nf storm

ystormus adj stormy

ystrad (-au) nm/f vale, flat

ystranc (-iau) nf trick

ystrancio vb play tricks; jib

ystrodur (-iau) nf cart-saddle

ystryd (ystrydoedd) nf street

ystrydebol adj stereotyped

ystryw (-iau) nf wile, craft, ruse

ystrywgar adj wily, crafty

ystum (-iau) nm/f bend; form; posture; (pl) grimaces

ystumio vb bend, distort; pose

ystumog (-au) nf stomach

ystwr nm stir, noise, bustle, fuss

Ystwyll nm Epiphany

ystwyrian vb stretch and yawn, stir

ystwyth adj flexible, pliant, supple

ystwythder nm flexibility, pliancy

ystwytho vb make flexible; bend, soften

ystyfnig adj obstinate, stubborn

ystyfnigo vb behave obstinately

ystyfnigrwydd nm obstinacy

ystyr (-on) nf/m sense, meaning

ystyrgar *adj* thoughtful, meditative

ystyriaeth (**-au**) *nf* consideration, heed

ystyried *vb* consider, regard, heed

ystyriol *adj* mindful, heedful

ysu *vb* eat, consume; hanker; itch

yswain (**-weiniaid**) *nm* esquire

yswil *adj* shy, bashful, timid

yswildod *nm* shyness, bashfulness

yswiriant *nm* insurance

yswirio *vb* insure

yswaeth *adv* more's the pity

yw *vb* is, are

yw *npl*, *coll n* (**-en** *nf*) yew

ENWAU PERSONAU PERSONAL NAMES

Adda Adam
Anghrist Antichrist
Andreas Andrew
Awstin Augustine
Bartholomeus Bartholomew
Beda Bede
Bedwyr Bedivere
Beti, Betsan, Betsi Betty, Betsy
Buddug Boadicea; Victoria
Bwda Buddha
Cadi Catherine, Kate
Cadog, Catwg Cadoc
Cai Kay
Caradog Caratacos, Caractacus
Caswallon Cassivellaunus
Catrin Catherine
Cesar Caesar
Crist Christ
Cystennin Constantine
Dafydd, Dewi David
Edmwnt, Emwnt Edmund
Efa Eve
Elen Helen, Ellen
Eleias Elijah, Elias
Eliseus Elisha, Eliseus
Emrys Ambrose
Ercwlff Hercules
Eseia, Esay Isaiah
Esyllt Iseult
Fychan Vaughan
Fyrsil, Fferyll Virgil
Ffowc Foulkes
Ffraid Bride, Bridget
Garmon Germanus
Geraint Gerontius
Gerallt Gerald
Glyndŵr Glendower
Gruffudd, Gruffydd Griffith
Gwallter Walter
Gwener Venus
Gwenffrewi, Gwenfrewi Winifred
Gwenhwyfar Guinevere
Gwilym William

Gwladus Gladys
Gwrtheyrn Vortigern
Harri Harry, Henry
Horas Horace
Hors Horsa
Hu, Huw Hugh
Iago James
Iau Jove, Jupiter
Iesu Grist Jesus Christ
Ieuan Evan
Ioan John
Iorwerth Edward
Iwan John
Lowri Laura
Luc Luke
Lleucu Lucy
Llwyd Lloyd
Llŷr Lear
Mabli Mabel
Mair Mary
Mali Molly
Mallt Maud, Matilda
Marc Mark
Marged, Margred Margaret
Mari Mary
Mawrth Mars
Mercher Mercury
Mererid Margaret
Meurig Morris
Mihangel Michael
Modlen, Magdalen Magdalene
Myrddin Merlin
Neifion Neptune
Ofydd Ovid
Oswallt Oswald
Owain Owen
Padrig Patrick
Pedr Peter
Peredur Perceval
Prys Price, Preece
Puw Pugh
Pyrs Pierce
Rheinallt Reginald

Rhisiart Richard
Rhobert Robert
Rhonwen Rowena
Rhydderch Roderick
Rhys Rees, Rice
Sadwrn Saturn
Sebedeus Zebedee
Selyf Solomon
Siân Jane
Siarl Charles
Siarlymaen Charlemagne

Sieffre Geoffrey
Siencyn Jenkin
Siôn John
Sioned Janet
Siôr, Siors George
Steffan Stephen
Timotheus Timothy
Tomos Thomas
Tudur Tudor
Twm Tom
Wmffre Humphrey

ENWAU LLEOEDD PLACE NAMES

Aberdâr Aberdare
Aberdaugleddyf Milford Haven
Aberddawan Aberthaw
Abergwaun Fishguard
Aberhonddu Brecon
Abermo, Bermo Barmouth
Aberpennar Mountain Ash
Abertawe Swansea
Aberteifi Cardigan
Afon Menai Menai Straits
Amwythig Shrewsbury
Arberth Narberth
Babilon Babylon
Breudeth Brawdy
Brycheiniog Brecknock
Brynbuga Usk
Bryste, Caerodor Bristol
Caer Chester
Caerdroea Troy
Caerdydd Cardiff
Caerefrog York
Caerfaddon Bath
Caerfyrddin Carmarthen
Caergaint Canterbury
Caergrawnt Cambridge
Caergybi Holyhead
Caergystennin Constantinople
Caerhirfryn Lancaster, Lancashire
Caerliwelydd Carlisle
Caerloyw Gloucester
Caerlŷr Leicester (shire)
Caerllion Caerleon
Caernarfon Caernarvon
Caersallog Salisbury
Caerwrangon Worcester
Caer-wynt Winchester
Caer-Wysg Exeter
Caint Kent
Calfaria Calvary
Casllwchwr Loughor
Cas-mael Puncheston
Casnewydd Newport, Mon.
Castell-Nedd Neath

Castellnewydd Newcastle
Ceinewydd New Quay
Ceredigion Cardiganshire
Cernyw Cornwall
Clawdd Offa Offa's Dyke
Clwyd North East Wales
Coed-duon Blackwood
Conwy Conway
Côr y Cewri Stonehenge
Croesoswallt Oswestry
Crucywel Crickhowell
Cydweli Kidwelly
Dinas Basing Basingwerk
Dinbych Denbigh
Dinbych-y-pysgod Tenby
Donaw Danube
Drenewydd Newtown
Dyfed Demetia, South West Wales
Dyfnaint Devon
Dyfrdwy Dee
Efrog York
Eryri Snowdonia
Fflandrys Flanders
Fflint Flint
Gâl Gaul
Glynebwy Ebbw Vale
Gwent South East Wales
Gwlad-yr-haf Somerset
Gwy Wye
Gwynedd North West Wales
Gŵyr Gower
Hafren Severn
Hendy-gwyn Whitland
Henffordd Hereford
Hwlffordd Haverfordwest
Iâl Yale
Lacharn, Talacharn Laugharne
Lerpwl Liverpool
Llanandras Presteigne
Llanbedr Pont Steffan Lampeter
Llandaf Landaff
Llandudoch St Dogmaels
Llaneirwg St Mellons

Llanelwy St Asaph
Llaneurgain Northop
Llanfair-ym-Muallt Builth
Llangatwg Cadoxton
Llangrallo Coychurch
Llanilltud Fawr Llantwit Major
Llanllieni Leominster
Llansawel Briton Ferry
Llanymddyfri Llandovery
Llwydlo Ludlow
Llyn Tegid Bala Lake
Maesyfed Radnor
Manaw Isle of Man
Manceinion Manchester
Meirionnydd Merioneth
Môn Anglesey
Morgannwg Glamorgan
Mynwy Monmouth
Mynyw St David's
Nanhyfer, Nyfer Nevern
Pennarlâg Hawarden
Pen-y-Fantach Mumbles Head
Penbedw Birkenhead
Pen-bre Pembrey
Penfro Pembroke
Penrhyn Gobaith Da Cape of Good Hope
Pen-y-bont ar Ogwr Bridgend
Pontarfynach Devil's Bridge
Pont-y-pŵl Pontypool
Porthaethwy Menai Bridge
Porthmadog Portmadoc
Powys Mid Wales
Rhuthun Ruthin
Rhydychen Oxford
Sain Ffagan St Fagans
Sili Sully
Solfach Solva
Tafwys Thames

Treamlod Ambleston
Trecelyn Newbridge
Trefaldwyn Montgomery
Trefdraeth Newport, Pem
Treforus Morriston
Trefyclo Knighton
Trefynwy Monmouth
Treffynnon Holywell
Tyddewi St David's
Tywi Towy
Wdig Goodwick
Wrecsam Wrexham
Wysg the Usk
Y Bont-faen Cowbridge
Y Fenni Abergavenny
Y Gelli (Gandryll) Hay
Y Gogarth Great Orme
Y Mot New Moat
Y Rhws Rhoose
Y Waun Chirk
Ynys Bŷr Caldey Island
Ynys Dewi Ramsey Island
Ynys Echni Flat Holm
Ynys Enlli Bardsey Island
Ynys Gybi Holy Island
Ynys Lawd South Stack
Ynys Seiriol Puffin Island
Ynysoedd Erch Orkney Islands
Ynysoedd Heledd The Hebrides
Ynysoedd y Moelrhoniaid The Skerries
Ynys y Garn Guernsey
Ynys Wyth Isle of Wight
Yr Wyddfa Snowdon
Yr Wyddgrug Mold
Ystrad-fflur Strata Florida
Ystrad Marchell Strata Marcella
Ystumllwynarth Oystermouth
Y Trallwng Welshpool

ENGLISH-WELSH DICTIONARY

A

a, an *adj*: **a man** dyn. **an ass** asyn
aback *adv* yn ôl. **taken a.** wedi synnu
abandon *vt* rhoi'r gorau i, gadael
abandoned *adj* wedi ei adael, ofer, afradlon
abase *vt* darostwng, iselhau, gostwng
abash *vt* cywilyddio
abate *vb* gostwng, lleihau; gostegu
abattoir *n* lladd-dy
abbess *n* abades
abbey *n* abaty, mynachlog
abbot *n* abad
abbreviate *vt* byrhau, talfyrru
abbreviation *n* byrfodd
abdicate *vb* ymddeol, ymddisgwyddo
abdomen *n* bol
abdominal *adj* perthynol i'r bol
abduct *vt* dwyn ymaith drwy drais, cipio
aberration *n* cyfeiliorn, gwyriad
abet *vt* cefnogi, cynorthwyo, ategu
abeyance *n* dirymedd dros dro, oediad
abhor *vt* ffieiddio, casáu
abhorrence *n* ffieidd-dod, atgasrwydd, atgasedd
abide *vb* aros, trigo; goddef
abiding *adj* arhosol, gwastadol
ability *n* gallu, medr
abject *adj* distadl, dirmygedig
ablative *n* abladol
ablaze *adv* ar dân, yn wenfflam
able *adj* abl, galluog
ablution *n* golchiad; puredigaeth
abnormal *adj* anghyffredin, annormal
aboard *adv* ar fwrdd (llong)

abode *n* annedd, trigfa, cartrefle
abolish *vt* diddymu, dileu
abominable *adj* ffiaidd
abomination *n* ffieidd-dra
aborigines *npl* cyn-drigolion
abort *vi* erthylu, atal
abortion *n* erthyliad; erthyl
abortive *adj* seithug, ofer
abound *vi* amlhau, heigio; ymhelaethu
about *prep* am, oddeutu, tua ♦ *adv* oddeutu, o gwmpas
above *prep* uwch, uwchlaw ♦ *adv* fry
abrasive *adj* yn peri traul; annymunol
abreast *adj* ochr yn ochr, cyfystlys
abridge *vt* talfyrru, cwtogi
abroad *adv* allan, ar led, ar daen, dros y dŵr
abrogate *vt* diddymu, dileu
abrupt *adj* disymwth, sydyn, swta; serth
abscess *n* cornwyd, casgliad, crynhofa
abscond *vi* rhedeg i ffwrdd, dianc
absence *n* absenoldeb
absent *adj* absennol ♦ *vt* absenoli.
a.-minded *adj* anghofus
absenteeism *n* absenoliaeth
absolute *adj* cwbl, hollol; diamodol ♦ *n* diamod, absolwt
absolutely *adv* yn hollol
absolution *n* gollyngdod; maddeuant
absolve *vt* rhyddhau, gollwng; maddau
absorb *vt* yfed, llyncu, sugno, sychu
absorbent *adj* amsugnol ♦ *n*

amsugnydd

absorption n llynciad, sychiad

abstain vb ymatal, ymgadw

abstemious adj cymedrol, sobr

abstention n ymataliad

abstinence n dirwest, ymataliad

abstinent adj cymedrol, sobr

abstract vt tynnu, haniaethu, crynhoi ♦ adj haniaethol ♦ n crynodeb

abstraction n haniaeth; synfyfyrdod

abstruse adj tywyll, dyrys, astrus

absurd adj gwrthun, afresymol

abundance n digonedd, helaethrwydd

abundant adj aml, helaeth, digonol

abuse vt camddefnyddio, camdrin; difrio

abuse n camddefnydd; difriaeth

abusive adj sarhaus, gwatwarus

abysmal adj diwaelod, dwys, enbyd

abyss n y dyfnder, agendor

academic, -al adj athrofaol, academig

academy n ysgol, athrofa, academi

accede vi cytuno, cydsynio

accelerate vt cyflymu, chwimio

accelerator n ysbardun, chwimiadur

accent n acen; llediaith ♦ vt acennu

accentuate vt acennu; pwysleisio

accept vt derbyn (yn gymeradwy)

acceptable adj derbyniol, cymeradwy

acceptance n derbyniad

access n dyfodfa, dyfodiad, mynedfa, mynediad

accessary n cynorthwywr, cefnogydd

accessible adj hygyrch; hawdd dod ato

accession n esgyniad (i'r orsedd)

accessory adj cynorthwyol,

cyfranogol; atodol

accidence n ffurfiant

accident n damwain, anap

accidental adj damweiniol

accidentally adv yn ddamweiniol

acclaim vt datgan cymeradwyaeth

acclamation n bloddest, cymeradwyaeth

accommodate vt cymhwyso; lletya

accommodating adj cyfaddasol

accommodation n lle, llety

accompaniment n cyfeiliant

accompanist n cyfeilydd

accompany vb hebrwng; cyfeilio

accomplice n cynorthwywr mewn trosedd

accomplish vt cyflawni, cwblhau

accomplished adj medrus

accomplishment n medr, dawn, camp

accord vb cytuno; cyflwyno ♦ n cydfod

accordance n : in a. with yn unol â

according adv: a. to yn ôl

accordingly adv felly, gan hynny

accordion n acordion

accost vt cyfarch

account vb cyfrif ♦ n cyfrif; hanes

accountable adj cyfrifol, atebol

accountant n cyfrifydd

accountancy n cyfrifyddiaeth

account number n rhif cyfrif

accredit vt coelio, credu; awdurdodi

accrue vi deillio, codi, digwydd

accumulate vb casglu, pentyrru, cronni

accumulator n cronadur

accuracy n cywirdeb

accurate adj cywir

accurately adv yn gywir

accursed adj melltigedig, melltigaid

accusation n cyhuddiad

accusative adj gwrthrychol

(gram.); cyhuddol
accuse vt cyhuddo
accustom vt arfer, ymarfer, cynefino
accustomed adj cyfarwydd, cyffredin
ace n as; mymryn
ache vi poeni, gwynio ♦ n poen, cur
achieve vt cyflawni, gorffen, cwpláu, cwblhau
achievement n cyflawniad, camp
acid adj siarp, sur ♦ n suryn, asid
acidic adj asidig
acknowledge vt cydnabod, cyfaddef
acknowledgment n cydnabyddiaeth
acorn n mesen
acoustic adj clybodig
acoustics npl acwsteg
acquaint vt hysbysu, ymgydnabod
acquaintance n cydnabod, cydnabyddiaeth, adnabyddiaeth
acquainted adj cydnabyddus, cynefin, cyfarwydd
acquiesce vi dygymod, cydsynio
acquire vt cael, ennill
acquisition n caffaeliad
acquit vt rhyddhau
acre n erw, cyfair, acer
acrid adj chwerw, llymsur
acrimonious adj chwerw, sarrug, cecrus
acrobat n acrobat
across adv, prep yn groes, ar draws; trosodd
acrylic adj acrylig
act vb gweithredu, actio ♦ n act, gweithred, deddf
action n gweithred, gweithrediad
activate vb gweithredoli
active adj bywiog; gweithredol
activity n gweithgarwch, gweithgaredd
actor n actor, actiwr
actress n actores

actual adj gwir, gwirioneddol
actually adv mewn gwirionedd
actuary n ystadegydd, cyfrifydd
actuate vt ysgogi, cymell, cyffroi
acumen n treiddgarwch, craffter
acute adj llym, tost; craff
A.D. abbr O.C.
adage n dihareb, dywediad
adamant n adamant, diemwnt
adapt vt cyfaddasu
adapter n adaptydd
add vb chwanegu, atodi; adio
adder n neidr, gwiber
addict vt ymroddi, gorddibynnu
addiction n ymroddiad, gorddibyniaeth, tueddiad
addition n ychwanegiad
additional adj ychwanegol
additive n adiolyn
address vb annerch; cyfeirio ♦ n anerchiad; cyfeiriad
adduce vt dwyn ymlaen; nodi
adept n un cyfarwydd; campwr
adequate adj digonol
adhere vi ymlynu, glynu wrth
adhesion n glyniad, ymlyniad
adhesive adj glynol, ymlynol ♦ n adlyn, glud
adieu excl bydd wych! ffarwel!
adjacent adj cyfagos, gerllaw
adjective n ansoddair
adjoin vt cydio, cyffwrdd â
adjourn vt gohirio, oedi
adjudge vt dyfarnu, barnu
adjudicate vt beirniadu, barnu
adjudicator n beirniad
adjunct n atodiad, ychwanegiad
adjure vt tynghedu, tyngu
adjust vt cymhwyso, addasu, unioni
ad-lib adv yn rhydd, difyfyr
administer vt gweinyddu
administration n gweinyddiaeth
administrative adj gweinyddol
admirable adj rhagorol, campus
admiral n llyngesydd
admiralty n morlys

admiration *n* edmygedd
admire *vt* edmygu
admission *n* derbyniad; addefiad
admit *vt* derbyn; addef, cyfaddef
admittance *n* derbyniad; trwydded
admixture *n* cymysgiad, cymysgedd
admonish *vt* rhybuddio, ceryddu
admonition *n* rhybudd, cerydd
ad nauseam *adv* hyd syrffed
ado *n* helynt, heldrin, ffwdan
adolescence *n* llencyndod, adolesens
adolescent *n* adolesent, llencyn, llances
adopt *vb* mabwysiadu
adoption *n* mabwysiad
adore *vt* addoli
adorn *vt* addurno
adrift *adv* yn rhydd, diangor
adroit *adj* medrus, deheuig, hyfedr
adulation *n* gweniaith, truth
adult *n* (un) mewn oed, oedolyn
adulterate *vt* llygru
adulterer *n* godinebwr
adulteress *n* godinebwraig
adultery *n* godineb
advance *vb* symud ymlaen; dyrchafu; rhoi benthyg ♦ *n* benthyg, echwyn
advanced *adj* ar y blaen
advancement *n* dyrchafiad; lles, budd
advancing *adj* cynyddol, ar gynnydd
advantage *n* mantais
advantageous *adj* manteisiol
advent *n* dyfodiad; yr Adfent
adventure *n* antur, anturiaeth
adverb *n* adferf
adversary *n* gwrthwynebydd
adverse *adj* adfydus, gwrthwynebus, croes
adversity *n* adfyd, drygfyd
advert *n* hysbyseb
advertise *vt* hysbysu, hysbysebu
advertisement *n* hysbysiad,
hysbyseb
advertiser *n* hysbysydd
advertising *adj* hysbysebol
advice *n* cyngor, cyfarwyddyd
advisable *adj* doeth, buddiol
advise *vt* cynghori, annog; hysbysu
advisedly *adv* ar ôl ystyried, yn bwyllog
advisory *adj* ymgynghorol
advocate *n* eiriolwr, bargyfreithiwr ♦ *vt* eiriol, dadlau, cefnogi, pleidio
adze *n* neddau, neddyf
aerial *adj* awyrol, wybrol
aeroplane *n* awyren
aerosol *n* erosol
aesthetic *adj* esthetig
aesthetics *n* estheteg
afar *adv* pell, hirbell
affable *adj* hynaws, caruaidd, clên
affair *n* achos; mater; helynt
affect *vt* effeithio; cymryd arno, ffugio
affectation *n* mursendod, rhodres, ffug
affection *n* serch, cariad; clefyd, haint; affeithiad (*gram.*)
affectionate *adj* serchog, caruaidd
affiliate *vt* mabwysiadu, tadogi; uno
affinity *n* cyfathrach; tebygrwydd
affirm *vb* haeru, taeru; sicrhau, gwirio
affirmation *n* cadarnhad
affirmative *adj* cadarnhaol
affix *vt* atodi, gosod
afflict *vt* cystuddio
affliction *n* cystudd, adfyd
affluence *n* cyfoeth, digonedd
affluent *adj* goludog, cyfoethog, cefnog
afford *vt* rhoddi; fforddio
afforestation *n* coedwigaeth
affray *n* ymryson, ffrwgwd, ysgarmes
affront *vt* sarhau, tramgwyddo ♦ *n*

sarhad

afield adv: **far a.** ymhell i ffwrdd

aflame adv ar dân

afloat adv yn nofio; ar daen, ar led

afoot adv ar droed

afraid adj ag ofn arno, ofnus

afresh adv o'r newydd, eilwaith

Africa n Affrica

after prep, conj wedi, ar ôl, yn ôl ♦ adv wedyn

after-care n gofal wedyn, ôl-ofal

after-effects n ôl-effeithiau

afterlife n y byd a ddaw

aftermath n adladd, adlodd

afternoon n prynhawn

afters n y cwrs terfynol

afterthought n syniad diweddar

afterwards adv wedi hynny, wedyn

again adv eilwaith, drachefn, eto

against prep erbyn, yn erbyn

age n oed, oedran; oes; henaint ♦ vb heneiddio

aged adj hen, oedrannus

agency n goruchwyliaeth, cyfrwng, asiantaeth

agenda n agenda

agent n goruchwyliwr; gweithredydd, cynrychiolydd

aggravate vt gwneuthur yn waeth

aggregate n cyfanswm, crynswth

aggression n ymosodiad, gormes

aggressive adj ymosodol, ymwthiol, gormesol

aggrieve vt blino, tramgwyddo

aghast adj syn, brawychedig

agile adj heini, sionc, gwisgi

agitate vt cynhyrfu, aflonyddu, cyffroi

agnostic n agnostig, anffyddiwr

ago adv yn ôl. **long a.** ers talm

agog adv yn awchus

agonizing adj mewn gwewyr meddwl

agony n ing, poen

agrarian adj tirol, gwledig

agree vi cytuno; dygymod; cyfateb

agreeable adj clên, dymunol, hyfryd

agreement n cytundeb

agricultural adj amaethyddol

agriculture n amaethyddiaeth

aground adv ar lawr, ar dir, i dir

ahead adv ymlaen, o flaen

aid vt cynorthwyo, helpu ♦ n cymorth, cynhorthwy

ail vb clafychu; blino, poeni

ailment n dolur, afiechyd, anhwyldeb

aim vb anelu, amcanu ♦ n amcan, nod

air n awyr; osgo; cainc, alaw ♦ vt awyru

aircraft n awyren

airforce n llu awyr

airline n cwmni hedfan

airlock n aerglo

airport n maes glanio

air mail n post awyr

airtight adj aerglos, aerdyn

aisle n ystlys eglwys; llwybr; eil

ajar adj cilagored

akin adj perthynol, perthnasol

alack excl och fi!

alacrity n bywiogrwydd, parodrwydd

alarm vt dychrynu ♦ n braw, dychryn; rhybudd; larwm

alarm-clock n cloc larwm

alas excl och!

albeit conj er, er hynny, eto

album n albwm; record hir

alcohol n alcohol

alcoholic adj, n alcoholig, meddwyn

alcove n cilfach wely; hafdy, deildy, alcof

alder n gwernen

ale n cwrw

alert adj esgud, effro, gwyliadwrus

algebra n algebra

Algeria n Algeria

alias adv mewn modd, dan enw arall

alibi n dadlau bod mewn man arall

alien adj estronol ♦ n estron

alight vi disgyn

align vb cyfunioni

alike adj yr un fath ♦ adv yn gyffelyb

aliment n maeth, ymborth

alimony n alimoni

alive adv, adj yn fyw, byw

alkali n alcali

alkaline adj alcalaidd

all adj holl; oll, i gyd ♦ adv yn hollol ♦ n y cwbl, y cyfan; pawb

allay vt lleddfu, lliniaru; tawelu

all clear adv yn glir

allege vt honni, haeru

allegedly adv yn honedig

allegiance n teyrngarwch, gwrogaeth

allegory n alegori

allergic adj alergig

allergy n alergedd

alleviate vt ysgafnhau, esmwytho

alley n llwybr, ale

alliance n cyfathrach, cynghrair

allied adj cynghreiriol

alliteration n cyflythreniad, cyseinedd

all-night adj drwy'r nos

allocate vt cyfleu, rhannu, dosbarthu

allot vb gosod, penodi

allotment n cyfran; rhandir

all-out adj yn llwyr, a'i holl egni

allow vt caniatáu, goddef

allowance n goddefiad; dogn; lwfans

alloy n aloi

allude vi cyfeirio, sôn

allure vt hudo, denu, llithio

allusion n crybwylliad, cyfeiriad (at)

alluvium n llifbridd, dolbridd

ally vt cynghreirio ♦ n cynghreiriad

almighty adj hollalluog, hollgyfoethog

almond n almon

almoner n elusennwr

almost adv bron, agos, braidd

alms n elusen, cardod

aloft adv yn uchel, fry, i fyny

alone adv, adj unig, ar ei ben ei hun

along adv ymlaen; ar hyd. **all a.** o'r cychwyn

aloof adv, adj yn cadw draw; pell

aloud adv yn uchel, yn groch

alphabet n egwyddor, abiéc

alphabetical adj yn nhrefn yr wyddor

Alps npl: **the A.** yr Alpau

already adv eisoes, yn barod

also adv hefyd

altar n allor

alter vb newid, altro

alteration n newid, cyfnewidiad

altercation n ymryson, ffrae

alternate adj bob yn ail ♦ vi digwydd bob yn ail; eilio

alternating adj bob yn ail

alternative n dewis arall

alternatively adv o ddewis arall

although conj er

altitude n uchder

alto n alto

altogether adv oll, i gyd, yn gyfan gwbl

aluminium n alwminiwm

always adv yn wastad(ol), bob amser

a.m. abbr a.m.

amalgamate vb cymysgu, cyfuno, uno

amanuensis n ysgrifennydd dros arall

amass vt casglu, cronni, pentyrru

amateur n amatur

amateurish adj trwsgl, anfedrus, amaturaidd

amatory adj carwriaethol

amaze vt synnu, rhyfeddu, aruthro

amazement n syndod

amazing adj rhyfeddol

ambassador n llysgennad

amber n ambr

ambidextrous *adj* deheuig â'i
  ddwy law
ambiguity *n* amwysedd
ambiguous *adj* amwys
ambition *n* uchelgais
ambitious *adj* uchelgeisiol
amble *vi* rhygyngu ♦ *n* rhygyng
ambulance *n* ambiwlans
ambush *n, vb* cynllwyn, rhagod
ameliorate *vt* gwella, diwygio
amenable *adj* hydrin; atebol;
  cyfrifol
amend *vb* gwella, diwygio, cywiro
amendment *n* gwelliant
amends *n* iawn
amenity *n* hyfrydwch; hynawsedd
America *n* yr Amerig
American *adj* Americanaidd ♦ *n*
  Americanwr
amiable *adj* hawddgar, serchus
amicable *adj* cyfeillgar
amid, -st *prep* ynghanol, ymhlith,
  ymysg
amiss *adv* ar fai, o'i le
amity *n* cyfeillgarwch
ammonia *n* amonia
ammunition *n* arlwy rhyfel; pylor,
  etc
amnesty *n* maddeuant
amok *adv* yn wyllt, dilywodraeth
among, -st *prep* ymhlith, ymysg,
  rhwng
amorous *adj* hoff o garu,
  carwriaethus
amorphous *adj* di-ffurf, amorffus
amount *vi* cyrraedd; codi ♦ *n* swm
amour *n* carwriaeth
ample *adj* helaeth, eang; cyflawn,
  digon
amplify *vt* helaethu, ehangu
amputate *vt* torri aelod, trychu
amulet *n* peth a wisgir fel swyn
amuse *vt* difyrru, diddanu
amusement *n* difyrrwch,
  digrifwch
an Gwêl a
anachronism *n* camamseriad

anaemia *n* diffyg gwaed
anaemic *adj* di-waed, diwryg
anaesthesia *n* dideimladrwydd
anaesthetic *adj, n* anesthetig
analogy *n* cyfatebiaeth,
  cydweddiad
analyse *vt* dadansoddi, dadelfennu
analysis (-yses) *n* dadansoddiad
analyst *n* dadansoddwr
analytical *adj* dadansoddol
anarchic, -al *adj* anarchol
anarchist *n* anarchydd, terfysgwr
anarchy *n* anhrefn, aflywodraeth,
  anarchaeth
anathema *n* anathema
anatomy *n* anatomeg
ancestor *n* cyndad, (*pl*) hynafiaid
ancestry *n* ach, achau; hynafiaid
anchor *n* angor ♦ *vb* angori
anchoress, -ite *n* meudwy, ancr
ancient *adj* hen, hynafol; oesol
ancillary *adj* ategol, cynorthwyol
and *conj* a, ac
anecdote *n* hanesyn, chwedl
anew *adv* o'r newydd
angel *n* angel
anger *n* dicter, llid ♦ *vt* digio, llidio
angle *n* ongl ♦ *vi* genweirio,
  pysgota
Anglican *adj* perthynol i Eglwys
  Loegr, Anglicanaidd
angling *n* pysgota
angry *adj* dig, llidiog
anguish *n* ing
angular *adj* onglog
animadvert *vi* beirniadu, ceryddu,
  sennu
animal *n* anifail, mil ♦ *adj*
  anifeilaidd
animate *adj* byw ♦ *vt* bywhau;
  ysgogi
animation *n* bywiogrwydd
animosity *n* gelyniaeth, digasedd
animus *n* drwgdeimlad, gelyniaeth
ankle *n* migwrn, ffêr, swrn
annals *npl* cofnodion blynyddol
annex *vt* cysylltu, cydio;

meddiannu

annihilate vt diddymu, difodi

annihilation n diddymiant, difodiant

anniversary n pen blwydd; cylchwyl flynyddol

annotate vb gwneud nodiadau

announce vt datgan, cyhoeddi

announcement n cyhoeddiad, hysbysiad

announcer n cyhoeddwr

annoy vt poeni, blino, cythruddo

annoyance n blinder, poendod

annoying adj traffferthus, blinderus

annual adj blynyddol

annuity n blwydd-dal

annul vt diddymu, dileu, dirymu

anoint vt eneinio, iro

anomaly n peth croes i reol, afreolaidd-dra

anon adv yn union, toc, yn y man

anonymity n cyfrif dienw

anonymous adj dienw, anhysbys

anorak n anorac

another pron, a arall

answer vb ateb ♦ n ateb, atebiad

answerable adj atebol, cyfrifol

ant n morgrugyn

antagonism n gelyniaeth, gwrthwynebiaeth

antagonist n gwrthwynebydd

Antarctic n: the A. Antarctica

antarctic adj o gylch y pegwn deheuol

ante- prefix cyn, o flaen, rhag- ♦ n rhagflaenydd

antecedent adj blaenorol

antediluvian adj cynddilywaidd

antelope n gafrewig, antelop

antenatal adj cyn-geni

anterior adj blaen, blaenorol, cyn-

anthem n anthem

anthology n blodeugerdd

anthracite n glo caled, glo carreg

anthropology n anthropoleg

anti-, ant- prefix gwrth-, yn erbyn

antibiotic n, adj gwrthfiotig

antichrist n anghrist

anticipate vt achub y blaen, disgwyl

anticlimax n disgynneb

antics npl munudiau, ystumiau, maldod, stranciau

antidote n gwrthwenwyn

antifreeze n, adj gwrthrew, direwyn

antipathy n gwrthnaws; casineb

antipodes npl pellafoedd byd, eithafoedd

antiquarian adj hynafiaethol ♦ n hynafiaethydd

antiquated adj hen a di-les

antique adj hen, hynafol, henffasiwn

antique n hen beth

antique-shop n siop hen bethau

antiquity n hynafiaeth; y cynoesoedd

anti-Semitism n gwrth-Iddewiaeth

antiseptic n, adj antiseptig

antisocial adj gwrthgymdeithasol

antithesis (-es) n gwrthgyferbyniad

antler n cainc o gorn carw, rhaidd

anvil n eingion, einion

anxiety n pryder

anxious adj pryderus, awyddus

any adj un, unrhyw, rhyw, peth, dim

anybody pron unrhyw un, rhywun

anyone pron rhywun

anything pron dim, rhywbeth, rhywfaint

anywhere adv rhywle

apace adv ar garlam, ar ffrwst, ar frys

apart adv o'r neilltu, ar wahân

apartheid n aparteid

apartment n rhandy, llety

apathetic adj difraw, difater, didaro

apathy n difrawder, difaterwch

ape n epa ♦ vt dynwared

aperture n bwlch, twll, agorfa

apex n blaen, brig, pen, copa

aphis (aphides) n pryf gwyrdd

aphorism n gwireb, dihareb

apiece adv yr un, ar wahân, un bob un

apocalypse n datguddiad

apocryphal adj anghanonaidd, apocryffaidd

apologize vi ymddiheuro, ymesgusodi

apology n ymddiheuriad, esgusawd

apoplexy n parlys mud, strôc

apostasy n gwrthgiliad

apostate n gwrthgiliwr

apostle n apostol

apostolic, -al adj apostolaidd

apostrophe n sillgoll, collnod (')

apothecary n apothecari, fferyllydd

appal vt brawychu, digalonni

appalling adj arswydus, gwarthus

apparatus n offer, aparatws

apparel n dillad, gwisg

apparent adj amlwg, eglur

apparently adv mae'n debyg

apparition n drychiolaeth, ysbryd

appeal vi apelio, erfyn ♦ n apêl

appear vi ymddangos, ymrithio

appearance n ymddangosiad

appease vt llonyddu, tawelu, dofi

appellation n enw, teitl

append vt atodi, ychwanegu

appendicitis n enyniad y coluddyn crog, apendiseitis

appendix n atodiad, ychwanegiad

appertain vi perthyn

appetite n archwaeth, chwant, awydd

appetizer n lluniaeth i greu blas, blasyn

applaud vt cymeradwyo, curo dwylo

applause n cymeradwyaeth

apple n afal. a. of the eye cannwyll llygad

appliance n offeryn, dyfais

applicant n ymgeisydd

application n cymhwysiad; cais; ymroddiad

applied adj cymwysedig

apply vb cymhwyso; ymroi; cynnig (am), ymgeisio

appoint vb gosod, penodi, pennu

appointment n cyhoeddiad; penodiad

apportion vt rhannu, dosbarthu

apposite adj addas, priodol

appraise vt prisio

appreciate vt prisio, gwerthfawrogi

appreciation n gwerthfawrogiad

appreciative adj gwerthfawrogol

apprehend vt ymaflyd mewn; dirnad; ofni

apprehension n dirnadaeth; ofn

apprehensive adj ofnus, pryderus

apprentice n prentis, dysgwr ♦ vt prentisio

apprise vt hysbysu; tafoli

approach vb nesáu, dynesu ♦ n dyfodfa

approachable adj hawdd mynd ato

approbation n cymeradwyaeth

appropriate vt meddiannu ♦ adj priodol, addas

approval n cymeradwyaeth

approve vt cymeradwyo; profi

approximate vi agosáu ♦ adj agos

approximately adv oddeutu, tua, yn agos i

appurtenance n peth perthynol

apricot n bricyllen

April n Ebrill

apron n (ar) ffedog, barclod

apt adj tueddol; cymwys, parod

aquarium n pysgodlyn, pysgoty

aquatic adj dyfrol, dyfriog

aqueduct n dyfrffos

arable adj: **a. land** tir âr

arbiter n dyddiwr, brawdwr, beirniad

arbitrament n rhaith, dedfryd

arbitrary adj gormesol, mympwyol

arbitrate *vb* cyflafareddu,
athrywyn
arbour *n* deildy
arc *n* bwa, arc
arcade *n* arcêd
arch *n* bwa, pont; nen ♦ *vt* pontio
arch- *prefix* arch-, carn-, prif-
archaeology *n* archaeoleg
archaic *adj* hynafol, henaidd
archangel *n* archangel
archbishop *n* archesgob
archdeacon *n* archddiacon,
archddiagon
archdruid *n* archdderwydd
archer *n* saethydd, saethwr
archery *n* saethyddiaeth
archipelago *n* twr ynysoedd,
ynysfor
architect *n* pensaer
architecture *n* pensaerniaeth
archive *n* archif
archway *n* ffordd fwaol
Arctic *n*: the A. yr Artig
arctic *adj* gogleddol
ardent *adj* gwresog, poeth,
angerddol
ardour *n* angerdd, aidd
arduous *adj* llafurus, blin, caled
area *n* arwynebedd, wyneb
Argentina *n* Ariannin
argue *vb* dadlau, ymresymu
argument *n* dadl, ymresymiad
arid *adj* sych, crin, cras, gwyw
aright *adv* yn iawn, yn briodol
arise *vi* cyfodi, codi
aristocracy *n* pendefigaeth
aristocrat *n* pendefig, gŵr mawr
aristocratic *adj* pendefigaidd,
bonheddig
arithmetic *n* rhifyddeg
arithmetician *n* rhifyddgwr
ark *n* arch
arm *n* braich; cainc
arm *n* arf ♦ *vb* arfogi
armament *n* offer rhyfel;
arfogaeth
armchair *n* cadair freichiau

armed *adj* arfog
armful *adj* coflaid, ceseiliaid
armistice *n* cadoediad
armour *n* arfogaeth, arfwisg
armoured *adj* wedi ei amddiffyn
armoury *n* arfdy
armpit *n* cesail
armrest *n* man i orffwys braich
army *n* byddin
aroma *n* perarogl(au)
aromatic *adj* peraroglaidd, pêr,
persawrus
around *adv, prep* am, o amgylch
arouse *vt* deffro(i), dihuno; cyffroi
arraign *vt* cyhuddo o flaen brawdle
arrange *vb* trefnu
arrangement *n* trefn, trefniad,
trefniant
arrant *adj* dybryd, cywilyddus
array *vt* trefnu, cyfleu; gwisgo ♦ *n*
trefn; gwisg
arrears *npl* ôl-ddyled
arrest *vt* atal; dal, dala, restio
arrival *n* dyfodiad, cyrhaeddiad
arrive *vi* cyrraedd, dyfod
arrogance *n* balchder, traha
arrogant *adj* balch, trahaus
arrogate *vt* hawlio, trawshawlio
arrow *n* saeth
arsenal *n* arfdy, ystordy neu ffatri
arfau
arson *n* llosgiad, llosg
art *n* celfyddyd; ystryw
artefact *n* celflun
artery *n* rhedweli
artful *adj* ystrywgar, dichellgar,
cyfrwys
art gallery *n* oriel gelf
arthritis *n* gwynegon, crydcymalau
article *n* erthygl; nwydd; bannod
articulate *vb* cymalu; cynanu ♦ *adj*
â meddwl clir, trefnus
artifice *n* dyfais; ystryw, dichell
artificer *n* saer, crefftwr,
celfyddydwr
artificial *adj* celfyddydol; gosod,
dodi, ffug

artillery n offer rhyfel, magnelau
artisan n crefftwr
artist n celfyddydwr, arlunydd, artist
artistic adj celfydd, celfyddgar, artistig
as conj, adv megis, fel; cyn, mor; â, ag
asbestos n ystinos, asbestos
ascend vb esgyn, dringo, dyrchafu
ascendancy n goruchafiaeth, uchafiaeth
ascension n esgyniad, dyrchafael
ascent n esgynfa, rhiw, gorifyny
ascertain vt cael gwybod, mynnu gwybod
ascetic n meudwy ♦ adj meudwyaidd, ymgosbol, asgetig
ascribe vt cyfrif i, priodoli, rhoddi
ash n onnen, onn
ash (-es) n lludw, ulw
ashamed adj ar arno gywilydd
ashore adv i'r lan, ar y lan
ashtray n plat lludw
aside adv o'r neilltu
ask vb gofyn, holi; ceisio
askance adv yn llygatraws, yn gam
askew adv ar osgo, ar letraws
aslant adv ar ei ogwydd, ar oledd
asleep adj yng nghwsg, yn cysgu
asparagus n merllys, asbaragws
aspect n golwg, golygwedd, wyneb, agwedd
aspen n aethnen
asperity n gerwindeb, llymder
asperse vt taenellu; gwaradwyddo
aspersion n difriad, enllib
asphyxiate vt mygu, tagu
aspirate vt seinio ag anadl ♦ n yr (h)
aspiration n dyhead
aspire vi dyheu
aspirin n asbrin
ass n asyn; asen
assail vt ymosod ar, rhuthro ar
assailant n ymosodwr

assassin n bradlofrudd, llofrudd
assassinate vt bradlofruddio
assault n ymosodiad ♦ vt ymosod
assay n praw(f) ♦ vb profi; cynnig, ceisio
assemble vb cynnull, ymgynnull
assembly n cynulliad, cymanfa
assent vi cydsynio ♦ n cydsyniad
assert vt haeru, honni, mynnu
assess vt trethu, prisio, asesu
assessment n asesiad
assessor n aseswr, cyfeisteddwr
asset n ased
assets npl eiddo, meddiannau
assiduous adj dyfal, diwyd
assign vt gosod, penodi; trosglwyddo
assimilate vb cymathu; tebygu
assist vb cynorthwyo, cymorth, helpu
assistance n cymorth
assistant n cynorthwyydd
assize n brawdlys
associate vb cymdeithasu, cyfeillachu, cysylltu ♦ n cydymaith
association n cymdeithas, cymdeithasfa
assort vb trefnu, dosbarthu
assorted adj amryfath
assortment n dosbarthiad, pigion
assuage vt llonyddu, lliniaru, lleddfu
assume vt cymryd ar; tybied; honni
assumption n tyb(iaeth), bwriant, honiad, dyrchafiad (Mair i'r nefoedd)
assurance n sicrwydd; hyder, hyfder
assure vt sicrhau; yswirio
asterisk n serennig, seren (*)
asthma n caethder, diffyg anadl, y fogfa
asthmatic adj byr ei wynt, caeth ei frest
astonish vt synnu

astound *vt* synnu, syfrdanu
astral *adj* serol
astray *adv* ar gyfeiliorn, ar grwydr
astride *adv* â'r traed ar led
astrologer *n* sêr-ddewin
astrology *n* sêr-ddewiniaeth
astronaut *n* gofodwr
astronomer *n* seryddol, seryddwr
astronomy *n* seryddiaeth
astute *adj* craff, cyfrwys, call
asunder *adv* ar wahân, yn ddryllliau
asylum *n* noddfa. **lunatic a.** gwallgofdy
at *prep* yn, wrth, ger, ar
atheist *n* anffyddiwr
Athens *n* Athen
athlete *n* mabolgampwr
athletics *npl* mabolgampau
atlantic *adj* atlantaidd ♦ *n:* **the A. (Ocean)** Môr Iwerydd
atlas *n* llyfr mapiau, atlas
atmosphere *n* awyrgylch
atom *n* mymryn, gronyn, atom
atomic *adj* atomig
atone *vi* gwneuthur iawn
atonement *n* iawn, cymod
atrocious *adj* erchyll, anfad, ysgeler
attach *vb* gosod, glynu; atafaelu
attachment *n* ymlyniad, serch
attack *vt* ymosod ar ♦ *n* ymosodiad
attain *vt* ennill; cyrraedd; cael gafael
attainment *n* cyrhaeddiad
attempt *vt* ceisio, cynnig ♦ *n* cynnig, ymgais
attend *vb* gweini; ystyried; dilyn, mynychu
attendance *n* gwasanaeth; presenoldeb
attendant *n* gweinydd ♦ *adj* yn dilyn, ynghlwm wrth
attention *n* sylw, ystyriaeth
attentive *adj* astud, ystyriol
attenuate *vt* teneuo, lleihau
attest *vb* tystio, gwirio; ardystio

attic *n* nenlofft, nenlawr
attire *vt* gwisgo ♦ *n* gwisg, dillad
attitude *n* ystum, agwedd, osgo
attorney *n* twrnai
attract *vt* tynnu, atynnu, denu, hudo
attraction *n* atyniad
attractive *adj* atyniadol
attribute *n* priodoledd
attribute *vt* priodoli, cyfrif i
attrition *n* rhathiad, treuliad, traul
attune *vt* hwylio, cyweirio
auburn *adj* gwinau, browngoch
auction *n* arwerthiant, ocsiwn
auctioneer *n* arwerthwr
audacious *adj* hy, digywilydd, haerllug
audacity *n* hyfdra, ehofndra, beiddgarwch
audible *adj* hyglyw, clywadwy
audience *n* gwrandawyr, cynulleidfa
audio-visual *adj* clyweledol
audit *vt* archwilio cyfrifon ♦ *n* archwiliad
audition *n* clywelediad
auditor *n* gwrandawr; archwilydd
auger *n* taradr, ebill
augment *vt* ychwanegu, atodi
augur *n* dewin ♦ *vb* darogan; argoeli
August *n* Awst
august *adj* urddasol, mawreddog
aunt *n* modryb
aura *n* naws, awyrgylch
aural *adj* clywedol
auspices *npl* nawdd
auspicious *adj* yn argoeli'n dda, ffafriol
austere *adj* gerwin, llym, tost, caled
austerity *n* gerwindeb, llymder
Australia *n* Awstralia
Australian *n* Awstraliad ♦ *adj* Awstralaidd
Austria *n* Awstria
Austrian *n* Awstriad ♦ *adj*

Awstriaidd

authentic *adj* dilys, gwir

author *n* awdur, awdwr

authoritarian *adj* awdurdodus

authoritative *adj* awdurdodol

authority *n* awdurdod

authorize *vt* awdurdodi

auto- *prefix* hunan-, ym-

autobiography *n* hunangofiant

autocracy *n* unbennaeth

autocrat *n* unben; dyn awdurdodol

autograph *n* llofnod

automatic *adj* hunanysgogol, awtomatig

automation *n* awtomasiwn

automobile *n* cerbyd, modur

autonomy *n* ymreolaeth

autumn *n* hydref

auxiliary *adj* cynorthwyol, ategol ♦ *n* cynorthwywr

avail *vb* llesáu, tycio ♦ *n* lles, budd

available *adj* ar gael

avalanche *n* syrthfa, cwymp (eira, *etc*)

avarice *n* cybydd-dod, trachwant

avaricious *adj* cybyddlyd, ariangar

avenge *vt* dial cam

avenue *n* mynedfa, rhodfa

aver *vt* gwirio, haeru

average *n* canolbris; cyfartaledd; cyffredin

averse *adj* gwrthwynebol, gelynol; croesi

aversion *n* gwrthwynebiad; casbeth

avert *vt* troi heibio, gochel, osgoi

aviary *n* adarfy

avidity *n* awydd, awch, gwanc

avocation *n* gorchwyl, galwedigaeth

avoid *vt* gochel, osgoi, arbed

avouch *vt* gwirio, haeru; arddelwi

avow *vt* addef; cydnabod

await *vt* disgwyl, aros

awake *vb* deffro, dihuno ♦ *adj* effro

award *vt* dyfarnu ♦ *n* dyfarniad

aware *adj* hysbys, ymwybodol

awareness *n* arwybod, ymwybyddiaeth

awash *adj* llawn, cyforiog

away *adv* ymaith, i ffwrdd

awe *n* (parchedig) ofn ♦ *vt* rhoi arswyd

awful *adj* ofnadwy, arswydus

awhile *adv* am ennyd, am dro

awkward *adj* trwsgl, lletchwith, anghyfleus

awl *n* mynawyd

awning *n* cysgodlen, adlen

axe *n* bwyall, bwyell

axiom *n* gwireb

axis (**axes**) *n* echel, pegwn

axle *n* echel

ay *adv* ie

aye *adv* yn wastad(ol), byth

azure *n* glas y ffurfafen, asur ♦ *adj* asur

B

babble *vb* baldordd, clebran ♦ *n* baldordd

babe *n* baban, plentyn bach

baby *n* baban, maban, babi

babysitter *n* gwarchodwr babanod

bachelor *n* dyn dibriod, hen lanc; baglor

back *n* cefn ♦ *vb* cefnogi; bacio ♦ *adv* yn ôl

background *n* cefndir

backhander *n* tâl dirgel; ergyd â chefn y llaw

backpack *n* cefnbwn

backslide *vi* gwrthgilio

backward *adv* yn ôl, ar ôl ♦ *adj* hwyrfrydig; digynnydd; araf

backwater *n* dŵr disymud ar ymyl afon, lle o'r neilltu, dibwys, cwter gwsg

bacon *n* cig moch, bacwn

bad *adj* drwg, drygionus; gwael, sâl

badge *n* bathodyn
badger *n* mochyn daear, broch ♦ *vt* profocio, poeni
badminton *n* badminton
bad-tempered *adj* â thymer ddrwg
baffle *vt* drysu, siomi, trechu
bag *n* cwd, cod, bag
baggage *n* clud, celfi, pac
bagpipe *n* pibgod
bah *excl* pw!
bail *n* meichiau, gwystl ♦ *vt* mechnio
bail, bale *vt* hysbyddu cwch
bailiff *n* beili; hwsmon, goruchwyliwr
bait *vt* abwydo; baeddu, eirthio ♦ *n* abwyd
bake *vb* pobi, crasu
baker *n* pobydd
bakery *n* popty
balance *n* clorian, mantol; gweddill ♦ *vt* mantoli; cydbwyso
balanced *adj* cytbwys, cymesur
balcony *n* oriel, balcon
bald *adj* moel, penfoel
bale *n* pwn, sypyn, bwrn
baleful *adj* alaethus, gresynol, galarus
baler *n* byrnwr
balk, baulk *n* balc; siom ♦ *vt* balcio; siomi
ball *n* pêl, pellen
ball *n* dawns, dawnsfa
ballad *n* baled
ballast *n* balast
ball bearings *npl* berynnau pêl, pelferynnau
ballerina *n* balerina
ballet *n* bale
balloon *n* balŵn
ballot *n* balot, tugel
balm *n* balm, triagl
bamboozle *vb* twyllo, llygad-dynnu
ban *n* gwaharddi, ysgymuno
banal *adj* cyffredin, sathredig
banana *n* banana

band *n* band, rhwymyn; mintai; seindorf
bandage *n* rhwymyn ♦ *vb* rhwymo, rhwymynnu
bandbox *n* bocs hetiau
bandit *n* herwr, ysbeiliwr
bandy *vt* taflu (pêl, *etc*) yn ôl a blaen
bandy-legged *adj* coesgam
bane *n* dinistr, melltith
baneful *adj* dinistriol, andwyol
bang *vb* curo, dulio, clepian ♦ *n* ergyd, twrf
bangle *n* breichled
banish *vt* alltudio, deol
bank *n* mainc; rhes
bank *n* glan, torlan; traethell
bank *n* banc, ariandy ♦ *vb* bancio
banker *n* bancwr
bankrupt *n* methdalwr
bankruptcy *n* methdaliad
bank statement *n* datganiad banc, adroddiad banc
banner *n* baner, lluman
banns *npl* gostegion
banquet *n* gwledd ♦ *vb* gwledda
bantam *n* coriar, dandi
banter *n* ysmaldod, cellwair ♦ *vb* cellwair, profocio
baptism *n* bedydd
Baptist *n* Bedyddiwr
baptize *vt* bedyddio
bar *n* bar, bollt; rhwystr; traethell ♦ *vt* bario; eithrio
barb *n* barf; adfach
barbarian *n* barbariad, anwariad
barbaric *adj* barbaraidd
barbecue *n* rhostfa
barbed wire *n* weiar bigog
barber *n* barbwr
bard *n* bardd, prydydd
bare *adj* noeth, llwm, moel, prin ♦ *vt* dinoethi
barefooted *adj* troednoeth
barely *adv* prin, o'r braidd
bargain *n* bargen ♦ *vb* bargeinio
barge *n* bad mawr

bark n barc, llong, llestr
bark vi cyfarth, coethi ♦ n cyfarthiad
bark n rhisgl ♦ vt dirisglo, digroeni
barley n haidd, barlys
barm n burum, berem, berman
barmaid n barferch
barman n barmon
barn n ysgubor
barometer n hinfynegydd, baromedr
baron n barwn, arglwydd
baronet n barwnig
barrack n lluest, lluesty, gwersyllty
barrage n argae, clawdd
barrel n baril, casgen
barren adj diffrwyth; amhlantadwy
barricade n atalglawdd ♦ vt cau
barrier n atalfa, rhwystr, terfyn, ffin
barrister n bargyfreithiwr
barrow n berfa, whilber; crug
barter vb cyfnewid, ffeirio ♦ n cyfnewid
base adj isel, gwael, distadl, gau
base n sylfaen; bôn ♦ vt sylfaenu, seilio
baseball n pel-fâs
basement n islawr
bashful adj swil, gwylaidd
basic adj gwaelodol, sylfaenol
basin n basn, cawg, dysgl
basis (bases) n sail, sylfaen
bask vi ymheulo, torheulo
basket n basged, cawell
basketful n basgedaid
bass n bas, isalaw; bâs, draenogiad y môr
bastard n bastard, plentyn gordderch/siawns
baste vt iro, brasteru; ffusto, ffonodio
bastinado n, vt ffonodio gwadnau'r traed
bat n ystlum
bat n bat ♦ vi batio

batch n pobiad, ffyrnaid; swp, sypyn
bath n ymolchfa, badd, baddon; bath
bathe vb ymdrochi, ymolchi, golchi
bathroom n ystafell ymolchi
baton n llawffon, baton, arweinffon
battalion n byddin, mintai, bataliwn
batter vt curo, pwyo ♦ n defnydd crempog, cytew
battery n magnelfa; batri
battle n brwydr, cad ♦ vi brwydro
battlefield n maes y gad
battlement n canllaw, murganllaw.
battleship n llongryfel
bauble n ffril, tegan
baulk Gwêl **balk**
bawdy adj anllad, anweddus
bawl vi gweiddi, crochlefain, bloeddio
bay n bae
bay vb, n cyfarth. **to hold at b.** rhoi cyfarth
bay n llawryf
bay adj gwinau, gwineugoch
bayonet n bidog ♦ vt bidogi
bazaar n basâr
be vi bod
beach n traeth, traethell ♦ vt gyrru ar y traeth
beacon n gwylfa, goleudy; coelcerth
bead n glain. **beads** paderau
beadle n rhingyll
beak n pig, gylfin, duryn
beaker n cwpan, diodlestr â phig, bicer
beam n trawst, paladr; pelydryn ♦ vi pelydru
bean n ffäen, ffeuen
bear n arth; arthes
bear vt dwyn, cludo; geni; dioddef, goddef

beard n barf; col ŷd

bearing n ymddygiad; traul

beast n bwystfil, anifail

beat vt curo ♦ n cur, curiad

beatitude n gwynfyd

beautiful adj prydferth, hardd, teg

beauty n prydferthwch, harddwch, tegwch. **b. parlour** parlwr pincio

beaver n afanc, llostlydan

becalm vt tawelu, llonyddu

because adv, conj oherwydd, oblegid, o achos; gan, am

beck n amnaid, awgrym

beckon vb amneidio

become vb dyfod; gweddu

becoming adj gweddus

bed n gwely; cefn, pám

bedding n dillad gwely

bedeck vt addurno, trwsio

bedew vt gwlitho, gwlychu

bedfellow n cywely

bedlam n bedlam

bedraggled adj wedi caglo, dwyno; aflêr

bedrid(den) adj gorweiddiog

bedroom n ystafell wely, llofft

bedsitter n ystafell un gwely, ceginlofft

bedstead n pren neu haearn gwely

bee n gwenynen

beech n ffawydden

beef (**beeves**) n eidion; cig eidion, biff

beehive n cwch gwenyn

beeline n llinell unionsyth, ddiwyro

beer n cwrw

beestings npl llaeth newydd, llaeth toro

beet n betys

beetle n chwilen

beetroot n betys

befall vb digwydd

befit vb gweddu

before prep o flaen, gerbron, cyn ♦ adv o'r blaen

beforehand adv ymlaen llaw

befriend vt ymgeleddu, bod yn gefn

beg vb erfyn, deisyf, ymbil; cardota

beget vt cenhedlu, creu, peri

beggar n cardotyn ♦ vt tlodi, llymhau

begin vb dechrau

beginning n dechreuad

beguile vt hudo, twyllo; swyno, difyrru

behalf n plaid, rhan, achos, tu

behave vb ymddwyn

behaviour n ymddygiad

behead vt torri pen

behest n arch, archiad

behind adv, prep ar ôl, yn ôl, tu ôl, tu cefn

behold vt edrych, gweld ♦ vb imper wele

behove vt bod yn rhwymedig ar

beige adj beis

being n bod

belated adj diweddar; wedi ei ddal gan y nos

belch vb bytheirio

beleaguer vt gwarchae ar

belfry n clochdy

Belgium n Gwlad Belg

belie vt anwireddu, siomi

belief n cred, crediniaeth, coel

believe vb credu, coelio

believer n credwr, credadun

belittle vt bychanu

bell n cloch

belle n merch brydweddol, meinwen

bellicose adj rhyfelgar, ymladdgar

belligerent adj rhyfelog ♦ n rhyfelblaid

bellow vb rhuo, bugunad

bellows npl megin

belly n bol, bola; cest, tor ♦ vb bolio

belong vi perthyn

belongings npl meddiannau, eiddo

beloved adj annwyl, cu ♦ n anwylyd

below *adv, prep* is, islaw, isod, obry, oddi tanodd

belt *n* gwregys

bemoan *vt* galaru am, arwylo

bemused *adj* syfrdan

bench *n* mainc

bend *vb* plygu, camu ♦ *n* tro, camedd

beneath *adv, prep* is, tan, oddi tanodd

benediction *n* bendith

benefactor *n* cymwynaswr, noddwr

benefice *n* bywoliaeth eglwysig

beneficent *adj* daionus, llesfawr

beneficial *adj* buddiol, llesol

benefit *n* budd, lles, elw ♦ *vb* llesáu, elwa

benevolent *adj* daionus, haelionus

benighted *adj* a ddaliwyd gan y nos; tywyll

benign *adj* tirion, mwyn

bent *n* tuedd, gogwydd

benumb *vt* merwino, fferru, diffrwytho

bequeath *vt* cymynnu, cymynroddi

bequest *n* cymynrodd

bereave *vt* difuddio, amddifadu

beret *n* bere

Berlin *n* Berlin

berry *n* aeronen, mwyaren

berserk *adj* gwyllt, aflywodraethus

berth *n* lle llong; gwely llongwr; swydd

beseech *vt* atolygu, deisyf, erfyn

beseem *vt* gweddu

beset *vt* cynllwyn; amgylchynu

beside *prep* gerllaw, wrth, yn ymyl. **to be b. oneself** o'i bwyll

besides *adv, prep* heblaw, gyda

besiege *vt* gwarchae ar

besmirch *vt* llychwino, parddu

bespeak *vt* ymofyn ymlaen llaw

best *adj, adv* gorau

bestial *adj* bwystfilaidd

bestir *vt* cyffroi, ymysgwyd

bestow *vt* rhoddi, cyflwyno, anrhegu

bestride *vt* eisteddd neu gamu yn groes i

bet *n* bet, cyngwystl ♦ *vb* betio, dal am

betoken *vt* arwyddo, argoeli

betray *vt* bradychu

betrayal *n* brad

betroth *vt* dyweddio

better *adj* gwell, rhagorach ♦ *adv* yn well ♦ *vt* gwella

between, betwixt *prep* rhwng, cydrhwng

beverage *n* diod

bewail *vt* cwyno, cwynfan, galaru am

beware *vi* gochel, ymogelyd

bewilder *vt* drysu, mwydro, pensyfrdanu

bewitch *vt* rheibio

beyond *adv, prep* tu hwnt

bi- *prefix* dau-, deu-

bias *n* tuedd, gogwydd, rhagfarn ♦ *vt* tueddu

Bible *n* Beibl

bibliography *n* llyfryddiaeth

bibulous *adj* yfgar, llymeitgar

bicker *vi* ffraeo, ymrafaelio, ymgecru

bicycle *n* ceffyl haearn, deurod, beic

bid *vb* erchi; gwahodd; cynnig

bide *vb* aros, disgwyl

biennial *adj* dwyflynyddol

bier *n* elor

bifocals *npl* gwydrau deuffocal

big *adj* mawr; braisg

bigamy *n* dwywreigiaeth

bigheaded *adj* bras, mawreddog

bigot *n* penboethyn

bikini *n* bicini

bilberries *npl* llus

bile *n* bustl, geri

bilingual *adj* dwyieithog

bilingualism *n* dwyieithedd; dwyieithog

bill *n* bil; mesur; rhaglen;

hysbyslen

bill *n* pig, gylfin, duryn
billet *n* lletty (milwr) ♦ *vt* lletya
billiards *n* biliards
billion *n* biliwn
billow *n* ton, gwaneg, moryn ♦ *vi* tonni
billy-goat *n* bwch gafr
bin *n* cist
bind *vt* rhwymo, caethiwo
binge *n* gloddest, sbri
bingo *n* bingo
binoculars *n* deulygadur
biography *n* bywgraffiad, cofiant
biological *adj* biolegol
biology *n* bywydeg, bioleg
birch *n* bedw, bedwen; gwialen fedw ♦ *vt* chwipio
bird *n* aderyn
Biro *n* biro
birth *n* genedigaeth
birthday *n* pen-blwydd. **b. card** *n* carden pen-blwydd
birthmark *n* man geni
biscuit *n* bisgeden
bisect *vt* dwyrannu, rhannu
bisector *n* dwyrannydd
bisexual *adj* deurywiol
bishop *n* esgob
bishopric *n* esgobaeth
bison *n* ych gwyllt, bual
bit *n* tamaid; tipyn, dernyn; genfa, bit
bitch *n* gast
bite *vb* cnoi, brathu ♦ *n* cnoad, brath; tamaid
bitter *adj* chwerw, bustlaidd, tost
bittern *n* aderyn y bwn, bwmp y gors
bitterness *n* chwerwedd, chwerwder
bitumen *n* pyg
bituminous *adj* pyglyd
bizarre *adj* rhyfedd, od, chwithig
blab *vb* prepian, clepian ♦ *n* clepgi
black *adj* du ♦ *n* du, dyn du ♦ *vt* duo. **b. ice** *n* iâ du

blackberries *npl* mwyar duon
blackbird *n* aderyn du, mwyalchen
blackboard *n* bwrdd du
blackcurrant *n* cyrensen ddu ♦ *adj* cwrens du
blacken *vt* duo, pardduo; tywyllu
blackguard *n* dihiryn ♦ *vt* difrïo
blackleg *n* bradwr
blackmail *n* arian bygwth, blacmel
blacksmith *n* gof
bladder *n* pledren, chwysigen
blade *n* llafn; eginyn, blewyn
blame *vt* beio ♦ *n* bai
blameless *adj* di-fai
blanch *vt* gwynnu, cannu
bland *adj* mwyn, tyner, tirion
blandish *vt* gwenieithio, truthio
blank *adj* gwag, syn. **b. verse** mesur di-odl. **b. cheque** *n* siec wag
blanket *n* blanced, gwrthban
blare *vb* canu utgorn ♦ *n* sain utgorn
blarney *n* gweniaith, truth
blaspheme *vb* cablu, difenwi
blasphemy *n* cabledd, cabl
blast *n* chwa, chwythiad, deifiad ♦ *vt* deifio; saethu. **b. furnace** *n* ffwrnais chwythu
blatant *adj* stwrllyd, digywilydd, haerllug
blaze *n* fflam, ffagl ♦ *vi* fflamio, ffaglu
bleach *vb* cannu, gwynnu
bleak *adj* oer, digysgod, noeth, noethlwm
blear *adj* pŵl, dolurus, dyfriog
bleat *vb* brefu ♦ *n* bref
bleed *vb* gwaedu
blemish *vt* anafu, anurddo ♦ *n* anaf, bai, mefl
blend *vb* cymysgu ♦ *n* cymysgedd
bless *vt* bendithio
blessed *adj* bendigedig, gwyn ei fyd
blessing *n* bendith
blight *n* malltod ♦ *vt* mallu, deifio

blind adj dall, tywyll ♦ vt dallu ♦ n llen, bleind

blindness n dallineb

blink vb cau'r llygaid, ysmicio, amrantu

bliss n gwynfyd, dedwyddyd

blister n chwysigen, pothell ♦ vb pothellu

blithe adj llawen, llon, hoenus

blitz n blits

blizzard n ystorm erwin o wynt ac eira

bloat vb chwyddo, chwythu

blob n ysmotyn, bwrlwm

block n plocyn, cyff ♦ vt cau, rhwystro

blockade n gwarchae ♦ vb gwarchae ar

blockhead n penbwl, hurtyn

blonde adj o bryd golau

blood n gwaed; gwaedoliaeth. **b. pressure** n pwysedd gwaed

bloody adj gwaedlyd

bloom n blodeuyn; gwawr, gwrid ♦ vi blodeuo

blossom n blodeuyn ♦ vi blodeuo

blot n ysmotyn du, blot, mefl ♦ vb blotio

blotch n ysmotyn, blotyn, ystremp

blouse n blows

blow n dyrnod, ergyd

blow vb chwythu

blow-dry vb chwythu'n sych

bludgeon n pastwn

blue adj, n glas ♦ vt glasu

bluff adj garw, brochus

blunder n amryfusedd ♦ vb amryfuso

blunt adj pŵl, di-fin; plaen ♦ vt pylu

blur n ysmotyn, ystaen

blurb n broliant

blurt vt rhuthro dywedyd

blush vi cochi, gwrido ♦ n gwrid

bluster vi trystio, brochi ♦ n brawl, broch

blustery adj stormus, rhuadus

boar n baedd

board n bwrdd, bord; ymborth ♦ vb byrddio

boarding house n llety

boast n ymffrost ♦ vb ymffrostio

boat n bad, cwch

bobbin n gwerthyd

bobby n plismon

bode vt darogan, argoeli

body n corff

bog n cors, mignen, siglen

boggle vi petruso; rhusio, ffwndro

bogus adj ffug, gau, ffuantus

bogy, -ey n bwbach, bwci, bwgan

boil n cornwyd, casgliad

boil vb berwi

boiler n pair, crochan

boisterous adj terfysglyd, trystiog, brochus

bold adj hy, eofn; hyderus; eglur

bollard n bolard

bolster n gobennydd ♦ vt ategu

bolt n bollt ♦ vb bolltio; dianc; trafflyncu

bomb n bom

bombast n chwyddiaith

bombastic n chwyddedig

bona fide adj o'r iawn ryw, dilys, didwyll

bond n rhwymyn; ysgrifrwym ♦ adj caeth

bondage n caethiwed

bone n asgwrn

bonfire n coelcerth, banffagl

Bonn n Bonn

bonnet n bonet

bonny adj braf, nobl

bonus n bonws, ychwanegiad

booby n hurtyn, penbwl

book n llyfr

boom n bŵm

boom vb trystio, utganu ♦ n trwst, swae

boon n ffafr, bendith, caffaeliad

boor n taeog

boost vb gwthio, hybu

boot n botasen, esgid

booth n bwth, lluest, lluesty, caban

booty n ysglyfaeth, anrhaith, ysbail

booze vi diota, meddwi ♦ n diod feddwol

border n ffin, goror, ymyl ♦ vb ymylu

bore vb tyllu, ebillio ♦ n twll

bore n pla, dyn diflas ♦ vt blino, diflasu, llethu

bored adj wedi syrffedu ar beth, wedi alaru

boring adj diflas, annifyr, llethol

born adj wedi ei eni

borough n bwrdeistref

borrow vt benthyca

bosom n mynwes, côl

boss n meistr

botany n llysieueg

botch n ystomp ♦ vb ystompio, bwnglera

both adj, pron, adv y ddau, ill dau

bother vb blino, trafferthu ♦ n helynt, trafferth

bottle n potel, costrel ♦ vt potelu, costrelu. **b. opener** n agorwr poteli

bottom n gwaelod, godre, tin

bough n cainc, cangen

boulder n carreg fawr, clogfaen

bounce vb neidio, adlamu; bostio, ymffrostio

bound n terfyn, ffin, cyffin ♦ vt ffinio

bound vi llamu, neidio

boundary n ffin, terfyn

bounty n daioni, haelioni, ced

bouquet n blodeuglwm, pwysi

bout n sbel, term; ornest, ffrwgwd

bow n bwa; dolen

bow vb plygu, crymu, ymgrymu ♦ n moesymgrymiad

bow n pen blaen llong, bow

bowels npl ymysgaroedd, perfedd

bower n deildy

bowl n cawg, basn

bowler n het galed; bowliwr

box n bocs, pren bocs

box n bocs, blwch, cist; sedd, côr; bwth

box n bonclust ♦ vb taro bonclust; paffio. **b. office** n swyddfa docynnau

boy n bachgen, hogyn, mab, gwas

boycott n, vb ymwrthod â pherthynas a chydweithrediad, boicot(io)

boyfriend n cariadfab, anwylyd

boyhood n bachgendod, mebyd

brace n rhwymyn; pâr ♦ vt tynhau, cryfhau

bracelet n breichled

bracket n braced, cromfach

bracken n rhedyn ungoes

brag n brol, ymffrost, bocsach ♦ vb brolio, ymffrostio

braid n pleth, brwyd ♦ vt plethu, brwydo

brain n ymennydd

brake n dryslwyn, prysglwyn

brake n brêc ♦ vt brecio

bramble n miaren

bran n eisin, bran, rhuddion

branch n cangen, cainc ♦ vi canghennu

brand n pentewyn; nod ♦ vt gwarthnodi

brandish vb ysgwyd, chwifio

brandy n brandi

brash adj byrbwyll, ehud

brass n pres, efydd

brassière n bronglwm

brat n crwt, crwtyn; croten

bravado n gwag-ymffrost, bocsach, gorchest

brave adj dewr, gwrol, glew ♦ vt herio

bravo excl da iawn! campus!

brawl vi ffraeo, terfysgu ♦ n ffrae, ffrwgwd

brawn n cnawd

bray vt pwyo, briwio, malurio

bray vi brefu (megis asyn), nadu

brazen adj haerllug, hy
Brazil n Brasil
breach n adwy, rhwyg, tor; trosedd
bread n bara
breadth n lled
break vb torri ♦ n toriad, tor
breakdown n salwch, colli iechyd; (car) torri lawr
breakfast n brecwast ♦ vb brecwasta
breakwater n morglawdd
breast n bron, dwyfron, mynwes ♦ vt wynebu, ymladd â
breath n anadl, gwynt
breathalyser n anadlydd, anadliadur
breathe vb anadlu, chwythu
breathing n anadliad; anadlu
breech n tin, bôn
breeches npl llodrau, clos
breed vb magu; epilio; bridio ♦ n rhywogaeth, brid
breeze n awel, awelan, chwa
brethren npl brodyr (ffigurol yn bennaf)
brevity n byrder, byrdra
brew vt darllaw, bragu
brewer n darllawydd, bragwr
bribe n llwgrwobrwy ♦ vt llwgrwobrwyo
brick n bricsen, priddfaen ♦ vt bricio
bride n priodferch, priodasferch
bridegroom n priodfab
bridesmaid n morwyn briodas
bridge n pont ♦ vt pontio
bridle n ffrwyn ♦ vt ffrwyno
brief adj byr
brier, briar n miaren, drysïen
brigade n brigâd, mintai, torf
brigand n ysbeiliwr, carnleidr, herwr
bright adj disglair, claer, gloyw, hoyw
brilliance n disgleirdeb
brilliant adj disglair, llachar ♦ n

gem
brim n ymyl, min, cyfor; cantel
brimstone n brwmstan
brindled adj brith, brych
brine n heli
bring vt dwyn, cyrchu, dyfod â, dod â
brink n min, ymyl, glan
brisk adj bywiog, heini, sionc
bristle n gwrychyn, gwrych ♦ vi codi gwrychyn
Britain n Prydain
British adj Prydeinig, Brytanaidd
Briton n Brython, Prydeiniwr
Brittany n Llydaw
brittle adj brau, bregus
broach vt agor baril, gollwng; agor ymddiddan
broad adj llydan; eang; bras
broaden vb lledu, ehangu
broccoli n brocoli, math o fresych
brochure n llyfryn
brogue n llediaith (Gwyddelod)
broil vt briwlio
broken adj toredig, briw, drylliedig
broker n brocer, dyn canol
broll n terfysg, ymrafael, ymryson
bronchitis n bronceitis
bronze n pres, efydd
brooch n tlws
brood n nythaid; hil, epil ♦ vi deor; synfyfyrio
brook n nant, cornant, afonig
broom n banadl; ysgub, ysgubell
broth n potes, cawl
brothel n puteindy
brother (-s, brethren) n brawd
brotherly adj brawdol. b. love brawdgarwch
brow n ael, talcen; crib
brown adj brown, llwyd, gwinau. b. paper n papur llwyd. b. sugar n siwgr coch
browse vi brigbori, pori, blewynna
bruise vb cleisio, ysigo ♦ n clais
brunette n gwineuferch

brunt n pwys a gwres, ergyd

brush n brws ♦ vt brwsio, ysgubo

brushwood n manwydd, prysgwydd

brusque adj cwta, anfoesgar, taeog

Brussels sprouts npl ysgewyll Brwsel

brutal adj creulon, bwysfilaidd

brute n anifail, creadur (direswm)

bubble n bwrlwm ♦ vb byrlymu

buccaneer n môr-leidr, môr-herwr

buck n bwch; coegyn ♦ vb llamsachu

bucket n bwced, ystwc

buckle n bwcl, gwäeg ♦ vb byclu, gwaegu

bud n blaguryn, eginyn ♦ vb blaguro, egino

budge vb syflyd, chwimio

budget n cwd, coden; cyllideb

buff adj llwydfelyn

buffalo n bual

buffet n cernod ♦ vt cernodio, baeddu

buffoon n digrifwas, croesan, ysgentyn

bug n drewbryf, bwg

bugbear n bwgan, bwbach, bwci

bugle n corn, utgorn

build vt adeiladu ♦ n corffolaeth

building n adail, adeilad, adeiladaeth

bulb n bwlb

bulge n chwydd ♦ vt chwyddo

bulk n swm, crynswth

bull n tarw

bulldozer n peiriant clirio ffordd, tarw dur

bullet n bwled, bwleden

bulletin n bwletin

bullfight n ymladd teirw

bullfinch n coch y barfau

bullion n aur neu arian clamp, bwliwn

bullock n bustach, eidion, ych

bull's eye n trawiad union

bully n gormeswr, bwli ♦ vt gormesu, erlid

bulrushes npl llafrwyn, hesg

bulwark n gwrthglawdd; canllaw

bumbailiff n bwmbeili

bumble-bee n cacynen

bump vb bwmpio, hergydio ♦ n bwmp, hergwd

bumper adj llawn, helaeth

bumpkin n lleban, llabwst, llelo

bumptious adj hunandybus, rhodresgar

bumpy adj aflonydd, anwadal, garw

bun n bynsen, bynnen, teisen

bunch n swp; cwlwm, pwysi ♦ vb sypio

bundle n bwndel, coflaid ♦ vt bwndelu

bungalow n tŷ unllawr, byngalo

bungle vb bwnglera, ystompio ♦ n bwnglerwaith

bunion n corn ar fys troed

bunker n bwncer

bunkum n lol, ffiloreg, truth

bunting n (defnydd) banerau

buoy n bwi ♦ vt cynnal, cadw rhag suddo

buoyant adj hynawf; calonnog

burden n baich ♦ vt beichio, llwytho

bureau n ysgrifgist; swyddfa

bureaucracy n biwrocratiaeth

burgess, burgher n dinesydd, bwrdais

burglar n torrwr tŷ, bwrgler

burial n claddedigaeth, angladd

burlesque n digrifwawd, gwatwargerdd

burly adj corfol, praff, mawr

burn vb llosgi, ysu ♦ n llosg, llosgiad

burnish vt caboli, llathru, gloywi

burrow n twll cwningen ♦ vb tyllu, tyrchu

bursar n bwrser, swyddog ariannol

bursary n amneriaeth, ysgoloriaeth

burst vb byrstio, ymrwygo, ymddryllio, torri ♦ n rhwyg
bury vt claddu
bus n bws
bush n perth, llwyn; prysgwydd, drysi
bushel n bwysel, mesur wyth galwyn
business n busnes, masnach, gwaith. **b. trip** n taith fusnes
businessman/woman n gŵr busnes/gwraig fusnes
bus-stop n atalfa bws, arosfan
bust n penddelw; mynwes
bustle vi trafferthu, ffwdanu ♦ n ffwdan
busy adj prysur
busybody n ymyrrwr, dyn busneslyd, trwyn
but conj, prep ond, eithr
butcher n cigydd ♦ vt cigyddio, lladd
butler n trulliad, bwtler
butt n nod, targed; cyff clêr
butt vt cornio, hyrddu, twlcio, hwylio
butt n casgen, baril
butter n ymenyn ♦ vt rhoi ymenyn ar
buttercup n blodyn yr ymenyn
butterfly n glöyn byw, iâr fach yr haf, pili-pala
buttermilk n llaeth enwyn
buttery n bwtri
buttock n ffolen
button n botwm ♦ vt botymu
buttress n ateg, gwanas ♦ vt ategu
buxom adj glandeg, gweddgar, nwyfus
buy vt prynu
buzz vb suo, sisial, mwmian ♦ n su, sŵn gwenyn
by prep gan, wrth, trwy, ger, gerllaw ♦ adv heibio, yn agos ♦ prefix rhag-, is-
by-election n isetholiad
by(e)-law n is-ddeddf

by-gone n yr hyn a fu
bypass n ffordd osgoi
by-product n isgynnyrch
bystander n un yn sefyll gerllaw
byword n ymadrodd cynefin, cyffredin

C

cab n cab
cabal n clymblaid, cabal ♦ vi clymbleidio
cabaret n cabare
cabbage n bresychen, bresych
cabin n caban ♦ vt cabanu, caethiwo
cabinet n cell, cist; cabinet
cable n rhaff fferf; cebl tanfor
cackle vi clegar
cactus n mwl ysgallen, cactws
cad n taeog, bryntyn, cenau
caddie n gwas golffwr
cadence n goslef, diweddeb
cadet n mab ieuengaf; cadlanc
café n tŷ bwyta, caffe
cage n cawell, caets ♦ vt cau, carcharu
cairn n carn, carnedd, crug
cajole vt twyllo drwy weniaith
cake n teisen, cacen ♦ vb torthi; caglu
calamity n adfyd, trallod, trychineb
calcine vb llosgi'n galch
calculate vb cyfrif, bwrw cyfrif, clandro
calculation n cyfrif
calculator n cyfrifiannell
calendar n calendr, almanac
calf (calves) n llo
calf n (of the leg) croth (coes)
calibre n calibr
call vb galw ♦ n galwad, galw; ymweliad
calling n galwedigaeth
callous adj croendew, dideimlad,

caled

calm adj tawel ♦ n tawelwch ♦ vb tawelu

calorie n calori, uned gwres

calumny n anair, enllib, athrod, cabl

calve vi bwrw llo

Calvinism n Calfiniaeth

camber n camber

Cambodia n Cambodia

Cambrian adj Cymreig

camel n camel

cameo n cameo

camera n ystafell; teclyn tynnu lluniau, camera

camouflage n cuddliw, dull o ddieithrio ♦ vb dieithrio, cuddio

camp n gwersyll ♦ vi gwersyllu

campaign n ymgyrch, rhyfelgyrch

campbed n gwely plyg

campsite n maes gwersylla

campus n campws

can n tyn, piser, stên ♦ vb gallu. **c. opener** n agorwr caniau

Canada n Canada

Canadian adj Canadaidd ♦ n Canadiad

canal n camlas; pibell

canary n caneri

Canary Islands npl: **the C.I.** yr Ynysoedd Dedwydd

cancel vt dileu, dirymu, diddymu

cancer n dafad wyllt, cancr, cranc

candid adj teg, onest, plaen

candidate n ymgeisydd

candle n cannwyll

candlestick n canhwyllbren

candour n onestrwydd, didwylledd

candy n candi

cane n corsen, cansen ♦ vt curo â chansen

canine adj perthynol i'r ci

canister n tun cadw te, bocs (te)

canker n cancr ♦ vb cancro

canned adj ar gadw mewn can tun

cannibal n canibal

cannon n magnel

canny adj call, cyfrwys, ffel

canoe n ceufad, canw

canon n canon, rheol

canopy n gortho, nenlen

cant n ffugsancteiddrwydd, rhagrith ♦ vi rhagrithio

cantankerous adj cwerylgar, cynhennus

cantata n cantata, cantawd

canteen n cantîn

canter vi rhygyngu ♦ n rhygyng

canticle n cantigl, canig, cân, emyn

canto n cân, adran o gân

canton n rhandir, talaith

canvas n cynfas, lliain bras

canvass vb trafod; ymofyn pleidleisiau, canfasio

canyon n ceunant, canion

cap n cap, capan ♦ vt capio

capable adj galluog, cymwys, cyfaddas

capacity n gallu, cymhwyster; cynnwys

cape n penrhyn, pentir, trwyn

cape n mantell, cêp

caper n pranc ♦ vi prancio

capital adj prif, pen ♦ n priflythyren; prifddinas; cyfalaf

capitalism n cyfalafiaeth

capital punishment n y gosb eithaf

capitulate vi ymostwng ar amodau

caprice n mympwy, chwilen

capsize vb dymchwelyd, troi

capsule n capswl

captain n capten

caption n pennawd, teitl

captivate vt swyno, hudo, denu

captive adj caeth ♦ n carcharor

captivity n caethiwed; caethglud

captor n daliwr, deiliad

capture n daliad ♦ vt dal

car n car, cerbyd. **c. wash** golffca geir

caravan n carafán; men. **c. site** n maes carafanau

carbine *n* dryll byr, byrddryll
carbohydrate(s) *n*
  carbohydrad(au)
carbon *n* carbon
carbuncle *n* carbwncl
carburettor *n* carburadur
carcass, -ase *n* celain, ysgerbwd
card *n* cerdyn, carden
card *vt* cribo gwlân
cardiac *adj* perthynol i'r galon
Cardiff *n* Caerdydd
cardigan *n* cardigan
cardinal *adj* prif, arbennig ♦ *n*
  cardinal
care *n* gofal, pryder ♦ *vi* gofalu,
  malio
career *n* gyrfa, hynt ♦ *vi* carlamu
careful *adj* gofalus, gwyliadwrus
careless *adj* diofal, esgeulus
caress *n* anwes, mwythau ♦ *vt*
  anwesu
caret *n* gwallnod, diffygnod (^)
caretaker *n* gofalwr
cargo *n* llwyth (llong), cargo
caricature *n* gwawdlun, digriflun
caring *adj* gofalus
carnage *n* galanastra, lladdfa
carnal *adj* cnawdol
carnation *n* blodyn cigliw
carnival *n* carnifal
carnivorous *adj* cigysol, rheibus
carol *n* carol ♦ *vi* caroli, canu
carouse *vi* gloddesta, cyfeddach
carp *vi* pigo beiau, cecru, cadw
  swn
car park *n* maes parcio
carpenter *n* saer coed
carpet *n* carped ♦ *vt* carpedu
carriage *n* cerbyd; cludiad;
  ymarweddiad
carrier *n* cariwr, cludydd. **c. bag** *n*
  cludfag
carrion *n* burgyn, celain, ysgerbwd
carrot *n* moronen
carry *vb* cario, cludo, cywain
cart *vb* men, troi, cert, cart, car
cartilage *n* madruddyn

carton *n* carton
cartoon *n* digriflun, cartwn
cartridge *n* cetrisen
carve *vt* cerfio, naddu; torri cig
cascade *n* rhaeadr
case *n* achos, cyflwr; dadl
case *n* cas, gwain; cist wydr
casement *n* ffenestr adeiniog,
  casment
cash *n* arian parod. **c. desk** *n* safle
  talu
cashier *n* ariannwr, trysorydd
cashier *vt* diswyddo
casing *n* plisgyn; casin
casino *n* casino
cask *n* casgen, baril
casket *n* cistan, prenfol, blwch
casserole *n* llestr coginio a dal
  bwyd
cassette *n* casét
cassock *n* llaeswisg ddu offeiriad,
  casog
cast *vb* bwrw, taflu ♦ *n* tafliad. **c.
  iron** haearn bwrw
caste *n* llwyth; gradd, braint; cast
castigate *vt* cystwyo
casting-vote *n* pleidlais y
  cadeirydd
castle *n* castell ♦ *vi* castellu
castrate *vt* disbaddu
casual *adj* damweiniol, achlysurol
casualty *n* un wedi ei anafu
casuistry *n* achosionaeth
cat *n* cath
cataclysm *n* dilyw, dylif,
  rhyfertiwy
catacomb *n* claddgell, claddogof
catalogue *n* catalog
catapult *n* blif, catapwlt
cataract *n* rhaeadr, sgwd; pilen
catarrh *n* llif annwyd, gormwyth
catastrophe *n* trychineb
catch *vt* dal ♦ *n* bach, clicied;
  dalfa
catching *adj* heintus
catchment area *n* dalgylch
catechism *n* holwyddoreg,

catecism

category *n* trefn, dosbarth

cater *vi* arlwyo, darmerth, darparu

caterpillar *n* lindys

cathartic *n* carthlyn

cathedral *n* eglwys gadeiriol

catholic *adj* catholig; pabyddol ♦ *n* catholigydd; pabydd

catkins *npl* cenawon cyll, cywion gwyddau

cattle *npl* gwartheg, da

caucus *n* clymblaid

caudle *n* sucan

cauldron *n* crochan, pair, callor

cauliflower *n* blodfresychen

causality *n* achosiaeth

cause *n* achos ♦ *vt* achosi, peri

causeway *n* sarn, cawsai

caustic *adj* ysol, llosg, deifiol

cauterize *vt* serio

caution *n* pwyll, gwyliadwriaeth; rhybudd ♦ *vt* rhybuddio

cautious *adj* gwyliadwrus

cavalcade *n* mintai o farchogion

cavalier *n* marchog, marchfilwr

cavalry *n* gwŷr meirch

cave *n* ogof

cavern *n* ceudwll, ogof

caviar(e) *n* grawn pysgod, cafiâr

cavil *vi* cecru

cavity *n* ceudod, gwagle

caw *vi* crawcian

cease *vb* peidio, darfod

cedar *n* cedrwydden

cede *vt* rhoi i fyny, gildio, trosglwyddo

ceiling *n* nen, nenfwd

celebrate *vt* clodfori; dathlu; gweinyddu

celebrated *adj* clodfawr, enwog, hyglod

celebrity *n* bri, enwogrwydd; gŵr o fri

celery *n* seleri

celestial *adj* nefol, nefolaidd

celibate *adj* dibriod

cell *n* cell

cellar *n* seler

cement *n* sment ♦ *vt* smentio; cadarnhau

cemetery *n* mynwent, claddfa

censer *n* thuser

censor *n* beirniad; sensor

censure *n* cerydd, sen ♦ *vt* ceryddu

census *n* cyfrifiad

cent *n* y ganfed ran o ddoler

centenarian *n* canmlwyddiad

centenary *n* canmlwyddiant

centigrade *adj* canradd, sentigred

central *adj* canol, canolog. **c. heating** *n* gwres canolog

centre *n* canol, canolfan, canolbwynt ♦ *vb* canolbwyntio

centre-forward *n* canolwr blaen

centre-threequarter *n* canolwr

centrifugal *adj* allgyrchol

centripetal *adj* mewngyrchol

centurion *n* canwriad

century *n* canrif

ceramic *adj* perthynol i grefft y crochenydd, ceramig

cereal *n* grawn, ŷd

cerebral *adj* ymenyddol

ceremony *n* seremoni, defod

certain *adj* sicr; neilltuol; rhyw, rhai

certainly *adv* yn sicr, yn siwr

certainty *n* sicrwydd

certificate *n* tystysgrif

certify *vt* hysbysu, tystio

cesspool *n* carthbwll

chafe *vb* rhwbio; llidio ♦ *n* llid, cythrudd

chaff *n* us, manus, mân us

chaffer *vi* edwica, bargeinio, bargenna

chaffinch *n* pinc, asgell fraith

chagrin *n* cythrudd, siom

chain *n* cadwyn ♦ *vt* cadwyno

chair *n* cadair ♦ *vt* cadeirio

chairman *n* cadeirydd

chalet *n* bwthyn (haf)

chalice *n* cwpan cymun, caregl

chalk n sialc ♦ vt sialcio

challenge n her, sialens ♦ vt herio, sialensio

chamber n ystafell, siambr

chamberlain n gwas ystafell, siambrlen

champ vt cnoi, dygnoi

champagne n gwin Champagne

champion n pencampwr; pleidiwr ♦ vt cymryd plaid

chance n damwain, siawns ♦ vt digwydd

chancel n cangell

chancellor n canghellor

chandelier n canhwyllyr

chandler n canhwyllydd, masnachydd

change vb newid, cyfnewid ♦ n newid

changing-room n ystafell newid

channel n sianel, gwely; rhigol

chant vt corganu ♦ n corgan, salmdon

chaos n tryblith, anhrefn

chap vt agennu, torri (am ddwylo)

chapel n capel

chaplain n caplan

chapter n pennod; cabidwl

char vb golosgi, deifio

character n cymeriad; nod, arwydd

characteristic adj nodweddiadol ♦ n nodwedd

charcoal n marwor, golosg, sercol

charge vb siarsio; cyhuddo; rhuthro; codi; llwytho ♦ n siars; gofal, cyhuddiad; rhuthr; pris; ergyd

charger n march rhyfel, cadfarch

chariot n cerbyd

charity n cariad; cardod, elusen

charlatan n un yn honni gwybodaeth; cwac

charm n swyn, cyfaredd ♦ vt swyno

charming adj cyfareddol, swynol, cwrtais

chart n siart

charter n siarter, breinlen ♦ vt breiniu; llogi. **c. flight** n hediad siartr

charwoman n morwyn wrth y dydd

chary adj gwagelog, gochelgar, gofalus

chase vt ymlid, erlid, hel ♦ n helwriaeth

chasm n hafn, ceunant, agendor

chaste adj diwair, pur, dillyn

chasten vt puro, coethi; ceryddu

chastise vb ceryddu, cosbi, cystwyo

chastity n diweirdeb, purdeb

chat vi sgwrsio, ymgomio ♦ n sgwrs, ymgom

chattel n catel

chatter vi trydar, cogor; clebran; rhincian

chatterbox n clebryn, cleben

chatty adj siaradus, parod am sgwrs

chauffeur n gyrrwr

cheap adj rhad, salw

cheat n twyll; twyllwr ♦ vt twyllo

check n rhwystr, atalfa ♦ vt atal, ffrwyno

cheek n grudd, boch; digwilydd-dra

cheeky adj digywilydd, haerllug, eg(e)r

cheer n calondid, cysur; arlwy ♦ vb llonni, sirioli, sirio

cheerful adj llon, siriol

cheers! excl iechyd da!

cheese n caws

chef n prif gogydd

chemical adj cemegol ♦ n cyffur

chemise n crys merch

chemist n fferyllydd; cemegwr

chemistry n cemeg

cheque n archeb (ar fanc), siec. **c. book** n llyfr siec; (col) llyfr main. **c. card** n carden siec

chequer vt amryliwio, britho

chequered adj brith, anwadal

cherish vt meithrin, coleddu, mynwesu

cherry n ceiriosen

cherub n ceriwb

chess n gwyddbwyll

chest n cist, coffr; brest

chestnut n castan

chevalier n marchog

chew vb cnoi. **c. the cud** cnoi cil

chewing gum n gwm cnoi

chick, chicken n cyw (iâr)

chicken-pox n brech yr ieir

chide vt ceryddu, dwrdio

chief adj pen, pennaf, prif ♦ n pennaeth

chieftain n blaenor, pennaeth

chilblain n llosg eira, cibwst, malaith

child (-ren) n plentyn

childhood n plentyndod, mebyd

Chile n Chile

chill n oerni, annwyd ♦ adj oer, anwydog ♦ vb oeri, fferru, rhynnu

chime n sain cloch neu gloc ♦ vb canu (clychau)

chimera n anghenfil; bwgan, bwbach

chimney n corn mwg, simnai

chin n gên

China n China, Tseina

china n llestri te (tsieni)

chink n agen, hollt

chip vb hacio, naddu ♦ n asglodyn, pric

chips npl sglodion

chiropodist n troedfeddyg

chirp vi yswitian, grillian, trydar

chisel n cŷn, gaing

chit n nodyn byr

chivalry n urddas marchog; sifalri

chives n cennin sifi

chocolate n siocled

choice n dewis, dewisiad ♦ adj dewisol, dethol

choir n côr; cafell

choke vb tagu; mygu; topio, cau

choler n geri, bustl; dicter, llid

cholera n y geri marwol, colera

choose vb dewis, dethol, ethol

chop vt torri ♦ n golwyth

choral adj corawl

chord n tant; cord

chore n y dwt

chorus n côr, cytgan, byrdwn, corws

Christ n Crist

christen vt bedyddio, enwi

Christendom n (gwledydd) Cred

Christian adj Cristnogol ♦ n Cristion

Christianity n Cristnogaeth

Christmas n Nadolig

Christmassy adj Nadoligaidd

chrome n crôm

chronic adj parhaol (am anhwyldeb)

chronicle n cronicl ♦ vt cronicio

chronology n amseryddiaeth

chrysanthemum n ffarwel haf

chubby adj wynepgrwn, tew

chuck vt taro dan yr ên; taflu, lluchio

chuckle vi chwerthin yn nwrn dyn

chum n cyfaill mebyd ♦ vi cyfrinachu

chunk n tafell dew, toc

church n eglwys, llan ♦ vt eglwysa

churchyard n mynwent

churl n taeog, costog, cerlyn

churlish adj afrynwiog, taeogaidd

churn n buddai ♦ vb corddi

chutney n picl cymysg

cider n seidr

cigar n sigâr

cigarette n sigarét

cincture n gwregys, rhwymyn

cinder n marworyn, colsyn

cine-camera n camera sine

cinema n sinema

cinnamon n sinamon

cipher n gwagnod (O); ysgrifen ddirgel ♦ vi cyfrif

circle n cylch ♦ vb cylchu

circuit n cylch; cylchdaith
circular adj crwn ♦ n cylchlythyr
circulate vb cylchredeg, lledaenu
circum- prefix cylch-, am-
circumcise vt enwaedu
circumference n cylchyn; cylchedd
circumflex n acen grom, to (ˆ)
circumlocution n cylchymadrodd
circumscribe vt cyfyngu
circumspect adj gwyliadwrus, gofalus
circumstance n amgylchiad
circumstantial adj amgylchus
circumvent vt twyllo
circus n syrcas
cistern n dyfrgist, pydew, sistern
citadel n castell, amddiffynfa, caer
cite vt gwysio; dyfynnu
citizen n dinesydd
city n dinas
civic adj dinesig
civil adj gwladol; moesgar
civilian n dinesydd (anfilwrol)
civilization n gwareiddiad
civilize vt gwareiddio
civil service n gwasanaeth sifil, gwasanaeth gwladol
civil war n rhyfel cartref
clack vi clecian, clepian, clegar
claim vt hawlio ♦ n hawl
clamber vi dringo, cribo
clammy adj gludiog, cleiog, toeslyd
clamour n gwaedd, dadwrdd ♦ vi crochlefain
clamp n ystyffwl, craff
clan n tylwyth, llwyth
clandestine adj lladradaidd
clang, clank vb cloncio ♦ n clonc
clap n twrf, trwst ♦ vb curo; taro; clepian
claret n claret
clarify vt gloywi, puro; egluro
clarinet n clarinet
clarion n utgorn
clash vb taro, gwrthdaro ♦ n

gwrthdrawiad
clasp n gwäeg, bach, clesbyn ♦ vt gwaegu; cofleidio
class n dosbarth ♦ vt dosbarthu
classic n clasur, campwaith, llên goeth ♦ adj clasurol
classical adj clasurol
classics npl clasuron
classify vb dosbarthu
classroom n ystafell ddosbarth
clatter vb clewtian, clepian, trystio ♦ n trwst
clause n adran, cymal
claw n crafanc, ewin ♦ vt crafangu, cripio
clay n clai
clean adj glân, glanwaith ♦ vt glanhau
cleaner n glanhawr, glanheydd
cleaning n glanhad, glanheuad
cleanly adv yn lân
cleanse vt glanhau
cleanser n glanhawr
clear adj clir, eglur, gloyw; croyw ♦ vt clirio
cleave vi glynu (wrth)
cleave vt hollti; fforchogi
clef n allwedd, cleff
cleft n hollt, agen
clement adj tyner, tirion, trugarog
clench vt cau yn dynn, clensio
clergy n offeiriaid
clergyman n clerigwr, offeiriad
clerical adj clerigol; perthynol i glerc
clerk n clerc
clever adj medrus, deheuig, clyfar
cleverness n medr, deheurwydd, clyfrwch
click vi clician, clepian ♦ n clic
client n cyflogydd cyfreithiwr, cwsmer
cliff n clogwyn, allt
climate n hinsawdd
climax n uchafbwynt
climb vb dringo
climbing adj dringol

clinch *vt* clensio; cau, cloi

cling *vi* glynu, cydio

clinic *n* meddygfa, clinig

clinical *adj* clinigol

clink *vi* tincian

clip *vt* cneifio, tocio, clipio

clique *n* clîc, clymblaid

cloak *n* mantell, clogyn, clog ♦ *vt* cuddio, celu

cloakroom *n* ystafell ddillad

clock *n* cloc

clod *n* tywarchen

clog *n* clocsen ♦ *vt* llesteirio; tagu; clocsio

cloister *n* clwysty

close *vb* cau; terfynu ♦ *n* diwedd, diweddglo

close *adj* agos, clòs; caeth, tyn

close *n* clas, clos, buarth, clwt, cae

closed shop *n* gwaith cyfyngedig, gwaith i rai yn unig

closet *n* cell, ystafell; geudy

close-up *n* llun agos

closure *n* cau, gorffen, darfod

clot *n* tolchen ♦ *vb* tolchi, ceulo

cloth *n* brethyn, lliain

clothe *vt* dilladu, gwisgo

clothes *npl* dillad, gwisgoedd

clothes peg *n* bachyn dillad

clothier *n* brethynnwr, dilledydd

clothing *n* dillad

cloud *n* cwmwl ♦ *vt* cymylu

clout *n* cernod, clewt; clwt ♦ *vt* clewtian; clytio

clover *n* meillion, clofer

clown *n* lleban; croesan, clown

club *n* pastwn; clwb ♦ *vb* pastynu; clybio

clue *n* pen llinyn, arwydd

clump *n* clwmp, clamp, cyff

clumsy *adj* trwsgl, anfedrus, lletchwith

cluster *n* clwstwr, swp ♦ *vb* casglu, tyrru

clutch *n* crafanc; gafael, (*pl*). hafflau ♦ *vb* crafangu

clutter *n* dadwrdd, helynt

co- *prefix* cyd-

coach *n* cerbyd; hyfforddwr ♦ *vb* hyfforddi

coagulate *vb* ceulo

coal *n* glöyn, glo

coalesce *vi* cyfuno, cyd-doddi

coalition *n* cyfuniad; cynghrair, clymblaid

coarse *adj* garw, aflednais; bras

coast *n* arfordir, glan ♦ *vi* hwylio gyda'r lan

coastal *adj* arfordirol

coastguard *n* gwyliwr y glannau

coastline *n* morlin

coat *n* cot. **c. hanger** *n* cambren (dillad). **c. of arms** *n* arfbais

coating *n* caen, golchiad

coax *vb* hudo, denu, perswadio

cobble, -stone *n* carreg balmant

cobbler *n* crydd, cobler

cobweb *n* gwe pryf cop, gwe'r cor

cock *n* ceiliog; mwdwl; cliced (dryll) ♦ *vb* mydylu; codi cliced

cockerel *n* cyw ceiliog, ceiliogyn

cock-eyed *adj* â llygad tro

cockles *npl* cocos, cocs, rhython

cockpit *n* sedd peilot; ymladdfan ceiliogod

cockroach *n* chwilen ddu

cock-sure *adj* gorbendant, gorhyderus

cocktail *n* coctêl

cocoa *n* coco

coconut *n* cneuen goco, coconyt

cod *n* y penfras; cod

code *n* côd

coerce *vb* gorfodi, gorthrechu

coercion *n* gorfodaeth, gorthrech

coffee *n* coffi

coffin *n* arch, ysgrin

cog *n* dant olwyn, còg

cogent *adj* cryf, grymus, argyhoeddiadol

cohabit *vi* cyd-fyw

cohere *vi* cydlynu

cohesion *n* cydlyniad

coil vb torchi ♦ n torch

coin n arian bath ♦ vb bathu

coincide vi cyd-ddigwydd, cyd-daro

coincidence n cyd-ddigwyddiad

coke n golosg, côc

colander n hidl

cold adj oer ♦ n oerfel, oerni, annwyd. **to catch a c.** dal annwyd

colic n bolwst, colig

collapse vi disgyn, cwympo ♦ n cwymp, methiant

collapsible adj plygadwy

collar n coler ♦ vb coleru. **c. bone** pont yr ysgwydd

collateral adj cyfochrog, cyfystlys

colleague n cydweithiwr

collect n colect ♦ vb crynhoi, hel, ymgynnull, casglu

collection n casgliad

collector n casglwr

college n coleg

collide vb gwrthdaro

collie n ci defaid

collier n glówr; llong lo

colliery n gwaith glo, pwll glo, glofa

collision n gwrthdrawiad

colloquial adj llafar, tafodieithol

colon n gorwahannod, colon (:); coluddyn mawr

colonel n cyrnol

colonial adj trefedigaethol

colony n trefedigaeth, gwladfa

colossal adj cawraidd, anferth

colour n lliw, baner ♦ vb lliwio; cochi. **c. bar** gwahanfur lliw. **c. blind** lliwddall

coloured adj lliw

colourful adj lliwgar

colouring n lliwiad

colourless adj di-liw

colt n ebol

column n colofn

columnist n newyddiadurwr, colofnydd

coma n hunglwyf, côma

comb n crib ♦ vb cribo

combat n brwydr, gornest ♦ vb brwydro

combination n cyfuniad

combine vb cyfuno. **c. harvester** cynaeafydd, combein

come vi dod, dyfod. **to c. across** dod ar draws. **to c. to light** dod i'r golwg. **to c. to an end** dod i ben. **to c. by** meddiannu. **to c. to pass** digwydd

comedian n comedïwr

comedy n comedi

comfort n cysur, diddanwch ♦ vt cysuro, diddanu

comfortable adj cysurus, cyffyrddus

comfortably adv yn gysurus, yn gyffyrddus

comic adj comic, digrif, ysmala

comma n rhagwahannod, atalnod, coma

command vb gorchymyn ♦ n gorchymyn, awdurdod

commandeer vb meddiannu

commander n cadlywydd, comander

commandment n gorchymyn

commando n mintai (o filwyr), un o'r fintai

commemorate vt coffáu, dathlu

commence vb dechrau

commend vt cymeradwyo, canmol

commensurate adj cymesur

comment vi sylwi, esbonio ♦ n sylw

commentary n sylwebaeth

commentator n esboniwr, sylwebydd

commerce n masnach

commercial adj masnachol

commiserate vt cydymdeimlo â, cyd-dosturio â

commission n comisiwn, dirprwyaeth ♦ vb comisiynu

commissionaire n porthor

commissioner n comisiynydd

commit vt cyflawni; traddodi;

cyflwyno

commitment n ymrwymiad; traddodiad

committee n pwyllgor

commodity n nwydd (masnachol)

common adj cyffredin ♦ n tir cyffredin, cytir, comin. **the C. Market** y Farchnad Gyffredin

commoner n cominwr, gwerinwr

commonplace adj dibwys, cyffredin

commons npl y cyffredin. **House of C.** Tŷ'r Cyffredin

common sense n synnwyr cyffredin

commonwealth n cymanwlad

commotion n cyffro, terfysg

communal adj cymunol, cymunedol

commune vi ymddiddan; cymuno ♦ n cymundod; comun

communicate vb cyfathrebu; cymuno

communication n cyfathrebiad, cysylltiad, neges

communion n cymun, cymundeb

communism n comiwnyddiaeth

communist n comiwnydd

community n cymdeithas, cymuned. **c. centre** canolfan gymuned

commute vt cymudo, pendilio

commuter n cymudwr, pendiliwr

compact n cytundeb, cyfamod; bag bach, compact ♦ adj cryno ♦ vt crynhoi. **c. disc** cryno ddisg

companion n cydymaith

companionship n cwmniaeth, cyfeillach

company n cymdeithas, cwmni. **keep c. with** cadw cwmni â

comparative adj cymharol

comparatively adv yn gymharol

compare vt cymharu, cyffelybu

comparison n cymhariaeth

compartment n adran, cerbydran

compass n cwmpawd; cwmpas ♦

vt amgylchu

compassion n tosturi

compatible adj cydweddol, cyson

compatriot n cydwladwr

compel vt cymell, gorfodi

compendium n crynodeb, talfyriad

compensate vt talu iawn, digolledu

compensation n iawndal

compete vi cystadlu

competence n cymhwysedd

competent adj cymwys, digonol

competition n cystadleuaeth

competitive adj cystadleuol

competitor n cystadleuydd

complacency n ymfoddhad

complacent adj hunan-foddhaus, digonol

complain vi cwyno, achwyn, grwgnach

complaint n cwyn, achwyniad; anhwyldeb

complement n cyflawnder, cyflenwad

complementary adj cyflenwol

complete adj cyflawn ♦ vt cyflawni

completely adv yn llwyr

completion n cwblhad

complex adj cymhleth, dyrys

complexion n gwedd, pryd, gwawr

compliance n cydsyniad

complicate vt cymhlethu; drysu

complicated adj cymhleth, dyrys

complication n cymhlethdod

compliment n cyfarchiad; canmoliaeth

comply vi cydsynio, ufuddhau

component n cydran, cyfansoddyn

compose vt cyfansoddi; cysodi; tawelu

composed adj hunanfeddiannol

composer n cyfansoddwr

composition n cyfansoddiad, traethawd

composure n tawelwch, hunan-feddiant

compound adj cyfansawdd ♦ n cymysg ♦ vb cymysgu

comprehend vt amgyffred, dirnad

comprehension n amgyffred, dirnadaeth

comprehensive adj cynhwysfawr. **c. school** Ysgol Gyfun

compress vt gwasgu, crynhoi ♦ n plastr

comprise vt amgyffred, cynnwys

compromise n cymrodedd, cyfaddawd ♦ vb cymrodeddu, cyfaddawdu

compulsion n gorfodaeth

compulsive adj trwy orfod, o anfodd

compulsory adj gorfodol

computer n cyfrifiadur. **c. operator** cyfrifiadurwr. **c. science** cyfrifianneg, cyfrifiaduraeg

comrade n cydymaith

concave adj ceugrwm

conceal vb cuddio, celu, dirgelu

concede vt caniatáu, addef

conceit n tyb, mympwy; hunanadyb, hunanoldeb, cysêt

conceited adj hunandybus, hunanol, balch

conceive vb dirnad; tybied, synied; beichiogi

concentrate vt crynodi, canolbwyntio

concentration n crynodiad, ymroddiad

concept n cysyniad

conception n syniad; beichiogiad

concern vt perthyn, ymwneud (â), gofalu (am), pryderu, bod a wnelo â ♦ n busnes, diddordeb; gofal, pryder

concerned adj yn teimlo pryder, pryderus, gofalus, yn ymboeni

concerning prep ynglŷn â, ynghylch

concert n cyngerdd ♦ vt cyd-drefnu

concerted adj cydunol, wedi ei gyd-drefnu

concertina n consertina

conclude vb diweddu; casglu, barnu

conclusion n diwedd; casgliad

conclusive adj terfynol

concoct vt llunio, dyfeisio

concoction n cymysgedd

concourse n tyrfa, torf

concrete adj diriaethol ♦ n concrit

concur vi cydredeg; cydgroesi; cytuno

concurrently adv yn gyfredol

concussion n cyd-drawiad, ysgytiad

condemn vt condemnio, collfarnu

condensation n cywasgiad, cyddwysedd

condense vb cywasgu, cyddwyso, cwtogi

condensed adj cyddwys

condition n cyflwr, ansawdd; amod ♦ vb cyflyru; amodi

conditional adj amodol

conditionally adv ar amod

conditioner n cyflyrydd

condole vi cydofidio, cydymdeimlo

condolence n cydymdeimlad

condom n condom. **condoms** npl (col) sachau dyrnu

condominium n cydlywodraeth, condominiwm

condone vt maddau, esgusodi, cymeradwyo

conduce vi arwain, tueddu

conducive adj tueddol i, â thuedd i

conduct n ymddygiad, ymarweddiad, tywys

conduct vt arwain

conductor n arweinydd; tocynnwr

cone n pigwrn, côn

confection n cyffaith

confectioner n cyffeithiwr

confer vb ymgynghori, cyflwyno

conference n cynhadledd

confess vb cyffesu, cyfaddef

confession n cyffesiad, cyffes

confetti n conffeti

confide *vb* ymddiried

confidence *n* ymddiried, hyder.
self-c. hunanhyder

confident *adj* hyderus

confidential *adj* cyfrinachol

confine *vt* cyfyngu, carcharu,
caethiwo

confined *adj* caeth, cyfyng

confinement *n* caethiwed, adeg
geni

confirm *vt* cadarnhau; conffirmio

confirmation *n* cadarnhad; bedydd
esgob, conffirmasiwn

confirmed *adj* cyson, arferol,
gwastadol, wedi ei gadarnhau

confiscate *vt* atafaelu

conflict *n* gwrthdrawiad, ymryson

conflict *vi* anghytuno, gwrthdaro

conflicting *adj* anghyson

conform *vb* cydymffurfio;
cydffurfio

confound *vt* cymysgu, drysu

confront *vt* wynebu

confrontation *n* gwrthdaro

confuse *vt* cymysgu, drysu

confused *adj* cymysg; didrefn;
dyrys; tywyll

confusion *n* anhrefn

confute *vt* gwrthbrofi, dymchwelyd

congeal *vb* rhewi, fferru, tewychu,
ceulo

congenial *adj* cydnaws, hynaws

congest *vb* cronni, gorlanw

congested *adj* gorlawn

congestion *n* gorlenwad, tagfa,
crynhoad

congratulate *vt* llongyfarch

congratulations *n*
llongyfarchiadau

congregate *vb* ymgynnull

congregation *n* cynulleidfa

congress *n* cyngres, cymanfa

conjunction *n* cysylltiad

conjunctivitis *n* llid yr amrant

conjure *vb* consurio

conjurer *n* consurwr

connect *vb* cysylltu, cydio

connected *adj* cysylltiedig,
cysylltiol

connection *n* cysylltiad,
perthynas. in c. with ynglŷn â

connive *vi* goddef, cau llygaid
rhag

conquer *vt* gorchfygu, trechu

conqueror *n* gorchfygwr,
concwerwr

conquest *n* buddugoliaeth,
concwest

conscience *n* cydwybod

conscientious *adj* cydwybodol

conscious *adj* ymwybodol

consciousness *n* ymwybyddiaeth

conscript *n* gorfodog, gŵr rhif ♦
vb gorfodi

conscription *n* gorfodaeth filwrol

consecrate *vt* cysegru

consecutive *adj* olynol

consent *vi* cydsynio ♦ *n* cydsyniad,
caniatâd

consequence *n* canlyniad

consequently *adv* o ganlyniad

conservation *n* cadwraeth,
gwarchodaeth

conservative *adj* ceidwadol ♦ *n*
ceidwadwr

conservatory *n* tŷ gwydr

conserve *vt* cadw, diogelu,
amddiffyn

consider *vb* ystyried

considerable *adj* cryn

considerate *adj* ystyriol, tosturiol

consideration *n* ystyriaeth

considering *prep* ag ystyried

consign *vt* traddodi, trosglwyddo

consist *vi* cynnwys

consistency *n* cysondeb

consistent *n* cyson

consolation *n* cysur, diddanwch

console *vt* cysuro, diddanu

consonant *adj* cysain; cyson ♦ *n*
cytsain

conspicuous *adj* amlwg

conspiracy *n* bradwriaeth, brad,
cynllwyn

conspire *vb* bradfwriadu, cynllwynio

constable *n* cwnstabl, heddgeidwad

constant *adj* cyson

constantly *adv* yn gyson

constipate *vt* rhwymo

constipated *adj* rhwym

constipation *n* rhwymedd

constituency *n* etholaeth

constituent *adj* cyfansoddol ♦ *n* etholwr; cyfansoddyn

constitution *n* cyfansoddiad

constitutional *adj* cyfansoddiadol

constraint *n* cyfyngydd, cyfyngiad

construct *vt* ffurfio, llunio, adeiladu, saernio

construction *n* adeiladwaith, lluniad; cystrawen

constructive *adj* ymarferol, adeiladol

construe *vt* cyfieithu; dehongli

consul *n* ynad, conswl; consul

consulate *n* consuliaeth

consult *vb* ymgynghori

consultant *n* ymgynghorwr

consume *vb* treulio, difa, ysu; nychu

consumer *n* prynwr, treuliwr, defnyddiwr

consummate *adj* perffaith, cyflawn

consummate *vt* perffeithio, cyflawni

consumption *n* traul; darfodedigaeth

contact *n* cyffyrddiad, cyswllt. c. lenses *npl* gwydrau cyffwrdd

contagious *adj* heintus

contain *vt* cynnwys, dal

container *n* cynhwysydd

contaminate *vt* halogi, llygru, heintio

contemplate *vb* ystyried, myfyrio; bwriadu

contemporary *adj* cyfoes(ol) ♦ *n* cyfoeswr

contempt *n* dirmyg, diystyrwch. c. of court dirmyg llys

contemptuous *adj* dirmygus

contend *vb* ymryson, ystadlu

contender *n* cystadleuydd

content *adj* bodlon ♦ *vt* bodloni

content *n* cynnwys

contented *adj* bodlon

contention *n* cynnen, ymryson

contentment *n* bodlonrwydd

contents *npl* cynnwys, cynhwysiad

contest *n* cystadleuaeth, ymryson

contest *vb* amau, ymryson, ymladd

contestant *n* cystadleuydd

context *n* cyd-destun

continent *adj* cymedrol; diwair

continent *n* cyfandir

continental *adj* cyfandirol

contingency *n* damwain, digwyddiad

continual *adj* parhaus, gwastadol

continuation *n* parhad

continue *vb* parhau, para, dal (i)

continuous *adj* parhaol, di-fwlch, di-dor

contort *vt* gwyrdroi, dirdynnu

contour *n* amlinell, cyfuchlinedd

contra- *prefix* gwrth-, croes-

contraband *adj, n* (nwyddau) gwaharddedig

contraceptive *n* cyfarpar gwrthgenhedlu

contract *n* cytundeb, cyfamod

contract *vb* byrhau; cytuno, cyfamodi

contraction *n* talfyriad, cywasgiad

contractor *n* contractwr, adeiladydd

contradict *vt* gwrth-ddweud

contraption *n* dyfais

contrary *adj* gwrthwyneb, croes. on the c. i'r gwrthwyneb

contrast *n* gwrthgyferbyniad ♦ *vb* gwrthgyferbynnu

contribute *vb* cyfrannu

contribution *n* cyfraniad

contributor *n* cyfrannwr
contrive *vb* dyfeisio, llwyddo, trefnu
control *vt* llywodraethu, rheoli ♦ *n* rheolaeth, awdurdod. **self c.** hunan-reolaeth
controversial *adj* dadleuol
controversy *n* dadl
convalesce *vi* ymadfer, gwella
convene *vi* galw, gwysio, cynnull
convenience *n* cyfleustra, hwylustod
convenient *adj* cyfleus, gweddus, hwylus
convent *n* cwfaint, lleiandy
convention *n* confensiwn, cynhadledd
conventional *adj* confensiynol
conversant *adj* cyfarwydd, cynefin
conversation *n* ymddiddan, sgwrs
converse *vi* ymddiddan, ymgomio
converse *adj n* gwrthwyneb, cyferbyniol
conversion *n* tröedigaeth, tro
convert *vt* troi, newid, trosi. **converted** try trosgais
convertible *adj* trosadwy
convex *adj* crwm
convey *vt* cludo; trosi, trosglwyddo; cyfleu
conveyor belt *n* cludfelt
convict *vt* barnu'n euog, euogfarnu; argyhoeddi
convict *n* troseddwr
conviction *n* euogfarn; argyhoeddiad
convince *vt* argyhoeddi
convincing *adj* argyhoeddiadol
convulse *vt* dirgrynu, dirdynnu
cook *n* cogydd, cogyddes ♦ *vb* coginio, gwneud bwyd
cooker *n* cwcer. **pressure c.** gwascogydd, sosban wyllt
cookery *n* coginiaeth
cooking *n* coginiaeth
cool *adj* oeri, oeraidd; hunanfeddiannol ♦ *vb* oeri,

claearu
coop *n* cawell, cut ieir ♦ *vt* cutio
co-operate *vi* cydweithio, cydweithredu
co-operation *n* cydweithrediad
co-operative *n* cydweithfa ♦ *adj* cydweithredol
co-opt *vt* cyfethol
co-ordinate *n* cyfesuryn ♦ *vb* cyfesur, cyd-drefnu
cop *n* plismon ♦ *vt* dal
cope *n* copa, crib
cope *vi* ymdaro â, ymdopi â
copious *adj* helaeth, dibrin
copper *n* copr, copor
copse *n* prysgwydd, prysglwyn
copy *n* copi ♦ *vt* copïo
copyright *n* hawlfraint
coracle *n* cwrwgl
coral *n* cwrel
cord *n* cortyn, rheffyn, tennyn ♦ *vt* rheffynnu
cordial *adj* o galon, calonnog ♦ *n* cordial, gwirod
cordon *n* rhes, cadwyn
corduroy *n* melfaréd, rib
core *n* calon, perfedd, craidd
cork *n* corc, corcyn ♦ *vt* corcio
corkscrew *n* corcsgriw
cormorant *n* mulfran, bilidowcar
corn *n* ŷd, llafur
corn *n* corn (ar droed)
corned beef *n* corn-biff
corner *n* congl, cornel, cil ♦ *vt* cornelu. **c. kick** cic gornel
cornet *n* corned
cornflakes *npl* creision ŷd
cornflour *n* blawd corn
coronation *n* coroniad
coroner *n* crwner
coronet *n* coronig
corporal *adj* corfforol
corporate *adj* yn un corff, corfforedig
corporation *n* corfforaeth; cest
corporeal *adj* corfforol; materol
corps *n* corfflu

corpse *n* corff (marw), celain

corpuscle *n* corffilyn

correct *adj* cywir ♦ *vt* cywiro, ceryddu

correction *n* cywiriad; cerydd

correspond *vi* cyfateb; gohebu

correspondence *n* cyfatebiaeth; gohebiaeth

correspondent *n* gohebydd

corridor *n* coridor

corrode *vb* cyrydu, ysu, rhydu, treulio

corrugated *adj* rhychiog, gwrymiog

corrupt *adj* llygredig, pwdr ♦ *vb* llygru

corruption *n* llygredigaeth

corset *n* staes

cosmetic *n* cosmetig

cost *vi* costio ♦ *n* cost, traul

costly *adj* drudfawr, drud, prid

costume *n* gwisg, costiwm

cosy *adj* cysurus, clyd

cot *n* gwely bychan, cot

cottage *n* bwthyn

cotton *n* cotwm; edau. **c. wool** gwlân cotwm

couch *n* glwth, soffa ♦ *vb* gorwedd

cough *n* peswch ♦ *vb* pesychu

council *n* cyngor. **c. house** tŷ cyngor

councillor *n* cynghorwr

counsel *n* cyngor ♦ *vt* cynghori

counsellor *n* cynghorwr, cyfarwyddwr

count *n* cyfrif ♦ *vb* rhifo, cyfrif. **c. the cost** bwrw'r draul

count *n* iarll

countenance *n* wynepryd; cefnogaeth ♦ *vt* cefnogi

counter *n* cownter

counter- *prefix* gwrth- ♦ *adj* croes ♦ *adv* yn erbyn, yn groes

counteract *vt* gwrthweithio

counterfeit *n* ffug, twyll ♦ *adj* gau, ffug ♦ *vt* ffugio

counterfoil *n* gwrthddalen

countermand *vt* gwrthorchymyn

counterpane *n* cwrlid, cwilt gwely

counterpart *n* rhan gyfatebol, cymar

countess *n* iarlles

countless *adj* aneirif, di-rif

country *n* gwlad, bro ♦ *adj* gwladaidd, gwledig. **c. music** canu gwlad

countryman *n* gwladwr

countryside *n* cefn gwlad

county *n* sir, swydd

coup *n* ergyd, trawiad, dymchwel, llwyddiannus

couple *n* cwpl ♦ *vt* cyplu, cyplysu

couplet *n* cwpled

coupon *n* cwpon

courage *n* gwroldeb, dewrder

courier *n* cennad; tywyswr

course *n* cwrs, hynt ♦ *vt* hela, ymlid. **of c.** wrth gwrs. **in the c.** **of** yn ystod. **in due c.** yn ei bryd. **crash c.** cwrs carlam

court *n* llys; cwrt; cyntedd ♦ *vt* caru

courteous *adj* cwrtais

courtesy *n* cwrteisrwydd, cwrteisi

courtier *n* gŵr llys, llyswr

courtly *adj* llysaidd, boneddigaidd

court-martial *n* cwrt-marsial ♦ *vt* dodi ar brawf

courtship *n* carwriaeth

courtyard *n* buarth, cwrt, clos, iard

cousin *n* cefnder; cyfnither

cove *n* cil, cilfach

covenant *n* cyfamod ♦ *vb* cyfamodi

cover *vt* gorchuddio, toi; amddiffyn ♦ *n* gorchudd, clawr. **c.** **charge** *n* tâl am wasanaeth. **book** **c.** clawr llyfr. **to take c.** cuddio, cysgodi

covert *adj* cêl, cudd, dirgel

covert *n* lloches; prysglwyn

covet *vt* chwennych, chwenychu

cow *n* buwch. **barren c.** myswynog

milking c. buwch odro. **c. in calf** buwch gyflo

coward n llwfrddyn, llwfryn, llwfrgi

cowardice n llwfrdra

cowardly adj llwfr

cowboy n cowboi

cower vi swatio, cyrcydu

cowl n cwcwll, cwfl

cowpox n brech y fuwch

cowslip n briallu Mair

coxswain n llywydd cwch, cocs

coy adj swil, gwylaidd

crab n cranc

crab (apple) n afal sur, afal crabas

crack vb cracio, hollti ♦ n crac

cracker n cracer; bisgeden

crackle vi clindarddach

cradle n crud, cawell; cadair fagu

craft n crefft; cyfrwystra, dichell; llong, bad

craftsman n crefftwr

craftsmanship n crefftwriaeth

crafty adj cyfrwys, dichellgar

crag n craig, clegr, clogwyn

cram vb gorlenwi, stwffio, saco

cramp n cwlwm gwythi, cramp; creffyn ♦ vt caethiwo, gwasgu

cramped adj clós

cranberries npl llugaeron

crane n garan, crëyr, crychydd, craen ♦ vt estyn (gwddf)

cranium (-ia) n benglog

crank n cranc; mympwywr ♦ vi cam-droi; troi

crankshaft n camwerthyd, crancsiafft

cranny n agen, hollt, agennig

crape n crêp

crash n, vb gwrthdaro, cwympo ♦ n gwrthdrawiad, cwymp. **c. helmet** n helmed ddiogelwch

crate n cawell

crater n safn llosgfynydd; ceudod, cawg

cravat n cadach gwddf, crafat

crave vb crefu, deisyf, chwennych, dyheu

craving n blys, chwant

crawl vi ymlusgo, cropian; crafu

crayon n creon

craze n ysfa

crazy adj penwan, gorffwyll, o'i gof

creak vi gwichian

cream n hufen

creamery n hufenfa

creamy adj hufennog

crease n ôl plygiad, plyg ♦ vt crychu

create vt creu

creation n cread, creadigaeth

creative adj creadigol

creator n crëwr, creawdwr

creature n creadur

crèche n meithrinfa

credence n cred, coel, ffydd

credentials npl credlythyrau

credible adj credadwy, hygoel, hygred

credit n coel, cred; clod, credyd ♦ vt coelio. **c. card** cerdyn credyd

creditor n credydwr

credulous adj hygoelus

creed n credo

creek n cilfach

creep vi ymlusgo, cropian

creeper n dringiedydd

creepy adj iasol

cremate vt amlosgi

crematorium n amlosgfa

crêpe n crêp

crescent n hanner lleuad; cilgant ♦ adj cynyddol

cress n berwr

crest n crib; mwng; arwydd ar arfbais

Crete n Creta

crevice n agen, hollt, rhigol

crew n criw, gwerin llong; haid

crib n preseb; caban; gwely plentyn ♦ vt copïo

cricket n criced; cricsyn

crime n trosedd

criminal adj troseddol ♦ n troseddwr

crimson adj, n rhuddgoch

cringe vi cynffonna, ymgreinio

crinkle vb crychu ♦ n crych, plyg

cripple n cloff, efrydd ♦ vt cloffi, efryddu

crisis (**crises**) n argyfwng

crisp adj cras, crych

crisps npl creision tatws

criterion (-ia) n maen prawf, safon

critic n beirniad

critical adj beirniadol; pryderus; peryglus

criticism n beirniadaeth

criticize vt beirniadu

croak vi crawcian ♦ n crawc

crochet vb crosio ♦ n crosiet, gwaith crosio

crockery n llestri

crocodile n crocodil

crocus n saffrwn, crocus

croft n tyddyn, crofft

crony vi cyfaill agos, cydymaith

crook n crwca, bagl, ffon fugail; troseddwr

crooked adj crwca, cam

crop n cnwd, cynnyrch; crombil ♦ vt tocio, torri

cross n, adj croes ♦ vb croesi

cross-cut vb trawsdorri

cross-examine vt croesholi

crossing n croesfan

cross-road n croesffordd

cross-section n trawsdoriad

crosswise adv ar groes

crossword n croesair

crotchet n crosied

crouch vi cyrcydu ♦ n cwrcwd

crow n brân

crow vi canu fel ceiliog; ymffrostio

crow-bar n trosol, bar haearn

crowd n torf, tyrfa ♦ vb tyrru, heidio

crowded adj llawn o bobl

crown n coron; corun ♦ vt coroni

crucial adj hanfodol, terfynol

crucifix n croeslun

crucifixion n croeshoeliad

crucify vt croeshoelio

crude adj cri, crai; llymrig, amrwd

cruel adj creulon

cruelty n creulondeb

cruet n criwed

cruise vi morio ♦ n mordaith

cruiser n gwiblong

crumb n briwsionyn

crumble vb briwsioni, malurio ♦ n briwsiongrwst

crumbly adj briwsionllyd

crumpet n crymped; lefren

crumple vb crychu, gwasgu

crunch vb creinsio

crupper n pedrain, crwper, pen ôl

crusade n rhyfel y groes, croesgad

crush vb gwasgu, llethu ♦ n gwasgiad, torf

crust n crawen, crofen, crystyn

crutch n bagl, ffon fagl

crux n craidd

cry vb llefain, wylo, crio ♦ n llef, sgrech, cri

cryptic adj dirgel, cyfrin

crystal n grisial ♦ adj grisialaidd

crystallisation n crisialiad

cub n cenau

cube n ciwb ♦ vb ciwbio

cubic adj ciwbig. **c. root** gwreiddyn ciwb

cubicle n cuddygl

cuckoo n cog, cwcw; gwirionyn

cucumber n cucumer

cud n cil

cuddle vb anwylo, anwesu, tolach

cue n awgrym; ciw

cuff n torch llawes

cuff vt cernodio ♦ n cernod, dyrnod

cul-de-sac n pen ffordd, heol hosan

cull vt dewis, pigo

culminate vi cyrraedd ei anterth, diweddu

culmination n anterth

culpable adj beius, camweddus
culprit n troseddwr,
    drwgweithredwr
cult n addoliad, cwlt
cultivate vt diwyllio, trin, meithrin
cultural adj diwylliannol
culture n diwylliant; gwrtaith
cultured adj diwylliedig, coeth
cumbersome adj afrosgo, beichus
cunning adj dichellgar, cyfrwys ♦
    n cyfrwystra
cup n cwpan
cupboard n cwpwrdd
cup-tie n gornest gwpan
curate n curad
curator n curadur
curb n genfa, atalfa; cwrbyn ♦ vt
    ffrwyno
curd n caul, ceuled; caws
curdle vb ceulo, cawsio, cawsu
cure n iachâd, gwellhad;
    meddyginiaeth ♦ vb iachâu,
    gwella; halltu
curfew n hwyrgloch
curiosity n cywreinrwydd,
    chwilfrydedd
curious adj cywrain; chwilfrydig;
    hynod
curl n cwrl, cudyn ♦ vb cyrlio
curlew n gylfinir
curly adj cyrliog, crych
currants npl grawn Corinth,
    cwrens. **currant bread** bara brith
currency n arian breiniol
current adj rhedegol, cyfredol,
    cyfoes ♦ n ffrwd, llif. **c. account**
    cyfrif cyfredol. **c. affairs** materion
    cyfoes
currently adv ar hyn o bryd
curriculum n cwricwlwm. National
    C. Cwricwlwm Cenedlaethol
curry vt trin lledr ♦ n cyrri. **to c.
    favour** cynffonna, ceisio ffafr
curse n melltith, rheg ♦ vb
    melltithio, rhegi
cursory adj brysiog, diofal
curt adj cwta, byr, cryno

curtail vt cwtogi, talfyrru; prinhau
curtain n llen
curtsy n cyrtsi
curve n camu, gwyro, troi ♦ n
    tro; cromlin
cushion n clustog
custard n cwstard
custodian n ceidwad
custody n dalfa, cadwraeth
custom n defod; cwsmeriaeth; toll
customary adj arferol
customer n cwsmer
customs npl y tollau. **c. officer** n
    swyddog tollau
cut vb torri ♦ n toriad, archoll,
    briw. **c. back** torri yn ôl. **c. in**
    torri ar draws. **c. out** torri allan.
    c. through torri trwodd
cute adj ciwt, cyfrwys
cuticle n croen, pilen, cwticl
cutlery n cwtleri
cutlet n golwyth, cydled
cycle n cylch; cyfres; beic ♦ vb
    seiclo
cycling n beicio
cyclist n beiciwr
cyclone n trowynt
cygnet n cyw alarch, alarchen
cylinder n rhol; silindr
cymbal n symbal
cynic n gwawdiwr, sinig
cynical adj gwawdlyd, dirmygus
cynicism n coegni, gwawd
cyst n coden
cystitis n llid y bledren
Czechoslovakia n Tsiecoslofacia

D

dab vt dabio ♦ n dab
dabble vb dablo
dad, dada, daddy n tad, tada,
    tyta, dada
daffodil n cenhinen Bedr
daft adj hurt, gwirion
dagger n dagr, bidog

daily adj dyddiol, beunyddiol ♦ adv beunydd, bob dydd

dainty n danteithfwyd, amheuthun ♦ adj danteithiol, dillyn, del

dairy n llaethdy. **d. products** cynhyrchion llaeth

dais n esgynlawr, llwyfan

daisy n llygad y dydd

dale n dyffryn, glyn, dôl, cwm, bro

dam n argae, cronfa ♦ vt argáu, cronni

dam n mamog, mam (anifail)

damage n niwed, difrod ♦ vt niweidio, difrodi. **damages** npl iawn

damn vb damnio, rhegi, melltithio

damnation n damnedigaeth

damned adj colledig

damp adj llaith ♦ n lleithder ♦ vb lleitho

damson n eirinen ddu

dance vb dawnsio ♦ n dawns. **folk d.** dawns werin. **public folk d.** twmpath dawns

dancer n dawnsiwr

dandelion n dant y llew

dandruff n marwdon, cen

Dane n brodor o Ddenmarc, Daniad

danger n perygl, enbydrwydd

dangerous adj peryglus, enbyd

dangle vb hongian; siglo

dapper adj del, twt, sionc, heini

dare vb beiddio, mentro

dare-devil n un byrbwyll, un mentrus

daring adj beiddgar, mentrus ♦ n beiddgarwch

dark adj tywyll ♦ n tywyllwch, nos

darken vb tywyllu

darkness n tywyllwch

darling n anwylyd, cariad ♦ adj annwyl

darn vt cyweirio, trwsio ♦ n cyweiriad, trwsiad

dart n dart, picell, saeth ♦ vb dartio, rhuthro

dash vb rhuthro, chwalu, chwilfriwio ♦ n rhuthr; llinell (—)

dashboard n dashfwrdd

data npl data

date n dyddiad, amseriad; datysen (ffrwyth) ♦ vb dyddio. **out of d.** henffasiwn, wedi dyddio. **up to d.** hyd yn hyn, cyfoes

dated adj dyddiedig

daub vt dwbio, iro

daughter n merch. **daughter-in-law** merch yng nghyfraith

dawdle vi ymdroi, swmera

dawn vi gwawrio, dyddio ♦ n gwawr

day n diwrnod, dydd. **by d.** liw dydd. **today** heddiw. **next d.** trannoeth. **the d. before yesterday** echdoe

day-break n gwawr, toriad dydd

day-dream vb pensynnu, synfyfyrio

daylight n golau dydd

day-time n y dydd

daze vt synnu, syfrdanu; dallu

dazzle vb disgleirio, pelydru; dallu

dazzling adj disglair, llachar

deacon n diacon, blaenor

dead adj marw; difywyd ♦ adv hollol. **the d. y meirw. d. centre** yn ei ganol. **d. tired** wedi blino 'n lân. **d. heat** cwbl gyfartal

deaden vb lleddfu, marweiddio

deadlock n methu symud mlaen na nôl

deadly adj marwol, angheuol

Dead Sea n the D. Sea y Môr Marw

deaf adj byddar

deafen vb byddaru

deafness n byddardod

deal vb delio, trin ♦ n trafodaeth, dêl. **a great d.** llawer iawn. **to d. with** ymwneud â

dealer n masnachwr

dean n deon

dear adj annwyl, cu, hoff; drud ♦ n

annwylyd, cariad. **d. me** o'r
annwyl!

death *n* angau, marwolaeth, tranc.
Black D. y Pla Du

deathly *adj, adv* fel angau,
angheuol, marwol

death rate *n* cyfradd marw

debar *vt* atal, lluddias, cau allan

debase *vt* iselu, darostwng, llygru

debate *vb* dadlau, ymryson ♦ *n*
dadl

debit *n* debyd

debt *n* dyled

debtor *n* dyledwr

decade *n* degawd

decadence *n* dirywiad, adfeiliad

decapitate *vt* torri pen

decay *vi* dadfeilio, pydru ♦ *n*
dadfeiliad

decease *n* tranc, marwolaeth ♦ *vi*
marw, trengi

deceased *n* ymadawedig,
trancedig

deceit *n* twyll, dichell, hoced

deceive *vt* twyllo, hocedu, siomi

December *n* Rhagfyr

decent *adj* gweddus, gweddaidd

deception *n* twyll, ffug, dichell

deceptive *adj* twyllodrus,
dichellgar

decide *vb* penderfynu

decided *adj* pendant, penderfynol

decidedly *adv* yn siŵr, yn ddiau

deciduous *adj* collddail

decimal *adj* degol ♦ *n* degolyn. d.
system system ddegol. **d. point**
pwynt degol. **recurring** d. degolyn
cylchol

decipher *vt* datrys, dehongli

decision *n* penderfyniad

decisive *adj* penderfynol, pendant

deck *n* bwrdd llong, dec. **d. chair** *n*
cadair haul

deck *vt* trwsio, addurno

declaration *n* datganiad; cau
batiad

declare *vb* mynegi, datgan,
cyhoeddi

decline *vb* dadfeilio; gwrthod ♦ *n*
dadfeiliad; darfodedigaeth

decompose *vb* pydru, braenu;
dadelfennu

decorate *vt* addurno, arwisgo

decoration *n* addurn, tlws

decorator *n* addurnwr, peintiwr tai

decoy *n* hud, magl ♦ *vt* hudo,
llithio

decrease *vb* lleihau, gostwng ♦ *n*
lleihad

decree *n* gorchymyn, dyfarniad ♦
vb gorchymyn, dyfarnu

dedicate *vt* cysegru, cyflwyno

dedication *n* cysegriad, cyflwyniad

deduce *vt* tynnu, casglu,
diddwytho

deduct *vt* tynnu ymaith, didynnu

deduction *n* diddwythiad, didyniad

deed *n* gweithred

deem *vt* meddwl, ystyried, barnu

deep *adj* dwfn; dwys ♦ *n* dwfn,
dyfnder. **d. freeze** *n* rhewgell. **d.
litter** gwasarn

deepen *vb* dyfnhau, trymhau,
dwysáu

deeply *adv* yn ddwys

deer (deer) *n* carw, hydd

deface *vt* difwyno, anurddo, hagru

default *n* diffyg, gwall, pall, meth
♦ *vb* methu, torri

defeat *vt* gorchfygu, trechu ♦ *n*
gorchfygiad

defect *n* diffyg, nam

defective *adj* diffygiol

defence *n* amddiffyn, amddiffyniad

defenceless *adj* diamddiffyn

defend *vt* amddiffyn

defendant *n* diffynnydd

defender *n* amddiffynnwr

defer *vb* oedi, gohirio

defiance *n* her, herfeiddiad

defiant *adj* herfeiddiol

deficient *adj* diffygiol, prin, yn
eisiau

deficit *n* diffyg

defile vi symud yn rhes ♦ n culffordd, bwlch, ceunant
defile vt halogi, difwyno
define vt diffinio
definite adj penodol, pendant
definitely adv yn bendant, heb os
definition n diffiniad
deflate vb dadchwythu
deflect vb gwyro, osgoi
deform vt anffurfio, hagru, afluniedidio
deformed adj afluniaidd, anffurf
deformity n anffurfiad
defraud vt twyllo, hocedu; ysbeilio
defray vt talu (treuliau)
defrost vt dadrewi (fridge)
defroster n dadrewydd
deft adj medrus, hylaw, deheuig
defunct adj marw, trancedig
defy vt beiddio, herfeiddio, herio
degenerate vi dirywio ♦ adj dirywiedig
degrade vt diraddio, difreinio
degree n gradd
dehydrate vt dihydradu
dehydration n dihydrad
de-ice vb toddi
deign vb ymostwng, teilyngu
deity n duwdod; duw
deject vt digalonni
dejected adj digalon
delay vb oedi, gohirio ♦ n oediad
delectable adj hyfryd, hyfrydlon
delegate vt dirprwyo ♦ n dirprwy, cynrychiolydd
delete vt dileu
deliberate vb ystyried yn bwyllog ♦ adj pwyllog, bwriadol
deliberately adv yn fwriadol
delicacy n amheuthun, danteithfwyd. **delicacies** danteithion
delicate adj tyner; cain; gwanllyd
delicious adj danteithiol, blasus
delight n difyrru; ymhyfrydu ♦ n hyfrydwch
delightful adj hyfryd, braf

delinquency n bai, trosedd
delinquent n troseddwr, tramgwyddwr ♦ adj troseddol, tramgwyddus
delirious adj wedi drysu, yn drysu, gwallgof
deliver vt traddodi; gwaredu, danfon; cludo
deliverance n gwaredigaeth
delivery n traddodiad; danfoniad
dell n glyn, pant, ceunant, cwm
delude vt twyllo, hudo
deluge n dilyw, dylif ♦ vt gorlifo
delusion n twyll, cyfeiliornad; lledrith
delve vb cloddio, palu, ymchwilio
demand vt gofyn, hawlio, mynnu ♦ n gofyn, hawl
demean vt ymddwyn
demeanour n ymddygiad
demented adj gwallgof, gorffwyll
demesne n treftadaeth, tiriogaeth; bro
demi- prefix hanner
demise n marwolaeth
democracy n gweriniaeth, democrat, democratiaeth
democrat n gwerinydd, gweriniaethwr
democratic adj gwerinol, democratig
demolish vt dymchwelyd, distrywio
demonstrate vb arddangos, profi; gwrthdystio
demonstration n arddangosiad, gwrthdystiad
demonstrator n arddangoswr, gwrthdystiwr
demote vb darostwng
demur vi codi gwrthwynebiad, petruso
demure adj swil, gwylaidd
den n ffau, gwâl, lloches
denial n gwadiad; nacâd, gwrthodiad. **self-d.** hunanymwadiad

Denmark n Denmarc
denomination n enw, enwad
denote vt arwyddo, dynodi, hynodi
denounce vt lladd ar, cyhuddo, condemnio
dense adj tew, dwys; pendew, hurt
density n dwysedd, trwch
dent n tolc ♦ vt tolcio
dental adj deintiol
dentist n deintydd
dentistry n deintyddiaeth
dentures npl dannedd gosod/dodi
deny vt gwadu, gomedd, gwrthod
deodorant n diaroglydd
depart vi ymadael; cychwyn
department n adran, dosbarth. d.
store n siop adrannol
departure n ymadawiad; cychwyniad
depend vi dibynnu
dependable adj dibynadwy
dependant n dibynnydd
dependent adj dibynnol
depict vt darlunio
deplete vt gwacáu, gwagu, hysbyddu
depopulate vt diboblogi
deport vt alltudio
deportation n alltudiaeth
deportment n ymddygiad, ymarweddiad
deposit vt dodi i lawr; adneuo; gwaddodi ♦ n adnau, blaendal; gwaddod. **d. account** n cyfrif cadw
depot n storfa; gorsaf
depreciate vb dibrisio
depredation n anrheithiad
depress vt gostwng, iselu; digalonni
depressed adj digalon, iselfryd
depression n iselder (ysbryd); dibwysiant (tywydd); pant; dirwasgiad (diwydiant)
deprivation n enbydrwydd, amddifadedd, colled
deprive vt amddifadu
deprived adj amddifadus

depth n dyfnder
deputation n dirprwyaeth
deputise vt dirprwyo
deputy n dirprwy
derail vb taflu oddi ar gledrau
derelict adj wedi ei adael, diberchen, diffaith
deride vt gwatwar, gwawdio
derision n gwatwar, gwawd, dirmyg
derive vb derbyn, cael; tarddu, deillio
derogatory adj amharchus, difriol, dilornus, gwawdus
descant n desgant, cyfalaw
descend vi disgyn
descent n disgyniad, disgynfa; hil, ach
describe vt disgrifio, darlunio
description n disgrifiad, darluniad
desecrate vt digysegru, halogi
desert n haeddiant
desert adj diffaith, anial ♦ n diffeithwch
desert vb gadael, cefnu ar; encilio
deserter n enciliwr, ffoadur
deserve vb haeddu, teilyngu
deserving adj haeddiannol, teilwng
design n arfaeth; cynllun ♦ vb arfaethu; cynllunio
designer n cynllunydd, dylunydd
desirable adj dymunol, dewisol
desire vb dymuno ♦ n dymuniad, chwant
desk n desg
desolate adj anghyfannedd, diffaith ♦ vt anghyfanheddu
despair n anobaith ♦ vi anobeithio
desperate adj diobaith, anobeithiol; gorffwyll
desperation n anobaith, enbydrwydd, gorffwylltra
despicable adj dirmygedig, ffiaidd
despise vt dirmygu, diystyru
despite prep er, er gwaethaf
despoil vt anrheithio, ysbeilio
despondent adj digalon, isel-

ysbryd

despot n unben, gormeswr

dessert n pwdin, melysfwyd

destination n cyrchfan, pen y daith

destiny n tynged, tynghedfen

destitute adj anghenus, amddifad

destroy vt distrywio, difetha, dinistrio

destroyer n dinistrydd; distrywlong

destruction n distryw, dinistr

detach vt datod, gwahanu, dadgysylltu

detached adj ar wahân

detachment n adran; didoliad; mintai (o filwyr)

detail n manylyn, (pl) manylion ♦ vb manylu, neilltuo. **in d.** yn fanwl

detain vt cadw, atal, caethiwo

detect vt canfod, darganfod, datgelu

detection n darganfyddiad, datgeliad

detective n carchariad, ataliad

detention n carchariad, ataliad

deter vt cadw rhag, atal, rhwystro

detergent n golchydd

deteriorate vb dirywio, gwaethygu

determination n penderfyniad

determine vb penderfynu, pennu

determined adj penderfynol

deterrent n atalrym, ataliad

detest vt ffieiddio, casáu, atgasu

detour n cylch

detract vt tynnu oddi wrth, bychanu

detriment n colled, niwed, anfantais

detrimental adj niweidiol, colledus, o anfantais

devaluation n gwerthostyngiad, datbrisiad

devastate vt diffeithio, difrodi

devastating adj difrodus

develop vb datblygu

developing adj datblygol, ar ei brifiant

development n datblygiad

device n dyfais

devil n diafol, diawl, cythraul

devilish adj dieflig

devious adj diarffordd, troellog; cyfeiliornus

devise vt dyfeisio

devoid adj amddifad

devolution n datganoli

devote vt cysegru, cyflwyno, ymroddi

devoted adj ffyddlon, ymroddgar

devotion n defosiwn, ymroddiad

devour vt ysu, difa, traflyncu

devout adj duwiol, crefyddol, defosiynol

dew n gwlith ♦ vb gwlitho

diabetes n clefyd melys/siwgr

diabetic adj, n diabetig

diabolical adj dieflig

diagnosis n diagnosis

diagonal n croeslin ♦ adj croeslinol

diagram n darlun eglurhaol, diagram

dial n deial ♦ vb deialu

dialect n tafodiaith

dialogue n ymddiddan, deialog, sgwrs

diameter n tryfesur, diamedr

diamond n diemwnt

diaphragm n llengig; diaffram

diarrhoea n rhyddni, dolur rhydd

diary n dyddiadur, dyddlyfr

dice n dis

dictate vb arddywedyd, gorchymyn

dictate n arch, galwad, gorchymyn

dictation n arddywediad

dictatorship n unbennaeth

dictionary n geiriadur

diddle vt twyllo, hocedu

die vi marw, trengi, trigo, darfod

diehard n un di-ildio

diesel n disel

diet n ymborth, lluniaeth, deiet

dietetics n deieteg
differ vi gwahaniaethu
difference n gwahaniaeth
different adj gwahanol
differentiate vb gwahaniaethu
difficult adj anodd, caled
difficulty n anhawster
diffident adj petrusgar, anhyderus
dig vb palu, cloddio, ceibio
digest vb treulio, toddi; cymathu
digest n crynhoad
digestion n treuliad, traul
digit n digid, bys
digital adj digidol
dignified adj urddasol
dignify vt anrhydeddu, urddasu
dignity n urddas, teilyngdod
digress vi gwyro, crwydro
dike, dyke n clawdd, ffos; argae
dilapidate vb adfeilio, malurio
dilapidated adj adfeiliedig
dilemma n dilema
diligence n diwydrwydd, dyfalwch
diligent adj diwyd, dyfal
dilute vt cymysgu â dwfr, teneuo,
gwanhau
dim adj pŵl, aneglur ♦ vb tywyllu,
cymylu
dimension n mesur, maintioli,
dimensiwn
diminish vb lleihau, prinhau
diminutive adj bychan; bachigol;
n bachigyn
dimmer n pylydd
dimple n pannwl, pant ♦ vb panylu
din n twrf, dadwrdd, mwstwr
dine vi ciniawa
diner n ciniawr
dinghy n dingi
dingle n cwm, glyn, pant
dingy adj tywyll, dilewyrch;
tlodaidd
dining room n ystafell fwyta
dinner n cinio. **d. jacket** n cot
ginio, cot giniawa
dint n tolc; grym ♦ vt tolcio
diocesan adj esgobaethol ♦ n esgob

diocese n esgobaeth
dioxide n deuocsid
dip vb trochi, gwlychu; gostwng ♦
n trochfa
diphthong n deusain, dipton
diploma n tystysgrif, diploma
diplomacy n diplomyddiaeth
diplomat n diplomydd
diplomatic adj diplomyddol
dire adj dygn, arswydus, echryslon
direct adj union, uniongyrchol ♦ vt
cyfarwyddo, cyfeirio
direction n cyfarwyddyd; cyfeiriad
directly adv yn union, yn ddi-oed
director n cyfarwyddwr
directory n cyfarwyddiadur
dirge n galarnad, marwnad
dirt n baw, llaid, llaca
dirty adj budr, brwnt ♦ vt budro,
diwyno, maeddu
disability n anabledd
disable vt analluogi
disabled adj anabl
disadvantage n anfantais
disagree vi anghytuno
disagreeable adj annymunol, cas
disappear vi diflannu
disappearance n diflaniad
disappoint vt siomi
disappointed adj siomedig
disappointment n siomedigaeth
disapprove vb anghymeradwyo
disarm vb diarfogi
disarmament n diarfogiad
disarray n anhrefn ♦ vb anrhefnu
disaster n trychineb, aflwydd
disband vb dadfyddino; gwasgaru
disbelief n anghrediniaeth, angoel
disc n disg(en)
discard vt rhoi heibio, gwrthod
discern vt canfod, dirnad
discerning adj deallus, craff
discharge vb dadlwytho, rhyddhau
♦ n gollyngdod, rhyddhad,
gollwng
discipline n disgyblaeth ♦ vt
disgyblu

disclaim *vt* diarddel, gwadu

disclose *vt* dadlennu, datguddio

disclosure *n* datguddiad, dadleniad

disco *n* disgo

discomfit *vt* gorchfygu, dymchwelyd

discomfort *vt* anghysuro ♦ *n* anghysur

discompose *vt* aflonyddu, cyffroi

disconcert *vt* aflonyddu, cyffroi, tarfu

disconnect *vb* datgysylltu

disconsolate *adj* digysur, anniddan, galarus

discontent *n* anfodlonrwydd

discontented *adj* anfodlon

discontinue *vt* torri, atal

discord *n* anghytgord

discount *n* disgownt

discourage *vt* digalonni

discourteous *adj* anghwrtais

discover *vt* darganfod, canfod

discovery *n* darganfyddiad

discredit *n* anfri, anghlod, amarch ♦ *vt* anghoelio; amau, difrio

discreet *adj* call, synhwyrol, pwyllog

discrepancy *n* anghysondeb

discretion *n* barn, pwyll, synnwyr

discriminate *vb* gwahaniaethu

discrimination *n* gwahaniaethu, rhagfarn, anffafriaeth

discursive *adj* crwydrol, anghysylltiol

discuss *vt* trin, trafod

discussion *n* trafodaeth, sgwrs

disdain *vb* diystyru, dirmygu, diystyrwch ♦ *n* dirmyg

disease *n* afiechyd, clefyd, clwyf

disembark *vb* glanio

disengage *vb* datgyweddu, rhyddhau

disentangle *vt* datod, datrys

disestablish *vt* datgysylltu

disfigure *vt* anffurfio, anharddu, hagru

disgrace *vt* gwaradwyddo ♦ *n* gwaradwydd, gwarth

disgraceful *adj* gwaradwyddus, gwarthus

disguise *n* dieithrio, ffugio, lledrithio ♦ *n* rhith, dieithrwch

disgust *n* diflastod, ffieidd-dod ♦ *vt* diflasu, ffieiddio

disgusting *adj* ffiaidd, brwnt, gwrthun

dish *n* dysgl; dysglaid

dishcloth *n* cadach llestri

dishearten *vt* digalonni

dishevelled *adj* anhrefnus, aflêr, anniben

dishonest *adj* anonest

dishonour *n* amarch, gwarth ♦ *vb* amharchu

dishwasher *n* peiriant golchi llestri

disillusion *vb* dadrithio

disincentive *n* gwrthgymhelliant

disinfect *vb* diheintio

disinfectant *n* diheintydd

disintegrate *vb* datod, chwalu

disinterested *adj* heb ddiddordeb, diduedd

disjointed *adj* datgymalog

disk *n* disg(en)

dislike *vt* casáu ♦ *n* casineb

dislocate *vt* rhoi o'i le, datgymalu

dislodge *vt* symud, syflyd, gwared

dismal *adj* tywyll, dilewyrch, digalon

dismay *n* brawychu, siomi, digalonni ♦ *n* braw, siom, chwithdod

dismiss *vt* gollwng; diswyddo

dismount *vb* disgyn, dymchwelyd

disobedience *n* anufudd-dod

disobedient *adj* anufudd

disobey *vb* anufuddhau

disorder *n* anhrefn; anhwyldeb ♦ *vt* anhrefnu

disorderly *adj* afreolus, anniben

disown *vt* gwadu, diarddel

disparage *vt* amharchu, bychanu, difrio

disparaging adj amharchus, gwaradwyddus

disparity n anghyfartaledd, rhagor

dispatch vb anfon; diweddu ♦ n neges

dispel vt chwalu, gwasgaru

dispensary n fferyllfa

dispense vb rhannu; gweinyddu; hepgor

disperse vb gwasgaru, chwalu, taenu

dispirit vt digalonni, llwfrhau

dispirited adj digalon, gwangalon

display vt arddangos ♦ n arddangosiad

displease vt anfodloni, anfoddio, digio

displeasure n anfodlonrwydd, dicter

disposable nappies npl clytiau untro

dispose vt hepgor, gwaredu

disposition n anianawd

disprove vt gwrthbrofi

dispute vb dadlau, ymryson ♦ n dadl

disqualify vb difreinio, atal

disquiet vb anesmwytho

disregard vt diystyru, esgeuluso ♦ n diystyrwch, esgeulustra

disreputable adj gwarthus, amharchus

disrespect n amarch

disrupt vt rhwygo, amharu

dissatisfaction n anfodlonrwydd

dissatisfy vt anfodloni

dissect vb difynio, trychu; dadansoddi

disseminate vt hau, taenu, lledaenu

dissent vi anghytuno ♦ n anghytundeb; ymneilltuaeth

dissertation n traethawd

dissimilar adj annhebyg, gwahanol

dissipate vt chwalu, gwasgaru, afradloni

dissociate vt anghysylltu,

gwahanu, diaelodi

dissolute adj afradlon, ofer

dissolution n ymddatodiad, datodiad, diddymiad

dissolve vb toddi, datod; datgorffori, diddymu

distance n pellter

distant adj pell, pellennig, oeraidd

distaste n difiastod, cas

distend vt estyn, lledu, chwyddo

distil vb distyllu, dihidlo

distillery n distyllty

distinct adj gwahanol; eglur

distinction n arbenigrwydd, rhagoriaeth, gwahaniaeth

distinctive adj gwahanrodol, arbennig

distinguish vb gwahaniaethu; hynodi

distinguished adj enwog, amlwg

distort vt ystumio, anffurfio, gwyrdroi

distract vb tynnu ymaith, drysu, mwydro

distraction n dryswch, diffyg sylw

distress n cyfyngder, ing, trallod

distressing adj trallodus, blin, poenus

distribute vt rhannu, dosbarthu

distribution n dosbarthiad, rhaniad

distributor n dosbarthydd, dosbarthwr

district n dosbarth, ardal, rhandir. **d. council** cyngor dosbarth

distrust n drwgdybiaeth ♦ vb drwgdybio

disturb vt aflonyddu, cyffroi

disturbance n aflonyddwch, cyffro, terfysg

disturbed adj blinderus, cynhyrfus

ditch n ffos

ditto adv eto, yr un, yr un peth

dive vi ymsuddo, deifio

diverse adj gwahanol; annhebyg

diversion n difyrrwch, adloniant; dargyfeiriad

divert vt dargyfeirio, difyrru

divide vb rhannu, dosbarthu, gwahanu ♦ n gwahanfa

divided adj rhanedig

dividend n buddran; difidend

divine adj dwyfol ♦ n diwinydd ♦ vb dewinio, dyfalu

divinity n duwdod; diwinyddiaeth

division n rhan, rhaniad; cyfraniaeth. **long d.** n rhannu hir

divorce vt ysgar(u) ♦ n ysgariad

divorced adj wedi ysgaru

divulge vt datguddio, dadlennu

dizzy adj penysgafn, pensyfrdan

DJ n troellwr

do vb gwneud, gwneuthur

docile adj dof, hywedd, hydrin

dock n (dail) tafol

dock vt tocio, cwtogi

dock n doc, porthladd ♦ vt docio; cwtogi

dockyard n iard longau

doctor n doctor, meddyg; doethor, doethur

doctrine n athrawiaeth

document n ysgrif, gweithred, dogfen

documentary adj dogfennol

dodge vb osgoi, twyllo ♦ n cast, ystryw

doe n ewig

dog n ci ♦ vb dal i ddilyn

dogged adj cyndyn, ystyfnig

dogmatic adj athrawiaethol; awdurdodol, pendant

dole n dôl, dogn. **on the d.** yn ddiwaith, ar y clwt ♦ vt dogni, rhannu

doleful adj trist, prudd, galarus

doll n dol, doli

dollar n doler

dolphin n dolffin

domain n tiriogaeth, maes

dome n cromen, cryndo

domestic adj teuluaidd, cartrefol; gwâr, dof

dominant adj trech

dominate vb dominyddu

dominion n rheolaeth; dominiwn, tiriogaeth

don vt gwisgo (dilledyn) ♦ n athro (coleg)

donate vt rhoddi

donation n rhodd

donkey n asyn, mul

donor n rhoddwr

doodle vb dwdlan

doom n dedfryd, barn, tynged ♦ vt dedfrydu, tynghedu, collfarnu

doomsday n dydd barn

door n drws, dôr, porth

doorkeeper n porthor

doorstep n rhiniog, trothwy

doorway n porth, drws

dope n cyffur ♦ vb rhoi cyffur

dormant adj ynghwsg; di-rym

dormitory n ystafell gysgu, hundy

dose n dogn ♦ vt dogni

dot n dot ♦ vt dotio

dote vi dotio, gwirioni, ffoli, dylu

double adj, n dwbl ♦ vb dyblu, plygu. **d. glazing** gwydro dwbl, ffenestri dwbl. **d. flat** meddalnod dwbl

double-bass n bas dwbl

double-dealing n twyll

doubt vb amau, petruso ♦ n amheuaeth, (pl) amheuon

doubtful adj amheus, petrus

doubtless adv yn ddiamau, diau

dough n toes

doughnut n toesen

douse vb trochi; diffodd

dove n colomen

dowdy adj aflêr, anniben

down n manblu

down n gwaun, rhos, mynydd-dir

down adv i lawr, i waered. **d. and out** digalon, truenus

downcast adj digalon, prudd

downfall n cwymp, codwm, dinistr

downpour n tywalltiad, pistylliad ♦ vb tywallt, pistyllio

downright adj diamheuol

downstairs n y llawr ♦ adv ar y llawr

downwards adv i lawr, i waered

dowry n gwaddol

doze vi hepian ♦ n cyntun

dozen n deuddeg, dwsin

drab adj llwydaidd, salw

draft n drafft, braslun ♦ vb drafftio braslunio

drag vb llusgo ♦ n car llusg

dragon n draig

dragon-fly n gwas y neidr

drain n traen, carthffos

drain vb draenio, diferu, yfed. **draining board** bwrdd diferu

drainage n draeniad. **d. basin** dalgylch afon

drake n ceiliog hwyad, meilart

drama n drama

dramatic adj dramatig

dramatise vb dramadeiddio, dramodi

dramatist n dramodydd

drape vt gwisgo, gorchuddio

draper n dilledydd

drastic adj cryf, llym, trwyadl

draught n dracht, llymaid, drafft(en); tynfa (llong)

draughts npl drafftiau

draughtsman n drafftsmon, lluniedydd

draw n atyniad, tynfa ♦ vb tynnu, llusgo; lluniadu, darlunio. **d. to scale** graddluniadu. **drawn game** gêm gyfartal

drawback n anfantais

drawer n drâr, drôr

drawing n lluniad, llun

drawing room n ystafell groeso

drawl vb llusgo (geiriau)

dread n ofni, arswydo ♦ n ofn, arswyd

dreadful adj ofnadwy

dream vb breuddwydio ♦ n breuddwyd

dreamy adj breuddwydiol

dreary adj llwm, diflas, digysur

dredge vb glanhau

dregs npl gwaddod, gwaelodion, gwehilion

drench vt gwlychu; drensio

dress vb gwisgo, dilladu ♦ n gwisg

dresser n dreser, gwisgwr

dressing n dresin. **salad d.** dresin salad. **d. gown** gwn gwisgo

dressmaker n gwniadwraig

dressmaking n gwniadwaith ♦ vb gwneud dillad

dribble n dribl(ad), drefl ♦ vb driblo, dreflu, glafoerio

drier n peiriant sychu

drift n drifft, lluwch; tuedd ♦ vb drifftio, lluwchio

drill vb drilio ♦ n dril

drink vb yfed ♦ n diod, llymaid

drinker n yfwr, diotwr

drinking water n dŵr yfed

drip vb diferu, defnynnu ♦ n diferiad

dripping adj diferol ♦ n toddion, saim

drive n dreif, gyriant, cymhelliad ♦ vb dreifio, gyrru

drivel vi glafoerio, driflan, dreflu ♦ n glafoerion

driver n gyrrwr

driving adj trwm, â grym y tu ôl iddo, grymus ♦ n gyrru

driving licence n trwydded yrru

drizzle vb briwlan ♦ n glaw mân

droll adj digrif, ysmala

drone n gwenynen ormes; diogyn

droop vi llaesu, ymollwng; nychu

drop n diferyn, dafn, cwympiad ♦ vb diferu, cwympo, gollwng. **d. goal** gôl adlam

drought n tywydd sych, sychder, sychdwr

drover n porthmon, gyrrwr

drown vb boddi

drowsy adj cysglyd, marwaidd, swrth

drudgery n caledwaith, slafdod

drug n cyffur

druid *n* derwydd
drum *n* tabwrdd, drwm ♦ *vb* tabyrddu
drunk *adj* meddw, brwysg
drunkard *n* meddwyn
dry *adj* sych, hysb, cras ♦ *vb* sychu. **d. cleaners** *n* sych lanhawyr
dryness *n* sychder, craster
dry rot *n* sych-bydredd, tyllau pryfed
dual *adj* deuol. **d. carriageway** ffordd ddeuol
dub *vt* urddo, galw, llysenwi; dwbio, lleisio (ffilm)
dubious *adj* amheus, petrus
Dublin *n* Dulyn
duchess *n* duges
duchy *n* dugiaeth
duck *n* hwyad, hwyaden
duck *vb* trochi; gostwng pen, gwyro
duckling *n* cyw hwyaden
dud *n* ffugbeth
due *adj* dyledus, dyladwy ♦ *n* dyled, haeddiant
duel *n* gornest
duet *n* deuawd
duke *n* dug
dull *adj* dwl, hurt; marwaidd; diflas; cymylog; pŵl ♦ *vb* pylu, lleddfu
dumb *adj* mud
dumbfound *vt* syfrdanu, drysu
dummy *n* dymi; delw; ffug-bas (rygbi) ♦ *vb* ffug-basio
dump *n* dymp, storfa ♦ *vb* dympio
dumpling *n* tymplen, poten
dunce *n* hurtyn, twpsyn, penbwl
dune *n* twyn
dung *n* tom, tail
dungarees *npl* dyngaris
dungeon *n* daeardy, daeargell, dwnsiwn
dupe *n* gwirionyn ♦ *vt* twyllo
duplex *adj* dwplecs
duplicate *adj* dyblyg ♦ *n* copi ♦ *vt* dyblygu

duplicity *n* dichell, rhagrith
durable *adj* parhaol, parhaus, cryf
duration *n* parhad
duress *n* gorfodaeth
during *prep* yn ystod
dusk *n* cyfnos, gwyll
dust *n* llwch ♦ *vt* taenu neu sychu llwch, dwstio
dustbin *n* bin sbwriel
duster *n* cadach, dwster
dustman *n* dyn lludw
dusty *adj* llychlyd
Dutch *n* Iseldireg. **Dutchman** *n* Iseldirwr
dutiful *adj* ufudd, ufuddgar
duty *n* dyletswydd; toll. **customs d.** tolldal. **import d.** toll fewnforio. **export d.** toll allforio
dwarf *n* cor, corrach ♦ *adj* corachaidd
dwell *vi* trigo, preswylio
dwelling *n* annedd, preswyl
dwindle *vi* darfod, lleihau, dirywio
dye *vb* lliwio, llifo ♦ *n* lliw, lliwur
dyke *n* morglawdd, cob
dynamic *adj* dynamig
dynamics *n* dynameg

E

each *adj, pron* pob, pob un. **e. other** ei gilydd
eager *adj* awyddus. awchus
eagle *n* eryr
ear *n* clust, dolen; tywysen. **earache** clust dost
earl *n* iarll
early *adj* cynnar, bore, boreol ♦ *adv* yn fore
earmark *vt* clustnod, nod clust ♦ *vb* clustnodi, neilltuo
earn *vt* ennill, elwa
earnest *adj* difrif, difrifol, taer
earnest *n* ern, ernes ♦ *vb* gwystl
earnings *npl* enillion

earphone n ffôn clust
earring n clustlws
earshot n clyw
earth n daear, pridd ♦ vt priddo
earthenware npl llestri pridd
earthly adj daearol, ar wyneb daear
earthquake n daeargryn
ease n esmwythdra, esmwythyd; rhwyddineb ♦ vb esmwytho
easel n isl
east n dwyrain ♦ adj dwyreiniol. E. Germany Dwyrain yr Almaen
Easter n y Pasg
eastern adj dwyreiniol
eastwards adj, adv tua'r dwyrain
easy adj hawdd, rhwydd
easy-chair n cadair esmwyth
easy-going adj didaro, di-hid
eat vt bwyta, ysu
eaves npl bargod, bondo
eavesdrop vb clustfeinio
ebb n trai ♦ vi treio
eccentric adj od, hynod; echreiddig
ecclesiastic adj eglwysig ♦ n clerigwr
echo n atsain, carreg ateb ♦ vb atseinio
eclipse n eclips, diffyg, clip ♦ vb tywyllu
ecology n ecoleg
economic adj economaidd
economical adj cynnil, darbodus
economics n economeg
economize vb cynilo
economy n cynildeb, darbodaeth, economi
ecstasy n gorfoledd, gorawen, hwyl
edge n min, ymyl, ymyl ♦ vb minio; hogi; symud. to be on e. bod ar bigau'r drain
edible adj bwytadwy
edict n cyhoeddiad, gorchymyn
Edinburgh n Caeredin
edit vt golygu, paratoi i'r wasg

edition n argraffiad
editor n golygydd
editorial adj golygyddol
educate vt addysgu
education n addysg
educational adj addysgol
eel n llysywen
eerie adj iasol, annaearol
effect n effaith; canlyniad ♦ vt effeithio. after-effects sgil-effeithiau
effective adj effeithiol
effectiveness n effeithiolrwydd
effeminate adj merchetaidd
efficiency n effeithlonrwydd
efficient adj effeithiol, cymwys
effort n ymdrech, ymgais
effusive adj teimladol, arddangosiadol
e.g. adv abbr er enghraifft, e.e.
egg n wy. scrambled e. cymysgwy
egg vt annog, annos
egg cup n cwpan wy
egg shell n masgl/plisgyn wy
ego n ego, yr hunan
egoism n myfiaeth, egoistiaeth
egotism n hunanoldeb
egotist n un hunanol
Egypt n yr Aifft
eiderdown n cwrlid plu
eight adj, n wyth
eighteen adj, n deunaw, un deg wyth
eighth adj wythfed
eighty adj n pedwar ugain, wyth deg
Éire n Iwerddon Rydd, Gweriniaeth Iwerddon
either adj un o'r ddau ♦ conj naill ai ♦ adv, conj na, nac, ychwaith
ejaculate vb saethu; gweiddi; ebychu
eject vt byrw allan; diarddel
eke vt estyn allan; hel neu grafu
elaborate adj llafurfawr, manwl
elaborate vb manylu
elapse vi mynd heibio, treiglo

elastic adj hydwyth, ystwyth. **e. band** n cylch lastig

elated adj gorawenus, calonnog

elation n gorawen

elbow n elin, penelin

elder n henuriad, hynafgwr ♦ adj hŷn

elderly adj oedrannus

eldest adj hynaf

elect vt ethol, dewis ♦ adj etholedig

election n etholiad; etholedigaeth

elector n etholwr

electorate n etholaeth

electric adj trydanol, electrig. **e. blanket** n blanced drydan. **e. fire** n tân trydan

electrician n trydanwr

electricity n trydan

electrify vt gwefreiddio, trydanu

electronic adj electronig

elegant adj cain, dillyn, lluniaidd

elegy n marwnad, galarnad

element n elfen

elementary adj elfennol

elephant n cawrfil, eliffant

elevate vt dyrchafu, codi

eleven adj, n un ar ddeg

eleventh adj unfed ar ddeg

elf (elves) n ellyll, coblyn

elicit vb mynnu gan

eligible adj cymwys, etholadwy, dewisol

eliminate vt dileu, deol

elm n llwyf, llwyfen

elongate vt hwyhau, estyn

elongated adj hirgul

eloquent adj huawdl

else adv arall, amgen, pe amgen

elsewhere adv mewn lle arall

elude vt osgoi

elusive adj di-ddal, gwibiog, ansafadwy

emaciate vt teneuo, culhau, curio

emaciated adj tenau, curiedig

emanate vi deillio, tarddu, llifo

emancipate vt rhyddfreinio, rhyddhau

embankment n clawdd, cob

embargo n gwaharddiad

embark vb mynd neu osod ar long; hwylio. **to e. on** ymgymryd â, dechrau

embarrass vt rhwystro, drysu

embarrassed adj mewn penbleth, trafferthus

embarrassing adj dyrys, anffodus

embarrassment n chwithedd, embaras

embassy n llysgenhadaeth

embed vb mewnosod

embers npl marwor, marwydos

embezzle vt celcio, darnguddio, lladrata

embitter vt chwerwi

emblem n arwyddlun

embody vt corffori

emboss vt boglynnu

embrace vt cofleidio; cynnwys ♦ n cofleidiad

embroider vt brodio

embroidery n brodwaith

embryo n cynelwad, embryo

emend vt cywiro, diwygio

emerald n emrallt

emerge vi dyfod allan, dyfod i'r golwg, ymddangos

emergence n ymddangosiad

emergency n cyfyngder, taro, argyfwng. **in an e.** mewn taro

emigrate vi allfudo, ymfudo

eminent adj enwog, amlwg, o fri

emit vt rhoddi neu fwrw allan

emotion n cyffro, teimlad, emosiwn

emotional adj emosiynol

empathy n empathi

emperor n ymerawdwr, ymherodr

emphasis n pwys, pwyslais

emphasize vt pwysleisio

emphatic adj pwysleisiol, pendant

empire n ymerodraeth

empirical adj empeiraidd

employ vt cyflogi; arfer, defnyddio ♦ n gwasanaeth

employee *n* gŵr cyflog
employer *n* cyflogwr
employment *n* cyflogaeth, gwaith
empower *vt* awdurdodi, galluogi
empress *n* ymerodres
empty *adj* gwag, coeg ♦ *vb* gwagu,
arllwys, gwacáu, dihysbyddu
empty-handed *adj* gwaglaw
emulate *vt* ymgystadlu â; efelychu
emulsion *n* emwlsiwn
enable *vt* galluogi
enact *vt* deddfu, ordeinio; cyflawni
enchant *vt* swyno, cyfareddu, hudo
enclose *vt* amgáu
enclosed *adj* amgaeëdig
enclosure *n* lle caeëdig, lloc
encompass *vt* amgylchu, cylchynu
encore *n* encôr ♦ *adv* eto
encounter *vt* cyfarfod, taro ar ♦ *n*
ymgyfarfod, brwydr
encourage *vt* cefnogi, calonogi,
annog
encouragement *n* cefnogaeth,
calondid, anogaeth
encroach *vi* llechfeddiannu
encyclopaedia *n* gwyddoniadur
end *n* diwedd; diben ♦ *vb* diweddu,
dibennu, terfynu. **e. point** pwynt
terfyn. **from e. to e.** o ben bwy
gilydd
endanger *vt* peryglu
endear *vt* anwylo
endeavour *vi* ymdrechu ♦ *n*
ymdrech
ending *n* diwedd, dibeniad,
terfyniad
endless *adj* diddiwedd
endorse *vt* cefnogi, arnodi,
ardystio
endorsement *n* arnodiad,
ardystiad
endow *vt* gwaddoli, cynysgaeddu,
donio
endowment *n* gwaddol,
cynhysgaeth
endurance *n* dygnwch
endure *vb* parhau; dioddef,

goddef
enemy *n* gelyn
energetic *adj* grymus, egniol
energy *n* ynni, egni
enforce *vt* gorfodi
enforcement *n* gorfodaeth
engage *vb* ymrwymo, dyweddio;
cyflogi; ymladd
engaged *adj* ymrwymedig, wedi
dyweddio; prysur
engagement *n* ymrwymiad,
dyweddïad; brwydr
engaging *adj* deniadol
engender *vt* achosi, peri
engine *n* peiriant, injan
engineer *n* peiriannydd
engineering *n* peirianneg
England *n* Lloegr
English *adj* Saesneg, Seisnig ♦ *n*
Saesneg. **E. Channel** Môr Udd
Englishman (**-men**) *n* Sais (*pl*
Saeson)
engrave *vt* ysgythru
engraving *n* ysgythrad
engulf *vt* llyncu
enhance *vb* chwanegu, mwyhau,
chwyddo, hyrwyddo
enjoy *vt* mwynhau; meddu
enjoyable *adj* pleserus
enjoyment *n* mwynhad
enkindle *vt* ennyn
enlarge *vt* ehangu, helaethu
enlighten *vt* goleuo; hysbysu
enlightened *adj* goleuedig; golau
enlist *vb* ymrestru, listio; ennill
enmity *n* gelyniaeth
enormity *n* anfadrwydd,
ysgelerder
enormous *adj* dirfawr, anferth,
enfawr
enough *adj*, *n*, *adv* digon
enquire *vb* ymofyn, ymholi, gofyn,
holi
enquiry *n* ymholiad
enrage *vt* ffyrnigo, cynddeiriogi
enrich *vt* cyfoethogi
enrol *vt* cofrestru

enrolment n cofrestrad

ensign n lluman, baner; llumanwr

enslave vt caethiwo

ensue vi dilyn, canlyn

ensure vt diogelu, sicrhau

entail vt gorfodi, gofyn

entangle vt drysu, maglu, rhwydo

enter vb mynd i mewn, treiddio; cofnodi

enterprise n anturiaeth, menter

enterprising adj anturiaethus, mentrus

entertain vt difyrru, adlonni; croesawu

entertainer n difyrrwr, diddanwr

entertaining adj difyrrus, diddan

entertainment n difyrrwch, adloniant

enthrall vb swyno

enthrone vt gorseddu

enthusiasm n brwdfrydedd

enthusiastic adj brwdfrydig, eiddgar

entice vb hudo, denu, llithio

entire adj cyfan, hollol, llwyr

entirely adv yn gyfan gwbl, yn llwyr

entirety n cyfanrwydd

entrails npl perfedd, ymysgaroedd

entrance n mynediad, mynedfa. e. fee tâl mynediad

entrance vt swyno

entreat vt erfyn, ymbil, deisyf

entrust vt ymddiried

entry n mynediad, mynedfa; cofnodiad

envelop vt amgáu

envelope n amlen

envious adj cenfigennus

environment n amgylchedd, amgylchfyd

environmental adj amgylchol

envisage vb rhagweld

envoy n cennad, negesydd

envy n cenfigen, eiddigedd ♦ vt cenfigennu, eiddigeddu

epic adj arwrol, arwraidd ♦ n

arwrgerdd, epig

epidemic adj heintus ♦ n haint

epiglottis n epiglotis

epilepsy n epilepsi

Epiphany n Yr Ystwyll

episcopate n esgobaeth

episode n digwyddiad, gogyfran, episôd

epistle n epistol, llythyr

epitaph n beddargraff

epitome n crynodeb, talfyriad

equable adj gwastad, cyson, tawel

equal adj cyfartal ♦ n cydradd ♦ vt bod yn gyfartal. without e. heb ei ail

equality n cydraddoldeb, cyfartaledd

equalize vb cydraddoli, cyfartalu

equally adv yn ogystal â, yn llawn, yn gyfartal

equanimity n tawelwch, anghyffro

equate vt cyfartalu, cymharu

equation n hafaliad. simple e. hafaliad syml. quadratic e. n hafaliad dwyradd. simultaneous e. n hafaliad cydamserol

equator n y cyhydedd

equatorial adj cyhydeddol

equestrian adj marchogol ♦ n marchog

equilateral adj hafalochrog

equilibrium n cydbwysedd, cymantoledd

equip vt taclu, paratoi, cymhwyso, cyfarparu

equipment n cyfarpar, offer

equipoise n cydbwysedd

equivalent adj cyfwerth, cyfartal

equivocal adj amwys

era n cyfnod

eradicate vt difodi, difa

erase vt dileu, rhwbio allan

eraser n dilëydd, rwber

erect adj syth, unionsyth ♦ vt codi, adeiladu

ermine n carlwm

erode vb ysu, treulio, erydu

erosion n erydiad

erotic adj serchol, nwydol, erotig

err vi cyfeiliorni

errand n neges, cenadwri

erratic adj ansefydlog, crwydraidd

error n cyfeiliornad, camgymeriad; bai, gwall. **in e.** ar gam

erupt vb echdorri, torri allan

eruption n echdoriad, tarddiad

escalator n escaladur

escapade n pranc, direidi

escape vb dianc, osgoi ♦ n dihangfa

escort vt hebrwng ♦ n gosgordd

especial adj arbennig, neilltuol

especially adv yn arbennig, yn enwedig

espionage n ysbiaeth

esquire n yswain, ysgwier

essay n ymgais; traethawd, ysgrif

essay vt profi, ymgeisio

essence n hanfod; rhinflas

essential adj hanfodol, anhepgor ♦ n hanfod, anghenraid

essentially adv yn hanfodol

essentials npl hanfodion, anhepgorion

establish vt sefydlu

establishment n sefydliad

estate n stad, ystad, eiddo. **industrial e.** stad ddiwydiannol

esteem vt parchu, edmygu, cyfrif ♦ n parch, bri

estimate vt, n amcangyfrif

estimation n amcangyfrif, parch, bri

estrange vt dieithrio

estuary n aber

et cetera adv ac yn y blaen

eternal adj tragwyddol, bythol

eternally adv yn dragwyddol, yn oes oesoedd, byth bythoedd

eternity n tragwyddoldeb

ethical adj moesegol

ethics npl moeseg

Ethiopia n Ethiopia

ethnic adj ethnig, cenhedlig

ethos n ethos, naws, natur

etiquette n moesau, arfer

etymology n geirdarddiad

eucharist n cymun, cymundeb

Europe n Ewrob, Ewrop

European adj Ewropeaidd ♦ n Ewropead

evacuate vt ymgilio, ymadael (â)

evade vt gochelyd, osgoi

evangelical adj efengylaidd

evangelist n efengylydd

evangelize vt efengylu

evaporate vb ymageru, anweddu

evaporated milk n llaeth anwedd(og)

evasion n osgoad, gocheliad

eve n min nos, noswyl

even adj gwastad, llyfn; cyfartal ♦ adv hyd yn oed. **e. number** eilrif

evening n noswaith, yr hwyr, min nos. **e. class** n dosbarth nos. **e. dress** n gwisg ffurfiol

evensong n prynhawnol weddi, gosber

event n digwyddiad. **in the e. of** os bydd

eventful adj llawn digwyddiadau

eventuality n achlysur, digwyddiad posibl

eventually adv o'r diwedd

ever adv bob amser, erioed, byth. **e. and anon** byth a hefyd

evergreen n adj bythwyrdd, anwyw

everlasting adj tragwyddol, bythol

evermore adv byth, byth bythoedd

every adj pob

everybody pron pawb, pob un

everyday adj bob dydd, beunyddiol

everyone pron pawb, pob un

everything pron popeth

everywhere adv ym mhobman

evict vt troi allan, dadfeddiannu

evidence n tystiolaeth, prawf

evident adj amlwg, eglur

evil adj drwg, drygionus ♦ n drwg, drygioni

evoke vt galw neu dynnu allan; gwysio

evolution n esblygiad

evolve vb datblygu; esblygu

ewe n dafad, mamog

ex- prefix allan o; cyn-

exact adj manwl, cywir, union

exact vt hawlio, mynnu

exacting adj manwl, gorthrymus

exactly adv yn union, i'r dim

exaggerate vt chwyddo, gorliwio

exaggeration n gormodiaith, gorliwiad

exalt vt dyrchafu, mawrygu

examine vt arholi, archwilio

examination n arholiad, archwiliad

examiner n arholwr, archwiliwr

example n esiampl, enghraifft

exasperate vt llidio, cythruddo

exasperation n llid, cythrudd

excavate vt cloddio

exceed vt rhagori ar, bod yn fwy na

exceedingly adv tros ben, tra

excel vb rhagori

excellent adj rhagorol, ardderchog, godidog, campus

except prep ac eithrio, eithr, namyn, oddieithr, heblaw

exception n eithriad

exceptional adj eithriadol

excerpt n dyfyniad, detholiad

excess n gormod, gormodedd

excessive adj gormodol, eithafol

exchange vt cyfnewid, ffeirio ♦ n cyfnewid, cyfnewidfa. **e. rate** cyfradd cyfnewid

exchequer n trysorlys

excise n toll ♦ vt gosod toll

excite vt cynhyrfu, cyffroi

excited adj cynhyrfus

excitement n cynnwrf

exciting adj cyffrous

exclaim vt llefain, gweiddi, bloeddio, ebychu

exclamation n llef, gwaedd,

ebychiad. **e. mark** ebychnod

exclude vt cau allan, bwrw allan

exclusion n gwaharddiad, gwrthodiad

exclusive adj cyfyngedig

excommunicate vt esgymuno

excrement n carth, tom, baw

excrete vt ysgarthu

excruciating adj dirdynnol

excursion n gwibdaith, pleserdaith

excuse vt esgusodi ♦ n esgus

execute vt cyflawni, gweithredu; dienyddio

execution n cyflawniad, dienyddiad

executioner n dienyddiwr

executive adj gweithiol, gweithredol ♦ n gweithredwr. **e. committee** pwyllgor gwaith

executor n ysgutor

exemplify vt egluro, dangos, enghreifftio

exempt adj rhydd, esgusodol ♦ vt rhyddhau, esgusodi

exercise n ymarfer, ymarferiad ♦ vb ymarfer. **e. book** llyfr ysgrifennu, ymarfer

exert vt ymegnïo, ymdrechu

exertion n ymdrech, ymroddiad

exhale vb anadlu allan

exhaust vt disbyddu, diffygio, gwacáu ♦ n disbyddwr, gwacáwr. **e. (pipe)** n pibell nwyon

exhausted adj lluddedig, blin, disbyddedig, wedi ymládd

exhaustion n gorluddeb

exhaustive adj trwyadl

exhibit vt dangos, arddangos

exhibition n arddangosfa; ysgoloriaeth

exhilarate vt llonni, sirioli, bywiogi

exile n alltud; alltudiaeth ♦ vt alltudio

exist vi bod, bodoli

existence n bod(olaeth), hanfod. **e. in** mewn bod, ar glawr

exit n allanfa ♦ vb mynd allan,

ymadael
exodus n ymadawiad
exonerate vt esgusodi
exorbitant adj afresymol, gormodol
exotic adj estron, egsotig
expand vb lledu, ehangu, datblygu
expanse n ehangder
expansion n ehangiad, ymlediad
expect vb disgwyl
expectancy n disgwyliad
expectation n disgwyliad
expediency n hwylustod
expedient adj hwylus, cyfleus ♦ n ystryw
expedite vt hyrwyddo, hwyluso
expedition n ymgyrch, alldaith
expel vt bwrw allan, diarddel
expend vt gwario, treulio
expenditure n gwariant
expense n traul, cost
expenses npl treuliau
expensive adj drud, costus
experience n profiad ♦ vt profi
experienced adj profiadol
experiment n arbrawf ♦ vi arbrofi
expert n arbenigwr ♦ adj medrus, deheuig
expertise n medr, dawn, arbenigaeth
expire vb anadlu allan; darfod, marw
expiry n diwedd, terfyn
explain vt egluro, esbonio
explanation n eglurhad, esboniad
explanatory adj eglurhaol, esboniadol
explicit adj eglur, manwl, echblyg
explode vb ffrwydro, chwalu
exploit n camp, gorchest ♦ vt gweithio, gwneud elw o, ymelwa ar
exploitation n ymelwad
explore vt fforio, chwilio
explorer n fforiwr
explosion n ffrwydriad; tanchwa
explosive n ffrwydrydd/yn ♦ adj

ffrwydrol
exponent n esboniwr, dehonglwr
export vt allforio ♦ n allforyn
exporter n allforiwr
expose vt amlygu, dinoethi
expound vt esbonio
express vt mynegi, datgan ♦ adj cyflym, clir ♦ n trên cyflym
expression n mynegiant
expressly adv yn unig swydd, yn benodol
expulsion n diarddeliad
exquisite adj odiaeth, rhagorol; coeth
extempore adv, adj byrfyfyr, o'r frest
extend vb estyn, ymestyn; ehangu
extension n helaethiad, ehangiad, (ym)estyniad
extensive adj ymestynnol, helaeth
extent n ehangder, maint, hyd, mesur. **to some e.** i raddau
extenuate vt lleihau, lleddfu; esgusodi
exterior adj allanol ♦ n tu allan
exterminate vt difodi, dileu
external adj allanol
extinct adj wedi diffodd, wedi darfod, diflanedig
extinguish vt diffodd; diddymu, dileu
extinguisher n diffoddwr
extol vt moli, moliannu, clodfori
extort vt cribddeilio, gwasgu
extortionate adj gormodol
extra adj ychwanegol ♦ adv tu hwnt, dros ben ♦ n peth dros ben, ychwanegiad
extract vt echdynnu, tynnu; dyfynnu, rhinio ♦ n echdyniad; dyfyniad; rhin, darn
extracurricular adj allgyrsiol
extramural adj allanol
extraordinary adj hynod, anghyffredin
extravagant adj gwastraffus, afradlon

extreme adj i'r eithaf, eithafol ♦ n eithaf

extremely adv dros ben, gor-

extremity n pen, eithaf; cyfyngder

extrovert adj allblyg, alltro ♦ n alltroedydd, person allblyg

eye n llygad; crau; dolen ♦ vt llygadu, sylwi ar, gwylio

eyeball n cannwyll y llygad

eyebrow n ael

eyelashes npl blew yr amrant

eye-level n llinell orwel

eyelid n amrant

eye-opener n agoriad llygad

eyesight n golwg

eyesore n hyllbeth

eyewitness n llygad-dyst

F

fable n chwedl, dameg; anwiredd

fabric n adail, adeilad, defnydd

fabricate vt llunio, dyfeisio, ffugio

fabrication n ffug, anwiredd

fabulous adj chwedlonol, diarhebol

face n wyneb, wynepryd ♦ vb wynebu. **f. cloth** n clwtyn ymolchi. **f. value** arwynebwerth

facilitate vt hwyluso, hyrwyddo

facility n hwylustod, cyfleustra, rhwyddineb

fact n ffaith, gwirionedd. **as a matter of f.** mewn gwirionedd

factor n ffactor, elfen, nodwedd. **prime f.** ffactor cysefin

factory n ffatri

factual adj ffeithiol

faculty n cynneddf; cyfadran

fad n mympwy, chwilen

fade vb diflannu, gwywo; colli ei liw

fag n/vb slafio, ymlâdd, blino ♦ n caledwaith, lludded; gwas bach

fail vi ffaelu, methu, pallu, diffygio. **without f.** yn ddi-ffael

failure n methiant, pall,

aflwyddiant

faint adj llesmeiriol, gwan, llesg ♦ vi llewygu ♦ n llesmair, llewyg

fair n ffair

fair adj teg, glân; gweddol; golau

fairly adv yn deg/lân, yn weddol

fairness n glendid, tegwch

fairy n un o'r tylwyth teg

fairy-tale n stori hud, chwedl werin

faith n ffydd, cred, coel

faithful adj ffyddlon, cywir

faithfully adv yn ffyddlon, yn gywir. **yours f.** yr eiddoch yn gywir

fake n ffug ♦ vb ffugio

falcon n hebog, curyll

fall vi cwympo, syrthio ♦ n cwymp. **f. out** cweryla. **f. through** methu

fallacy n cyfeiliornad, gwall

fallow n braenar ♦ vt braenaru

false adj gau, ffug, ffals, twyllodrus. **f. teeth** dannedd gosod/dodi

falter vb petruso, methu, pallu

fame n enwogrwydd, clod, bri

familiar adj cynefin, cyfarwydd

familiarity n cynefindra

family n teulu, tylwyth

famine n newyn

famish vb newynu, llwgu

famous adj enwog

fan n gwyntyll; ffan ♦ vt gwyntyllio, chwythu

fanatic n penboethyn, ffanatig

fanaticism n penboethni, ffanatigiaeth

fanciful adj ffansïol

fancy n dychymyg, ffansi, serch ♦ vt dychmygu, ffansïo, serchu. **f. dress** gwisg ffansi

fang n ysgithr, dant, pig, blaen

fantastic adj ffantastig, rhyfeddol

fantasy n ffantasi

far adj pell (ennig) ♦ adv ymhell. **as f. as** hyd at

farce n ffars

fare n cost, pris; ymborth ♦ vb bod,

dod ymlaen, byw

farewell *excl* yn iach, ffarwel ♦ *n* ffarwel. **to bid f.** canu'n iach

farm *n* fferm ♦ *vt* amaethu, ffarmio

farmer *n* ffarmwr, ffermwr, amaethwr. **Young Farmers' Club** Clwb y Ffermwyr Ifainc

farmhouse *n* ffermdy

farming *n* ffermio. **intensive f.** ffermio dwys

farmyard *n* buarth, clos

fascinate *vt* hudo, swyno

fascinating *adj* hudol, swynol

fascism *n* ffasgaeth

fashion *n* ffasiwn, arfer, dull ♦ *vt* llunio, gwneud

fashionable *adj* ffasiynol

fast *vi* ymprydio ♦ *n* ympryd

fast *adj* tyn, sownd; buan, cyflym, clau

fasten *vb* sicrhau, cau, clymu, ffasno

fastener *n* ffasnydd

fastening *n* ffasnin

fastidious *adj* cysetlyd

fat *adj* tew, bras ♦ *n* braster, bloneg, saim

fatal *adj* angheuol, marwol; andwyol

fatality *n* trychineb, marwolaeth

fate *n* tynged, ffawd ♦ *vt* tynghedu

fateful *adj* tyngedfennol

father *n* tad ♦ *vt* tadogi

father-in-law *n* tad-yng-nghyfraith

fatherly *adj* tadol

fathom *n* gwryd ♦ *vt* plymio

fatigue *n* lludded, blinder ♦ *vt* lluddedu, blino

fatten *vb* tewhau, pesgi

fatty *adj* seimlyd, brasterog

fatuous *adj* ynfyd, ffôl

fault *n* bai, diffyg, nam, anaf. **at f.** ar fai

faultless *adj* di-fai, perffaith

faulty *adj* gwallus, diffygiol

favour *n* ffafr, cymwynas ♦ *vt*

ffafrio. **in f. of** o blaid

favourable *adj* ffafriol

favourite *adj*, *n* ffefryn ♦ *adj* hoff

fawn *n* elain ♦ *adj* llwyd

fawn *vi* cynffonna, gwenieithio

fear *n* ofn, braw, arswyd ♦ *vb* ofni, arswydo

fearful *adj* ofnus, brawychus, arswydus

feasible *adj* dichonadwy

feast *n* gwledd, gŵyl ♦ *vb* gwledda

feat *n* camp, gorchest

feather *n* pluen, plufyn ♦ *vt* pluo, plufio

feature *n* arwedd, nodwedd

February *n* Chwefror, Mis Bach

federal *adj* cynghreiriol, ffederal

fee *n* ffi, tâl, cyflog

feeble *adj* gwan, eiddil

feed *vb* porthi, ymborthi, bwydo ♦ *n* porthiant, ffid, ymborth, gwledd

feedback *n* adborth, ymateb ♦ *vb* adborthi

feel *vb* teimlo, clywed, profi

feeler *n* teimlydd; ymchwiliad

feeling *n* teimlad, synhwyriad

feign *vb* cymryd arno, ffugio

fell *vb* cwympo, cymynu ♦ *n* croen; ffridd, rhos

fellow *n* cymar; cymrawd ♦ *prefix* cyd-

fellowship *n* cymdeithas, cyfeillach; cymrodoriaeth

felt *n* ffelt ♦ *vb* ffeltio

female *adj*, *n* benyw

feminine *adj* benywaidd, benywol

feminist *n* ffeminist

femur *n* ffemwr

fence *n* clawdd, ffens ♦ *vb* cau, amgáu

fencing *n* ffensio, cleddyfaeth

fend *vb* cadw draw; ymdaro, ymdopi

ferment *n* eples, cynnwrf ♦ *vb* eplesu, cynhyrfu

fermentation *n* eplesiad

fern *n* rhedynen, rhedyn

ferocious *adj* ffyrnig, gwyllt, milain

ferret *n* ffured ♦ *vt* ffuredu, chwilota

ferry *n* porth, fferi ♦ *vb* cludo dros

ferry-boat *n* ysgraff

fertile *adj* ffrwythlon, toreithiog

fertilisation *n* ffrwythloniad

fertility *n* ffrwythlonder

fertilize *vb* ffrwythloni; gwrteithio

fertilizer *n* gwrtaith

fervent *adj* brwd, gwresog, tanbaid, taer

fester *vi* crawni, gori, crynhoi

festival *n* gŵyl, dydd gŵyl. **singing f.** cymanfa ganu

festive *adj* llawen, llon

festivity *n* rhialtwch, miri, ysbleddach

fetch *vt* cyrchu, hôl, ymofyn, nôl

fête *n* gŵyl, miri ♦ *vi* gwledda

feud *n* cynnen, ffiwd

feudal *adj* ffiwdal

feudalism *n* ffiwdaliaeth

fever *n* twymyn, clefyd, gwres

feverish *adj* â thwymryn

few *adj* ychydig, prin, anaml

fiancé(e) *n* darpar-ŵr/wraig

fib *n* anwiredd, celwydd

fibre *n* edefyn, ffibr

fibreglass *n* ffibr gwydrog

fickle *adj* anwadal, oriog, gwamal

fiction *n* ffuglen

fictitious *adj* ffug, ffugiol

fiddle *n* ffidil, crwth ♦ *vi* canu'r ffidl; ffidlan

fidelity *n* ffyddlondeb, cywirdeb

fidget *vt* ffwdanu, aflonyddu ♦ *n* un ffwdanus, un aflonydd

field *n* cae, maes ♦ *vb* maesu

field marshal *n* maeslywydd

field work *n* gwaith maes

fiend *n* cythraul, ellyll, ysbryd drwg

fierce *adj* ffyrnig, milain; tanbaid

fiery *adj* tanllyd, tanbaid

fifteen *adj*, *n* pymtheg

fifth *adj*, *n* pumed

fifty *adj*, *n* hanner cant, deg a deugain

fig *n* ffigysen

fight *vb* ymladd, cwffio, brwydro, rhyfela ♦ *n* ymladdfa, brwydr

fighter *n* ymladdwr, brwydrwr

fighting *n* ymladd

figment *n* creadigaeth (y dychymyg)

figurative *adj* ffigurol, cyffelybiaethol

figure *n* ffigur; llun, ffurf ♦ *vb* cyfrif; llunio; ymddangos. **f. of speech** troad ymadrodd

figurehead *n* arweinydd (mewn enw)

file *n* ffeil, rhathell; rhes ♦ *vb* ffeilio, rhathu

fill *vb* llenwi ♦ *n* llenwad, llonaid, gwala

fillet *n* llain, ffiled. **f. steak** *n* stêc ffiled

filling *n* llenwad, mewnyn

filly *n* eboles

film *n* pilen, caenen; ffilm ♦ *vb* ffilmio, gwneud ffilm. **f. strip** stribed ffilm

filter *n* hidl, hidlydd ♦ *vb* hidlo, ffiltro. **f. tip** *n* hidl difaco

filth *n* brynti, budreddi, baw

filthy *adj* brwnt, budr, aflan

filtrate *n* hidlif ♦ *vb* hidlo

fin *n* adain, asgell, ffin

final *adj* terfynol, olaf. **semi-f.** cynderfynol

finale *n* ffinale, diweddglo

finally *adv* o'r diwedd, yn olaf

finance *n* cyllid ♦ *vb* cyllido, codi arian

financial *adj* cyllidol, ariannol

find *vt* darganfod ♦ *n* darganfyddiad

finding *n* darganfyddiad, dedfryd

fine *adj* main; mân; gwych; braf

fine *n* dirwy ♦ *vt* dirwyo

finery *n* gwychder**

finger n bys ♦ vt bysio, bodio. **little
f.** bys bach. **third f.** bys y fodrwy.
middle f. y bys canol
fingerprint n bysbrint, ôl bys
finicky adj cysetlyd, gorfanwl
finish n diweddu, gorffen,
cwblhau ♦ n diwedd; gorffeniad
finished adj gorffenedig
finite adj meidrol
Finland n y Ffindir
fir n ffynidwydden
fire n tân ♦ vb tanio, ennyn. **wild f.**
tân gwyllt. **f. precautions**
rhagodion tân
firearm n arf-tân
firebrigade n brigâd dân
fire engine n peiriant tân
fire escape n grisiau tân
fire-extinguisher n diffoddydd tân
fireguard n sgrin dân
fireman n taniwr, diffoddwr tân
fireplace n lle tân
fireside n aelwyd
firewood n coed tân, cynnud
fireworks npl tân gwyllt
firm n cwmni, ffyrm ♦ adj cadarn,
diysgog
firmly adv yn gadarn, yn ddiysgog
first adj cyntaf, blaenaf, prif ♦ adv
yn gyntaf. **f. aid** n cymorth
cyntaf. **f. class** adj dosbarth
cyntaf. **f. floor** n llawr cyntaf. **f.-
hand** adj o lygad y ffynnon. **f.-rate**
adj campus, ardderchog, rhagorol
fish n pysgodyn, pysgod ♦ vb
pysgota. **f. and chips** pysgodyn a
sglodion
fisherman n pysgotwr
fishing n pysgota
fishing rod n genwair, gwialen
bysgota
fishmonger n gwerthwr pysgod
fishy adj amheus; pysgodol
fist n dwrn
fit n llewyg, ffit, mesur
fit adj ffit, addas, cymwys,
gweddus; abl, iach ♦ vb ffitio,

gweddu, taro
fitful adj anwadal, gwamal
fitment n cynhalydd
fitness n ffitrwydd, addasrwydd
fitter n ffitiwr
fitting n ffitiad ♦ vb ffitio ♦ adj
priodol, gweddus, addas. **fittings**
mân daclau, ffitiadau
five adj pum ♦ n pump
fix vb sicrhau, sefydlu, gosod ♦ n
cyfyngder, cyfyng-gyngor
fixation n sefydlogiad, sefydledd
fixed n sefydlog
fixture n gosodyn, peniant (byd
chwarae)
fizz vi sïo
fizzle vb hisian, sïo
fizzy adj byrlymog
flabbergast vt synnu, syfrdanu
flabby adj llipa, llac, llaes
flag n baner, lluman; fflagen ♦ vb
llumanu; llaesu
flake n fflaw, caenen; pluen (eira)
flamboyant adj coegwych
flame n fflam ♦ vi fflamio, ffaglu
flame-resistant adj gwrthfflam
flan n fflan
flank n ystlys, ochr ♦ vb ymylu,
ystlysu
flannel n gwlanen
flap n llabed, fflap ♦ vb fflapio
flare vb fflêr, fflach; fflerio, fflachio
flash vb fflachio ♦ n fflach
flashback n ôl-fflach
flashlight n fflachlamp
flashy adj gorwych
flask n costrel, fflasg
flat n fflat, gwastad; meddalnod ♦
adj fflat, gwastad, lleddf ♦ vb
fflatio
flatten vb gwastatáu
flatter vt gwenieithio
flattery n gwenieith
flatulence n gwynt (yn y cylla)
flaunt vb fflawntio, rhodresa
flavour n blas, cyflas ♦ vt blasu,
cyflasu

flavouring n cyflasyn

flaw n bai, diffyg, nam

flax n llin

flaxen adj golau, o lin

flay vt blingo

flea n chwannen

flee vb ffoi, cilio, dianc, diflannu

fleece n cnu ♦ vt cneifio; ysbeilio

fleet n llynges, fflyd ♦ adj cyflym, buan

fleeting adj diflanedig

flesh n cig, cnawd. **f. and blood** cig a gwaed. **f. and bones** cnawd ac esgyrn

flex n fflecs

flexible adj hyblyg, ystwyth

flick vt cyffwrdd â blaen chwip, cnithio

flier n ehedwr

flight n hediad, ffo, rhes

flighty adj gwamal, penchwiban

flimsy adj tenau, simsan, bregus

flinch vi cilio yn ôl, gwingo, llwfrhau

fling vt taflu, bwrw, lluchio ♦ n rhwysg, taflïad

flint n callestr, carreg dân, fflint

flip vb cnithio ♦ n cnith

flippant adj tafodrydd, gwamal

flipper n asgell

flirt vb cellwair caru, fflyrtan ♦ n fflyrten, fflyrtyn

flit vi gwibio

float n arnofyn, fflôt, trol ♦ vb arnofio

flock n diadell, praidd ♦ vi heidio

flog vt fflangellu, chwipio

flood n llif, dilyw, cenllif ♦ vt llifo, gorlifo

floodlight n llifolau ♦ vb llifoleuo

floor n llawr ♦ vt llorio; methu. **ground f.** daearlawr. **first f.** llawr cyntaf

flop n methiant, ymollwng

flora n fflora, planhigion

floral adj fflurol

florid adj blodeuog

florist n tyfwr neu werthwr blodau

flounce vi swalpio, ysboncio ♦ n llam, ysbonc

flounder n lleden fach ♦ vb ymdrybaeddu, ffwndro

flour n blawd, can

flourish vb blodeuo; ffynnu; ysgwyd ♦ n rhwysg; cân cyrn

flout vb gwawdio, wftfio, diystyru

flow n llifo, llifeirio ♦ n llif, llanw

flow chart n siart rhediad

flower n blodeuyn, blodyn ♦ vi blodeuo. **flowerpot** pot blodau

flowery adj blodeuog

flu n ffliw, anwydwst

fluctuate vi codi a gostwng, amrywio, anwadalu

flue n pibell simnai, ffliw

fluency n huodledd, llithrigrwydd

fluent adj llithrig, rhugl

fluff n fflwcs, fflwff ♦ vb bwnglera, methu

fluid adj hylif, llifol ♦ n hylif, llifydd

fluke n pry'r afu; ffliwc, lwc

fluoride n ffliworid

flurry n cyffro, ffwdan

flush n gwrid; rhuthr dŵr ♦ adj cyfwyneb, gorlawn ♦ vb gwrido, cochi; gorlifo

fluster vb ffwdanu, cyffroi ♦ n ffwdan, cyffro

flute n ffliwt

flutter vb dychlamu, siffrwd ♦ n dychlamiad, siffrwd

fly n gwybedyn, cleren, pryf

fly vb ehedeg, ehedfan; ffoi ♦ n pryf, cleren, copis. **f. into a passion** ymwylltio, gwylltu

flying adj hedegog, cyflym

flyover n pontffordd, trosffordd

foal n ebol, eboles ♦ vb bwrw ebol. **in f.** cyfebol

foam n ewyn ♦ vi ewynnu, glafoerio

focus n canolbwynt, ffocws ♦ vb canolbwyntio

fodder n porthiant, ebran

foe n gelyn

fog n niwl

foggy adj niwlog

foil vt rhwystro, trechu ♦ n ffoil, ffwyl, dalen

fold n plyg; corlan ♦ vb plygu, corlannu

folder n plygell

folding n plygiant

foliage n dail, deiliant

folio n ffolio

folk npl pobl, gwerin

folklore n llên gwerin

folk song n cân werin

follow vb canlyn, dilyn

follower n dilynwr, canlynwr

following adj dilynol, canlynol ♦ n dilyniad, canlynwyr

folly n ffolineb, ynfydrwydd

fond adj hoff, annwyl

fondle vt anwylo, anwesu

font n bedyddfaen

food n bwyd, ymborth, lluniaeth. tinned f. bwyd tun. f. poisoning n gwenwyn bwyd

fool n ffŵl, ynfytyn ♦ vb ynfydu, twyllo

foolhardy adj rhyfygus

foolish adj ffôl, ynfyd, annoeth

foot (feet) n troed; troedfedd ♦ vb troedio. f. and mouth disease n clwyf y traed a'r genau. f. rot clwy'r traed

football n pêl-droed

footballer n peldroediwr

footbrake n brêc troed

footbridge n pont gerdded, pompren

foothold n gafael troed, troedle

footing n sylfaen, safle

footlights npl golau'r godre

footman n gwas (â lifrai)

footmark n ôl troed

footnote n troednodiad

footpath n llwybr troed

footprint n ôl troed

footstep n cam, ôl troed

footway n troedffordd

footwear n troedwisg

for prep i, at, am, dros, er ♦ conj canys, oblegid, oherwydd, gan, achos

forage n bwyd (anifail), porthiant ♦ vb chwilio am fwyd

forasmuch conj yn gymaint ag, am, gan, oherwydd

foray n cyrch, rhuthr ♦ vb gwneud cyrch, rhuthro

forbid vt gwahardd, gwarafun, gomedd

forbidden adj gwaharddedig

force n grym; trais ♦ vt gorfodi. centrifugal f. grym allgyrchol. centripetal f. grym mewngyrchol. the forces y lluoedd arfog

forceful adj grymus, egniol

forceps n gefel fain

forcible adj nerthol, effeithiol

ford n rhyd ♦ vt rhydio

fore adj blaen, blaenaf ♦ adv ymlaen ♦ prefix cyn-, rhag-, blaen-. to the f. amlwg, blaenllaw

forearm n elin ♦ vb rhagarfogi

forebode vt rhagargoeli, rhagarwyddo, darogan

foreboding n rhagargoel

forecast n rhagolygon, rhagolwg ♦ vb rhagddweud, darogan

forefather n cyndad

forefinger n mynegfys

forefront n lle blaen ♦ adj blaen

forego vb hepgor. **foregone conclusion** penderfyniad ymlaen llaw

foreground n blaendir

forehead n talcen

foreign adj estron, tramor. f. affairs materion tramor

foreigner n estron, tramorwr

foreman n fforman

foremost adj blaenaf ♦ adv ym mlaenaf

forensic adj fforensig

forerunner n rhagredegydd

foresee vt rhagweld, rhagwybod

foreseeable adj rhagweladwy

foreshadow vb rhagarwyddo, rhagargoeli

foresight n rhagweledigaeth

forest n coedwig, fforest ♦ vt coedwigo, fforestu

forestall vt achub y blaen

forestry n coedwigaeth. f. commission Comiswn Coedwigo

foretaste n rhagflas ♦ vb rhagbrofi

foretell vt rhagfynegi, darogan

forever adv am byth

foreword n rhagair, rhagymadrodd

forfeit n fforffed, fforffed ♦ vt fforffedu, colli

forge n gefail, ffwrn ♦ vb gofannu; ffugio

forget vt anghofio

forgetful adj anghofus

forgive vt maddau

forgiveness n maddeuant

forgo vt gadael, hepgor, mynd heb

fork n fforch, fforc ♦ vb fforchio

forlorn adj amddifad, truan, anobeithiol

form n ffurf; mainc; ffurflen ♦ vb ffurfio. application f. ffurflen gais

formal adj ffurfiol, defodol

former adj blaenaf, blaenorol

formerly adv gynt, yn flaenorol

formidable adj arswydus, ofnadwy, grymus

formula n rheol, fformwla

forsake vt gadael, ymadael â, gwrthod, cefnu ar

fort n caer, castell, amddiffynfa

forte n cryfder ♦ adj uchel, cryf

forth adv allan, ymlaen. **and so f.** ac felly yn y blaen

forthcoming adj ar ddod, gerllaw

forthright adj union, plaen

forthwith adv yn ddioed, ar unwaith

fortify vt cadarnhau, cryfhau

fortitude n gwroldeb, dewrder

fortnight n pythefnos

fortnightly adj, adv bob pythefnos

fortress n amddiffynfa, caer, castell

fortunate adj ffodus, ffortunus

fortunately adv yn ffodus, yn lwcus

fortune n ffawd; ffortun

fortune teller n un sy'n dweud ffortun

forty adj, n deugain

forum n fforwm

forward n blaenwr ♦ adj eofn, hy; blaen ♦ adv ymlaen ♦ vb anfon ymlaen; hwyluso, hyrwyddo. **inside f.** mewnwr. **wing f.** blaenasgellwr

fossil n ffosil ♦ adj ffosilaidd

fossilise vb ffosileiddio

foster vt magu, meithrin, coleddu

foster-child n plentyn maeth

foster-mother n mamfaeth

foul adj aflan; annheg; afiach ♦ n ffowl(en) ♦ vb ffowlio, llychwino. **f. play** anfadwaith. **f. throw** camdaflu

found vt dechrau, sylfaenu, sefydlu

foundation n sail, sylfaen

founder vb ymddryllio, suddo ♦ n sylfaenydd

foundry n ffowndri, efail

fountain n ffynnon, ffynhonnell

four adj, n pedwar (f pedair)

foursome n pedwarawd

fourteen adj, n pedwar (pedair) ar ddeg

fourth adj pedwerydd (f pedwaredd)

fowl n dofednyn, ffowlyn, ffowl

fox n cadno, llwynog

foyer n cyntedd

fraction n ffracsiwn. **improper f.** ffracsiwn pendrwm. **vulgar f.** ffracsiwn cyffredin. **proper f.** ffracsiwn bondrwm

fracture n toriad, drylliad ♦ vt torri, dryllio
fragile adj brau, bregus
fragment n dryll, darn, briwsionyn
fragrance n perarogl, persawr
frail adj brau, bregus, gwan, eiddil
frame n ffrâm; agwedd ♦ vt fframio, llunio. **f. of mind** agwedd meddwl
framework n fframwaith
franchise n etholfraint ♦ vb etholfreinio
frank adj didwyll, agored
frankincense n thus
frantic adj cyffrous, gwallgof
fraternal adj brawdol
fraternity n brawdoliaeth
fraud n twyll, hoced
fraudulent adj twyllodrus
fraught adj llwythog, llawn
fray n ymryson, ymgiprys, ffrae, rhaflad ♦ vb treulio, rhaflo
freak n mympwy, peth od
freckle n brych, brychni
free adj rhydd; hael; di-dâl, rhad ♦ vb rhyddhau
freedom n rhyddid, rhyddfraint
free expression n rhyddfynegiant
freehold adj rhydd-ddaliadol
free kick n cic rydd
freely adv yn rhydd, yn hael
freemason n saer rhydd
free trade n masnach rydd
free verse n mesur rhydd, y wers rydd
free will n ewyllys rydd, o'i fodd
freeze vb rhewi, fferru
freeze-dry vb sychrewi
freezer n rhewgist, rhewgell
freezing point n rhewbwynt
freight n llwyth llong ♦ vt llwytho llong
French adj Ffrengig ♦ n Ffrangeg. **F. beans** npl ffa Ffrengig
Frenchman n Ffrancwr
Frenchwoman n Ffrances
frenzy n gorffwylltra, cynddaredd

frequency n amider, mynychder
frequent adj mynych, aml ♦ vt mynychu
frequently adv yn fynych, yn aml
fresh adj ffres, crai, cri, croyw, newydd
freshen vb ffresáu, ireiddio
freshness n ffresni, creider, irder
fret vb sorri, poeni ♦ n soriant, trallod, ffret
friar n brawd, mynach
friction n ffrithiant, ymrafael
Friday n dydd Gwener
fridge n oergell, rhewadur
friend n cyfaill, ffrind
friendly adj cyfeillgar
friendship n cyfeillgarwch
frieze n ffris
fright n dychryn, ofn, braw
frighten vb dychrynu, brawychu, codi ofn ar
frightful adj dychrynllyd, brawychus
frigid adj oer, rhewllyd; oeraidd, oerllyd. **f. zone** n cylchfa rew
frill n ffril
fringe n ymyl, ymylwe, rhidens ♦ vb ymylu, rhidennu. **f. benefits** n cilfanteision
frisk vt prancio
fritter vt afradu, ofera, gwastraffu
frivolous adj gwamal; diystyr, disylwedd
frizzy adj crychlyd
fro adv: **to and f.** yn ôl ac ymlaen
frock n ffrog
frog n llyffant (melyn), broga; bywyn, ffroga
frolic vi prancio, campio ♦ n pranc
from prep o, oddi, oddi wrth, gan
front n wyneb, blaen, ffrynt, talcen ♦ vb wynebu ♦ adj blaen. **f. door** drws ffrynt. **f. page** tudalen blaen. **f. room** ystafell (ffrynt)
frontier n ffin, terfyn, goror
frost n rhew
frostbite n ewinrhew

frosty adj rhewllyd

froth n ewyn ♦ vi ewynnu

frown vi cuchio, gwgu ♦ n cuwch, gwg

frozen adj wedi rhewi

frugal adj cynnil, darbodus

fruit n ffrwyth, ffrwythau. **f. juice** sudd ffrwyth. **f. salad** salad ffrwythau

fruiterer n gwerthwr ffrwythau

fruitful adj ffrwythlon, toreithiog

fruition n ffrwythloniad

frustrate vt rhwystro, llesteirio

frustration n llesteiriant

fry vb ffrio ♦ n afu, sil, silod. **small f.** n pobl ddibwys

frying-pan n ffrimpan, padell ffrio

fudge n cyffug

fuel n tanwydd; cynnud. **f. cell** cynudydd

fugitive adj ar ffo, diflanedig ♦ n ffoadur

fulfil vt cyflawni

fulfilment n cyflawniad

full adj llawn, cyflawn ♦ n llonaid

full-back n cefnwr

fuller n pannwr

full stop n atalnod

fulltime adj llawn amser

fully adv yn gyfan gwbl, yn gyflawn, yn hollol

fulsome adj ffiaidd, diflas (am weniaith, etc)

fumble vb palfalu, bwnglera

fume n tarth, mwg; llid ♦ vb mygu; llidio, sorri

fun n difyrrwch, digrifwch, hwyl

function n swydd, swyddogaeth; ffwythiant (mathemateg)

functional adj swyddogaethol, ffwythiannol, defnyddiol

fund n cronfa, trysorfa

fundamental adj sylfaenol

funeral n angladd, cynhebrwng, claddedigaeth

fungus n ffwng

funnel n twmffat, twndis, corn

funny adj digrif, ysmala; rhyfedd, hynod

fur n blew, ffwr; cen. **f. coat** n cot ffwr

furious adj cynddeiriog, ffyrnig, gwyllt

furlong n ystad, wythfed ran milltir

furnace n ffwrn, ffwrnais

furnish vt dodrefnu, rhoddi

furnishings npl dodrefn

furniture n dodrefn, celfi

furrow n cwys, rhych ♦ vt cwyso, rhychu

furry adj blewog

further adj pellach ♦ adv ymhellach ♦ vt hyrwyddo. **f. education** addysg bellach

fury n cynddaredd, ffyrnigrwydd

fuse n ffiws, toddyn, diogelydd ♦ vb ffiwsio

fuss n ffwdan, helynt, stŵr ♦ vb ffwdanu

fussy adj ffwdanus

futile adj ofer, di-les

future adj, n dyfodol

fuzzy adj blewog, aneglur

G

gabble vb bregliach, clebran ♦ n cleber

gable n piniwn, talcen tŷ

gadget n dyfais

Gaelic n Gaeleg ♦ adj Gaelaidd

gaff n bach pysgota

gag n smaldod; safnglo ♦ vb smalio; safngloi, cau ceg

gaiety n llonder, difyrrwch, miri

gaily adv yn llawen

gain vb ennill, elwa ♦ n ennill, elw, budd

gait n cerddediad, osgo

gale n awel, gwynt cryf; tymestl

gall n bustl, chwydd ♦ vb dolurio, blino. **g. bladder** n coden y bustl.

g. **stones** cerrig y bustl
gallant adj gwrol, dewr ♦ n carwr
gallery n oriel, llofft
galley n rhwyflong; galï
gallon n galwyn
gallop n carlam ♦ vb carlamu
gallows n crocbren
galore n, adv digonedd
galvanize vt galfaneiddio, galfanu;
symbylu
gamble vb hapchwarae, gamblo ♦
n gambl
game n chwarae, camp;
helwriaeth ♦ adj calonnog, dewr,
glew
game-keeper n cipar
gammon n palfais (mochyn);
ffwlbri, lol
gander n ceiliagwydd, clacwydd
gang n mintai, torf, haid, gang
gangster n troseddwr
gangway n tramwyfa, eil, ale;
pont
gaol n carchar ♦ vt carcharu
gap n bwlch, adwy
gape vi rhythu, syllu ♦ n rhythiad
garage n modurdy, garej
garbage n ysgarthion, ysbwriel,
sothach
garble vt darnio, llurgunio
garden n gardd ♦ vi garddio
gardener n garddwr
gardening n garddwriaeth
gargle n golch gwddf ♦ vb golchi
gwddf
garish adj coegwych
garland n coronbleth, garlant,
talaith
garlic n garlleg
garment n dilledyn, gwisg
garnish vt addurno, harddu
garrison n gwarchodlu, garsiwn
garrulous adj tafodrydd, siaradus
garter n gardas, gardys ♦ vb
gardysu
gas n nwy ♦ vb gwenwyno â nwy.
g. **cooker** ffwrn nwy. g. **fire** tân

nwy. g. **ring** cylch nwy
gash n archoll, hollt, hac ♦ vt
archolli, hacio
gasket n gasged
gas-mask n mwgwd nwy
gasometer n tanc nwy
gasp vb ebychu, anadlu'n drwm
gate n porth, llidiart, clwyd, gât,
iet ♦ vb porthio, porthellu
gate-crasher n ymyrrwr
gatehouse n porthordy
gateway n mynedfa
gather vb casglu, cynnull, crynhoi,
hel
gathering n casgliad, cynulliad
gaudy adj coegwych, gorwych
gauge n mesur; llcai; meidrydd ♦
vt mesur, meidryddu
Gaul n Gâl
Gaulish n Galeg
gaunt adj llwm, tenau
gauntlet n dyrnfol, maneg ddur. **to
throw down the g.** herio
gauze n rhwyllen, gaws, meinwe
gay adj llon, bywiog, ofer, hoyw
gaze vi edrych, syllu, tremio ♦ n
golwg, trem
gazette n newyddiadur
(swyddogol)
gazetteer n geiriadur daearyddol
GCSE n abbr TGAU = Tystysgrif
Gyffredin Addysg Uwchradd
gear n gêr, offer, taclau ♦ vb
taclu, harneisio
gearbox n gergist, blwch gêr,
gerbocs
gelignite n geligneit
gem n glain, gem, tlws
gender n cenedl
genealogy n achau; achyddiaeth
general adj cyffredin, cyffredinol ♦
n cadfridog. g. **election** n etholiad
cyffredinol
generalize vb cyffredinoli
generally adv yn gyffredinol
generate vt cenhedlu, cynhyrchu,
generadu

generation n cenhedliad;
cenhedlaeth, to

generator n cynhyrchydd;
generadur

generosity n haelioni

generous adj hael, haelionus,
haelfrydig

genetic adj genetig

genetics n geneteg

Geneva n Genefa

genial adj hynaws, rhadlon, tyner,
tirion

genital adj cenhedlol. **genitals** npl
organau cenhedlu

genius n athrylith

genteel adj bonheddig,
boneddigaidd

gentle adj bonheddig; mwyn, tyner

gentleman n gŵr bonheddig

gently adv yn dyner, addfwyn; gan
bwyll

gentry npl bonedd

gents npl toiledau dynion

genuine adj dilys, diffuant, pur

geography n daearyddiaeth

geology n daeareg

geometry n geometreg

geriatrics n geriatreg

germ n hedyn, eginyn, germ

German adj Almaenaidd ♦ n
Almaenwr; Almaeneg. **G. measles**
y frech Almeinig

Germany n yr Almaen

germinate vi egino, atyfu

germination n eginiad, atyfiant

gesture n ystum, arwydd, mosiwn

get vb cael, caffael, ennill. **to g. on
with it** bwrw arni, bwrw iddi

geyser n geyser

Ghana n Ghana

ghastly adj erchyll, gwelw

gherkin n gercin

ghost n ysbryd, drychiolaeth,
bwgan

giant n cawr ♦ adj cawraidd

gibberish n cleber, baldordd

gibe vb gwawdio ♦ n gwawd

giblets npl giblets, syrth gŵydd

Gibraltar n Gibralter

giddiness n pendro

giddy adj penfeddw, penchwiban

gift n rhodd, dawn, anrheg, gwobr

gifted adj dawnus, talentog

gigantic adj cawraidd, dirfawr,
anferth

giggle vb lledchwerthin, giglan

gill n tageli; gil, chwarter peint

gimmick n gimig

gin n jin; hoenyn

ginger n sinsir

gingerly adj, adv gochelgar,
gwyliadwrus

gipsy, gy- n sipsi

giraffe n siráff

girder n trawst

girdle n gwregys, rhwymyn ♦ vt
gwregysu

girl n merch, geneth, hogen

girlfriend n cariadferch, anwylyd

girth n cengl; cylchfesur, cwmpas

gist n cnewyllyn pwnc, ergyd,
sylwedd

give vb rhoddi, rhoi. **g. up** rhoi'r
gorau i

glacier n rhewlif, iâen, glasier

glad adj llawen, llon, balch

gladiator n cleddyfwr, ymladdwr

gladly adv yn llawen, â phleser

glamorous adj swynol, cyfareddol,
hudol

glamour n swyn, cyfaredd, hud

glance vb ciledrych, tremio ♦ n
cipolwg, trem, cip

gland n chwarren, cilchwyrnen,
gland

glare vb disgleirio; rhythu ♦ n
disgleirdeb, tanbeidrwydd

glass n gwydr; gwydraid; pl
gwydrau, sbectol

glassy adj gloyw, pŵl

glaze vt gwydro; scleinio ♦ n
sclein, gwydredd

glazier n gwydrwr

gleam n pelydryn, llewyrch ♦ vi

pelydru, llewyrchu

glean vb lloffa

glebe n clastir, tir eglwys

glee n llonder, hoen; rhangan

glen n glyn, cwm, dyffryn

glib adj llyfn, llithrig, rhugl, ffraeth

glide vi llithro, llifo ♦ n llithr, llithrad

gliding n, vb llithran

glimmer vi llewyrchu'n wan ♦ n llewyrchyn, llygedyn

glimpse n trem, cipolwg

glint vb fflachio ♦ n fflach, llewyrch

glisten vi disgleirio

glitter vi tywynnu, pelydru ♦ n pelydriad

gloat vb llawenhau

global adj hollfydol, cyffredinol

globe n pêl, belen

gloom n caddug, prudd-der, tywyllwch

gloomy adj prudd, digalon, tywyll

glorify vt gogoneddu

glorious adj gogoneddus

glory n gogoniant ♦ vi ymffrostio, gorfoleddu

gloss n disgleirdeb arwynebol, sglein; glôs, esboniad

glossary n geirfa

glossy adj llathraidd

glove n maneg

glow vi twymo, gwrido ♦ n gwres, gwrid

glower vi cuchio, gwgu

glue n glud ♦ vt gludio, asio

glum adj prudd, digalon, trist

glut vt gorlenwi, glythu ♦ n gormodedd, gorlawnder

glutton n glwth

gluttony n glythineb

gnarled adj cnotiog, ceinciog, garw

gnat n gwybedyn, cylionen

gnaw vb cnoi, deintio, cnewian

gnome n gwibrel; ysbryd, coblyn

go vi mynd, cerdded, rhodio ♦ n

tro

goad n swmbwl ♦ vt symbylu

goal n gôl, nod, bwriad. **g. posts** npl pyst gôl. **g. shooter** saethwr

goalkeeper n golgeidwad, golwr

goat n gafr

goblin n ellyll, coblyn, bwgan

god n duw. G. Duw

godchild n mab bedydd, merch fedydd

goddess n duwies

godfather n tad bedydd

godhead n duwdod

godly adj duwiol

godmother adj mam fedydd

godsend n caffaeliad

goggles npl gwydrau

gold n aur ♦ adj aur, euraid

golden adj euraid

goldfish npl eurbysg, pysgod aur

goldsmith n gof aur, eurych

golf n golff. **g. links** maes golff. **g. course** n maes golffio

golfer n golffwr

gong n gong, cloch fwyd

good adj da, daionus; cryn ♦ n da, daioni, lles. **g. morning** bore da. **g. afternoon** prynhawn da. **g. evening** noswaith dda. **g. night** nos da. **g. enough** digon da, no **g.** dim gwerth, da i ddim. G. Friday Dydd Gwener y Groglith. **g. humour** natur dda

good-bye excl, n da bo chi, yn iach! ffarwel

good-looking adj golygus

goodly adj hardd, teg

good-natured adj hynaws, rhadlon

goodness n daioni

goods npl nwyddau, eiddo

goodwill n ewyllys da; braint (masnachol)

goose (**geese**) n gŵydd

gooseberry n eirinen Fair, gwsbersen

gooseflesh n croen gŵydd

gore n gwaed, gôr ♦ vb cornio

gorge n hafn, ceunant ♦ vb safnio, trafiyncu

gorgeous adj ysblennydd, gwych

gorilla n gorila

gorse n eithin

gory adj gwaedlyd

gosling n cyw gwydd

gospel n efengyl

gossip n clec, clonc, clebryn, clebran ♦ vb clebran, clecian, hel straeon

gout n gowt, cymalwst

govern vb llywodraethu, rheoli, llywio

governess n athrawes

government n llywodraeth

governor n llywodraethwr

gown n gŵn

grab vb crafangu, cipio ♦ n gwanc, crap

grace n gras, rhad, graslonrwydd; gosgeiddrwydd ♦ vt harddu, prydferthu, addurno

graceful adj graslon, rhadlon; gosgeiddig, lluniaidd

gracious adj graslon, grasol, rhadlon, hynaws

grade n gradd, safon ♦ vb graddio

gradient n graddiant

gradual adj graddol

gradually adv yn raddol

graduate vb graddio, graddoli ♦ n gŵr gradd, graddedig

graduation n graddedigaeth, graddnod

graffiti n graffiti

graft n impyn, hunan-les ♦ vt impio, grafftio

grain n grawn, gronyn; mymryn; graen ♦ vb graenu, graenio

gram n gram

grammar n gramadeg. **g. school** n ysgol ramadeg

grammatical adj gramadegol

granary n ysgubor

grand adj mawreddog, ardderchog, crand; prif, uchel

grandchild n ŵyr, wyres. **great g.** n gorwyr(es)

granddaughter n wyres

grandfather n taid, tad-cu. **great g.** n hen daid, hen-dad-cu

grandmother n nain, mam-gu

grandson n ŵyr

granite n gwenithfaen, ithfaen

grant vt rhoddi, caniatáu ♦ n rhodd, grant. **to take for granted** cymryd yn ganiataol

granulated adj gronynnog

granule n gronynnell

grapefruit n grawnffrwyth

grapes n grawnwin

graph n graff

graphic adj graffig; byw

graphics npl graffigwaith, graffeg

grapple n gafl, gafaelfach ♦ vb gafaelyd, mynd i'r afael â

grasp vb gafael; amgyffred ♦ n gafael, amgyffrediad

grasping adj trachwantus

grass n glaswellt, porfa

grasshopper n ceiliog y rhedyn, sioncyn y gwair

grate n grat ♦ vb rhygnu, crafellu; merwino

grateful adj diolchgar; dymunol

grater n grater, crafellydd

gratify vt boddio, boddhau

grating adj garw, cras ♦ n gratin

gratitude n diolchgarwch

gratuity n cildwrn, rhodd

grave adj difrifol, dwys

grave n bedd, beddrod

gravel n graean, gro, grafel

gravestone n beddfaen, carreg fedd

graveyard n mynwent

gravitate vi disgyrchu, treiglo

gravity n disgyrchiant; pwysigrwydd. **centre of g.** craidd disgyrchiant

gravy n grefi, isgell, sew

graze vb pori; crafu, rhwbio, ysgythru

grease n saim, iraid ♦ vt iro, seimio

greaseproof adj gwrthsaim

greasy adj seimllyd, ireidlyd

great adj mawr. **g. many** llawer iawn

greatly adv yn fawr

Greece n Groeg

greed n trachwant, gwanc

greedy adj barus, trachwantus, gwancus

Greek n Groeg; Groegwr ♦ adj Groegaidd

green adj gwyrdd, glas, ir ♦ vb glasu

greenery n gwyrddlesni

greengrocer n gringroser, gwerthwr llysiau

greenhouse n tŷ gwydr

Greenland n Grønland

greet vt annerch, cyfarch

greeting n cyfarchiad

grenade n grenâd

grey adj llwyd, llwydwyn, glas

greyhound n milgi

grid n grid, alch. **g. reference** cyfeirnod grid

grief n gofid, galar, hiraeth

grievance n cwyn

grieve vb gofidio, galaru, hiraethu

grievous adj gofidus, poenus, blin, dirifol

grill n gril, gridyll ♦ vb grilio, gridyllu. **mixed g.** gril cymysg

grille n gril, dellt

grim adj sarrug, milain, dirifol

grimace n ystum ♦ vi ystumio

grimy adj budr, brwnt, diraen

grin vb lledwenu ♦ n gwên

grind vb malu (ŷd etc); llifo (arf), llifanu

grip n gafael, gwasgu ♦ n gafael, crap

grisly adj erch, erchyll, hyll, milain

gristle n madruddyn, gwythi

grit n grit, grud, graean; pybyrwch

groan vi, n griddfan

grocer n groser

groceries npl nwyddau

groin n cesail morddwyd, gwerddyr

groom n priodfab; gwastrawd ♦ vb trwsio

groove n rhigol, rhych ♦ vt rhigoli, rhychu

grope vi ymbalfalu

gross n gros; crynswth ♦ adj bras, aflednais. **g. profit** elw gros

grotto n groto

ground n llawr, daear, tir; sail; gwaelod ♦ vt daearu, llorio. **g. floor** n daearlawr

groundless adj di-sail

groundwork n sylfaen, sail

group n grŵp, twr, bagad ♦ vt grwpio. **discussion g.** cylch trafod

grouse n grugiar ♦ vb grwgnach

grove n llwyn, celli

grovel vi ymgreinio

grow vb tyfu, prifio, cynyddu, codi

grower n tyfwr

growing adj yn tyfu

growl vi chwyrnu

growth n twf, tyfiant, cynnydd

grub n pryf, cynrhonyn; bwyd ♦ vb dadwreiddio

grubby adj budr, brwnt

grudge vt gwarafun, grwgnach ♦ n dig, cenfigen, cas

gruesome adj erchyll, hyll, ffiaidd

gruff adj sarrug, garw, swta

grumble vi grwgnach, tuchan

grumpy adj sarrug, diserch

grunt vi rhochian ♦ n rhoch

guarantee n gwarant, ernes ♦ vt gwarantu, mechnïo

guard n gard, gwarchodydd; sgrin ♦ vb gwarchod

guarded adj gwyliadurus, gofalus

guardian n gwarcheidwad

guerilla n herfilwr

guess vb dyfalu, dyfeisio ♦ n

amcan
guesswork n dyfaliad
guest n gwestai, gŵr/gwraig (g)wadd
guffaw n crechwen ♦ vb crechwenu
guidance n cyfarwyddyd
guide n arweinydd ♦ vt arwain, cyfarwyddo
guide book n teithlyfr
guide-dog n arweingi
guide-lines npl canllawiau
guild n cymdeithas, corfforaeth, urdd
guile n twyll, dichell, ystryw
guillotine n gilotin
guilt n euogrwydd, bai
guilty adj euog
guinea pig n mochyn cwta
guise n dull, modd, rhith, diwyg
guitar n gitâr
gulf n gwlff, geneufor; gagendor
gull n gwylan; gwirionyn ♦ vt twyllo
gullet n corn gwddf, sefnig
gullible adj hygoelus
gully n rhigol, ffos
gulp vt llawcian, traflyncu ♦ n llawc, traflwnc
gum n gwm, glud ♦ vt gymio, gludio
gumboots npl esgidiau rwber
gums npl cig y dannedd, gorchafanau, crib y dannedd, gorfant
gun n gwn, dryll
gunner n gynnwr
gunpowder n powdr gwn
gunshot n ergyd gwn
gunsmith n gof gynnau (bach)
gurgle vi byrlymu
gush vb ffrydio, llifeirio ♦ n ffrwd, hyrddwynt
gust n chwythwm
gusto n awch, blas, sêl
gut n perfeddyn, coluddyn ♦ vt diberfeddu; difrodi, ysbeilio

gutter n ffos, cwter, cafn
guttural adj gyddfol
guzzle vb llawcio, traflyncu
gym n campfa
gymnasium n gymnasiwm, campfa
gymnast n mabolgampwr
gynaecologist n gynaecolegydd
gynaecology n gynaecoleg
gypsy n sipsi
gyrate vi troi, chwyrlïo

H

ha excl ha!
haberdashery n dilladach, siop ddillad
habit n arferiad; anian; gwisg ♦ vt gwisgo, dilladu
habitable adj cyfannedd, cyfanheddol
habitat n cartref, cynefin
habitation n trigfa, preswylfa
habitual adj arferol, cyson
habituate vt arfer, cynefino
hack vb hacio, torri ♦ n hac
hack n hurfarch; cystog, slâf
hackneyed adj ystrydebol, cyffredin
hades n annwfn
haddock n corbenfras, hadog
haemorrhage n gwaedlif
haemorrhoids npl clwyf y marchogion
haft n carn
hag n gwrach, gwiddon
haggard adj gwyllt, curiedig
haggle vi bargeinio'n daer
hail n cenllysg, cesair ♦ vb bwrw cesair
hail excl henffych well ♦ vb cyfarch, galw
hair n gwallt, blew, rhawn. **hair's breadth** trwch y blewyn. **h. splitting** hollti blew
hairbrush n brws gwallt

haircut n triniaeth gwallt, toriad, crop

hairdresser n triniwr gwallt

hair dryer n sychwr gwallt

hair spray n chwistrelliad gwallt; chwistrellydd gwallt

hairy adj blewog

hake n cegddu

hale adj iach, cryf, hoenus

half (halves) n hanner

half-back n hanerwr

half-breed adj cymysgryw

half-dead adj lledfyw

half-hearted adj diawydd, llugoer

halfpenny n dimai

halibut n halibwt

hall n llys, neuadd, plas; cyntedd

hallmark n dilysnod

hallo excl heló

hallow vt cysegru, sancteiddio

Halloween n nos Galangaeaf

hallucination n geuddrych, rhithwelediad

halo n corongylch, gogoniant, halo, lleugylch

halt vb sefyll ♦ n safiad; gorsaf, arosfa

halter n cebystr, tennyn

halve vt haneru

ham n morddwyd, ham

hames npl mynci

hamlet n pentref

hammer n morthwyl, mwrthwl, gordd ♦ vb morthwylio

hammock n hamog, gwely crog

hamper n rhwystro, llesteirio

hamstring n llinyn y gar

hand n llaw; (of clock) bys ♦ vt estyn, trosglwyddo. **hand-off** n hwp llaw. **in-hand** adj ar waith. **to be on h.** bod â llaw

handbag n bag llaw

handbook n llawlyfr

handbrake n brec llaw

handcuff n gefyn llaw

handful n dyrnaid, llond llaw

handicap n rhwystr, llestair,

anfantais; blaen. **handicapped children** plant dan anfantais

handicraft n crefft

handiwork n gwaith llaw

handkerchief n cadach poced, hances, macyn, neisied

handle n carn, coes, troed, dolen, clust, dwrn ♦ vt trin, trafod. **to fly off the h.** colli tymer

handlebars npl cyrn

handmade adj wedi ei wneud â llaw

handmaid, -en n llawforwyn

handrail n canllaw

handsome adj golygus, hardd, prydferth; hael

handwriting n llawysgrifen

handy adj hylaw, deheuig, cyfleus

hang vb crogi, hongian, dibynnu

hangar n awyrendy

hang-gliding vb barcuta

hangover n blinder ddoe, pen mawr

hank n cengl

hanker vi blysio, crefu, dyheu, hiraethu

hanky-panky n twyll, dichell ♦ adj twyllodrus, dichellgar

hap n hap, damwain

haphazard adj, adv damweiniol, ar siawns

happen vi digwydd

happily adv yn hapus

happiness n dedwyddwch, hapusrwydd

happy adj dedwydd, hapus

happy-go-lucky adj didaro, di-hid

harangue n araith, arawd ♦ vb areithio

harass vt poeni, blino, gofidio

harassment n poen, blinder

harbour n porthladd, harbwr ♦ vb llochesu

hard adj caled, anodd. **h. of hearing** trwm ei glyw. **to be h. done by** cael cam. **h. headed** hirben

hardboard n caledfwrdd

harden vb caledu

hardener n caledwr

hardness n caledwch

hardship n caledi

hard shoulder n llain galed

hard-up adj prin o arian

hardware n nwyddau metel

hardwood n pren caled

hardy adj caled, cryf, gwydn; hy, eofn

hare n ysgyfarnog, ceinach

harebrained adj byrbwyll, gwyllt

harelip n bylchfin, gwefus fylchog

hark excl gwrando! clyw! **h. back** dychwelyd

harlot n putain

harm n niwed, drwg, cam ♦ vt niweidio, drygu

harmful adj niweidiol

harmless adj diniwed, diddrwg

harmonious adj cytûn

harmonise vb cytgordio, cytuno

harmony n harmoni, cynghanedd

harness n harnais, gêr ♦ vt harneisio

harp n telyn ♦ vi canu'r delyn

harpoon n tryfer ♦ vt tryferu

harrow n og ♦ vt llyfnu; rhwygo, dryllio

harrowing adj dychrynllyd, ofnadwy, deifiol

harry vt difrodi, blino

harsh adj garw, gerwin, aflafar

harshness n craster, gerwindeb

hart n hydd

harvest n cynhaeaf ♦ vt cynaeafu

harvester n cynaeafwr. **combine h.** n combein

hash n briwgig; cymysgfa, cybolfa

hasp n hesben

haste n brys, hast ♦ vi brysio, prysuro

hasten vb brysio, prysuro, hastu

hastily adv yn frysiog

hasty adj brysiog, byrbwyll

hat n het

hatch vb deor, gori ♦ n deoriad

hatch n gorddrws, rhaghddor, dôr

hatchery n deorfa

hatchet n bwyell (fach)

hate vt casáu ♦ n cas, casineb

hateful adj cas, atgas

hatred n cas, casineb, digasedd

haughtiness n balchder, traha, ffroenucheledd

haughty adj balch, ffroenuchel, trahaus

haul vb tynnu, llusgo, halio ♦ n dalfa

haulage n cludiad, cludiant

haulier n haliwr

haunch n morddwyd, pedrain

haunt vt cyniwair, mynychu; trwblu, aflonyddu ♦ n cyniweirfa, cynefin, cyrchfa

have vt cael, meddu. **I h. blue eyes** mae llygaid glas gennyf. **I h. a cold** mae annwyd arnaf

haven n hafan, porthladd

haversack n ysgrepan

havoc n hafog, difrod

hawk n hebog, cudyll, curyll ♦ vb heboca

hawk vt gwerthu o dŷ i dŷ, pedlera

haws npl crawel y moch, criafol y moch

hawthorn n draenen wen

hay n gwair

hayfever n clefyd y gwair

hayrick n tas wair

hazard n perygl, llestair, antur ♦ vt anturio, peryglu

hazardous adj peryglus, enbydus

haze n niwl, tarth, tawch

hazel n collen ♦ adj gwinau golau

haziness n aneglurder

hazy adj aneglur, niwlog

he pron ef, efe; efo, fo, o

head n pen ♦ vb blaenori, penio

headache n dolur (cur) yn y pen, pen tost

header n peniad

headgear n penffest, penwisg

heading n pennawd
headlamp n lamp fawr
headland n pentir, penrhyn; talar
headline n pennawd, teitl, hedin
headlong adv pendramwnwgl
headmaster n prifathro
headmistress n prifathrawes
headphone n ffôn pen
headquarters npl pencadlys
headstrong adj cyndyn
headway n cynnydd
heal vb iacháu, meddyginiaethu
health n iechyd. **h. food shop** n siop bwyd iach. **H. Service** n y Gwasanaeth Iechyd
healthy adj iach, iachus
heap n crug, pentwr ♦ vt crugio, pentyrru
hear vb clywed
hearing n clyw
hearing aid n cymorth clywed
hearken vi gwrando, clustfeinio
hearsay n sôn, siarad ♦ adj o ben i ben, ail-law
hearse n hers
heart n calon
heart-ache n ing, dolur calon
heart attack n trawiad
heartburn n dŵr poeth
hearten vb calonogi
hearth n aelwyd
heartland n perfeddwlad
hearty adj calonnog, cynnes
heat n gwres, poethder, (sport) rhagras ♦ vb twymo, poethi
heater n gwresogydd
heath n rhos, rhostir
heathen adj paganaidd ♦ n pagan
heather n grug
heating n gwres
heave vb codi, dyrchafu; chwyddo; taflu ♦ n hwb
heaven n nef, nefoedd
heavenly adj nefol, nefolaidd
heavily adv yn drwm, yn drymaidd
heavy adj trwm, trymaidd, trymllyd

heavyweight n (sport) pwysau trwm
Hebrew n Hebrëwr; Hebraeg ♦ adj Hebraeg; Hebreig
heckle vb ymyrryd
hectare n hectar
hedge n clawdd, gwrych, perth
hedgehog n draenog
heed vt ystyried, talu sylw ♦ n ystyriaeth
heel n sawdl ♦ vb sodli
heifer n anner, heffer, treisiad
height n uchder, uchelder, taldra
heinous adj dybryd, anfad, ysgeler
heir n etifedd, aer
heiress n etifeddes, aeres
helicopter n hofrennydd
hell n uffern
hellish adj uffernol
hello excl helô!, hylô!, clyw!, gwrando!
helm n llyw; llywyddiaeth
helmet n helm
help vt helpu, cymorth, cynorthwyo ♦ n help, cymorth, cynhorthwy
helper n cynorthwywr, helpwr
helpful adj defnyddiol, cymwynasgar, gwasanaethgar, buddiol
helping n dogn, cyfran (o fwyd)
helpless adj diymadferth
helter-skelter adv blith-draphlith
hem n hem, ymyl ♦ vt hemio
hemi- prefix hanner
hemisphere n hemisffer
hemlock n cegid
hemp n cywarch
hen n iâr
hence adv o gyllt yma ♦ excl ymaith!
henceforth, -forward adv rhag llaw, mwyach, o hyn ymlaen
henchman n gwas, canlynwr, cefnogydd
hepatitis n llif yr afu, hepatitis
her pron ei, hi, hithau
herald n herald ♦ vt cyhoeddi;

rhagflaenu

herb n llysieuyn, sawr-lysieuyn
herbal adj llysieuol
herbicide n llysieiddiad
herd n gyr, cenfaint, gre ♦ vb heidio
here adv yma
hereditary adj etifeddol
heredity n etifeddeg
heresy n heresi, gau athrawiaeth
heretic n heretic, camgredwr
heritage n etifeddiaeth, treftadaeth
hermit n meudwy
hernia n bors, hernia, torllengig
hero n arwr, gwron
heroic adj arwrol
heroine n arwres
heron n crëyr, crychydd
herring n pennog, ysgadenyn
hesitant adj petrusgar
hesitate vi petruso
hesitation n petruster
heterodox adj anuniongred
heterodoxy n anuniongrededd
heterogeneous adj anghydryw, afryw, heterogenus
heterosexual n anghyfunryw
hew vt naddu, torri, cymynu
hewer n cymynwr, torrwr
hexa- prefix chwech
heyday n anterth
hiatus n hiatws
hibernate vi gaeafu
hiccup n yr ig ♦ vi igian
hide vb cuddio, celu, ymguddio
hide n croen
hide-and-seek n chwarae mig
hideous adj hyll, erchyll
hiding place n cuddfan, lloches
hierarchy n gradd, offeiriadaeth
higgle vi taeru, bargenna
high adj uchel; mawr; cryf; llawn
highbrow adj uchel-ael
high chair n cadair ar gyfer plentyn
highland n ucheldir
highly adv yn fawr, yn uchel

highness n uchelder
high-priest n archoffeiriad
high-spirited adj calonnog, nwyfus
high water n pen llanw
highway n priffordd, ffordd fawr
highwayman n lleidr penffordd
hijack vb cipio
hike vb crwydro ♦ n taith gerdded
hilarious adj llawen, llon, siriol, hoenus
hill n bryn, allt, gorifyny
hillock n bryncyn, ponc, twmpath
hilly adj bryniog, mynyddig
hilt n carn cleddyf
him pron ef, efe, yntau
hind adj ôl
hind n ewig
hinder vt rhwystro, atal, lluddias, llesteirio
hindrance n rhwystr, llestair, lludd
hinge n colyn drws ♦ vb troi, dibynnu
hint n awgrym ♦ vt awgrymu
hinterland n cefnwlad
hip n clun, pen uchaf y glun
hippie n hipi
hips npl egroes
hire n cyflogi, hurio, llogi ♦ n cyflog, hur
hiss vb chwythu, sïo, hysio, hisian
historian n hanesydd
historic adj hanesyddol
historical adj hanesyddol
hit vb taro ♦ n ergyd, trawiad
hitch vb bachu ♦ n cwlwm; atalfa, rhwystr
hitchhike vb bodio
hitchhiker n bodiwr
hither adv yma, hyd yma, tuag yma
hitherto adv hyd yma, hyd yn hyn
hive n cwch gwenyn. **h. off** vb rhannu, trosglwyddo, newid
hoar adj llwyd, penllwyd ♦ n llwydrew, barrug
hoard n cronfa, cuddfa ♦ vt cronni

hoarfrost n barrug, llwydrew
hoarse adj cryg, cryglyd
hoax vt twyllo ♦ n cast, tric, twyll
hob n pentan
hobble vb hercian
hobby n difyrwaith, hobi
hobby horse n ceffyl pren; hoff beth
hobgoblin n bwbach, bwci, bwgan
hoe n hof ♦ vb hofio
hog n mochyn
hoist vt codi, dyrchafu
hold vb dal, credu; atal; cadw ♦ n gafael, dalfa
hold n ceudod llong, howld
holdall n celsach
holding n deiliadaeth; tyddyn
hold up n (robbery) lladrad arfog; (in traffic) rhwystr
hole n twll, ffau
holiday n gŵyl, dygwyl
holiness n sancteiddrwydd
Holland n Isalmaen
hollow adj cau, gwag ♦ n ceudod, pant ♦ vt tyllu, cafnio
holly n celyn, celynnen
holocaust n lladdfa
holster n gwain
holy adj sanctaidd, glân
Holy Ghost/Spirit n Ysbryd Glân
homage n gwrogaeth
home n, adj cartref ♦ adv adref. **at h.** gartref
homeland n mamwlad
homeless adj digartref
homely adj cartrefol
home rule n ymreolaeth, hunan-lywodraeth
homesick adj hiraethus
homestead n tyddyn
homework n gwaith cartref
homicide n dynleiddiad, llofruddiaeth
homily n pregeth, homili
homogeneous adj cydryw, homogenus
homosexual n gwrywgydiwr

homosexuality n gwrywgydiaeth
hone n carreg hogi, hôn ♦ vb hogi
honest adj (g)onest, didwyll
honesty n (g)onestrwydd
honey n mêl
honeycomb n dil mêl, crwybr ♦ vt tyllu, britho
honeymoon n mis mêl
honeysuckle n gwyddfid
honorary adj mygedol
honour n anrhydedd ♦ vt anrhydeddu
honourable adj anrhydeddus
hood n cwfl, cwcwll
hoodwink vt dallu, twyllo
hoof n carn
hook n bach; cryman ♦ vb bachu
hooker n bachwr
hooligan n adyn, dihiryn
hoop n cylch, cant ♦ vt cylchu, cantio
hoot vb hwtian, hwtio ♦ n hŵt
hop vb hercian ♦ n llam, herc
hope n gobaith ♦ vb gobeithio
horde n torf, haid, mintai
horizon n gorwel
horizontal adj llorwedd
hormone n hormon
horn n corn ♦ vt cornio, twlcio
horned adj corniog
hornet n gwenynen feirch, cacynen
horoscope n horosgôp
horrible adj erchyll, ofnadwy
horrid adj erchyll, echrydus, anferth
horrify vt brawychu
horror n arswyd, erchylltod
horse n march, ceffyl
horsehair n rhawn
horseman n marchog
horsemanship n marchogaeth
horseplay n direidi
horseshoe n pedol
horticultural adj garddwriaethol
horticulture n garddwriaeth
horticulturist n garddwriaethwr
hose (hose) n hosan; (hoses)

pibell ddŵr
hospitable adj lletygar, croesawus
hospital n ysbyty
hospitality n lletygarwch, croeso
host n llu, byddin
host n lletywr, gwesteiwr
hostage n gwystl
hostel n llety efrydwyr, neuadd breswyl
hostess n croesawferch
hostile adj gelyniaethus
hot adj poeth, twym, brwd, gwresog
hotbed n magwrfa
hotch-potch n cymysgfa, cybolfa
hotel n gwesty
hotelier n gwestywr
hot-headed adj penboeth, byrbwyll
hot-water bottle n jar/potel dŵr twym
hound n bytheiad, helgi ♦ vt hela, erlid, annos
hour n awr
house n tŷ, annedd ♦ vb lletya
household n teulu, tylwyth
householder n deiliad tŷ
housekeeper n gofalyddes
housewife n gwraig tŷ
housing n tai
hovel n penty, hofel
hover vi hofran
hovercraft n hofrenfad
how adv pa mor, pa fodd, pa sut, sut
howbeit adv er hynny
however adv pa fodd bynnag, sut bynnag
howl vi udo, oernadu ♦ n udiad, oernad
hoyden n rhampen, hoeden
hub n both olwyn; canolbwynt
hubbub n mwstwr
huddle vb tyrru, gwthio
hue n gwawr
huff n sorri, tramgwyddo ♦ n soriant
hug vt cofleidio, gwasgu

huge adj anferth, enfawr, dirfawr
hulk n corff llong, llong foel, hwlc
hull n corff llong; cibyn, plisgyn
hullabaloo n dadwrdd, helynt, halibalŵ
hum vb mwmian ♦ n si, sibrwd
human adj dynol
humane adj tirion, tosturiol, trugarog
humanism n dyneiddiaeth
humanist n dyneiddiwr
humanistic adj dyneiddiol
humanitarian n dyngarwr
humanitarianism n dyngaroldeb
humanity n dynoliaeth, dynolryw
humble adj gostyngedig, ufudd ♦ vt darostwng
humble-bee n cacynen
humbug n twyll, ffug, hoced; twyllwr ♦ vt twyllo
humdrum adj diflas
humid adj llaith
humiliate vt bychanu, gwaradwyddo, darostwng, iselu
humiliation n darostyngiad
humility n gostyngeiddrwydd
humour n hwyl, donioldeb ♦ vt boddio
hump n crwmach, crwmp, crwb
hunch n syniad, tybiaeth
hunch backed adj cefngrwm
hundred adj cant, can ♦ n cant; cantref
Hungary n Hwngari
hunger n newyn, chwant bwyd ♦ vi newynu
hungry adj newynog
hunk n cwiff(yn)
hunt vb hela, erlid ♦ n helwriaeth, hela
hunter n heliwr; ceffyl hela
hunting n hela
hurdle n clwyd
hurl vt hyrddio
hurly-burly n hwrli-bwrli, dwndwr
hurricane n corwynt
hurried adj brysiog

hurry vb brysio ♦ n brys
hurt vb niweidio, dolurio, brifo ♦ n niwed, dolur
hurtful adj niweidiol
hurtle vb gwrthdaro, chwyrlïo
husband n gŵr, priod ♦ vt cynilo
husbandry n amaethyddiaeth, hwsmonaeth
hush excl ust ♦ vb distewi ♦ n distawrwydd
husk n plisgyn, cibyn ♦ vt plisgo
husky adj sych, cryglyd
hussy n maeden
hustings n hwstyng, llwyfan etholiad
hustle vb gwthio, prysuro
hut n bwth, caban, cwt
hutch n cwt cwningen, cwb
hyacinth n croeso haf
hybrid adj croesryw
hydration n hydradiad
hydraulic adj hydrolig
hydraulics n hydroleg
hydro- prefix dwfr
hydroelectric adj hydroelectrig
hydrophobia n hydroffobia
hygiene n iechydaeth, gwyddor glendid
hymn n emyn ♦ vb emynu
hyper- prefix gor-, tra-
hyperbole n gormodiaith
hypermarket n archfarchnad
hyphen n cyplysnod, cysylltnod (-)
hypnotism n swyngwsg, hypnotiaeth
hypnotize vt swyno, rheibio
hypochondria n pruddglwyf, y felan
hypocrisy n rhagrith
hypocrite n rhagrithiwr
hypothesis (-theses) n damcaniaeth
hyssop n isop
hysteria n y famwst, hysteria
hysterical adj hysterig

I

I pron mi, myfi; fi, i; minnau, innau
ice n iâ, rhew ♦ vt taenu (megis) â rhew
iceberg n mynydd rhew
ice cream n hufen iâ
Iceland n Gwlad yr Iâ
ice lolly n loli iâ
ice rink n llain iâ
icicle n clöyn iâ, cloch iâ, pibonwy
icing n eising
icy adj rhewllyd
idea n drychfeddwl, syniad
ideal adj delfrydol, ideal ♦ n delfryd
idealism n delfrydiaeth
idealist n delfrydiwr
idealistic adj delfrydol
idealize vb delfrydu
identical adj yr un (yn union)
identify vt adnabod (fel yr un); uniaethu
identikit (picture) n tebyglun
identity n unfathiant, hunaniaeth
idiocy n gwiriondeb, penwendid
idiom n priod-ddull, idiom
idiosyncrasy n tymer, anianawd
idiot n gwirionyn, hurtyn
idle adj segur, ofer ♦ vb segura, ofera
idleness n segurdod, diogi
idol n eilun
idolater n eilunaddolwr
idolatry n eilunaddoliaeth
idolise vb addoli, gwirioni
idyll n bugeilgerdd; canig
if conj os, pe
igloo n iglw
ignite vb ennyn, tanio, cynnau
ignition n taniad
ignoble adj anenwog, isel, gwael, salw
ignominious adj gwarthus,

gwaradwyddus

ignorance n anwybodaeth

ignorant adj anwybodus

ignore vt anwybyddu, diystyru

il- prefix di-, an-

ill adj drwg; gwael, claf ♦ adv yn ddrwg ♦ n drwg, niwed

ill-advised adj annoeth, ffôl

illegal adj anghyfreithlon

illegible adj annarllenadwy, aneglur

illegitimate, illicit adj anghyfreithlon

illiterate adj anllythrennog

illness n afiechyd, anhwylder, anhwyldeb

illogical adj afresymegol

ill-timed adj anamserol

ill-treat vb camdrin

illuminate vt goleuo, addurno

illumination n golau, esboniad

illusion n rhith, lledrith, rhithganfyddiad

illustrate vt egluro; darlunio

illustration n eglureb; darlun

illustrative adj darluniol, eglurhaol

illustrious adj enwog, hyglod

ill-will n gelyniaeth, casineb

im- prefix di-, an-

image n delw, llun; delwedd

imagery n delweddaeth

imaginary adj dychmygol

imagination n dychymyg, darfelydd

imaginative adj dychmygus

imagine vt dychmygu, tybio

imbalance n anghydbwysedd

imbecile adj, n (un) penwan

imbue vt trwytho

imitate vt dynwared, efelychu

immaculate adj difrycheulyd, pur, glân

immaterial adj dibwys

immature adj anaeddfed

immediate adj agos, presennol

immediately adv ar unwaith

immemorial adj er cyn cof

immense adj anferth, eang, dirfawr

immerse vt trochi, suddo

immigrant n mewnfudwr

immigrate vi mewnfudo

imminent adj gerllaw, agos, wrth y drws

immobile adj diymod, disymud

immoral adj anfoesol

immortal adj anfarwol

immortality n anfarwoldeb

immortalize vb anfarwoli

immovable adj diysgog, ansymudol

immune adj rhydd rhag

immunization n gwrth-heintiad

immunize vb gwrtheintio

immure vt caethiwo, carcharu

immutable adj anghyfnewidiol, digyfnewid

imp n dieflyn, cenau

impact n ardrawiad, gwrthdrawiad

impair vt amharu

impale vt trywanu

impart vt cyfrannu, rhoddi

impartial adj diduedd, amhleidiol, teg

impassable adj na ellir mynd heibio iddo

impasse n ataliad, pen draw

impassioned adj brwd, hwyliog, cyffrous

impassive adj digyffro, didaro

impatient adj diamynedd

impeach vt cyhuddo, cwyno yn erbyn, uchelgyhuddo

impeccable adj di-fai

impede vt atal, rhwystro, llesteirio

impediment n atalfa, rhwystr, nam

impel vt gyrru, hyrddio, cymell

impending adj agos, gerllaw

imperative n gorchymyn ♦ adj gorchmynnol, gorfodol

imperfect adj amherffaith

imperial adj ymerodrol

imperil vt peryglu

imperious adj awdurdodol, trahaus

impermeable adj anathraidd

impersonal adj amhersonol

impersonate vt personoli, cynrychioli, portreadu (person)

impertinent adj amherthnasol; digywilydd

imperturbable adj tawel, digyffro

impervious adj na ellir ei dreiddio, anhydraidd

impetuous adj byrbwyll, nwydwyllt

impetus n cymhelliad, symbyliad

impinge vi taro yn erbyn, gwrthdaro, cyffwrdd â

impious adj annuwiol, diras

implacable adj anghymodlon

implant vt plannu, gwreiddio

implement n offeryn, arf ♦ vb gweithredu

implication n ymhlygiad, goblygiad

implicit adj dealledig; ymhlyg, goblygedig

implore vt atolygu, ymbil, erfyn, crefu

imply vt arwyddo, awgrymu

impolite adj anfoesgar

import vt mewnforio ♦ n (pl) mewnforion; arwyddocâd; pwys

importance n pwys, pwysigrwydd

important adj pwysig

importer n mewnforiwr

importune vt dyfal geisio, taer erfyn

impose vb gosod ar; twyllo

imposing adj llethol, mawreddog

impossibility n amhosibilrwydd

impossible adj amhosibl

impostor n twyllwr

imposture n twyll, hoced

impotence n anallu, analluedd

impotent adj di-rym, analluog

impound vt ffaldio; atafaelu

impoverish vt tlodi, llymhau

impracticable adj anymarferol

imprecate vt rhegi, melltithio

impregnable adj cadarn, di-syfl

impregnate vt ffrwythloni; trwytho

impress vt argraffu, pwyso, dylanwadu ♦ n argraffiad

impression n argraff

impressionable adj hawdd ei argyhoeddi

impressive adj trawiadol

imprint vt argraffu ♦ n argraff, delw

imprison vt carcharu

improbable adj annhebygol

impromptu adj, adv ar y pryd, byrfyfyr

improper adj anweddus

improve vb gwella, diwygio

improvement n gwelliant

improvise vb addasu ar y pryd

imprudent adj digywilydd, haerllug

impulse n cymhelliad, ysgogiad

impulsive adj byrbwyll

impunity n bod heb gosb. with i. yn ddi-gosb

impure adj amhur, aflan

impute vt cyfrif i; priodoli; bwrw ar

in prep yn, mewn, i mewn, o fewn

in- prefix di-, an-

inability n anallu

inaccessible adj anhygyrch

inaccurate adj anghywir, anfanwl

inaction n segurdod

inadequate adj annigonol

inadmissible adj annerbyniol

inadvertent adj anfwriadol, amryfus

inane adj gwag, gwageddus, ofer

inanimate adj difywyd, dienaid

inappropriate adj anaddas

inasmuch adv yn gymaint (â)

inaudible adj anhyglyw, na ellir ei glywed

inaugurate vt urddo, cysegru, agor, dechrau

inauguration n agoriad, dechreuad

inborn adj cynhenid, greddfol

inbreed vb mewnfrido

incandescent adj gwynias
incantation n swyn, swyngyfaredd
incapable adj analluog
incapability n anallu
incapacitate vt anghymhwyso, analluogi
incarcerate vt carcharu
incarnation n ymgnawdoliad
incendiary adj llosg ♦ n bom tân
incense n arogldarth
incense vt llidio, cythruddo
incentive adj cymelliadol ♦ n cymhelliad
inception n dechreuad, agoriad
incessant adj di-baid, di-dor
incest n llosgach
inch n modfedd
incident n digwyddiad
incidental adj digwyddiadol, achlysurol
incidentally adv gyda llaw
incinerate vb llosgi'n ulw
incineration n llosgiad llwyr
incinerator n llosgydd, ffwrnais
incipient adj dechreuol
incise vt torri, trychu
incisive adj llym, miniog
incite vt annog, cyffroi, annos
inclement adj gerwin, garw, drycinog
inclination n tuedd, gogwydd
incline vb tueddu, gogwyddo ♦ n llethr
include vt cynnwys
including prep gan gynnwys
inclusive adj cynwysedig, gan gynnwys
incognito adj yn ddirgel, dan ffugenw
incoherent adj digyswllt, anghysylltus
income n incwm. **i. tax** treth incwm
incompatible adj anghytûn
incompetent adj anghymwys
incomplete adj anghyflawn
incomprehensible adj

annealladwy
incongruous adj anghydweddol, anaddas
inconsistency n anghysondeb
inconsistent adj anghyson
inconspicuous adj anamlwg
incontestable adj diymwad, diamheuol
inconvenience n anghyfleustra
inconvenient adj anghyfleus
incorporate vb corffori, ymgorffori
incorporated adj corfforedig
incorrect adj anghywir
incorrigible adj anwelladwy
increase vb cynyddu ♦ n cynnydd
incredible adj anhygoel, anghredadwy
incredulity n anghrediniaeth
incredulous adj anghrediniol
increment n cynnydd, ychwanegiad
incriminate vt cyhuddo, euogi
incubate vb gori, deor
incubator n deorydd
incumbent adj rhwymedig ar ♦ n periglor, offeiriad, clerigwr
incur vt rhedeg i ddyled; achosi
incursion n cyrch
indebted adj dyledus
indecent adj anweddus
indecision n petruster
indecisive adj amhendant
indeed adv yn wir; iawn, dros ben
indefatigable adj diflin, dyfal
indefinite adj amhenodol, amhendant
indelible adj annileadwy
indelicate adj afiednais
indemnify vb digolledu
indemnity n iawn
indented adj bylchog, danheddus
indenture n cytundeb, cyfamod
independence n annibyniaeth
independent adj annibynnol ♦ n annibynnwr
indescribable adj annisgrifiadwy
indeterminate adj amhenodol,

penagored

index *n* mynegai; mynegfys

India *n* India

Indian *adj* Indiaidd ♦ *n* Indiad

indicate *vt* dangos, arwyddo

indicative *adj* arwyddol, mynegol

indicator *n* dangosydd

indict *vt* cyhuddo

indifference *n* difaterwch, difrawder

indifferent *adj* difater; dibwys

indigenous *adj* cynhenid

indigent *adj* anghenus, tlawd, rheidus

indigestion *n* diffyg traul, camdreuliad

indignant *adj* dig, digofus, dicllon

indignation *n* dig, digofaint, llid

indignity *n* amarch, sarhad, anfri

indirect *adj* anuniongyrchol

indiscreet *adj* annoeth

indiscriminate *adj* diwahaniaeth

indispensable *adj* anhepgorol

indisposed *adj* anhwylus

indisputable *adj* diamheuol

indissoluble *adj* annatod

indistinct *adj* aneglur, anhyglyw, bloesg

indite *vt* cyfansoddi, traethu

individual *adj* unigol ♦ *n* un, unigolyn

indoctrinate *vt* trwytho (ag athrawiaeth), credorfodi

indoctrination *n* credorfodaeth

indolence *n* seguryd, syrthni

indolent *adj* segur, swrth, dioglyd

indomitable *adj* anorchfygol, di-ildio

indoor *adj, adv* dan do

indubitable *adj* diamheuol

induce *vt* darbwyllo, denu, cymell

inducement *n* anogiad

induct *vt* sefydlu; anwytho

induction *n* anwythiad

indulge *vb* boddio; maldodi

indulgence *n* ymfoddhad; maldod

indulgent *adj* ffafriol, maldodus

industrial *adj* diwydiannol, gweithfaol

industrialize *vb* diwydianu

industrious *adj* diwyd, dyfal, gweithgar

industry *n* diwydrwydd; diwydiant

inebriate *vt* meddwi ♦ *n* meddwyn

inedible *adj* anfwytadwy

ineffable *adj* anhraethol, anhraethadwy

ineffective *adj* aneffeithiol

inefficiency *n* anallu

inefficient *adj* analluog

ineligible *adj* anghymwys

inept *adj* heb fod yn taro, gwrthun, gwirion

inequality *n* anghysondeb

inert *adj* swrth, diynni, diegni

inertia *n* anegni, inertia

inestimable *adj* amhrisiadwy

inevitable *adj* anochel, anesgorol

inexhaustible *adj* dihysbydd

inexorable *adj* di-ildio, anhyblyg

inexpensive *adj* rhad

inexperience *n* diffyg profiad

inexperienced *adj* amhrofiadol, dibrofiad

infallible *adj* anffaeledig

infallibility *n* anffaeledigrwydd

infamous *adj* gwaradwyddus, gwarthus

infancy *n* mabandod, mebyd, maboed

infant *n* maban, baban; un dan oed

infantry *n* gwŷr traed, milwyr traed

infatuate *vt* gwirioni, ffoli, dwlu

infatuated *adj* wedi ffoli, wedi gwirioni

infect *vt* heintio, llygru

infection *n* haint

infectious *adj* heintus

infer *vt* casglu

inferior *adj* is, israddol ♦ *n* isradd

inferiority *n* israddoldeb

inferiority complex *n* cymhleth y

taeog
infernal *adj* uffernol, dieflig
infertile *adj* anffrwythlon
infertility *n* anffrwythlondeb
infest *vt* bod yn bla, heigiannu
infidel *n* anffyddiwr
infidelity *n* anffyddlondeb
infield *adj* mewnfaes
infinite *adj* anfeidrol
infinitesimal *adj* anfeidrol fach, gorfychan
infinitive *adj* annherfynol ♦ *n* berfenw
infirm *adj* egwan, gwan, gwanllyd
infirmary *n* ysbyty, clafdy
infirmity *n* gwendid, llesgedd
inflame *vb* ennyn, cyffroi, llidio
inflamed *adj* llidus
inflammable *adj* hylosg, hyfflam
inflammation *n* enyniad, enynfa, llid
inflatable *adj* y gellir ei chwyddo neu ei chwythu
inflate *vt* chwyddo
inflation *n* chwyddiant
inflect *vt* ffurfdroi; treiglo
inflexible *adj* anhyblyg
inflexibility *n* anhyblygrwydd
inflict *vt* peri, gweinyddu (cosb, poen, *etc*)
influence *n* dylanwad ♦ *vt* dylanwadu
influenza *n* ffliw
influx *n* dylifiad
inform *vb* hysbysu
informal *adj* anffurfiol
information *n* gwybodaeth, hysbysrwydd
infra- *prefix* is-
infra-red *adj* is-goch
infrastructure *n* seilwaith
infrequent *adj* anaml
infringe *vt* torri, troseddu
infuriate *vt* ffyrnigo, cynddeiriogi
infuse *vt* tywallt, arllwys; trwytho
infusion *n* trwyth, hydreiddiad
ingenious *adj* medrus, cywrain,

celfydd
ingenuous *adj* didwyll, diddichell
ingenuousness *n* didwylledd, diffuantrwydd
ingrained *adj* wedi greddfu; cynhenid
ingratiate *vt* ennill ffafr
ingratitude *n* anniolchgarwch
ingredients *npl* cynhwysion, defnyddiau
inhabit *vt* cyfaneddu, trigo, preswylio
inhabitable *adj* cyfannedd, trigadwy
inhabitant *n* preswyliwr
inhale *vt* anadlu
inhere *vi* glynu, ymlynu, bod
inherent *adj* cynhenid, greddfol
inherit *vt* etifeddu
inheritance *n* etifeddiaeth
inheritor *n* etifedd, etifeddwr
inhibit *vt* gwahardd, atal
inhibition *n* ataliad, atalnwyd
inhibitor *n* atalydd
inhuman *adj* annynol, creulon
inimical *adj* gelyniaethus
inimitable *adj* digyffelyb
iniquitous *adj* drwg, traws
iniquity *n* anwiredd, camwedd
initial *adj* dechreuol ♦ *n* llythyren gyntaf
initiate *vt* egwyddori; derbyn; dechrau
initiative *n* cynhoredd, menter
inject *vt* chwistrellu
injection *n* chwistrelliad, pigiad
injunction *n* gorchymyn, gwaharddiad
injure *vt* niweidio, anafu
injury *n* niwed, cam, anaf
injustice *n* anghyfiawnder, cam
ink *n* inc ♦ *vt* incio
inkling *n* awgrym, arwydd
inland *adj* canoldirol ♦ *n* canoldir.
I. Revenue *n* Cyllid y Wlad
inlet *n* cilfach, bae
inmate *n* trigiannydd, preswylydd

inmost adj nesaf i mewn, dyfnaf

inn n tafarn, tafarndy, gwesty

innate adj cynhenid, cynhwynol, greddfol

inner adj mewnol

innings npl batiad

innkeeper n tafarnwr

innocence n diniweidrwydd

innocent adj diniwed, gwirion, dieuog

innocuous adj diniwed, diberygl

innovate vi newid, cyflwyno

innovation n newyddbeth

innuendo n ensyniad

innumerable adj aneirif, afrifed, dirifedi, di-rif

inoculate vt brechu

inoculation n brechiad

inoffensive adj di-ddrwg

inordinate adj anghymedrol, di-rôl

inorganic adj anorganig

input n mewnbwn, cyfraniad

inquest n cwest; trengholiad

inquire vb ymofyn, ymholi, gofyn, holi

inquiry n ymholiad

inquisition n ymchwiliad; chwillys

inquisitive adj ymofyngar, holgar

in-road n cyrch

insane adj gwallgof, gorffwyll, ynfyd

insanitary adj aflachus, brwnt

insatiable adj anniwall

inscribe vt arysgrifio

inscription n arysgrif

inscrutable adj anolrheiniadwy, anchwiliadwy

insect n pryf, trychfil

insensibility n dideimladrwydd

insensible adj dideimlad

insert vb mewnosod

in-service adj mewn swydd

inside n tu mewn ♦ adj mewnol ♦ prep y tu mewn i ♦ adv i mewn, o fewn

inside-forward n mewnwr

inside-half n mewnwr

inside-out adv o chwith

inside-right n mewnwr de

insidious adj llechwraidd

insight n mewnwelediad

insignificance n dinodedd

insignificant adj di-nod, distadl, dibwys

insincere adj annidwyll, ffuantus, rhagrithiol

insincerity n annidwylledd

insinuate vb ensynio

insipid adj diflas, merfaidd

insist vi mynnu

insolence n haerllugrwydd

insolent adj haerllug

insolvent adj methdalus, wedi torri

insomnia n anhunedd

inspect vt arolygu, archwilio

inspector n arolygwr

inspiration n ysbrydoliaeth

inspire vb ysbrydoli

instability n ansadrwydd

install vt sefydlu, gorseddu

instalment n cyfran, rhandal

instance n enghraifft ♦ vt enwi, nodi

instant adj taer, ebrwydd ♦ n eiliad, moment. i. coffee n coffi powdr

instantaneous adj yn y fan; disymwth

instantly adv ar drwiad

instead adv yn lle

instep n mwnwgl troed, cefn troed

instigate vt annog, cymell

instil vt argymell

instinct n greddf

institute n athrofa

institution n sefydliad

instruct vt hyfforddi

instruction n hyfforddiant

instructor n hyfforddwr

instrument n offeryn

insubordinate adj anufudd, gwrthryfelgar

insufferable adj annioddefol

insufficient adj annigonol

insular adj ynysol, cul

insulate vt ynysu, inswleiddio

insult vt sarhau ♦ n sarhad

insuperable adj anorfod, anorchfygol

insurance n yswiriant. **i. policy** n polisi yswiriant

insure vb yswirio

insurgent adj gwrthryfelgar ♦ n gwrthryfelwr

insurrection n terfysg, gwrthryfel

intact adj cyfan, dianaf

integral adj cyfan, cyflawn

integrate vb cyfannu

integrity n cywirdeb, gonestrwydd

intellect n deall

intellectual n deallusyn ♦ adj deallus, deallgar

intelligence n deallgarwch, deallusrwydd; hysbysrwydd

intelligent adj deallus

intelligible adj dealladwy

intend vt bwriadu, amcanu, golygu

intense adj angerddol, dwys

intensive care unit n uned ofal arbennig

intent adj dyfal, diwyd, astud

intent n bwriad, amcan; ystyr; diben

intention n bwriad

intentional adj bwriadol

inter vt claddu, daearu

inter- prefix rhwng, cyd

interaction n rhyngweithiad

interbreed vb rhyngfridio

intercede vi cyfryngu, eiriol

intercept vt rhyng-gipio, rhwystro, rhagod

intercession n cyfryngdod, eiriolaeth

interchange vt cyfnewid, ymgyfnewid

intercourse n cyfathrach

interdict vt gwahardd ♦ n gwaharddiad

interest n budd, buddiant; diddordeb; llog ♦ vt diddori

interested adj â chanddo ddidordeb

interesting adj diddorol

interests npl diddordebau

interface n cydwyneb

interfere vi cyfryngu, ymyrryd, ymhél

interference n ymyrraeth

interim adj dros dro ♦ n cyfamser

interior adj mewnol ♦ n tu mewn, canol, perfeddwlad

interject vt ebychu

interlock vb cyd-gloi

interloper n ymwthiwr, ymyrrwr

interlude n egwyl; anterliwt

intermediary n canolwr, cyfryngwr

intermediate adj canol, canolradd

intern vt carcharu

internal adj mewnol

international adj cydwladol, rhyngwladol

interpolate vt dodi i mewn, rhyngosod

interpolation n rhyngosodiad

interpose vb gosod rhwng, cyfryngu, rhyngwthio

interpret vt dehongli; cyfieithu

interpretation n dehongliad; cyfieithiad

interpreter n lladmerydd, cyfieithydd

interrelation n cydberthynas

interrogate vt holi

interrogative adj gofynnol

interrupt vt torri ar, torri ar draws, ymyrryd

intersect vb croesi ei gilydd; croesdorri

intersection n croesdoriad

intersperse vb gwasgaru, britho

interval n egwyl, saib

intervene vi ymyrryd

interview n cyfweliad ♦ vb cyfweld

intestines npl perfedd, coluddion

intimacy n agosatrwydd
intimate adj cyfarwydd, agos ♦ n cydnabod
intimate vt arwyddo, hysbysu
intimidate vt dychrynu, brawychu
into prep i, i mewn i
intolerable adj annioddefol
intonation n tonyddiaeth, goslef
intone vt llafarganu
intoxicate vt meddwi
intoxication n meddwdod
intractable adj anhydrin, afreolus
intransitive adj cyflawn (gramadeg)
intrepid adj di-ofn, diarswyd, gwrol, dewr
intricate adj dyrys, cymhleth, astrus
intrigue vi, n cynllwyn
intrinsic adj priodol, hanfodol
introduce vt cyflwyno
introduction n cyflwyniad, rhagarweiniad
introductory adj dechreuol, agoriadol, rhagarweiniol
introspection n mewnsylliad
introvert adj mewnblyg
intrude vb ymyrryd
intruder n ymyrrwr, ymwthiwr
intrusion n ymwthiad, ymyrraeth
intuition n sythwelediad
inundate vt gorlifo, boddi
inundation n gorlifiad
inure vt cyfarwyddo, caledu
invade vt goresgyn
invalid adj di-rym, annilys
invalid n un afiach, un methedig
invaluable adj amhrisiadwy
invariable adj gwastad, dieithriad
invariably adv yn ddieithriad
invasion n goresgyniad
invective n difrïaeth, cabledd
invent vt dyfeisio, dychmygu
inventory n rhestr, stocrestr
inverse adj (yn y) gwrthwyneb, yn groes
inversion n gwrthdro

invert vt troi wyneb i waered, gwrthdroi
inverted commas npl dyfynodau
invest vt buddsoddi; arwisgo
investigate vt chwilio, archwilio, ymchwilio
investigation n ymchwiliad
investigator n ymchwiliwr
investiture n arwisgiad
investment n buddsoddiad
investor n buddsoddwr
invidious adj annymunol
invigilate vb arolygu
invigilator n arolygwr, gwyliwr
invigorate vt cryfhau, grymuso
invincible adj anorchfygol
inviolable adj dihalog, cysegredig
invisible adj anweledig, anweladwy
invitation n gwahoddiad
invite vt gwahodd
invoice n anfoneb
involuntary adj o anfodd, anfwriadol
involve vt drysu; cynnwys, ymwneud
involvement n ymwneud, ymglymiad
inward adj mewnol
iodine n iodin
ion n ïon
ionisation n ïoneiddiad
ionise vb ïoneiddio
iota n mymryn, iod, gronyn
ir- prefix di-, an-
Iran n Iran
Iraq n Iraq
irate adj dig, llidiog
Ireland n Iwerddon
iris n enfys; elestr
Irish adj Gwyddelig ♦ n Gwyddeleg
irksome adj blin, trafferthus, diflas
iron n, adj haearn ♦ vt smwddio
ironic adj eironig
ironing board n bwrdd smwddio
ironmonger n gwerthwr nwyddau haearn
irony n eironi

irradiate vt arbelydru
irradiation n arbelydredd
irrational adj direswm, afresymol
irreconcilable adj anghymodion
irrefutable adj anatebadwy
irregular adj afreolaidd
irregularity n afreoleidd-dra
irrelevant adj amherthnasol
irreparable adj anadferadwy
irreproachable adj diargyhoedd, di-fai
irresistible adj anorchfygol
irretrievable adj anadferadwy
irrevocable adj di-alw-yn-ôl
irrigate vt dyfrhau
irritable adj croendenau, anniddig, llidiog
irritate vt blino, poeni, cythruddo
is vi mae, sydd, yw, ydy(w), oes
island, isle n ynys
islet n ynysig
isolate vt neilltuo, gwahanu
isolated adj wedi ei neilltuo, wedi ei wahanu
isolation n neilltuaeth, arwahanrwydd
Israel n Israel
Israelite n Israeliad
issue n llif; agorfa, arllwysfa; hilogaeth, plant; canlyniad, pwnc mewn dadl ♦ vb tarddu, deillio; rhoi allan, cyhoeddi
isthmus n culdir
it pron efe, fe, ef, efo, fo, o; hi
Italian adj Eidalaidd ♦ n Eidalwr; (LING) Eidaleg
italic adj italig
italicize vb italeiddio
italics npl llythrennau italaidd
Italy n Yr Eidal
itch n ysu, cosi ♦ n y crafu, ysfa
item n peth, pwnc, darn, tamaid
iterate vt ailadrodd
itinerant adj teithiol
itinerary n taith, teithlyfr
itinerate vi teithio, cylchdeithio
itself pron ei hun, ei hunan

ivory n ifori
ivy n eiddew, iorwg

J

jab n jab, pigiad ♦ vb procio, gwanu
jabber vi bragawthan, clebran ♦ n clebar
jack n jac
jackass n asyn gwryw; hurtyn
jackdaw n corfran, jac-y-do
jacket n siaced
jade vt blino, lluddedu
jagged adj danheddog, ysgithrog
jail n carchar
jam n jam; tagfa
jam vt jamio, tagu
Jamaica n Jamaica
jangle vi clochdar
janitor n porthor
January n Ionawr
Japan n Nihon, Japán, Siapán
Japanese adj Siapaneaidd ♦ n Siapanead; (LING) Siapaneg
jar n anghytsain; anghydfod ♦ vb rhygnu
jar n jar
jargon n ffregod, bregiaith, jargon
jaundice n y clefyd melyn
jaunt vi gwibio, rhodio ♦ n gwibdaith
jaunty adj llon, bywiog, talog
javelin n picell, gwaywffon
jaw n gên, cern; (pl) safn
jay n sgrech y coed
jazz n jas
jealous adj eiddigus, cenfigennus, gwenwynllyd
jealousy n cenfigen, eiddigedd
jeans n jîns
jeep n jîp
jeer vb gwawdio, gwatwar
jelly n jeli
jellyfish n slefen fôr
jeopardy n perygl, enbydrwydd

jerk n plwc, ysgytiad ♦ vb plycio, ysgytio

jerkin n siercyn, siaced

jersey n siersi

Jerusalem n Caersalem, Jerwsalem

jest n cellwair, ysmaldod ♦ vi cellwair, ysmalio

Jesus n Iesu

jet n ffrwd, jet; muchudd ♦ vb ffrydio, pistyllio

jettison vt taflu (llwyth) dros y bwrdd

jetty n jeti, glanfa

Jew n Iddew

jewel n gem, tlws

jeweller n gemydd

jewellery n gemwaith, gemau

Jewish adj Iddewig

jib n hwyl flaen llong, jib

jib vi nogio, strancio

jig n dawns fywiog, jig

jig-saw n jig-so

jilt vt siomi cariad

jingle n rhigwm, tinc ♦ vb tincial

job n tasg, gorchwyl, gwaith

Job Centre n Canolfan Gwaith

jobless adj diwaith

jockey n joci

jocose adj cellweirus, direidus, ysmala

jocular adj ffraeth, ysmala

jog vb loncian

jogger n lonciwr

join vb cydio, cysylltu, uno, ymuno, asio

joiner n asiedydd, saer coed

joint n cyswllt, cymal ♦ adj cyd. **j. of meat** darn o gig

joist n dist, trawst

joke n cellwair, maldod ♦ vb cellwair, ysmalio

jolly adj braf, difyr, llawen

jolt n ysgytiad ♦ vb ysgytio

Jordan n Iorddonen

jostle n hergwd ♦ vb gwthio

jot n iod, tipyn ♦ vt nodi

jotter n nodlyfr

journal n newyddiadur

journalism n newyddiaduraeth

journalist n newyddiadurwr

journey n taith, siwrnai ♦ vt teithio

jovial adj llon, llawen

joy n llawenydd, gorfoledd

joyful adj llon, llawen, gorfoleddus

J.P. Gwêl **justice of the peace**

jubilant adj gorfoleddus

jubilee n jiwbili

Judaism n Iddewaeth

judge n barnwr, beirniad ♦ vb barnu, beirniadu

judg(e)ment n barn, brawd, dyfarniad; dedfryd

judicial adj barnwrol, ynadol

judiciary n barnwyr gwlad, barnwriaeth

judicious adj call, synhwyrol, doeth

jug n jwg

juggle vb siwglo

juggler n siwglwr

juice n sug, sugn, sudd, nodd

juicy adj llawn sudd

July n Gorffennaf

jumble vb cymysgu, cyboli ♦ n cymysgfa, cybolfa

jumble sale n ffair sborion

jump vb neidio, llamu ♦ n naid, llam

jumper n neidiwr; siwmper

jumpy adj ofnus

junction n cydiad; uniad; cyffordd

juncture n cyfwng, cyswllt

June n Mehefin

jungle n jyngl, coedwig; drysi

junior adj iau, ieuengach; ieuaf. **j. school** n ysgol iau

junk n sothach

jurisdiction n awdurdod

juror, juryman n rheithiwr

jury n rheithgor

just adj cyfiawn, uniawn, teg ♦ adv yn union; prin, braidd; newydd. **j. now** gynnau(fach)

justice n cyfiawnder; ynad, ustus.
  j. of the peace n ynad heddwch
justify vt cyfiawnhau
jut vi taflu allan, ymwthio
juvenile adj ieuanc

K

kale n cêl, celys
kangaroo n cangarŵ
keel n gwaelod llong, trumbren,
  cilbren
keen adj craff, llym, awchus, brwd
keep vb cadw, cynnal ♦ n cadw;
  amddiffynfa
keeper n ceidwad
keepsake n cofrodd
kennel n cenel, cwb ci, cwt ci
kerb n cwrbyn
kerchief n cadach, neisied, hances,
  macyn
kernel n cnewyllyn
kestrel n cudyll
kettle n tegell
kettle-drum n tympan
key n agoriad, allwedd; cywair. **k.
  ring,** n cylch allweddi. **k. worker** n
  gweithiwr allweddol
keyboard n allweddell
keyhole n twll clo
khaki n, adj. k. caci
kick vb cicio, gwingo ♦ n cic
kid n myn; hogyn, plentyn, crwt
kidnap vt herwgipio
kidney n aren. **k. beans** npl ffa
  dringo, cidnebêns
kill vt lladd
killer n lladdwr
killing n lladd
kiln n odyn
kilo n cilo
kilogram n cilogram
kilometre n cilomedr
kilowatt n cilowat
kin n perthynas, tras, carennydd
kind n rhyw, rhywogaeth, math

kind adj caredig
kindergarten n ysgol feithrin
kindle vb ennyn, cynnau
kindly adj caredig, hynaws, tirion
kindness n caredigrwydd
kindred n perthynas; perthynasau
  ♦ adj perthynol
king n brenin
kingdom n teyrnas
kingfisher n glas y dorlan
kink n cinc
kiosk n ciosg, bwth
kipper n ciper, ysgadenyn hallt
  (neu sych)
kirk n eglwys (Albanaidd)
kiss vt cusanu ♦ n cusan
kit n cit, pac
kitchen n cegin. **k. garden** n gardd
  lysiau
kitchenette n cegin fach
kite n barcut
kitten n cath fach ♦ vb bwrw
  cathod
kleptomania n ysfa ladrata
knack n cnac, medr
knacker n prynwr hen geffylau,
  nacer
knapsack n ysgrepan
knave n cnaf, dihiryn
knead vt tylino
knee n glin, pen-lin, pen-glin
kneel vi penlinio
knell n cnul
knickers npl nicers
knife (knives) n cyllell
knight n marchog ♦ vt urddo yn
  farchog
knighthood n urdd farchog
knit vb gwau; clymu
knitting needle n gwaell
knob n cnap, cnwc; dwrn
knock vb cnocio, taro, curo ♦ n
  cnoc, ergyd
knot n cwlwm; cymal, cwgn,
  cainc ♦ vt clymu
know vb gwybod, adnabod
knowing adj gwybodus

knowingly adv yn fwriadol
knowledge n gwybodaeth
knowledgeable adj gwybodus
knuckle n cymal, migwrn, cwgn

L

label n llabed, label ♦ vt llabedu,
enwi
labial adj gwefusol
labialize vb gwefusoli
laboratory n labordy
laborious adj llafurus
labour n llafur; gwewyr esgor ♦ vb
llafurio. **the L. Party** Y Blaid
Lafur. **l. force** n llafurlu
labourer n gweithiwr, labrwr
labyrinth n drysfa
lace n las, les; carrai ♦ vb cau
(esgidiau)
lacerate vt rhwygo, llarpio, dryllio
darnio
lack n eisiau, diffyg, gwall ♦ vb
bod mewn eisiau
lackadaisical adj diynni, llipa
laconic adj byreiriog, byr, cwta
lacquer n lacer ♦ vb lacro
lad n bachgen, hogyn, llanc
ladder n ysgol; rhwyg (mewn
hosan)
lade vt llwytho
ladies npl toiledau merched
ladle n lletwad, llwy
lady n arglwyddes; boneddiges,
bonesig
ladybird n buwch goch gota
lag vi llusgo ar ôl, ymdroi, llercian
lagging n ynysydd, lagin
lagoon n morlyn, lagŵn
lair n gwâl, lloches, ffau
laity n lleygwyr
lake n llyn
lamb n oen ♦ vb bwrw ŵyn, wyna
lame n cloff ♦ vt cloffi
lament vb galaru, cwynfan, cwyno
lamentation n galar, galarnad

laminate adj haenog ♦ vb haenogi,
lamineiddio, laminadu
lamp n lamp, llusern
lampoon n dychangerdd,
gogangerdd ♦ vb dychanu
lamppost n polyn lamp
lampshade n lamplen
lance n gwaywffon, picell ♦ vt
lansio, agor dolur
lance corporal n is-gorpral
land n tir, gwlad ♦ vb tirio, glanio
landing n glaniad, glanio; glanfa;
pen y grisiau
landlady n perchennog llety,
gwraig llety
landlord n meistr tir; lletywr,
tafarnwr
landscape n tirlun
lane n lôn, wtre, beidr
language n iaith. **l. laboratory** n
labordy iaith
languid adj egwan, llesg
languish vi nychu, dihoeni, llesgáu
languor n llesgedd, nychdod
lank adj cul, tenau, main, llipa
lanky adj meindal
lantern n llusern
lap n arffed, glin
lap vb plygu, lapio ♦ n plyg, tro,
cylch
lap vb llepian, lleibio
lapel n llabed
lapse n cwymp, methiant, gwall ♦
vi llithro, cwympo, methu
larceny n lladrad
larch n llarwydden
lard n bloneg ♦ vt blonegu
larder n bwtri, pantri
large adj mawr, helaeth, eang,
maith
largely adv gan mwyaf
lark n ehedydd
lark n sbort, difyrrwch, miri ♦ vi
cellwair, prancio
larva (-ae) n cynrhonyn, larfa
laryngitis n gwddf tost, laringitis
larynx n afalfreuant, bocs llais

lascivious   273   lease

lascivious adj anllad, trythyll, anniwair
lash n llach, fflangell ♦ vb llachio, fflangellu; rhwymo
lass n llances
lasso n dolneraff, lasw ♦ vt dolneraffu
last adj olaf, diwethaf ♦ adv yn olaf, yn ddiwetha. **at l.** o'r diwedd. **l. night** neithiwr. **l. week** yr wythnos ddiwethaf
last vi parhau, para
latch n clicied ♦ vt clicedu
late adj hwyr, diweddar. **l. developers** plant hwyrgynnydd
lately adv yn ddiweddar
latent adj dirgel, cudd
later adv wedyn, eto, yn ddiweddarach
lateral adj ochrol
latest adj diweddaraf
lath n eisen, dellten
lathe n turn
lather n trochion ♦ vb seboni, trochioni; golchi
Latin adj, n Lladin
Latin America n America Ladin
latitude n lledred; penrhyddid
latter adj diwethaf
lattice n dellt, rhwyllwaith
laud vt canmol, clodfori, moli
laudable adj canmoladwy
laugh vb chwerthin ♦ n chwerthiniad
laughable adj chwerthinllyd, digrif
laughing stock n cyff gwawd
laughter n chwerthin
launch vb lansio
launderette n landret, golchdy
laundry n golchdy; dillad golch
laureate adj llawryfog
laurel n llawryf
lavatory n tŷ bach, ymolchfa, ystafell ymolchi
lavender n lafant
lavish adj hael, afradlon, gwastraffus ♦ vb afradu,

gwastraffu
lavishness n haelioni, afradlonedd
law n cyfraith, deddf. **l. and order** cyfraith a threfn. **l. of the land** cyfraith gwlad
lawful adj cyfreithlon
lawgiver adj deddfroddwr
lawless adj digyfraith
lawlessness n anghyfraith
lawn n lawnt, llannerch. **l. tennis** n tenis (lawnt)
lawnmower n peiriant torri porfa
lawsuit n cyngaws, cyfraith
lawyer n cyfreithiwr, twrnai
lax adj llac, esgeulus, diofal
laxative n carthlyn
lay n cân, cerdd
lay vt gosod, dodi; dodwy
lay adj lleyg
layby n gorffwysfan
layer n haen
laze vb diogi, segura
laziness n diogi
lazy adj diog, dioglyd
lea n doldir, dôl
lead n plwm
lead vb arwain, tywys ♦ n blaenoriaeth
leader n arweinydd; erthygl flaen
leadership n arweinyddiaeth
leaf (**leaves**) n deilen, dalen
leaflet n taflen
league n cynghrair ♦ vi cynghreirio
leak n agen, coll ♦ vi gollwng, diferu, colli
lean adj main, tenau, cul ♦ n cig coch
lean vb pwyso, gogwyddo
leap vb neidio, llamu ♦ n naid, llam. **l. year** n blwyddyn naid
leapfrog n chwarae naid
learn vb dysgu
learned adj dysgedig, hyddysg
learner n dysgwr
learning n dysg, dysgeidiaeth
lease n prydles ♦ vt prydlesu

leasehold n prydles
leash n cynllyfan, tennyn ♦ vt cynllyfanu
least adj lleiaf. **at l.** o leiaf
leather n lledr
leave n cennad, caniatâd
leave vb gadael, ymadael
leaven n lefain ♦ vt lefeinio
Lebanon n Libanus
lecherous adj trythyll, anllad
lechery n trythyllwch, anlladrwydd
lectern n darllenfa
lecture n darlith ♦ vb darlithio
lecturer n darlithydd
ledge n silff, ysgafell; crib
ledger n llyfr cyfrifon
lee n ochr gysgodol, cysgod gwynt
leech n gelen
leek n cenhinen
leer vi cilwenu
lees npl gwaddod, gwaelodion
left adj aswy, chwith
left-handed adj llawchwith
left-handedness n llawchwithedd
left luggage n lle cadw bagiau
leg n coes
legacy n etifeddiaeth, cymynrodd
legal adj cyfreithiol, cyfreithlon
legalize vb cyfreithloni
legation n llysgenhadaeth
legend n chwedl
legible adj darllenadwy, eglur
legion n lleng, llu
legislate vi deddfu
legislation n deddfwriaeth
legislative adj deddfwriaethol
legitimate adj cyfreithlon
leisure n hamdden
leisurely adj hamddenol
lemon n lemwn
lemonade n diod lemwn, lemonêd
lend vt benthyca, rhoi benthyg
length n hyd, meithder
lengthen vb estyn, hwyhau
lengthy adj hir, maith
leniency n tiriondeb, tynerwch
lens n lens. **concave l.** lens

ceugrwm. **convex l.** lens amgrwm
Lent n y Grawys
lentil n corbysen, lentil
leonine adj llewaidd
leopard n llewpart
leper n dyn gwahanglwyfus, gwahanglaf
leprosy n gwahanglwyf
less adj, adv llai
lessee n prydlesai
lessen vb lleihau
lesson n gwers; llith
lest conj rhag, rhag ofn, fel na
let vt gadael, goddef; gollwng; gosod, rhentu
lethal adj marwol, angheuol
lethargy n cysgadrwydd, syrthni
letter n llythyren; llythyr
letterbox n bocs llythyrau
lettering n llythreniad
lettuce n letysen
level n, adj lefel, gwastad ♦ vt lefelu, gwastatáu. **spirit l.** n lefelydd
level crossing n croesfan
level-headed adj pwyllog
lever n trosol
leveret n ysgyfarnog ieuanc, lefren
Levite n Lefiad
levity n ysgafnder, gwamalrwydd
levy vt codi, trethu ♦ n treth
lewd adj anllad, anweddus
lexicographer n geiriadurwr
lexicon n geiriadur
liability n cyfrifoldeb, rhwymedigaeth
liable adj atebol
liaison n cyswllt
liar n gŵr celwyddog, celwyddgi
libel n athrod, enllib ♦ vt athrodi, enllibio
liberal adj hael, rhyddfrydig, rhyddfrydol ♦ n rhyddfrydwr
liberate vt rhyddhau
liberation n rhyddhad
liberty n rhyddid
librarian n llyfrgellydd

library n llyfrgell
Libya n Libya
licence n trwydded; penrhyddid.
driving l. n trwydded yrru
license vt trwyddedu
licensed adj trwyddedig
licentious adj penrhyd, ofer,
anllad
lick vt llyfu, llyo; curo
lid n caead, clawr
lie n celwydd, anwiredd ♦ vi dweud
celwydd
lie vi gorwedd
liege adj ffyddlon, ufudd
lieutenant n is-gapten; rhaglaw
life (lives) n bywyd, einioes, oes,
buchedd, hoedl
lifebelt n nofdorch, gwregys achub
lifeboat n bad achub
lifeguard n achubwr
life insurance n yswiriant bywyd
life jacket n siaced achub
lifeless adj difywyd, marw(aidd)
lifetime n oes, einioes, hoedl
lift vt codi, dyrchafu ♦ n codiad;
lifft
ligament n giewyn, gewyn
light n golau, goleuni ♦ adj golau ♦
vb goleuo, cynnau
light adj ysgafn
light bulb n bwlb golau
lighter n goleuydd, taniwr
light-footed adj ysgafndroed
light-headed adj penchwiban
light-hearted adj ysgafnfryd
lighthouse n goleudy
lightning n mellt, lluched
lightning conductor n cludydd
mellt
lightship n goleulong
like adj tebyg, cyffelyb
like vb caru, hoffi
likeable adj hoffus; dymunol
likelihood n tebygolrwydd
likely adj, adv tebygol, tebyg
liken vt cyffelybu
likeness n tebygrwydd

likewise adv yn gyffelyb, yn yr un
modd
lilac n lelog
lily n lili, alaw
lily-of-the-valley n lili'r
dyffrynnoedd
limb n aelod, cainc
lime n calch
limekiln n odyn galch
limelight n amlygrwydd
limestone n carreg galch
limit n terfyn, ffin ♦ vt cyfyngu
limited adj cyfyngedig
limp adj llipa, ystwyth, hyblyg
limp vi hercian, cloffi
limpet n brenigen, llygad maharen
line n llin, llinell, lein, rhes;
llinach ♦ vt llinellu, rhesu
lineage n ach, llinach
linear adj llinellog, llinellaidd,
llinol, unionlin. **l. equation**
hafaliad llinol
linen n lliain
line-out n lein, llinell
liner n leiner
linesman n llumanwr
linger vb ymdroi, aros
lingo n iaith ddieithr, cleber
linguist n ieithydd
linguistics n ieithyddiaeth
liniment n ennaint, eli
lining n leinin
link n dolen, cyswllt ♦ vb cydio,
cysylltu
linnet n llinos
lino n leino
linseed n had llin, llinad
lintel n capan drws, lintel
lion n llew
lip n gwefus, min, gwefl
lipstick n minlliw
liquid n llyn, hylif ♦ adj gwlyb,
hylif
liquidate vb talu, clirio (dyled),
dirwyn i ben, diddymu, dileu
liquidize vb hylifo
liquor n diod, gwirod

lisp *n* bloesgni ♦ *vb* siarad yn floesg

list *n* rhestr, llechres ♦ *vt* rhestru

list *n* gogwydd, goledd ♦ *vi* pwyso, gwyro, gogwyddo

listen *vi* gwrando

listener *n* gwrandawr

listless *adj* llesg, diynni

listlessness *n* llesgedd

litany *n* litani

literacy *n* llythrennedd

literal *adj* llythrennol

literary *adj* llenyddol

literature *n* llenyddiaeth

lithe, lithesome *adj* ystwyth, hyblyg

lithograph *n* lithograff

litigate *vb* cyfreithio

litmus *n* litmws

litre *n* litr

litter *n* elorwely; ysbwriel, gwasarn; torllwyth, tor

little *adj* bach, bychan; mân, ychydig ♦ *n* ychydig, tipyn

liturgy *n* litwrgi

live *adj* byw, bywiol, bywiog

live *vi* byw

livelihood *n* bywoliaeth

livelong *adj* maith, hirfaith

lively *adj* bywiog, hoyw, heini, sionc

liven *vb* bywiogi

liver *n* iau, afu

livery *n* lifrai

living *n* bywoliaeth; personiaeth

lizard *n* madfall, modrchwilen

load *n* llwyth ♦ *vb* llwytho

loaf (loaves) *n* torth

loaf *vb* ystelcian, sefyllian, diogi

loafer *n* diogyn, segurwr

loam *n* tywotglai, marl, priddglai

loan *n* benthyg, benthyciad

loath, loth *adj* anewyllysgar, anfodlon

loathe *vt* ffieiddio, casáu

loathsome *adj* atgas, ffiaidd

lobby *n* cyntedd, porth, lobi

lobster *n* cimwch

local *adj* lleol. **l. government** *n* llywodraeth leol

locality *n* lle, safle, ardal, cymdogaeth

locate *vt* lleoli, sefydlu, gosod

location *n* lleoliad

loch *n* llyn

lock *n* clo; llifddor ♦ *vb* cloi, cau

lock *n* cudyn; (*pl*) gwallt

locked *adj* ar glo, ynghlo, dan glo

locker *n* cwpwrdd clo

locomotion *n* ymsymudiad

locomotive *adj* ymsymudol ♦ *n* peiriant rheilffordd

locust *n* locust

lodge *n* lluest, llety; cyfrinfa ♦ *vb* lletya

lodger *n* lletywr

lodging *n*, **lodgings** *npl* llety

loft *n* taflod, llofft

lofty *adj* uchel, aruchel, dyrchafedig

log *n* cyff, boncyff, pren

loggerheads *npl* benben

logic *n* rhesymeg

logical *adj* rhesymegol

loin *n* llwyn, lwyn

loiter *vi* ymdroi, loetran, sefyllian

loll *vi* gorweddian, diogi

lollipop *n* lolipop

London *n* Llundain

loneliness *n* unigrwydd

lonely *adj* unig

long *adj*, *adv* hir, maith, llaes

long *vi* hiraethu, dyheu

longevity *n* hirhoedledd, hiroes

long-headed *adj* call, hirben

longing *n* hireath, dyhead

longitude *n* hydred

longitudinal *adj* hydredol

long sight *n* golwg hir

long-suffering *adj* hirymarhous ♦ *n* hirymaros

long-term *adj* yn y tymor hir

long-winded *adj* hirwyntog

look *vb* edrych, syllu ♦ *n*

edrychiad, golwg
looking-glass *n* drych
lookout *n* gwyliwr
loom *n* gwŷdd
loom *vi* ymrithio, ymddangos
loon *n* gwirionyn, dihiryn
loop *n* dolen ♦ *vb* dolennu
loophole *n* dihangdwll
loose *adj* rhydd, llac ♦ *vt* gollwng
loosen *vb* rhyddhau, llacio
loot *n* anrhaith, ysbail ♦ *vb*
ysbeilio, anrheithio
looter *n* ysbeiliwr, anrheithiwr
lop *vt* tocio
lopsided *adj* unochrog,
anghymesur, anghyfartal
lord *n* arglwydd ♦ *vb*
arglwyddiaethu
lord mayor *n* arglwydd faer
lordship *n* arglwyddiaeth
lore *n* dysg, llên, traddodiad
lorry *n* lori. **l. driver** *n* gyrrwr lori
lose *vb* colli
loss *n* colled
lost property office *n* swyddfa
eiddo coll
lot *n* coelbren, rhan, tynged. **a l.**
llawer
lotion *n* golchdrwyth, eli
lottery *n* hapchwarae, raffl
lotus *n* alaw'r dŵr
loud *adj* uchel, croch. **l. speaker** *n*
corn siarad
lounge *n* lolfa ♦ *vi* segura,
gorweddian
louse (**lice**) *n* lleuen
lousy *adj* lleuog, brwnt
lout *n* lleban, llabwst, delff
love *n* cariad, serch ♦ *vt* caru
loveliness *n* prydferthwch
lovely *adj* hawddgar, teg, hyfryd
lover *n* cariad, carwr
loving *adj* cariadus, serchog
loving-kindness *n* trugaredd,
cariad
low *adj* isel
low *vi* brefu ♦ *n* bref (buwch)

lower *vb* gostwng, darostwng, iselu
lower *vi* gwgu, duo, hel cymylau
lowliness *n* gostyngeiddrwydd
lowly *adj* isel, iselfrydig,
gostyngedig
low tide *n* llanw isel; trai
low water *n* trai, distyll
loyal *adj* teyrngar
loyalty *n* teyrngarwch, ffyddlondeb
lozenge *n* losin
lubricate *vt* iro, llithrigo, seimio
lucid *adj* eglur, clir
luck *n* lwc, damwain, hap, ffawd
lucky *adj* ffodus, lwcus
ludicrous *adj* chwerthinllyd,
gwrthun
lug *vb* llusgo, tynnu
luggage *n* clud, bagiau, celfi
luggage rack *n* silff eiddo
lukewarm *adj* claear, llugoer
lull *vt* suo, gostegu ♦ *n* gosteg
lullaby *n* hwiangerdd
lumbago *n* llwynwst
lumber *n* llanastr, anialwch
lumber *vb* pentyrru; llusgo
luminous *adj* golau, disglair,
llachar
lump *n* lwmp, clamp, clap, talp. **l.
sum** cyfandaliad
lunacy *n* lloerigrwydd,
gwallgofrwydd
lunatic *n* lloerig, gwallgofddyn
lunch *vb* ciniawa (ganol dydd)
lunch, luncheon *n* byrbryd, cinio
canol dydd
lung *n* ysgyfaint
lunge *n* hergwd, gwth, rhuthr
lurch *n* cyfyngder, dryswch, trybini
♦ *vi* gwegian
lure *n* hud ♦ *vt* hudo, denu
lurid *adj* erchyll, erchliw,
fflamgoch
lurk *vi* llercian, llechu
luscious *adj* melys
lush *adj* toreithiog, ffrwythlon
lust *n* chwant, trachwant ♦ *vi*
trachwantu

lustre n gloywder, disgleirdeb, llewyrch
lusty adj heini, cryf, pybyr, grymus
Luxembourg n Luxembourg
luxuriant adj toreithiog, bras, ffrwythlon
luxurious adj moethus
luxury n moeth, moethusrwydd, amheuthun
lying adj celwyddog
lyre n telyn gron
lyric adj telynegol ♦ n telyneg

M

mace n brysgyll, byrllysg
macerate vb meddalu, mwydo; nychu, curio
machine n peiriant
machinery n peiriannau
mackerel n macrell
mackintosh n cot law
mad adj cynddeiriog, gwallgof, gwyllt, ynfyd
madden vb gwallgofi, ffyrnigo
made-to-measure adj wedi ei dorri gan deiliwr
madman n ynfytyn, gwallgofddyn
madness n ynfydrwydd, gwallgofrwydd
madrigal n madrigal
magazine n ystorfa, arfdy; cylchgrawn
maggot n cynrhonyn
magic adj cyfareddol ♦ n hud, dewiniaeth, swyngyfaredd
magician n swynwr, dewin
magistrate n ynad
magnanimous adj mawrfrydig
magnet n magned
magnetic adj magnetig
magnificent adj gwych, ysblennydd
magnify vt mawrhau, mwyhau, chwyddo

magnifying-glass n chwyddwydr
magnitude n maint, maintioli
magpie n pi, pia, pioden, piogen
maid n merch, morwyn
maiden name n enw morwynol
mail n y post
mail n arfwisg
maim vt anafu, anffurfio, llurgunio
main n prif bibell; prif gebl; cefnfor. **in the m.** yn bennaf, gan mwyaf
main adj pennaf, prif, mwyaf. **m. road** n priffordd, ffordd fawr
mainland n y tir mawr
mainly adv yn bennaf
mainstay n prif gynhaliaeth
maintain vt dal, cynnal, maentumio
maintenance n cynhaliaeth, gofalaeth
maize n indrawn, injan corn
majesty n mawrhydi, mawredd
majestic adj mawreddog, urddasol
major adj mwy, mwyaf, pennaf ♦ n uwchgapten
majority n mwyafrif; oedran llawn
make vt gwneud, gwneuthur, peri ♦ n gwneuthuriad
maker n gwneuthurwr, creawdwr
making n gwneuthuriad, ffurfiad
make-up n colur
malady n drwg, anhwyldeb, dolur
male n, adj gwryw
malevolence n malais
malevolent adj drygnaws, maleisus
malformation n camffurfiad
malice n malais
malign vt enllibio, difrïo, pardduo
malignant adj llidiog, adwythig, gwyllt
mallet n gordd
malnutrition n gwallfaethiad, camluniaeth
malt n brag ♦ vb bragu
maltreat vb cam-drin
maltreatment n camdriniaeth

mammal n mamal
mammoth n mamoth ♦ adj anferth
man (men) n dyn, gŵr
manacle n gefyn ♦ vt gefynnu
manage vb trin, llywodraethu, rheoli; ymdaro, ymdopi, llwyddo
manageable adj hydrin
management n rheolaeth, goruchwyliaeth
manager n goruchwyliwr, rheolwr
mandate n gorchymyn, arch
mane n mwng
mange n clafr, clefri, brech y cŵn
manger n mansier, preseb
mangle vt llurgunio
mangle n mangl
manhood n dyndod
mania n gwallgofrwydd, gorawydd
maniac n gwallgofddyn
manifest adj amlwg ♦ vt amlygu, dangos
manifesto n datganiad, maniffesto
manifold adj amryw, amrywiol
manipulate vt trin, trafod
mankind n dynolryw
manly adj dynol, gwrol
manner n modd; moes
mannerism n dullwedd
mannerly adj boneddigaidd, moesgar
manners npl moesau
manor n maenor, maenol
manse n tŷ gweinidog, mans
manservant n gwas
mansion house n trigfan y maer
manslaughter n dynladdiad
mantelpiece n silff ben tân
mantle n mantell ♦ vt mantellu
manual adj perthynol i'r llaw ♦ n llawlyfr
manufacture n gwaith, nwydd ♦ vt gwneuthur, gwneud
manure n tail, gwrtaith, achles ♦ vt teilo, gwrteithio, achlesu
manuscript n llawysgrif
many adj aml, sawl, llawer. **as m.** cymaint, cynifer. **how m.** sawl

map n map
maple n masarnen
mar vt difetha, andwyo, hagru
maraud vb ysbeilio, anrheithio
marble n marmor, mynor; marblen
March n (mis) Mawrth
march vb ymdeithio ♦ n ymdaith
march n mers, goror, cyffin
marchioness n ardalyddes
mare n caseg
margarine n margarin
margin n ymyl, cwr, goror
marigold n gold Mair, gold
marine adj morol ♦ n môr-filwr; llynges
mariner n morwr, llongwr, mordwywr
marital n priodasol
maritime adj morol, arforol
mark n nod, marc ♦ vt nodi, marcio, craffu, sylwi
market n marchnad ♦ vb marchnata
maroon vb rhoi a gadael ar ynys anial
marquis n ardalydd
marriage n priodas
married adj priod
marrow n mêr. **vegetable m.** n pwmpen
marry vb priodi
Mars n Mawrth
marsh n morfa, cors, mignen
marshal n cadlywydd, marsialydd ♦ vt byddino, trefnu
mart n mart
martial adj milwraidd, milwrol
martinet n disgyblwr llym
martyr n merthyr ♦ vt merthyru
martyrdom n merthyrdod
marvel n rhyfeddod ♦ vi rhyfeddu, synnu
marvellous adj rhyfeddol, gwych
marxism n marcsiaeth
marxist adj marcsaidd
mascara n masgara, colur llygaid

masculine adj gwryw, gwrywaidd

mash n cymysg, stwns ♦ vt stwnsio

mask n mwgwd ♦ vt mygydu, cuddio

mason n saer maen, masiwn, meiswn

mass n pentwr, talp, crynswth, mas; (pl) y werin

mass n offeren

massacre n cyflafan ♦ vt cyflafanu

massive adj anferth

mast n hwylbren

master n meistr, athro, capten (llong) ♦ vt meistroli

masterpiece n campwaith, gorchest

mastery n meistrolaeth, goruchafiaeth

masticate vt cnoi, malu

mastiff n gafaelgi, cystowci, catgi

mat n mat ♦ vt matio, plethu

match n matsen

match n cymar; priodas; ymrysonfa, gêm ♦ vb cystadlu; cyfateb

matchless n digymar, digyffelyb

mate n cymar, cydymaith; mêt ♦ vt cymharu

material adj materol; o bwys ♦ n defnydd

materialism n materoliaeth

maternal adj mamol; o du'r fam

maternity n mamolaeth

mathematics npl mathemateg

matins npl boreol weddi, plygain

matriculate vb ymaelodi mewn prifysgol, matricwleiddio

matrimony n priodas

matron n gwraig briod, meistres, matron, modron

matter n mater; crawn ♦ vi bod o bwys

mattock n caib, matog

mattress n matras

mature adj aeddfed; mewn oed ♦ vb aeddfedu

maturity n aeddfedrwydd

maul vt baeddu, pwyo ♦ n sgarmes

mauve n lliw porffor, piws

maxim n dihareb, gwireb, rheol

maximum n uchafswm, uchafrif, uchafbwynt

May n Mai. **M. Day** n Calan Mai

may n blodau drain gwynion

maybe adv efallai, hwyrach, dichon

mayor n maer

mayoress n maeres

me pron myfi, mi, fi, i; minnau

mead n medd

meadow n dôl, gwaun, gweirglodd

meagre adj cul, tenau, prin, tlodaidd, llwm

meal n blawd

meal n pryd o fwyd

meals on wheels npl pryd ar glud

mean n cyfrwng, modd; canol; cymedr

mean vt meddwl, golygu, bwriadu

mean adj gwael, isel, crintach, iselwael

meander n ystum (afon) ♦ vi dolennu, troelli, ymdroelli

meaning n ystyr, meddwl

meanness n cybydd-dod, crintachrwydd

means npl cyfrwng, modd(ion), cyfoeth. **by all m.** ar bob cyfrif, wrth gwrs

meantime, -while adv yn y cyfamser

measles npl y frech goch

measure vt, n mesur

measurement n mesur, mesuriad

meat n ymborth, bwyd; cig

mechanic n peiriannydd

mechanical adj peiriannol, peirianyddol, mecanyddol

mechanics npl mecaneg

mechanism n peirianwaith

medal n bathodyn, medal

meddle vi ymyrryd, busnesa, ymhél

media *npl* cyfryngau

mediaeval *adj* canoloesol

medial *adj* canol, canolog

mediate *vi* canoli, cyfryngu

medical *adj* meddygol

medicine *n* meddyginiaeth; ffisig, moddion

mediocre *adj* canolig, cyffredin

meditate *vb* myfyrio

meditation *n* myfyrdod

Mediterranean *n*: **the M.** y Môr Canoldir

medium *n* canol; cyfrwng ♦ *adj* canol, canolig

medley *n* cymysgfa, cybolfa; cymysgedd, cadwyn o alawon

meek *adj* llariaidd, addfwyn

meekness *n* addfwynder

meet *vb* cyfarfod, cwrdd ♦ *adj* addas

meeting *n* cyfarfod, cyfarfyddiad

melancholy *adj* prudd, pruddglwyfus ♦ *n* pruddglwyf, y felan

mêlée *n* ymgiprys, ysgarmes

mellifluous *adj* melyslais, melysber

mellow *adj* aeddfed, meddal ♦ *vb* aeddfedu

melody *n* peroriaeth, melodi

melt *vb* toddi, ymdoddi

member *n* aelod. **M. of Parliament** *n* Aelod Seneddol

membership *n* aelodaeth

membrane *n* pilen, croenyn

memento *n* cofarwydd

memoir *n* cofiant

memorable *adj* cofiadwy, bythgofiadwy

memorandum *n* cofnod, cofnodiad

memorial *adj* coffadwriaethol ♦ *n* coffadwriaeth; cofeb; deiseb

memorise *vt* dysgu ar gof

memory *n* cof; coffadwriaeth

menace *n* bygythiad ♦ *vt* bygwth

menagerie *n* milodfa, sioe (siew) anifeiliaid

mend *vb* gwella, cyweirio, trwsio, helpu

mendacity *n* anwiredd, celwydd

mendicant *adj* cardotaidd, cardotyld ♦ *n* cardotyn

menial *adj* gwasaidd, isel ♦ *n* gwas

meningitis *n* llid yr ymennydd

menstruation *n* y misglwyf

mensuration *n* mesureg

mental *adj* meddyliol

mention *vt* crybwyll, sôn ♦ *n* crybwylliad

mentor *n* cynghorwr, cyfarwyddwr

menu *n* bwydlen, arlwy

mercantile *adj* marchnadol, masnachol

mercenary *adj* ariangar, chwannog i elw ♦ *n* huriwr, milwr cyflog

merchandise *n* marsiandiaeth

merchant *n* masnachwr, marsiandwr

merciful *adj* trugarog, tosturiol

mercifully *adv* drwy drugaredd

merciless *adj* didrugaredd

mercuric *adj* mercurig

mercury *n* arian byw, mercwri

mercy *n* trugaredd

mere *adj* unig, pur, moel, noeth, hollol

mere *n* llyn, llwch

merge *vb* soddi, suddo, colli, ymgolli, uno

merger *n* ymsoddiad, cyfuniad, ymdoddiad, uniad

meridian *n* nawn; cyhydedd; anterth

merit *n* haeddiant, teilyngdod ♦ *vt* haeddu, teilyngu

mermaid *n* môr-forwyn

merriment *n* digrifwch, difyrrwch

merry *adj* llawen, llon

merry-go-round *n* ceffylau bach

mesh *n* masgl, magl, rhwydwaith

mess *n* saig; llanastr, annibendod ♦ *vb* bwyta; ymhél; maeddu

message *n* cenadwri, neges

messenger *n* cennad, negesydd

messieurs (Messrs) *npl* meistri

metabolism *n* metaboleg, metabolaeth

metal *n* metel ♦ *adj* metelaidd

metamorphosis (-ses) *n* trawsffurfiad, metamorffosis

metaphor *n* trosiad

metaphysics *n* metaffiseg

mete *vb* mesur

meteor *n* seren wib

meter *n* mesurydd; medr

method *n* trefn, method, dull

meticulous *adj* gorfanwl

metonymy *n* trawsenwad

metre *n* mesur, mydr

metrical *adj* mydryddol

metric system *n* system fedrig

metropolis *n* prifddinas

mettle *n* metel, anian, ysbryd

mew *vi* mewian

Mexico *n* México

miasma *n* tawch heintus

Michaelmas *n* gŵyl Fihangel

microbe *n* trychfilyn, meicrob

micro-chip *n* meicro-sglodyn

microphone *n* meicroffon, meic

microscope *n* chwyddwydr, meicrosgop

microwave *n* meicrodon. **m. oven** ffwrn meicrodon

mid *adj* canol

midday *n* canol dydd, hanner dydd

middle *n, adj* canol

middle-aged *adj* canol oed

middling *adj* canolig, gweddol, symol

midge *n* gwybedyn

midget *n* corrach

midnight *n* canol nos, hanner nos

midriff *n* llengig

midst *n* canol, plith

midsummer *n* canol haf. **M. Day** *n* gŵyl Ifan

midwife (-wives) *n* bydwraig

mien *n* golwg, pryd, gwedd, agwedd

might *n* nerth, cadernid, gallu

mighty *adj* cadarn, galluog, nerthol

migrant *n* mudwr, ymfudwr, crwydrwr ♦ *adj* mudol, crwydrol

migrate *vi* symud, mudo

migration *n* mudiad, ymfudiad

milch *adj* blith, llaethog

mild *adj* tyner, tirion, mwyn; gwan, ysgafn

mildew *n* llwydi, llwydni

mildness *n* tynerwch, tiriondeb, mwynder

mile *n* milltir

mileage *n* milltiredd

milestone *n* carreg filltir

militant *adj* milwriaethus

military *adj* milwrol

militate *vi* milwrio

milk *n* llaeth, llefrith ♦ *vt* godro

milkman *n* dyn llaeth

milkshake *n* ysgytlaeth, llaeth 'di guro

Milky Way *n*: **the M.W.** Y Llwybr Llaethog, Caer Wydion

mill *n* melin ♦ *vt* melino, malu

millennium *n* mil blynyddoedd

miller *n* melinydd

millimetre *n* milimedr

milliner *n* hetwraig

million *n* miliwn

millionaire *n* miliynydd

millstone *n* maen melin

mime *n* meim

mimic *vt* dynwared, gwatwar

mimicry *n* dynwarededd

mince *vt* malu ♦ *n* briwgig, briwfwyd

mind *n* meddwl, bryd, cof ♦ *vb* gofalu, cofio

mine *n* mwynglawdd, pwll

miner *n* mwynwr, glöwr

mineral *adj* mwynol ♦ *n* mwyn

mineral water *n* dŵr pistyll

mingle *vb* cymysgu, britho

mingy *adj* cybyddlyd, crintach

miniature *n* mân ddarlun ♦ *adj* bychan

minimize vt lleihau, bychanu
minimum n lleiafswm, isafrif
mining n mwyngloddiaeth.
　opencast m. n mwyngloddio brig
minister n gweinidog ♦ vb
　gwasanaethu, gweinidogaethu
ministry n gweinidogaeth,
　gweinyddiaeth, gwasanaeth
minnow n pilcodyn, pilcyn, sildyn,
　silcyn
minor adj llai, lleiaf, lleddf; un
　dan oed
minority n maboed, mebyd;
　lleiafrif
minster n mynachlog; eglwys
　gadeiriol
minstrel n clerwr, cerddor
mint n bathdy ♦ vt bathu
mint n mintys
minus adj, pron llai, heb, yn fyr o
　♦ n minws
minute adj bach, bychan, mân;
　manwl
minute n munud; cofnod. **m. book**
　n llyfr cofnodion
minx n coegen, mursen, maeden
miracle n gwyrth
miraculous adj gwyrthiol
mirage n rhithlun, lleurith
mire n lliaid, llaca, tom, baw
mirror n drych ♦ vt adlewyrchu
mirth n llawenydd, digrifwch,
　afiaith
mis- prefix cam-
misadventure n anffawd,
　damwain
misanthropist n dyngasâwr
misapprehension n
　camddealltwriaeth
misbehave vi cymmddwyn
misbehaviour n camymddygiad
miscarriage n erthyliad. **m. of
　justice** n aflwyddo cyflawnder
miscarry vi erthylu; aflwyddo;
　colli
miscellaneous adj amrywiol
mischance n anffawd, damwain

mischief n drwg, drygioni, direidi
mischievous adj drygionus,
　direidus
misconception n camsyniad,
　cam-dyb
misconduct n camymddygiad ♦ vb
　camymddwyn
misdeed n drwgweithred,
　camwedd
misdemeanour n camwedd,
　trosedd
miser n cybydd
miserable adj truenus, gresynus,
　anhapus
misery n trueni, gresyni, adfyd
misfortune n anffawd, aflwydd
misgivings npl amheuon, ofnau
misguide vb camarwain
mishandle vb cam-drin
mishap n anap, anffawd, aflwydd
misinterpret vb camesbonio
misjudge vb camfarnu, camddeall
mislead vb camarwain, twyllo
misnomer n camenw
misprint n cambrint ♦ vb
　camargraffu
misread vb camddarllen
misrepresent vt camddarlunio,
　camliwio
miss vt methu, ffaelu, colli ♦ n
　meth
missal n llyfr offeren
missile n saethyn, tafleryn
missing adj yn eisiau, yngholl, ar
　goll
mission n cenhadaeth
missionary n cenhadwr ♦ adj
　cenhadol
missive n llythyr
misspell vb camsilafu
mist n niwl, nudden; tarth; caddug
mistake vt camgymryd, methu ♦ n
　camgymeriad, gwall
mistletoe n uchelwydd
mistress n meistres; athrawes;
　Mrs
mistrust vt drwgdybio, amau

misty *adj* niwlog

misunderstanding *n* camddealltwriaeth

mite *n* hatling; mymryn, tamaid

mitigate *vt* lleddfu, lliniaru, lleihau

mitre *n* meitr

mix *vb* cymysgu

mixture *n* cymysgedd, cymysgfa

moan *n, vb* ochain, griddfan, udo

moat *n* ffos (castell)

mob *n* torf, tyrfa, haid ♦ *vt* ymosod ar, baeddu

mobile *adj* symudol, symudadwy; mudol (cemeg)

mobilize *vt* dygyfor, byddino

mock *vb* gwatwar ♦ *adj* gau, ffug

mockery *n* gwatwar; ffug

mode *n* modd, dull

model *n* cynllun, patrwm ♦ *vt* llunio

moderate *adj* cymedrol ♦ *vt* cymedroli

moderation *n* cymedroldeb

modern *adj* modern, diweddar

modernize *vb* moderneiddio

modest *adj* gwylaidd; diymhongar

modesty *n* gwylder, gwyleidd-dra

modify *vt* newid, lleddfu

modulate *vb* cyweirio neu reoli llais

moiety *n* hanner, hanereg

moist *adj* llaith, gwlyb

moisture *n* lleithder, gwlybaniaeth, gwlybwr

moisturizer *n* lleithydd

molar *n* cilddant

mole *n* man geni

mole *n* gwadd, twrch daear

mole *n* morglawdd

molecule *n* molecwl ♦ *adj* molecylig

molehill *n* pridd y wadd

molest *vt* molestu, aflonyddu, blino

mollify *vt* meddalu, tyneru, dyhuddo

mollycoddle *vb* maldodi

molten *adj* tawdd

moment *n* moment; pwys, pwysigrwydd

momentum *n* momentwm

monarch *n* brenin, teyrn, penadur

monarchy *n* brenhiniaeth

monastery *n* mynachlog, mynachdy

monastic *adj* mynachaidd

Monday *n* dydd Llun

monetary *adj* ariannol

money *n* arian, pres

mongrel *adj* cymysgryw ♦ *n* mwngrel

monitor *n* monitor

monk *n* mynach

monkey *n* mwnci

mono- *prefix* un-

monogamy *n* unwreigiaeth

monoglot *adj* uniaith ♦ *n* person uniaith

monolith *n* maen hir

monologue *n* ymson

monopoly *n* monopoli

monosyllable *n* gair unsill

monotheism *n* undduwiaeth

monotone *adj, n* unsain, un-dôn

monotonous *adj* undonog

monotony *n* undonedd, unrhywiaeth

monsoon *n* monswn

monster *n* anghenfil; clamp ♦ *adj* anferth

monstrous *adj* angenfilaidd, anferth, gwrthun

month *n* mis

monthly *adj* misol ♦ *n* misolyn

monument *n* cofadail, cofgolofn

mood *n* hwyl, tymer; modd

moody *adj* oriog, cyfnewidiol

moon *n* lleuad, lloer. **harvest m.** *n* lleuad fedi

moonlight *n* golau leuad

moonshine *n* ffiloreg, ffwlbri, lol

moor *n* morfa, rhos, gwaun

moor *vt* angori, bachu, sicrhau

moorhen *n* iâr fach y dŵr

moorland *n* rhostir, gweundir
mop *n* mop ♦ *vt* mopio, sychu
mope *vi* pendrymu, delwi
moraine *n* marian
moral *adj* moesol ♦ *n* moeswers, addysg
morality *n* moesoldeb
morals *npl* moesau
morass *n* cors, mignen
morbid *adj* afiach
mordant *adj* brathog, llym
more *adj* mwy, ychwaneg, rhagor ♦ *adv* mwy, mwyach
moreover *adv* heblaw hynny, hefyd
moribund *adj* ar farw, ar dranc
morning *n* bore ♦ *adj* bore, boreol
Morocco *n* Moroco
morose *adj* sur, sarrug, afrywiog, blwng
morphology *n* ffurfianneg, morffoleg
morrow *n* trannoeth
morsel *n* tamaid, tameidyn
mortal *adj* marwol, angheuol ♦ *n* dyn marwol
mortar *n* cymrwd, morter; breuan, morter
mortgage *n* morgais, arwystl ♦ *vt* morgeisio, arwystlo
mortify *vb* marwhau; blino, siomi
mortise *n* mortais ♦ *vt* morteisio
mortuary *n* marwdy
mosaic *adj* brith, amryliw ♦ *n* brithwaith, mosaig
Moscow *n* Moscow
mosque *n* mosg
moss *n* mwswgl, mwsogl
most *adj* mwyaf, amlaf
mostly *adv* gan mwyaf, fynychaf
mote *n* brycheuyn, llychyn
moth *n* gwyfyn
mother *n* mam. **m.-in-law** *n* mam yng nghyfraith, chwegr
motion *n* symudiad, ysgogiad; cynigiad
motive *adj* symudol, ysgogol ♦ *n*

cymhelliad, amcan, motif
motley *adj* brith, cymysg
motor *n* modur
motor cycle *n* beic modur
motorist *n* modurwr
motorway *n* traffordd
mottle *vt* britho, brychu
motto *n* arwyddair
mould *n* pridd, daear, gweryd ♦ *vt* priddo
mould *n* mold; delw ♦ *vt* moldio, llunio, delweddu
mould *n* llwydni, llwydi
moulder *vi* malurio, adfeilio
moult *vb* bwrw plu, mudo
mound *n* twmpath, clawdd, crug
mount *n* mynydd, bryn
mount *vb* esgyn, dringo, codi, mynd ar gefn; gosod
mountain *n* mynydd
mountaineer *n* mynyddwr
mourn *vb* galaru
mournful *adj* galarus, dolefus, alaethus
mourning *n* galar; galarwisg
mouse (mice) *n* llygoden ♦ *vb* llygota
moustache *n* trawswch, mwstas
mouth *n* genau, safn, ceg ♦ *vb* cegu, safnu
move *vb* symud, syflyd; cymell; cynnig; cyffroi
movement *n* symudiad; ysgogiad
mow *vt* lladd (gwair) ♦ *n* mwdwl, medel
MP *n abbr* AS (aelod seneddol)
much *adj* llawer ♦ *adv* yn fawr
mucilage *n* glud, llys, llysnafedd
muck *n* tail, tom, baw ♦ *vt* tomi, baeddu
mucus *n* llys, llysnafedd
mud *n* mwd, llaid, llaca, baw
muddle *vi* drysu ♦ *n* dryswch
mug *n* cwpan, godart
mulberry *n* morwydden
mule *n* mul, bastart mul
mullion *n* post ffenestr

multi- *prefix* aml, lluosog
multifarious *n* amryfath, lluosog
multiple *adj* amryfal ♦ *n* cynhwysrif, lluosrif
multiplicand *n* lluosrif, lluosyn
multiplication *n* amlhad, lluosogiad, lluosiad
multiplicity *n* lluosogrwydd
multiply *vb* amlhau, lluosogi, lluosi
multi-storey *adj* aml-lawr
multitude *n* lliaws, tyrfa
mumble *vb* grymial, mynglal
mummy *n* mwmi
mumps *n* clwy'r pennau, y dwymyn doben
munch *vt* cnoi
mundane *adj* bydol, daearol
municipal *adj* dinesig, bwrdeisiol
munificent *adj* hael, haelionus
munitions *npl* arfau neu offer rhyfel
mural *adj* murol ♦ *n* murlun
murder *vt* llofruddio ♦ *n* llofruddiaeth
murderer *n* llofrudd
murky *adj* tywyll, cymylog, dudew
murmur *vb, n* murmur, grwgnach
muscle *n* cyhyr, cyhyryn
muscular *adj* cyhyrog
muse *n* awen, awenydd
muse *vi* myfyrio, synfyfyrio
museum *n* amgueddfa
mushroom *n* madarch
music *n* miwsig, cerdd, cerddoriaeth, peroriaeth
musical *adj* cerddorol
musician *n* cerddor
mussel *n* misglen. **mussels** *npl* cregyn gleision
must *vb def* rhaid
mustard *n* mwstart
muster *n* casglu, cynnull, byddino ♦ *n* cynulliad, mwstwr
musty *adj* wedi llwydo, hendrwm, mws
mutable *adj* anwadal, cyfnewidiol
mutate *vb* treiglo (llythrennau)

mutation *n* cyfnewidiad, treiglad
mute *adj* mud ♦ *n* mudan
muteness *n* mudandod
mutilate *vt* anafu, hagru, llurgunio
mutiny *n* terfysg, gwrthryfel
mutter *vb* myngial, grymial, mwmian
mutton *n* cig dafad, cig mollt, cig gwedder
mutual *adj* cyd, o boptu, y naill a'r llall
muzzle *n* genau, ffroen; pennor ♦ *vt* cau safn, rhoi taw ar
my *pron* fy
myriad *n* myrdd
myrmidon *n* anfadwas, dihiryn
myrrh *n* myrr
myrtle *n* myrtwydd
myself *pron* myfi fy hun
mysterious *adj* dirgel, rhyfedd, dirgelaidd
mystery *n* dirgelwch
mystic *n* cyfriniwr, cyfrinydd
mystify *vt* synnu, syfrdanu
myth *n* dameg, chwedl, myth
mythology *n* chwedloniaeth

N

nab *vb* cipio, dal
nadir *n* isafbwynt, ory
nag *vb* cecru, ffraeo, cadw sŵn ♦ *n* ceffyl
nail *n* hoel, hoelen; ewin ♦ *vt* hoelio. **n. file** *n* ffeil/rhathell ewinedd
naïve *adj* diniwed, diddichell, gwirion
naked *adj* noeth
namby-pamby *adj* merf, merfaidd, llipa
name *n* enw ♦ *vt* enwi, galw
namely *adv* sef, nid amgen
namesake *n* cyfenw
nanny *n* nani
nap *vi* cysgu, pendwmpian ♦ *n*

cyntun

nape n gwar, gwegil
napkin n napcyn, cadach, cewyn
nappy n cewyn, clwt
narcotic adj narcotig ♦ n moddion
cwsg
narrate vt adrodd (hanes)
narrative n hanes, chwedl, stori
narrow adj cul, cyfyng ♦ vb
culhau, cyfyngu
nasal adj trwynol
nasty adj cas, brwnt, budr, ffiaidd
natal adj genedigol
nation n cenedl
national adj cenedlaethol
nationalism n cenedlaetholdeb
nationalist n cenedlaetholwr
nationality n cenedl,
cenedligrwydd
nationalization n gwladoliad
nationalize vb gwladoli,
cenedlaetholi
native ♦ n brodor ♦ adj brodorol;
cynhenid
nativity n genedigaeth
natural adj anianol, naturiol
naturalist n naturiaethwr
naturalize vb naturioli, breinio,
cywladu, brodori
nature n anian, natur; naturiaeth
naught n dim
naughtiness n drygioni, direidi
naughty adj drwg, drygionus
nausea n clefyd y môr; cyfog;
ffieidd-dod
nauseous adj cyfoglyd, ffiaidd,
atgas
nautical adj morwrol, mordwyol
naval adj llyngesol, morol
nave n corff eglwys
nave n both, bwl
navel n bogail
navigate vt morio, mordwyo,
llywio
navvy n cloddiwr, ceibiwr
navy n llynges
nay adv na, nage; nid hynny yn

unig

naze n trwyn, penrhyn, pentir
neap adj, n: **n. tide** nêp, llanw isel
near adj, adv, prep agos, ger,
gerllaw ♦ vb agosáu, nesu
nearby adv gerllaw, yn ymyl
nearly adv bron
nearness n agosrwydd
neat adj del, destlus, twt, trefnus;
pur
nebula (-ae) n niwlen; niwl sêr
nebulous adj niwlog
necessarily adv o
angenrheidrwydd
necessary adj angenrheidiol
necessitate vt gorfodi, gwneud yn
angenrheidiol
necessitous adj anghenus, rheidus
necessity n angen, anghenraid,
rhaid
neck n gwddf, mwnwgl, gwar
necklace n mwclis
necromancy n dewiniaeth
nectar n neithdar
need n, vb (bod mewn) angen,
eisiau
needful adj rheidiol, angenrheidiol
needle n nodwydd; gwaell
needlework n gwniadwaith
needless adj afreidiol,
dianghenraid
nefarious adj anfad, drygionus,
ysgeler
negation n nacâd, gwadiad,
negyddiad
negative adj nacaol, negyddol
neglect vt esgeuluso ♦ n
esgeulustra
negligence n esgeulustod
negligent adj esgeulus
negotiate vb trafod, trefnu, negodi
negotiation n trafodaeth, cyd-
drafodaeth
negro n dyn du, negro
neigh vi gweryru ♦ n gweryriad
neighbour n cymydog
neighbourhood n cymdogaeth

neither conj na, nac, ychwaith ♦
adj, pron na'r naill na'r llall, nid
yr un o'r ddau

Nemesis n dialedd

neo- prefix newydd, diweddar

nephew n nai

nepotism n neigaredd

nerve n giewyn, gewyn, nerf ♦ vt
gwroli

nervous adj gieuol; nerfus, ofnus

nest n nyth ♦ vb nythu

nestle vb nythu, gwasgu'n glos at

nestling n aderyn bach, cyw

net n rhwyd, rhwyden

net adj union, cywir, net ♦ vt
rhwydo

netball n pêl rwyd

nether adj isaf

Netherlands npl: **the N.** yr
Iseldiroedd

nettle n danadl ♦ vt pigo; llidio

network n rhwydwaith

neuralgia n gieuwst

neurasthenia n nerfwst

neuritis n newritis

neurosis n newrosis

neuter adj diryw

neutral adj amhleidiol ♦ n
amhleidydd

neutrality n newtraliaeth,
amhleidiaeth

neutralize vt dieffeithio, dirymu

never adv ni ... erioed, ni ... byth

nevertheless adv, conj eto, er
hynny

new adj newydd. **N. Year** n Y
Calan, Y Flwyddyn Newydd. **N.
York** n Efrog Newydd. **N. Zealand**
n Seland Newydd

newcomer n newydd-ddyfodiad

newness n newydd-deb

news n newydd, newyddion, hanes

newsagent n gwerthwr papurau
newyddion

newspaper n papur newydd,
newyddiadur

newt n madfall, genau-goeg,

modrchwilen

next adj nesaf ♦ adv yn nesaf

nib n blaen, nib

nibble vb deintio, cnoi

nice adj neis, hardd, tlws; manwl,
cynnil

niche n cloer, cilfach

nickname n llysenw ♦ vt llysenwi

niece n nith

niggard n cybydd ♦ adj cybyddlyd,
crintach

nigger n dyn du (mewn dirmyg)

nigh adj, adv agos

night n nos; noson, noswaith. **by n.**
liw nos. **dead of n.** cefn nos. **n.
club** n clwb nos

nightdress n gwn nos, coban

nightfall n y cyfnos, yr hwyr

nightingale n eos

nightmare n hunllef

nil n dim

nimble adj gwisgi, heini, sionc

nimbleness n sioncrwydd

nincompoop n penbwl, gwirionyn

nine adj, n naw

nineteen adj, n pedwar (pedair) ar
bymtheg, un deg naw

ninety adj, n deg a phedwar ugain,
naw deg

ninth adj nawfed

nip vb brathu, cnoi; deifio

nipple n diden, teth, tethan

nit n nedden

nitrate n nitrad

nitre n neitr

nitrogen n nitrogen

nitrous adj nitrus

no adj ni ... neb, dim ♦ adv ni, etc
dim; nac oes, nage, naddo

nobility n bonedd, urddas,
mawredd

noble adj ardderchog, urddasol,
pendefigaidd ♦ n pendefig

nobleman n pendefig

nobody n neb

nocturnal adj nosol, gyda'r nos

nod vb amneidio; pendrymu ♦ n

amnaid

noise n swn, twrf, trwst

noisome adj niweidiol, atgas, ffiaidd

noisy adj swnllyd

nomad n nomad, crwydrwr ♦ adj crwydrol

nom de plume n ffugenw

nomenclature n cyfundrefn enwau

nominal adj enwol, mewn enw

nominate vt enwi, enwebu

nomination n enwebiad

nominative adj enwol

non- prefix an-, di-

nonagenarian n un deng mlwydd a phedwar ugain

non-alcoholic adj dialcohol

nonce n: for the n. am y tro

nonchalance n difrawder, difaterwch

nonchalant adj didaro, difater

nonconformist n anghydffurfiwr, ymneilltuwr

nonconformity n anghydffurfiaeth, ymneilltuaeth

nondescript adj anodd ei ddarlunio, od

none pron neb, dim, dim un

nonentity n dyn dibwys, neb

nonplus vt drysu, dymchwelyd

nonsense n lol, dyli, gwirioneb

non-violence n didreisedd

non-violent adj di-drais, didrais

noodle n gwirionyn, ffwlcyn; nwdl

nook n congl, cornel, cilfach

noon n nawn, hanner dydd, canol dydd

noose n clwm rhedeg, magl

nor conj na, nac

normal adj rheolaidd, cyffredin, safonol

normality n normalrwydd

north n gogledd ♦ adj gogleddol. N. Pole n Pegwn y Gogledd. N. Sea n Môr y Gogledd

northern adj gogleddol. N. Ireland n Gogledd Iwerddon

Norway n Norwy

nose n trwyn ♦ vb trwyno, ffroeni, gwyntio

nosebleed n gwaedlif o'r trwyn

nosegay n blodeuglwm, pwysi

nostalgia n hiraeth

nostril n ffroen

not adv na, nac, nad, ni, nid

notable adj nodedig, hynod, enwog

notary n nodiadur, nodiedydd

notation n nodiant

notch n rhic, bwlch, hecyn, rhwgn, rhint

note n nod, nodyn ♦ vt nodi, sylwi

noted adj nodedig, hynod, enwog

note pad n pad ysgrifennu

notepaper n papur ysgrifennu

noteworthy adj nodedig

nothing n dim. n. at all dim byd, dim o gwbl

notice n sylw, rhybudd ♦ vt sylwi

noticeboard n hysbysfwrdd

notify vt hysbysu, rhoi rhybudd

notion n tyb, amcan, syniad

notoriety n enw gwael

notorious adj hynod, carn, rhemp

notwithstanding conj er ♦ prep er, er gwaethaf

nought n dim; gwagnod (0)

noun n enw

nourish vt maethu, meithrin

nourishing adj maethlon

nourishment n maeth

novel adj newydd ♦ n nofel

novelist n nofelydd

November n Tachwedd

novice n newyddian, nofis

now adv, conj n yn awr, yr awron, yrwan, weithian, bellach. just n. gynnau. n. and then yn awr ac yn y man

nowadays adv yn y dyddiau hyn

nowhere adv dim yn unlle

noxious adj niweidiol, afiach

nozzle n ffroenell

nuclear adj niwclear

nucleus n cnewyllyn, bywyn

nude *adj* noeth, noeth lymun
nudge *vt* pwnio, penelino
nugatory *adj* ofer, disylwedd, dirym
nugget *n* clap aur
nuisance *n* pla, poendod, budreddi
null *adj* diddim, dirym, ofer
numb *adj* diffrwyth, cwsg ♦ *vt* fferru, merwino
number *n* nifer, rhif, rhifedi; rhifyn ♦ *vt* rhifo, cyfrif. **n. plate** *n* plat rhif car, plat cofrestru
numeral *n* rhifol, rhifnod
numeration *n* cyfrifiad
numerator *n* rhifiadur
numerical *adj* rhifiadol
numerous *adj* niferog, lluosog, aml
nun *n* lleian, mynaches
nurse *n* mamaeth, gweinyddes, nyrs ♦ *vt* magu, meithrin, nyrsio
nursery *n* magwrfa, meithrinfa
nurture *n* maeth, magwraeth, meithriniad ♦ *vt* maethu, meithrin
nut *n* cneuen; gwain, gweinell
nutcracker *n* gefel gnau
nutriment *n* maeth
nutrition *n* maeth, maethiad
nutritious *adj* maethlon
nutshell *n* plisgyn (masgl) cneuen
nuzzle *vb* trwyno, turio, ymwasgu
nylon *n* neilon

O

oaf *n* delff, hurtyn, awff, llabwst
oak *n* derwen; derw
oakum *n* carth, breisgion
oar *n* rhwyf
oat *n* ceirchen, (*pl*) ceirch
oatcake *n* bara ceirch, teisen geirch
oath *n* llw
oatmeal *n* blawd ceirch
obdurate *adj* caled, cyndyn,

ystyfnig, anhyblyg
obedience *n* ufudd-dod
obedient *adj* ufudd
obese *adj* tew, corffol
obey *vb* ufuddhau
obituary *n* marwgoffa
object *n* gwrthrych; amcan ♦ *vb* gwrthwynebu
objection *n* gwrthwynebiad
objectionable *adj* annymunol
objective *adj* gwrthrychol ♦ *n* amcan, nod
obligation *n* dyled, rhwymau
oblige *vt* rhwymo; boddio; gorfodi
obliging *adj* caredig, cymwynasgar
oblique *adj* lleddf, gŵyr, ar osgo
obliterate *vt* dileu
oblivion *n* angof, ebargofiant
oblong *adj* hirgul ♦ *n* oblong
obnoxious *adj* atgas, ffiaidd
obscene *adj* serth, anllad, anniwair, brwnt
obscure *adj* tywyll; anhysbys ♦ *vt* tywyllu
obsequious *adj* gwasaidd, cynffongar
observation *n* sylw; sylwadaeth
observatory *n* arsyllfa
observe *vb* sylwi, arsyllu; cadw
observer *n* sylwedydd, arsyllwr
obsolete *adj* anarferedig, ansathredig
obstacle *n* rhwystr, atalfa
obstinate *adj* cyndyn, ystyfnig, gwrthnysig
obstreperous *adj* trystiog, afreolus
obstruct *vt* cau, tagu; rhwystro, lluddio
obtain *vt* cael, caffael, ennill
obtrude *vb* gwthio ar, ymwthio
obtrusive *adj* ymwthgar
obtuse *adj* pŵl, di-fin, hurt. **o. angle** ongl aflem
obvious *adj* eglur, amlwg
occasion *n* achlysur ♦ *vt* achlysuro
occasional *adj* achlysurol, anaml

occidental *adj* gorllewinol

occult *adj* cudd, dirgel, cêl, cyfrin

occupation *n* gwaith, galwedigaeth; meddiant

occupy *vt* meddu, meddiannu; llenwi; dal

occur *vi* digwydd; taro i'r meddwl

occurrence *n* digwyddiad

ocean *n* môr, cefnfor, cyfanfor, eigion

o'clock *adv* o'r gloch

octagon *n* wythongl

octave *n* wythawd, octef

octavo *adj* wythblyg ♦ *n* llyfr wythblyg

October *n* Hydref

octogenarian *n* gŵr pedwar ugain mlwydd oed

odd *adj* od, hynod. o. number odrif

odds *npl* ots, gwahaniaeth; mantais

ode *n* awdl

odious *adj* atgas, cas, ffiaidd

odium *n* atgasrwydd; gwaradwydd; bai

odour *n* arogl, aroglau, sawr

of *prep* o; gan; am; ynghylch. o. course *prep* wrth gwrs

off *adv* ymaith, i ffwrdd ♦ *prep* oddi, oddi wrth, oddi ar. o. and on yn awr ac yn y man

offal *n* syrth, gwehilion, perfedd

offence *n* tramgwydd, trosedd, camwedd

offend *vb* tramgwyddo, troseddu, pechu; digio

offender *n* troseddwr

offensive *adj* tramgwyddus, atgas, ffiaidd; ymosodol

offer *vb* cynnig, cyflwyno; offrymu ♦ *n* cynnig

offering *n* offrwm, aberth

office *n* swydd; swyddfa

officer *n* swyddog, swyddwr

official *adj* swyddogol ♦ *n* swyddog

officiate *vi* gweinyddu

officious *adj* ymyrgar, busneslyd

offside *n* camochr, camsefyll ♦ *vb* camochri, camsefyll

offspring *n* hiliogaeth, epil, hil, plant

oft, often *adv* yn aml, yn fynych

ogle *vb* cilwenu, ciledrych

ogre *n* anghenfil, bwystfil, cawr

oh *excl* O!

oil *n* olew, oel ♦ *vt* iro, oelio

oil rig *n* llwyfan olew

ointment *n* ennaint, eli

okay *excl* popeth yn iawn

old *adj* hen, oedrannus. of o. gynt. o. age henaint, henoed. o. and infirm hen a methedig. o.-fashioned *adj* henffasiwn, od. o. stager *n* hen law

olive *n* olewydden

omelette *n* crempog wyau

omen *n* argoel, arwydd, rhagarwydd

ominous *adj* argoelus, bygythiol

omission *n* gwall

omit *vt* gadael allan, esgeuluso

on *prep* ar, ar warthaf ♦ *adv* ymlaen

once *adv* unwaith; gynt

one *adj*, *n* un. o.-way *adj* unffordd (*street, traffic*)

onion *n* wynwynyn, wnionyn

only *adj* unig ♦ *adv* yn unig; ond

onset *n* ymosodiad, cyrch; cychwyn

onslaught *n* ymosodiad, rhuthr, cyrch

onus *n* baich, dyletswydd, cyfrifoldeb

onward *adj*, *adv*, onwards *adv* ymlaen

ooze *n* llaid, llysnafedd ♦ *vi* chwysu

opaque *adj* afloyw, tywyll

open *adj* agored ♦ *vb* agor, ymagor

open-air *n*, *adj* awyr agored

opencast *n* (*coal*) (glo) brig

opening *n* agoriad, agorfa

operate vb gweithredu, gweithio

operation n gweithrediad; gweithred, triniaeth lawfeddygol

operator n gweithredydd, trafodwr

opiate n cysglyn

opinion n tyb, meddwl, barn, opiniwn

opponent n gwrthwynebydd

opportune adj amserol, cyfleus

opportunity n cyfle, egwyl

oppose vt gwrthwynebu, cyferbynnu

opposite adj, adv, prep gwrthwyneb, cyferbyn

opposition n gwrthwynebiad, gwrthblaid

oppress vt gorthrymu, llethu

optician n optegydd

optimism n optimistiaeth

optimist n optimist

option n dewisiad, dewis

or conj neu, ai, ynteu, naill ai

oracle n oracl

oral adj geneuol, llafar, anysgrifenedig

orally adv ar lafar

orange n oren, oraens ♦ adj melyngoch

oration n araith, anerchiad

orator n areithiwr, areithydd

orb n pêl, pelen, pellen; y llygad

orbit n rhod, tro, cylchdro, chwyldro

orchard n perllan

orchestra n cerddorfa

ordain vt ordeinio, urddo

ordeal n prawf llym

order n trefn; gorchymyn, archeb; urdd ♦ vb ordeinio, trefnu, gorchymyn; archebu; urddo. **in o. that** er mwyn

orderly adj trefnus ♦ n gwas milwr

ordinal adj trefnol

ordinarily adv fel rheol

ordinary adj cyffredin, arferol

ordination n ordeiniad, urddiad

ore n mwyn

organ n organ, offeryn

organist n organydd

organization n trefn; cyfundrefn; trefniadaeth

organize vb trefnu

organized adj trefnus. **o. by** trefnwyd gan

organizer n trefnydd

orgy n gloddest, cyfeddach

oriental adj dwyreiniol ♦ n dwyreiniwr

orientate vb cyfeirio

orifice n genau, ceg, agorfa

origin n dechreuad, tarddiad

original adj, n gwreiddiol

originality n gwreiddioldeb

originate vb dechrau, tarddu

ornament n addurn ♦ vt addurno

ornate adj addurnedig, mawrwych

ornithology n adaryddiaeth, adareg

orphan adj, n amddifad

orthodox adj uniongred

orthography n orgraff

oscillate vb siglo, dirgrynu, osgiladu

ostensible adj ymddangosiadol, proffesedig

ostentation n rhodres

ostentatious adj rhodresgar

ostracize vt diarddel, alltudio

ostrich n estrys

other adj, pron arall, llall, amgen

otherwise adv amgen

otter n dyfrgi, dwrgi

ounce n owns

our pron ein, ein ... ni

oust vt disodli

out adv allan, i maes

outcast n alltud, digartref, gwrthodedig

outcome n canlyniad, ffrwyth

outcrop n brig, cribell ♦ vb brigo

outcry n gwaedd; dadwrdd; gwrthdystiad

outdo vt rhagori ar, trechu

outdoor adj yn yr awyr agored

outer adj allanol, nesaf allan, cyrion

outing n pleserdaith, gwibdaith

outlandish adj dieithr, estronol, anghysbell, diarffordd

outlast vb goroesi

outlaw n herwr

outlay n traul, cost

outlet n allfa

outline n amlinelliad, braslun; amlinell ♦ vb amlinellu

outlive vb goroesi

outlook n rhagolwg, argoel; golygfa

outset n dechrau, dechreuad

outside n tu allan, tu faes ♦ adj, adv allan(ol), oddi allan ♦ prep tu allan i, tu faes i

outside-forward n blaenwr mas

outside-half n maswr

outside-left n asgellwr chwith

outside-right n asgellwr de

outskirts npl cyrrau, maestrefi

outstanding adj amlwg; dyledus

outward adj allanol

outwards adv tuag allan

outweigh vt gorbwyso

oval adj hirgrwn

ovary n wygell, wyfa, ofari

ovation n cymeradwyaeth

oven n ffwrn, popty

over prep uwch, tros ♦ adv gor, rhy, tra

overall adj o ben i ben ♦ n troswisg

overbearing adj gormesol

overcast adj cymylog

overcharge vt gorbrisio, codi gormod

overcoat n cot fawr/uchaf

overcome vt gorchfygu, trechu, cael y gorau ar

overdo vb gorwneud

overflow n gorlif(iad) ♦ vb gorlifo

overhead adj, adv uwchben

overheat vi gorboethi

overload vb gorlwytho

overlook vb edrych dros; esgeuluso

overnight adv dros nos

overpopulate vb gorboblogi

overpower vb trechu

overrun vb goresgyn

overseas adv tramor, dros y môr

overtake vt goddiweddyd

overthrow n dymchweliad ♦ vt dymchwelyd

overture n cynnig; agorawd

overturn vt troi, dymchwelyd

overwhelm vt llethu, gorlethu

overwork vb gorweithio

owe vt bod mewn dyled

owl n tylluan, gwdihŵ

own adj eiddo dyn ei hun, priod ♦ vt meddu; arddel, addef

owner n perchen, perchennog

ox (-en) n ych, eidion

oxide n ocsid

oxygen n ocsigen

oyster n llymarch, wystrysen

P

pace n cam, camre; cyflymdra ♦ vb camu, cerdded

pacific adj heddychol, tawel

Pacific Ocean n Môr Tawel

pacifism n heddychiaeth

pacifist n heddychwr

pacify vt heddychu, tawelu

pack n pac, swp, pwn ♦ vb pacio, pynio

package n pecyn, bwndel, sypyn

packed lunch n tocyn, pryd wedi ei bacio

packet n sypyn, paced

pact n cyfamod, cynghrair

pad n pad ♦ vt padio

paddle n padl, rhodl, rhwyf ♦ vb rhodli, padlo

paddling pool n pwll padlo

paddock n marchgae, cae bach

padlock n clo clap, clo clwt, clo

egwyd

pagan *n* pagan ♦ *adj* paganaidd

page *n* tudalen

pageant *n* pasiant

pail *n* ystwc, crwc, bwced

pain *n* poen, gwayw, dolur ♦ *vt* poeni

painful *adj* poenus

painkiller *n* lleddfydd poen, lladdwr poen, dofydd poen

painstaking *adj* gofalus, trylwyr, diwyd

paint *n* paent, lliw ♦ *vt* peintio, lliwio

painter *n* peintiwr; arlunydd

painting *n* llun, darlun

pair *n* pâr, dau, cwpl ♦ *vb* gwelwi

Pakistan *n* Pakistan

palace *n* plas, palas, palasty

palaeo-, paleo- *prefix* hen, hynafol

palatable *adj* archwaethus, blasus

palate *n* taflod y genau; blas, archwaeth

palatial *adj* palasaidd, gwych

palaver *n* cleber, baldordd ♦ *vb* clebran, baldorddi

pale *adj* gwelw, llwyd, glas, gwelwlas ♦ *vb* gwelwi

pale *n* pawl, cledr; clawdd, ffin

Palestine *n* Palestina

palisade *n* palis, gwalc

pall *vb* diflasu

pallet *n* gwely gwellt, matras

pallid *adj* gwelw, llwyd

pallor *n* gwelwedd

palm *n* palf, cledr llaw ♦ *vt* palfu

palm *n* palmwydden. **P. Sunday** Sul y Blodau

palpable *adj* amlwg, dybryd, teimladwy

palpitate *vi* curo, dychlamu

palsy *n* parlys ♦ *vt* parlysu, diffrwytho

paltry *adj* distadl, gwael, pitw

pamper *vt* mwytho, maldodi

pamphlet *n* pamffled, llyfryn

pan- *prefix* oll-

pan *n* padell

pancake *n* crempog, cramwythen, ffroisen

pandemonium *n* dadwrdd, terfysg, mwstwr

pander *vb* porthi, gweini

pane *n* cwar, cwarel, paen

panegyric *n* molawd

panel *n* panel

pang *n* gloes, gwasgfa, brath, gwayw

panic *n* dychryn, panig

pansy *n* trilliw, llysiau'r Drindod

pant *vi* dyheu

pantaloons *npl* llodrau

panties *npl* pantos

pantomime *n* pantomeim

pantry *n* bwtri, pantri

pants *npl* pants

papacy *n* pabaeth

papal *adj* pabaidd

paper *n* papur ♦ *vb* papuro. **blotting p.** *n* papur sugno. **tissue p.** *n* papur sidan. **brown p.** *n* papur llwyd

paperback *n* llyfr clawr meddal

paperclip *n* clip papur

papist *n* pabydd

papyrus (-i) *n* papurfrwyn

par *n* cyfartaledd, llawn werth

parable *n* dameg

parachute *n* parasiwt

parade *n* rhodfa; rhodres, rhwysg

paradise *n* paradwys, gwynfa, gwynfyd

paradox *n* gwrthddywediad, paradocs

paradoxical *adj* paradocsaidd

paradoxically *adv* yn baradocsaidd

paraffin *n* paraffin

paragraph *n* paragraff

parallel *adj* cyfochrog, cyflin, paralel

paralyze *vt* parlysu, diffrwytho

paralysis *n* parlys

paralytic *adj*, *n* claf o'r parlys

paramount *adj* pen, pennaf, prif

paramour n gordderch
parapet n canllaw, rhagfur
paraphernalia npl meddiannau, taclau, celfi, petheuach
paraphrase n aralleiriad ♦ vt aralleirio
parasite n un yn byw ar gefn un arall, cynffonnwr
parcel n parsel, swp, sypyn
parch vb crasu, deifio, golosgi, sychu
parched adj cras, crasboeth
parchment n memrwn
pardon n maddeuant, pardwn ♦ vt maddau, pardynu
parent n tad neu fam, (pl) rhieni
parenthesis (-ses) n sangiad, ymadrodd rhwng cromfachau
pariah n dyn ysgymun
parings npl pilion, creifion
Paris n Paris
parish n plwyf ♦ adj plwyf, plwyfol
parishioner n plwyfolyn, (pl) plwyfolion
parity n cydraddoldeb, cyfartaledd
park n parc, cae, coetgae ♦ vb parcio
parking meter n amserydd parcio, rheolydd parcio
parking ticket n tocyn parcio
parlance n ymadrodd, iaith
parliament n senedd
parliamentary adj seneddol
parlour n parlwr
parochial adj plwyfol
parody n parodi ♦ vb gwatwar, dynwared
parole n gair, addewid, parôl
parricide n tadladdiad; tadleiddiad
parrot n parot, perot
parry vt osgoi, gochelyd, troi heibio
parse vt dosbarthu
parsimonious adj crintach, cybyddlyd
parsimony n crintachrwydd
parsley n persli

parsnip n panasen
parson n person, offeiriad
part n rhan; parth; plaid ♦ vb rhannu, parthu; gwahanu; ymadael
partake vb cyfrannu, cyfranogi
partial adj rhannol; pleidiol, tueddol
participate vb cyfranogi
participle n rhangymeriad
particle n mymryn, gronyn; geiryn
particular adj neilltuol, penodol; manwl ♦ n pwnc, (pl) manylion
parting n ymadael
partisan n pleidiwr
partition n canolfur, gwahanfur, palis
partly adv mewn rhan, yn rhannol
partner n partner; cymar
partridge n petrisen
part-time adj rhan amser
party n plaid; parti, mintai
pass vb mynd heibio, llwyddo, pasio; treulio, bwrw ♦ n cyflwr, sefyllfa; bwlch; trwydded. **to p. away** vb marw. **reverse p.** n pas wrthol
passable adj y gellir mynd heibio iddo; purion
passage n tramwyfa; mordaith; cyfran
passenger n teithiwr
passing n ymadawiad, tranc, pasio ♦ adj yn pasio, diflannol
passion n dioddefaint; gwŷn, nwyd
passionate adj angerddol, nwydwyllt
passive adj goddefol
Passover n y Pasg
passport n trwydded deithio, pasbort
past adj, n gorffennol ♦ prep wedi ♦ adv heibio
paste n past ♦ vt pastio, gludio
pastern n egwyd
pasteurize vb pasteureiddio
pasteurized adj wedi ei

basteureiddio

pastime n difyrrwch, adloniant

pastor n bugail (eglwys), gweinidog

pastoral adj bugeiliol ♦ n bugeilgerdd

pastry n pasteiod, pasteiaeth, tarten; crwst

pasture n porfa ♦ vb porfelu, pori

pasty n pastai

pat vt patio, pratio, canmol ♦ adj parod, cymwys, priodol

patch n clwt, darn ♦ vt clytio

patchwork n clytwaith

paten n plat cymundeb

patent adj agored, cyhoedd, amlwg; breintiedig ♦ n breintlythyr

paternal adj tadol

paternoster n pader

path n llwybr

pathetic adj gresynus, pathetig

pathological adj patholegol

pathos n teimlad, dwyster

patience n amynedd

patient adj amyneddgar, dioddefus ♦ n dioddefydd, claf

patriarch n patriarch

patrimony n treftadaeth; gwaddol

patriot n gwladgarwr

patriotic adj gwladgarol

patrol n gwyliadwriaeth, gwylfa, patrôl

patron n noddwr

patronage n nawdd, nawddogaeth

patronize vt noddi, nawddogi

patronizing adj nawddogol

patronymic n tadenw

patter vb curo (fel glaw ar ffenestr)

patter n padera ♦ n clebar, siaradach

pattern n patrwm, cynllun

paucity n prinder

paunch n bol, cest

pauper n dyn tlawd, tlotyn

pause n saib, seibiant, hoe ♦ vi

aros, sefyll, ymbwyllo

pave vt palmantu

pavement n palmant, pafin

pavilion n pabell, pafiliwn

paw n palf, pawen, ♦ vb paifu, pawennu

pawky adj direidus

pawn n gwystl, (CHESS) gwerin ♦ vt gwystlo

pay vb talu ♦ n tâl, cyflog, pae, hur. **back p.** ôl-dâl

payment n taliad, tâl

pea n pysen

peace n heddwch, tangnefedd ♦ excl gosteg!, ust!

peaceful adj heddychol, tangnefeddus, llonydd

peach n eirinen wlanog

peacock n paun

peak n pig; crib, copa; uchafbwynt

peal n sain clychau; twrf (taran) ♦ vb canu

peanut n cneuen ddaear

pear n gellygen

pearl n perl

peasant n gwladwr, gwerinwr

peasantry n gwerin

peat n mawn

pebble n carreg lefn, cerrigyn, gröyn

peck vb pigo, cnocellu ♦ n cnoc, pigiad

peculiar adj priod, priodol; hynod

peculiarity n hynodrwydd

pecuniary adj ariannol

pedagogue n athro plant, ysgolfeistr

pedal n pedal ♦ vb pedalu

pedant n pedant

pedantic adj pedantig

peddle vb pedlera

pedestal n troed, bôn, gwaelod

pedestrian adj ar draed, pedestrig ♦ n gŵr traed, cerddwr. **p. crossing** n croesfan

pedigree n ach, achau, bonedd

pedlar *n* pedler

pee *n* pisiad ♦ *vb* pisio

peel *n* pil, croen, rhisgl ♦ *vb* pilio, plicio, crafu

peep *vi* cipedrych, sbio ♦ *n* cipolwg, cip

peer *vi* ciledrych, syllu

peer *n* gogyfurdd, cydradd; pendefig

peevish *adj* anniddig, blin, piwis

peg *n* hoel bren, peg ♦ *vt* pegio

Peking *n* Peking

pelf *n* golud

pellet *n* peled, pelen, haelsen

pelt *vt* lluchio, taflu, peledu, baeddu

pelvis *n* pelfis

pen *n* pin, ysgrifbin ♦ *vt* ysgrifennu

pen *n* lloc, ffald, cwt ♦ *vt* ffaldio, llocio

penal *adj* penydiol

penalize *vb* cosbi

penalty *n* cosb, cosbedigaeth. **p. (kick)** *n* cic gosb

penance *n* penyd

pence *npl* ceiniogau, pres

pencil *n* pwyntil, pensel, pensil. **p. sharpener** *n* naddwr pensiliau

pendant *n* tlws

pending *prep* hyd, nes, yn ystod

pendulous *adj* yn hongian, yn siglo

pendulum *n* pendil

penetrate *vb* treiddio; dirnad

penfriend *n* cyfaill llythyru

penguin *n* pengwin

penicillin *n* penisilin

peninsula *n* gorynys

penis *n* cala, pidyn

penitence *n* edifeirwch

penitent *adj* edifar, edifarus, edifeiriol

penitentiary *n* carchar

penknife (**-knives**) *n* cyllell boced

pen name *n* ffug enw

pennant, pennon *n* penwn, banner

penniless *adj* heb geiniog

penny (**pence, pennies**) *n* ceiniog

pension *n* blwydd-dal, pensiwn

pensioner *n* pensiynwr

pensive *adj* synfyfyriol, meddylgar

pent *adj* wedi ei gau i mewn, caeth

Pentateuch *n* pumllyfr Moses

penult *n* goben

people *n* pobl, gwerin ♦ *vt* pobli, poblogi

pepper *n* pupur

peppermint *n* mintys poethion; botwm gwyn

per *prep* trwy, wrth, yn ôl

peradventure *adv* efallai

perceive *vt* canfod, gweld, dirnad, deall

percentage *n* hyn a hyn y cant, canran

perceptible *adj* canfyddadwy

perception *n* canfyddiad, canfod

perceptive *adj* yn gallu dirnad

perch *n* perc; clwyd ♦ *vb* clwydo

perchance *adv* efallai, hwyrach

percolate *vb* hidlo, diferu

percussion *n* trawiad, gwrthdrawiad. **p. band** seindorf daro

peremptory *adj* pendant, awdurdodol

perennial *adj* drwy'r flwyddyn; bythol, lluosflwydd

perfect *adj* perffaith ♦ *vt* perffeithio

perfection *n* perffeithrwydd

perfectly *adv* yn berffaith

pervervid *adj* brwd, tanbaid

perfidy *n* brad, dichell, ffalster

perforate *vt* tyllu

perforated *adj* tyllog

perforation *n* twll

perforce *adv* o orfod, drwy drais

perform *vb* cyflawni; chwarae, perfformio

performance *n* perfformiad

performer *n* perfformiwr

perfume *n* perarogl, persawr ♦ *vt* perarogli

perfunctory *adj* o raid, diofal, esgeulus

perhaps *adv* efallai, hwyrach, ond odid, dichon

peril *n* perygl, enbydrwydd

perimeter *n* amfesur, perimedr

period *n* cyfnod; cyfadran (miwsig); diweddnod; misglwyf

periodic *adj* cyfnodol

periodical *n* cyfnodolyn

peripatetic *adj* crwydrol, cylchynol, peripatetig

peripheral *adj* ymylol

periphery *n* ymylon, cylchfesur

periphrastic *adj* cwmpasog

perish *vi* colli, trengi, marw, darfod; llygru

periwinkle *n* gwichiad

perjure *vt*: **p. oneself** tyngu anudon

perjury *n* anudon, anudoniaeth

perk *n* mantais. **to p. up** bywhau, adfywio

perky *adj* bywiog, eofn, hyf

permanent *adj* parhaol, arhosol, sefydlog

permeate *vt* treiddio, trwytho

permissible *adj* wedi ei ganiatáu

permission *n* caniatâd, cennad

permissive *adj* goddefol. **the p. society** y gymdeithas oddefol

permit *vb* caniatáu ♦ *n* trwydded

peroration *n* diweddglo araith, perorasiwn

perpendicular *adj* syth, unionsyth

perpetrate *vt* cyflawni (rhyw ddrwg)

perpetual *adj* parhaol, parhaus, bythol

perpetuate *vt* parhau, anfarwoli

perplex *vt* drysu, cythryblu, trallodi

persecute *vt* erlid

persevere *vi* dyfalbarhau

persist *vi* dal ati; mynnu, taeru,

dyfalbarhau

persistent *adj* dyfal, taer, cyndyn, parhaus

person *n* person

personable *adj* golygus, prydweddol, hawddgar

personal *adj* personol. **p. assistant** *n* cynorthwyydd personol

personality *n* personoliaeth

personally *adv* yn bersonol

perspective *n* persbectif, safbwynt

perspiration *n* chwys

perspire *vb* chwysu

persuade *vt* darbwyllo, perswadio

pert *adj* eofn, tafodrydd

pertain *vi* perthyn

pertinent *adj* perthynol, cymwys

perturb *vt* cyffroi, aflonyddu, cythruddo

peruse *vt* darllen, chwilio

pervade *vt* treiddio, trwytho

perverse *adj* gwrthnysig, trofaus, croes

pervert *vt* gwyrdroi, llygru, camdroi ♦ *n* cyfeiliornwr

pessimism *n* pesimistiaeth

pessimist *n* pesimist

pest *n* pla, haint, poendod

pester *vt* blino, aflonyddu, poeni

pestilence *n* haint, pla

pet *n* anwylyn, ffafryn ♦ *adj* llywaeth, swci ♦ *vt* anwesu, canmol

petal *n* petal

petite *adj* bychan

petition *n* deisyfiad; deiseb, petisiwn

petitioner *n* deisebwr

petrel *n* aderyn drycin

petrified *adj* stond

petrify *vb* parlysu

petroleum *n* petroliwm

petrol pump *n* pwmp petrol

petrol station *n* gorsaf betrol

petticoat *n* pais

petty *adj* bach, bychan, mân, gwael

petulant adj anniddig, anfoddog, anynad

pew n eisteddle, côr, sedd

pewit, peewit n cornicyll, cornchwiglen

pewter n piwter

phantom n rhith, drychiolaeth

Pharisee n Pharisead

pharmacy n fferylliaeth; fferyllfa

pharynx n sefnig

phase n golwg, gwedd, agwedd; tro

pheasant n ceiliog coed, coediar, ffesant

phenomenon (-na) n ffenomen; rhyfeddod

phial n ffiol

philander vi gwamalio caru

philanthropist n dyngarwr

philanthropy n dyngarwch

Philippines n Pilipinas

Philistine n Philistiad

philology n ieitheg

philosopher n athronydd

philosophical adj athronyddol

philosophy n athroniaeth

phlegm n cornboer, llysnafedd, fflem

phlegmatic adj difraw, digyffro, difywyd

phobia n ffobia

phone n ffôn, teleffon ♦ vb ffonio. **p. book** n cyfeiriadur ffôn. **p. box** n caban ffôn. **p. call** n galwad ffôn

phonetic adj seinegol

phonetician n seinegydd

phonetics n seineg

phoney adj ffug

phonology n ffonoleg

phosphorus n ffosfforws

photocopier n llungopïwr

photocopy n llungopi ♦ vb llungopïo

photograph n llun, ffotograff

photographer n ffotograffydd

photography n ffotograffiaeth

phrase n ymadrodd; cymal ♦ vt geirio

phraseology n geiriad, geirweddiad

physical adj corfforol, materol; ffisegol. **p. education** n addysg gorfforol

physician n meddyg, ffisigwr

physicist n ffisegydd/wr

physics n ffiseg

physiology n ffisioleg

physiotherapy n ffisiotherapi

physique n corffolaeth, cyfansoddiad

piano n piano

pick n caib ♦ vb ceibio

pick vb pigo, dewis, dethol ♦ n dewis

pickaxe n caib

picket n polyn, cledren; gwyliwr, gwyliadwriaeth, picedwr ♦ vb picedu

pickle n picl, heli ♦ vt piclo, halltu

picnic n picnic

pickpocket n pigwr pocedi, codleidr

pictorial adj darluniadol

picture n llun, darlun, pictiwr. **p. book** llyfr lluniau

picturesque adj darluniaidd, gwych, byw

pie n pastai. **p. chart** n siart olwyn

piebald adj brith; brithryw

piece n darn, dryll, rhan ♦ vt clytio, asio, uno

piecemeal adv bob yn damaid

pied adj brith, brithliw

pier n piler; pier

pierce vb brathu, gwanu, trywanu

piety n duwioldeb

piffle n lol, oferedd, gwegi

pig n mochyn ♦ vb porchellu, bwrw perchyll

pigeon n colomen

pigeonhole n cloer

pigeon-house n colomendy

piggy bank n cadw-mi-gei, blwch cynilo

pig-headed adj pendew, ystyfnig

pigment n paent, lliw

pigsty n twlc mochyn

pigtail n pleth

pike n gwaywffon; penhwyad

pile n crug, pentwr ♦ vt pentyrru

pile n pawl, cledr

pile n blew, cedor

piles npl clwyf y marchogion

pilfer vb chwiwladrata

pilgrim n pererin

pilgrimage n pererindod

pill n pelen, pilsen

pillage n ysbail, anrhaith ♦ vt ysbeilio, anrheithio

pillar n colofn, piler. **p. box** n bocs postio

pillion n sgil

pillory n rhigod, pilwri

pillow n gobennydd, clustog. **p. case** n cas gobennydd

pilot n cyfarwyddwr llongau, peilot

pimple n ploryn, tosyn

pin n pin ♦ vt pinio, hoelio

pinafore n brat, piner

pincers npl gefel, pinsiwrn

pinch vb pinsio, gwasgu; cynilo ♦ n pins, pinsiad; gwasgfa, cyfyngder

pincushion n pincas, pincws

pine n pinwydden

pine vi dihoeni, nychu, curio

pineapple n afal pîn

pinion n asgell, adain ♦ vt torri esgyll

pink adj, n pinc

pinpoint vb pinbwyntio

pint n peint

pioneer n arloeswr, arloesydd

pious adj duwiol, duwiolfrydig, crefyddol

pip n hedyn afal, etc

pipe n pib, pibell ♦ vb canu pibell

piping adj: **p. hot** chwilboeth

piquant adj pigog, llym, tost

pique vt llidio, cyffroi; ymfalchïo ♦ n soriant

pirate n môr-leidr

piss vb pisio

pissed adj meddw

pistol n llawddryll, pistol

pit n pwll, pydew ♦ vt pyllu. **coal p.** pwll glo

pitch n pyg ♦ vt pygu

pitch vb bwrw; gosod; taro (tôn) ♦ n gradd, mesur, traw

pitcher n piser, ystên, cawg

pitchfork n picfforch, picwarch: seinfforch

piteous adj truenus, gresynus

pitfall n magl, perygl

pith n bywyn; mwydion; mêr; grym, sylwedd

pithy adj cryno, cnawd, cnwysfawr

pitiful adj truenus, tosturiol

pitiless adj didostur, didrugaredd

pittance n dogn, cyfran (annignol)

pity n tosturi, trueni, gresyn ♦ vt tosturio, gresynu

pivot n colyn, pegwn

placable adj cymodlon, hynaws

placard n murlen, hysbyslen

placate vt cymodi, heddychu, dyhuddo

place n lle, man, mangre ♦ vt cyfleu, gosod. **to take p.** digwydd. **in the first p.** yn y lle cyntaf

placid adj araf, tawel, llonydd

plagiary n llên-ladrad; llên-leidr

plague n pla, haint ♦ vt poeni, blino

plaice n lleden

plaid n plod

plain adj plaen, eglur ♦ n gwastadedd

plaintiff n achwynwr, hawlydd

plait n pleth ♦ vt plethu

plan n cynllun, plan ♦ vt cynllunio, planio

plane adj, n gwastad, lefel

plane n plaen; awyren ♦ vt plaenio

planet n planed

plank n astell, estyllen, planc

planning n cynllunio. **p. permission** n caniatâd cynllunio

plant n planhigyn, llysieuyn; offer; ffatri ♦ vt plannu

plaster n plaster ♦ vt plastro

plastic n, adj plastig. **p. bag** cwdyn plastig

plat n darn o dir, clwt, lawnt

plate n plat; llestri aur, etc ♦ vt golchi â metel

plateau n gwastadfan uchel

platform n llwyfan, esgynlawr

platitude n sylw hen a diflas, gwireb

platoon n platŵn

platter n plat, dysgl, noe

plaudit n banllef o gymeradwyaeth

plausible adj teg neu resymol yr olwg, ffals

play vb chwarae; canu (offeryn) ♦ n chwarae

player n chwaraewr

playful adj chwareus

playground n chwaraele

playgroup n grŵp chwarae

playing field n maes chwarae

plaything n tegan

playwright n dramodydd

plea n ple, dadl, hawl; esgus

plead vb pledio, dadlau, eiriol, ymbil

pleasant adj hyfryd, pleserus, difyr, siriol

please vb boddhau, boddio, rhyngu bodd. **if you p.** os gwelwch yn dda

pleased adj boddhaus, bodlon, hapus. **p. to meet you** mae'n dda gen i gwrdd â chi

pleasing adj dymunol

pleasure n pleser, hyfrydwch

pleat n plet, pleten ♦ vt pletio

plebeian n gwerinwr, gwrêng

plebiscite n pleidlais y bobl

pledge n gwystl, ernes ♦ vt gwystlo

plenary adj llawn, cyflawn, diamodol

plenty n digon, helaethrwydd

plethora n gorgyflawnder

pleurisy n eisglwyf, plewrisi

pliable, pliant adj ystwyth, hyblyg

pliers npl gefel fechan

plight n cyflwr, drych, anghyflwr

plight vt addo, gwystlo

plod vb troedio, ymlafnio, llafurio, slafio

plot n darn o dir; brad, cynllwyn; cynllun, plot, ystofiad ♦ vb cynllwyn; cynllunio

plotter n cynllwynwr

plough n aradr, gwŷdd ♦ vb aredig, troi

ploy n cynllun, strategaeth

pluck vt tynnu; pluo ♦ n glewder

plucky adj dewr, gwrol, glew

plug n topyn, plwg ♦ vt topio, plygio

plum n eirinen

plumage n plu

plumber n plymwr

plumbing n gwaith plymwr

plume n pluen, plufyn ♦ vt pluo, plufio

plummet n plymen

plump adj tew, llyfndew, graenus ♦ vb pleidleisio i un (yn unig)

plunder n ysbail, anrhaith ♦ vt ysbeilio, anrheithio

plunge n plymiad ♦ vb plymio, trochi, bwrw

pluperfect adj gorberffaith

plural adj lluosog

plus n plws, ychwaneg ♦ prep, adj ychwanegol

plush n plwsh

ply vb arfer, defnyddio, gyrru; poeni

plywood n pren haenog (tair-haen, pum-haen)

pneumatic adj â'i lond o wynt, awyrog

pneumonia n llid yr ysgyfaint, niwmonia

poach vb herwhela, potsio

poach vt berwi (wy) heb ei blisg
poacher n herwheliwr, potsiwr
pock n brech, ôl brech
pocket n poced, llogell ♦ vt pocedu. **p. knife** cyllell boced. **p. money** arian poced
pod n coden, plisgyn, masgl, cibyn
podgy adj byrdew
poem n cerdd, cân
poet n bardd, prydydd
poetry n barddoniaeth, prydyddiaeth
poignant adj llym, tost, ingol, aethus, awchlym
point n pwynt; man; blaen ♦ vb pwyntio; blaenllymu; dangos. **p. of view** n safbwynt. **to be on the p. of doing sth** bod ar fin gwneud rhywbeth. **to get the p.** deall. **there's no p. (in doing)** does dim diben gwneud. **to p. out** nodi
pointed adj pigfain
pointedly adv yn llym
pointer n cyfeirydd; mynegfys
pointless adj dibwynt, diystyr, gwag
poise vb mantoli; hofran ♦ n ystum, osgo
poison n gwenwyn ♦ vt gwenwyno
poisoning n gwenwyno
poisonous adj gwenwynig
poke vb gwthio, pwnio, procio
poker n pocer
poky adj cyfyng, gwael
polar adj pegynol
pole n pawl, polyn; pegwn
polemic adj dadleuol ♦ n dadl
police n heddlu. **p. car** n car heddlu. **p. station** n gorsaf heddlu
policeman n heddwas, heddgeidwad, plismon
policewoman n heddferch, plismones
policy n polisi
polish vb cwyro, caboli, gloywi, llathru ♦ n cwyr
polite adj moesgar, boneddigaidd

politic adj call, cyfrwys, doeth, buddiol
political adj gwleidyddol
politician n gwleidydd, gwleidyddwr
politics n gwleidyddiaeth
poll n pen, copa; pôl ♦ vb cneifio; pleidleisio, polio. **p. tax** treth y pen, treth gymunedol
pollen n paill
polling booth n bwth pleidleisio
polling day n dydd pleidleisio
polling station n gorsaf bleidleisio
pollute vt halogi, difwyno, llygru
pollution n llygredd
polo neck n jersi polo
polygamy n amlwreigiaeth
polysyllable n gair lluosill
polytechnic n polytechnig
pomegranate n pomgranad
pomp n rhwysg
pompous adj rhwysgfawr, balch
pond n llyn, pwll
ponder vb ystyried, myfyrio, pwyso
ponderous adj pwysfawr, trwm
pong n drewdod
pontiff n archoffeiriad; y Pab
pontoon n ysgraff
pony n merlyn, poni, merlen. **p. trekking** merlota
pooh excl pw!
pool n pwll, llyn
pool n cronfa; pwll ♦ vt cydgyfrannu
poor adj tlawd, truan, gwael, sâl
poorly adj sâl, gwael, claf
pop vb ffrwydro, ysgortio; picio, plannu, taro
pope n pab
popery n pabyddiaeth
pop-gun n gwn clats
poplar n poplysen
poppy n pabi (coch), llygad y bwgan
populace n gwerin, gwerinos
popular adj poblogaidd

population n poblogaeth
populous adj poblog
porcelain n porslen
porch n porth, cyntedd
porcine adj mochaidd
porcupine n ballasg
pore n twll chwys
pore vi astudio, myfyrio, synfyfyrio
pork n cig moch, porc
porker n mochyn, porcyn
porous adj tyllog
porpoise n llamhidydd
porridge n uwd
port n porth, porthfa, porthladd
port n ochr aswy llong wrth edrych ymlaen
port n gwin Oporto, gwin coch
portable adj cludadwy
portcullis n porthcwlis
portent n argoel; rhyfeddod, gwyrth
porter n porthor
portfolio n cas papurau, portffolio; swydd
porthole n ffenestr llong; gyndwll
portion n rhan, cyfran, gwaddol
portly adj tew, corffol
portrait n llun, darlun
portray vt portreadu, darlunio
Portugal n Portiwgal
pose vb sefyll, ymddangos, cymryd ar ♦ n ystum, rhodres
posh adj hardd, coeth
position n safle, sefyllfa, swydd
positive adj cadarnhaol, pendant, posidiol
posse n mintai, torf
possess vt meddu, meddiannu
possession n meddiant
possessor n perchen, perchennog
possibility n posibilrwydd
possible adj posibl, dichonadwy
possibly adv dichon, efallai
post n post, cledr ♦ vt gosod, cyhoeddi
post n post, llythyrfa; safle, swydd

♦ vb postio
post- prefix wedi, ar ôl
postage n cludiad (llythyr, etc.)
postal adj post
postal order n archeb bost
postbox n bocs postio
postcard n cerdyn post
postcode n côd post
poster n hysbyslen, poster
posterior adj ar ôl, ôl
posterity n cenedlaethau'r dyfodol, hiliogaeth
postgraduate adj graddedig
posthumous adj ar ôl marw
postman n postmon
postmark n postfarc
postmaster n postfeistr
post office n llythyrdy, swyddfa'r post
postpone vt gohirio, oedi
postscript n ôl-ysgrif
posture n agwedd, ystum, osgo
postwar adj ar ôl y rhyfel
posy n blodeuglwm, pwysi
pot n pot, potyn; crochan ♦ vb potio
potato (-oes) n taten, pytaten
potency n nerth, grym
potent adj cryf, galluog, grymus, nerthol
potential adj dichonadwy, dichonol ♦ n potensial
pothole n ceubwll
potion n dogn, llymaid, llwnc
pottage n cawl, potes
potter n crochenydd
potter vb diogi, ymdroi, sefyllian, swmera
pottery n llestri pridd; gwaith llestri pridd; priddweithfa
potty n pot
pouch n cod, coden, cwd ♦ vb cydu
poultice n powltis
poultry n dofednod, ffowls
pounce vb disgyn ar, dyfod ar warthaf
pound n pwys; punt

pound n ffald ♦ vt ffaldio

pound vb pwyo, pwnio, malu, malurio

pour vb tywallt, arllwys; bwrw

pout vi pwdu, sorri, terru, monni

poverty n tlodi

poverty-stricken adj tlawd, llwm

powder n powdr, llwch, pylor ♦ vt powdro

powdered milk n llaeth powdr

powder room n ystafell bincio

power n gallu, nerth, grym, awdurdod; pŵer

power cut n toriad yn y cyflenwad

power failure n pall ar y cyflenwad

powerful adj nerthol, grymus

powerless adj dirym

power station n pŵerdy

pox n brech

practicable adj dichonadwy

practical adj ymarferol

practice vi arfer, arferiad, ymarferiad

practise vb arfer, ymarfer

practising adj ymarferol; yn dilyn ei swydd

practitioner n meddyg; cyfreithiwr

prairie n gwastatir, gweundir, paith

praise vt canmol, moli ♦ n canmoliaeth, mawl

pram n coets, pram

prance vi prancio

prank n cast, ystranc, pranc

prawn n corgimwch

pray vb gweddïo. **I p. thee** atolwg

prayer n gweddi

pre- prefix cyn-, rhag-, blaen-

preach vb pregethu

preacher n pregethwr

preamble n rhagymadrodd, rhaglith

precarious adj ansicr, peryglus, enbyd

precaution n rhagofal, rhagocheliad, gofal

precede vb blaenori, blaenu, rhagflaenu

precedence n blaenoriaeth

precedent n cynsail

precentor n arweinydd y gân, codwr canu

preceptor n athro, hyfforddwr

precinct n cyffin, rhodfa

precious adj gwerthfawr, prid, drud

precipice n dibyn, diffwys, clogwyn

precipitate vt bwrw, hyrddio ♦ vi gwaddodi, gwaelodi ♦ adj byrbwyll, anystyriol

précis n crynodeb

precise adj penodol, manwl

preclude vt cau allan, atal, rhwystro

precocious adj hen o'i oed, henaidd, henffel

precondition n rhagamod

precursor n rhagredegydd, rhagflaenydd

predatory adj anrheithgar, ysglyfaethus

predecessor n rhagflaenydd

predestination n rhagarfaethiad

predicament n cyflwr, helynt, sefyllfa

predicate vt haeru, honni ♦ n traethiad

predict vb rhagfynegi, rhagddywedyd, proffwydo

predilection n hoffter, tuedd, tueddfryd

predominate vi bod yn bennaf neu yn fwyaf, arglwyddiaethu, rhagori

pre-eminent adj ar y blaen i bawb

preen vb pincio, harddu

preface n rhagymadrodd, rhaglith

prefect n rhaglaw; swyddog

prefer vt dewis yn hytrach, bod yn well gan

preferable adj gwell

preference n dewis, hoffter,

ffafraeth, blaenoriaeth

preferential *adj* ffafriol

preferment *n* dyrchafiad, codiad

prefix *vt* rhagddodi ♦ *n* rhagddodiad

pregnancy *n* beichiogaeth

pregnant *adj* beichiog, llawn

prehistoric *adj* cynhanesiol

prejudice *n* rhagfarn; niwed ♦ *vt* rhagfarnu, niweidio

prejudiced *adj* rhagfarnllyd

prelate *n* esgob, prelad

preliminary *adj* arweiniol, rhagarweiniol

prelude *n* rhagarweiniad; preliwd (cerdd.)

premarital *adj* cyn priodi

premature *adj* anaeddfed, cynamserol

premier *adj* blaenaf, pennaf, prif ♦ *n* prifweinidog

première *n* blaenberfformiad

premise *n* rhagosodiad; (*pl*) adeiladau, *etc* ♦ *vt* rhagosod

premium *n* gwobr, tâl, taliad

preoccupied *adj* wedi ymgolli

preoccupy *vt* rhagfeddiannu; llenwi, ymgolli

prepaid *adj* wedi ei dalu ymlaen llaw, rhagdalwyd

preparation *n* paratoad, darpariaeth

preparatory *adj* rhagbaratoawl

prepare *vb* paratoi, darparu, darbod, arlwyo

prepared *adj* parod; effro

preposition *n* arddodiad

preposterous *adj* afresymol, gwrthun

prerequisite *n* rhagangenraid

prerogative *n* braint, rhagorfraint

presage *n* argoel, rhagargoel ♦ *vt* argoeli

presbyter *n* henuriad, offeiriad

Presbyterian *adj* Henadurol, Presbyteraidd ♦ *n* Presbyteriad

presbytery *n* henaduriaeth; tŷ

offeiriad Pabyddol

prescience *n* rhagwybodaeth

prescribe *vb* gorchymyn, cyfarwyddo

prescription *n* cyngor, cyfarwyddyd, presgripsiwn

presence *n* gŵydd, presenoldeb

present *adj*, *n* presennol

present *n* anrheg ♦ *vt* anrhegu; cyflwyno; dangos

presentiment *n* rhagargoel

presently *adv* yn fuan

preserve *vt* cadw, diogelu ♦ *n* jam

preside *vi* llywyddu

president *n* llywydd, arlywydd

press *vb* gwasgu ♦ *n* gwasg; gwryf; cwpwrdd

pressing *adj* taer, dwys

pressure *n* gwasgiad, gwasgfa, pwys

prestige *n* bri, dylanwad, braint

presumable *adj* y gellir ei dybio

presumably *adv* yn ôl pob tebyg, gellid tybio

presume *vb* tybio, tebygu; beiddio, rhyfygu

presumption *n* rhyfyg; tyb

presumptuous *adj* rhyfygus

pretence *n* rhith, esgus, ffug

pretend *vb* ffugio, cymryd ar, cogio; proffesu; honni hawl

pretension *n* honiad, hawl

preter- *prefix* tu hwnt i, mwy na

pretext *n* esgus, cochl

pretty *adj* tlws, del, pert ♦ *adv* cryn, go

prevail *vi* tycio, ffynnu; gorfod, trechu

prevalent *adj* cyffredin; nerthol

prevent *vt* rhagflaenu; atal, rhwystro

preview *n* rhagolwg

previous *adj* blaenorol, cynt

prey *n* ysglyfaeth, aberth ♦ *vi* ysglyfaethu

price *n* pris, gwerth ♦ *vt* prisio. **p. list** *n* rhestr prisiau, taflen brisiau; telerau *npl*

prick *n* pigyn, swmbwl ♦ *vb* pigo; picio, codi

prickle *n* draen ♦ *vb* pigo, tymhigo

pride *n* balchder ♦ *vt* balchio, ymfalchio

priest *n* offeiriad

priesthood *n* offeiriadaeth

prig *n* sychfoesolyn, mursennwr, coethyn

prim *adj* cymen, cymhenllyd

primary *adj* prif, cyntaf, cysefin; cynradd. **p. school** *n* ysgol gynradd

primate *n* archesgob

prime *adj* prif, cyntaf; gorau ♦ *n* anterth

prime *vt* llwytho, llenwi, cyflenwi

primer *n* llyfr cyntaf, cynlyfr

primeval *adj* cynoesol, cyntefig

primitive *adj* cyntefig; garw, amrwd

primordial *adj* cyntefig, cysefin

primrose *n* briallen, (*pl*) briallu

prince *n* tywysog

principal *adj* prif ♦ *n* pen; prifathro; corff

principality *n* tywysogaeth

principle *n* egwyddor, elfen

print *n* argraff, print, ôl ♦ *vb* argraffu, printio

printed *adj* argraffedig, wedi ei argraffu

prior *adj* cynt, blaenorol ♦ *n* prior, priol

priority *n* blaenoriaeth

priory *n* priordy, mynachdy

prise, prize *vt* dryllio'n agored â throsol

prism *n* prism

prison *n* carchar, carchardy

prisoner *n* carcharor

pristine *adj* hen, cyntefig, cysefin

private *adj* preifat, cyfrinachol, personol. **p. enterprise** *n* ymroddiad unigol

privation *n* amddifadrwydd, diffyg

privilege *n* braint, rhagorfraint

privy *adj* dirgel, cudd, cyfrin ♦ *n* geudy

prize *n* gwobr ♦ *vt* prisio, gwerthfawrogi

prize *n* ysbail, caffaeliad, gwobr

pro- *prefix* am, yn lle; o blaid

probability *n* tebygolrwydd

probable *adj* tebygol, tebyg

probate *n* prawf ewyllys

probation *n* prawf

probe *n* profiedydd ♦ *vt* profi, chwilio

probity *n* uniondeb, cywirdeb

problem *n* pwnc, drysbwnc, problem

procedure *n* trefn, arfer, defod, dull

proceed *vi* mynd, deillio, tarddu; erlyn ♦ *n* (*pl*) enillion, elw

process *n* gweithrediad, goruchwyliaeth, dull

procession *n* gorymdaith; deiliiad

proclaim *vt* cyhoeddi, datgan

proclamation *n* cyhoeddiad, proclamasiwn

proclivity *n* gogwydd, tuedd

proconsul *n* rhaglaw

procrastinate *vi* oedi, gohirio

procreate *vt* cenhedlu

procure *vb* ceisio, caffael, cael

prod *vt* procio, pwnio, symbylu

prodigal *adj* afradlon, hael

prodigious *adj* aruthrol, anferth

prodigy *n* rhyfeddod, gwyrth

produce *vt* cynhyrchu, epilio; dwyn ♦ *n* cynnyrch, ffrwyth

product *n* cynnyrch, ffrwyth

production *n* cynhyrchiad; (*pl*) cynhyrchion

profane *adj* anghysegredig, halogedig ♦ *vt* anghysegru, halogi

profess *vb* proffesu, arddel

profession *n* proffes, galwedigaeth

professional *adj* proffesiynol

professor *n* proffeswr; athro

proffer *vt*, *n* cynnig

proficient adj hyddysg, cyfarwydd

profile n ystlyslun, cernlun

profit n budd, lles, elw, proffid ♦ vb llesáu, proffidio

profiteer vi gwneud elw

profligate adj afradlon, ofer

profound adj dwfn, dwys, angerddol

profundity n dyfnder

profuse adj hael, helaeth, toreithiog

progenitor n cyndad

progeny n hil, epil, hiliogaeth

prognostic n argoel, rhagarwydd

programme n rhaglen

progress n cynnydd; taith ♦ vi cynyddu

progressive adj cynyddgar, progresif

prohibit vt gwahardd

project n bwriad, cynllun; project

project vb bwrw; bwriadu; ymestyn; taflunio (ffilm)

projectile n teflyn

projector n taflunydd

proletariat n gwerin, gwrêng

prolific adj epiliog, ffrwythlon, toreithiog

prolix adj maith, amleiriog

prologue n rhagair, prolog

prolong vt hwyhau, estyn

promenade n rhodfa ♦ vb rhodianna

prominent adj yn sefyll allan, amlwg

promise n addewid ♦ vb addo, argoeli

promissory adj addewidiol

promontory n pentir, penrhyn

promote vt hyrwyddo, meithrin, dyrchafu

promoter n hyrwyddwr

prompt adj parod, buan ♦ vt cofweini; cymell

promptitude n parodrwydd

promulgate vt cyhoeddi, lledaenu

prone adj â'i wyneb i waered; tueddol

prong n fforch, pig fforch

pronominal adj rhagenwol

pronoun n rhagenw

pronounce vb cynanu, yngan; cyhoeddi, datgan

pronunciation n cynaniad

proof n prawf; proflen

prop n ateg, post, prop ♦ vt ategu

propaganda n propaganda

propagate vt epilio, cenhedlu; lledaenu

propel vt gyrru ymlaen, gwthio

propensity n tuedd, tueddfryd, gogwydd

proper adj priod, priodol, gweddus

property n priodoledd; eiddo; priodwedd (cemeg)

prophecy n proffwydoliaeth

prophesy vb proffwydo

prophet n proffwyd

propinquity n agosrwydd, cyfnesafrwydd

propitiate vt cymodi, dyhuddo

propitiation n cymod, iawn

propitious adj tirion, ffafriol

proportion n cyfartaledd, cyfrannedd

proportional adj cyfrannol

proportionate adj cymesur

proposal n cynnig

propose vb cynnig, bwriadu

proposition n cynigiad; gosodiad

propound vt cynnig, gosod gerbron

proprietor n perchen, perchennog

propriety n priodoldeb, gwedduster

propulsion n gwthiad, gyriad

prorogue vt gohirio

prosaic adj rhyddieithol, cyffredin

proscribe vt deol, diarddel, gwahardd

prose n rhyddiaith

prosecute vt erlyn, dilyn, dwyn ymlaen

prosecutor n erlynydd

proselyte n proselyt

prosody n mydryddiaeth

prospect n rhagolwg, golwg, golygfa

prospectus n rhaglen, hysbyslen, prosbectws

prosper vb llwyddo, tycio, ffynnu

prosperity n llwyddiant, hawddfyd, ffyniant

prostitute n putain ♦ vt darostwng

prostrate adj yn gorwedd ar ei wyneb; ar lawr yn lân ♦ vt bwrw i lawr; ymgrymu

protect vt amddiffyn, noddi

protection n amddiffyn, nawdd, diogelwch

protective adj amddiffynnol

protector n amddiffynnydd

protest vb gwrthdystio ♦ n gwrthdystiad

prototype n cynddelw, cynllun

protract vt estyn, hwyhau

protrude vb gwthio allan

protuberance n chwydd

proud adj balch

prove vb profi

provender n ebran, gogor, porthiant

proverb n dihareb

provide vt darparu

providence n rhagluniaeth, darbodaeth

provident adj darbodus

providential adj rhagluniaethol

province n talaith, tiriogaeth; cylch, maes

provision n darpariaeth. **provisions** npl darbodion; ymborth

proviso n amod

provocation n anogaeth, cyffroad, cythrudd

provoke vt annog, cyffroi, cythruddo, profocio

provost n maer, profost

prow n pen blaen bad neu long

prowess n dewrder, glewder, grymuster

prowl vi ysglyfaetha, prowlan

proximate adj nesaf, agos at; agos

proximity n agosrwydd

proxy n dirprwy

prude n mursen, coegen

prudence n pwyll, synnwyr, callineb

prudent adj pwyllog, synhwyrol, call, doeth

prune n eirinen sech

Prussia n Prwsia

pry vi chwilota, chwilenna

psalm n salm

psalmody n caniadaeth y cysegr, salmyddiaeth

psalter n llyfr salmau, sallwyr

pseudo- prefix gau, ffug

pseudonym n ffugenw

pshaw excl wfft, pw, och, ffei

psychiatrist n seiciatrydd

psychological adj seicolegol, meddyliol

psychology n seicoleg

puberty n aeddfedrwydd oed, blaenlencyndod, puberdod

public adj cyhoeddus ♦ n y cyhoedd. **p. house** n tŷ tafarn. **p. library** n llyfrgell gyhoeddus

publican n publican; tafarnwr

publicity n cyhoeddusrwydd

publish vt cyhoeddi

pucker vb crychu, crybachu

pudding n pwdin

puddle n corbwll; pydew, llaca

puerile adj bachgennaidd, plentynnaidd

puff n pwff, chwa, chwyth ♦ vb pwffio, chwythu

pugilist n paffiwr, ymladdwr

pugnacious adj ymladdgar, cwerylgar

puissant adj galluog, grymus, nerthol

pull vt tynnu ♦ n tynfa, tyniad

pullet n cywen

pulley n chwerfan, troell, pwli

pullover n gwasgod wlân

pulmonary adj ysgyfeiniol

pulp n bywyn, mwydion

pulpit n pulpud

pulsate vb curo (megis y galon)

pulse n curiad y galon, curiad y gwaed

pulse n pys, ffa, etc

pulverize vt malu yn llwch, chwilfriwio

pummel vt pwnio, dyrnodio, curo

pump n sugnedydd, pwmp ♦ vb pwmpio

pumpkin n pwmpen

pun n gair mwys, mwysair

punch n pwns; dyrnod ♦ vb pwnsio, dyrnodio

punctilious adj cysetlyg, gorfanwl

punctual adj prydlon

punctuate vt atalnodi

puncture n twll ♦ vt tyllu

pundit n ysgolhaig, doethwr

pungent adj llym, llymdost, siarp

punish vt cosbi, ceryddu; poeni

punishment n cosb, cosbedigaeth

punitive adj cosbol

puny adj eiddil, bychan, tila, pitw

pupil n ysgolhaig, ysgolor, disgybl; cannwyll llygad

puppet n delw, dol, pyped; gwas

puppy n ci bach

purblind adj cibddall, coegddall

purchase vt prynu, pwrcasu ♦ n pryniant, pwrcas

pure adj pur, noeth

purgative adj carthol ♦ n carthlyn

purgatory n purdan

purge vt puro, glanhau, carthu, coethi ♦ n carthlyn

purification n puredigaeth

purify vt puro, coethi, glanhau

Puritan n Piwritan

purity n purdeb

purl vi crychleisio, byrlymu

purlieu n cyffin, ffin, cymdogaeth

purloin vt lladrata, dwyn

purple adj, n porfforor

purport n ystyr, rhediad, ergyd ♦ vt arwyddo, proffesu, honni

purpose n pwrpas, bwriad, arfaeth ♦ vt bwriadu, arfaethu

purr vb canu crwth, grwnan

purse n pwrs, cod ♦ vb crychu

pursue vb dilyn, erlyn, erlid, ymlid

pursuit n ymlidiad; ymchwil, gorchwyl

purulent adj crawnllyd, gorllyd

purvey vb darparu lluniaeth, darmerth

purview n amcan, maes, cylch

pus n crawn, gôr

push vb gwthio ♦ n gwth, ysgŵd; ymdrech

pushchair n coets

puss n titw, pws; ysgyfarnog

pustule n ploryn, llinoryn

put vb gosod, dodi, rhoddi, rhoi

putative adj tybiedig, cyfrifedig

putrefaction n pydredd, madredd

putrefy vb pydru, madru

putrid adj pwdr, mall

putty n pwti ♦ vt pwtio

puzzle n dryswch, penbleth, pos ♦ vb drysu, pyslo

pygmy n corrach

pyjamas npl gwisg nos, gŵn nos

pyramid n pyramid, bera

pyre n cynnau angladdol, coelcerth

pyrotechnic adj, n (o natur) tân gwyllt

Q

quack n crachfeddyg, cwac

quack vi cwacian

quadrangle n pedrongl

quadrant n cwadrant

quadruped n pedwarcarnol

quadruple adj pedwarplyg

quadruplet n pedrybled

quaff vb drachtio, cofftio, yfed

quagmire n siglen, cors, mignen, sybwll

quail n sofliar

quaint adj od, henffasiwn
quake vi crynu
Quaker n Crynwr
qualification n cymhwyster;
cymhwysiad
qualified adj cymwys
qualify vt cymhwyso, cyfaddasu
quality n ansawdd, rhinwedd
qualm n petruster, amheuaeth
quandary n penbleth, cyfyng-
gyngor
quantity n swm, maint, mesur
quarantine n cwarant, neilltuaeth
quarrel n ymrafael, ffrae, cweryl ♦
vi ffraeo
quarry n chwarel, cloddfa, cwar ♦
vb cloddio
quarry n ysglyfaeth
quart n chwart, cwart
quarter n chwarter, cwarter; cwr,
man; trugaredd; (pl.) llety. **a q.
of an hour** chwarter awr. **q. final**
rownd gogynderfynol. **quarter-
sessions** n llys chwarter
quartet, -te n pedwarawd
quarto adj, n (llyfr) pedwarplyg
quartz n creigrisial, cwarts
quash vt diddymu, dirymu
quaver vi cwafrio, crynu ♦ n
cwafer
quay n cei
queen n brenhines
queer adj od, hynod, digrif,
ysmala
quell vt llonyddu, gostegu,
darostwng
quench vt diffodd, dofi, torri
quern n llawfelin, breuan
querulous adj cwynfanllyd, blin
query n holiad, gofyniad ♦ vb holi,
amau
quest n ymchwil, ymchwiliad,
cwest
question n gofyniad, cwestiwn ♦ vt
holi, amau
questionable adj amheus
question mark n gofynnod

questionnaire n holiadur
queue n cynffon, cwt, ciw
quibble n geirddadl, mân-ddadl ♦
vi geirddadlau, mân-ddadlau,
hollti blew
quick adj byw; buan, cyflym, clau.
to the q. i'r byw
quicken vb cyflymu
quicksilver n arian byw
quid n punt
quiescent adj distaw, llonydd,
digyffro
quiet adj llonydd, tawel, distaw ♦ n
llonyddwch, tawelwch ♦ vt
llonyddu, tawelu
quill n pluen, plufyn, cwilsyn
quilt n cwilt, cwrlid ♦ vt cwiltio
quintet n pumawd
quintuplet n pumled
quip n gair ffraeth, ateb parod
quit vt gadael, symud ♦ adj rhydd
quits adj yn gyfartal
quite adv cwbl, llwyr, hollol
quiver n cawell saethau
quiver vi crynu, dirgrynu
quixotic adj mympwyol, gwyllt
quiz vt holi, pyslo, profocio
quoit n coeten, coetan
quondam adj wedi bod, gynt, hen
quorum n nifer gofynnol, corwm
quota n rhan, cyfran, dogn, cwota
quotation n dyfyniad; prisiant
quote vt dyfynnu; nodi (prisiau)
quoth vt meddai, ebe

R

rabbi n rabi
rabbit n cwningen
rabble n ciwed, tyrfa ddireol
rabid adj cynddeiriog
rabies n y gynddaredd
race n ras, gyrfa, rhedfa ♦ vi rasio
race n hil
racial adj hiliol
racism n hiliaeth

rack n rac, clwyd, rhestl; arteithglwyd ♦ vt arteithio, dirdynnu

racket n twrf, mwstwr; raced (tennis etc.)

racy adj blasus; arab, ffraeth

radiant adj disglair, llachar, tanbaid

radiate vb pelydru, rheiddio

radiation n ymbelydredd

radiator n rheiddiadur

radical adj gwreiddiol, cynhenid; trylwyr ♦ n rhyddfrydwr, radical

radio n radio

radioactive adj ymbelydrol

radio station n gorsaf radio

radish n rhuddygl, radis

radius (-ii) n cylch; radius

raffle n raffl

raft n cludair, ysgraff, rafft

rafter n tulath, ceibren, trawst

rag n carp, clwt

rag doll n doli glwt

rage n cynddaredd ♦ vi terfysgu, cynddeiriogi

ragged adj carpiog, bratiog

raid n rhuthr, cyrch ♦ vb anrheithio, ysbeilio

rail n canllaw, cledren, rheilen ♦ vb cledru

rail vi difrïo, difenwi, cablu

raillery n difyrrwch, cellwair

railway n rheilffordd. r. station n gorsaf reilffordd

raiment n dillad, gwisg

rain n glaw ♦ vb glawio, bwrw glaw

rainbow n enfys

raincoat n cot law

rainy adj glawog

raise vt codi, cyfodi, dyrchafu

raisin n rhesinen

rake n cribin, rhaca ♦ vb cribinio, crafu, rhacanu

rally vb atgynnull; adgyfnerthu, gwella ♦ n cynulliad

ram n hwrdd, maharen ♦ vt hyrddio, pwnio

ramble vi gwibio, crwydro ♦ n gwib

rampant adj uchel ei ben, rhonc

rampart n caer, rhagfur, gwrthglawdd

ramshackle adj bregus, candryll

rancid adj â blas cryf arno, drewllyd

rancour n digasedd, chwerwder

random n antur, siawns, damwain ♦ adj damweiniol

range n amrediad; cwmpas; ystod; lle tân â ffwrn ♦ vb rhestru, cyfleu; crwydro

ranger n coedwigwr, ceidwad parc

rank n rheng, gradd ♦ vb rhestru. the r. and file y bobl gyffredin

rank adj mws; gwyllt, bras; rhonc, noeth

rankle vi gori, madru; cnoi, llidio

ransack vt chwilio, chwilota, ysbeilio

ransom n pridwerth ♦ vt prynu, gwaredu

rant vi bragaldian, brygawthan

rap n cnoc, ergyd ♦ vt cnocio, curo

rap n gronyn, mymryn, blewyn

rapacious adj rheibus, ysglyfaethus

rape vt treisio ♦ n trais

rapid adj cyflym, buan, chwyrn, gwyllt

rapist n treisiwr

rapture n perlewyg, gorawen, afiaith

rare adj anaml, prin; godidog; tenau

rascal n dihiryn, cnaf, gwalch, cenau

rash adj byrbwyll, rhyfygus, anystyriol

rash n brech, tarddiant

rasher n ysglisen, sleisen, tafell, golwyth

rasp vb rhasglio, crafu, rhygnu

raspberry n afanen, mafonen

rat n llygoden fawr, llygoden
ffrengig ♦ vi llygota
rate vt ffraeo, dwrdio, dweud y
drefn
rate n cyflymder; treth; cyfradd
(of interest)
rateable value n gwerth
trethiannol
ratepayer n trethdalwr
rather adv braidd, hytrach, go, lled
ratify vt cadarnhau
ratio n cyfartaledd; cymhareb
ration n dogn, saig ♦ vt dogni
rational adj rhesymol
rationale n rhesymwaith
rationalization n rhesymoliad
rationalize vb rhesymoli
rattle vb rhuglo, trystio ♦ n rhugl,
rhwnc
raucous adj cryg, garw, aflafar
ravage vt anrheithio, diffeithio,
difrodi
rave vi gwallgofi, ynfydu,
gwynfydu
ravel vb drysu; dad-weu, datod
raven n cigfran
ravenous adj rheibus, gwancus
ravine n hafn, ceunant
raving adj ynfyd, dwl, gwallgof
ravish vt treisio, cipio; swyno,
hudo
ravishing adj deniadol iawn
raw adj amrwd; crai, cri; noeth,
dolurus, garw; dibrofiad ♦ n cig
noeth, dolur
ray n paladr, pelydryn
ray n cath fôr
raze vt llwyr ddymchwelyd, dileu
razor n ellyn, rasal ♦ vt eillio. **r.
blade** n llafn ellyn
re prep ym mater, mewn perthynas
â
re- prefix ad-, ail-
reach vb cyrraedd, estyn ♦ n
cyrraedd
react vi adweithio
reaction n adwaith

reactionary adj adweithiol
reactor n adweithydd
read vb darllen
readable adj darllenadwy
reader n darllenydd
readily adv yn barod, yn ddiffwdan
reading n darllen
readjustment n atgywiriad,
addasiad
ready adj parod, rhwydd
reafforestation n ailfforestiad
real adj gwir, real, go-iawn
reality n gwirionedd, sylwedd;
dirwedd, realiti
realize vt sylweddoli; troi yn arian
really adv gwir, hollol, mewn difrif
realm n teyrnas, gwlad, bro
reap vb medi
reappear vi ailymddangos
rear n cefn, pen ôl, ôl
rear vb codi, magu; codi ar ei
draed ôl
reason n rheswm ♦ vb rhesymu
reasonable adj rhesymol
reassurance n calondid
reassure vt calonogi, cysuro
rebate n ad-daliad
rebel vi gwrthryfela ♦ n
gwrthryfelwr
rebellion n gwrthryfel
rebound vi adlamu ♦ n adlam
rebuff n nacâd, sen ♦ vt nacáu,
sennu
rebuke vt ceryddu ♦ n cerydd, sen
rebut vt gwrthbrofi,
gwrthddywedyd
recall vt galw yn ôl; galw i gof,
cofio
recant vb datgyffesu
recapitulate vt ailadrodd (yn
gryno)
recede vi encilio, cilio yn ôl
receipt n derbyniad; derbynneb
receive vt derbyn
receiver n derbynydd
recent adj diweddar
receptacle n llestr; cynheiliad

(llysieueg)
reception n derbyniad, croeso. **r. desk** n man croeso, man derbyn
receptionist n croesawferch, croesawydd
recess n cil, encil; cilfach; gwyliau
recessional adj, n (emyn) ymadawol
recipe n cyfarwyddyd; rysáit
recipient n derbyniwr, derbynnydd
reciprocal adj cilyddol
reciprocate vb talu'n ôl, cydgyfnewid; cilyddu
recital n adroddiad, datganiad
recitation n adroddiad
recite vb adrodd
reck vb gofalu, ystyried
reckless adj anystyriol, rhyfygus, dibris
reckon vb cyfrif, barnu, bwrw
reclaim vt adennill, diwygio
recline vb lledorwedd, gorwedd, gorffwys
recluse n meudwy, ancr
recognition n adnabyddiaeth, cydnabyddiaeth
recognize vt adnabod, cydnabod
recoil vi adlamu, gwrthneidio, cilio
recollect vt galw i gof, atgofio, cofio
recommend vt cymeradwyo, argymell
recompense vt ad-dalu, gwobrwyo, talu
reconcile vt cymodi, cysoni
recondite adj dwfn, cudd, cêl, tywyll
recondition vt atgyflyru, ail-wneud
reconnaissance n rhagchwiliad
reconnoitre vt chwilio, archwilio
record vt cofnodi, recordio ♦ n cofnod, record
recorder n (LAW) cofiadur; (MUS) recordydd
recording n recordiad
recount vt adrodd

re-count vb ailgyfrif
recoup vb digolledu
recourse n cyrchfa. **to have r. to** mynd at, defnyddio
recover vb cael yn ôl, adennill; ymadfer; adferiad
recreation n difyrrwch, adloniant
recruit n recriwt; newyddian ♦ vt codi gwŷr; adennill
rectangle n petryal
rectangular adj petryalog
rectify vt unioni, cywiro; puro, coethi
rectilinear adj unionlin
rector n rheithor
rectory n rheithoriaeth; rheithordy
recuperate vb adfer, ymadfer, cryfhau, gwella
recur vi ailddigwydd, dychwelyd
recurrence n ail-ddigwyddiad, ail-ymddangosiad
recurring adj cylchol
recusant n anghydffurfiwr
red adj, n coch, rhudd
redeem vt prynu (yn ôl), gwaredu
redemption n prynedigaeth
redeploy vb adleoli
redeployment n adleoliad, trawsgyflogaeth
red herring n (met) ysgyfarnog
redirect vt ailgyfeirio
redo vb ail-wneud
redolent adj yn sawru o
redoubtable adj i'w ofni; pybyr
redress vt unioni ♦ n iawn (am gam)
Red Sea n: the R.S. y Môr Coch
reduce vt lleihau, gostwng; rhydwytho
reduced adj gostyngol
reduction n lleihad, gostyngiad
redundancy n anghyflogaeth
redundant adj gormodol; anghyflog, digyflog
reed n cawnen, corsen, calaf; pibell
reef n plyg hwyl, riff ♦ vt plygu

hwyl

reef *n* creigle (yn y môr), creigfa, riff

reek *n* mwg, tarth, drewdod ♦ *vb* mygu, drewi

reel *n* ril ♦ *vb* dirwyn

reel *vi* troi, chwyldroi ♦ *n* dawns

refectory *n* ffreutur

refer *vb* cyfeirio, cyfarwyddo

reference *n* cyfeiriad; geirda

refill *n* adlenwad ♦ *vt* adlenwi

refine *vb* puro, coethi

reflect *vb* adlewyrchu; myfyrio

reflection *n* adlewyrchiad, myfyrdod, ailfeddwl

reflex *n* adweithred, atgyrch

reflexive *adj* atblygol

reform *vb* diwygio, gwella ♦ *n* diwygiad

reformation *n* diwygiad

reformatory *n* ysgol ddiwygio

refrain *vb* ymatal

refrain *n* byrdwn

refresh *vb* adfywio, dadebru, adlonni

refresher course *n* cwrs adolygu

refreshing *adj* adfywiol

refreshments *npl* ymborth, lluniaeth

refrigerate *vt* rheweiddio, cadw'n oer

refrigerator *n* rhewgell, oergell

refuge *n* noddfa, lloches

refugee *n* ffoadur

refund *n* ad-daliad ♦ *vb* ad-dalu

refurbish *vb* adnewyddu

refusal *n* gwrthodiad, nacâd

refuse *vb* gwrthod

refuse *n* ysbwriel, gwehilion, sothach

refute *vt* gwrthbrofi, datbrofi

regal *adj* brenhinol

regard *vb* edrych ar, ystyried ♦ *n* sylw, parch, hoffter

regarding *prep* ynglŷn â, ynghylch

regardless *adj* heb ofal, diofal

regenerate *vt* aileni

régime *n* trefn, cyfundrefn

regiment *n* catrawd

region *n* ardal, bro, gwlad

regional *adj* rhanbarthol

register *n* cofrestr ♦ *vt* cofrestru

registered *adj* cofrestredig

registrar *n* cofrestrydd

registration *n* cofrestriad. **r. number** *n* rhif cofrestru, rhif trethiant

registry *n* cofrestrfa

regret *vt* gofidio, edifaru ♦ *n* gofid

regular *adj* rheolaidd, cyson

regulate *vt* rheoleiddio, llywio, rheoli

regulation *n* rheol, trefniant

rehabilitate *vt* adfer i fri neu fraint, ailsefydlu

rehabilitation *n* adferiad

rehearsal *n* rihyrsal, practis

rehearse *vt* adrodd; ymarfer ymlaen llaw

reign *vi* teyrnasu ♦ *n* teyrnasiad

reimburse *vt* talu yn ôl, ad-dalu

rein *n* afwyn, awen ♦ *vt* ffrwyno

reindeer *n* carw

reinforce *vt* atgyfnerthu

reinstate *vt* adfer i safle neu fraint

reiterate *vt* ailadrodd, mynychu

reject *vt* gwrthod, bwrw ymaith

rejection *n* gwrthodiad

rejoice *vb* llawenhau, gorfoleddu

rejoin *vb* ateb, gwrthateb

rejoinder *n* ateb, gwrthateb

rejuvenate *vb* adfywiogi, adnewyddu

relapse *vi* ailglafychu, ailymhoelyd, atglafychu

relate *vb* adrodd, mynegi; perthyn

related *adj* yn perthyn; wedi ei ddweud

relating to *prep* yn ymwneud â

relation *n* adroddiad; perthynas

relationship *n* perthynas

relative *adj* perthnasol ♦ *n* perthynas, yn perthyn. **r. pronoun** *n* rhagenw perthynol

relax *vb* llacio, llaesu, ymollwng

relaxing *adj* ymlaciol

relay *n* cyfleuwad newydd, cyfnewid; darlledu ♦ *vb* ailosod. **r. race** *n* ras gyfnewid

release *vt* rhyddhau, gollwng ♦ *n* rhyddhad

relegate *vt* alltudio, deol, darostwng

relent *vi* tyneru, tirioni, llaesu

relevant *adj* perthnasol

reliable *adj* y gellir dibynnu arno, dibynadwy

reliance *n* ymddiried, dibyniaeth, hyder, pwys

relic *n* crair, (*pl*) gweddillion

relief *n* cynhorthwy; gollyngdod, ymwared; tirwedd

relieve *vt* cynorthwyo; esmwytho, ysgafnhau; rhyddhau, gollwng

religion *n* crefydd

religious *adj* crefyddol

relinquish *vt* gollwng, gildio, gwadu

relish *n* blas; enllyn, mwyniant ♦ *vb* blasio, hoffi

reluctance *n* amharodrwydd, anfodlonrwydd

reluctant *adj* anfodlon, anewyllysgar

rely *vi* hyderu, ymddiried, dibynnu

remain *vi* aros, parhau, gorffwys

remainder *n* gweddill, rhelyw

remains *npl* olion, gweddillion

remand *vt* aildraddodi. **r. home** *n* cartref i droseddwyr ifanc

remark *vb* sylwi ♦ *n* sylw

remarkable *adj* nodedig, hynod, rhyfedd, syn

remedial *n* adferol; meddyginiaethol

remedy *n* meddyginiaeth ♦ *vt* meddyginiaethu, gwella

remember *vt* cofio

remembrance *n* cof, coffa, coffadwriaeth

remind *vt* atgofio, atgoffa, cofio

reminiscence *n* atgof

remiss *adj* esgeulus, diofal, llac

remission *n* maddeuant

remit *vb* maddau; arafu, peidio; anfon

remittance *n* taliad

remnant *n* gweddill, gwarged

remonstrance *n* cwyn, gwrthdystiad

remonstrate *vi* ymliw, gwrthdystio

remorse *n* edifeirwch, gofid, atgno

remote *adj* pell, pellennig, anghysbell

remotely *adv* o bell

removable *adj* symudadwy, y gellir ei symud

removal *n* symudiad, diswyddiad

remove *vb* symud, dileu; mudo

remunerate *vt* talu, gwobrwyo

renaissance *n* dadeni

rend *vb* rhwygo, dryllio, llarpio

render *vb* talu; datgan; gwneud; troi, cyfieithu

rendezvous *n* cyrchfa, man cyfarfod

renegade *n* gwrthgiliwr

renew *vt* adnewyddu

renounce *vt* ymwrthod, ymwadu, gwadu

renovate *vt* adnewyddu

renown *n* clod, bri, enwogrwydd

rent *n* rhwyg

rent *n* ardreth, rhent ♦ *vt* ardrethu, rhentu

rental *n* rent

repair *vi* cyrchu, mynd

repair *vi* atgyweirio, trwsio ♦ *n* cywair

reparation *n* iawn, ad-daliad

repartee *n* ateb parod

repatriate *vb* adfer i'w wlad ei hun

repeal *vt* diddymu ♦ *n* diddymiad

repeat *vb* ailadrodd, ailgyflawni

repel *vt* bwrw yn ôl

repent *vb* edifarhau, edifaru

repentance *n* edifeirwch

repetition n ailadroddiad

repetitive adj ailadroddus

replace vb ailosod, dodi'n ôl; cymryd lle (arall)

replacement n un sy'n cymryd lle arall

replay vb ailchwarae

replenish vt ail-lenwi, diwallu

replete adj llawn, cyflawn, gorlawn

replica n copi cywir, cyflun

reply vi ateb ♦ n ateb, atebiad

report vt adrodd, hysbysu ♦ n adroddiad; swn ergyd

reporter n gohebydd

repose vb gorffwys ♦ n gorffwys

repository n ystorfa, trysorfa

reprehend vt ceryddu, argyhoeddi

represent vt portreadu; cynrychioli

representative adj yn cynrychioli ♦ n cynrychiolydd

repress vt atal, gostegu, llethu

repression n ataliad, darostyngiad, gwrthodiad

reprimand n cerydd ♦ vt ceryddu

reprisal n dial

reproach vt ceryddu, gwaradwyddo, edliw ♦ n gwaradwydd

reproduce vt atgynhyrchu, epilio

reproduction n atgynhyrchiad, copi; epiliad

reproof n cerydd

reprove vt ceryddu, argyhoeddi

reptile n ymlusgiad

republic n gweriniaeth, gwerinlywodraeth

repudiate vt diarddel, diarddelwi, gwadu

repugnant adj croes, atgas, gwrthun

repulse vt bwrw'n ôl; nacáu ♦ n gwrthergyd

repulsion n gwrthnysedd

repulsive adj atgas, ffiaidd

reputable adj parchus, cyfrifol

reputation n gair, cymeriad, enw da

repute vt cyfrif, tybied ♦ n parch, bri

request n cais ♦ vt ceisio, gofyn

requiem n offeren dros y meirw; galargerdd

require vt gofyn, mynnu

requisite adj gofynnol, angenrheidiol

requisition n archeb ♦ vb hawlio

requite vt talu, gwobrwyo, talu'r pwyth

rescind vt diddymu, dirymu

rescue vt achub ♦ n achubiad

research n ymchwil, ymchwiliad ♦ vb ymchwilio

resemblance n tebygrwydd

resemble vt tebygu i

resent vt tramgwyddo, digio, cymryd yn chwith

resentful adj digofus, llidiog

resentment n dig, dicter

reservation n cadw, cadfa

reserve vt cadw yn ôl, cadw wrth gefn ♦ n yr hyn a gedwir, cronfa; swildod

reserved adj swil; wedi ei gadw; r. seat sedd gadw

reservoir n cronfa, llyn

reshuffle vb aildrefnu

reside vi preswylio

residential adj preswyl

residue n gweddill

resign vt rhoi i fyny, ymddiswyddo, ymddeol

resignation n ymddiswyddiad; ymostyngiad

resilience n hydwythder, ystwythder

resilient adj hydwyth, ystwyth

resin n ystor, rhwsin

resist vb gwrthsefyll, gwrthwynebu

resistance n gwrthwynebiad, gwrthsafiad

resolute adj penderfynol

resolution n penderfyniad

resolve vb penderfynu ♦ n

penderfyniad
resonant *adj* atseiniol
resort *vi* cyrchu ♦ *n* cyrchfa;
ymwared
resound *vb* atseinio, diasbedain
resource *n* sgil, dyfais; (*pl*)
adnoddau
respect *vt* parch ♦ *n* golwg; parch
respectable *adj* parchus
respectful *adj* boneddigaidd, yn
dangos parch
respective *adj* priodol, ar wahân
respite *n* oediad, saib, seibiant,
hamdden
resplendent *adj* disglair,
ysblennydd
respond *vi* ateb, ymateb; porthi
response *n* ateb, atebiad
responsibility *n* cyfrifoldeb
responsible *adj* atebol, cyfrifol
responsive *adj* ymatebol
rest *n, vb* gorffwys ♦ *n* (*music*)
tawnod
rest *vi* aros, parhau ♦ *n* gweddill
restaurant *n* tŷ bwyta, bwyty
restful *adj* tawel, llonydd, esmwyth
restitution *n* adferiad; iawn
restive *adj* ystyfnig, ystranclyd,
noglyd, diamynedd
restless *adj* aflonydd, rhwyfus
restore *vt* adfer; atgyweirio
restrain *vt* atal, ffrwyno
restrained *adj* cynnil, gochelgar,
cymhedrol
restraint *n* atalfa, ffrwyn,
caethiwed
restrict *vt* cyfyngu, caethiwo
restriction *n* cyfyngiad
result *n* deillio, canlyn ♦ *n*
canlyniad
resume *vt* ailddechrau
résumé *n* crynodeb
resumption *n* ailddechreuad
resurgent *adj* yn ailgodi, yn ailfyw
resurrection *n* atgyfodiad
resuscitate *vb* adfywhau, dadebru
retail *vt* manwerthu, adwerthu ♦ *n*

adwerth
retailer *n* mân-werthwr
retain *vb* cadw, dal; llogi
retaliate *vb* talu'n ôl, talu'r pwyth,
dial
retaliation *n* dial
retard *vb* rhwystro, oedi
retch *vi* cyfogi, chwydu
retentive *adj* yn dal heb ollwng;
gafaelgar
reticent *adj* tawedog, distaw
retina *n* rhwyden y llygad, retina
retinue *n* gosgordd, gosgorddlu
retire *vi* ymneilltuo, encilio, cilio,
ymddeol
retired *adj* wedi ymddeol
retirement *n* ymddeoliad
retiring *adj* swil
retort *vb* gwrthateb ♦ *n* ateb
parod; ritort (*cemeg*)
retrace *vb* mynd yn ôl dros yr un
ffordd, dychwelyd
retract *vb* tynnu'n ôl
retrain *vb* ailhyfforddi
retreat *vi* cilio, encilio, ffoi ♦ *n*
encil, ffo
retrench *vb* cwtogi, cynilo
retribution *n* ad-daledigaeth, cosb,
dial
retrieve *vt* olrhain; adennill, adfer
retrogress *vi* mynd yn ôl, dirywio
retrospect *n* ad-drem, adolwg
return *vb* dychwelyd ♦ *n*
dychweliad; elw, enillion. **r.**
(**ticket**) *n* tocyn dwyffordd
reveal *vt* datguddio, amlygu,
dangos
revel *vi* gloddesta; ymhyfrydu ♦ *n*
gloddest
revelry *n* miri
revenge *vb, n* dial
revenue *n* cyllid, enillion, incwm
reverberate *vb* taro'n ôl; atseinio
revere *vt* parchu, anrhydeddu
reverence *n* parch, parchedigaeth
reverend *adj* parchedig
reverent *adj* parchus, gŵyl,

gwylaidd

reversal n dymchweliad, cwymp

reverse adj gwrthwyneb, chwith ♦ vb troi, gwrthdroi ♦ n gwrthdro, aflwydd. **r. charge call** n galwad y telir amdani'r pen arall. **r. (gear)** n gêr ôl

revert vb troi yn ôl, dychwelyd

review vt adolygu ♦ n adolygiad

reviewer n adolygydd

revile vt difenwi, cablu, gwaradwyddo

revise vt cywiro, diwygio

revision n cywiriad; adolygiad

revival n adfywiad, diwygiad

revive vb adfywio, adnewyddu

revoke vb galw yn ôl, diddymu, dirymu

revolt vb gwrthryfela ♦ n gwrthryfel

revolting adj gwrthnaws, atgas, ffiaidd

revolution n chwyldro, chwyldroad

revolutionary adj chwildroadol ♦ n chwildrowr

revolve vb troi, amdroi, cylchdroi

revolver n llawddryll

revulsion n atgasedd

reward n gwobr ♦ vt gwobrwyo

reword vb ailysgrifennu, ailddweud

rhapsody n hwyl, ymfflamychiad

rhetoric n rhetoreg, rhethreg

rheumatism n cryd cymalau, gwynegon

rhinoceros n rhinoseros

rhombus n rhombws

rhubarb n rhiwbob

rhyme n odl, rhigwm ♦ vb odli, rhigymu

rhythm n rhythm, rhediad

rib n asen, eisen

ribald n masweddwr ♦ adj masweddol

ribbon n rhuban, ysnoden

rice n reis

rich adj cyfoethog, goludog, bras

riches npl cyfoeth, golud

richness n cyfoethogrwydd, braster, ffrwythlonrwydd

rick n tas

rickets npl y llech(au)

rickety adj simsan, bregus

rid vt gwared

riddle n dychymyg, pos

riddle n rhidyll ♦ vt rhidyllio, gogrwn

ride vb marchogaeth, marchocáu

rider n marchogwr; atodiad

ridge n grwn, trum, cefn, crib

ridicule n gwawd ♦ vt gwawdio, chwerthin am ben

ridiculous adj chwerthinllyd

riding n marchogaeth

riding school n ysgol farchogaeth

rife adj aml, cyffredin, rhemp

riff-raff n gwehilion y bobl, dihirod

rifle vt anrheithio, ysbeilio

rifle n dryll, reiffl

rift n agen, hollt, rhwyg

rig vb rigio, taclu ♦ n rig

right adj iawn, uniawn; deau ♦ adv yn iawn ♦ vt unioni, cywiro ♦ n iawnder, hawl. **r. angle** n ongl sgwâr. **rights and customs** braint a defod. **r. wing** (POL) asgell dde

righteous adj cyfiawn

righteousness n cyfiawnder

rightful adj cyfreithlon, iawn, teg

rigid adj anhyblyg, manwl, caeth

rigmarole n ffregod, rhibidirês

rigour n llymder

rile vt cythruddo, ffyrnigo, llidio

rim n ymyl, cylch, cant

rind n pil, croen, crawen, rhisgl

ring n modrwy, cylch ♦ vb modrwyo

ring vb canu cloch, atseinio; modrwyo ♦ n swn cloch, tinc. **wedding r.** n modrwy briodas. **r. road** n cylchffordd

rinse vt golchi, trochi

riot n terfysg, gloddest ♦ vi terfysgu

rip *vb* rhipio, rhwygo, datod ♦ *n* rhwyg. **r.-off** *n* lladrad amlwg

ripe *adj* aeddfed

ripple *n* crych ♦ *vb* crychu

rise *vi* codi, cyfodi ♦ *n* codiad

risk *n* perygl, enbydrwydd ♦ *vt* peryglu, anturio, mentro

rite *n* defod

ritual *adj* defodol ♦ *n* defod

rival *n* cydymgeisydd ♦ *vb* cystadlu

river *n* afon

rivet *n* rhybed, hem, rifet ♦ *vb* rhybedu, hemio, rifetio

rivulet *n* afonig, nant, cornant

road *n* ffordd, heol; angorfa. **r. map** *n* map ffyrdd, map moduro. **r. works** *n* gwaith cynnal y ffordd

roam *vi* crwydro, gwibio

roar *vi* rhuo ♦ *n* rhu, rhuad

roast *vb* rhostio, crasu, pobi, digoni

rob *vt* lladrata, ysbeilio

robber *n* lleidr, ysbeiliwr

robbery *n* lladrad

robe *n* gwisg, gŵn

robin *n* brongoch

robust *adj* cadarn, cryf, grymus

rock *vb* siglo

rock *n* craig

rockery *n* gardd gerrig

rocket *n* roced

rocky *adj* creigiog; sigledig

rod *n* gwialen, llath

rodent *n* cnofil

roe *n* iyrches, ewig

roe *n* grawn pysgod, gronell

roebuck *n* iwrch

rogue *n* gwalch, cnaf

role *n* rhan, tasg, cymeriad

roll *vb* rholio, treiglo ♦ *n* rhôl. **r. call** *n* galw enwau (ar restr)

rolling *adj* tonnog. **r. pin** *n* rholbren. **r. stock** *n* rholstoc

Roman *n* Rhufeiniwr ♦ *adj* Rhufeinaidd, Rhufeinig. **R. Catholic** *n* Pabydd

romance *n* rhamant ♦ *vi* rhamantu

Romania *n* Românîa

romantic *adj* rhamantus

Rome *n* Rhufain

romp *vi* rhampio ♦ *n* rhamp; rhampen

rood *n* rhwd; y grog, y groes

roof *n* to, nen ♦ *vt* toi

rook *n* ydfran, brân

room *n* lle; ystafell. **r. service** *n* gwasanaeth ystafell

roomy *adj* helaeth, eang

roost *n* clwyd ♦ *vi* clwydo

rooster *n* ceiliog

root *n* gwraidd, gwreiddyn ♦ *vb* gwreiddio; diwreiddio

rope *n* rhaff ♦ *vt* rhaffu, rhwymo

rosary *n* paderau, llaswyr

rose *n* rhosyn. **r. hips** *npl* egroes

rosette *n* ysnoden

rostrum *n* llwyfan, areithfa

rosy *adj* rhosynnaidd, gwritgoch, disglair

rot *vb* pydru, braenu ♦ *n* pydredd; lol

rota *n* rhod, trefn

rotate *vi* troi, cylchdroi, chwyldroi

rote *n* tafod-leferydd

rotten *adj* pwdr, pydredig, sâl

rouge *n* lliw coch, gruddliw

rough *adj* garw, gerwin, bras

round *n* crwn ♦ *n* crwn, cylch, tro, rownd ♦ *adv, prep* o glych, o amgylch ♦ *vb* crynio, rowndio

roundabout *n* cylchdro, cylchfan, cylch ogylch; ceffylau bach ♦ *adj* o amgylch, cwmpasog

rouse *vb* dihuno, deffroi, cyffroi

rout *n* rhawt; ffo, dymchweliad ♦ *vb* ymlid, dymchwelyd

route *n* ffordd, llwybr, hynt

routine *n* defod, arfer

rove *vb* crwydro, gwibio

roving *adj* crwydrol

row *n* rhes, rhestr

row *vb* rhwyfo

row *n* terfysg, cythrwfl, ffrae

rowan *n* criafol

rowdy *adj* trystiog, afreolus
rowel *n* troell ysbardun, rhywel
rowing boat *n* cwch rhwyfo
royal *adj* brenhinol
royalty *n* brenhiniaeth; toll, tâl, breindal
rub *vb* rhwbio, rhathu, iro, crafu
rubber *n* rwber
rubbish *n* ysbwriel, sothach; lol. **r. bin** *n* bin ysbwriel. **r. dump** *n* tomen ysbwriel
rubble *n* rhwbel
ruby *n* rhuddem ♦ *adj* coch, rhudd
ruck *n* pentwr, crynswth, haid, ysgarmes
rucksack *n* rhychsach
ruction *n* helynt, terfysg
rudder *n* llyw
ruddy *adj* coch, gwridog, gwritgoch
rude *adj* anfoesgar; anghelfydd, garw
rudiment *n* egwyddor, elfen
rue *vt* galaru, gofidio, edifaru
rueful *adj* trist, truenus, gresynus
ruffian *n* adyn, anfadyn, dihiryn
ruffle *vb* crychu, cyffroi, aflonyddu
rug *n* hugan
rugby *n* rygbi
rugged *adj* garw, gerwin, clogyrnog
ruin *n* distryw, dinistr; adfail ♦ *vb* difetha, andwyo
rule *n* rheol, llywodraeth; riwl ♦ *vb* rheoli, llywodraethu; llinellu
ruler *n* llywodraethwr; pren mesur, rhiwl
ruling *n* dyfarniad, barn ♦ *adj* llywodraethol, mewn grym
rum *n* rym ♦ *adj* od, rhyfedd
rumble *vi* trystio, tyrfu, godyrfu
rummage *vb* chwalu a chwilio, chwilota
rumour *n* chwedl, gair, sôn, achlust
rump *n* tin, bôn, cwman, cloren
rumple *vt* crychu, sybachu

rumpus *n* helynt, terfysg
run *vb* rhedeg, llifo ♦ *n* rhediad, rhedfa. **in the long r.** yn y pen draw
rung *n* ffon ysgol
rupture *n* rhwyg; tor llengig ♦ *vb* rhwygo
rural *adj* gwledig, gwladaidd
ruse *n* ystryw, dichell
rush *n* brwynen, pabwyryn
rush *vb* rhuthro ♦ *n* rhuthr. **r. hour** *n* awr brysur
russet *adj* llwytgoch
Russia *n* Rwsia
rust *n* rhwd ♦ *vb* rhydu
rustic *adj* gwladaidd, gwledig ♦ *n* gwladwr
rusticate *vt* anfon adref am dymor
rustle *vi* siffrwd, chwithrwd, rhuglo
rusty *adj* rhydlyd
rut *n* rhych, rhigol
ruthless *adj* didostur, diarbed, creulon
rye *n* rhyg

S

Sabbath *n* Sabath, Saboth
sabotage *n* difrod bwriadol ♦ *vb* difrodi
sacerdotal *adj* offeiriadol
sack *n* sach, ffetan ♦ *vt* sachu; difrodi; diswyddo
sackcloth *n* sachlen, sachliain
sacrament *n* sacrament, ordinhad
sacred *adj* cysegredig, glân, sanctaidd
sacrifice *n* aberth, offrwm ♦ *vt* aberthu
sacrilege *n* halogiad, cysegrysbeiliad
sad *adj* trist, athrist, prudd, digalon
saddle *n* cyfrwy ♦ *vt* cyfrwyo; beichio

saddler n cyfrwywr

sadness n tristwch, prudd-der

safe adj diogel, dihangol, saff ♦ n cell, cist, cloer

safety n diogelwch. **s. belt** gwregys diogelwch. **s. pin** pin cau

saffron n saffrwm ♦ adj melyn

sag vb segio, segian, sagio, ymollwng

sage adj doeth ♦ n gŵr doeth

sage n saets

Sahara n Sahara

sail n hwyl ♦ vb hwylio, morio, mordwyo

sailing n hwylio. **s. boat** n llong hwylio

sailor n morwr, llongwr

saint n sant

sake n mwyn. **for the s. of** er mwyn

salary n cyflog

sale n gwerth, gwerthiant, arwerthiant

salient adj amlwg

saline adj heliaidd, hallt ♦ n heli

saliva n haliw, poer, dŵr anadl

sallow adj melyn afiach

salmon n eog, gleisiad, samwn

saloon n neuadd, salwn

salt n halen, halwyn (cemeg) ♦ adj hallt ♦ vt halltu. **s. cellar** n llestr halen. **s. water** n dŵr hallt, dŵr y môr

salty adj hallt

salute vt cyfarch; saliwtio ♦ n cyfarchiad; saliwt

salvation n iachawdwriaeth. **S. Army** Byddin yr Iachawdwriaeth

salve n eli, ennaint ♦ vt elïo, lleddfu; achub

same adj yr un, yr unrhyw, yr un fath

sample n sampl, enghraifft ♦ vt samplu, samplo

sanctify vt sancteiddio

sanctimonious adj ffug-sanctaidd, sych-dduwiol

sanction n caniatâd; cosb; sancsiwn (moeseg) ♦ vt caniatáu; cosbi

sanctity n sancteiddrwydd

sanctuary n cysegr; noddfa, nawdd

sand n tywod ♦ vt tywodi. **s. castle** n castell tywod

sandpaper n papur gwydrog

sandpit n pwll tywod

sandwich n brechdan

sandy adj tywodlyd; melyngoch

sane adj iach, call, synhwyrol

sanitary adj iechydol. **s. towel** n tywel misglwyf, tywel iechydol

sanitation n iechydaeth

sanity n iechyd meddwl, iawn bwyll

Santa Claus n Siôn Corn

sap n nodd, sudd, sugn ♦ vt sugno, hysbyddu

sap vb tangloddio, diseilio

sapling n pren ieuanc

sapphire n saffir ♦ adj glas

sarcasm n gwawdiaith, coegni, gair du

sarcastic adj gwawdlym, coeglyd, brathog

sardine n sardîn

sash n gwregys; ffrâm ffenestr

satchel n sachell, cod lyfrau

sate vt digoni, llenwi, diwallu

satellite n canlynwr, cynffonnwr; lleuad; lloeren

satiate vt digoni, diwallu, syrffedu

satin n satin, pali

satire n dychan, gogan

satirize vb dychan, goganu

satisfaction n bodlonrwydd; iawn

satisfactory adj boddhaol; iawnol

satisfy vt bodloni, diwallu, digoni

saturate vt trwytho, mwydo

Saturday n dydd Sadwrn

sauce n saws; haerllugrwydd

saucepan n sosban

saucer n soser

saucy adj digywilydd, haerllug

Saudi Arabia n Saudi Arabia
saunter vi rhodianna, ymdroi, swmera
sausage n selsig, selsigen
savage adj gwyllt, ffyrnig, milain, anwar ♦ n dyn gwyllt, anwariad, anwarddyn
save vb achub, arbed, gwaredu; cynilo ♦ prep oddieithr, ond
saving adj achubol, darbodus
savings npl cynilion
saviour n achubwr, gwaredwr, iachawdwr
savour n sawr, blas ♦ vb sawru
savoury n blasusfwyd; adj sawrus
saw n llif ♦ vb llifio
sawdust n blawd llif
sawmill n melin lifio
say vb dywedyd, dweud
saying n dywediad, ymadrodd, gair
scab n crachen, cramen; clafr
scabies n y crafu
scaffold n ysgaffald; dienyddle
scald vt ysgaldio, sgaldan(u) ♦ n ysgaldiad
scale n clorian, tafol, mantol
scale n graddfa ♦ vb dringo
scale n cen ♦ vb cennu; digennu, pilio
scallop n gylfgragen; gwlf ♦ vt gylfu, minfylchu
scalp n copa, croen y pen ♦ vt penfingo
scamp n cnaf, gwalch, dihiryn
scamper vi ffoi, carlamu, brasgamu
scan vb corfannu; sganio, edrych, chwilio
scandal n tramgwydd, gwarth, enllib
Scandinavia n Llychlyn
scanner n sganydd
scant, -y adj prin
scapegoat n bwch dihangol
scapegrace n dyn diras, oferwr, dihiryn

scar n craith ♦ vt creithio
scarce adj, adv prin
scarcely adv prin, braidd, odid, nemor
scare vt brawychu, tarfu ♦ n dychryn
scared adj wedi cael ofn, wedi rhuso, wedi brawychu
scarf n crafat, sgarff
scarlatina n y dwymyn goch
scarlet adj ysgarlad
scarp n llethr
scathe vt deifio, anafu, niweidio
scathing adj deifiol, miniog
scatter vb gwasgaru, chwalu, taenu
scavenger n carthwr, carthydd
scene n lle; golwg, golygfa
scenery n golygfa
scenic adj hardd, golygfaol
scent n arogl, aroglau, trywydd; perarogl ♦ vt arogli
sceptic n amheuwr
sceptical adj amheugar
sceptre n teyrnwialen
schedule n atodlen, cofrestr, taflen
scheme n cynllun; cynllwyn ♦ vb cynllunio
schism n rhwyg, ymraniad, sism
scholar n ysgolhaig, ysgolor
scholarly adj ysgolheigaidd
scholarship n ysgolheictod; ysgoloriaeth
scholastic adj athrofaol
school n ysgol, ysgoldy ♦ vt disgyblu
schoolbook n llyfr ysgol
schoolboy n bachgen ysgol
schoolchildren npl plant ysgol
schooldays npl dyddiau ysgol
schoolgirl n merch ysgol
schoolmaster n athro
schoolmistress n athrawes
schooner n ysgwner
sciatica n clunwst
science n gwyddor, gwyddoniaeth
scientific adj gwyddonol

scientist n gwyddonydd
scissors npl siswrn
scoff n gwawd ♦ vi gwawdio, gwatwar
scold vb dwrdio, tafodi, ceryddu, cymhennu ♦ n cecren
scone n sgon
scoop n lletwad ♦ vt cafnu, cafnio
scope n ergyd, bwriad; cylch, cwmpas, lle
scorch vb deifio, llosgi, greidio, rhuddo
score n hac, rhic; cyfrif, dyled; sgôr; ugain
score vb rhicio, cyfrif, sgori(o)
scorn n dirmyg ♦ vb dirmygu, gwatwar
scorpion n ysgorpion
Scot n Ysgotyn, Albanwr
scotch vt hacio, darnio, trychu
Scotch adj Ysgotaidd, Albanaidd
scot-free adj croeniach, dianaf
Scotland n Yr Alban
Scottish adj Albanaidd
scoundrel n cnaf, dihiryn
scour vt carthu, ysgwrio
scour vb rhedeg; chwilio
scourge n fflangell, pla ♦ vt fflangellu
scout n sgowt, ysbïwr ♦ vt sgowta, ysbio
scowl vb cuchio, gwgu ♦ n cilwg, gwg
scraggy adj esgyrnog, tenau, cul, salw
scramble vi, n ciprys, ymgiprys.
  scrambled egg n cymysgwy
scrap n tamaid, tameidyn, dernyn
scrapbook n llyfr lloffion
scrape vb crafu ♦ n helynt, helbul, crafiad
scratch vb crafu, cripio
scrawl vb ysgriblo, ysgrafio
scream vi ysgrechain ♦ n ysgrech, gwawch
screech vi ysgrechain ♦ n ysgrech
screen n llen, cysgod; sgrin ♦ vt

cysgodi
screw n sgriw, hoel dro ♦ vb ysgriwio
screwdriver n tyrnsgriw
scribble n ysgribl ♦ vb ysgriblo, ysgriblan
script n llawysgrif, ysgrif, sgript
scripture n ysgrythur
scroll n rhôl, plyg llyfr
scrub n prysgwydd; ysgwrfa ♦ vt ysgwrio
scruff n gwar, gwegil
scrum(mage) n sgrym, ysgarmes
scruple n petruster (moesol) ♦ vi petruso
scrupulous adj gwyliadwrus, manwl
scrutinize vt chwilio, archwilio
scrutiny n archwiliad
scuffle vi, n ymgiprys, ymryson
scull n rhwyf unllaw, rhodl ♦ vb rhodli
scullery n cegin fach, cegin gefn
sculptor n cerflunydd
sculpture n cerfluniaeth; cerflun ♦ vb cerfio, torri
scum n sgum; gwehilion, sorod
scurf n cen, mardon
scurrilous adj bustlaidd, brwnt, difriol
scurry vi ffrystio ♦ n ffrwst, ffwdan
scurvy adj crachlyd, crach ♦ n llwg
scutter vi ffoi, diengyd
scuttle n llestr glo
scuttle vt tyllu llong i'w suddo
scuttle vi heglu ffoi, dianc
scythe n pladur
sea n môr, cefnfor; moryn. **s. water** n dŵr y môr
seaboard n morlan, glan y môr
seafood n bwyd môr
seagull n gwylan
seal n morlo
seal n sêl, insel ♦ vt selio
sea level n lefel y môr

seam *n* gwniad, gwrym; haen, gwythïen; craith
seaman *n* morwr, llongwr
seamstress *n* gwniadwraig, gwniadyddes
seamy *adj* annymunol
seance *n* seawns
seaplane *n* awyren fôr
sear *adj* sych, crin, gwyw ♦ *vt* serio, deifio
search *vb* chwilio, profi ♦ *n* ymchwil
seashore *n* glan y môr
seasickness *n* salwch y môr
seaside *n* glan y môr
season *n* tymor, amser, pryd, adeg ♦ *vb* tymheru; halltu. **high/low s.** *n* tymor prysur/llac
seasonal *adj* tymhorol
season ticket *n* tocyn tymor
seat *n* sedd, sêt, eisteddle ♦ *vi* eistedd
seat belt *n* gwregys diogelwch
seaweed *n* gwymon, gwmon
seaworthy *adj* addas i'r môr, diogel
secede *vi* ymneilltuo, encilio; torri'n rhydd, ymwahanu
secession *n* ymneilltuad, enciliad; ymwahaniad
seclude *vt* cau allan, neilltuo
second *adj* ail ♦ *n* ail; eiliad ♦ *vt* eilio. **s. class** *n* ail ddosbarth, isradd
secondary *adj* eilradd, uwchradd. **s. school** *n* ysgol uwchradd
second-hand *adj* ail-law
secret *adj* dirgel, cyfrinachol ♦ *n* cyfrinach
secretary *n* ysgrifennydd. **S. of State** *n* Ysgrifennydd Gwladol
secretive *adj* yn celu, tawedog
sect *n* sect, enwad
sectarian *adj* enwadol, cul
section *n* toriad, trychiad; rhan, adran
sector *n* sector

secular *adj* bydol; lleygol; seciwlar
secure *adj* sicr, diogel ♦ *vt* sicrhau, diogelu
security *n* diogelwch, sicrwydd, gwystl
sedate *adj* tawel, digyffro ♦ *vb* rhoi i gysgu, tawelu
sedative *adj* lleddfol, lliniarol
sedge *n* hesg
sediment *n* gwaelodion, gwaddod
sedition *n* terfysg, brad, gwrthryfel
seduce *vt* llithio, hudo, twyllo
seductive *adj* llithiol, deniadol
see *n* esgobaeth
see *vb* gweld, canfod
seed *n* had, hedyn ♦ *vb* hadu, hedeg
seedy *adj* hadog; salw; sâl, anhwylus
seek *vb* ceisio, ymofyn, chwilio
seem *vi* ymddangos
seemly *adj* gweddus, gweddaidd, addas
seep *vb* diferu, gollwng
seer *n* gweledydd
seesaw *n* siglenydd
seethe *vb* berwi, byrlymu
segment *n* darn, rhan, segment
segregate *vt* didoli, neilltuo, gwahanu
seize *vb* gafael mewn, atafaelu, dal, achub
seizure *n* daliad; strôc
seldom *adv* anfynych, anaml
select *vt* dewis, dethol
self (selves) *n* hun, hunan ♦ *prefix* hunan-, ym-
self-catering *adj* hunan arlwy
self-conscious *adj* hunanymwybodol, swil
self-contained *adj* annibynnol, ar wahân
self-control *n* hunanlywodraeth
self-employed *adj* hunangyflogedig
self-evident *adj* amlwg, eglur

self-government *n* ymreolaeth
self-interest *n* hunan-les
selfish *adj* hunanol
self-possessed *adj* hunanfeddiannol
self-respect *n* hunan-barch
self-sacrifice *n* hunanaberth
selfsame *adj* yr un, yr unrhyw
self-satisfied *adj* hunanddigonol
self-service *n* hunanwasanaeth
self-sufficient *adj* hunanddigonol, hy
sell *vb* gwerthu; siomi ♦ *n* siom
seller *n* gwerthwr
sellotape *n* selotâp
semblance *n* tebygrwydd, rhith
semi- *prefix* hanner, lled, go
semicolon *n* gwahannod (;)
seminary *n* athrofa, ysgol
sempiternal *adj* bythol, tragwyddol
senate *n* senedd
send *vt* anfon, danfon, gyrru
senile *adj* hen a methedig, heneiddiol
senior *adj* hŷn ♦ *n* hynaf
seniority *n* blaenoriaeth
sensation *n* ymdeimlad, teimlad; cyffro, ias, syndod
sensational *adj* iasol, cyffrous
sense *n* synnwyr, pwyll, ystyr
senseless *adj* dienaid, disynnwyr, hurt
sensible *adj* synhwyrol; teimladwy
sensitive *adj* teimladwy, croendenau; hydeiml
sensual *adj* cnawdol; trythyll, chwantus
sensuous *adj* teimladol, synhwyrus
sentence *n* brawddeg; barn, dedfryd ♦ *vt* dedfrydu
sententious *adj* doetheiriog
sentiment *n* syniad, teimlad
sentry *n* gwyliwr, gwyliedydd
separate *adj* ar wahân ♦ *vb* gwahanu, neilltuo, ysgar; ymwahanu

separation *n* gwahaniad
sept- *prefix* saith, seith-
September *n* Medi
septic *adj* braenol, pydrol, madreddol
sepulchre *n* bedd, beddrod
sequel *n* canlyniad
sequence *n* trefn, dilyniad
sequester *vt* neilltuo; atafaelu
serenade *n* hwyrgan, nosgan ♦ *vt* hwyrganu
serene *adj* teg; tawel, digynnwrf
sergeant *n* rhingyll, sarsiant
serial *adj* cyfresol, bob yn rhifyn ♦ *n* stori gyfres
series *n* rhes, cyfres
serious *adj* difrifol
seriously *adv* yn ddifrifol
sermon *n* pregeth
serpent *n* sarff
serrated *adj* danheddog
serum *n* serwm
servant *n* gwas; morwyn
serve *vb* gwasanaethu, gweini
service *n* gwasanaeth, oedfa; llestri. **s. charge** *n* tâl am wasanaeth
serviceable *adj* gwasanaethgar, defnyddiol
serviette *n* napcyn
servile *adj* gwasaidd
session *n* eisteddiad; sesiwn; tymor
set *vb* gosod, dodi; plannu; sadio; sefydlu; machlud ♦ *n* set; impyn, planhigyn
settee, settle *n* sgiw, setl
setting *n* lleoliad, safle; machludiad
settle *vb* sefydlu; penderfynu; cytuno, setlo; plwyfo; talu
settlement *n* cytundeb; gwladfa
seven *adj*, *n* saith
seventeen *adj*, *n* dau (dwy) ar bymtheg, un deg saith
seventh *adj* seithfed
seventy *adj*, *n* deg a thrigain,

saith deg

sever *vb* gwahanu, datod, torri

several *adj* amryw; gwahanol

severance *n* gwahaniad, datgysylltiad

severe *adj* caled, tost, llym, gerwin

severity *n* llymder, gerwindeb

sew *vb* gwnïo, pwytho

sewage *n* carthffosiaeth, carthion

sewer *n* ceuffos, carthffos

sewing machine *n* peiriant gwnïo

sex *n* rhyw

sex education *n* addysg ryw

sextet *n* chwechawd

sexton *n* clochydd; torrwr beddau

sexual *adj* rhywiol

shabby *adj* carpiog, gwael, aflêr

shack *n* caban

shackle *n* hual, gefyn, llyffethair

shade *n* cysgod; ysbryd ♦ *vt* cysgodi

shadow *n* cysgod ♦ *vt* cysgodi

shadowy *adj* cysgodol, rhithiol

shady *adj* cysgodol; amheus

shaft *n* paladr, saeth; llorp, braich; pwll; gwerthyd

shaggy *adj* cedenog, blewog

shake *vb* ysgwyd, siglo, crynu

shaky *adj* ansad, crynedig

shallow *adj* bas ♦ *n* basle, beisle

sham *n* ffugio ♦ *adj* ffug, gau, coeg ♦ *n* ffug, ffugbeth

shambles *n* galanastra

shame *n* cywilydd, gwaradwydd, gwarth ♦ *vb* cywilyddio, gwaradwyddo

shamefaced *n* swil, gwylaidd

shameful *adj* cywilyddus, gwarthus

shampoo *vt* golchi pen ♦ *n* siampŵ

shank *n* coes, gar, esgair; paladr

shanty *n* caban, bwthyn, penty

shape *n* siâp, llun ♦ *vt* siapio, llunio

shapeless *adj* aflunaidd, di-lun

shapely *adj* siapus, lluniaidd, gosgeiddig

share *n* rhan, cyfran ♦ *vb* rhannu; cyfranogi

share *n* swch aradr

shareholder *n* cyfranddaliwr

shark *n* siarc, morgi; twyllwr

sharp *adj* siarp, llym, miniog ♦ *n* llonnod (cerdd)

sharpen *vb* hogi, minio, awchlymu

sharpener *n* naddwr

sharper *n* siarpwr

sharply *adv* yn sydyn

shatter *vb* dryllio, chwilfriwio; ysigo

shave *vb* eillio, torri barf; rhasglio

shavings *npl* naddion

shawl *n* siôl

she *pron* hi ♦ *adj, prefix* benyw

sheaf (**sheaves**) *n* ysgub

shear *vt* cneifio; siero

shears *npl* gwellau

sheath *n* gwain; (*contraceptive*) maneg atal cenhedlu

sheathe *vt* gweinio

shed *n* penty, sied

shed *vt* tywallt; gollwng; colli; dihidlo, bwrw

sheen *n* disgleirdeb, llewyrch, gwawr

sheep (**sheep**) *n* dafad

sheer *vi* gwyro or y ffordd, cilio

sheer *adj* pur, glân, noeth, syth, serth

sheet *n* llen; cynfas; hwylraff; taflen

shekel *n* sicl

shelf (**shelves**) *n* silff, astell

shell *n* cragen; plisgyn, masgl; tân-belen

shellfish *n* cregynbysg

shelter *n* cysgod, lloches ♦ *vb* cysgodi, llochesu; ymochel; llechu

shelve *vi* llechweddu, llethru

shelve *vt* gosod naill ochr, troi o'r neilltu

shepherd *n* bugail ♦ *vt* bugeilio

sheriff *n* sirydd, siryf

sherry *n* sieri

Shetland *n* Shetland

shield *n* tarian ♦ *vt* cysgodi, amddiffyn

shift *vb* newid, symud; ymdaro ♦ *n* newid; tro, stem, shifft

shilling *n* swllt

shilly-shally *n* anwadalwch

shimmer *vi* tywynnu, caneitio, rhithio

shin *n* crimog, crimp coes

shindy *n* helynt, ffrwgwd, terfysg

shine *vb* disgleirio, llewyrchu, tywynnu ♦ *n* disgleirdeb, sglein, llewyrch

shingle *n* graean, gro

shingle *n* peithynen; estyllen

shingles *npl* yr eryr, yr eryrod

shiny *adj* gloyw, disglair

ship *n* llong ♦ *vt* trosglwyddo

shipping *n* llongau (gwlad)

shipshape *adj, adv* taclus, trefnus, twt

shipwreck *n* llongddrylliad

shire *n* sir

shirk *vt* gochel, osgoi

shirt *n* crys

shiver *vi* crynu

shiver *vb* dryllio, chwilfriwio

shoal *n* haig ♦ *vi* heigio

shoal *n* basle, beisle

shock *n* sioc, ergyd, ysgytiad ♦ *vt* ysgytio; tramgwyddo

shocking *adj* arswydus, ysgytiol

shoddy *n* brethyn eilban ♦ *adj* ffug, gwael

shoe *n* esgid; pedol ♦ *vt* pedoli

shoehorn *n* seisbin, siasbi

shoelace *n* carrai/lasen esgid

shoemaker *n* crydd

shoe shop *n* siop esgidiau

shoot *vb* tarddu, blaguro; saethu ♦ *n* ysbrigyn, blaguryn

shooting *n* saethu

shop *n* masnachdy, siop ♦ *vb* siopa

shopkeeper *n* siopwr

shopper *n* prynwr

shopping *n* siopa

shore *n* glan, traeth

short *adj* byr, cwta, prin

shortage *n* prinder, diffyg

short circuit *n* cylchedd byr

shortcoming *n* diffyg, bai

short cut *n* llwybr tarw, llwybr llygad, ffordd fer

shorthand *n* llaw-fer

shorts *npl* trowsus cwta

shot *n* ergyd; saethwr

shoulder *n* ysgwydd, palfais ♦ *vt* ysgwyddo. **s. blade** *n* sgapwla, pont yr ysgwydd

shout *vb* bloeddio, gweiddi ♦ *n* bloedd, gwaedd

shove *vb* gwthio

shovel *n* llwyarn ♦ *vt* rhofio

show *vb* dangos, arddangos ♦ *n* arddangosfa, sioe, siew

shower *n* cawod, cawad ♦ *vb* cawodi, bwrw

shred *n* llarp, cerpyn ♦ *vb* rhwygo, torri'n fân

shrew *n* cecren, gwraig anynad; llyg

shrewd *adj* ffel, craff, call, cyfrwys

shriek *vb* ysgrechian ♦ *n* ysgrech

shrill *adj* llym, main, meinllais

shrimp *n* berdysen ♦ *vi* berdysa

shrine *n* ysgrin; creirfa; cysegr, seintwar

shrink *vb* crebachu, tynnu ato, cilio

shrivel *vb* crychu, crebachu

shroud *n* amdo, amwisg; (*pl*) rhaffau hwylbren ♦ *vt* amdoi, cuddio, celu

Shrove Tuesday *n* Mawrth Ynyd

shrub *n* prysgwydden, llwyn

shrug *vb* codi'r ysgwyddau

shudder *n* crynfa, echryd, arswyd ♦ *vi* crynu, arswydo

shuffle *vb* siffrwd; llusgo; gwingo,

gwamalu

shun vt gochelyd, osgoi

shunt vb troi o'r neilltu, symud o'r ffordd, siyntio

shut vb cau ♦ pl caeëdig

shutter n caead, clawr, gwerchyr

shuttle n gwennol (gwëydd)

shuttlecock n gwennol

shy adj swil ♦ vi osgoi, rhusio

siblings npl plant

sick adj claf; yn chwydu, â chyfog arno; wedi diflasu

sickbay n canolfan iechyd

sickening adj atgas, diflas, cyfoglyd

sickle n cryman

sickly adj afiach, nychlyd

side n ochr, ystlys; tu, plaid ♦ vi ochri

sidestep vb ochrgamu

sidetrack vt troi o'r neilltu

sideways adv tua'r ochr, yn wysg ei ochr

sidle vi cerdded yn wysg ei ochr, gwyro

siege n gwarchae

sieve n gogr, gwagr, rhidyll, sife

sift vt gogrwn, nithio, hidlo, rhidyllu

sigh vb ochneidio ♦ n ocheaid

sight n golwg, golygfa ♦ vt gweld

sightseeing n taith i weld y wlad

sign n arwydd, argoel ♦ vb arwyddo, llofnodi

signal adj hynod ♦ n arwydd

signatory adj arwyddol ♦ n arwyddwr

signature n llofnod

significance n arwyddocâd, ystyr

significant adj arwyddocaol; o bwys

signify vb arwyddo, arwyddocáu

signpost n mynegbost, arwyddbost

silence n taw, distawrwydd ♦ vt rhoi taw ar

silent adj distaw, tawedog, mud

silhouette n llun du, cysgodlun,

silwet

silicon n silicon. **s. chip** sglodyn silicon

silk n sidan

silky adj sidanaidd

sill n sil

silly adj gwirion, ffôl, disynnwyr

silt n gwaelodion, llaid ♦ vb gwaelodi, tagu

silver n arian ♦ vt ariannu. **s. paper** n papur arian

silversmith n gof arian

silvery adj ariannaid(d)

similar adj tebyg, cyffelyb

simile n cyffelybiaeth, cymhariaeth

simmer vi lledferwi, goferwi

simper vi cilwenu, glaswenu

simple adj syml, unplyg; gwirion, diniwed

simplicity n symlrwydd, unplygrwydd

simplify vt symleiddio

simulate vt ffugio, dynwared

simultaneous adj cyfamserol, ar y pryd

sin n pechod ♦ vb pechu

since conj gan, yn gymaint ♦ prep er, er pan

sincere adj diffuant, didwyll, pur

sinew n gewyn, giewyn

sing vb canu

singe vt deifio

singer n canwr, cantwr, cantores

singing n canu

single adj sengl, dibriod, gweddw. **s. bed** n gwely sengl. **s.-minded** adj unplyg, cywir. **s. room** n ystafell sengl

singlet n gwasgod wlanen, crys isaf

singular adj unigol; hynod

sinister adj ysgeler; chwithig

sink vb soddi, suddo ♦ n sinc

sinner n pechadur

sinuous adj dolennog, troellog

sip vt llymeitian ♦ n llymaid,

llymeidyn

siphon *n* siffon

sir *n* syr

siren *n* corn, seiren

sirloin *n* llwyn eidion

sissy *n* cadi(ffan)

sister *n* chwaer

sister-in-law *n* chwaer yng nghyfraith

sit *vb* eistedd

site *n* safle, lle ♦ *vb* lleoli

sitting *n* eisteddiad

situated *adj* yn sefyll, wedi ei leoli

situation *n* lle, safle; sefyllfa

six *adj*, *n* chwech

sixteen *adj*, *n* un ar bymtheg, un deg chwech

sixth *adj* chweched

sixty *adj*, *n* trigain, chwe deg

sizable *adj* gweddol fawr

size *n* maint, maintioli

sizzle *vb* ffrio

skate *n* cath för

skate *n* sgêt ♦ *vb* ysglefrio

skateboard *n* bwrdd sglefrio

skein *n* cengl, sgain

skeleton *n* ysgerbwd; amlinelliad

sketch *n* llun, braslun ♦ *vb* braslunio, tynnu

skewer *n* gwaell, gwachell

ski *n* sgi ♦ *vb* sgio

skid *vb* llithro (naill ochr)

skier *n* sgïwr

skiff *n* ysgafnfad, ceubal, sgiff

skill *n* medr, medrusrwydd

skilled *adj* medrus, crefftus

skim *vb* tynnu, codi (hufen)

skimmed milk *n* llaeth glas, llaeth sgim

skimp *vb* crintachu, cybydda

skimpy *adj* crintach

skin *n* croen ♦ *vb* blingo

skinny *adj* tenau; prin, crintach

skip *vi* llamu, sgipio

skipper *n* capten llong

skipping-rope *n* rhaff sgipio

skirmish *n* ysgarmes

skirt *n* godre, sgyrt ♦ *vt* dilyn gyda godre

skit *n* gogan

skittish *adj* nwyfus, gwantan, anwadal

skittles *npl* ceilys

skulk *vi* llechu, techu

skull *n* penglog

skunk *n* drewgi

sky *n* wybren, wybr, awyr

skylark *n* ehedydd

skylight *n* ffenestr do

slab *n* llech

slack *adj* llac, diofal, esgeulus ♦ *n* glo mân

slacken *vb* llacio, llaesu

slag *n* sorod, slag

slake *vt* torri (syched), slecio

slam *vb* cau yn glats, clepian

slander *n* enllib ♦ *vt* enllibio

slang *n* iaith sathredig, slang ♦ *vt* difrio

slant *vb* gwyro, gogwyddo ♦ *n* gogwydd

slanting *adj* ar oledd/osgo

slap *vt* clewtian ♦ *n* clewt(en), palfod

slapdash *adj* ffwrdd-â-hi, rhywsutrywfodd

slash *n* slaes, hac ♦ *vt* slasio, chwipio

slate *n* llech, llechen

slate *vt* sennu, difrio

slattern *n* slwt, slebog, sopen

slaughter *n* lladdedigaeth, lladdfa ♦ *vt* lladd

slaughterhouse *n* lladd-dy

slave *n* slaf, caethwas ♦ *vi* slafio

slavery *n* caethiwed, caethwasanaeth

slay *vt* lladd

sled, sledge, sleigh *n* car llusg, sled

sledgehammer *n* gordd

sleek *adj* llyfn, llyfndew, graenus

sleep *vb* cysgu, huno ♦ *n* cwsg, hun

sleeper *n* (*person*) cysgwr; pren
neu ddefnydd arall i ddal y
cledrau

sleeping bag *n* sach gysgu

sleeping pill *n* pilsen gysgu

sleepy *adj* cysglyd

sleet *n* eirlaw

sleeve *n* llawes

sleight *n* deheurwydd, cyfrwystra,
dichell

slender *adj* main, eiddil, prin

slice *n* tafell, ysglisen ♦ *vt* tafellu,
ysglisio

slick *adj* llyfn, tafodrydd, slic

slide *vb* llithro, sglefrio ♦ *n*
llithren, sleid

slight *adj* ysgafn, eiddil, prin ♦ *vt*
diystyru ♦ *n* diystyrwch, sarhad

slightly *adj* yn fain; ychydig

slim *adj* main, eiddil

slime *n* llaid, llaca; llys,
llysnafedd

sling *vt* taflu, lluchio ♦ *n* ffon dafl

slip *vb* llithro, dianc; gollwng ♦ *n*
slip

slipper *n* llopan, sliper

slippery *adj* llithrig, diafael, di-
ddal

slipshod *adj* anniben

slipway *n* llithrfa

slit *vb* hollti, agennu, rhwygo ♦ *n*
hollt

slither *vb* ymlusgo, llithro

slobber *vb* glafoerio, slobran

sloe *n* eirinen ddu fach, draenen
ddu

slog *vb* gweithio'n galed

sloop *n* slŵp

slop *n* (*pl*) golchion ♦ *vb* gwlychu,
trochi

slope *n* llethr, gogwydd ♦ *vb*
gogwyddo

sloppy *adj* lleidiog, tomlyd;
meddal, masw; anniben

slot *n* agen, twll

sloth *n* diogi, seguryd, syrthni

slouch *vb* llaesu, ymollwng;

cerdded yn aflêr

sloven *n* dyn aflêr, slebog

slovenly *adj* anniben

slow *adj* araf, hwyrfrydig,
hwyrdrwm ♦ *vb* arafu

slowly *adj* yn araf (deg)

sludge *n* llaid, llaca

slug *n* gwlithen, malwoden

sluggish *adj* diog, dioglyd, swrth

sluice *n* llifddor

slum *n* slym

slumber *vb* hepian, cysgu ♦ *n* cwsg

slump *n* cwymp, gostyngiad;
dirwasgiad

slur *vb* difrïo ♦ *n* llithriad, cyflusg
(cerdd.); anfri

slush *n* llaid, llaca, eira gwlyb

slut *n* slwt, slebog

sly *adj* cyfrwys, ffals, dichellgar,
tan din

smack *n* blas ♦ *vi* blasu, blasio,
archwaethu

smack *n* smac, palfod ♦ *vb* smacio,
chwipio

smack *n* llongan, smac

small *adj* bach, bychan, mân, main

smallholder *n* tyddynnwr

small-pox *n* y frech wen

smart *vi* gwynio, dolurio, llosgi ♦ *n*
gwŷn, dolur ♦ *adj* llym, bywiog;
ffel, ffraeth; crand

smash *vb* torri, malu, chwilfriwio

smattering *n* gwybodaeth fas,
crap

smear *vt* iro, dwbio

smell *n* arogl, aroglau ♦ *vb* arogli

smile *vb* gwenu ♦ *n* gwên

smirch *vt* llychwino, difwyno

smirk *vi* cilwenu, glaswenu ♦ *n*
cilwen

smith *n* gof

smithy *n* gefail (gof)

smog *n* smog, mwgwl

smoke *n* mwg ♦ *vb* mygu, ysmygu,
smocio

smoked *adj* wedi ei fygu

smoky *adj* myglyd

smooth adj llyfn, esmwyth ♦ vt llyfnhau

smother vb mygu, llethu

smoulder vi mudlosgi

smudge n baw, staen, smotyn ♦ vb difwyno, trochi

smug adj hunanol, cysetlyd

smuggle vt smyglio

smut n parddu, huddygl, smotyn; siarad aflan

smutty adj aflan, brwnt

snack n tamaid, byrbryd. **s. bar** n lle am damaid

snag n rhwystr, maen tramgwydd

snail n malwoden, malwen

snake n neidr

snap vb clecian, torri'n glats; tynnu llun ♦ n clec

snare n magl, croglath ♦ vt maglu, rhwydo

snarl vi ysgyrnygu, chwyrnu

snatch vb cipio ♦ n cip, crap; tamaid

sneak vi llechian ♦ n llechgi

sneaking adj llechwraidd, cachgïaidd

sneer vb gwawdio, glaswenu ♦ n gwawd, glaswen

sneeze vi tisian

sniff vb ffroeni, gwyntio

snigger vb glaswerthin

snip vb torri, cynhinio ♦ n demyn, toriad

snipe n gïach

snippet n tamaid, cynhinyn

snob n crechyn (pl. crachach), snob

snobbish adj crachaidd, snoblyd

snooker n snwcer

snooze vb hepian ♦ n cyntun

snore vi chwyrnu

snort vi ffroeni, ffroenochi

snotty adj cas

snout n trwyn anifail, duryn

snow n eira, ôd ♦ vb bwrw eira, odi

snowball n pelen eira

snowdrift n lluwch

snowflake n pluen eira

snow plough n aradr eira

snub vt sennu ♦ n sen

snub adj pwt, smwt

snub-nosed adj trwyn smwt

snuff vb ffroeni, snwffian ♦ n trwynlwch, snisyn

snug adj cryno, clyd, diddos

snuggle vb ymwasgu at; llochi, anwesu

so adv, conj fel, felly; mor, cyn

soak vb mwydo, sucio; slotian

soap n sebon ♦ vb sebono. **s. opera** n opera sebon. **s. powder** n powdr golchi

soapy adj sebonllyd

soar vi ehedeg, esgyn

sob vi igian, beichio ♦ n ig, ebwch

sober adj sobr, sad ♦ vb sobri

sobriety n sobrwydd

so-called adj dywededig

soccer n pêl-droed, y bêl gron

sociable adj cymdeithasgar

social adj cymdeithasol. **s. club** n clwb cymdeithasol. **s. security** n nawdd cymdeithasol. **s. work** n gwaith cymdeithasol

socialism n sosialaeth

socialist n sosialydd

society n cymdeithas, cyfeillach

sociology n cymdeithaseg

sock n hosan

socket n twll, crau, soced

sod n tywarchen

soda water n dŵr soda

sodden adj wedi mwydo, soeglyd

sofa n glwth, esmwythfainc, soffa

soft adj meddal, tyner; distaw; gwirion. **s. drink** n diod ysgafn

software n meddalwedd

soggy adj gwlyb, lleidiog

soil n pridd, daear, gweryd

soil vt difwyno, baeddu ♦ n baw, tom

solace n cysur, diddanwch ♦ vt cysuro, diddanu

solar adj heulog, solar

solder n sawdring, sawdur, sodr ♦ vt asio, sawdurio, sodro

soldier n milwr

sole adj unig, unigol, un

sole n gwadn ♦ vt gwadnu

sole (fish) n lleden chwithig

solemn adj difrifol, dwys

sol-fa n sol-ffa ♦ vb solffeuo

solicit vt erfyn, ymofyn; llithio

solicitor n cyfreithiwr

solid adj caled, sylweddol, solet, cadarn

solid n solid

solidarity n undod

solitary adj unig; anghyfannedd

solitude n unigedd

solo n unawd

soloist n unawdydd

soluble adj toddadwy, hydawdd

solution n dehongliad, esboniad; toddiant

solve vt datrys, dehongli

solvent adj yn gallu talu, di-ddyled ♦ n toddfa

sombre adj tywyll, prudd

some adj rhai, rhyw, peth, ychydig ♦ pron rhywrai, rhywfaint ♦ adv ynghylch, tua, rhyw

somebody pron = someone

somehow adv rywfodd, rhywsut

someone pron rhywun

somersault n trosben ♦ vb troi tin dros ben, pen dra mwnwgl

something n rhywbeth

sometime adv rywbryd, gynt

sometimes adv weithiau, ar brydiau, ambell waith

somewhat adv go, lled, braidd

somewhere adv (yn) rhywle

son n mab

song n cân, cathl, cerdd

sonic adj sonig

son-in-law n mab yng nghyfraith

sonnet n soned

soon adv buan, ebrwydd, clau

sooner adv (time) ynghynt, yn

gynt; (preference): **I would s. do** byddai'n well gennyf wneud; **s. or later** yn hwyr neu'n hwyrach

soot n huddygl, parddu

soothe vt lliniaru, lleddfu, dofi, tawelu

sop n tamaid (wedi ei wlychu)

sophism n soffyddiaeth

sophist n soffydd

sophistical adj soffyddol

sophisticated adj soffistigedig

sopping adj gwlyb diferu

soppy adj teimladol; mwydlyd

soprano n soprano

sorcerer n swynwr, dewin

sorcery n swyngyfaredd, dewiniaeth

sordid adj brwnt, cybyddlyd, gwael

sore adj tost, blin, dolurus ♦ n dolur

sorrow n tristwch, gofid, galar ♦ vi tristáu, gofidio

sorry adj drwg gan, edifar; salw

sort n modd; math, bath ♦ vt trefnu, dosbarthu

sortie n cyrch

sorting office n swyddfa ddosbarthu

so-so adv gweddol

sot n diotyn, meddwyn

soul n enaid

soul-destroying adj yn fwrn llethol

sound n sain, sŵn, trwst ♦ vb seinio

sound vb plymio, chwilio

sound n culfor, swnt

sound adj iach, iachus, dianaf, cyfan, dilys. **s. effects** npl effeithiau sain

soundboard n seinfwrdd

soundly adv yn drwm, yn llwyr

soundproof adj yn gwrthsefyll sŵn

soup n potes, cawl

sour adj sur ♦ vb suro

source n ffynhonnell, tarddiad

south *n* deau, de. **S. Africa** *n* De
Affrica
southern *adj* deheuol
souvenir *n* cofrodd
sovereign *adj* pen ♦ *n* penadur;
sofren
Soviet *adj* Sofietaidd
Soviet Union *n*: **the S.U.** yr
Undeb Sofietaidd
sow *n* hwch
sow *vt* hau
soya *n* soya. **s. beans** *npl* ffa soya
space *n* lle, gwagle, gofod, encyd,
ysbaid
spaceman *n* gofodwr
spaceship *n* llong ofod
spacious *adj* eang, helaeth
spade *n* rhaw, pâl
Spain *n* Hisbaen
span *n* rhychwant ♦ *vt* rhychwantu
spaniel *n* adargi, sbaniel
Spanish *adj* Sbaenaidd ♦ *n*
Sbaeneg
spank *vt* slapio, smacio, palfodi,
chwipio tin
spanner *n* sbaner
spar *vi* cwfflo, paffio
spar *n* polyn, cledren, ceibren
spare *adj* prin; tenau; sbâr ♦ *vt*
arbed; hepgor
sparerib *n* sbarib, asen-frân
sparing *adj* cynnil, prin
spark *n* gwreichionen
sparkle *vi* gwreichioni, serennu,
pefrio
sparkling *adj* gloyw, llachar;
byrlymog
sparrow *n* aderyn y to
sparse *adj* tenau, prin, gwasgarog
spasm *n* pwl, gwayw, brath
spate *n* llifeiriant sydyn
spatter *vb* tasgu
spawn *n* grawn, gronell; grifft; sil
♦ *vb* silio, bwrw grawn
speak *vb* llefaru, siarad
speaker *n* llefarydd, siaradwr
spear *n* gwaywffon, picell ♦ *vt*

trywanu
special *adj* neilltuol, arbennig
specialist *n* arbenigwr
speciality *n* arbenigrwydd
species (**species**) *n* rhywogaeth
specific *adj* priodol, penodol,
pendant
specify *vt* enwi, penodi
specimen *n* enghraifft, cynllun
specious *adj* teg yr olwg, rhithiol
speck *n* brycheuyn, ysmotyn
speckle *vt* britho, brychu
spectacle *n* drych, golygfa; (*pl*)
sbectol
spectator *n* edrychwr, gwyliwr
spectre *n* drychiolaeth
spectrum (**-ra**) *n* spectrwm
speculate *vi* dyfalu; anturio,
mentro
speculation *n* dyfaliad; antur,
menter
speech *n* llafar, lleferydd, parabl,
ymadrodd; araith
speed *n* cyflymder, buander ♦ *vb*
prysuro, cyflymu. **s. limit** *n*
ataliad cyflymder
speedometer *n* mesurydd
cyflymdra
spell *n* cyfaredd, swyn
spell *n* sbel, hoe, ysbaid
spell *vt* sillafu
spend *vb* treulio, gwario, bwrw
spendthrift *n* afradwr, oferwr,
gwastraffwr
sperm *n* had
spew *vb* chwydu
sphere *n* cronnell, sffêr, pêl;
cylch, maes
spice *n* perlysiau, peraroglau,
sbeis
spick-and-span *adj* fel y pin
spicy *adj* blasus; ffraeth, diddorol;
coch
spider *n* cor, corryn, pryf copyn
spike *n* pig, hoel, cethren
spikenard *n* ysbignard, nard
spill *vb* colli, tywallt

spin vb nyddu, troi, troelli

spinach n pigoglys, sbinais

spindle n gwerthyd; echel

spin-dryer n trowasgwr

spine n asgwrn cefn; draen, pigyn

spinner n nyddwr

spinning top n top tro

spinning-wheel n troell

spin-off n mantais

spinster n merch ddibriod, hen ferch

spiral adj fel cogwrn tro, troellog

spirant adj llaes ♦ npl llaesion

spire n meindwr, pigwrn, pigdwr

spirit n ysbryd; gwirod

spirited adj calonnog, nwyfus, ysbrydol

spiritual adj ysbrydol

spiritualist n ysbrydegydd

spit n bêr

spit n poeri

spite n sbeit, malais ♦ vt sbeitio

spiteful adj maleisus, sbeitlyd

spittle n poer, poeryn

spittoon n llestr poeri

splash vb sblasio, tasgu

spleen n y dúeg; pruddglwyf; natur ddrwg, gwenwyn

splendid adj ysblennydd, gwych, campus

splendour n ysblander, gwychder

splint n dellten, ysgyren, sblint

splinter vb ysgyrioni ♦ n ysgyren, fflaw

split vb hollti, rhannu, gwahanu

spoil n ysbail, anrhaith ♦ vb ysbeilio, ysbwylio, difetha

spoke n adain olwyn, sbogen, braich

spokesman n llefarwr, llefarydd

spoliation n ysbeiliad, ysbwyliad

sponge n sbwng ♦ vb ysbyngu

sponsor n mach, hyrwyddwr, noddwr; tad bedydd, mam fedydd

spontaneous adj gwirfoddol, digymell

spook n ysbryd, bwgan, bwci

spool n gwerthyd

spoon n llwy ♦ vb llwyo; caru

spoonful n llwyaid

spoor n brisg, ôl

sporadic adj achlysurol, gwasgarog

spore n had (rhedyn, etc)

sport n sbort, chwarae, difyrrwch, cellwair, hwyl

sportive adj chwareus, nwyfus

sports npl mabolgampau, chwaraeon

spot n man, lle, llecyn; brycheuyn, ysmotyn ♦ vt mannu, brychu, ysmotio ♦ adj ar y pryd

spotless adj difrycheulyd, glân

spotted adj brith, brych

spouse n priod

spout vt pistyllio, ffrydio ♦ n pistyll

sprain vt ysigo

sprawl vi ymdaenu, ymdreiglo, ymrwyfo

spray n gwlith, tawch, trochion ♦ vt taenellu; chwistrellu

spray n ysbrigyn, cainc; chwystrellydd

spread vb lledu, taenu, lledaenu, gwasgaru

spree n sbri

sprig n brigyn, ysbrigyn

sprightly adj bywiog, hoenus, nwyfus

spring vb tarddu, codi, deillio; llamu, neidio ♦ n ffynnon; llam; sbring; gwanwyn, **s.-clean** vt glanhau'r gwanwyn

springy adj sbongar

sprinkle vb taenellu, ysgeintio

sprint vb gwibio

sprinter n gwibiwr

sprit n sbryd

sprite n ysbryd, bwgan, bwci

sprout vb tarddu, egino, glasu

sprouts npl (Brussels) ysgewyll Brysel

spruce adj twt, taclus, smart;

crand ♦ *n* pyrwydden
spry *adj* sionc, heini, hoyw
spur *n* ysbardun, swmbwl ♦ *vb* ysbarduno, symbylu
spurious *adj* ffug, gau, annilys
spurn *vb* cicio, dirmygu, tremygu
spurt *n* ysbonc
sputter *vb* poeri siarad, baldorddi
spy *n* ysbiwr ♦ *vb* ysbio
squabble *vi* cweryla, ffraeo ♦ *n* ffrwgwd, ffrae
squad *n* carfan, mintai
squadron *n* sgwadron
squalid *adj* brwnt, bawlyd, budr
squall *vi* ysgrechain ♦ *n* gwawch; storm o wynt
squalor *n* brynti
squander *vt* gwastraffu, afradu
square *adj.* *n* sgwâr, petryal
squash *vt* gwasgu, llethu ♦ *n* sboncen. **orange s.** sudd oren
squat *vi* swatio, cyrcydu
squawk *vi* gwawchio ♦ *n* gwawch
squeak *vi* gwichian ♦ *n* gwich
squeal *vi* gwichian
squeamish *adj* dicra, misi
squeeze *vb* gwasgu
squelch *vt* llethu, gostegu, rhoi taw ar
squib *n* tanen wyllt, fflachen; gogan, dychan
squint *vb* ciledrych, cibedrych ♦ *n* llygaid croes
squire *n* ysgweier, yswain
squirm *vb* gwingo
squirrel *n* gwiwer
squirt *vb* chwistrellu, tasgu ♦ *n* chwistrell, gwn dŵr
stab *vb* brathu, gwanu, trywanu
stable *n* ystabl
stable *adj* diysgog, sefydlog, safadwy, sad
stack *n* tas, bera; corn simnai, stac
staff *n* ffon; erwydd; staff
stag *n* carw, hydd
stage *n* pwynt; gradd, lefel; llwyfan

stage-coach *n* y goets fawr
stagger *vb* honclan, gwegian; syfrdanu
stagnant *adj* llonydd, marw
stagnate *vi* cronni, sefyll
staid *adj* sad, sobr
stain *vb* ystaenio, llychwino ♦ *n* staen
stained glass window *n* ffenestr liw
stainless *adj* difrycheulyd, gloyw
stair *n* gris, staer
stake *n* polyn, pawl, ystanc; cyngwystl
stale *adj* hen, hendrwm; diflas, mws
stalk *vb* torsythu, rhodio'n benuchel, mynd ar drywydd
stalk *n* paladr, gwelltyn, coes
stall *n* côr; stondin; talcen glo ♦ *vb* stolio
stalls *npl* (*in cinema, theatre*) seddau; stondinau
stallion *n* march, stalwyn
stalwart *adj* cadarn, pybyr, dewr
stamen *n* brigeryn
stamina *n* saf, ynni
stammer *vb* bloesgi, siarad ag atal arno
stamp *n* stamp, delw, argraff ♦ *vb* stampio; curo traed
stampede *n* chwalfa, rhuthr
stanch *vt* atal, sychu (*gwaed*)
stanchion *n* annel, ateg, post, gwanas
stand *vb* sefyll, bod, aros ♦ *n* safiad; eisteddle; stondyn
standard *n* lluman, baner; post; safon
stanza *n* pennill
staple *n* prif nwydd; edefyn (*gwlân, etc*)
staple *n* ystwffwl, stapal
stapler *n* styffylwr
star *n* seren ♦ *vb* serennu
starch *n* starts

stare vb llygadrythu, synnu
stark adj syth, moel, rhonc ♦ adv hollol
starling n aderyn drudwy, drudwen, aderyn yr eira
starry adj serennog
start vb dechrau, cychwyn, codi, rhusio, tasgu
startle vt brawychu, dychrynu, rhusio
starvation n newyn
starve vb newynu; fferru, rhynnu
state n ystad, cyflwr, ansawdd; rhwysg; gwladwriaeth; talaith
state vt mynegi, datgan; penodi
stately adj urddasol, mawreddog
statement n mynegiad, datganiad, haeriad
statesman (men) n gwladweinydd
station n gorsaf, stesion; safle, sefyllfa
stationary adj sefydlog
stationer n gwerthwr papurau
stationer's n (shop) siop bapurau
stationmaster n gorsaf-feistr
statistics npl ystadegau
statue n delw, cerfddelw, cerflun
stature n uchder, taldra, corffolaeth
status n safle, braint, statws
statute n deddf, cyfraith, ystatud
staunch adj pybyr, cywir
stave n estyllen, erwydd ♦ vt astellu; dryllio. **s. off** cadw draw
stay vb aros; ategu; atal ♦ n arhosiad; ateg; (pl) staes
stead n lle
steadfast adj diysgog
steadily adv yn bwyllog, yn gyson
steady adj sad, diysgog; cyson, gwastad
steak n golwyth, stec
steal vb dwyn, lladrata, cipio
stealth n lladrad. **by s.** yn ddistaw bach
stealthy adj lladradaidd
steam n ager, anwedd, stêm, tarth

♦ vb ageru
steamer n agerlong, stemar
steed n march, ceffyl
steel n dur ♦ vt caledu
steelworks n gwaith dur
steep adj serth ♦ n dibyn, clogwyn, llethr
steep vt rhoi yng ngwlych, mwydo, sucio
steeple n clochdy
steer n bustach
steer vb llywio; cyfeirio
steering n llywio
steering wheel n llyw
stem n paladr, corsen, coes, bôn; ach; pen blaen
stem vt gwrthsefyll, gwrthladd, atal
stench n drewdod, drycsawr
stenography n llaw-fer
step n camu; cerdded ♦ n cam; gris
step- prefix llys-
stepdaughter n llysferch
stepfather n llystad
stepmother n llysfam, mam wen
stepsister n llyschwaer
stepson n llysfab
stereotype n ystrydeb ♦ vt ystrydebu
sterile adj diffrwyth, sych
sterilize vb diffrwythloni, diheintio
sterling n ysterling; diledryw, diffuant
stern adj llym, penderfynol
stern n starn, pen ôl llong
stethoscope n corn meddyg
stevedore n llwythwr a dadlwythwr llongau
stew vb araf ferwi, stiwio ♦ n stiw
steward n stiward, goruchwyliwr, distain
stick n pren, ffon, pric, gwialen
stick vb glynu; gwanu, brathu
sticky adj gludiog, glynol; anodd
stiff adj syth, anystwyth, anhyblyg, ystyfnig

stiffen vb sythu, ystyfnigo

stifle vt mygu, tagu, diffodd

stigma n gwarthnod, stigma

stile n camfa, sticil, sticill

still n distyllfa, stil

still adj llonydd; marw ♦ vb llonyddu

still adv eto, er hynny; byth

stilt n ystudfach

stilted adj annaturiol; mawreddog

stimulant n symbylydd; gwirod

stimulate vt symbylu

stimulus (-li) n symbyliad, swmbwl

sting vb pigo, brathu, colynnu ♦ n colyn

stingy adj crintach, cybyddlyd

stink vi, n drewi

stinking adj drewllyd

stint vt cynilo, cybydda ♦ n prinder

stipend n cyflog, tâl

stipulate vb amodi, mynnu

stir vb cyffroi, cynhyrfu, symud ♦ n stŵr, cynnwrf

stirrup n gwarthol

stitch n pwyth; gwayw, pigyn ♦ vt pwytho, gwnïo

stoat n carlwm

stock n cyff; stoc, ystôr. **stocks** npl cyffion

stock exchange n cyfnewidfa stoc

stocking n hosan

stocky adj cadarn, cryf, cydnerth

stodgy adj toeslyd, trymllyd, diflas

stoke vb edrych ar ôl tân, tanio

stole n ystola

stolid adj swrth, digyffro

stomach n cylla, stumog

stone n carreg, maen ♦ vt llabyddio

stool n ystôl

stoop vb plygu, crymu, gwargrymu, ymostwng

stop vb atal, rhwystro; stopio; cau; aros, sefyll ♦ n atalfa; atalnod

stoppage n (pay) ataliad, (strike) streic

stopper n topyn, caead

storage n stôr, storfa

store n ystôr, ystorfa ♦ vt ystorio

storey, story n uchdwr, llofft, llawr

stork n ciconia, chwibon

storm n (y)storm, tymestl

stormy adj stormus, tymhestlog, garw

story n hanes, chwedl, stori; celwydd

stout adj tew, ffyrf; pybyr, gwrol, glew

stove n stof, ffwrn

stow vb pacio, dodi o'r neilltu

stowaway n teithiwr cudd

straddle vt bongamu, lledu'r traed

straggle vi crwydro, gwasgaru

straggler n crwydryn

straight adj union, syth

straighten vb unioni

straightforward adj syml; didwyll, gonest

straightway adv yn y fan, yn syth

strain vb straenio, streiflo, ysigo; tynhau; hidlo ♦ n straen

strainer n hidl(en)

strait adj cyfyng, cul, caeth ♦ n cyfyngder; culfor

strand n traeth, traethell, tywyn

strand n cainc (rhaff), edau

strange adj dieithr, estronol, rhyfedd

stranger n dyn dieithr, estron

strangle vt tagu, llindagu

strap n strap, cengl

strategic adj strategol

strategy n strategaeth

stratum (-ta) n haen

straw n gwellt; gwelltyn, blewyn

strawberry n mefysen, syfien

stray vi crwydro, cyfeiliorni

streak n llinell, rhes, rhesen; stremp ♦ vb gwibio

stream n ffrwd ♦ vb ffrydio, llifo

streamer n rhuban, baner

street n heol, ystryd

strength n cryfder, nerth, grym

strengthen vb cryfhau, nerthu

strenuous adj egniol, ymdrechgar

stress n pwys, straen, caledi

stretch vb estyn, tynhau ♦ n estyniad

stretcher n trestl, stretsier

strew vt gwasgaru, sarnu, chwalu, taenu

strict adj cyfyng, caeth, llym

stricture n cyfyngiad; cerydd, sen

stride vb camu, brasgamu ♦ n cam

strife n cynnen, ymryson, ymrafael

strike vb taro; gostwng ♦ n taro, streic

striker n streiciwr

striking adj trawiadol, hynod

string n llinyn, tant, cortyn

stringent adj caeth, llym, tyn

strip n llain, llafn, llefnyn. **film s.** striplun, stribed ffilm

strip vb diosg, ymddiosg, ymddihatru

stripe n rhes, rhesen; gwialennod

striped adj rhengog, rhesenog; â llinellau amliw ar hyd-ddo

stripling n glaslanc, llanc, llencyn

strive vi ymdrechu; ymryson

stroke n dyrnod, ergyd, trawiad; llinell

stroke vt llochi, dylofi, pratio, canmol

stroll vi crwydro, rhodianna

strong adj cryf, grymus, cadarn

stronghold n amddiffynfa, cadarnle

structure n adail, adeilad, saerniaeth, adeiledd, strwythur

struggle vi gwingo; ymdrechu ♦ n ymdrech

strut vi torsythu

stub n bonyn

stubble n sofl

stubborn adj cyndyn, ystyfnig

stuck-up adj ffroenuchel

stud n boglwm, boglyn, styden

stud n gre

student n myfyriwr, efrydydd

studio n stiwdio

study n astudiaeth, efrydiaeth, npl efrydiau; myfyrgell, stydi ♦ vb myfyrio, efrydu, astudio

stuff n defnydd, stwff ♦ vb stwffio, gwthio

stuffing adj (bed) fflocys; (CULIN) stwffin

stuffy adj myglyd, trymllyd, trymaidd

stumble vb tramgwyddo, baglu, syrthio

stump n bonyn, boncyff

stun vt syfrdanu, byddaru, hurtio

stunt vt crabio

stunted adj crablyd

stupefy vt syfrdanu, hurtio

stupendous adj aruthrol

stupid adj hurt, pendew, dwl, twp

stupor n syfrdandod, syrthni

sturdy adj talgryf, pybyr, cadarn, cryf

stutter vi siarad ag atal arno, bloesgi

sty n cwt, cut, twlc

style n dull, arddull; cyfenw, teitl ♦ vt cyfenwi

stylish adj dillyn, trwsiadus

stylus n (of record player) nodwydd

suave adj mwyn, tirion, hynaws, rhadlon

sub- prefix tan-, is-, go-

subconscious n isymwybod ♦ adj isymwybodol

subdue vt darostwng; lleddfu

subject adj darostyngedig; caeth; ufudd ♦ n deiliad; pwnc, testun; goddrych

subject vt darostwng, dwyn dan

subjective adj goddrychol

subjugate vt darostwng

subjunctive adj dibynnol

sublime adj aruchel, arddunol

submarine adj tanforol ♦ n llong

danfor

submerge vb soddi, suddo
submission n ymostyngiad;
ufudd-dod; cyflwyniad
submissive adj gostyngedig, ufudd
submit vb ymostwng,
ymddarostwng; datgan barn;
cyflwyno
subnormal adj isnormal
subordinate adj israddol ♦ vt
darostwng
subpoena n gwŷs
subscribe vb tanysgrifio, cyfrannu
subscription n tanysgrifiad,
cyfraniad
subsequent adj canlynol, dilynol
subsequently adv wedyn, ar ôl
hynny
subside vi eilydd, ymollwng;
darfod
subsidiary adj israddol;
ychwanegol, atodol
subsidy n arian cymorth,
cymhorthdal
subsist vb byw, bod, bodoli,
ymgynnal
subsistence n cynhaliaeth
subsoil n isbridd
substance n sylwedd, defnydd; da
substantial adj sylweddol
substantiate vt profi, gwirio
substitute n eilydd, cynrhprwy, un
yn lle arall ♦ vt rhoi yn lle
subterfuge n ystryw, cast
subterranean adj tanddaearol
subtle adj cyfrwys, craff
subtract vt tynnu ymaith
suburb n maestref
subvert vt dymchwelyd, gwyrdroi
subway n isffordd
succeed vb dilyn, canlyn, llwyddo,
ffynnu
success n llwyddiant, llwydd,
ffyniant
successful adj llwyddiannus
successfully adv yn llwyddiannus
succession n dilyniad, olyniaeth

successive adj dilynol, olynol
succinct adj byr, cryno
succour vt swcro, ymgeleddu ♦ n
swcr, ymgeledd
succulent adj ir, iraidd, noddlyd
succumb vi ymollwng dan, ildio,
marw
such adj cyfryw, y fath, cyffelyb
suck vb sugno, dyfnu; llyncu, yfed
suckle vt rhoi bron, sugno
suction n sugn, sugniad,
sugndyniad
sudden adj sydyn, disymwth,
disyfyd
suds npl trochion sebon, sucion
sue vb erlyn; erfyn, deisyf
suede n swêd
suet n gwêr, swyf, siwed
suffer vb goddef, dioddef, gadael
sufferer n dioddefydd
suffering n dioddef
suffice vb bod yn ddigon, digoni
sufficient adj digon, digonol
suffix n olddodiad
suffocate vb mygu, tagu
suffrage n pleidlais
suffuse vt taenu, gwasgaru,
ymledu
sugar n siwgr ♦ vt siwgro
suggest vt awgrymu
suggestion n awgrym, awgrymiad
suicide n hunanladdiad
suit n cwyn, cyngaws, hawl;
deisyfiad, cais; siwt, pâr ♦ vb
ateb, siwtio, gweddu, taro
suitable adj addas, cyfaddas,
cymwys
suitably adv yn addas
suitcase n bag dillad
suite n cyfres; gosgordd, nifer
suitor n cwynwr; cariadfab
sulk vi sorri, pwdu, mulo
sullen adj sarrug, cuchio, blwng
sully vt difwyno, llychwino
sulphur n sylffwr
sultan n swltan
sultry adj mwrn, mwll, clòs

sum *n* swm ♦ *vt* crynhoi, symio

summarize *vb* crynhoi

summary *adj* byr, cryno ♦ *n* crynodeb

summer *n* haf

summerhouse *n* tŷ haf

summit *n* pen, copa, crib

summon *vt* gwysio, dyfynnu

summons *n* gwŷs, dyfyn

sump *n* swmp

sumptuous *adj* moethus

sun *n* haul ♦ *vt* heulo

sunbathe *vb* torheulo, bolaheulo

sunbeam *n* pelydryn

sunburn *n* llosg haul

Sunday *n* dydd Sul

sunder *vt* ysgaru, gwahanu

sundry *adj* armryw, amrywiol

sunflower *n* blodyn yr haul

sunglasses *npl* sbectol haul

sunny *adj* heulog

sunshine *n* heulwen

sunstroke *n* ergyd (yr) haul

suntan *n* lliw haul

sup *vb* llymeitian; swpera, swperu ♦ *n* llymaid

super- *prefix* uwch, goruwch, gor-, tra-, ar-

superannuation *n* ymddeoliaeth, pensiwn

superb *adj* ysblennydd, godidog

supercilious *adj* balch, ffroenuchel

superficial *adj* arwynebol, bas

superfine *adj* coeth

superfluous *adj* gormodol, afreidiol

superintend *vt* arolygu

superintendent *n* arolygwr, arolygydd

superior *adj* uwch, gwell, rhagorach; uwchraddol ♦ *n* uchafiad, uwchradd

superiority *n* rhagoriaeth

superlative *adj* uchaf; eithaf

supermarket *n* archfarchnad

supernatural *adj* goruwchnaturiol

supersede *vt* disodli

superstition *n* coelgrefydd, ofergoeliaeth

superstitious *adj* coelgrefyddol, ofergoelus

supervene *vi* digwydd

supervise *vt* arolygu

supervision *n* arolygiaeth

supine *adj* diofal, didaro, swrth

supper *n* swper

supplant *vt* disodli

supple *adj* ystwyth, hyblyg

supplement *n* atodiad ♦ *vt* atodi

supplementary *adj* atodol, ychwanegol

suppliant *n* ymbiliwr, erfyniwr

supplicate *vb* erfyn, ymbil, deisyf

supplier *n* cyflenwr, cyflenwydd

supply *vt* cyflenwi, cyflawni ♦ *n* cyflenwad

support *vt* cynnal ♦ *n* cynhaliaeth

supporter *n* cefnogwr, cefnogydd

suppose *vt* tybio, tybied, bwrw

suppository *n* tawddgyffur

suppress *vt* llethu, gostegu; atal; celu

suppurate *vi* crawni, gori

supreme *adj* goruchaf, prif, pennaf

sur- *prefix* gor-

surcharge *n* gordal, gordoll ♦ *vb* codi gormod

sure *adj, adv* siwr, sicr; diamau, diau

surely *adv* yn sicr, yn ddiau

surety *n* mach, meichiau, gwystl

surf *n* traethfor, beiston; goreuwyn ♦ *vb* brigo, brigdonni

surface *n* wyneb, arwynebedd, caen

surfeit *n* syrffed ♦ *vb* alaru, syrffedu

surge *vi* ymchwyddo ♦ *n* ymchwydd

surgeon *n* llawfeddyg

surgery *n* llawfeddygaeth; meddygfa, llys meddyg

surgical *adj* llawfeddygol

surly *adj* sarrug, afrywiog

surmise *n* tyb ♦ *vt* tybied, amau

surmount *vt* mynd dros, gorchfygu, trechu

surname *n* cyfenw ♦ *vt* cyfenwi

surpass *vt* rhagori ar, trechu

surplice *n* gwenwisg

surplus *n* gweddill, gormod, gwarged

surprise *n* syndod ♦ *vt* synnu

surprising *adj* syn, rhyfedd

surrender *vb* traddodi, ildio

surreptitious *adj* lladradaidd, llechwraidd

surrogate *n* dirprwy, rhaglaw esgob

surround *vt* amgylchu, amgylchynu

surroundings *npl* amgylchoedd

surveillance *n* arolygiaeth, gwyliadwriaeth

survey *vt* edrych, arolygu; mesur ♦ *n* arolwg

survival *n* goroesiad

survive *vb* goroesi

survivor *n* goroeswr

susceptible *adj* parod i, tueddol i

suspect *vt* drwgdybio, amau ♦ *n* un a ddrwgdybir

suspend *vt* crogi; gohirio, atal

suspended sentence *n* dedfryd wedi'i gohirio

suspense *n* pryder, petruster, oediad

suspension *n* ataliad. **s. bridge** *n* pont grog

suspicion *n* drwgdybiaeth, amheuaeth

suspicious *adj* drwgdybus, amheus

sustain *vt* cynnal; dioddef, goddef

sustained *adj* parhaus, cyson

sustenance *n* cynhaliaeth, ymborth, bwyd

swagger *vb* rhodresa, torsythu, swagro

swallow *n* gwennol

swallow *vt* llyncu ♦ *n* llwnc

swamp *n* cors ♦ *vt* gorlifo, boddi

swan *n* alarch

swank *vi* bocsachu, rhodresa ♦ *n* bocsach

swap *vb* ffeirio

swarm *n* haid ♦ *vi* heidio, heigio

swarm *vb* dringo

swarthy *adj* melynddu, croenddu, tywyll

swat *vb* taro

swathe *vt* rhwymo, rhwymynnu

sway *vb* siglo, gwegian; llywio ♦ *n* llywodraeth, swae

swear *vb* tyngu, rhegi

sweat *n* chwys ♦ *vb* chwysu

sweater *n* cot wlan, sweter

sweaty *adj* chwyslyd

swede *n* rwden, sweden

Swede *n* Swediad

Sweden *n* Sweden

Swedish *adj* Swedaidd

sweep *vb* ysgubo ♦ *n* ysgubiad; ysgubwr

sweeping *adj* ysgubol

sweet *adj* melys, pêr, peraidd ♦ *n* pwdin

sweeten *vb* melysu; pereiddio

sweetheart *n* cariad

sweetmeat *n* fferin, melysyn

swell *vb* chwyddo ♦ *n* chwydd, ymchwydd; gŵr mawr

swelling *n* chwydd(i)

swelter *vi* crasu; lluddedu, dyddfu

sweltering *adj* llethol, tesog

swerve *vi* gwyro, osgoi, cilio, troi

swift *adj* cyflym, buan, chwyrn, clau

swift *n* gwennol ddu

swig *n* llymaid, dracht ♦ *vb* drachtio

swill *n* golchion; bwyd sur ♦ *vb* golchi; slotian

swim *vb* nofio ♦ *n* nawf

swimmer *n* nofiwr

swimming *n* nofio

swimmingly *adv* yn braf, yn hwylus

swimming pool *n* pwll nofio

swimsuit *n* dillad nofio, gwisg nofio

swindle *vb* twyllo, hocedu ♦ *n* twyll

swine (swine) *n* mochyn

swing *vb* siglo ♦ *n* sigl, siglen, swing

swinge *vt* llachio, baeddu

swirl *vb* troi, chwyldroi, chwyrndroi

swish *vb* chwipio

switch *n* swits, botwm ♦ *vb* troi, newid

swivel *n* bwylltid ♦ *vb* troi

swollen *adj* chwyddedig, wedi chwyddo

swoon *vt* llewygu, llesmeirio ♦ *n* llewyg

swoop *vb* dyfod ar warthaf, disgyn

swop *vt* cyfnewid, ffeirio

sword *n* cleddyf, cleddau, cledd

sycamore *n* sycamorwydden

syllable *n* sillaf

syllabus *n* rhaglen, maes llafur

syllogism *n* cyfresymiad

symbol *n* arwyddlun, symbol, symlen (estheteg)

symbolism *n* symboliaeth

symmetrical *adj* cymesur

symmetry *n* cymesuredd

sympathetic *adj* cydymdeimladol

sympathize *vi* cydymdeimlo

sympathy *n* cydymdeimlad

symphony *n* symffoni

symposium (-ia) *n* trafodaeth, cynhadledd

symptom *n* arwydd

synagogue *n* synagog

synchronize *vb* cyfamseru, cydamseru

syncopation *n* trawsacen (cerdd)

syncope *n* marwlewyg; syncopé

syndicate *n* cwmni

synod *n* cymanfa, senedd, synod

synonym *n* (gair) cyfystyr

synopsis (-ses) *n* cyfolwg; crynodeb

syntax *n* cystrawen

synthesis (-ses) *n* cyfosodiad, synthesis

Syria *n* Syria

syringe *n* chwistrell ♦ *vt* chwistrellu

syrup *n* sudd; triagl (melyn)

system *n* cyfundrefn; trefn, system

systematic *adj* cyfundrefnol

systematize *vb* cyfundrefnu

T

tab *n* tafod, llabed

tabby *n* cath frech, cath fenyw

tabernacle *n* tabernacl, pabell

table *n* bwrdd, bord; tabl, taflen

tableau *n* golygfa (ddramatig)

table-cloth *n* lliain bord (bwrdd)

tableful *n* bordaid, byrddaid

tablespoon *n* llwy fwrdd

tablet *n* llechen, llech; tabled

table tennis *n* tennis bwrdd, ping pong

taboo *n* ysgymunbeth; gwaharddiad, tabŵ

tabular *adj* taflennol

tabulate *vt* tablu, taflennu

tacit *adj* dealledig (ond heb ei grybwyll)

taciturn *adj* tawedog

tack *n* tac, pwyth, brasbwyth ♦ *vb* tacio

tackle *n* taclau, offer, tacl (mewn rygbi), taclad ♦ *vb* ymosod ar, taclo

tackler *n* taclwr

tact *n* tact, callineb, doethineb

tactful *adj* doeth, pwyllog, synhwyrol

tactician *n* tactegydd

tactics *npl* cynlluniau, tactegau

tactile *adj* cyffyrddol

tactless *adj* di-dact, annoeth

tadpole *n* penbwl, penbwla
tag *n* pwyntl; clust, dolen
tail *n* cynffon, llosgwrn, cwt
tailback *n* cwt, tagfa
tailor *n* teiliwr
taint *vb* llygru, heintio, difwyno ♦ *n* llwgr, ystaen, mefl
take *vb* cymryd, derbyn, cael
talcum *n* talcwm
tale *n* chwedl, hanes, stori, clec, clep
talent *n* talent
talisman *n* swynbeth, swyn, cyfaredd
talk *vb*, *n* siarad
talkative *adj* siaradus
tall *adj* tal, hir, uchel
tallness *n* taldra
tallow *n* gwêr
tally *n* cyfrif ♦ *vb* cyfateb, cytuno
talon *n* ewin, crafanc (aderyn)
tambourine *n* tambwrin
tame *adj* dof, gwâr ♦ *vt* dofi
tamper *vi* ymhel(â), ymyrryd(â)
tampon *n* tampwn
tan *vb* trin lledr; llosgi, melynu
tangent *n* tangiad, llinell gyffwrdd
tangible *adj* cyffyrddadwy, sylweddol
tangle *vb* drysu, cymysgu ♦ *n* dryswch, cyfanheddion
tank *n* dyfrgist, tanc
tankard *n* diodlestr, tancr
tanker *n* tancer, llong olew
tannery *n* barcerdy, crwynfa, tanerdy
tantalize *vt* poeni, poenydio, pryfocio
tantamount *adj* cyfwerth, cyfystyr
tantrums *npl* stranciau, nwydau
tap *vb* taro yn ysgafn
tap *n* tap, feis ♦ *vt* tapio, gollwng
tape *n* tâp, incil
tape measure *n* tâp mesur
tape-recorder *n* recordydd tâp, peiriant recordio, arnodydd
taper *n* cannwyll gŵyr, tapr ♦ *vb*

meinhau, tapro
tapestry *n* tapestri
tape-worm *n* llyngeren
tapioca *n* tapioca
tar *n* tar; llongwr, morwr
tardy *adj* hwyrfrydig, araf, diweddar, ymarhous
target *n* nod, targed
tariff *n* toll; rhestr taliadau, rhestr prisiau
tarmac *n* tarmac
tarnish *vb* pylu, cymylu, llychwino
tarpaulin *n* tarpolin
tarry *vb* aros, oedi, tario; trigo, preswylio
tart *n* tarten, pastai
tart *adj* sur, surllyd
tartan *n* brithwe, plod
task *n* gorchwyl, tasg ♦ *vt* rhoi tasg, trethu, llethu
tassel *n* tusw, tasel
taste *vb* chwaethu, blasu, profi ♦ *n* blas; chwaeth
tatter *n* rhecsyn, cerpyn
tattered *adj* carpiog
tattle *vb* clebran, clegar ♦ *n* cleber, baldordd
tattoo *n* tatŵ ♦ *vb* torri llun (yn y croen)
taunt *vt* edliw, dannod, gwatwar ♦ *n* gwaradwydd, sen
taut *adj* tyn
tautologous *adj* ailadroddol, cyfystyrol
tautology *n* tawtologaeth, ailadrodd, cyfystyredd
tavern *n* tafarn, tafarndy, tŷ tafarn
tawdry *adj* coegwych
tawny *n* melynddu, melyn
tax *n* treth ♦ *vt* trethu; cyhuddo
taxi *n* tacsi. **t. rank** *n* lloc dacsi
taxidermist *n* stwffiwr anifeiliaid
tea *n* te
tea-bag *n* bag te, cwdyn te
teacup *n* disgl de, cwpan te
tea-leaves *n* dail te

tea-party n teparti
teach vt dysgu, addysgu
teacher n athro
teaching n dysgeidiaeth; dysgu
teak n tîc
team n gwedd, pâr, tîm
teapot n tebot
tear n deigryn, deigr
tear vb rhwygo, llarpio ♦ n rhwyg
tearful adj dagreuol
tease vt pryfocio, plagio, poeni
teaser n poenwr, poenydiwr
teaspoon n llwy de
teaspoonful n llond llwy de
teat n teth, diden, bron
technical adj technegol
technician n technegydd
technique n techneg
technological adj technolegol
technology n technoleg
teddy (bear) n arth anwes, tedi
tedious adj blin, anniben, poenus
tedium n diflastod, blinder
teem vb epilio, hilio, heigio
teenager n un yn yr arddegau
teens n arddegau
teethe vi torri dannedd
teetotaller n llwyrymwrthodwr, titotal
telecast n telediad
telecommunication n cysylltiad trwy'r teliffon, telegyfathrebaeth
telegram n teligram
telegraph n teligraff ♦ vb teligraffio
teleology n dibenyddiaeth
telepathy n telepathi
telephase n olgyfnwr
telephone n teliffon, ffôn. t. box n bocs ffonio. t. call n galwad ffôn. t. directory cyfeirlyfr ffôn
telescope n ysbienddrych, telisgob
televise vb teledu
television n teledu
tell vb dweud, traethu, adrodd, mynegi; cyfrif, rhifo
telltale n clepgi, clepiwr,

clepwraig
temerity n rhyfyg, hyfdra
temper n tymer, naws ♦ vt tymheru
temperament n anianawd
temperamental adj gwamal, oriog, di-ddal
temperance n dirwest
temperate adj cymedrol; tymherus
temperature n tymheredd
tempest n tymestl
tempestuous adj tymhestlog
temple n teml
temple n arlais
temporal adj tymhorol
temporary adj dros amser, tymhoroi
temporize vi oedi, anwadalu
tempt vt temtio, profi
tempter n temtiwr
temptation n temtiad, temtasiwn
ten adj, n deg
tenable adj daliadwy, y gellir ei ddal; diffynadwy
tenacious adj tyn ei afael, gwydn, gludiog, cyndyn
tenacity n cyndynrwydd
tenant n deiliad, tenant
tench n tens
tend vb tendio, gweini
tend vi tueddu, cyfeirio, symud
tendance n sylw, gofal, tendans
tendency n tuedd, gogwydd
tendentious adj pleidiol, pleidgar
tender adj tyner, tirion, mwyn; meddal
tender vb cynnig, cyflwyno ♦ n cynnig
tenderness n tynerwch
tendon n gewyn
tendril n tendril
tenement n annedd, rhandy
tenet n daliad, barn, tyb
tenfold adj dengwaith
tennis n tennis. **t. ball** n pêl dennis. **t. court** n cwrt tennis. **t. racket** n

raced tennis

tenon n tyno

tenor n cyfeiriad, tuedd, rhediad; tenor

tense adj tyn, dirdynnol, dwys, angerddol

tense n amser (berf)

tension n tyndra, pwys, tyniant

tent n pabell

tentacle n tentacl, braich

tentative adj arbrofiadol, dros dro; ansicr

tenter-hook n bach deintur. **on tenter-hooks** ar bigau'r drain

tenth adj degfed

tenuous adj tenau, main, prin

tenure n deiliadaeth

tepid adj claear

tercentenary n trichanmlwyddiant

term n terfyn; term; teler, amod; tymor ♦ vt galw, enwi

terminal adj terfynol, termol

terminate vb terfynu

termination n terfyniad

terminology n termynoleg

terminus n terfyn

termites npl morgrug gwynion

tern n môr-wennol

terrace n rhes dai, teras

terrain n tir, bro, ardal

terrestrial adj daearol

terrible adj dychrynllyd, ofnadwy, arswydus

terrier n daeargi

terrific adj dychrynllyd, arswydus

terrify vt brawychu, dychrynu

terrifying adj brawychus, dychrynllyd

territorial adj tiriogaethol

territory n tir, tiriogaeth

terror n dychryn, braw, arswyd, ofn

terrorise vb dychrynu, brawychu

terrorist n terfysgwr, brawychwr

terror-stricken adj wedi ei ddychrynu

terse adj byr a chryno

terseness n byrdra

test n prawf ♦ vt profi

testament n testament, cyfamod, ewyllys

testator n cymynnwr

tester n profwr

testicle n caill, carreg

testify vb tystio

testimonial n tysteb, tystlythyr

testimony n tystiolaeth; profiad

testy adj afrywiog, ffrom, croes

tetanus n gên glo, tetanws

tether n rhaff, tennyn ♦ vt clymu

text n testun, adnod

textbook n gwerslyfr

textile adj gweol

textual adj testunol

texture n gwe, gwead, cyfansoddiad

Thailand n Gwlad Thai

than conj na, nag

thank vt, n diolch

thankful adj diolchgar

thankless adj diddiolch

thanks npl diolch, diolchiadau

thanksgiving n diolchgarwch

that pron dem hwn (hon) yna (acw), honna, honno, hynny ♦ rel a, y(r) ♦ adj hwn, hon, yma, yna, acw ♦ conj mai, taw

thatch n to, to, gwellt ♦ vt toi

thatcher n töwr (â gwellt, etc)

thaw vb dadlaith, dadmer, meirioli, toddi

the adj yr, y

theatre n theatr, chwaraedy; maes, golygfa

theatrical adj theatraidd

thee pron ti, tydi, tithau

theft n lladrad

their pron eu

theirs pron yr eiddynt, eiddynt hwy

theism n duwiaeth, theistiaeth

theist n un sy'n credu yn Nuw

them pron hwy, hwynt, hwythau

theme n testun, pwnc, thema

themselves pron eu hunain

then *adv* y pryd hwnnw, yna ♦ *conj* yna

thence *adv* oddi yno, o hynny

thenceforth *adv* o'r amser hwnnw ymlaen

theocracy *n* theocratiaeth

theologian *n* diwinydd

theological *adj* diwinyddol

theology *n* diwinyddiaeth

theorem *n* theorem

theoretical *adj* damcaniaethol, mewn theori

theorise *vb* damcaniaethu

theory *n* damcaniaeth, tyb

therapeutic *adj* iachaol, meddygol

therapy *n* therapi

there *adv* yna, yno, acw; dyna, dacw

thereafter *adv* wedyn

thereat *adv* ar hynny, yna

thereby *adv* trwy hynny

therefore *conj* gan hynny, am hynny

therefrom *adv* oddi yno

therein *adv* yno, ynddo

thereupon *adv* ar hynny

therewith *adv* gyda hynny

thermal *adj* thermol, gwresol, brwd

thermometer *n* thermomedr, mesurydd gwres

these *adj pl* y rhai hyn, y rhai yma

thesis (-ses) *n* gosodiad; traethawd, thesis

they *pron* hwy, hwynt, hwynt-hwy

thick *adj* tew, praff, trwchus

thicken *vb* tewhau, tewychu

thicket *n* prysglwyn, llwyn

thick-headed *adj* pendew, hurt, twp

thickness *n* trwch, tewder

thick-skinned *adj* croendew

thief (**thieves**) *n* lleidr

thieve *vi* lladrata, dwyn

thigh *n* clun, morddwyd

thimble *n* gwniadur

thin *adj* tenau, cul, main; anami, prin ♦ *vb* teneuo

thine *pron* eiddot ti; dy

thing *n* peth, dim

think *vb* meddwl

thinker *n* meddyliwr

third *adj* trydydd, trydedd

thirst *n* syched ♦ *vi* sychedu

thirteen *adj, n* tri (tair) ar ddeg, un deg tri (tair)

thirty *adj, n* deg ar hugain, tri deg

this *adj, pron* hwn, hon, hyn

thistle *n* ysgallen

thither *adv* yno, tuag yno

thong *n* carrai

thorax *n* y ddwyfron, y frest, thoracs

thorn *n* draen, draenen; pigyn, swmbwl

thorny *adj* dreiniog, pigog

thorough *adj* trwyadl, trylwyr

thoroughbred *adj* tryryw, o rywogaeth dda

thoroughfare *n* tramwyfa

thorough-going *adj* trwyadl

thoroughness *n* trylwyredd

those *adj pl* y rhai hynny, y rhai yna

thou *pron* ti, tydi, tithau

though *conj* er, pe, cyd

thought *n* meddwl

thoughtful *adj* meddylgar, ystyriol

thoughtless *adj* difeddwl, anystyriol

thousand *adj, n* mil

thraldom *n* caethiwed

thrall *n* caethwr, caethwas

thrash *vt* dyrnu, ffusto, curo

thread *n* edau, edefyn

threadbare *adj* llwm, treuliedig, wedi treulio

threat *n* bygwth, bygythiad

threaten *vt* bygwth

threatening *adj* bygythiol

three *adj, n* tri, tair

three-cornered *adj* trichornel

threefold *adj* triphlyg

three-legged adj teircoes

threepence n tair ceiniog, pisyn tair

thresh vt dyrnu, ffusto

thresher n dyrnwr, ffustwr

threshold n trothwy, rhiniog, hiniog

thrice adv teirgwaith

thrift n darbodaeth, cynildeb

thriftless adj gwastraffus

thrifty adj darbodus, cynnil, diwastraff

thrill vb gwefreiddio ♦ n ias, gwefr

thriller n stori iasoer

thrilling adj cyffrous, gwefreiddiol

thrive vi llwyddo, ffynnu; prifio

throat n gwddf

throb vi dychlamu, curo

throe n dolur, poen, gloes, gwewyr

thrombosis n clot mewn gwythien, thrombosis

throne n gorsedd, gorseddfainc

throng n tyrfa, torf ♦ vb tyrru, heidio

throstle n bronfraith

throttle n corn gwynt, corn gwddf, sbardun ♦ vt llindagu

through prep trwy ♦ adv trwodd

throughout prep trwy, trwy gydol ♦ adv trwodd

throw n tafliad ♦ vb taflu, bwrw, lluchio

thrower n taflwr

thrush n bronfraith

thrush n llindag, gân

thrust n vb gwthio, gwanu, brathu ♦ n gwth

thud n twrf, sŵn trwm

thug n lladdgawr, dihiryn

thumb n bawd ♦ vt bodio

thump n dyrnodio, pwnio, dulio

thumping adj aruthrol

thunder n taran(au), tyrfau, trystau ♦ vb taranu

thunderbolt n llucheden

thunderstorm n storm dyrfau

Thursday n dydd Iau

thus adv fel hyn, felly

thwart vt croesi, gwrthwynebu

thwart vb rhwystro

thy pron dy, 'th

thyme n teim

thyroid n thiroid

tiara n talaith, coron, coronig

tibia n asgwrn y grimog

tick vi tipian, ticio ♦ n tipian, tic

tick vt marcio, ticio ♦ n nod, marc, tic

tick n lliain gwely, tic

ticket n tocyn, ticed. **t. collector** n tocynnwr. **t. office** n swyddfa docynnau

tickle vb goglais, gogleisio ♦ n goglais

ticklish n gogleisiol; anodd, dyrys

tide n llanw, teid; amser, pryd. **high/low t.** n penllanw, trai

tidiness n taclusrwydd

tidings npl newyddion, chwedlau

tidy adj taclus, twt, trefnus, destlus

tie vt clymu, rhwymo ♦ n cwlwm, cadach

tier n rhes, rheng

tiff n ffrae fach

tiger n teigr, dywalgi

tight adj tyn, cryno, twt; cyfyng

tighten vb tynhau

tightness n tyndra

tights npl teits

tigress n teigres

tile n priddlech, teilsen

till prep, conj hyd

till vt trin, amaethu, llafurio

tiller n coes llyw; llafurwr, triniwr

tilt vb gogwyddo; gosod (â gwaywr)

tilth n triniaeth tir, âr

timber n coed, pren

time n amser ♦ vt amseru

timely adj amserol, prydlon

timepiece n cloc, wats

timetable n amserlen

timid adj ofnus, ofnog, llwfr

timidity n ofnusrwydd

timing n amseriad

timorous adj ofnus, ofnog

tin n alcam, tun

tincture n lliw

tinfoil n ffoel alcam

tinge vt lliwio, arlliwio ♦ n arlliw, gwawr

tingle vi ysu, llosgi, merwino

tinker n tincer; eurych ♦ vb tincera

tinkle vb tincian

tinned adj mewn tun, tun

tint n lliw, arlliw, gwawr ♦ vt lliwio

tinted adj wedi ei liwio

tinworker n gweithiwr tun, gweithiwr alcam

tiny adj bychan, bach, pitw

tip n blaen, pen ♦ vt blaenu

tip vb troi, dymchwelyd; gwobrwyo ♦ n tip, tomen; cyngor; gwobr, cil-dwrn

tipple vb llymeitian, diota

tippler n diotwr, meddwyn

tipsy adj meddw, penfeddw, brwysg

tiptoe n: on t. ar flaenau ei draed

tip-top adj campus, penigamp

tirade n araith lem

tire vb blino, lluddedu, diffygio

tire, tyre n cant, cylch, teiar

tired adj blinedig

tiredness n blinder

tireless adj diflino

tiresome adj blin, diflas, plagus

tiro, tyro n newyddian, dechreuwr

tissue n gwe, meinwe; defnydd cnawd

tissue paper n papur sidan

titanic adj cawraidd, anferth, aruthrol

titbit n tamaid blasus, amheuthun

tithe n degwm ♦ vt degymu

titivate vb pincio, ymbincio

title n teitl, hawl, hawlfraint

titled adj â theitl

title-deed n dogfen hawlfraint

title-page n wyneb-ddalen

titmouse n gwas y dryw, yswidw

titter vi cilchwerthin, chwerthinial

tittle n gronyn, mymryn, tipyn

tittle-tattle n cleber

titular adj yn rhinwedd teitl; mewn enw

to prep i, at, hyd, er mwyn, wrth, yn

toad n llyffant du dafadennog

toadstool n caws llyffant, bwyd y boda, madarch

toady n cynffonnwr ♦ vt cynffonna

toast n tost; llwncdestun ♦ vb tostio, crasu

toaster n tostiwr

tobacco n tybaco, baco

tobacconist n gwerthwr tybaco

toboggan n tybogan, sled fach, car llusg

today adv heddiw

toddle vi cropian

toddler n plentyn bach

toe n bys troed; blaen carn ceffyl

toe-cap n blaen esgid

toffee n taffi, cyflaith

together adv ynghyd, gyda'i gilydd

toil vi llafurio, poeni ♦ n llafur

toilet n trwsiad, gwisgiad; ystafell ymolchi, tŷ bach. **t. paper** n papur tŷ bach. **t. water** n dŵr Groeg

token n arwydd, argoel; tocyn

tolerable adj goddefol; gweddol, symol, cymhedrol

tolerant adj goddefgar

tolerate vt goddef

toleration n goddefgarwch

toll n toll, treth

toll vb canu (cloch, cnul)

tollbooth n tollfa

tomato n tomato

tomb n bedd, beddrod

tomboy n hoeden, rhampen

tom-cat n gwrcath, cwrcyn

tome n cyfrol (fawr)

tomfool n ynfytyn, pen-ffŵl

tomfoolery n ynfydrwydd, ffwlbri

tomorrow adv yfory

tomtit n gwas y dryw, yswidw

ton n tunnell

tonality n tonyddiaeth

tone n tôn, oslef ♦ vb tyneru, lleddfu

tongs npl gefel

tongue n tafod; tafodiaith, iaith

tonic n meddyginiaeth gryfhaol, tonic. **t. water** n dŵr tonig

tonnage n pwysau llwyth (llong); toll

tonsil n tonsil

tonsillitis n llid y tonsil

tonsure n corun, tonsur

tonight adv heno

too adv rhy; hefyd. **t. much** gormod

tool n arf, erfyn

toot vb canu corn

tooth (**teeth**) n dant

toothache n dannoedd

toothbrush n brws dannedd

toothed adj danheddog

toothless adj diddannedd, mantach

toothpaste n sebon dannedd, past dannedd

toothpick n pic dannedd

toothsome adj danteithiol, blasus

top n pen, brig, copa ♦ vt tocio; rhagori ar

top-heavy adj pendrwm

topic n pwnc

topical adj amserol

topography n daearyddiaeth leol

topple vb syrthio, cwympo, dymchwel

topsyturvy adv wyneb i waered, yn bendramwnwgl

torch n fflach, tors, ffagl

torch-light n golau tors

torment n poen, poenedigaeth ♦ vt poeni, poenydio

tormentor n poenydiwr

torn adj wedi ei rwygo, rhwygedig

tornado n hyrddwynt, corwynt

torpedo n torpedo

torpid adj marwaidd, cysglyd, swrth

torrent n cenllif, llifeiriant, rhyferthwy

torrential adj llifeiriol, trwm

torrid adj poeth, crasboeth

torso n corff (heb y pen a'r aelodau), torso

tortoise n crwban

tortoise-shell n cragen crwban, trilliw (am gath)

tortuous adj troellog, trofaus

torture n dirboen, artaith ♦ vt arteithio

torturer n arteithiwr

tory n tori, ceidwadwr ♦ adj toriaidd

toryism n toriaeth

toss vb taflu, lluchio, bwrw

total adj hollol, cyflawn ♦ n cyfan, cyfanswm

totalitarian adj totalitaraidd

totalitarianism n totalitariaeth

totality n cyfanrwydd

totally adv yn llwyr, yn gyfan, yn ei grynswth

totter vi honcian, siglo, gwegian

touch vb teimlo, cyffwrdd ♦ n teimlad

touched adj dan deimlad

touching adj teimladwy

touch-line n yr ystlys

touchstone n maen prawf, safon

touchy adj croendenau

tough adj gwydn, caled, cyndyn

toughen vb gwneud yn wydn, cryfhau

tour n tro, taith

tourism n twristiaeth

tourist n teithiwr, ymwelydd, twrist. **t. office** n swyddfa twristiaid

tournament n twrnamaint

tourniquet n offeryn i atal gwaed

tousle vt dragio, anhrefnu

tousled adj anniben
tout vi poeni pobl am archebion, gwasgu ar
tow n carth
tow vt llusgo, tynnu
toward, -s prep tua, tuag at
towel n lliain sychu, tywel
tower n twr ♦ vi esgyn, ymgodi, sefyll yn uchel
town n tref. t. **centre** n canol(y) dref. t. **clerk** n clerc y dref. t. **council** n cyngor y dref. t. **hall** n neuadd y dref
township n trefgordd
toxic adj gwenwynig
toy n tegan ♦ vi chwarae, maldodi
trace n tres; ôl, trywydd
trace vt olrhain, dilyn ♦ n ôl
tracery n rhwyllwaith (maen, etc)
trachea n breuant, corn gwynt, pibell wynt
track n ôl, brisg; llwybr ♦ vt olrhain
tracksuit n tracwisg
tract n ardal, rhandir
tract n traethodyn
tractable adj hydyn, hydrin, hywedd
traction n tyniad, tyniant, llusgiad
trade n masnach; crefft ♦ vb masnachu
trade-mark n nod masnach
trader n masnachwr
trade-union n undeb llafur
trade-wind n gwynt y dwyrain, cylchwynt
tradition n traddodiad
traditional adj traddodiadol
traduce vt cablu, difenwi, enllibio
traffic vb masnachu, traffnidio ♦ n masnach, trafnidiaeth. t. **jam** n tagfa. t. **warden** n warden traffig
traffic-lights npl goleuadau traffig
tragedy n trasiedi, trychineb
tragic adj trychinebus, alaethus
trail n llusg, brisg, ôl ♦ vb llusgo
trailer n ôl-gerbyd, ôl-gart, cart;

rhaglun (ffilm)
train vb hyfforddi, ymarfer ♦ n gosgordd; godre; trên, cerbydres
trained adj hyfforddedig, cymwys, wedi ei hyfforddi
trainer n hyfforddwr
training n hyfforddiant, disgyblaeth. t. **shoes** npl esgidiau ymarfer
trait n nodwedd, (pl) teithi
traitor n bradwr, teyrnfradwr
trajectory n taflwybr
trammel n rhwyd; hual ♦ vt llyffetheirio, hualu
tramp vb crwydro, trampio ♦ n crwydryn
trample vb sathru, sangu, mathru
trance n llewyg, llesmair, perlewyg
tranquil adj tawel, llonydd, digyffro
tranquility n tawelwch, llonyddwch
tranquillizer n tawelyn, tawelydd
trans- tran-, tra- prefix tros-, tra-
transact vt trafod, gwneud, trin
transaction n trafodaeth
transactions n trafodion
transcend vt rhagori ar, trarhagori
transcendent adj tra-rhagorol
transcendental adj trosgynnol
transcribe vt copïo
transcriber n adysgrifiwr, copïwr, copïydd
transcript n copi, adysgrifiad
transept n croes (eglwys)
transfer vt trosglwyddo ♦ n trosglwyddiad
transference n trosglwyddiad
transfiguration n gweddnewidiad
transfigure vt gweddnewid
transfix vt trywanu, gwanu
transform vt trawsffurfio
transformation n trawsffurfiad
transformer n newidydd
transfusion n trosglwyddiad (gwaed), trallwysiad (gwaed)

transgress *vt* troseddu
transgression *n* trosedd, camwedd
transgressor *n* troseddwr
transient *adj* diflanedig, darfodedig
transit *n* mynediad dros, trosiad
transition *n* trosiad, trawsgyweiriad
transitional *adj* ar newid, tros dro
transitive *adj* anghyflawn (*gram*)
transitory *adj* diflanedig, darfodedig
translate *vt* cyfieithu
translation *n* cyfieithiad
transliterate *vt* trawslythrennu
translucent *adj* tryloyw
transmigrate *vi* trawsfudo
transmission *n* trosglwyddiad
transmit *vt* anfon, trosglwyddo
transmitter *n* trosglwyddydd
transmitting-station *n* gorsaf drosglwyddo
transmute *vt* trawsnewid
transparency *n* tryloywder
transparent *adj* tryloyw
transpire *vb* dyfod yn hysbys, digwydd
transplant *vt* trawsblannu
transport *vt* trosglwyddo; alltudio ♦ *n* trosglwyddiad; cludiant; perlewyg, gorawen
transpose *vt* trawsddodi, trawsgyweirio
transubstantiation *n* trawssylweddiad
transverse *adj* croes, traws
trap *n* trap, magl; car bach ♦ *vt* dal, maglu
trapeze *n* trapis
trappings *npl* harnais, gêr
trash *n* sothach, gwehilion, ffwlbri, ysbwriel
travail *vi* trafaelu ♦ *n* trafael, llafur
travel *vb* teithio, trafaelio ♦ *n* teithio, (*pl*) teithiau. **t. agent** *n* asiant teithio
traveller *n* teithiwr, trafaeliwr. **t.'s**

cheque *n* siec deithio
travelling *adj* teithiol
traverse *vb* mynd ar draws, croesi
travesty *n* parodi
trawl *vb* llusgrwydo ♦ *n* llusgrwyd
trawler *n* llong bysgota
tray *n* hambwrdd
treacherous *adj* twyllodrus
treachery *n* brad, bradwriaeth
treacle *n* triagl
tread *vb* sathru, sengi, troedio ♦ *n* sang
treadmill *n* troell droed
treason *n* brad, bradwriaeth
treasonable *adj* bradwrus
treasure *n* trysor ♦ *vt* trysori
treasurer *n* trysorydd
treasury *n* trysorfa, trysordy, y Trysorlys
treat *vb* trin; tretio; traethu ♦ *n* gwledd, amheuthun
treatise *n* traethawd
treatment *n* triniaeth, ymdriniaeth
treaty *n* cyfamod, cytundeb
treble *adj* triphlyg ♦ *n* trebl ♦ *vb* treblu
tree *n* pren, coeden
trefoil *n* meillionen, meillion
trek *vi* mudo ♦ *n* mud, mudo
trellis *n* delltwaith
tremble *vi* crynu, echrydu, arswydo
tremendous *adj* dychrynllyd, ofnadwy, anferth
tremor *n* crynfa, cryndod, ias
tremulous *adj* crynedig
trench *n* ffos, rhigol, rhych ♦ *vb* ffosi
trenchant *adj* llym, miniog
trencher *n* trensiwr, treinsiwr, plat
trend *vi* tueddu ♦ *n* tuedd, gogwydd
trepidation *n* cryndod, ofn, dychryn
trespass *vi* troseddu ♦ *n* trosedd
trespasser *n* tresmaswr
tress *n* cudyn gwallt, tres

trestle n trestl
tri- prefix tri
triad n tri, (pl) trioedd
trial n prawf, profedigaeth, treial
triangle n triongl
triangular adj trionglog
tribal adj llwythol
tribe n llwyth, tylwyth, gwehelyth
tribulation n trallod, cystudd
tribunal n brawdle, llys, tribiwnlys
tributary adj dan deyrnged ♦ n rhagafon, isafon, cainc
tribute n teyrnged, treth
trice n munudyn, chwinciad
trick n tric, cast, ystryw ♦ vt castio
trickery n dichell, twyll, ystryw
trickle vi diferu, diferynnu
trickster n twyllwr, castiwr
tricky adj ystrywgar; anodd
tricycle n treisigl
trident n tryfer
triennial adj bob tair blynedd
trifle n gronyn, mymryn; gwaelbeth ♦ vt ofera, cellwair
trifling adj diwerth, dibwys
trigger n cliced, triger
trigonometry n trigonomeg
trill vb crychleisio, cwafrio ♦ n crychlais
trillion n triliwn
trilogy n cyfres o dair (nofel, drama etc)
trim adj taclus, twt, del ♦ vb taclu, trwsio ♦ n diwyg, trefn
trinity n trindod
trinket n tegan, tlws
trio n triawd
trioxide n triocsid
trip vb tripio, maglu; disodli ♦ n trip, tro
tripartite adj teiran
tripe n tripa
triple adj triphlyg
triplet n tripled
tripod n trybedd
trite adj cyffredin, sathredig

triumph n gorfoledd, buddugoliaeth ♦ vi gorfoleddu; buddugoliaethu
triumphal adj buddugol
triumphant adj buddugoliaethus
triumvirate n llywodraeth tri (Rhufain)
trivet n trybedd
trivial adj distadl, dibwys, diwerth
trolley, -y n troli
troop n byddin, torf, mintai ♦ vb tyrru. **troops** npl lluoedd, minteioedd
trooper n milwr (ar farch)
trophy n gwobr, tlws
tropic n trofan
tropical adj trofannol
trot vb tuthio, trotian ♦ n tuth, trot
troubadour n trwbadŵr, bardd telynegol
trouble vt blino, trafferthu ♦ n blinder, trallod, helbul, trafferth
troubled adj aflonydd, anesmwyth, pryderus, ofnus, dyrys
troubles npl trafferthion, helbulon, pryderon, ofnau
troublesome adj blinderus, trafferthus
trough n cafn
trounce vt ffonodio, cystwyo, baeddu
troupe n mintai o berfformwyr
trousers npl llodrau, trowsus, trwser
trousseau n dillad priodasferch
trout n brithyll
trow vb tybied, meddylied, credu
trowel n trywel
truant n triawnt, mitsiwr
truce n cadoediad
truck n trwc, gwagen
truck vb cyfnewid, ffeirio
truckle vi plygu, ymostwng, ymgreinio
truculent adj ffyrnig, milain
trudge vb cerdded yn ffwdanus, trwmgerdded
true adj gwir, cywir

truism *n* gwireb, gwiredd
truly *adv* yn wir, yn ddiau, yn gywir
trump *vb* utganu; twyllo, ffugio ♦ *n* trwmp
trumpery *n* sothach, ffwlbri ♦ *adj* coeg, gwacsaw
trumpet *n* utgorn, corn, trwmped
truncheon *n* pastwn, trensiwn
trundle *vb* treiglo, rholio
trunk *n* cyff, cist; corff; duryn, trwnc
trunks *npl* trons
truss *vb* gwneud bwndel; gwaellu (ffowlyn)
trust *n* ymddiried, ymddiriedaeth, coel; ymddiriedolaeth ♦ *vb* hyderu, ymddiried, coelio
trustee *n* ymddiriedolwr
trusteeship *n* ymddiriedolaeth
trustworthy *adj* y gellir dibynnu arno
trusty *adj* ffyddlon, cywir, teyrngar
truth *n* gwir, gwirionedd
truthful *adj* geirwir
truthfulness *n* geirwiredd
try *vb* profi, cynnig, ceisio, treio
trying *adj* poenus, anodd, blin
tryst *n* oed
T-shirt *n* crys-T
tub *n* twba, twb, baddon
tuba *n* tiwba
tube *n* pib, pibell, tiwb, corn
tuber *n* cloronen, taten
tuberculosis *n* darfodedigaeth, dicáu, dicléin
tubular *adj* tiwbaidd. **t. bridge** céubont
tuck *vt* cwtogi, plygu ♦ *n* plyg, twc
Tuesday *n* dydd Mawrth
tuft *n* cogyn, tusw, cudyn
tug *vb* llusgo, tynnu
tuition *n* addysg, hyfforddiant
tulip *n* tiwlip
tumble *vb* cwympo ♦ *n* codwm, cwymp

tumbler *n* gwydryn
tumid *adj* chwyddedig
tummy *n* bola
tumour *n* chwydd, casgliad, cornwyd
tumult *n* terfysg, cynnwrf
tumultuous *adj* terfysglyd
tuna *n* tiwna
tune *n* tôn, tiwn, cywair ♦ *vb* cyweirio
tuneful *adj* soniarus
tunic *n* crysbais, siaced
Tunisia *n* Tunisia
tunnel *n* ceuffordd, twnnel
turban *n* twrban
turbid *adj* afloyw, cymysglyd, lleidiog
turbine *n* twrbin
turbot *n* twrbot
turbulence *n* terfysg, cynnwrf
turbulent *adj* terfysglyd, afreolus
turf *n* tywarchen
turgid *adj* chwyddedig
Turk *n* Twrc
turkey *n* twrci
Turkey *n* Twrci
Turkish *adj* Twrcaidd
turmoil *n* trafferth, ffwdan, berw
turn *vb* troi ♦ *n* tro, trofa
turncoat *n* gwrthgiliwr
turner *n* turniwr
turning *n* tro; tröedigaeth
turning point *n* trobwynt
turnip *n* erfinen, meipen
turnout *n* cynulliad
turnover *n* cyfanswm busnes
turnpike *n* tollborth, tyrpeg
turnstile *n* camfa dro
turntable *n* trofwrdd
turpentine *n* twrpant, turpant
turpitude *n* gwarth, ysgelerder
turquoise *n* maen glas (gwerthfawr)
turret *n* twred, tyryn
turtle *n* crwban môr
turtle, -dove *n* turtur
tusk *n* ysgithrddant, ysgithr

tussle *n* ymgiprys, ysgarmes
tut *excl* twt!
tutelage *n* hyfforddiant, nawdd
tutor *n* athro, hyfforddwr ♦ *vt* hyfforddi
tutorial *adj* tiwtorial
twaddle *n* lol, ffiloreg
twang *vb* clecian, swnio ♦ *n* sŵn, llediaith
tweed *n* brethyn gwlân, twid
tweezers *n* gefel fach
twelfth *adj* deuddegfed
twelve *adj, n* deuddeg, un deg dau
twentieth *adj* ugeinfed
twenty *adj, n* ugain
twice *adv* dwywaith
twiddle *vt* chwarae bodiau, cellwair
twig *n* brigyn, ysbrigyn, impyn
twilight *n* cyfnos, cyfddydd
twill *n* brethyn caerog
twin *n* gefell
twine *n* llinyn ♦ *vb* cyfrodeddu, cordeddu
twinge *n* cnofa, brath, gwayw
twinkle *vi* serennu, pefrio
twinkling *n* chwinciad, amrantiad
twirl *vb* chwyrndroi, chwyldroi, nydd-droi
twist *vb* nyddu, nydd-droi, cyfrodeddu; troi, gwyrdroi ♦ *n* tro; edau gyfrodedd
twit *n* dannod, edliw; un ffôl
twitch *vb* tymhigo, brathgnoi ♦ *n* tymig
twitch *n* gwayw, brath, plwc ♦ *vb* brathu, tynnu'n sydyn, plycio
twitter *vi* trydar
two *adj, n* dau, dwy
two-faced *adj* dauwynebog
twofold *adv* deublyg
two piece *n* deuddarn
tympan *n* tabwrdd, tympan
type *n* math, teip
typescript *n* teipysgrif
typewriter *n* teipiadur, peiriant teipio

typhoid *n* twymyn yr ymysgaroedd
typhoon *n* corwynt
typhus *n* twymyn heintus, teiffws
typical *adj* arwyddol, nodweddiadol
typify *vt* arwyddo, nodweddu
typist *n* teipydd
typographical *adj* argraffyddol
typography *n* argraffwaith
tyranny *n* tra-arglwyddiaeth, gormes
tyrannize *vb* gormesu, treisio
tyrant *n* gormesteyrn, gormeswr
tyre *n* teiar
tyro *n* newyddian, dechreuwr

U

ubiquitous *adj* ym mhob man, hollbresennol
udder *n* pwrs, cadair, piw
ugh *excl* ach! ych y fi!
ugly *adj* hagr, hyll
ugliness *n* hagrwch, hylldra
ulcer *n* casgliad, cornwyd, wiser
Ulster *n* Ulster
ulterior *adj* tu draw i, tu hwnt i, pellach; cudd
ultimate *adj* diwethaf, olaf, eithaf
ultimately *adv* o'r diwedd
ultimatum *n* y gair olaf, y rhybudd olaf
ultra *adj* eithafol ♦ *prefix* tu hwnt i, gor-
ultramodern *adj* modern iawn
umbrage *n* tramgwydd
umbrella *n* ymbrelo, brela, ambarél, ymbarél
umpire *n* dyfarnwr, canolwr
un- *prefix* an-, am-, ang-, af-, di-, heb
unable *adj* analluog
unaccented *adj* diacen
unacceptable *adj* anghymeradwy, annerbyniol
unaccompanied *adj* heb gwmni;

heb gyfeiliant
unaccountable adj anesboniadwy
unaccustomed adj anghyfarwydd,
anghynefin
unacquainted adj anghyfarwydd
unadulterated adj pur, digymysg
unaffected adj naturiol; heb ei
effeithio gan
unanimity n unfrydedd
unanimous adj unfrydol
unanimously adv yn unfryd
unarmed adj diamddiffyn, heb
arfau
unassailable adj diysgog
unassuming adj diymhongar
unattainable adj anghyraeddadwy
unavoidable adj anorfod
unaware adj anymwybodol
unawares adv yn ddiarwybod
unbearable adj annioddefol
unbecoming adj anweddus,
anweddaidd
unbeliever n anghredadun,
anffyddiwr
unbelieving adj anghrediniol
unbiassed adj diduedd
unblemished adj di-nam, dinam
unbounded adj diderfyn
unbridled adj heb ei ffrwyno
unbroken adj di-dor
unbutton vb datod, datfotymu
uncalled (for) adj di-alw-amdano
uncanny adj rhyfedd, dieithr,
annaearol
uncle n ewythr
unclean adj brwnt, aflan
uncomfortable adj anghysurus
uncommon adj anghyffredin
uncompromising adj di-ildio,
digyfaddawd, cyndyn
unconcerned adj difater, didaro
unconditional adj diamod
unconfirmed adj heb ei gadarnhau
unconquerable adj anorchfygol
unconscionable adj digydwybod,
afresymol
unconscious adj anymwybodol

unconstitutional adj
anghyfansoddiadol
uncontaminated adj di-lwgr, pur
uncontrollable adj aflywodraethus
unconventional adj
anghonfensiynol
uncouth adj trwsgl, lletchwith,
garw, amrwd
uncover vb datguddio
unction n eli; eneiniad, arddeliad,
hwyl
unctuous adj seimlyd; rhagrithiol
uncultivated adj heb ei feithrin
undamaged adj heb ei niweidio
undecided adj petrus, mewn
penbleth
undefended adj diamddiffyn
undefiled adj dihalog, pur
undefined adj amhenodol,
annelwig
undeniable adj anwadadwy
under prep tan, is, islaw ♦ adv
tanodd, oddi tanodd ♦ prefix is-,
tan-
undercurrent n islif
underestimate vb prisio'n rhy isel
undergraduate n myfyriwr
israddedig
underground adj tanddaearol
underhand adj llechwraidd, tan
din
underline vb tanlinellu, pwysleisio
undermine vb tanseilio
underneath adv oddi tanodd ♦ prep
tan
underpass n ffordd danddaearol,
tanffordd
underrate vb tanbrisio, iselbrisio
understand vt deall, dirnad
understanding n amgyffred,
dealltwriaeth
undertake vb ymgymryd
undertaker n ymgymerydd; saer
(coffinau)
undertaking adj ymrwymiad
undertone n islais
underworld n annwn

undeserved adj anhaeddiannol

undesirable adj annymunol

undeveloped adj heb ei ddatblygu

undeviating adj diwyro

undignified adj anurddasol, diurddas

undisciplined adj diddisgyblaeth

undisputed adj diamheuol

undisturbed adj llonydd, tawel, digyffro

undo vt dadwneud; datod; andwyo, difetha

undoing n distryw, dinistr

undoubted adj diamheuol

undress vb dadwisgo

undue adj amhriodol

undulate vi tonni

unearned adj heb ei ennill

unearthly adj annaearol

uneasiness n anesmwythder, pryder

uneasy adj anesmwyth, aflonydd, pryderus

unedifying adj di-fudd, anadeiladol

uneducated adj annysgedig

unemployed adj di-waith, segur

unemployment n diweithdra, anghyflogaeth

unending adj diddiwedd

unendurable adj anniodefol

unequal adj anghyfartal

unequalled adj digymar, dihafal

unequivocal adj diamwys

unerring adj sicr

uneven adj anwastad

uneventful adj diddigwyddiad

unexpected adj annisgwyliadwy

unfailing adj di-feth

unfair adj annheg

unfairness n annhegwch

unfaithful adj anffyddlon

unfamiliar adj anghyfarwydd

unfasten vb datod

unfathomable adj annealladwy

unfavourable adj anffafriol

unfeeling adj dideimlad

unfettered adj dilyffethair

unfinished adj anorffenedig

unfit adj anghymwys; aflach

unfitting adj amhriodol

unflinching adj diysgog, dewr

unfold vb datblygu

unforeseen adj heb ei ragweld

unforgiving adj anfaddeugar

unfortunate adj anffodus

unfortunately adj yn anffodus

unfounded adj di-sail

unfrequented adj anhygyrch, unig

unfriendly adj anghyfeillgar

unfrock vb diarddel

unfulfilled adj heb ei gyflawni

unfurnished adj diddodrefn

ungainly adv afrosgo, trwsgl

ungentlemanly adj anfonedidgaidd

ungodly adj annuwiol, drwg

ungrammatical adj anramadegol

ungrateful adj anniolchgar

unguarded adj ar awr wan

unguent n ennaint, eli

unhallowed adj halogedig

unhappiness n anhapusrwydd

unhappy adj anhapus

unharmed adj dianaf

unhealthy adj aflach

unheeding adj diofal

unhesitating adj dibetrus

unhorse vb taflu oddi ar geffyl

unicorn n uncorn, unicorn

unification n uniad

uniform adj unffurf ♦ n gwisg swyddogol

uniformity n unffurfiaeth

unify vt unoli, uno

unilateral adj unochrog

unimpaired adj dianaf

unimpeded adj dirwystr

unimportant adj dibwys

uninspired adj diawen

unintelligent adj anneallus

unintelligible adj annealladwy

unintentional adj anfwriadol

uninteresting adj anniddorol

union n undeb; uniad

unionism n undebaeth

unionist *n* undebwr; unoliaethwr
(Iwerddon)
unique *adj* dihafal, digymar
unison *n* unsain, unseinedd
unit *n* un, rhif un; uned; undod
Unitarian *n* Undodwr ✧ *adj*
Undodaidd
Unitarianism *n* Undodiaeth
unite *vb* uno, cyfuno, cyduno,
cydio
united *adj* unol, unedig. **U. States
(of America)** *n* yr Unol Daleithiau
United Kingdom *n:* the U.K. y
Deyrnas Unedig
unity *n* undod
universal *adj* cyffredinol
universe *n* bydysawd
university *n* prifysgol
unjust *adj* anghyfiawn, annheg
unjustly *adv* ar gam
unkempt *adj* heb ei gribo, aflêr,
anniben
unkind *adj* angharedig
unknown *adj* anadnabyddus,
anenwog
unlace *vb* datod
unlawful *adj* anghyfreithlon
unlearned *adj* annysgedig
unless *conj* oni, onid
unlettered *adj* anllythrennog
unlike *adj* annhebyg
unlikely *adj* annhebygol
unlimited *adj* diderfyn
unload *vb* dadlwytho
unlock *vb* datgloi
unlucky *adj* anlwcus
unmanageable *adj* aflywodraethus
unmannerly *adj* anfoesgar
unmarried *adj* dibriod
unmask *vb* dinoethi
unmatched *adj* digymar
unmerciful *adj* didrugaredd
unmistakable *adj* digamsyniol
unmixed *adj* digymysg
unnatural *adj* annaturiol
unnecessary *adj* dianghenraid
unobserved *adj* heb ei weld

unobtrusive *adj* anymwthiol
unoccupied *adj* gwag
unopened *adj* heb ei agor
unopposed *adj* yn
ddiwrthwynebiad
unorthodox *adj* anarferol,
anuniongred
unpack *vb* dadbacio
unpaid *adj* di-dâl, didal
unparalleled *adj* digyffelyb
unpardonable *adj* anfaddeuol
unpatriotic *adj* anwlatgar
unpleasant *adj* annymunol
unpolluted *adj* dihalog, pur
unpopular *adj* amhoblogaidd
unpopularity *n* amhoblogrwydd
unpractical *adj* anymarferol
unprejudiced *adj* diragfarn
unprepared *adj* amharod
unprincipled *adj* diegwyddor
unprofitable *adj* amhroffidiol
unprotected *adj* diamddiffyn
unpublished *adj* anghyhoeddedig
unqualified *adj* heb gymhwyster
unquestionable *adj* diamheuol
unready *adj* amharod
unreasonable *adj* afresymol
unrelated *adj* amherthnasol; heb
berthyn
unremitting *adj* dyfal
unrestrained *adj* dilywodraeth
unripe *adj* anaeddfed
unrivalled *adj* digymar
unruffled *adj* tawel
unruly *adj* afreolus
unsafe *adj* anniogel
unsatisfactory *adj* anfoddhaol
unsatisfied *adj* anfodlon
unsatisfying *adj* annigonol
unscathed *adj* dianaf
unscrew *vt* agor; llacio; datroi
unscrupulous *adj* diegwyddor
unseasonable *adj* annhymorol
unseat *vb* troi o'i swydd; taflu
(ceffyl)
unseemly *adj* anweddaidd
unseen *adj* anweledig

unsettled *adj* ansefydlog
unshaken *adj* diysgog, cadarn
unsighted *adj* heb allu gweld
unsightly *adj* diolwg, blêr
unskilful *adj* anfedrus
unskilled *adj* anghelfydd
unsociable *adj* anghymdeithasgar
unsolicited *adj* heb ei ofyn
unsound *adj* diffygiol, cyfeiliornus
unsparing *adj* diarbed, hael
unspeakable *adj* anhraethol
unstable *adj* ansefydlog
unstained *adj* dilychwin
unsteadiness *n* ansadrwydd
unsteady *adj* ansefydlog
unsubstantial *adj* ansylweddol
unsuccessful *adj* aflwyddiannus
unsuitable *adj* anaddas
unsullied *adj* dilychwin
unsurmountable *adj* anorchfygol
unsurpassed *adj* diguro
unsuspecting *adj* heb amau dim
untainted *adj* di-lwgr, pur
untangle *vb* datrys
unthankful *adj* anniolchgar
unthinking *adj* difeddwl
untidy *adj* anniben
untie *vb* datod
until *prep, conj* hyd, hyd oni, nes, tan
untimely *adj* anamserol
untiring *adj* diflino
unto *prep* i, at, hyd at, wrth
untold *adj* di-ben-draw
untoward *adj* anffodus, cyndyn
untrodden *adj* disathr
untrue *adj* celwyddog
unusual *adj* anarferol, anghynefin; anghyffredin; newydd; dieithr
unutterable *adj* anhraethadwy
unvarying *adj* digyfnewid, cyson
unveil *vb* dadorchuddio
unversed *adj* anhyddysg
unwarranted *adj* heb ei warantu
unwary *adj* diofal
unwell *adj* anhwylus
unwholesome *adj* afiach

unwieldy *adj* afrosgo
unwilling *adj* anfodlon, amharod
unwise *adj* annoeth
unwittingly *adj* yn ddiarwybod
unworthiness *n* annheilyngdod
unworthy *adj* annheilwng
unwounded *adj* dianaf, cyfan
unyielding *adj* di-ildio
up *adj, prep* i fyny, i'r lan
upbringing *n* magwraeth
upheaval *n* cyffro, terfysg
uphill *adj* i fyny
uphold *vb* cynnal
upholsterer *n* dodrefnwr, clustogwr
upkeep *n* cynhaliaeth
upland *n* ucheldir, blaenau
uplifting *adj* dyrchafol
upon *prep* ar, ar warthaf, ar uchaf
upper *adj* uwch, uchaf
uppermost *adj, adv* uchaf
upright *adj* syth, union, unionsyth
uprising *n* terfysg, gwrthryfel
uproar *n* terfysg, cythrwfl, dadwrdd
uproot *vb* diwreiddio
upset *vb* troi, dymchwelyd, cyffroi, gofidio
upshot *n* swm, canlyniad, diwedd
upside-down *adj, adv* (â'i) wyneb i waered
upstairs *n* llofft
upstart *n* crach fonheddwr
upward *adj, adv*, **upwards** *adv* i fyny
uranium *n* wraniwm
urban *adj* dinasol, dinesig
urbane *adj* hynaws, mwyn, boneddigaidd
urbanize *vb* gwneud yn drefol
urchin *n* draenog; crwtyn
urethra *n* pibell ddŵr o'r bledren
urge *vb* cymell, annog
urgency *n* brys
urgent *adj* taer, pwysig, yn gofyn brys
urine *n* troeth, trwnc, piso

urn *n* wrn
us *pron* ni, nyni, ninnau; 'n
usage *n* arfer, defod, triniaeth
use *n* iws, arfer, defnydd, gwasanaeth, diben ♦ *vb* iwsio, arfer, defnyddio
used *adj* arferedig, mewn arfer, cynefin; (*car*) ail-law
useful *adj* defnyddiol
useless *adj* diwerth
user *n* defnyddiwr
usher *n* rhingyll; isathro; tywysydd ♦ *vt* arwain i mewn, dwyn ymlaen
usual *adj* arferol, cynefin
usurer *n* usuriwr
usurp *vt* trawsfeddiannu
usurper *n* trawsfeddiannwr
usury *n* usuriaeth, ocraeth
utensil *n* offeryn, llestr
uterus *n* croth, bru
utilitarian *adj* defnyddiol
utilitarianism *n* llesyddiaeth
utility *n* defnyddioldeb, budd, lles
utilization *n* defnydd
utilize *vt* defnyddio
utmost *adj* eithaf, pellaf
utopia *n* gwlad ddelfrydol (ddychmygol)
utopian *adj* defrydol, anymarferol
utter *adj* eithaf, pellaf; hollol, llwyr
utter *vt* yngan, traethu, dywedyd
utterance *n* parabl, ymadrodd, lleferydd
uttermost *adj* eithaf, pellaf
U-turn *n* tro pedol
uvula *n* tafod bach, tafodig
uvular *adj* tafodigol

V

vacancy *n* lle gwag, swydd wag, gwacter
vacant *adj* gwag; syn, synfyfyriol, hurt

vacate *vt* ymadael â, gadael yn wag
vacation *n* seibiant, gwyliau
vaccinate *vt* brechu, bufrechu, torri'r frech
vaccination *n* y frech, brechiad
vaccine *n* brech
vacillate *vi* anwadalu, bwhwman
vacuous *adj* gwg, syn, hurt
vacuum *n* gwag, gwagle, gwactod
vacuum cleaner *n* sugnydd llwch
vacuum flask *n* thermos, jac
vagabond *n* crwydryn, dihiryn
vagary *n* mympwy
vagrancy *n* crwydro
vagrant *adj* crwydrol ♦ *n* crwydryn
vague *adj* amwys, amhenodol
vagueness *n* amwysedd
vain *adj* balch, coegfalch; ofer
vale *n* dyffryn, glyn, bro, cwm, ystrad
valediction *n* ffarwel
valentine *n* falant, folant
valet *n* gwas
valiant *adj* dewr, dewrwych, gwrol, glew
valid *adj* digonol, dilys, cyfreithlon, iawn
validate *vb* cadarnhau, dilysu
validity *n* dilysrwydd
valley *n* dyffryn, cwm, glyn
valour *n* dewrder, gwroldeb, glewder
valuable *adj* gwerthfawr
valuation *n* prisiad
value *n* gwerth ♦ *vt* gwerthfawrogi, prisio
valuer *n* prisiwr
valve *n* falf
vampire *n* sugnwr gwaed
van *n* blaen cad, y rheng flaenaf
van *n* men, fan
vandal *n* fandal
vandalism *n* fandaliaeth
vane *n* ceiliog gwynt
vanguard *n* blaen cad, blaenfyddin
vanilla *n* fanila

vanish *vi* diflannu, darfod

vanity *n* gwagedd, gwegi, coegfalchder

vanquish *vt* gorchfygu, trechu

vanquisher *n* gorchfygwr

vantage *n* mantais

vapid *adj* diflas, merf, marwaidd, egr

vaporize *vb* anweddu

vaporous *adj* llawn tarth

vapour *n* tawch, tarth, ager, anwedd

variable *adj* cyfnewidiol, anwadal, oriog

variable *n* newidyn (rhifyddiaeth)

variance *n* anghytundeb, anghydfod, amrywioldeb

variant *n* amrywiad

variation *n* amrywiad

varicose *adj* chwyddedig (am wythiennau)

varied *adj* amrywiol

variegated *adj* brith, brithliw

variety *n* amrywiaeth

various *adj* gwahanol, amrywiol

varnish *n* barnais, farnais ♦ *vt* barneisio, farneisio

varnisher *n* farneisiwr

vary *vb* amrywio; newid

vase *n* cwpan, cawg

vaseline *n* faselin, eli

vassal *n* caethddeiliad, taeog, aillt, deiliad

vast *adj* dirfawr, anferth

vastness *n* mawredd, ehangder

vat *n* cerwyn

Vatican *n* plas y Pab

vaticinate *vb* proffwydo, darogan

vaticination *n* proffwydoliaeth, darogan

vault *n* daeargell, claddgell; cromen ♦ *vb* neidio, llamu

vaulted *adj* bwaog

vaunt *vb* ymffrostio, bostio, brolio

veal *n* cig llo

vector *n* fector

veer *vb* troi, cylchdroi; trawshwylio

vegetable *adj* llysieuol ♦ *n* llysieuyn ymborth

vegetarian *n* llysieuwr

vegetate *vi* tarddu, tyfu; ofera

vegetation *n* tyfiant llysiau, llystyfiant

vehemence *n* angerdd

vehement *adj* angerddol, tanbaid

vehicle *n* cerbyd; cyfrwng, moddion

veil *n* gorchudd, llen ♦ *vt* gorchuddio

vein *n* gwythien

velar *adj* felar

veldt *n* anialdir, maestir

vellum *n* memrwn

velocity *n* buander, cyflymder, buanedd (mathemateg)

velvet *n* melfed

venal *adj* llygredig, anonest

vend *vt* gwerthu

vendor *n* gwerthwr

veneer *n* argaen, wynebiad; rhith, ffug

venerable *adj* hybarch

venerate *vt* parchu, anrhydeddu

venereal *adj* gwenerol

Venetian blind *n* llen Fenis

vengeance *n* dial, dialedd

vengeful *adj* dialgar

venial *adj* maddeuadwy, esgusodol

venison *n* cig carw, fenswn

venom *n* gwenwyn

venomous *adj* gwenwynig

venous *adj* gwythennol

vent *n* agorfa, twll, arllwysfa ♦ *vt* arllwys, gollwng

ventilate *vt* awyru, gwyntyllu

ventilation *n* awyriad, gwyntylliad

ventilator *n* awyrydd, gwyntyllydd

ventriloquism *n* tafleisiaeth

ventricle *n* bolgell y galon, fentrigl

venture *n* anturiaeth, mentr ♦ *vb* anturio, mentro

venturesome *adj* mentrus, anturus

venue *n* man cyfarfod

Venus n Gwener, duwies serch
veracious adj cywir, geirwir, gwir
veracity adj geirwiredd
verandah n feranda
verb n berf
verbal adj berfol; geiriol
verbally adv mewn geiriau, gair
   am air
verbatim adv air am air, air yng
   ngair
verbiage n amleiriaeth,
   geiriogrwydd
verb-noun n berfenw
verbose adj amleiriog
verbosity n geiriogrwydd
verdant adj gwyrddlas, gwyrdd
verdict n dyfarniad, dedfryd,
   rheithfarn
verdure n gwyrddlesni
verge n min, ymyl ♦ vi ymylu
verger n byrllysgydd, eglwyswas
verfication n gwireddiad
verify vt gwiro, gwireddu
verily adv yn wir, yn ddiau
verisimilitude n tebygolrwydd
veritable adj gwironeddol
verity n gwir, gwirionedd
vermilion adj fermiliwn, lliw cochlyd
vermin npl pryfed, pryfetach;
   llygod, etc
vernacular adj cynhenid, brodorol
   ♦ n iaith y wlad
vernal adj gwanwynol
veronica n feronica, llysiau
   Llywelyn
versatile adj amrywdawn
versatility n amlochredd
verse n gwers, adnod, pennill;
   prydyddiaeth
versed adj cyfarwydd, hyddysg
versify vb mydru, prydyddu, prydu
version n cyfieithiad, trosiad;
   esboniad
vers libre n gwers rydd
versus prep yn erbyn
vertebra (-brae) n un o gymalau'r
   asgwrn cefn

vertebrate n anifail ag asgwrn
   cefn
vertex (-tices) n pen, crib, copa
vertical adj syth, unionsyth, plwm
vertigo n y bendro, y ddot
vervain n llysiau hudol, y ferfain
verve n bywyd, egni, asbri
very adj, adv iawn, pur, tra;
   diamheuol
vespers npl gosber
vessel n llestr
vest n gwasgod, crys isaf ♦ vb
   arwisgo, cynysgaeddu
vestal adj gwyryfol ♦ n lleian,
   gwyry
vested adj yn ymwneud ag eiddo
vestibule n porth, cyntedd
vestige n ôl, ôl troed, brisg
vestigial adj gweddilliol, ôl
vestment n gwisg, defodwisg
vestry n festri
vesture n gwisg, dilledyn, dillad
vet vb arholi, archwilio ♦ n
   meddyg anifeiliaid
vetch n pys llygod
veteran n un hen a chyfarwydd
veterinary adj milfeddygol. **v.**
   surgeon meddyg anifeiliaid,
   milfeddyg
veto (-oes) n gwaharddiad ♦ vb
   gwahardd
vex vt blino, poeni, poenydio,
   cythruddo
vexation n blinder, gofid
vexed adj blin, dig
vexing adj blin, plagus
via prep trwy, ar hyd
viable adj abl i fodoli, dichonadwy
viaduct n pontffordd, fforddbont
vial n ffiol
viand n bwyd, ymborth
vibrant adj dirgrynol
vibrate vb crynu, dirgrynu
vibration n dirgryniad
vicar n ficer
vicarage n ficeriaeth; ficerdy
vicarious adj dirprwyol, mechnïol

vice *n* drygioni, drygedd, bai, gwŷd
vice *n* gwasg, feis
vice- *prefix* rhag-, is-
vice-admiral *n* is-lyngesydd
vice-chairman *n* is-gadeirydd
vice-chancellor *n* is-ganghellor
vice-president *n* is-lywydd
viceroy *n* rhaglaw
vice-versa *adv* i'r gwrthwyneb
vicinity *n* cymdogaeth
vicious *adj* drygionus, gwydus
viciousness *n* drygioni, sbeit
vicissitude *n* cyfnewidiad, tro
victim *n* aberth, ysglyfaeth
victimise *vb* erlid, gormesu
victor *n* gorchfygwr
victorious *adj* buddugol, buddugoliaethus
victory *n* buddugoliaeth
victual *n* (*pl*) bwyd, lluniaeth ♦ *vt* bwydo
victualler *n* gwerthwr bwyd. **licensed v.** *n* tafarnwr
vide *vb* gwêl
videlicet (**viz**) *adv* sef, h.y.
vie *vi* cystadlu, cydymgais
Vienna *n* Wien
Vietnam *n* Fietnam
view *n* golygfa, barn ♦ *vt* edrych
viewer *n* gwyliwr (teledu)
viewpoint *n* safbwynt
vigil *n* noswyl, gwylnos
vigilant *adj* gwyliadwrus
vignette *n* addurn, llun
vigorous *adj* grymus, egnïol
vigour *n* grym, nerth, egni, ynni
viking *n* môr-leidr (o Lychlyn gynt)
vile *adj* gwael, brwnt
vileness *n* brynti
vilify *vt* pardduo, difrïo
villa *n* fila
village *n* pentref
villager *n* pentrefwr
villain *n* cnaf, adyn, dihiryn
villainous *adj* anfad, ysgeler

villainy *n* anfadwaith
vim *n* grym, ynni
vindicate *vt* amddiffyn, cyfiawnhau
vindication *n* cyfiawnhad
vindictive *adj* dialgar
vindictiveness *n* dialedd
vine *n* gwinwydden
vinegar *n* finegr
vineyard *n* gwinllan
vintage *n* cynhaeaf gwin
vintner *n* gwinwr, gwinydd
viola *n* fiola
violate *vt* torri, troseddu, treisio, trochi
violation *n* treisiad, trosedd
violence *n* ffyrnigrwydd, trais
violent *adj* gwyllt, tanbaid, angerddol
violet *n* fioled, crinllys
violin *n* ffidil
violinist *n* feiolinydd, ffidler
violoncello *n* basgrwth
viper *n* gwiber
viper's bugloss *n* tafod y bwch
virago *n* cecren
virgin *n* gwyry, morwyn
virginal *n* tyrginal ♦ *adj* gwyryfol, morwynol
virile *adj* gwrol, egnïol
virility *n* gwrolaeth, gwroldeb
virtual *adj* rhinweddol
virtually *adv* i bob pwrpas
virtue *n* rhinwedd
virtuoso *n* un celfydd, carwr celfyddyd
virulence *n* gwenwyn, caseb
virulent *adj* gwenwynig, ffyrnig
virus *n* gôr, crawn; gwenwyn, firws
visa *n* fisa
visage *n* wyneb, wynepryd
vis-à-vis *adv* wyneb yn wyneb, gyferbyn
viscid *adj* gwydn, gludiog
viscount *n* is-iarll
visible *adj* gweladwy, gwel:dig
vision *n* gweledigaeth, golwg,

gweled

visionary *n* breuddwydiwr ♦ *adj* breuddwydiol

visit *vt* ymweld, gofwyo ♦ *n* ymweliad

visitation *n* ymweliad, archwiliad

visitor *n* ymwelwr, ymwelydd

visor *n* miswrn, mwgwd

vista *n* golygfa

visual *adj* gweledol, golygol. **v. aids** cyfarpar gweled

visualise *vb* gwneud yn weledig, disgrifio, dychmygu

vital *adj* bywiol, bywydol, hanfodol

vitality *n* bywyd, bywiogrwydd

vitalize *vb* bywiocáu, bywiogi

vitamin *n* fitamin

vitiate *vt* llygru, difetha, dirymu

vitreous *adj* gwydrol, gwydraidd

vitriol *n* fitriol, asid sylffurig

vitriolic *adj* fitriolaidd, atgas, chwerw

vituperate *vt* cablu, difenwi, difrio

vituperative *adj* difriol

vivacious *adj* bywiog, heini, nwyfus

vivacity *n* hoen, nwyf

viva voce *adv* ar lafar

vivid *adj* byw, clir, llachar, tanbaid

vividness *n* eglurder

vivify *vt* bywhau, bywiocáu

vivisection *n* bywdrychiad, bywddifyniad

vixen *n* cadnawes, llwynoges

viz. *adv* sef (talfyriad o *videlicet*)

vizier *n* swyddog gwlad (Mohametanaidd)

vocable *n* gair

vocabulary *n* geirfa

vocal *adj* lleisiol, llafarol, llafar

vocalist *n* lleisiwr, cantor

vocalize *vt* llafarseinio; llafarogi

vocally *adv* a'r llais

vocation *n* galwad, galwedigaeth

vocative *adj* cyfarchol

vociferate *vb* crochlefain, gweiddi

vodka *n* fodca

vogue *n* arfer, ffasiwn, bri

voice *n* llais, lleferydd; stad (*gram.*)

voiced *adj* llafarog, lleisiol

voiceless *adj* dilais, mud

void *adj* gwag; ofer, di-rym ♦ *n* gwagle ♦ *vt* gwagu, gollwng; gwacau

volatile *adj* hedegog, anwadal, gwamal, ysgafn, cyfnewidiol

volcanic *adj* folcanig

volcano *n* llosgfynydd, mynydd tân

vole *n* llygoden y maes

volition *n* ewyllysiad, ewyllys

volley *n* cawod o ergydion; taro pêl yn yr awyr

volt *n* uned grym trydan, folt

voltage *n* grym trydan

voluble *adj* rhugl, ymadroddus

volume *n* cyfrol; swm, crynswth, folum (cemeg), cyfaint (mathemateg)

voluminous *adj* mawr, helaeth

voluntary *adj* gwirfoddol

volunteer *n* gwirfoddolwr ♦ *vb* gwirfoddoli

voluptuary *n* pleserwr, glythwr

voluptuous *adj* glwth, trythyll

voluptuousness *n* trythyllwch

vomit *vb* chwydu, cyfogi

voracious *adj* gwancus, rheibus

vortex *n* trobwll, chwyldro

votary *n* addunwr, diofrydwr; pleidiwr

vote *n* pleidlais ♦ *vb* pleidleisio

voter *n* pleidleisiwr

votive *adj* addunedol, addunol

vouch *vb* gwirio, gwarantu

vouchsafe *vt* caniatáu, rhoddi

vow *n* adduned, diofryd ♦ *vb* addunedu

vowel *n* llafariad. **v. affection** affeithiad. **v. mutation** gwyriad

voyage *n* mordaith ♦ *vb* mordeithio, morwyo

voyager *n* mordeithiwr

vulcanize *vb* caledu rwber

vulgar *adj* cyffredin; isel, di-foes, aflednais

vulgarism *n* ymadrodd aflednais

vulgarity *n* diffyg moes

Vulgate *n* Y Fwlgat

vulnerable *adj* archolladwy, hyglwyf, hawdd ei niweidio

vulture *n* fwltur

W

wad *n* sypyn, wad

wadding *n* wadin

waddle *vi* siglo, honcian

wade *vb* beisio, rhydio

wader *n* rhydiwr

wadi *n* gwely afon (sy'n dueddol i sychu)

wafer *n* afrifaden

waft *vt* chwifio, cludo, dygludo

wag *vb* ysgwyd, siglo, honcian

wag *n* cellweiriwr, wag

wage *vt* gwneuthur, dwyn ymlaen

wage *n* cyflog, hur

wager *n* cyngwystl ♦ *vt* cyngwystlo

waggish *adj* cellweirus

waggle *vb* siglo

wagon *n* men, gwagen

wagtail *n* sigl-i-gwt

waif *n* plentyn digartref

wail *vb* cwynfan, wylofain, udo

wainscot *n* palis

waist *n* gwasg, canol

waistcoat *n* gwasgod

wait *vb* aros; gweini ♦ *n* arhosiad

waiter *n* gweinydd

waiting *n* aros, sefyll

waiting room *n* ystafell aros

waitress *n* gweinyddes

wake *vb* deffro ♦ *n* gwylmabsant; gwylnos

wake *n* ôl, brisg

wakefulness *n* anhunedd

waken *vb* deffro, dihuno

Wales *n* Cymru

walk *vb* cerdded, rhodio ♦ *n*

rhodfa; tro

walker *n* cerddwr

walkie-talkie *n* set radio symud a siarad

walking *n* cerddediad; cerdded. **w. stick** ffon gerdded

walkover *n* goruchafiaeth hawdd, digystadleuaeth

wall *n* mur, gwal, pared ♦ *vt* murio

wallaby *n* cangarŵ bach

wall-cress *n* berwr y fagwyr

wallet *n* ysgrepan, gwaled

wallflower *n* llysiau'r fagwyr, blodau'r fagwyr, blodau mamgu

wallop *vt* curo, llachio, wado

wallow *vi* ymdreiglo, ymdrybaeddu

wallpaper *n* papur wal

walnut *n* cneuen Ffrengig

walrus *n* morfarch

waltz *n* wols

wan *adj* gwelw, gwelwlas, llwyd

wand *n* gwialen, llath, hudlath

wander *vb* crwydro, gwibio, cyfeiliorni

wanderer *n* crwydryn

wandering *adj* ar grwydr

wanderlust *n* elfen grwydro

wane *vi* darfod, treio, cilio, lleihau

wangle *vb* dyfeisio

want *n* angen, eisiau, diffyg ♦ *vb* bod mewn angen

wanting *adj* yn eisiau

wanton *adj* anllad, trythyll; diachos

wantonness *n* anlladrwydd

war *n* rhyfel ♦ *vb* rhyfela

warble *vb* telori

warbler *n* telor

ward *n* gwart, gward; gwarchodaeth ♦ *vt* gwarchod, amddiffyn

warden *n* gwarden, gwarcheidwad

wardenship *n* gwardeniaeth

warder *n* gwarchodwr, gwyliwr

wardrobe *n* cwpwrdd dillad,

gwardrob

ware n nwydd; llestri, wâr

warehouse n ystordy, ystorfa, warws

warfare n milwriaeth, rhyfel

wariness n pwyll, gwyliadwriaeth

warlike adj rhyfelgar, milwraidd, milwrol

warm adj cynnes ✦ vb cynhesu

warmonger n rhyfelgi

warmth n cynhesrwydd

warn vt rhybuddio

warning n rhybudd

warp n ystof, dylif ✦ vb gwyro, lleddfu

warrant n gwarant, awdurdod ✦ vt gwarantu, cyfreithloni

warrantor n gwarantydd

warren n cwningar, parc cwningod

warrior n rhyfelwr

warship n llong rhyfel

wart n dafad, dafaden

wary adj gwyliadwrus, gochelgar

was vi oedd, bu

wash vb golchi ✦ n golchiad, golchfa; golchion

washable adj golchadwy

washing n golch

washing machine n peiriant golchi

washing powder n powdr golchi

washing-up liquid n sebon golchi llestri

wasp n cacynen, gwenynen feirch

wassail n gwasael

waste vb difrodi, gwastraffu, treulio ✦ n gwastraff, traul

wasteful adj gwastraffus

wastepaper basket n basged sbwriel

wastrel n oferwr, oferddyn

watch vb gwylio, gwylied, gwarchod ✦ n gwyliadwriaeth; oriawr, oriadur, wats

watchful adj gwyliadwrus

watchmaker adj oriadurwr, trwsiwr watsys

watchman n gwyliwr

watch-night n gwylnos

watchword n arwyddair, cyswynair

water n dwfr, dŵr ✦ vb dyfrhau

water-cock n tap

watercolour n paent (i'w gymysgu â dŵr); dyfrliliw

watercress n berwr dŵr

waterfall n rhaeadr, pistyll, cwymp dŵr, sgwd

waterhen n iâr fach y dŵr

watering place n lle i anifeiliaid gael dŵr; tref ffynhonnau

waterlogged adj llawn dŵr

watermark n dyfrnod

waterproof adj diddos

watershed n trum, gwahanfa ddŵr

water skiing n sglefrio ar ddŵr

watertight adj diddos, heb ollwng dŵr neu leithder

water wagtail n sigwti fach y dŵr

watt n wat, uned pŵer trydan

wattle n clwyd, pleiden; tagell ceiliog

wave vb chwifio; tonni ✦ n ton

waver vi anwadalu, petruso, gwamalu

wax n cwyr ✦ vt cwyro

wax vi cynyddu, tyfu

wax-candle n cannwyll gŵyr

waxworks npl arddangosfa delwau cwyr

way n ffordd, modd, arfer

wayfarer n fforddolyn, teithiwr, tramwywr

wayfaring tree n ysgawen y gors

waylay vt cynllwyn, rhagod

wayside n ymyl y ffordd

wayward adj cyndyn, ystyfnig, gwrthnysig

we pron ni, nyni, ninnau

weak adj gwan, egwan

weaken vb gwanhau, gwanychu

weakling n un gwan, edlych, ewach

weakly adj gwanllyd
weak-minded adj diniwed, gwirion
weakness n gwendid
weal n llwydd, llwyddiant, lles
weald n fforest; gwlad agored
wealth n golud, cyfoeth, da
wealthy adj cyfoethog
wean vt diddyfnu
weapon n arf
wear vb gwisgo, treulio ♦ n traul; gwisg
weariness n blinder
weary adj blin, blinedig ♦ vb blino
weasel n gwenci, bronwen
weather n tywydd, hin ♦ vt dal, dioddef
weather-beaten adj ag ôl y tywydd arno
weatherglass n baromedr
weathervane n ceiliog gwynt
weave vb gwau, gweu
weaver n gwehydd
web n gwe
webbing n webin
web-footed adj â thraed gweog
wed vb priodi, ymbriodi
wedding n priodas
wedge n cŷn, gaing, lletem ♦ vt cynio; gwthio i mewn
wedlock n ystad briodas, priodas
Wednesday n dydd Mercher
wee adj bach, bychan, pitw
weed n chwynnyn, chwyn ♦ vb chwynnu
week n wythnos
weekday n diwrnod gwaith
weekend n dros y Sul, penwythnos
weekly n wythnosolyn (cylchgrawn) ♦ adj wythnosol ♦ adv yn wythnosol
weep vb wylo, wylofain, llefain
weevil n gwyfyn yr ŷd
weft n anwe
weigh vb pwyso; codi (angor)
weight n pwys, pwysau
weighty adj pwysig, trwm
weir n cored

weird adj annaearol, iasol
welcome excl, n croeso ♦ vt croesawu ♦ adj derbyniol, dymunol
weld vt asio
welfare n llwydd, lles
welfare state n gwladwriaeth les
well adv yn dda ♦ adj da, iach ♦ excl wel
well n ffynnon, pydew
well-balanced adj cytbwys
wellbeing n lles, budd
well-bred adj boneddigaidd
well-fed adj mewn cas cadw da
wellingtons npl esgidiau glaw
well-off adj cefnog, da ei fyd
Welsh adj Cymreig (o ran teithi); Cymraeg (o ran iaith) ♦ n Cymraeg
Welshman n Cymro
Welshwoman n Cymraes
welt n gwald, gwaldas
welter vi ymdrybaeddu
wen n wen
wench n geneth, llances
wend vt mynd, cerdded
werewolf n bleidd-ddyn
Wesleyan adj Wesleaidd
west n gorllewin ♦ adj gorllewinol. **W. Germany** n Gorllewin yr Almaen. **W. Indies** npl: **the W.I.** India'r Gorllewin
westerly adj gorllewinol, o'r gorllewin
western adj gorllewinol
westwards adv tua'r gorllewin
wet adj gwlyb ♦ vt gwlychu ♦ n gwlybaniaeth
wetness n gwlybaniaeth
wetting n gwlychfa
wether n molit, gwedder
whack vb llachio, baeddu, ffonodio
whale n morfil
wharf n porthfa, llwythfa
what adj, pron yr hyn; pa beth, pa faint
whatever pron beth bynnag

whatsoever *pron* pa beth bynnag
wheat *n* gwenith
wheedle *vt* denu, hudo, llithio, truthio
wheel *n* olwyn, rhod, troell ♦ *vt* olwyno, powlio
wheelbarrow *n* berfa (drol), whilber
wheelchair *n* cadair olwyn
wheelwright *n* saer troliau
wheeze *vi* gwichian ♦ *n* gwich
wheezy *adj* gwichlyd
whelk *n* chwalc, gwalc
whelp *n* cenau
when *adv* pan, pa bryd
whence *adv* o ba le, o ba un
whenever *adv* pa bryd bynnag
where *adv* ym mha le; yn y lle, lle
whereabouts *adv* ymhle
whereas *conj* gan, yn gymaint â
whereby *adv* trwy yr hyn
wherefore *adv* paham, am hynny
wherein *adv* yn yr hyn
whereof *adv* y ... amdano
whereon *adv* ar yr hwn
wheresoever, wherever *adv* pa le bynnag
whereto *adv* y ... iddo
whereupon *adv* ar hynny
wherewithal *n* modd, arian
wherry *n* ysgraff, ceubal, porthfad
whet *vt* hogi, minio, awchlymu
whether *conj* ai, pa un ai
whetstone *n* carreg hogi, hogfaen, agalen
whey *n* maidd, gleision
which *pron* pa un, pa rai; a ♦ *adj* pa
whichever *pron, adj* pa un bynnag
whiff *n* chwiff, pwff, chwyth, chwa
Whig *n* Chwig, Rhyddfrydwr
while *n* ennyd, talm, amser ♦ *vt* treulio ♦ (hefyd whilst) *adv* cyhyd, tra
whim *n* mympwy, chwim
whimper *vb* swnian crio

whimsical *adj* ysmala, mympwyol
whimsicality *n* bod yn fympwyol
whin *n* eithin
whinchat *n* clochdar yr eithin
whine *vb* swnian crio, cwynfan
whinny *vi* gweryru
whip *vb* chwipio, ffrewyllu, fflangellu ♦ *n* chwip, ffrewyll, fflangell
whiphand *n* llaw uchaf
whippet *n* corfilgi
whipping *n* chwipiad, fflangelliad
whir *vi* chwyrndroi, chwyrnu
whirl *vb* chwyrlïo, chwyrnellu, chwyrndroi
whirligig *n* chwyrligwgan, chwyrnell
whirlpool *n* pwll tro, trobwll
whirlwind *n* trowynt, corwynt
whisk *n* tusw ♦ *vb* ysgubo; chwyrlïo
whiskered *adj* blewog, barfog
whiskers *npl* blew, barf
whisky *n* chwisgi
whisper *vb, n* sibrwd, sisial
whist *n* chwist
whistle *vb* chwibanu ♦ *n* chwiban, chwibanogl, chwit
whit *n* tipyn, gronyn, mymryn
white *adj* gwyn, can, cannaid
whiten *vb* gwynnu, cannu
whiteness *n* gwynder, gwyndra
whitewash *n* gwyngalch ♦ *vb* gwyngalchu
whither *adv* i ba le
whiting *n* gwyniad
whitlow *n* ffelwm, ffalwm, ewinor, bystwn
whitlow grass *n* llysiau'r bystwn
Whit Monday *n* Llungwyn
Whitsun(day) *n* Sulgwyn
Whitsuntide *n* dros y Sulgwyn
whittle *vt* naddu, lleihau
whiz *vi* sïo, chwyrnellu, chwyrlïo
who *pron* a, pwy
whoever *pron* pwy bynnag
whole *adj* cyfan, holl; iach,

holliach ♦ n cyfan
wholehearted adj â'i holl galon
wholemeal adj â'r grawn cyfan, cyflawn
wholeness n cyfanrwydd
wholesale n cyfanwerth ♦ adj yn y crynswth
wholesaler n cyfanwerthwr
wholesome adj iach, iachus, iachusol
wholly adv yn hollol, yn gyfan gwbl, yn llwyr
whom pron a (y, yr)
whomsoever pron pwy bynnag
whoop vi bloeddio, banllefain ♦ n bloedd
whooping cough n pas
whop vt ffusto, baeddu
whopper n un mawr
whopping adj mawr iawn
whore n putain, hŵr
whorl n tro, troell, sidell
whortleberry n llus, llusi duon bach
whose pron y ... ei, eiddo pwy? pwy biau?
whosoever pron pwy bynnag
why adv paham, pam
wick n pabwyr, pabwyryn, wic
wicked adj drwg, drygionus, ysgeler
wickedness n drygioni
wicker n gwaith gwiail
wickerwork n plethwaith, basgedwaith
wicket n wiced, clwyd, llidiart
wide adj llydan, eang, helaeth; rhwth
wide-awake adj effro, ar ddihun
widely adj yn eang
widen vb lledu, llydanu
widespread adj cyffredinol
widgeon n wiwell
widow adj gweddw ♦ n gwraig weddw, gwidw
widowed adj gweddw
widower n gwidman

widowhood n gweddwdod
width n lled, ehangder
wield vt llywio, rheoli; ysgwyd, arfer, trin
wife (wives) n gwraig, gwraig briod, priod
wig n gwallt gosod, perwig, wig
wigging n ceryid
wild adj gwyllt ♦ n diffeithle
wilderness n anialwch
wildfire n tân gwyllt
wildness n gwylltineb
wile n dichell, ystryw, cast
wilful adj gwirfoddol, bwriadol; ystyfnig
wilfully adv o fwriad
wilfulness or U.S. **willfulness** n ystyfnigrwydd
wiliness n dichell, cyfrwystra
will vt ewyllysio, mynnu ♦ n ewyllys
willing adj ewyllysgar, bodlon
willingly adj o wirfodd
willingness n parodrwydd
will-o-the-wisp n jacolantern
willow n helygen, pren helyg
willowherb n helyglys
willowy adj helygaidd, gosgeiddig
willpower n grym ewyllys
willy-nilly adv bodlon neu beidio, o fodd neu anfodd
wily adj cyfrwys, dichellgar
wimple n gwempl
win vb ennill
wince vi gwingo
winch n wins
wind n gwynt
wind vb dirwyn, troi
windbag n clebryn
windfall n lwc, ffawd dda
windflower n anemoni, blodyn y gwynt
windless adj di-wynt, llonydd
windmill n melin wynt
window n ffenestr
windowpane n cwarel
windpipe n breuant, y bibell wynt

windscreen n ffenestr flaen
windscreen wiper n braich law
windward adj tua'r gwynt
windy adj gwyntog
wine n gwin
wineglass n gwydr gwin
wing n adain, asgell; asgellwr (rygbi)
wing-commander n asgell-gomander
winged adj adeiniog
wing-forward n blaenasgellwr
wink vb wincio, cau llygad ♦ n winc; hunell
winner n enillydd
winning adj enillgar, deniadol
winnings npl enillion
winnow vt nithio, gwyntyllio
winnower n nithiwr
winsome adj serchog, deniadol
winter n gaeaf ♦ vb gaeafu
wintry adj gaeafol
wipe vt sychu
wire n gwifr, gwifren
wireless n radio
wirepulling n cynllwyn, dylanwadu, 'tynnu gwifrau'
wiring n weiro
wiry adj gwydn, caled
wisdom n doethineb
wise adj doeth
wiseacre n doethyn, ffwlcyn
wish vb dymuno, chwennych ♦ n dymuniad
wishbone n asgwrn tynnu
wishful adj awyddus. **w. thinking** breuddwyd gwrach
wishywashy adj gwan, di-asgwrn-cefn
wisp n tusw
wistful adj awyddus, hiraethus
wit vb: **to w.** sef, hynny yw, nid amgen
wit n synnwyr; arabedd; gŵr ffraeth
witch n dewines, gwrach
witchcraft n dewiniaeth

with prep â, ag, gyda, gydag, efo, gan
withdraw vb tynnu yn ôl, encilio; codi arian
withdrawal n enciliad
withe n gwden, gwialen helyg
wither vb gwywo, crino
withering adj gwywol, crin
withhold vt atal, cadw yn ôl
within adv, n, prep i mewn, o fewn
without prep heb, di- ♦ adv, n tu allan
withstand vt gwrthsefyll
witless adj disynnwyr, ynfyd, ffôl
witness n tyst; tystiolaeth ♦ vb tystio
wits npl synhwyrau
witticism n ffraethair, ffraetheb
wittiness n ffraethineb
wittingly adv trwy wybod, yn fwriadol
witty adj arab, arabus, ffraeth
wizard n swynwr, dewin
wizardry n dewiniaeth, hud
wizened adj gwyw, crin, sybachog
woad n glaslys
wobble vi siglo, honcian, anwadalu
wobbly adj sigledig
woe n gwae
woebegone adj athrist
wolf (wolves) n blaidd
wolfsbane n llysiau'r blaidd
woman (women) n y gwraig, merch
womanliness n rhinweddau benywaidd
womanly adj gwreigaidd, benywaidd
womb n croth, bru
wonder n rhyfeddod, syndod ♦ vi rhyfeddu, synnu
wonderful, wondrous adj rhyfeddol
wont vb, n arfer ♦ adj arferol
woo vt caru; deisyf
wood n coed, coedwig; pren

woodbine n gwyddfid
woodcock n cyffylog
woodcutter n torrwr coed
wooded adj coedog
wooden adj o goed, o bren; trwsgl, trwstan
woodland n coetir
woodlark n ehedydd y coed
wood-louse (-lice) n gwrach y lludw, mochyn y coed, tyrchyn llwyd
woodpecker n taradr y coed
wood-pigeon n ysguthan
wood sage n chwerwlys yr eithin, saets gwyllt
wood sorrel n surran y coed
woodwind npl chwythoffer pren
woodwork n gwaith coed, gwaith saer
woof n anwe
wool n gwlân
woollen adj gwlanog, gwlân
woolly adj gwlanog
woolsack n sedd yr Arglwydd Ganghellor
word n gair ♦ vt geirio
wording n geiriad
wordy adj geiriog, amleiriog
work n gwaith, gweithred, gorchwyl ♦ vb gweithio
worker n gweithiwr
workhouse n tloty, wyrcws
working adj yn gweithio, gwaith
workman n gweithiwr
workmanlike adj gweithgar, diwyd
workmanship n saerniaeth, crefft
workshop n gweithdy
world n byd
worldly adj bydol
worldwide adj byd-eang
worm n pryf, abwydyn; llyngyren ♦ vb ymnyddu
wormwood n wermod
worn-out adj wedi blino; wedi treulio
worried adj pryderus, gofidus
worry vb cnoi, baeddu, blino,

poeni, poenydio ♦ n pryder, blinder
worse adj gwaeth
worsen vb gwaethygu
worship n addoliad ♦ vb addoli
worshipper n addolwr
worst vt gorchfygu, trechu
worsted n edafedd hirwlan, wstid
worth n gwerth, teilyngdod
worthless adj diwerth
worthy adj teilwng ♦ n gŵr o fri
wound n archoll, clwyf ♦ vt archolli, clwyfo
wraith n cyhiraeth, cyheuraeth
wrangle vb cecru, cweryla, ffraeo ♦ n ffrae, ymryson
wrap vt plygu, amdoi, lapio
wrapping paper n papur lapio
wrasse n gwrachen y môr
wrath n llid, digofaint, soriant
wrathful adj digofus, llidiog, dig
wreak vt tywallt, dial (llid)
wreath n torch
wreck n llongddrylliad ♦ vb llongddryllio
wren n dryw, dryw bach
wrench vt rhwygo ymaith, tyndroi ♦ n tyndro
wrestle vi ymgodymu, ymaflyd codwm
wrestler n ymgodymwr, taflwr codwm
wretch n adyn, truan; gwalch, dihiryn
wretched adj truan, truenus, gresynus
wriggle vb gwingo, ymnyddu
wright n saer
wring vt troi, gwasgu
wrinkle n crych, crychni ♦ vb crychu
wrinkle n awgrym, hysbysrwydd
wrinkled adj crychiog
wrist n arddwrn
wristband n rhwymyn llawes
wristwatch n wats arddwrn, wats fraich, oriawr

writ n: Holy W. yr Ysgrythur Lân
write vb ysgrifennu
writer n ysgrifennwr, awdur
writhe vb ymnyddu, gwingo
writing n ysgrifen; ysgrifennu
writing paper n papur ysgrifennu
wrong adj cyfeiliornus, cam, anghywir, o'i le ♦ n cam ♦ vt gwneud cam â, niweidio, drygu
wrongdoing n trosedd, camwedd
wrongful adj anghyfiawn, ar gam
wroth adj dig, dicllon, digofus, llidiog
wrought adj: w. iron haearn gyr
wry adj cam, gwyrgam

X

xenophobia n senoffobia
X-rays npl pelydrau X
xylophone n seiloffon

Y

yacht n llong bleser, iot
yachtsman n hwyliwr iot
yap vi clepian, cyfarth
yard n llath, llathen; hwyl-lath
yard n iard, buarth, cadlas, clos
yarn n edau, edafedd; stori, chwedl
yawl n bad mawr, cwch llong
yawn vi dylyfu gên, agor ceg
ye pron chwi, chwychwi; chwithau
yea adv ie, yn wir
year n blwyddyn, blwydd
yearling n anifail blwydd
yearly adv blynyddol
yearn vi hiraethu, dyheu
yearning n hiraeth
yeast n burum, berem, berman
yell vb ysgrechain ♦ n ysgrech, nâd
yellow adj, n melyn
yellowhammer n y benfelen, melyn yr eithin

yelp vi cyfarth, gogyfarth, cipial
yeoman n gwrêng, iwmon; amaethwr
yeomanry n meirchfilwyr
yes adv ie, do, oes, etc
yesterday n, adv doe
yet conj, adv er hynny, eto
yew n yw, ywen
Yiddish n Almaeneg Iddewaidd
yield vb ildio, gildio, ymroddi, rhoddi ♦ n cynnyrch
yoghurt n iogwrt
yoke n iau, gwedd ♦ vb ieuo
yokefellow n cymar
yokel n lleban, gwladwr, taeog
yolk n melyn wy, melynwy
yonder adj acw, draw ♦ adv dacw, acw, draw
yore n y dyddiau gynt, y cynfyd
you pron chi, chwi, 'ch; chwychwi; chwithau
young adj ifanc, ieuanc
younger adj iau
youngest adj ieuaf, ifancaf
youngster n bachgennyn, plentyn
your pron eich, 'ch
yours pron eiddoch. yr eiddoch
yourself pron eich hun(an)
yourselves pron eich hunain
youth n ieuenctid, mebyd; llanc. y. hostel n gwesty ieuenctid
youthful adj ieuanc, ieuengaidd
Yugoslavia n Iwgoslafia
Yule n Nadolig
Yuletide n tymor y Nadolig

Z

Zambia n Zambia
zeal n sêl, aidd, eiddgarwch, brwdfrydedd
zealot n gwynfydwr, penboethyn
zealous adj selog, eiddgar, brwdfrydig
zebra n sebra
zenana n gwragedd-dy, gwreicty

zenith *n* entrych; anterth
zephyr *n* awel dyner (o'r gorllewin)
zero *n* dim, diddim, gwagnod (0), sero
zest *n* awch, blas, afiaith
zigzag *adj*, *n* igam-ogam
Zimbabwe *n* Zimbabwe
zinc *n* sinc

zip *n* sip
zither *n* sither
zodiac *n* sidydd
zone *n* gwregys, cylch, rhanbarth
zoo *n* sw
zoological *adj* swolegol
zoologist *n* swolegydd
zoology *n* milofyddiaeth, swoleg